"I Can't Help It….I'M ITALIAN!"

by

Fran Vitello Murphy

To Diane,
God bless you &
Buono Fortuna,
Fran Vitello Murphy

xulon PRESS

This book is dedicated to my parents and grandparents who taught me the importance of family closeness, and instilled in me a love for each and every member of my family, past, present...and even future.

This book is also dedicated to my husband who has made my life complete, and who has given to this family his total love and devotion.

ACKNOWLEDGEMENTS

To Terry, Jack, and Steve, for their love, and for their enthusiasm for this book. Their encouragement meant so much to me. And to Steve for all his help.

To my brother Joe, for letting me pick his brain whenever I needed to. Reminiscing with him was pure joy. His input was most important to me.

To my sister Dorothy, for her excitement and enthusiasm for this book being written. As a published writer herself, her advice and input were much needed and greatly appreciated. The laughter *and* the tears were a cathartic for both of us.

Last, but not least, this book could <u>never</u> have been written if not for the love and patience of my husband John. His advice and corrective criticism was invaluable to me. His encouragement helped me to make this book and the characters in it come alive.

*****

I will be forever grateful to my wonderful family for their support, and for the faith they had in me.

ABOUT THE AUTHOR

Fran Murphy lives in South Weymouth, Massachusetts with her husband John. She and John are members of the Community Baptist Church in Weymouth.

Fran loves books, and works in the library of her church. She enjoys reading biographies, but also enjoys a good novel. James Michener and Jan Karon are two of her favorite authors.

One of the great passions of Fran's life (besides her grandchildren) has been the women's Bible study she has taught every Tuesday morning since 1990. She also, from time to time, teaches a course called "Woman, You've Been Deceived," a study for married Christian women.

"I Can't Help It...I'M ITALIAN!" is Fran's first book. She has also written numerous poems.

"Thou, O Lord, dost abide forever; and Thy name to all generations." This will be written for the generation to come; that a people yet to be created may praise the Lord."
~Psalm 102:12, 18

"Against the assault of laughter, nothing can stand."
~Mark Twain

"Weeping may endure for a night, but joy cometh in the morning."

~Psalm 30:5b (KJV)

"God has made laughter for me; everyone who hears will laugh with me."
~Genesis 21:6

CONTENTS

"I Can't Help It....I'M ITALIAN!"

by

Fran Vitello Murphy

PROLOGUE

"Leave Sicily? Why would we do that? Our families are here; everything we know and love is here. No, Pietro, I don't want to leave our home. What will we do when we get there? They won't understand us; they won't speak our language. Please, my husband, don't do this to us." "But there's a better life waiting for us in America, Fiessa. I just know it… I feel it. You need to trust me….. We're going!" In November 1913 Pietro and his family embarked on a frightening journey to an unknown land, and a totally uncertain future. Crocifessa was heartbroken…and terrified.

Ethel had a feisty spirit and loved a little excitement, not that there was much of it on the farm in Manchester, England. The year was 1896; she was thirteen years old, and did not want to leave her beloved Old Ned. "What does America have that we don't have here in England?" "Opportunity Ethel! Opportunity!" her father said. "Hmm, AMERICA…. everyone *does* seem to want to go there. Maybe it won't be so bad."

Harry searched his heart…and his Bible for answers; he was confused and overwhelmed. He secretly cried often, and called out, "Why? Why Lord? What has happened to our life? What did we do wrong?"

"Why do you have to be so outspoken, Hon?" John asked. "Honestly, you're like a gumball machine; a thought comes into your mind, drops down onto your tongue, and comes right out of your mouth." "Well, I can't help it…I'M ITALIAN!"

Joe grinned. "You talk to him Dad… no decent person would." Andy howled with laughter.

*****

This is a story about my family and me. It's a nice family…a real nice family; I think you'll like them. There are happy times and there are sad times in this story, like most family's stories. For instance, my grandparents, who came to this country and lived in… Oh, well, that's in the story. Then there's my uncle and my dad who nearly drowned in…. Wait! That's in there too. There's also the time my dad, while shaving a man with a straight razor, threatened … Oops! That's there too. You'll love the time my brother…Hold on! That's in the story, too. You know something? I think you should come on inside, and meet them yourself.

I welcome you! My whole family welcomes you!

CHAPTER ONE
America: Molasses and Lemons

In a little town in Sicily, called Riesi, a young woman waited anxiously for her parents to return home. The year was 1902, and she was twenty years old; her name was Crocifessa Bellanti. Her parents were visiting the Vitello family in hopes of arranging a marriage for her with their son Pietro. Crocifessa had never actually met Pietro, though she had seen him in town a few times when she had gone with her parents. Her father had said, "Pietro comes from a good family; he would make a good husband for you, Crocifessa." She had quickly responded, "Why would Pietro want to marry me, Papa? He's handsome and I'm so plain; I'm sure he'd rather marry a pretty girl." "Don't be stupid!" her father had said. "If he's at all the man I believe he is, then he'll be wanting to marry someone who will make him a good wife. You, Crocifessa, could be that woman…. and besides, you're not so plain."

Right now, she realized, her parents were talking to Mr. and Mrs. Vitello, trying to convince them, and probably Pietro, too, that she and Pietro would make a good match. *"Oh, God,"* she thought, *"what if he or his parents won't agree with the match?"* Her face flushed and her eyes filled with tears as she thought how humiliated she would feel if he rejected her. *"How could I ever face him if I see him in town?"* "No!" Enough!" she said aloud, as if she were talking to someone there. "I'm not going to think about this anymore!" She walked out into the garden to get some air and to try not to think about it. She shivered. The temperature was changing;

it was becoming quite cool. She sat down on the stone bench among the flowers; she inhaled deeply, trying to get lost in their strong fragrance. "It's impossible not to think about it," she decided, so she began to pray, "Lord, if you let Pietro accept me, I promise I'll be a good wife to him always; help me to accept Your will." After a while she got up and went back into the house to try to keep herself busy.

Two more hours went by and finally Crocifessa heard her parents walking up the road and talking. She couldn't make out what they were saying, but just then she heard her mother sigh; it was a kind of loud sigh. Was that a good sign? She stood in the doorway watching them as they came up the stone walk. Her mother looked up and ran to her and hugged her. *"Maybe it's not a good sign,"* she thought. "It's all set!" her father cried. "You, my dear daughter will be married to Pietro Vitello five months from today." Crocifessa felt weak all over; she didn't know whether to laugh or to cry. Her heart was beating rapidly. *"Thank You Lord, for Your kindness,"* she silently prayed. *"Help me to live up to my promise to You."*

Crocifessa and Pietro saw each other whenever possible during those five months, always well chaperoned, of course. It was a difficult and somewhat embarrassing time for Crocifessa, as she was a very shy girl. Making conversation was not easy for her; she was always afraid she would say something foolish, or that he might laugh at her. "It's a very nice day today," she said, on one of their visits. "Nice? It's a wonderful day today!" Pietro exclaimed. "It's a good day to be alive!" He took her breath away with his exuberance.

Crocifessa soon learned that Pietro loved to talk; it seemed to come so easy to him. She was very content to let him. One day, when they were out walking, Pietro said, "You know, Fiessa, I really like to talk, and I like talking with you; you're a real good listener, but I'm not giving you much of a chance to talk." "Oh, that's all right," she said, "I like listening to you, Pietro." "...*Fiessa,* he called me... *how strange; no one's ever called me that.* She smiled to herself. *"Fiessa... I think I like it...yes, I like it."*

Crocifessa became more and more comfortable with Pietro as time went on. He loved to tell stories, some true, some made up. He had a marvelous sense of humor and kept her laughing. She, on the other hand, was gentle and sedate, qualities Pietro liked very much in her.

On one of their outings, with chaperones not far behind, they walked to town and bought some bread and cheese and some fruit, which they ate under a tree on the way home. The chaperones sat under a tree a little distance from them. Pietro discovered something about Crocifessa that he admired that day. She had surprised him at the market when she quietly and discreetly spoke up to the shopkeeper who was weighing the fruit with his hand still on the scale. Pietro wasn't aware of it until he heard Crocifessa's soft voice. *"Most young women would not have done that,"* he marveled. *"I never would have thought she had it in her. She saved me some money today... isn't she something?"*

Each meeting was a learning experience for Pietro and Crocifessa. One evening, as they sat in her garden, Pietro began to sing; ... out of the blue he started singing an old Italian folk song, a lively tune, quite loudly, as a matter of fact. Crocifessa sat there dumbfounded. "Come on, you must know this song," Pietro said. "Sing! Sing!" "Oh, no," she cried, "I can't sing!" "Sure you can sing; everyone can sing," Pietro said. "No, really, I can't," she insisted. "You just don't want to sing in front of me," he teased. "That's it, isn't it? Well, that's okay, Fiessa, I'll sing for the both of us; I love to sing!" "You have a nice voice," Crocifessa said shyly. "Thanks!" he said, and went right on singing. She was amazed at his candor. *"How can he like me?* She thought. *"I'm so different from him."*

About a month before the wedding Pietro asked Crocifessa, "Fiessa, what do you think? Do you like me? I mean, do you *want* to marry me?" "What? Oh!" Crocifessa was stunned. "I...I don't know; I'll do as my parents say." "That's not what I asked you; do you *like* me? Do you really *want* to marry me?" Pietro pressed. "Well, Pietro...do *you* want to marry *me?*" she asked cautiously, suddenly frightened at the way this conversation was going. "Of course I want to marry you, Silly," Pietro cried. I care a great deal for you, Fiessa; don't you know that?" "Oh!" she said, relieved. "Yes, Pietro, I do want to marry you, and yes, I like you, I like you very much." "Ah, good! Good!" he responded, and sat back and started whistling a tune. He never failed to surprise Crocifessa.

Pietro and Crocifessa were married in the spring of 1903. After spending a few days alone together, they spent time visiting each other's relatives and getting to know the families. They made their home in Riesi, close to both families.

They looked forward to having a family of their own, and the following year Crocifessa, with the help of a mid-wife, gave birth to a healthy baby boy; they called him Carmello. They wanted more children, but after four years passed without another pregnancy, they began to believe they couldn't have anymore.

Then, on June 24, 1909, with the help of the mid-wife, a beautiful baby boy was born to Crocifessa, a child she considered destined for greatness. He was born completely encased in the unbroken caul, the amniotic membrane surrounding the fetus. This was a rare occurrence, and thought to be a sign from God that the child had been chosen for something very special. Crocifessa was a devout Catholic, and she took this very seriously. He was christened Angelo, because to them he was an angel sent from God.

In November of 1911, a beautiful, dark haired baby girl was born to Crocifessa and Pietro. They named her Crocifessa. She was the joy of their life.

*****

"We're going to America!" Pietro announced one day. "What? America? How? What are you talking about?" Crocifessa cried. She knew that look on her husband's face; it told her that his mind was already made up, and she felt a kind of panic rising in her. "There's a boat going to America in November; we're going to be on it." "But leave Sicily? How can we do that Pietro? Our families are here; everything we know and love is here. I don't want to go on some huge boat to a place we know nothing about. What will we do when we get there? They won't understand us; they won't speak our language. Please, my husband, don't do this to us." "But there's a better life waiting for us in America, Fiessa. I just know it…I feel it. You need to trust me…. We're going!"

When Angelo was four and a half years old, his parents sold everything they had and took him and his brother Carmello, who was nine and a half, and his little sister Crocifessa, two, and boarded a ship bound for America. "America," as Pietro had been told, was a land of opportunity, "where the streets are paved with gold." Carmello was thrilled; he had heard about America and couldn't wait to get there. Angelo was happy because this was something strange and exciting, and he had never seen a 'boat' before…. His mother was terrified.

Being in steerage for over three weeks was a most horrible experience, but it was all Peter could afford. The strong smells were bad, and the lack of privacy was awful, but the worst thing was the occasional rat they would see. Crocifessa was positively miserable and spent most nights crying and sleepless.

After a trip that seemed to take forever, they landed at Ellis Island in New York on a very cool and damp day in November 1913. After going through customs and being processed and registered, they gathered up their luggage and their meager belongings. Pietro's brother, Giuseppe was supposed to meet them, but where was he? How would they ever be able to find him in the throng of people? Pietro said, "I've never seen so many people in one place before." He scanned the crowd of faces for a long time, but after awhile they all seemed to blend together. "*Oh, God, please make him be here,*" he thought, as a feeling of panic began to build in him…and then he heard it…. It was like music to his ears…"Pietro… Pietro!" He could hear his name being called, but in the cacophony of voices and people, Pietro could not tell where it was coming from. "It must be Giuseppe, but where is he?" said Pietro. Suddenly Carmello cried, "Over there! Over there! I see him, Pa, it's Uncle Giuseppe." Giuseppe was tall, which made it easier for them to see him in the crowd. How he spotted them was amazing, as Pietro was small, barely 5'3", and Crocifessa was only 4'10".

The joy was indescribable seeing Giuseppe amongst all these strangers. He was waving and jumping up and down and tears were streaming down his face. "Pietro! Crocifessa!" he called, as he made his way through the crowd. They hugged, they kissed and they cried. "Welcome to America, Brother!" He hugged Carmello and picked Angelo up and carried him. He had never seen little Crocifessa as she was born after he left Sicily. "Bella, bella bambina," he exclaimed when he crouched down to look at her… "Beautiful baby!" She was very shy and the noise and the crowd frightened her. She clung to her mother. Maria, Giuseppe's wife, hugged and kissed them all, and picked up little Crocifessa. She and Crocifessa, Sr. cried tears of joy and relief. "I can't wait to sit with you and have coffee, like we used to, and tell you all about life in America," Maria said. "I've missed you, Maria," Crocifessa said, as she wiped the tears from her eyes.

Giuseppe had come to America over two years earlier, and was living in New York City, where he worked stocking shelves and hanging up clothes in a small haberdashery shop. He and his wife were planning to move to Boston soon, as Giuseppe was promised a better job in a large clothing store. He loved working with clothes and fabrics, and had a strong sense of design and style. He wanted to work in a fine, modern clothing store. His dream was to own his own store one day, and he was certain he could make it happen.

Pietro was different from his brother when it came to work. He may have been small, but he was very strong and loved working outside with his hands. In Sicily he had been a foreman, working in a sulphur mine, and every spare minute he had he spent in his garden. He was very proud of his garden; he grew tomatoes, eggplant, peppers, zucchini, lettuce, and cucumbers, also basilicor (basil), rosemary, and oregano. Crocifessa would cook and preserve all that she could, and the rest Pietro would sell at the market. Besides his many vegetables, Peter kept the land around their home blooming with color with the variety of flowers he planted. He looked forward to starting his garden in their new home in America. Unfortunately, a garden was not in their immediate future.

Giuseppe had rented a two-room, furnished flat for Pietro and his family, not far from where they were living. It was the best he could get for cheap rent. He had filled the icebox and cupboards with food, and on the kitchen table Maria had placed a bottle of Chianti, a loaf of homemade Italian bread, a large chunk of Romano cheese, and a bowl of fresh fruit. The aroma filled the tiny apartment. It was a warm welcome, and Pietro and Crocifessa were very grateful. They poured the wine and Giuseppe drank a toast to them. "Buono fortuna! Brother, Good luck here in America," he cried. "We will eat, and drink wine together many times from now on, Pietro," Giuseppe said, and hugged his brother again.

They were all exhausted by the time Giuseppe and Maria left; it had been a long and tiring day. The children were already asleep. The apartment certainly wasn't what they had hoped for, but that night they thanked God for His protection and His provision.... and for *family*.

*****

Pietro and his family lived in New York City, in their two-room, cold water flat for eight months. Carmello was enrolled in public school, and Pietro got work wherever he could find it. Somehow they managed to make ends meet, but just barely.

One night while they were all sleeping, Crocifessa awoke suddenly, hearing her children crying. Carmello was yelling, "What is this? Ma! Pa! Help!" Angelo was wailing and little Crocifessa sat up whimpering. When their mother lit the lamp, she screamed, "Pietro, look!" The children were covered with bedbugs. They were squirming, jumping up and down and scratching at themselves, all the while screaming and crying. Neighbors came out into the hallway yelling, "What's all the noise? What's going on?" Crocifessa came out into the hall with the children, brushing them off and crying, "It's bedbugs; there's bedbugs in our beds." Most of the neighbors couldn't understand what she was saying. One Italian neighbor called out, "Oh, for heaven's sake, is that all? We all have bedbugs; there's nothing you can do about it. You'll get used to them; after awhile you won't even know they're there. Go back to bed! Some of us here would like to get some sleep!"

They came back inside and Carmello said, "I'm not getting back in that bed." He grabbed his pillow and a blanket, shook them out and said, "I'm sleeping in the kitchen." Angelo and little Crocifessa followed suit. Pietro and his wife went back to their bed after they lifted both mattresses and swept all over and around them. Peter was stomping on the bugs he could see. Crocifessa sniffed, as her eyes filled with tears, "I'll never get used to it! Between the cockroaches in the kitchen and the bedbugs in the bedroom, living here is becoming unbearable. I can't stand it, Pietro; I'm used to a clean home." " I know, Fiessa, I know, but we'll get through this. Things will change, you'll see," Pietro said... trying to convince himself, also.

Crocifessa cried often and begged her husband to take them back to Riesi, "where," she said, "we were happy, and things are clean. You could get your old job back at the sulphur mine, and the children would have a place to run and play, and go to school where they speak the same language, and no one looks down on them. Please, Pietro, you love Sicily as much as I do; won't you at least think about it?"

Pietro did think about it; he thought long and hard about it, but he had a vision of their life in America, and he was determined to see it become a reality. Go back now? It was inconceivable to him.

When, a few days later, his wife brought the subject up again, he said, "No, Fiessa, we're not going back to Riesi. I will always love Sicily, but we are staying! This country is our home now and we're going to make a good life here. We'll work hard, we'll save our money, and one day we'll own our own home. We'll have a nice yard where the children can play and where we can grow vegetables and flowers, and, one day we'll go back to Riesi and visit our families and see our beloved Sicily. I promise you, Fiessa, soon you'll be happy here in America."

Crocifessa didn't believe him. She didn't like America; all she had seen of it was filthy and depressing. She didn't like the people either; she couldn't speak their language, and she didn't think they wanted to speak to her anyway. She was lonely, and she knew she'd be even lonelier soon, as Maria and Giuseppe were talking about moving to some place called Boston. She felt that she would never see another happy day for the rest of her life.

*****

Ethel Mariah Bell was thirteen years old the day her parents told her they were all moving to America; the year was 1896. She was a precocious child, and she loved her life exactly the way it was. All she could think to respond was, "Leave England forever?

Why on earth for? What does America have that we don't have right here in Manchester?" "Opportunity! Ethel, opportunity!" her father answered. She didn't want to leave the small farm that had always been home to her, nor did she want to leave faithful Old Ned, the family workhorse. She loved Old Ned and couldn't imagine leaving him. "Can't we take him with us, Daddy, please?" "I'm sorry, dear, but that's not possible," her father said. "I've sold Ned to the Wilson's; they'll take good care of him." "What? You sold Old Ned? That's not fair, Daddy! It's just not fair!" she cried, as she ran out to the barn to console Old Ned.

When the day came to say goodbye to Old Ned, Ethel cried as she watched her neighbor tie him to the back of their wagon and lead him away. Her mother tried to console her by telling her stories that she had heard in town about life in America. "It will be such an adventure, traveling by ship to a new land, one you will tell your children and your grandchildren about one day." The key word was *adventure*. Ethel was not one to turn away from a challenge. She had a feisty spirit and loved excitement, not that there was much of it in Manchester. AMERICA…Everyone *did* seem to want to go there. Maybe it won't be so bad. Ethel decided she would look forward to this new adventure.

Ethel loved America; it was all she hoped it would be. She and her family settled in Boston, Massachusetts, where she went to school, made friends and grew up. When she was sixteen years old, she began working as a mid-wife. Mid-wifery was very common, as most people couldn't afford to have their babies in a hospital. Ethel was a tireless worker in everything she set her mind to, and mid-wifery was no exception. It required her to live with the family for at least three weeks. Her duties were to care for the husband and children and to minister to the needs of the mother before the baby was born. She would help deliver the baby, and then he or she was added to the duties of the mid-wife. It was hard work and long hours, and most times she was paid with vegetables and fruit or a knitted scarf or sweater. Now and then she was paid in cash, but those times were few and far between.

One day, a friend invited Ethel to a social at a Baptist church in Dorchester. While she was there, she was introduced to Harry E.

Dalton. He was a simple man, plain and quiet. He liked Ethel right away for her vivacity and gift of conversation. She liked him for his polite manners and simple honesty. Ethel decided to go to his church the following Sunday. They talked afterwards for quite a while. Harry asked her if she would consider seeing him again. "Are you asking me out on a date, Harry?" Ethel asked. Harry was perspiring quite a bit. "Well, I guess I am." "Well, it's fine with me," she said, "but you will have to come to my home and ask my father." "Oh, absolutely!" Harry said, "I wouldn't consider it any other way."

Ethel wrote her address on a piece of paper for Harry, and he showed up at her home the following night. She was surprised to see him so soon. Her father answered the door, and Harry became tongue-tied all of a sudden. He was nervous, and he felt like a fool.

"Yes?" Her father said, as he stood in the doorway looking at a very nervous Harry. Her father knew the signs; *This young man is here to ask for my permission to court one of my daughters. Kitty is already spoken for, so he's here for either Ethel, or Mae, or possibly Mabel. Mildred is too young, so I'm betting he's here for Ethel."* "Can I help you, young man?" He asked. Harry managed to compose himself and said, "Mr. Bell, my name is Harry Dalton, and I am here to ask for your permission to court your daughter Ethel." "You are; well, come in, Mr. Dalton, and we'll talk about it." Harry liked Ethel's parents, and they liked him. Ethel's mother brought in tea and after a while they called Ethel downstairs to join them. "Well, Harry," her father finally said, "you have my permission to spend time with my daughter." "Thank you, Sir," Harry said. He was glad it went well, and relieved that it was over.

Harry and Ethel began seeing each other on a regular basis, and liked each other more and more with each meeting. Ethel was everything Harry wasn't, and vice-versa. She was a lovely young lady, albeit outspoken and somewhat strong willed. It seemed to Harry that she feared absolutely nothing. She was not a religious woman, whereas he was a strong Christian, firm in his beliefs. He read his Bible every day and went to Bible studies, and on Sundays he went to services in the morning and in the evening. He loved God, and was a faithful follower of His Son, Jesus Christ. He was a kind and gentle man who had a deep respect for women. Ethel thought he was the finest man she had ever known.

Ethel and Harry soon fell in love, and were married in 1904. They made their home in South Boston, where Harry worked for the Walworth Co., a brass foundry. They were very happy, and looked forward to the future.

"We have a good life, don't we Harry?" Ethel said one evening as she and Harry were having dinner. "Of course we do," said Harry, I couldn't be happier, Hon. "Why do you ask?" "Well, because I believe it's going to get even better Harry." She smiled at him and said, "We're going to have a baby!" Harry was very pleased. "Are you absolutely sure?" he asked. "I'm a mid-wife Dear, remember? I'm sure!"

Ernest was born in June 1905, a healthy, robust baby, weighing over ten pounds.

Ethel was right... life did get better. They enjoyed their little son, Ernie; he was the delight of their lives. So when one day Ethel announced that they were going to have another child, Harry said, "I'm absolutely thrilled; could life get any better than this?"

Howard was born in 1907, a beautiful, healthy baby. A year and a half later he died from drinking milk that came from sick cows. Harry and Ethel were heartbroken.

Gladys was born in 1910, an adorable and sweet little girl. They were positively thrilled with her; she brought real joy back into their lives. Little Ernie, now five years old, was crazy about his little sister. Sadly, three years later, she contracted Meningitis and died. Harry and Ethel were devastated.

Harry searched his heart...and his Bible for answers; he was confused and overwhelmed. He secretly cried often, and called out, "Why? Why, Lord? What has happened to our life? What did we do wrong?" Ethel became withdrawn and depressed, but she somehow managed to carry on for Ernie's sake. Ernie was now eight years old and he too was feeling the sadness of his little sister's death. He missed her playfulness, and it bothered him how quiet the house seemed lately.

Ethel didn't cry very often, but when, five months after Gladys was buried, she found herself pregnant again, she sobbed, "I can't go through this again, Harry; I can't lose another child." "I know, Ethel. God has given us the grace to get this far; I can't believe He'll take another child from us. We *must* put our trust in Him." "I'm trying, Harry, but it's hard to have faith in anything right now, I'm hurting so." "I know, dear, I know." "*Please, God.... please,*" he whispered.

On July 30, 1914 Ethel gave birth to a healthy, beautiful baby girl. Harry said, "This one is sent from God, to comfort us Ethel, in this time of sadness, and give us back our joy. We have a son and a daughter; these two are here to stay, I just feel it." "I'm afraid to believe that, Harry," Ethel said. "I'm afraid even to love her; I don't want to love her if she's going to be taken away from me." "Oh, no, Ethel! You mustn't be afraid to love her. The Bible says that 'Love conquers all!' You must believe that." "I want to believe it, Harry, but I'm so afraid. I don't even want to give her a name, because then she becomes a real person to me. I couldn't stand to call her by name, and then have her...."No, Ethel," said Harry. "You mustn't say such things. I know this talk is coming out of your heartache and disappointment, but this child is here, and whatever the future holds, we'll handle it. God's promise in Hebrews 13:5 says, "*I will never desert you or forsake you.*" Whatever His reason, God has given her to us, and she's real, Ethel, and she has a right to be loved and cared for, regardless of what *could* happen." Harry went on to say, "She's our little girl, Hon, and we *will* name her...we'll give her a name of stability, one that will ensure her place in this world...a name that will fit her strength and her sweetness. We'll call her.... Ethel."

Harry never stopped praying for little Ethel. He begged God, for his wife's sake, to protect their little girl. He and Ethel, Sr. began to feel a little less worried about their daughter's health and safety when she turned five years old. But Harry kept up his prayer vigil every day and he thanked God every night, for this beautiful little girl He gave them.

Ethel continued to grow into a sweet, healthy and happy child. She was truly the joy of her parents' life.

*****

"We're moving to Boston!" Pietro announced, as he read the letter from his brother, Giuseppe, who was now living there. There's a large three-room apartment available in the North End of Boston. Giuseppe says the owner will hold it until he hears from us, but we need to let him know as soon as possible. He says that area is called 'Little Italy' because mostly Italians live there." Pietro was very excited. "This is good! This is *wonderful*!" he cried. "Carmello and Angelo and even little Crocifessa will be able to play with their own kind, and go to school with people who can understand them." "But, Pietro," Crocifessa said, "We don't know anything about this Boston place." "What did we know when we left Sicily?" said Pietro. "What did we know about New York or this dump we're living in? It's got to be better than this; and we'll be close to Giuseppe and Maria again. Think about it...three rooms, Fiessa...*two bedrooms*! We're going!

The apartment in the North End was like most apartments in Boston. It was a typical cold-water flat on the second floor with a wood stove in the kitchen for cooking and heating the apartment. There was no parlor but the kitchen was quite large, large enough to put a settee and a soft chair at the far end of it. An outhouse in back served all four apartments in the house. But having two bedrooms was like living in a palace compared to the apartment in New York. Angelo and Carmello shared a room and little Crocifessa slept in a crib in her parents' room. They had to keep the bedroom doors open at night or there'd be no heat in them, but considering what they had in New York, this was not an inconvenience at all.

Crocifessa was content with the new place and Pietro was content that she was content. They all loved the new apartment, and Crocifessa made it an attractive and comfortable home. Carmello and Angelo were enrolled in the local public school and were learning English. Despite his small stature, Peter, (as Pietro was now being called by the men he worked with), had a pick and shovel job putting in new streets. Work started at 7:00 a.m. and ended at 5:00 p.m. Peter was a hard laborer and strong as an ox, thanks to his years working in the sulphur mine. Working on the streets was hard work, but he would work as much overtime as he could get. Sometimes he and a few other men would work right into the night, with lanterns burning along the road to give some light to their work. Many nights, when he would arrive home around 10:00, he'd be too tired to eat. He would simply fall into bed and sleep until he had to get up in the morning and start over again. It was not an easy time for him, but he was determined to make a better life for his family, and he knew that in America he had the opportunity to work hard and make money whenever possible.

On Sundays Peter would sleep late, read his newspaper, and eat lots of Crocifessa's wonderful food. He was not a religious man and wouldn't go to church no matter how much his wife tried to shame him into it. He was a good man and felt that he was right with God, and if he wasn't, "then I'll go to hell and that's all there is to it," he would say.

It hurt Crocifessa to hear him talk like that, but every Sunday morning she would still try to convince him that he should go with her and the boys. "You're stubborn as a mule!" she would say, when he wouldn't budge. "Stay home! I don't care! God doesn't want heathens in His house anyway." But when Christmas and Easter came around, he knew he'd really be in hot water with his wife if he didn't go to church on those days. He'd act like he was making a huge sacrifice, but Crocifessa paid him no mind. She would be thankful for those two days, and for the rest of the year she would simply pray for his very stubborn soul.

Most Sunday afternoons Peter would go down the street and play bocchi with some of the men in the neighborhood. He loved taking Carmello and Angelo with him, and teaching them the secrets of being a good bocchi player. Peter had a good sense of humor and was well liked in the neighborhood. Later, when the sun went down, he'd go home and Crocifessa would make him something to eat again. He had the appetite of a huge man, yet he never gained an ounce. He'd relax with her and the boys and listen to the Italian radio station. He'd go to bed around nine o'clock in the evening and Monday morning he'd start his workweek again. He was making descent money, and Crocifessa was seeing to it that some of it was being saved every week. She didn't believe in putting money in banks, so she hid it in different places throughout the apartment. She would sew a few dollars into the hem of draperies and a few more would go down deep in the sugar or flour canister. Crocifessa's favorite hiding place for money was in a sock hanging between the leaves of the kitchen table. A long tablecloth was always in place, so "if robbers break in, they'll never notice it." She was a shrewd and faithful saver, and even Peter didn't know of all her little caches. Many times he thought back to that day in Riesi, when he was courting her, and she had spoken up to the shopkeeper at the market. He would smile and think, *"I made the right move, marrying this one."* Life was good, and things were definitely getting better. Boston wasn't a bad place to live at all. Carmello and Angelo were both doing well in school and making new friends. Little Crocifessa was a happy, pleasant child. She was enjoying having her mother all to herself during the hours her brothers were in school.

It was a bitter cold winter that year, and little Crocifessa had developed a bad cold with a hacking cough, and she started running a fever. When all the home remedies failed and the fever grew worse, Peter and Crocifessa bundled her up in blankets and took her to Boston City Hospital. "Pneumonia!" the doctor said.

The doctors and nurses did everything they could for little Crocifessa, but each day she kept getting worse. After five days in the hospital, sweet little Crocifessa lost her battle with Pneumonia. Crocifessa, Sr. cried hysterically. She was confused and frustrated. She couldn't communicate with the doctors. She wanted to know why her little girl died. She wanted to know if she could have done something to prevent her death. But the doctors who spoke to her and Peter didn't speak Italian. Peter tried hard to speak to the doctor, but the little broken English he knew was so limiting that he couldn't get the information he and his wife so desperately needed. He wished they had brought Carmello with them, as he understood English pretty well. 'Pneumonia!' He understood *that* word, and tried to make Crocifessa understand. She didn't.... she couldn't. Little Crocifessa was not quite three and a half years old.

The sadness was great in their little home on Salem Street. The boys were heartbroken and Crocifessa was devastated. She felt that this would never have happened to her little girl if only they had remained in Sicily. Peter did his best to comfort her, but for a long time she was inconsolable. Giuseppe and Maria spent a lot of time with her, and neighbors came and brought food and kindness, but a part of her died along with little Crocifessa. Peter knew it would take a long time before she would be herself again, *"if she will ever be herself again,"* he thought. He would be patient; he would try to be sensitive. Peter was suffering a lot; he missed his sweet little daughter. He wasn't one to show his feelings, and he wouldn't burden his wife with his pain. He took lots of walks around the block alone; it was his way.

Peter kept wondering if Crocifessa was right; maybe if they had remained in Sicily this never would have happened. He knew he couldn't think that way though; there was nothing they could have done to save their little girl's life. For his wife's sake he had to be strong... but he felt so very sad. He would do everything in his power to get his family through this terrible tragedy. Somehow deep down inside, he knew in time, life would be good again in America.... it just had to be.

*****

On January 18, 1919, when Angelo was nine and a half years old, like most children, he was in school doing his lessons, when all of a sudden an explosion rocked his school. Everyone screamed, thinking it was the school that had exploded. Teachers were trying to calm the children while they waited to hear what had happened. As it turned out, it wasn't the school at all. It was the Purity Distilling Company; the huge molasses tank had exploded. The children were dismissed from school and told to go straight home. *"Oh, Wow!* Angelo thought, *"I've got to see this."*

On his way over to North End Park, where he'd be able to see what had happened, the stench hit him like a sledgehammer. At about the same moment, he spotted his brother running full speed *away* from North End Park, along with lots of other people. "Mello! Mello! What's happening?" he cried. "Angelo, run! Run!" Mello yelled. "Why? What's going on?" "Don't ask questions," his brother yelled, "just run!" People were screaming and running. Firemen and police were yelling to the people to get off the streets. "Go to your homes... NOW!" Angelo started running and his brother slowed down until he caught up to him. "This is really exciting, Mello, huh!" Angelo said. "Nothing like this ever happened around here before." "Yeah!" Carmello cried. "It'll be even more exciting if that hot molasses catches up with us." Angelo looked back, and for the rest of his life he never forgot what he saw. A 'river' of molasses, about three feet deep, was making its way toward them. They quickened their pace.

Angelo and his brother arrived home just as their father was getting there. "Pa! Isn't this exciting?" Angelo said. "Oh, it's exciting all right, Son, but it's not good. This is a terrible thing that's happened and people could die. We'll know more about it tomorrow." The smell of molasses was overpowering as they walked up the stairs. "Oh, thank God you're home, all of you! I've been worried sick!" Said Crocifessa. "Come in! Come in! The police have been up and down the streets telling people to get to their homes and stay off the streets. Lord, I hope no one gets hurt. Well, take your coats off and come into the kitchen. I have chicken soup on the stove; it'll warm you up." "I don't think I can eat a bite," Peter said, "with that awful, burning smell of molasses in my nose; and believe me, not a one of us will get a wink of sleep tonight either." Peter ate two bowls of soup and a large chunk of bread, followed by two cups of coffee and a handful of almond cookies. After supper he fell sound asleep in his chair reading the newspaper. When Crocifessa woke him and told him to go to bed, he said, "Well, all right, but, what's the sense? Who can sleep tonight?"

All night long they heard the firemen and police working down near the distilling company. The cold temperature didn't make their work any easier. The U.S. Army sent soldiers to help, and the Red Cross volunteers worked through the night and for many weeks to come.

The stench of molasses kept Crocifessa, Carmello and Angelo awake most of the night. Peter's snoring didn't help either.

The next day the headline of the Boston Globe read: "MOLASSES TANK EXPLOSION INJURES 50 AND KILLS 10." Many wood buildings were demolished and cars and wagons were destroyed. Horses, dogs and cats were found dead, either crushed to death, or drowned in the thick molasses. The devastation was overwhelming.

The smell of molasses stayed in the air for many years; it was something Angelo would never forget. Whenever the Molasses Tank Explosion was mentioned, even thirty and forty years later, Angelo loved to tell the story about "the time he and his brother were nearly buried alive in hot molasses."

*****

When Carmello was almost eighteen years old, he was riding in a car one evening with some friends. They were driving too fast, and they collided with another car. No one was badly hurt except Carmello who had a sharp piece of metal protruding from him, and was bleeding badly. He was rushed to Boston City Hospital, and after close examination and X-rays taken, it was found that the metal piece had pierced his kidney. Further X-rays showed that it had also punctured his liver. The doctor-on-call that evening told Crocifessa and Peter that Carmello's condition was critical, and that they should prepare themselves for the worst. He said, "An operation won't help much, and it would be very expensive; he'd probably die on the operating table." Crocifessa was beside herself with grief. "I'm very sorry," the doctor said," but with or without the surgery, chances are, he's not going to make it." A nurse had heard that a famous Italian surgeon, Dr. Biondi, who dealt with these problems, was visiting Boston hospitals at the time. Crocifessa had heard of him when they were still in Sicily. He was from Naples and his fame had spread to Riesi. She was determined to seek him out and have him operate on Carmello. She was convinced that God had brought Dr. Biondi to America, and to Boston because of her son. The nurse at the hospital told Crocifessa which hospital this great surgeon would be visiting next. Crocifessa and Peter went to that hospital, and by some miracle they found him, and told him about Carmello's accident and his condition. He acted put out, like they were bothering him. Crocifessa had brought all the money she could lay her hands on; she took the "sock" money, and any other money she had hidden around the house. It amounted to almost two hundred dollars. She offered it to the doctor, and pleaded with him to come and operate on her son. Boston City Hospital was not next in his itinerary, and he was not one to change his plans, but Crocifessa begged and cried. She got down on her knees and sobbed, and promised him she would pray for good health and fortune for him for as long as she lived, if he would just come and help her son. He finally agreed to come to Boston City Hospital next, and see Carmello.

When Dr. Biondi came to the hospital, he examined Carmello and studied his X-rays. "I'm sorry," he said. "There's nothing can be done for him; he's going to die." He started to leave, and Peter said, "Wait! Aren't you even going to try?" "There's no sense in it," he said. "I'm pressed for time, and he's going to die anyway. Here is your money back; I'm afraid you'll need it for his funeral. I'm very sorry, but there's nothing I can do." Crocifessa became hysterical, almost screaming, and sobbing out of control, as he walked away from them, leaving them without hope, and with nowhere to turn.

The next day was the Catholic feast day of Our Lady of Sorrows, and in the North End, a parade was held in her honor. Crocifessa, heartbroken, and almost out of hope, fasted the entire day, and marched barefoot in the parade, begging the Lady to intercede to her Son, for Crocifessa's son. The parade wound its way through the streets of the North End, with Crocifessa and other women walking barefoot, offering this time as a sacrifice to God.

Women, more than men, did this, as they believed that Jesus' mother suffered for her Son, so she would understand their plight. It took the better part of the day, and Crocifessa was very tired when the parade ended. Her feet were sore, and cut in a few places, and bleeding a little. But Crocifessa believed that her sacrifice would touch the heart of God.

When Peter and Crocifessa and Angelo arrived at the hospital, Carmello was in a worse condition. Angelo broke down when he saw his older brother lying helpless in the bed. As they sat by his side, a doctor came in to examine him. "I'm glad you're here," he said. "I'm Dr. Christaldi; I've been taking care of Carmello, and I wanted to talk to you. I would like your permission to operate on your son." Angelo said, "What do you mean, doctor? I thought nothing could help him." Crocifessa kept pulling on Angelo's sleeve, "What is he saying?" "Doctor Christaldi, do you speak Italian?" Angelo asked. "No," he said, "My father was born in this country and my mother is Irish; I'm sorry." Angelo repeated in Italian what the doctor said. "Oh, Madre Deo," Crocifessa cried. "Can he help Carmello?" Peter was listening intently, and he understood. "Angelo, tell him that miserable big shot Dr. Biondi said that Carmello couldn't be helped." Angelo translated to the doctor what his father said. "I know, I know," he said. "But, I believe he might have been mistaken. I'm not saying I can save your son's life, but we'll never know if we don't take that chance. He's definitely going to die without surgery anyway. I'd like to at least try, if you will give your permission." Angelo translated and Peter said, "Si, si! He has no chance at all now; he's dying. Please, please try to save our son's life."

Carmello was operated on the following day, and the doctor had to remove his kidney; he repaired the liver as best he could. He told Crocifessa and Peter that they wouldn't know if he was going to make it for about three days. Crocifessa never put a piece of food in her mouth for the entire time; she drank water, that's all.

On the fourth day after the operation, Dr. Christaldi came into the room and told Crocifessa that he'd be trying to save *her* life if she didn't eat something right away. She said, "When I know my son is going to be all right, then I'll eat." Angelo translated. "Good!" the doctor said. "I'll see if the kitchen will send something up for you. Carmello has passed the crisis. We took some more X- rays this morning; his liver looks good, and he's healing beautifully. Mr. and Mrs. Vitello, your son is going to be fine. He'll be here for a while, though; I'm expecting that he'll be able to go home in about three weeks." "Gratsia, Deo! Gratsia!" Crocifessa cried over and over. She took the doctor's hand and kissed it three or four times. "Gratsia, Dottor, tanka you," she said, struggling with her English. Angelo was jumping up and down, laughing. "I knew he'd be all right!" he cried. "I just knew it!" Peter left the room, overcome by emotion. He walked around the hospital for a while. It was his way.

Three weeks later Carmello was home, recuperating rapidly, happy to be alive. Crocifessa believed without a doubt that the Lady had asked her Son to heal Carmello. She thanked Jesus every day for her son's life, and she prayed every day for good health and prosperity for that wonderful Dr. Christaldi, who had the kindness and the courage to take a chance.

*****

Mid-July, 1925 was, so far, a great year for young Ethel. She had good friends, was doing well in school and was about to turn eleven. Her life was happy; she enjoyed a close relationship with her parents, and adored her older brother, Ernie, who for the past two years was working as a copy boy for the Boston Globe newspaper. Her father was a kind man, deeply religious, with a very gentle spirit. Her mother was an outspoken, strong-minded woman with very little tolerance for foolishness or stupidity in anyone. Needless to say, she was the disciplinarian in the family, but she was also a good-hearted woman, who deeply loved her family. Ethel loved them both very much.

One evening, as she sat with her father in the living room, he read from the Bible to her. She had already memorized many passages in Scripture, and this evening he was helping her to memorize the twenty-third Psalm. "I'm very proud of you, Ethel," Harry said. "You're a good girl and very smart; I enjoy so much our time spent in the Word." "Me too, Daddy," she said. "Let's always read together." "I hope so, Honey," he said. "I hope so." Ethel felt a twinge of uneasiness, but she dismissed the feeling right away.

What her dad wasn't saying was that he knew he wasn't well, and when he began vomiting blood, Ethel's mom and Ernie rushed him to the hospital. The doctors ordered X-rays, blood tests, and many other tests. Ethel, Sr. was stunned by the results. "Lead Poisoning!" the doctor said. "He's a very sick man, Mrs. Dalton; he needs to be in a Tuberculosis sanitarium as soon as we can get him there." "This can't be!" she cried; "Why, my husband takes excellent care of himself, Doctor. He doesn't smoke or drink; he never has. How could he have gotten this?" He said, "Probably from so many years at the Foundry. It's unfortunate, but other men who have worked there have come down with the same illness. I'm really very sorry; I'll be glad to make all the arrangements to get your husband into the sanitarium for you if you wish." "I appreciate that, Doctor, but with Harry not able to work, we can't afford to keep him in a sanitarium." "I understand, Mrs. Dalton; then I'm afraid we'll have to get him into the Boston Hospital For Incurable Diseases." "Are you telling me that Harry will never get better?" Ethel asked. "It's hard to say," he said; "His X-rays show his lungs are in a real bad condition; we can only hope for the best. I'm afraid he'll be in the hospital along time, Mrs. Dalton. Go home now and try to get some rest. I'll take care of all the details." Ethel felt numb as she shook the doctor's hand and said good-bye.

Ernie noticed his mother trembling as they were leaving the hospital. "Don't worry, Mom, Dad will get better." Ernie said, "And in the meantime I'll be able to help you with the household expenses; we'll manage somehow." "I know you mean that, Ernie, but you don't make enough to support the three of us. I don't want *you* to worry either, Son. But, you're absolutely right, we *will* manage; we'll figure something out."

Young Ethel was shocked at the news. "A long time? How long, Mom?" "I don't know, Honey. We'll just take one day at a time, and pray; that's what Dad would want us to do. One thing you need to understand is that I'm going to have to go to work. I know I can get work as a mid-wife, but it will mean that I won't be home for two or three weeks at a time. It's not going to be easy for any of us, Ethel, and...well... I'm afraid I'm going to have to look into boarding schools for you." "Boarding school? You mean we won't be living together anymore?" Ethel cried. "Oh, Mom, when will I see you? When will I see Dad?" "Honey, I'll come and visit you when I'm between jobs," her mother said, "and Ernie will visit you and take you out on weekends whenever he can. I'll try very hard to work my jobs around your school vacations and holidays, and we'll visit Dad whenever possible. If we all pull together, we'll be fine; we need to be strong." "But, I'm scared, Mama," Ethel cried. "Please don't send me away to boarding school; I want to stay with you." "I know, Dear, it's not what I want either," her mom said. " But what we want is not what's important now; it's what we have to do to get through this. Life isn't always sweet like peaches and cream, Ethel; sometimes it's sour like lemons. But when it's sour like lemons, we add a little sugar, and do the best we can. We must be strong, Dear; what do you think your father would say to us?" "He'd tell us to trust God, and not to worry," said Ethel, tearfully. "Exactly!" her mother said. "And that's just what we'll do; we'll add a little sugar to the lemons, and trust God for the rest."

****

Angelo, Crocifessa and Carmello 1923

Pietro Vitello age 60

CHAPTER TWO
The Face of an Angel

Ingleside was situated on a little hill between East Boston and Revere, and had an excellent reputation. *"It looks like the boarding school where "Jane Eyre" lived,"* Ethel thought. *"Oh, God, please don't let my life be like Jane's."*

"I think you'll like it here, Ethel," said Miss Forbes, Head Mistress at Ingleside. She was very stern looking. Young Ethel was certain she was glaring at her as she said, "You obey the rules and you'll get along just fine." *"Oh, God, this is like Jane's boarding school."* " Come along now; say goodbye to your mother and brother." Ethel clung to her mother and Ernie until she knew she had to let them go. "You'll be okay, Sis," Ernie said. I'll be back next weekend to take you out; we'll do something fun." Ethel, Sr. was strong, but this was breaking her heart. She had just lost her husband, and in this moment she felt like she was losing her daughter, too. "All right, now," Miss Forbes said, "bring your things and I'll show you to your room and introduce you to your roommates. You'll be in a room with three other girls. It's Saturday, so they won't be in class."

Agnes, Ruth and Mary seemed like nice girls. They helped her unpack and get settled. The room was very large and in each corner there was a single bed, a night table, a small bureau and a small desk. "You've got the best corner," Mary said. "You've got the window right over your desk." It was a nice, bright room with white bedspreads and white curtains on the windows, and small floral rugs beside each bed. Each night table had a small lamp on it and each desk had a desk lamp. There were hooks and hangers for dresses and coats. It didn't look as bad as she thought it would. *"It's very clean"* she thought, *"It's almost attractive."*

Ethel was a shy girl, and didn't make friends easily, although her roommates were very friendly. She missed her father and mother and her brother. She didn't want to be anywhere but where they were. She didn't want to sleep in a room with three strangers, and she certainly didn't want to go to school and not go home afterward. Her mother was right; it wouldn't be easy. She could almost hear her father's voice, saying, "You're a good girl, Ethel; I'm very proud of you." *"I can do this, Dad,"* she thought. *"I can do this for you."*

*****

At fourteen Angelo quit school, with his parents' permission. Times were tough and they needed the money. After all, most kids he knew quit school before they were fourteen to go to work. "For pete's sake, why would anyone need more than eight years of school?" He got a job at the Commonwealth Thread Company in South Boston as a stock boy where Carmello used to work. He liked working more than going to school, and he felt like he was helping out. Carmello had been out of school for over five years and now worked as an apprentice in a barbershop. He hoped to own his own shop one day.

Work was slow for Peter at that time, so he welcomed the extra salaries coming into the house, and of course, Crocifessa put every spare penny in the sock between the leaves of the kitchen table.

At fifteen Angelo got a job working as a press feeder for Snowhill Press on Hanover Street in Boston. He worked there for two years. He left Snowhill to work for Lenox Press, which was located over Loews Theatre in Boston. He was only there about a year when they started laying off people; Angelo was one of them. He worked at a few odd jobs for a while but wasn't happy with any of them.

At eighteen Angelo decided to try his hand at boxing. Like his father, he was small, barely 5'4", and he learned at a very early age how to take care of himself. He had been in a few fights, and his friends thought he'd be a terrific boxer, so he joined a boxing gym and gave it a go. He was strong, well built and agile, and he won many of his sparring matches, but a barrage of blows to his handsome face soon made him decide that professional boxing was not for him.

Carmello, who now preferred to be called Charlie, finally got his own barbershop, located on Henley Street in Charlestown. Crocifessa gave him the "sock" money to help him get started. He was becoming known in the area and gaining new customers rapidly. He was content in his good fortune. Every now and then, (at his parents' insistence), Charlie would say to Angelo, "You should come and work with me, and learn the business." Angelo's response was always the same. "No thanks, Mello, that's one job I couldn't stand to do." "What do you have against barbering?" Charlie asked one day. "Shaving men's pimply faces, squeezing their blackheads when they want it done? I don't think so, Mello. If you can do it, you're a better man than I." "I can do it," Charlie said, "because it's a respectable line of work and it pays the bills. There are worse jobs you know; you shouldn't be so picky. "Yeah, yeah, I know," Andy said. "See ya later, Mello." "Okay Andy, take it easy. ....Oh, and call me Charlie, will ya?"

*****

Eventually Ethel came to love her time at Ingleside. She was a good student and did her lessons and her chores diligently. Her teachers liked her a lot and Agnes and Ruth became her good friends. She liked Mary too, but Mary always acted like she was a little better than they; there were times when she could be a little mean. She missed her parents and Ernie, but got to see them more often than she thought she would.

Ethel came to care a great deal for Miss Forbes, who turned out to be more than just Head Mistress; she was like a substitute mother. She was very kind to Ethel, especially when Harry's condition worsened. Ethel was so worried about her dad; the last time she saw him he looked real bad. "He's so thin!" she told Miss Forbes. A few months later Harry took a bad turn and went into a coma. Ernie picked her up and they went with their Mom, to see him. Young

Ethel cried all the way back to Ingleside. She prayed fervently that God would either heal her dad or take him home. A few days later Harry passed away peacefully, never gaining consciousness. He was buried in Salem, Massachusetts, where his family before him was buried. Ethel was fourteen years old, and she had lost her best friend.

In late July 1930 Ethel graduated from Ingleside with honors. It was a very special day; her mother and Ernie watched as she and fifteen other girls accepted their diplomas from Miss Forbes. She knew she would miss Miss Forbes a lot, but Ruth and Agnes promised to keep in touch with her. She and Ruth remained good friends for many years.

Ethel's mom was very proud of her. At sixteen Ethel was a lovely, intelligent girl. She looked forward to coming home to their new apartment on Bickford Street in Jamaica Plain. It would only be the two of them as Ernie had recently married Evelyn, an attractive girl of eighteen. He fell head over heels in love with her, and any faults she might have had, Ernie never noticed. He was deliriously happy, and loved his new position at the Globe. Ernie was now schoolboy sports (cub) reporter, covering all the high school games in and around Boston. He bought a second hand car, and felt like he was on top of the world.

Ethel and her mother struggled to make ends meet. Her mom took as many mid-wife jobs as she could get, but there was still very little money coming in. Ethel worked at a few odd jobs, hoping to find a better job all the while. Ernie helped out, but Evelyn had expensive tastes, so his salary didn't go as far as he would like.

One day Ethel asked her mother if she could invite her friend, Ruth Lovett over for lunch. They had very little food in the house at the time, and no money to buy more. But Ethel, Sr. said, "Sure, Honey, you invite Ruth for lunch; we'll manage." When Ruth came over that day, Ethel Sr. served poached egg on toast and tea for lunch. A few Saltine crackers with grape jelly on them became their dessert.

Ethel was very thankful for the nice lunch her mother set out. "Well, Ethel, Sr. said, "I'm glad you were pleased, dear. I hope it holds you 'til tomorrow, because that was tonight's supper. We have one piece of bread left for toast in the morning; we'll each have a half." Young Ethel laughed and said, "Oh, Mom, you're a doll; I'll be fine, but what about you?" "Me? Ha!" Ethel, Sr. said, "I can afford to go without a few meals. I'm too heavy as it is." "Mom," Ethel said, "I think you're perfect just the way you are." Her mother just grinned.

*****

In 1929 Peter and Crocifessa bought a three-family house at 952 Parker Street in Jamaica Plain. Peter's dream of owning his own home one day finally came true; no doubt because of all the money Crocifessa saved over the fifteen years they had been in America. They were very excited and couldn't wait to move into their new home. By that time Charlie had been married for a few years, and living nearby. He and his wife Margaret had a baby girl.

Charlie and Andy, (as Angelo now preferred to be called), hired a horse and wagon and made a couple of trips to the new house moving all their belongings. They moved into the first floor apartment, which was larger than any place they had lived before. On the first floor were the parlor, kitchen, dining room, two bedrooms and the bathroom; downstairs in the basement was another kitchen and dining room. Also downstairs was a large furnace and coal bin. It was Andy's job to make certain there was always plenty of coal in the furnace to keep all three apartments warm. "I hate shoveling coal into the furnace and emptying the ashes," Andy said, every time he did it. "It's such a filthy job; I wish Mello lived here, so we could *both* do the chores like we used to."

Peter and Crocifessa felt like rich landowners. The two other apartments upstairs were occupied by tenants, which helped pay the mortgage. The fact that the bank held a mortgage on Crocifessa's home was always a thorn in her side. She wanted to pay it up as soon as possible. She never did like banks; simply considered them a necessary evil. She was sure they were going to cheat her and Peter out of their money and their home. She continued to hide their money in the drapery hems and in the sock, which now hung between the leaves of the dining room table.

Andy decided to take his brother up on his offer to teach him the barbering business since there were no jobs around that he was interested in, or would pay a decent salary. He went to work with Charlie and became an excellent barber, all the while hating the work; but the tips made up for it, and the customers liked him a lot. Business was good and getting better all the time, although he and Charlie didn't always see eye to eye. They loved each other, and in many ways were real close, but there was always that little bit of animosity right there under the surface, ready to break out in an argument at the drop of a hat. They were quite different in many ways, always seeming to be in competition with each other. But at work Andy knew that Charlie was the boss, and he was grateful for his job and his week's pay.

Andy was always proud of his Sicilian heritage, but people like Al Capone, and so many other Mafia gangsters gave Sicilians a bad name. One day he was shaving a man who talked incessantly about the Mafia, and Sicilians in general. Andy became more and more aggravated as the man said that all Sicilians were 'cutthroats'. When he made the remark, "There isn't a Sicilian alive who wouldn't cut open your belly if he thought you swallowed a nickel," Andy held the straight razor against the man's throat and said, "I'm a Sicilian! Tell me, have you swallowed any nickels lately?" The man was absolutely terrified. He jumped up out of the chair and ran out of the shop with soap still on his face. Charlie grabbed the cape off of him as he ran out the door, and yelled, "And don't come back!" Andy and Charlie laughed 'til their sides ached; so did the other customers in the shop. "Well," Charlie said, "We lost a customer today, but thankfully, we'll never see that ignorant son-of-a-b.... again. To tell you the truth Andy, I can't remember when I've had such a good laugh." Every time they thought about it that day, they burst out laughing.

*****

Andy was walking up Bickford Street on his way home from work one day, when he noticed a very pretty girl sitting on her front stairs reading a magazine. *"She has the face of an angel,"* he said to himself. He stopped to talk with her and asked her what her name was. She said, "Ethel." "I'm Andy," he said. He noticed she was very shy, so he did most of the talking. She listened. When he was leaving he said, "Well, so long, Ethel; maybe I'll see you again some time." "It was nice talking to you, Andy," she said softly, as she lowered her eyes. *"She is so sweet,"* he thought. *"I'd really like to get to know her better."*

Each day, as Andy walked home along Bickford Street, he hoped that the 'angel' would be sitting out on her front steps. When she was they would chat. On weekends Andy would walk by with his little two-year-old niece, and just as he expected, Ethel was very taken with her. One day he asked Ethel if she would like to go to a movie some evening. "I would like that," she answered, "but I need to ask my mother." He wondered what his own mother would say about him going out with a girl who was not Sicilian…not even Italian.

"She's a nice girl, ah?" Crocifessa said. "Oh, yes, Mama, she's a real nice girl." "She's a Sicilian girl, ah?" "No, Ma, she's not Sicilian." "Ah, well, that's okay; she *is* Italian?" "Um, no… she's not Italian," Andy said. "What's the matter with you?" his mother cried. "Why can't you find a nice Italian girl like your brother did?"

Charlie had married Margaret, a fine Italian girl; not Sicilian, but what the heck, "Italian was better than Irish," as Crocifessa would say. It wasn't that she hated Irish people, or anyone else, for that matter. It was just that "Italians were so much nicer than other people." Of course, if anyone mentioned the Mafia, she would say, "Ha! They'll all burn in Hell! They're not true Sicilians, not even true Italians!" Charlie and Margaret were expecting their second child, and, of course, Crocifessa and Peter were thrilled.

"I like this girl, Mama," Andy persisted, "and I think you'll like her too, if you just give her a chance. She's very sweet, and she has the face of an angel." Finally Peter spoke up. "An angel, huh? Fiessa, this is America, and I'm sure there are just as many fine American girls as there are Italian girls for Angelo to choose from. I would prefer he go out with Italian girls, too, but he likes this girl, and she has the face of an angel." He smirked a little and continued. "I think we should trust his judgment, then we'll decide if he should date her or not. What do you think?" "Well, maybe," she said, "At least she's Catholic." Andy thought, *"Oh, well… Tomorrow's another day."*

*****

"What? You want to go out with an Italian?" cried Ethel's Mom. "Are you out of your mind? Don't you know that all Italian men beat their wives?" "Oh, Mom, where did hear that?" said Ethel. "That can't be true." "Of course it's true; why, everyone knows that. Ernie, talk some sense into your sister, will you?" "Where did you meet him, Sis?" Ernie asked. "Right out front," Ethel said. " He walks by every day on his way home. We've talked many times; he's really very nice." "Does he work?" "Oh, yes, Ernie, he's a barber," she answered. "A barber?" Ernie asked. "He must be a lot older than you." "Just a few years." said Ethel. She was feeling a little guilty because she had told Andy she was eighteen. She was almost seventeen, but she knew he wouldn't ask her out if he knew she was still only sixteen. She also knew her mother and Ernie wouldn't like her going out with a twenty one year old man. She felt right about going out with him, though; somehow, she knew it was a good thing. But she hated dishonesty, and knew she would have to tell Andy the truth. *" I'll tell him after our date Saturday night,"* she thought.

"You're young and inexperienced, Sis," Ernie continued. " You need to be very careful who you go out with; we just don't want to see you get hurt." "I heard that Italian men have horrible tempers," said Evelyn. "I don't know," Ernie said. "I work with two Italian men at the Paper, they seem okay. Ethel, do you really feel that he's a good man? I mean, one who can be trusted?" "Yes, Ernie, I do; I wouldn't consider going out with him if I didn't." "Okay! Ethel's not stupid, Mom." Ernie said. "I think we should give this *Andy* a chance. Who knows? He may turn out to be a really great guy. I don't think we should judge him before we've even met him. I mean, it's not like he's a Sicilian.... He isn't, is he Ethel?...Ethel?" *"Oh, God,"* Ethel thought...."*HELP!*"

*****

On Saturday evening Andy came to Ethel's house scrubbed, polished and wearing his best suit, his *only* suit, actually. He was nervous about meeting her mother and older brother, but he made a real good showing. Ernie was very impressed with Andy; he thought he was a real gentleman. But nothing was going to impress his mom. Andy was Italian, and that meant trouble, as far as she was concerned.

Andy and Ethel went to the Madison Theatre on Centre St. and saw "The Blue Angel", starring Marlene Dietrich and Emil Jannings. Andy bought popcorn and Cokes, and Ethel thought he was very charming. After the movie they stopped into the Busy Bee Spa, a little soda shop and variety store. They sat down at a booth and had a coke together. "I've really enjoyed this evening, Ethel," Andy said. "Do you think we can do this again soon?" "I've had a real nice time, Andy," she said. "It would be nice to go out with you again." "Great!" he said, "How about next Saturday night?" "Okay," Ethel said, "as long as it's alright with my mother and Ernie." Andy took Ethel home and said "good night" at her door. Oh, how he wanted to kiss her goodnight, but he wouldn't dare. *"She's so sweet,"* he thought, *"She might be offended if I try to kiss her on the first date."*

Ethel did tell Andy her age after their second date, but by this time Andy was crazy about her. She was very mature for her age and Andy felt strongly that there was something very special about their relationship.

Andy kissed Ethel on their third date. They were walking along Storrow Drive and sat down on a bench. There was no one else around. The moment was just right, and Andy knew it. He took her in his arms and kissed her softly on her lips. "I hope you didn't mind that," he said. Shyly, she answered, "No, Andy, I didn't mind at all." Ethel was sweet and innocent, and Andy swore to himself that he would never do anything to change that.

Andy and Ethel fell deeply in love very quickly. They dated only each other, and became engaged two years later. Andy bought Ethel a beautiful diamond engagement ring. Because of the Depression they waited another three years before they could see their way clear to get married. Ethel was working at the RussCraft Greeting Card Company, and living with her mom on Bickford Street, while Andy was working at the barbershop with Charlie, and living one street over on Parker Street with his parents. He and Ethel loved every moment they spent together, no matter where they were or what they were doing. They would go to the movies once a week, visit family, and now and then baby-sit so Margaret and Charlie could have a night out. Occasionally they'd get together with Sarah Butera and Pat (Pasquale) Provenzano. Sarah was a third or fourth cousin to Andy, and besides Margaret, she became Ethel's dearest friend. Pat and Sarah dated now and then, but made the decision to keep their relationship on a strictly friendship basis, although they loved each other dearly. Pat's mother was not a well woman, and since his father was deceased, and Pat was the only one left at home, he was her sole caregiver.

*****

In time, Crocifessa and Peter grew to love Ethel like she was their own daughter, despite the fact that she was '*Irish*', which, of course, she wasn't, but anyone who was not Italian was Irish to Peter and Crocifessa. Ethel learned to love them also. She decided that if she were ever going to be able to talk to them, she would have to learn Italian. She was working days at the card factory, so she signed up for a night course. Of course, it was pure Roman Italian that was taught, so she had some problems with the Sicilian dialect. They all had a few good laughs, when she would say something like, "Mi piaggia mangia fenestra," which, roughly translated meant, "I like to eat the window." She was a real good sport, and although embarrassed, she would laugh along with them when they told her what she had said. Ethel was a quick learner though, and soon she was speaking Sicilian like one of the family, although "with an *Irish* accent," as Crocifessa would say. She and Peter were very pleased that it meant so much to their future daughter-in-law to be able to speak their language. Of course, Andy was proud as a peacock.

Ethel's mom began to feel that Andy was probably a good man, and most likely would not beat her daughter. She learned to care for him in her own way but he was a Sicilian, so she was going to keep her eye on him. Ernie grew fond of Andy and enjoyed it when he was around. Andy liked Ernie and admired him a lot. He would read Ernie's article in the sports section of the Globe. He had never known a newspaper reporter, and it never failed to impress him every time he saw the name Ernest Dalton in print.

Ethel went to church every Sunday with Andy and his parents; her mother was not a religious woman, so she didn't mind at all. One day Andy said, "Ethel, my parents are giving me a hard time about the fact that you're not Catholic. You must know that they expect us to be married in the Catholic Church and to raise our children as Catholics." Ethel paused for a moment, and then said, "I've been doing a lot of thinking about that, Andy. Your church is the only church I go to, so I've decided to convert to Catholicism. I don't want anything to be different with us." "What?" Andy nearly screamed. He did not expect that response from her. Ethel smiled at his stunned reaction. "Will you come with me to speak to the priest about it?" "Will I? Yes! Yes! Of course!" Andy cried, " Oh, Ethel, you have just made everything perfect. I'm so happy, and you know my parents will be also." Crocifessa was ecstatic.

When the third floor tenants announced they were moving, Peter offered Charlie and Margaret the apartment. They were thrilled. "This way Margaret, we'll be able to save some money," Charlie said, " to buy our own home one day." Crocifessa wanted to keep her family together; she felt that with a three-family house, it could be done. It was what she and Peter wanted, and it would be a good start in life for Charlie and Andy and their wives.

Ethel and Andy were married on June 16, 1935 at Blessed Sacrament Church on Centre Street in Jamaica Plain. Margaret was Ethel's Maid-of-Honor. Her bridesmaids were Evelyn, Sarah, and Andy's cousin, Fanny Voltero. Charlie was his brother's best man; his cousin Carl Vitello and two friends served as ushers. The women wore long soft pink gowns and the men wore dark formal tuxedos. Everything was perfect until the Pastor laid down a few rules.........

For reasons no one could understand, the Pastor didn't seem to care much for Andy and Ethel. Andy thought that perhaps he didn't like Sicilians. Ethel thought maybe he didn't care for Baptists who became Catholic. He was a hard man and succeeded in making many things difficult for them. For instance, he wouldn't allow them to be married inside the altar; he refused to let them put a white runner down the aisle for the bride to walk on, and he wouldn't allow the organ to be played, so they had no music. Ethel walked down the long aisle of the church to meet her husband-to-be with no music playing...no "Here Comes the Bride"...nothing.

Ethel was not one to be shaken by the minor things in life. She had loved Andy from the moment he first spoke to her five years ago. She was not about to let anything or anyone ruin her wedding. She was nervous, but she walked slowly down the aisle, holding onto her brother Ernie's arm. As she came closer to Andy, she looked up and smiled at him. She took his breath away. *"She's the most beautiful creature I've ever seen,"* he thought. *"She really is an angel."* He was so filled up with happiness he thought he would burst. Tears came to his eyes as he thought, *" Thank you, Lord, for making someone so wonderful love me."* Ethel was thinking the same thing about Andy.

After the ceremony, Peter and Crocifessa had a simple reception planned at a hall nearby. There wasn't much money for extra things, but they had a caterer bring in some bottles of wine, some nice sandwiches and fancy cookies, and soft drinks and coffee. Ethel's mom couldn't afford to do much, but she had the wedding cake made.

The caterer had brought the food to the hall while the ceremony was going on. After he left, before the bridal party and the guests arrived, some people from the neighborhood, poor and hungry, came in and ate every sandwich and every cookie. The times were tougher on some than on others. Thankfully, they never touched the wedding cake. The wine, which was in the basement to stay cool was untouched also. Peter and Crocifessa were furious; Ethel, Sr. felt heartsick for her daughter. But nothing bothered Andy and Ethel that day. After five years of dating, their dream of being married to each other was now a reality. They were in their own little world, and to them everything was perfect.

The wedding guests enjoyed the wine, and the cake and coffee, and danced to the piano and accordion music. Andy and Ethel Vitello danced their first dance as husband and wife to the song, "I Love You Truly." It remained *their* song for the rest of their lives.

At one point during the reception, Ernie overheard his aunt say to his mom, "Well, Ethel, these Italians certainly do love their wine, don't they?" His mother heartily agreed, saying, "Mmm, they certainly do." Ernie just shook his head; then walked away chuckling, drinking a tall glass of wine.

Despite all the different problems they had with the wedding, and even the lack of food at the reception, it all turned out beautifully, and everyone had a real good time. Of course the wine probably *did* help.

Andy and Ethel went to New York on their honeymoon, paid for by Ernie. It was his wedding gift to them. They stayed at the Times Square Hotel. Neither of them had ever been far from home, so this was a great adventure for them. They were very moved at the sight of the Statue of Liberty. "I remember my parents crying when they first saw the Statue of Liberty," Andy said. "I think, after such a long trip, seeing it meant that we had finally arrived, and they were grateful the trip was over." "Do you remember Sicily at all?" Ethel asked. "Not very much," he said. "I was very young when we came here,".

They went to Ellis Island, and Andy tried to describe to Ethel what it was like when he and his family landed there twenty-one years earlier. "It must have been frightening, coming to a new country, not speaking the language," Ethel said. "I guess I was too young to understand what my parents were feeling," said Andy. "I remember my mother was scared to death, but it was fun and exciting for me and Charlie. Uncle Joe was there to meet us. Boy, was he a sight for sore eyes." "Why does your father call your uncle Joe, Giuseppe?" Ethel asked. "Because that's his real name," Andy said. "Giuseppe means Joseph in Italian." "Oh, I see," she said, "What's Mary's real name?" "It's Maria; not much different in English." "Your mother's name means crucifix, right?" Ethel asked. "Yeah, pretty awful, huh?" "Well, it's not a happy name," she said. "It's kind of sad." "I never really thought much about it, but you're right, it *is* a sad name." "Oh well," she said, "Angelo means angel; that's kind of nice." "Yeah, too bad the man doesn't fit the name, huh?" He grinned as he bent her backwards and kissed her neck. "Andy! Stop! People might see you!" He just laughed.

"You lived in a two-room, cold-water flat here in the city, didn't you?" Ethel asked. "Yeah, but I don't remember much about it, except the beds were loaded with bedbugs." "Oh, yuk!" cried Ethel. "That must have been awful." "Yeah, it was pretty bad," Andy said. "We were all in the same room. Charlie and I slept in a twin bed, Ma and Pa in another bed, and my little sister in a crib. I just remember scratching all over; Charlie was doing the same. Pa said there were cockroaches in the kitchen, too; I never saw them, though." "It must have been so crowded, all in the same room" said Ethel. "It was; I used to have to climb over Charlie to get out of bed, then squeeze between the crib and my parents' bed. We had to take down the door, and Ma put up a curtain because we couldn't open or close the door once all the beds were in there. I was just a kid; none of it bothered me, except the bugs, but it must have been torture for Ma. She cried a lot; I remember that. She really wanted to go back to Sicily, especially later, when we moved to Boston and my little sister died." "Oh Andy, I hope we never have to go through any of the heartaches our parents went through; I don't know how they ever endured such suffering." "I know Hon," he said. "But things are so much better today; we'll be fine. We're going to have a real good life, Ethel. I just know we are."

Ethel and Andy were enjoying their time in New York. They went to the Empire State Building. "Unbelievable!" was all Andy could say. "How did they ever build something so tall?" Ethel asked. They were simply in awe of everything. They had lunch at the famous Automat, and ate at some very nice restaurants. They went to a couple of shows, and Ethel was feeling all the while like they shouldn't be spending so much money. "It will be a long time before we do anything like this again," Andy said. "Besides, Ernie paid for the train fare and the hotel for the week. "We're going to live it up while we're here."

Each day was more wonderful than the last, and they hated to see it end. Ethel sent postcards to their families and close friends. They bought souvenirs for their parents, and Margaret and Charlie, Ernie and Evelyn (a little something special for Ernie), and Sarah and Pat. "Are you happy Hon?" Andy asked one afternoon, as they strolled through Central Park, eating peanuts and feeding the birds. "Oh, very happy Andy," Ethel said. He looked around, then took her in his arms and kissed her. "Ethel, You're the best thing that's ever happened to me; I love you more than life itself."

The highlight of their trip was Coney Island. They had so much fun going on all the rides and eating hot dogs and ice cream. They had their picture taken sitting on a half-moon. The photographer said, "All the honeymooners who come to Coney Island have their picture taken on the "honey-moon." Ethel thought, *"I'll cherish this picture all my life."*

Andy and Ethel spent a whole week in New York, and then took the train back to Boston. Ernie picked them up at South Station and drove them home; he was the only one they knew who could afford a car. Home, by the way, was the second floor at 952 Parker Street. Peter knew of an apartment for rent further down Parker St., so he told his tenants that he would like very much for Andy and Ethel to take it, but, if *they* were interested in it, it would be a little cheaper rent than they were paying him, and Andy and Ethel could move into their apartment. They jumped at the opportunity to pay a little less rent. Everyone was hurting because of the Depression. They went to speak to the owners of the house, took the apartment and moved into it three days later. They were very pleased. Needless to say, Peter and Crocifessa were thrilled. Family came first with them, and now all three apartments would be filled with their family. "That's the way it should be," said Crocifessa. She was very happy her family was all together. So were Ethel and Andy, and Margaret and Charlie.

Andy and Ethel loved their four-room apartment. The kitchen was huge, with built in cabinets and an icebox built into the wall. Off the kitchen was their bedroom, and off the parlor was a small room that they hoped would be a baby's room one day. The bathroom, which was tiny, contained a toilet and a tub, and was situated between the kitchen and the parlor. One could barely turn around in it. A door in their bedroom opened out to the back hall and led down to the backyard. Ethel happily made their apartment cozy and attractive.

****

**Andy and Ethel at Coney Island on their honeymoon,
June 1935**

CHAPTER THREE
What's In A Name?

It was 1937 and the house on Parker Street was buzzing with activity. Ethel was pregnant and Andy was ecstatic! Charlie and Margaret had three children, and Margaret was expecting their fourth. Ethel and Margaret had become very close friends; they were a great help to each other, and Crocifessa and Peter were happily looking forward to more grandchildren.

Margaret and Charlie's first child was a daughter, whom Crocifessa and Peter had said should be named after the father's mother. That was tradition, they said, in Italian families. Margaret and Charlie couldn't imagine naming their American-born child Crocifessa, so somehow they convinced his parents that in this country, 'Fiessa' means 'Frances'. It wasn't true, of course, but they felt this little deception was absolutely necessary. So, their first child was christened Frances, and everyone was happy, especially Ethel, who didn't have a drop of Italian blood in her. Many times over the next few months she thought, *"Thank God for Margaret and Charlie. Frances wouldn't be my first choice for a name, but if Andy and I have a little girl, I'll be happy to name her Frances, considering the alternative."*

Charlie and Margaret's second child was a boy and they named him Peter, after his grand- father. Their third child was also a boy and they named him Charles, Jr. Charlie said to Andy one day, "I love my family, but where the hell am I going to put four kids?" Andy said, "Well now, let me think… there's always the bathtub,

Mello." "Hey, now there's a thought," Charlie said. "Maybe I should be sleeping there." They both laughed.

Life was good and getting better all the time. Crocifessa and Peter were thoroughly enjoying grandparenthood.

*****

Ethel's mom was now living in Medford with Ernie. As it turns out, Ernie and Evelyn divorced due to reasons Ernie could not believe or face until he had to. He was very depressed; he couldn't sleep and hardly ate, and his job had suffered for a while. But, Ernie Dalton had been with the Boston Globe for many years and they valued him highly. They were willing to wait it out with him, and eventually he got back on his feet and buried himself in his work, which he loved. Ernie and Evelyn never had children, much to his regret; but he looked forward to his sister making him an uncle in a few months.

A blood test showed that Ethel's blood type was RH negative, and Andy's was B positive. The doctor said, "It's nothing for you to worry about, but when the baby's being born, there could be a problem." "A problem? What kind of problem?" Ethel asked. "Now, you don't need to be nervous about this," the doctor said. "If there *is* a problem, the procedure is to drain the baby's blood, while at the same time replacing it with fresh blood. Chances are, this won't happen, but if it does, we'll be prepared for it. "Don't be nervous?" Ethel said. "How do I do that?" "I really mean it, Ethel; you don't need to be concerned about it; it's not as uncommon as you might think. I'm telling you this now so that you won't be shocked when the time comes." Ethel could feel her heart pounding and the blood rushing to her head. *"Okay,"* she thought, *"The doctor's right; I can't do this to myself. I shouldn't worry over something that may not happen."* She remembered her father's favorite verses… Proverbs 3: 5, 6, *"Trust in the Lord with all your heart, and do not lean on your own understanding. In all your ways acknowledge Him and He will make your paths straight."* She decided to do what her dad always said to do… trust God for His protection. Andy tried hard not to show his fear over this. He was a passionate and emotional man, and he loved Ethel so much, that he feared for her a lot more than for the baby he didn't yet know.

One day Ethel said to Andy, "Honey, is it absolutely carved in stone that if we have a boy, we have to name him after your father?" "Oh! Oh!" Andy said, "What are you getting at?" "Well, I mean, Charlie and Margaret named their first son after him, so do you think he would be satisfied with that and not insist on us doing the same? I'm just asking, Dear, so please don't be upset." "I'm not upset, Honey," Andy said. "To be honest with you, I've been thinking a lot about that. I always thought if I ever had a son, I'd like to name him Joseph; I like the name a lot, and we both love St. Joseph." "I *love* the name Joseph," Ethel said. Oh, Andy, do you think we could? I mean, do you think your father will go along with it?" "I don't know Hon; I'm not sure how he'll take it, but, what the hell, all he can say is no.... very loudly. One of these days, I'll bring the subject up to Pa and see what happens. After all, like you said, Charlie did give him a namesake. Who knows, he just might go along with it." "Oh, thank you Andy, that's all I ask; and if he won't hear of it, then 'Peter' will be just fine." "Of course," Andy said, "if it's a girl, she's going to have to be named Frances; you do realize that, right? I might be able to get around Pa a bit.... but Ma? That's another story." "Oh, I've already accepted that, and it'll be fine," said Ethel. "'Course, two Frances Vitellos in one house could get mighty confusing. Oh, and Andy, could you *please* try to stop swearing before the baby comes?" "Yeah, I'll try," he mumbled.

*****

On April 27th, some time around eight o'clock in the morning, Ethel's labor started. Andy ran to Abie's variety store, which was a stone's throw away and used the public telephone to call the doctor. He said to get her to the hospital right away. He called a taxicab and ran home to help Ethel get ready. One hour later Ethel was in the labor room at St. Elizabeth Hospital in Brighton. The delivery room was ready for any problems that might occur. Andy was in the waiting room, pacing the floor and white as a sheet. He came close to tears many times in the ten hours he waited there. He wanted to hold his darling wife, and let her know that no matter what happened, he'd always be there for her. He prayed like he had never prayed before. Every once in a while, the doctor came out to let Andy know that, so far, everything was fine.

At a little after seven o'clock in the evening, Ethel delivered a perfect, healthy baby, and no problems during delivery. Ethel was fine, although exhausted. "You can go in to see her now, Andy," the doctor said. "Don't stay too long though; she needs her rest." Andy took off running. When he was half way down the corridor the doctor called out, "By the way, Andy, congratulations! It's a boy!" "Yahoo!" Andy shouted, "a boy!"

As Andy entered the room and saw Ethel laying there, his heart ached for her. She reached for him and he held her very gently. His eyes filled with tears, and he said, "I love you, Sweetheart, I love you so much. Are you in a lot of pain?" "Not too much," she said. "Have you seen the baby, Andy?" "No, not yet, I wanted to see you first." "It's a boy, Andy, and he's just perfect. I can't wait for you to see him. Go down to the nursery now Hon, before the nurse tells you that you have to leave. Take that card with you," she said, "the blue one on the table there; you'll need it to show to the nurse." "All right; don't go 'way!" he called, as he hurried out the door; I'll be right back." She smiled as she watched him go.

After he left, Ethel thought, *"Andy's going to be a wonderful father, I just know it."* She began thinking about her own dad. *"Oh, how I wish he was alive to see his beautiful grandson."* She remembered a scripture her Dad would say whenever someone had a new baby… Psalm 127: 3, *"Behold, children are a gift from the Lord; the fruit of the womb is a reward."* "Thank you, Lord," she whispered, "for your beautiful gift."

Andy walked down the corridor to the nursery. He held up the card that said, 'BABY BOY VITELLO'. The nurse went to one of the bassinets and picked up a baby wrapped in a blue blanket and walked to the window where Andy stood looking in. She smiled and opened the blanket so he could get a good look at the baby. He stood there staring at this beautiful little creature. Tears rolled down his cheeks unashamedly as the realization set in that this was his little boy, his very own son. He didn't think he could ever explain to anyone the joy he was feeling at that moment. "That's my son!" he mouthed to the nurse. She smiled again and nodded.

Andy used the public telephone in the hospital and called Abie at the store. Abie congratulated him and said, "Give my best to Ethel." He said he would go down and tell Peter and Crocifessa the good news. Andy thanked him and ran back to spend as much time as he could with Ethel. He knew a nurse would be in soon to tell him he had to leave.

Ethel smiled as Andy came back into the room. She knew the moment she looked at him that he had fallen in love with their new son. "He's beautiful!" Andy cried. "You sure make beautiful babies, Ethel." "No, *we* make beautiful babies; isn't he precious, Andy?" "He sure is, Hon; he's wonderful! By the way, have they told you how long you'll have to stay here?" "Well, Dr. Robinson thinks it will be around two weeks," she said. " I wish it could be sooner, Andy, but if I want to get better and be strong for you and the baby, I'd better take it nice and slow." "That's right, Hon; do whatever they tell you. Who knows? They just might let you come home sooner." "You should be okay Andy, with Ma and Margaret taking care of you." "Yeah, I'll be fine," he said.

Ethel was very weak and it was obvious that she was trying not to fall asleep, so Andy said, "I guess I should get going and let you get some rest. Besides, I'm sure the nurse is going to come any second and throw me out." "I am awfully tired, Andy." He kissed Ethel and said, "It's going to be awfully lonely at home, without my darling wife." "Lonely? You've got to be kidding," she said, forcing a tired laugh. "Ma and Pa are downstairs, Margaret and Charlie and the three kids are upstairs. I don't think you'll have time to be lonely, Hon." "Well," Andy said, "If you're not there, it's lonely."

Fridays were always busy at the barbershop; this day was especially so, as there were a lot of last minute drop-ins. It was about six-thirty and Andy hadn't eaten dinner yet. He had to wait a long time for the trolley and he was dragging. It felt good to finally sit and relax. His feet were killing him. He began thinking about his job and his future. He still hated barbering, although he never let his customers know that. Charlie was right though; it was a respectable job and it did pay the bills. Andy wanted more though; he wanted to be able to save some money so that one day he and Ethel could buy their own home and have a car, especially now that they had started a family.

The rhythm of the trolley was making him very sleepy; he could hardly keep his eyes open. *"I'd better concentrate on staying awake,"* he thought, *"or I'll miss my stop."* The conductor calling out "St. Elizabeth Hospital!" woke him with a start. *"Wow! I can't believe I fell asleep; I almost slept through my stop. Thank God that conductor has a loud voice,"* he thought. *"I'm not going to have much time to spend with Ethel as it is. Man, am I tired!"*

Andy was shocked as he walked into Ethel's room; she was listening to the radio and crying. "Oh, God, what's wrong?" He asked. He ran to her and held her close. She said, "Oh, Andy, listen." The announcer on the radio was saying, "Germany's great silver Hindenburg has exploded! The world's largest dirigible was ripped apart today by what is believed to have been a hydrogen gas leak as it was landing at the Lakehurst, New Jersey Landing Field. The American Zeppelin Company has placed the death toll to be at least thirty-four of the ninety-seven aboard, and many others were badly burned." "Oh no, that's awful!" Andy said. "Oh Andy, my heart aches for those poor people," said Ethel, "and for their families." She continued to weep softly, and finally said, "Andy, don't look at me, I look horrible. I'm feeling so weepy and emotional lately, and this Hindenburg explosion just tears me apart. I don't know what's wrong with me; it's not like I knew anyone on it. I'm just a big cry-baby lately." "There's nothing wrong with you, Hon," Andy said. "This is a horrible tragedy; I feel bad about it, too. And you don't look horrible to me, you still look beautiful." "Oh, sure!" was all she could manage to say when her eyes filled with tears again. "Have you forgotten what the doctor told you?" Andy continued. "He said this might happen. He said you might be feeling very emotional after the baby is born; that you might cry very easily." "I remember; I guess that's what this is then," she said. "But it's not like me to cry so easily. I'm really very happy, Andy; I'm feeling so much better, and the baby is just wonderful. I simply can't understand why I feel so sad; this is very strange." "I know, Hon, but it will pass, and you'll be back to your old self again." "I hope so," Ethel said, as she wiped another tear away…."I hate crying."

A few days later, Ethel was feeling much better, and was ready to leave the hospital. Ernie drove her and Andy and the baby home; everyone came out to greet them and to welcome Ethel and the new baby. Ethel put her little son in a bassinette in their bedroom and Crocifessa insisted she get right into bed. Crocifessa had made her 'famous' chicken soup and brought it upstairs to Ethel. "Nothing helps you feel better than a bowl of hot chicken soup," she said. "Mmm," Ethel said, as she put a spoonful into her mouth. "I love your chicken soup, Ma; it's absolutely delicious, and good for whatever ails you." "Buono! Mangia!" Crocifessa said. "Mmm," Ethel said again, as she took another spoonful. "Nothing like it! Gratsia, Ma." When the soup was gone Ethel slipped into a deep, contented sleep.

Crocifessa had more kindness and compassion than anyone Ethel had ever known. She cared about people, and didn't hesitate to ride the trolley, with a pan of chicken soup on her lap, to her sister-in-law, or some other relative who was sick and in need of some of her 'miracle chicken soup'. Many a sick neighbor also enjoyed her wonderful soup.

*****

Everyone was thrilled with the new baby, especially his cousin, Franny, who was now almost nine years old. She couldn't stop touching him and kissing him. She wanted to sit and rock him, which was fine with Ethel; her back was killing her from holding and nursing him.

Peter surprised Andy with his affection for his little grandson. He would hold him and kiss him on the head and sing to him. As Peter sat with the baby in his arms, Andy wondered how his father was taking the idea that they wanted the baby's name to be Joseph. Peter was hard to read; he didn't say much when Andy spoke to him about it. Andy wondered if his father was hurt or angry…."No," he thought, *"if he was angry, we'd know about it; that's one emotion he never hides. I just wish I knew what he was thinking. Maybe we should just forget about naming the baby Joseph. I mean, it's not all that important; Peter's a good name. I hope he's not upset; he's been so good to us, it's just not worth it."* Andy could hear his father singing softly to his little grandson.

Ernie came over again later in the afternoon and brought his mom to see her new little grandson. She stayed for a few days, and took care of her daughter and her little family. She wasn't about to let Crocifessa have all the fun.

Ethel Dalton was a very good woman, but she did have a critical nature, which drove Andy crazy at times. Sometimes it was all he could do to keep his mouth shut just to keep peace. But, for his wife's sake, he was respectful to his mother-in-law and he let a lot of things go by. But there were those other times when he just had to speak up, and of course, Ethel would be angry with him. But, it sure felt good to get a few things off his chest. It never changed anything, though; Andy and his mother-in-law were both stubborn, and they seemed to rub each other the wrong way more often than not. Yet, there was an underlying affection each felt for the other. Somehow, though, it seemed that neither of them would have been happy if they weren't at odds with each other once in a while. One thing they knew for certain… they had both met their match in the other.

Two weeks after Ethel and the baby came home from the hospital, Andy took his little son to Blessed Sacrament Church to have him baptized. Crocifessa and Peter went with him as they were to be the godparents; not that Andy and Ethel had much choice in the matter, as it was understood that the paternal grandparents, in Sicilian tradition, should be the godparents of the first grandchild. Ethel and Andy were fine with this arrangement because they knew that they'd be excellent godparents. Well, Crocifessa would be an excellent godmother; Peter would simply be an excellent grandfather. He'd leave the religious end to his wife. Ethel wanted to go to the church with them, but in the Catholic religion the mother didn't go to the baptism. It made no sense whatsoever to her, but she went along with it, knowing there was nothing she could do about it.

During the baptism, when the priest asked what the name of the baby would be, Peter answered unhesitatingly, "His name is *Joseph!*" Andy felt so much pride for his Dad at that moment. *"He's come a long way, God bless him."* Andy thought. The baptism was very nice despite the fact that baby Joseph screamed through the whole thing.

Back at home, Ethel and her mom and Margaret laid out a veritable feast for family and friends who were coming over to celebrate baby Joseph's Christening. Crocifessa made her 'famous' baked macaroni. Ethel often called it lasagna, so as not to confuse it with macaroni and cheese, but Crocifessa always referred to it as baked macaroni. It was her own recipe, similar to lasagna, but made with rigatoni pasta:

> *Crocifessa would sauté cauliflower, scallions and garlic in olive oil. It was poured into a large mixing bowl. She would then lightly cook sausage meat and put that in the bowl. While the rigatoni was par boiling, she would add to the mix ricotta cheese and eggs, salt and pepper. When the pasta was ready, she would drain it, pour it back into the pan and add the mix to it, and then layer it all in a large roasting pan with mozzarella cheese, her delicious spaghetti sauce, and grated Parmesan and Romano cheeses. She would then beat an egg and brush it all over the top, and bake it for about an hour or so, and... voila! Crocifessa's 'Famous' Baked Macaroni, a/k/a 'lasagna.'*

Margaret made her famous antipasto salad, and Ethel made some delicious chocolate-chip cookies (she didn't have a 'famous' dish yet). There was lots of fresh Italian bread, and a platter filled with different fruits. Ethel's mom had baked a lovely cake for the occasion, and coffee was perking, and wine was being chilled.

Ethel really appreciated Franny when something was going on; Franny loved watching her new little cousin. It gave Ethel a little respite when she needed it most. It was a lovely day for Ethel; she felt very happy surrounded by her and Andy's family and friends. She remembered another verse her father used to say: Psalm133: 1, *"Behold, how good and how pleasant it is for brethren to dwell together in unity."* She agreed, and silently thanked God for all His blessings.

One day, when 'Joey' was about six months old, Ethel was changing him on a blanket on the kitchen table. It was near supper-time and she had pasta cooking on the stove. All of a sudden the water in the pot began boiling over. She couldn't reach the stove from the kitchen table, so she quickly raced to the stove and turned down the gas. As she started to turn around she heard a loud thump. *"Oh God, no,"* she thought. As she turned completely she saw Joey on the floor; he was gasping and trying to cry but he couldn't. She screamed for Andy who was downstairs, as she picked up Joey and wrapped him in a blanket. He wasn't crying, in fact, he wasn't moving at all. Andy came flying up the stairs; he had never heard his wife scream like that. He knew before he got to the top of the stairs that something terrible had occurred. He could hear Ethel crying. "What happened?" He cried. "I...I think he's... unconscious, Andy." She became hysterical, sobbing between words. "Ethel, listen to me, what happened?" "I left him... for just a second; it was... only a second. He...fell off the table... and... he's not moving." "Oh God," Andy said, as he looked at Joey. He took him from Ethel's arms and shook him slightly, calling his name, but he wasn't responding. "We've got to get him to the hospital right away, Ethel." He ran to Abie's store and called Dr. Desimone. "Is he breathing, Andy?" "Yes," Andy said, "but he's not moving." The doctor said to get him right over to St. Elizabeth Hospital. "I'll meet you there," he said. Andy called a cab, then ran back home and tried to revive Joey. He still didn't respond. He was breathing; Andy was thankful for that.

A few moments later a police car pulled up. Andy ran downstairs and said to them, "Can you help us, please? Our baby has fallen and he's unconscious." "We know," one of the policemen said, "that's why we're here. We got a call from a doctor in Brighton and he told us what happened. Get your baby, sir, we'll get you to the hospital a lot quicker than a cab could." "Thank you! Thank you so much," Andy said as he ran back up the stairs. "Ethel! Ethel! The police are going to take us to the hospital; hurry! Hurry!" he cried. "Oh, thank God," she cried, as she ran downstairs carrying little Joey. "Don't you worry, Maam, we'll have you there in no time," the officer said, as he turned on the siren.

At home, Crocifessa prayed with all her heart for little Joey. Margaret and Charlie and the kids did the same. Peter was very quiet; he went outside and walked around the block a few times. It was his way. Crocifessa knew, in his heart, he was asking God to protect Joey.

By the time they got to the hospital Joey was awake but extremely listless. He had a bad lump on his head, and his eyes were somewhat dilated. Dr Desimone was waiting for them when they got there. He examined Joey and ordered X-rays of his body and his head. Ethel and Andy waited and prayed. Joey had to stay in the hospital to be watched closely. Andy and Ethel stayed in the waiting room all night, and slept from time to time in the chairs.

Dr. DeSimone came about eight o'clock in the morning. He ordered more X-rays of Joey's head. Later, he came into Joey's room and spoke to Ethel and Andy. "There are no broken bones," he said, "but there is some inflammation and fluid on his brain." "Oh, my God! What does that mean?" Ethel cried. Andy put his arm around Ethel and said, "How serious is it, doctor, and what needs to be done?" He was terribly frightened, but he didn't want Ethel to know how scared he was. Dr. Desimone said, "It could be very serious if we don't act right away. I've called in a specialist; what he's going to have to do is drill two tiny holes in the baby's skull, one on each side, and drain the fluid out to relieve the pressure." "Oh, my poor baby!" Ethel cried. "It's my fault… it's all my fault," she said. "If I hadn't left him to turn off the stove… this never would have happened." "Ethel," Dr. Desimone said, "this is what we doctors refer to as "a new mother's learning experience." Sometimes they're easy lessons and you laugh at them later, and sometimes they're harder lessons, and you wait them out with sweat and tears; you never laugh at those. This is one of those hard lessons, but I'm confident that Joey is going to be fine when this is all over. You're a good mother, Ethel; you mustn't blame yourself. You're not the first parent to take a chance, and you won't be the last." Ethel's eyes filled with tears; she just nodded. "Okay now!" Dr. Desimone went on. "You need to sign a form agreeing to this procedure, and then Dr. Jamison can get started. I'll bring him in so you can meet him, and he'll explain exactly what he's going to do." "Now tell me," Dr. Desimone asked.

"Have you eaten anything today?" "No," Andy said, "We haven't eaten since lunch yesterday." "I'm not hungry," said Ethel. "I don't think I could eat." "Well, whether you think you can or you can't, I'm ordering you to go down to the cafeteria and eat and drink something after the baby is taken into surgery. Do you trust me, Ethel?" "Yes," she said. "Then go and get something to eat; try the chicken salad; it's terrific. I know it sounds impossible, but try very hard not to worry. Your baby will be in excellent hands. Eat! I don't want you passing out; I don't think Andy needs that right now, either; right, Andy?" "That's for sure." Andy said.

Andy and Ethel did go to the cafeteria; they split a chicken salad sandwich, and each had a cup of coffee. Afterward, they went back upstairs and sat in Joey's room. "Dr. Jamison seems like a fine surgeon," Andy said, "and Dr. Desimone trusts him implicitly. I really do think that Joey's going to be O.K., Hon." "I hope so, Andy," she responded. "I don't think I could live with myself if he isn't." He said, "You just keep thinking about what Dr. Desimone said." "Which part? He said a lot of things," she answered. "The part where he said it wasn't your fault, Ethel; the part where he said that accidents like this happen to most people at some time or another; the part where he said that you are only human, and you'll learn a valuable lesson from this." "I know, Andy, you're right; I'm sorry I've been such a wreck. I just love Joey so much, I'd rather die than let anything happen to him." "I know that, Dear, I feel the same way, but let's try not to analyze this too much; it happened, and we're doing all we can for him." "Yes; thank you, Andy," Ethel said. "Oh, Lord, please take care of Joey." They held each other for a long time.

The longest three hours Andy and Ethel had ever spent was finally over. Dr. Jamison came into the room smiling. Andy and Ethel jumped up to greet him. "Well, everything went perfectly," he said. We got all the fluid out and the inflammation is going down. That's what we wanted, to relieve the pressure on the brain. I'm anticipating a complete recovery for your little boy. He'll have to stay here for a couple of days so we can watch him. I want to have another X-ray taken tomorrow, and then, if everything looks fine, he can go home the next day." "Oh, thank you, Doctor, thank you so much." Ethel said. Andy pumped his hand, thanking him profusely. "Can we see him now, Doctor?" Ethel asked. "In a little while," he said. "He'll be in the recovery room for a bit longer. I'll tell the nurse that you're waiting here in his room." "Thank you so much for everything," Ethel and Andy both said. "You're very welcome," he said, "it was my pleasure. I'll talk to you tomorrow."

When Dr. Jamison left the room, Andy sat down, put his hands over his face and broke into tears. He sobbed deep, painful sobs as Ethel held him, comforting him. "I knew this was killing you," Ethel said. "I know you, Andy; you were trying to be brave for my sake." He held her tightly, and said, "Our little boy is going to be all right, Hon; he's going to be all right." "Yes," she said. "We need to thank God right now, Andy." He held her hands and they prayed. Ethel remembered a verse her dad used to say, Psalm 46: 1, "*God is our refuge and our strength; a very present help in times of trouble.*" Andy said, "Amen."

When the nurse wheeled Joey into the room, Ethel gasped when she saw her baby's head all bandaged. She filled up with tears and just kept caressing him. The nurse said, "He's doing just fine, Mr. and Mrs. Vitello." "Is he really?" Ethel asked, "Because he looks so terrible." "Oh, all those bandages make it look so much worse than it is," the nurse replied; remember, he just came out of the anesthesia. He'll look a lot better tomorrow. He's going to sleep a lot now; you should go home and get some rest yourselves; you both look pretty tired." "I think you're right," Andy said. "I think we should go home, Hon, and get some rest. We'll come back first thing in the morning." "All right," Ethel said. "And, don't worry," the nurse said, "your doctor lives right across the street. If there was anything wrong, we would call him immediately." "Thank you," Ethel said. She felt a wave of relief take over her.

Andy and Ethel got to the hospital around 8:30 a.m. When they walked into Joey's room, he looked at them and smiled. The bandages had been removed and just two small bandages were on either side of his head. "Oh! He looks so much better," Ethel cried. "He's doing great," said Dr. Desimone as he walked into the room. "He had another X-ray this morning and it looks real good. He's alert and doesn't look any the worse for wear. He's a real little trooper, that one. As long as everything goes as expected, you'll be able to take him home tomorrow. I'll come by to see him the next day." "Oh, that's wonderful!" Ethel said. "Thank you so much, Doctor." "You're welcome;" he said, "I'll see you then."

Joey came home from the hospital the next day. The whole family came outside to welcome him home. Ernie had picked them up at the hospital and drove them home; he came back later with his mom. Neighbors dropped in to offer their help, and Franny couldn't do enough to help Ethel and Joey. Crocifessa had kept herself busy making her 'famous' chicken soup.

Later that evening, when Andy and Ethel were going to bed for the night, they looked at Joey sleeping peacefully in his crib. They just stared at him, without saying a word, and then they both leaned over and kissed his forehead. Five minutes later they were all sound asleep.

*****

In 1936 Peter and Crocifessa bought a little variety store called Bickford Variety. Peter was in his sixties and tired of working as a laborer. This was to be there retirement income, and of course, whatever money they could save Crocifessa would put into the 'sock'. Across the street from the store was the Jewish owned Bickford Bakery. Ethel often made hot pastrami sandwiches, so she would go there for their delicious rye bread, which she would have them slice nice and thick. She loved the smell of the bread baking when she walked in the door.

A narrow alley ran between Parker Street and Bickford Street. The store was right on the corner of the alley and Bickford Street. The Vitello house was at the other end of the alley on Parker Street. It was very convenient for them every morning and evening to just come out the door and walk down the alley. It was a terrific little store that catered to the many Italian families in the neighborhood. It carried just about anything you needed in the line of food, and if they didn't carry it, they would let you know which store in the area did.

There were about five little variety stores in the area of Parker Street, Bickford Street, and Bromley Park. It's amazing that Peter and Crocifessa were able to make a living from the store; but they made a good living from it. Jews owned at least three of those other variety stores. Diamond's was on the corner of Parker Street and Bromley Park; Abie's was on another corner of Parker Street and Bromley Park, and Saul's was up a little further on Parker Street, just to name a few. Then there was Christie's, a small Italian-owned meat market on another corner of Bromley Park and Parker Street. The Jewish-owned stores tried to cater to the Italian families, but as Peter would say, "How can a cat know what a dog likes to eat?"

The sense of smell was the sense a person was most thankful for upon entering the Vitello's store. They didn't carry meat, per se, but they did special order cold cuts like Genoa salami, bologna, mortadella, capicola and provolone for their steady customers. Parmesan and Romano cheeses were very popular. Peter would grind the cheese in a hand grinder attached to the three-inch thick solid wood counter. The ground cheese would fall onto a slice of wax paper, and Peter would fold the wax paper around it and put it in a paper bag, along with the customer's other purchases. Then Peter would total everything up on the bag and ring in the amount on the cash register. That old cash register was a beauty in itself. It was all cutout scrollwork and shined like it was pure silver, and had a loud ring to it when the drawer was opened.

On the right wall, when first entering the store, were see-through cases filled with all kinds of cookies. When a customer chose the cookies she wanted, Peter would put them in a paper bag and weigh them. Then he'd write the weight on the bag and total it up when the customer was finished shopping. Above the cookie cases were shelves that extended almost to the ceiling and went all around the entire store. They were loaded with canned goods and boxed items, like cereals, etc. Soaps, combs, pencils, brooms and all sorts of other miscellaneous items could also be found, either on shelves or hanging from hooks. On the left side was a large see-through case that held every kind of penny and nickel candy imaginable. It was a 'sweet-tooth's delight' for every kid who walked in with a nickel, or even just a penny; and if a parent couldn't spare a penny for candy,

Crocifessa would see to it that their child left with a piece of candy in his hand. Alongside the candy case were a couple of rough, hand-made shelves that held fresh Italian bread. They were never wrapped because they didn't hang around long. They were usually sold soon after they were delivered. If there were any loaves left over at the end of the day, Crocifessa would bring them home for the family. Also on the bread shelves were loaves of Bond and Wonder bread ('American' bread to Italians). There was a refrigerated case that held Coca-Cola, Moxie, ginger-ale, Dr. Pepper and various other soft drinks. For a nickel, you could quench a pretty big thirst.

An unpleasant sight, but absolutely necessary, was the flypaper that hung in several places from the ceiling; there were always lots of flies stuck to them; no one minded though, as it was a common sight in most food stores. Many people hung them in their homes. When flies covered most of the sticky area, the paper was discarded and a fresh one put up.

In the back of the store were two rooms, a kitchen and a bedroom, and a tiny room with a toilet in it. Crocifessa hung a curtain in the doorway to separate the store from the rooms. It was rather a nice set-up; when things were quiet in the store, Crocifessa and Peter would slip into the kitchen and make coffee and lunch and sit and eat, or read the newspaper. They always knew when someone came into the store because the bell hanging on the door would tinkle, announcing a customer. Often when a customer entered the store, he or she would hear Peter singing Italian songs. That man loved to sing, and customers got a kick out of it. Sometimes Andy and Charlie pitched in to help at the store on their days off.

The whole family loved the store, especially the grandkids, because Crocifessa would always give out penny candy. Peter was not always as generous as his wife; he would, more often than not, tell the kids, "No candy!" Go on home!" It might only be one o'clock in the afternoon, but in his very broken English, he would say, "Candy will spoil your appetite; you won't be able to eat your supper." His wife would always find a way to go out the back, through the kitchen and out into the alley, where she'd meet her grandchildren with a piece of candy for each of them. She would kiss their cheeks, and in her darling, extremely broken English, would say, "Nonja tolla

Papa; you hear me? No tolla Papa, okay?" It was always the same, as if Peter would get mad if he knew. He always knew, but never said anything. I think he felt that one 'soft-touch' in the family was enough.

Peter loved his grandchildren and he was very good to them, but Crocifessa had a heart of pure gold. Her family always came first, but she was also kind and giving to everyone, especially to those who had little. She was very careful with money, especially during the Depression years. But it was not uncommon for her, usually against Peter's wishes, to load up a box of food to send over to the family of a neighbor who was out of work. When Peter would protest, she would say, "No! We have it and they don't; they need to eat." He knew better than to argue with his wife when he knew she was right.

Early Saturday mornings Peter would take the streetcar and go into the North End, and buy cold cuts, wine, meat and fruit. He carried two large, leather shopping bags with strong leather handles; he thought that paper shopping bags were ridiculous. "Look at the handles on them," he would say, "they're so flimsy, they rip away from the bag with hardly anything in them." He would never be convinced of their usefulness. Many Saturdays, Andy or Charlie, whichever wasn't working at the barbershop that day, would go with him to give him a hand. Crocifessa would take care of the store 'til he got back. She didn't like being alone in the store, as her English wasn't as good as Peter's. His actually wasn't a lot better, but the customers seemed to understand his broken English better than Crocifessa's.

*****

It was June 22, 1938 and Andy was glued to the radio. Joe Louis was about to fight in a rematch of the 1936 bout, when Germany's Max Schmeling knocked out Louis, who was undefeated. Joseph Goebbels, Germany's Minister of Propaganda, had proclaimed Schmeling's victory a huge triumph for Germany and Hitlerism. "Schmeling's victory was not only sport," he had said, "It was a question of prestige for our race." Because professional boxing was one of the only sports that was integrated, win or lose, Joe Louis was a hero to black people everywhere.

Andy thought Joe Louis was the greatest fighter that ever lived. "I want Louis to show this Schmeling that an American, colored or white, is better than any Nazi boxer," he said to Charlie. Charlie had just come downstairs to listen to the fight with Andy. Andy found out later that Max Schmeling strongly opposed Naziism, but Andy didn't know that at the time of the fight, and all he wanted was to see Joe Louis knock this guy out. Ernie had been invited over but he declined, as boxing was not a sport he cared much for. Ethel put out some snacks and beer for them, put Joey to bed, and went upstairs to talk with Margaret.

A little while later Ethel heard Andy and Charlie yelling so loudly you could have heard them in the next town. She ran downstairs to tell them to be quiet or Joey would wake up. "Okay, okay, we'll be careful not to wake him," they both intoned. As Ethel was going back up the stairs she heard Andy yelling, "Knock him out, Joe! Come on, you've got him now! Kill that Nazi son of a b----" Charlie was yelling similar things. She ran downstairs again, very upset. "I can't believe my ears," she said. I'm ashamed of both of you. What if your son hears you?" "Ethel, Honey, you don't understand; this is boxing. I mean it's not something that most women..." The two boxers were at each other again; Andy's attention was riveted to the fight going on. Ethel just shook her head and said, "It's positively barbaric; I'm going back upstairs, but you have to keep your..." "Yahoo!" Andy and Charlie were out of their seats and jumping up and down. Ethel had to step back to keep from getting knocked over. "Five, six, seven, eight, nine, ten," they counted along with the referee. "He did it! He did it! He knocked out Schmelling in the first round!" Andy and Charlie were jumping up and down, hanging onto each other, laughing and still cheering as Ethel went to check on Joey again. Amazingly, he was still asleep. "Grown men!" Ethel said in sheer frustration. Andy grabbed Ethel and hugged her, and then said, "You talk to her Mello, no decent person would." Charlie laughed. Now this was not a mean thing to say, and they all knew it; it was just a silly thing Andy always said when he knew he was losing a simple argument with Ethel. Ethel said, "Andy, I'm serious!" "Oh, I know, Hon," Andy said. "You know I'm just kidding. We'll be quiet, I promise; we won't wake Joey."

Out in the hall, on her way upstairs, Ethel heard Andy saying, "Boy, I feel sorry for anyone who had money on Schmelling tonight." "Yeah," Charlie said, "You couldn't find a better fighter in the whole world than Joe Louis, that's for sure; the guy's unbeatable."

The last thing Ethel heard before she entered Margaret's apartment was Andy saying, "And he's a colored guy; can you beat that?" *"Unbelievable!"* She thought. Margaret was standing in the doorway shaking her head. "Crazy! They're both crazy!"

*****

One evening, just before Christmas, 1938, Margaret and Charlie came downstairs to have coffee with Andy and Ethel. Ethel was pregnant again; the baby was due in May. She was finally feeling well again, after suffering with morning sickness for over three months. But for the past month and a half she was feeling great, and able to keep her food down. She had made a chocolate cake and invited Charlie and Margaret down. She sent some cake upstairs for Franny, Peter and Junior (as young Charlie was called), and also for little Margie, who was born a couple of months after Joey. Franny was keeping an eye on her brothers and her little sister, while her mom and dad visited with Ethel and Andy downstairs.

They began talking about the Germans invading Austria. "What do think of Adolf Hitler?" Charlie asked. "I'm not sure," Andy said. "He's obviously a powerful leader, but there's something strange about him. He acts like all he wants is peace, but I'm not so sure that's really what's in his mind." "I don't like him!" Margaret said. I don't trust him; I don't know why, I just don't. I mean, look at that silly moustache he sports; I think he looks ridiculous. How can you trust anyone who looks like that?" Ethel laughed and agreed with Margaret. "It looks like he's got Czechoslovakia sown up, too, Charlie said. "I don't trust him either." "He was named this year's TIME magazine's Man of the Year," Ethel said.

"I heard that, too" Margaret said. "Can you believe that?" "Boy, I can think of a whole lot of other great men, besides Hitler that should have been TIME's Man of the Year," said Andy. "I mean, what's going on with the Jews over there? I mean, I'm no great lover of Jews, but it sure seems like Hitler hates them with a passion, and is hell-bent on making their lives miserable." "You know something?" Charlie said, "I'll bet we don't know the half of what's going on over there." "I think you're right, Mello." Andy said. "I just hope this country doesn't get involved in it." "Well, even though he wants to stay out of it," Ethel said, "I heard that President Roosevelt has requested Congress to increase funds for strengthening our armed forces. He said, "The United States needs to be adequately strong in self-defense.""" "Well, hopefully he's just taking precautions," Andy said. "He's a pretty smart guy; he'll keep us out of it."

"Ooh, Ethel," Margaret said, "Have you heard about that movie "Jezebel", starring Bette Davis? I think it's supposed to be real good." "Oh, yes," said Ethel. "I heard it's terrific." "I heard it's a little risqué," said Margaret." "Well, it's coming to the Madison next week," said Ethel. "Maybe we should go see it." "Yeah!" said Margaret, "I'm sure Ma will baby-sit for a couple of hours; let's definitely go." "Well, what do you say, Guys, is it a date?" Ethel asked. "Ooh, golly gee, Mello," Andy quipped. "We absolutely *must* go see it. I just couldn't bear it if I didn't see "Jezebel." Ethel and Margaret laughed, and said, "Oh, Andy, you're so silly." Charlie said, "Will somebody please tell me how we went from Hitler in Austria to Bette Davis in "Jezebel"?" Ethel and Margaret giggled like schoolgirls. "I just want to talk about something besides old ugly Hitler," Margaret said. "Okay, let's talk about baseball," Andy said, as he winked at Charlie. Charlie jumped right in with, "How about those Yankees, huh? Winning the World Series?" "Yeah," Andy said, "Chicago didn't have a chance." "Ohh," Margaret and Ethel just groaned. "You talk to him Margaret, no decent person would," Ethel said, giggling. "Hey, that's my line!" Andy quipped. They all started laughing.

****

CHAPTER FOUR
War!

On May 4th, 1939 Frances Ethel Vitello was born, respectfully named after her two grandmothers. She was a beautiful, healthy baby, with a pleasant disposition. Ethel had a much easier delivery than with her first, and again there were no problems at the time of birth. She also didn't experience any post-partum depression like she did when Joey was born. Ethel and Andy were thrilled with their little boy and new baby girl. Life was sweet!

Andy visited her every day and brought her flowers, just like he did two years ago. He was very tired, standing up most of the day, cutting hair, etc. and then catching the trolley to the hospital and trying not to fall asleep for fear of missing his stop. He'd spend an hour or so with Ethel, and go home, often times, to a crying two year old. He thanked God for his mom and Margaret, and Ethel's mom who took turns taking care of Joey, the house, the laundry and himself. Ernie was great, also; every few days he'd visit his sister in the hospital about an hour after Andy got there. Andy knew he timed it to give him a ride home. He never actually said that was his plan, but Andy knew it was; he appreciated it immensely, and told Ernie so. Of course, Ernie said it was just a coincidence.

Children were not allowed in the hospital, so one day, about a week after Frances was born, Ernie and his mom drove Andy to the hospital. They brought Joey with them, so while Ernie and his mom went in to see Ethel, Andy took Joey around to the side of the hospital, just beneath Ethel's window. A few minutes later Ernie brought his sister over to the window for a surprise. Ethel was so excited she cried, "Oh, Ernie, open the window, *please*! "It's a beautiful day," Ernie said as he opened the window. "Joey!' Joey!" she called. Joey looked up and started screaming, "Mommie! Mommie! Look, Daddy, it's Mommy!" "I know, Honey," Andy laughed, " that's why we're here, to see her." "Mommie, come down here," Joey called, "I want you!" "I can't come down right now, Honey, but I'll be home in a few days. I can't wait to hold you in my arms, Joey." "Me too," Joey cried. "Joey, we have to show Mommie your new dance," Andy said. He put Joey down and while Andy whistled a tune, Joey showed off his new dancing talent. Ethel laughed and clapped while Ernie and her mom cheered him on.

The visit from Joey made Ethel very happy, but Joey screamed something awful when it was time to say good-bye to Mommie. Ernie and his mom took Joey home while Andy spent time with Ethel. Joey screamed all the way home. "I don't know if this was such a good idea," Ernie said. "Oh, he'll be fine in a little while," Ethel, Sr. said. "It may not seem it right now, but believe me, this was good for the both of them."

A few days later, Ernie drove Ethel and Andy and their new baby girl home from the hospital. Everyone in the house ran out to the car to meet them. Little Joey ran into his mother's arms and said, "Don't you go 'way no more, Mommy." As soon as he saw his new baby sister, he started kissing her and saying, "my sissie...my baby." "Yes, Ethel said, " she's your baby sister, Honey."

Ethel's mom and Crocifessa could hardly wait to get their hands on their new little granddaughter. "Ooh! Let me hold that beautiful baby," her mom was saying. "Ah, bella bambina," Crocifessa cried. "Give me that beautiful baby girl." Ethel hesitated a moment, then placed the baby in her mother's arms. She knew Crocifessa may feel a little slighted, but, after all, she would get to see the baby every day, and her mom would be going home in a few days. Besides, Ethel, Sr. was *her* mom, and she sensed she was feeling a little like an outsider in this close, affectionate, and very expressive, Italian family. She needed to show her that she was still 'Number One Mom' in her daughter's eyes. Ethel, Sr. was very pleased.

They all went upstairs and Crocifessa brought up her 'famous' chicken soup, and everyone had a bowl; and while everyone was eating, Crocifessa was enjoying her little granddaughter. After a couple of minutes Ethel heard Ernie say, "Wow! This is the best chicken soup I've ever had." As she held her breath, waiting to hear her mother's response, Ethel heard her say, "My word Ernie, you're right; this is the best chicken soup I've ever tasted." Ethel was stunned, but she breathed a sigh of relief that her mother didn't take exception to Ernie's remark. After all, her mother had made chicken soup many times. She looked over at Andy and he was looking at her; he too looked shocked, but relieved. Crocifessa was in the other room changing the baby, but she could hear the conversation going on in the kitchen. She smiled and thought, *"Ethel Dalton is a good woman...and a fine judge of good food."*

"What's her name?" Joey asked, as he stared at his little sister. "Her name is Frances," Andy said. "Fancie," he said. Ethel smiled. "Say Fran-ces," she said. "Fan-cie," he said. They tried many times to get him to say Frances, but he just couldn't get his tongue around the 'Fr' and the 'ces' parts, so baby Frances became Fancie, and soon became Francie, not just to Joey, but to everyone.

*****

On Friday evening, September 1, 1939, as Ethel was cleaning up after supper, she heard Andy call from the living room, "Ethel come in here, listen to this." Andy was sitting on the edge of the coffee table, listening intently to the radio. Ethel stopped what she was doing and went into the living room. "What is it? What's wrong?" She asked. "I don't believe it!" Andy said. "That son of a b---- Hitler is dropping bombs all over the place. He's bombed Warsaw, and he's bombing other cities, too. Austria, Czechoslovakia, now Poland. I believe that tyrant is setting out to take over all of Europe." "Oh, that's terrible!" Ethel said. "He really is a tyrant, Andy; the way the Nazis are treating Jews over there, it's just a disgrace. They have to wear arm bands and the Star of David to show that they're Jewish, and they're being terribly mistreated and abused." "I've heard some awful stories, too Ethel. It's hard to believe someone could hate that

81

much. But, you know, it's possible that a lot of these stories are greatly exaggerated; you know how the press is." "Yes," Ethel said. "But it's also possible that these stories are greatly understated. I think your brother's right, Andy; I don't think we know the half of what's going on over there." "Mmm, It sure seems that way," Andy said. "Andy, you don't think Hitler has any idea of taking over this country, do you?" I mean, war would never come here, would it?" "Nah," The United States is too powerful a country," Andy said. "No one, not even Hitler would dare to make such a move. Nope, we have nothing to worry about here; this is the safest place in the world to live." "Well, thank God," Ethel said. "But…those poor people in Poland; what did they do to deserve this?" "I know, Hon." Andy wasn't saying so, but he wasn't quite as sure of things as he was twenty-four hours ago.

*****

Joey was an adorable, but very active toddler. He seemed to find ways to get hurt no matter how careful Ethel was. He was into every-thing, and there seemed to be no end to the mess he could make out of just about everything he touched. He could be the sweetest child on earth, until he didn't get his way, and then, what a temper he had; everyone on Parker Street could hear the screams. Ethel said one day, "He came into this world screaming, and has screamed every day since." Francie was now six months old, and a very easy baby to care for. She slept through the night at barely a month old and always awoke in a pleasant mood, whereas Joey always woke up hungry and yelling. He was going to make sure there was no chance that somebody might not hear him.

Some days Andy would have to work late. By the time he got home, Joey would be winding down and Ethel would be completely exhausted. Joey would leap into his arms and hug and kiss him. "Mommy, Daddy's home!" he would cry. Ethel would wearily smile and greet her husband. "I don't understand why you're so tired when I get home," he would say. "Joey is such a fun and loveable kid, and Francie is such a sweet baby. Maybe you ought to take some vita-mins or something, Hon, you know, build yourself up, so you're not so tired." "I *do* take vitamins," Ethel said, bristling slightly. "You have no idea, Andy, how a very active two and a half year old can wear you out." "Yeah, I guess; still, I'd rather have your job than mine," Andy said. "I'm on my feet all day, and they're killing me." "Oh, you poor dear!" Ethel said, as she took time out from cooking supper to wipe up the milk Joey spilled, and change Francie's very 'aromatic' diaper.

One day Andy was very sick with the worst cold he had ever had. He decided to stay home and "nip it in the bud." Unfortunately, he didn't get much rest that day, and "nipping it in the bud" became just a cliché. At about six o'clock in the evening, he said to Ethel, "I think I owe you an apology; this kid is unbelievable. Is he ever quiet? I mean, does he ever slow down?" Ethel just smiled. "He's actually been calmer than usual today; I've been trying to keep him quiet so you can get some rest." Andy just shook his head, "Unbelievable!" She poured Andy a glass of orange juice, and looked at him with a smile on her face; "but thanks," she said, "apology accepted."

A little while later, when Joey was finally exhausted, Ethel put him to bed. She and Andy looked at him as he slept, and thanked God for this precious, boisterous son of theirs. They also thanked Him for creating 'the need for sleep'. Andy decided that he would have to have no less than 105-degree temperature before he would stay home sick again. As he was dragging himself back into bed, Ethel heard him mumbling, "I don't know how she does it, and with a six month old to boot." She smiled again.

When Francie was a year and a half, she started running a slight fever, and wouldn't eat. She had a bad cough and was very list- less. This in itself wasn't alarming, as Ethel had seen her children with colds and coughs before; and fevers were fairly common with babies. Ethel called Dr. Desimone from Abie's, and he said "Dissolve a baby aspirin in a teaspoon of water and give it to her with some juice, and call me tomorrow if she's no better." It helped a little for a while, but when the fever went higher, Crocifessa said, "That baby needs to be in the hospital right away." "But Dr. Desimone said to wait and see how she is tomorrow," Ethel said. "She should be in the hospital!" Crocifessa said again. "Ma," Andy said, "she doesn't seem sick enough to be in the hospital. I'm sure she just has a bad cold."

"That's what your father and I thought, when our baby seemed only to have a bad cold." Crocifessa began to weep softly. "Mia bella bambina, mia bella bambina," she cried. "She has her name, she looks like her, and I'm telling you she's sick like her. Please, please take this baby to the hospital…now!" Crocifessa continued to cry, so Andy said, "All right, Ma, we'll take her to the hospital." Andy went to Abie's store and called a cab, and Dr. Desimone. "We're bringing the baby to the hospital," he said; "I think she's worse." "Okay Andy," the doctor said, "I'll meet you there." "Andy," Ethel said, as they rode to the hospital, "your mother was so adamant that we take Francie to the hospital; she scared me." "I know, Hon, she scared me too, but I've learned it's best to listen to her when she's that adamant about something. I don't know why, but when she's like this, she's almost always right. Let's just hope this time she's not.

At home, Crocifessa wept and prayed. Peter was quiet; he didn't say it, but his wife knew, in his own way, he was praying for his little granddaughter. He kept pacing the floor; then he went outside and walked around. Every now and then he would come back in the house and ask, "Any news?" When there wasn't, he'd pace some more, and then go for another walk. Crocifessa knew he was remembering back, and this was what he needed to do to deal with his fears. It was his way.

Ethel and Andy waited while the doctor examined little Francie and took X-rays of her lungs. When Dr. Desimone came back into the room, he said, "It's a good thing you didn't wait; your little girl has Pneumonia." "Oh, no!" Andy and Ethel said in unison. "We've caught it in time," he said, "and we're starting her on a powerful new drug. "Don't worry, she'll be fine." "Oh, thank God," Ethel said. "Andy, Ma was right!" "Yeah," Andy said, "It's really weird." "What's weird?" Dr. Desimone asked. "We had only been in this country about a year, when my little sister died of Pneumonia. Ma knew Francie had it too; she was positive." "Hmm, never underestimate the intuition of a grandmother," Dr. Desimone said. "Especially one who has lost a child. What year was that Andy?" "It was either

1914 or 1915," he said. "That must have been awfully hard on your parents, but things have changed a lot since then. You got her here in plenty of time, and she is going to be fine. And if all goes as I expect, you'll be able to take her home in a couple of days; I'll see her at home after that." "That's wonderful," Ethel said. "Thank you, Doctor." "You're welcome Ethel."

Crocifessa sobbed, "I knew it! I just knew it!" "It's Okay Ma, she's going to be fine," Andy said. "The doctor said it's in the early stages of Pneumonia. He's put her on a strong new medicine. It's not like years ago, Ma; children don't have to die from Pneumonia any more." Crocifessa just sobbed. Andy hugged his mother and Ethel came over and hugged her, too. Crocifessa kept saying, "Gratsia, Deo, gratsia."

Margaret and Charlie and Franny had just come downstairs. When they saw Crocifessa crying and everyone holding each other, Margaret began to weep. "Oh no!" she cried. Franny was close to hysteria, and Charlie stood there stunned. "Ethel turned around and said, "No, no, Margaret, Francie's going to be fine. She does have Pneumonia, but they caught it in time, thanks to Ma." She ran to Margaret and Franny and hugged them; they laughed and cried together. Charlie breathed a sigh of relief. Peter was nowhere to be found; it was his way. Andy went to look for him to bring him the good news.

Francie was healing quickly, and was able to come home in three days. They were *all* saying, "Thank you, Lord, thank you."

*****

One day while Andy was cutting a customer's hair, the man asked him if he had ever been in the armed forces. Andy said no, and the man said, "You better watch out; the army and the navy are sending men over seas and you could be recruited. We're going to be in a full scale, total world war pretty soon, you'll see." "But even if that happens," Andy said, "I'm not a kid anymore; I'm in my thirties now, married with two children. I can't leave my family to go to war. Besides, they're taking younger men." "Not anymore," the man said. They just raised it to married men; soon it will be married men with one, and then two children. If the army needs you, pal, you're going, and that's all there is to it." "Darn it," Andy said. "I knew I should have applied for a job at the shipyard when I had the chance. Now there are probably no jobs available that I can do. I mean, all I've ever done is barbering and printing; not much call for that in civil defense. Hey, I know; I did a little boxing when I was younger; I'll go over there and duke it out with Adolph. Oh well, "nothing ventured, nothing gained," as they say. I guess I'll just have to wait it out and hope for the best." He continued cutting the man's hair. "Look," the man said, "You go see Tom O'Brien; he's a politician and a pretty good guy. I've got his address here... somewhere..." He fumbled through his pockets and finally produced a card. "Ah, here it is," he said, and handed the card to Andy. "You go talk to him; he's gotten civil defense jobs for a lot of guys; he'll help you out if he can." "Thanks," Andy said, as he stared at the card. "I just might do that."

"Can you paint?" Tom O'Brien asked in a gruff, impatient voice. "Paint? Well, not really," Andy said. "I mean, I've painted a couple of walls in my apartment, but that's about it." "Good! You're now a painter! I'm going to give you a note; you take it to the personnel director at the Jeffries Point, East Boston shipyard." "Do you think I have a chance of getting the job?" Andy asked. "You've *got* the job, Andy! Now get going, and good luck." "Thank you! Thank you so much, Mr. O'Brien." "Don't mention it; glad to do it," he said.

"When can you start?" the personnel director asked. "Well," Andy said, " I need to give my boss some time to...." "Fine," he said, "Get yourself a coupla pair of coveralls and be here ready for work two weeks from today." "I will," Andy said, his mind reeling from the events of the last few hours. "I will, and thanks a lot."

When Andy arrived home, Ethel was waiting eagerly to learn how he made out at his meeting with Tom O'Brien. He ran up the stairs, threw his arms around her and kissed her; then picked her up and swung her around as she laughed with girlish pleasure. "Tell me! Tell me!" she yelled, "What happened?" He was so excited he couldn't stop hugging and kissing her. When he finally told her what Mr. O'Brien said, and also about his meeting with the personnel director at the shipyard, she was positively thrilled. "Oh Andy, that's wonderful!" she cried. "I'm so happy for you!" "For *us* Ethel!" he said, "For you and me and the kids!" Joey came running up to his dad and Andy scooped him up in his arms and kissed him. "Guess what, Joey!" Andy cried. "What, Daddy?" Joey asked excitedly. "We're going to be millionaires soon!" Andy laughed. "Joey, you tell Mommy that Daddy's going to be making twenty five dollars a week." Ethel gasped. "You're kidding, right?" she asked. "No I'm not, my darling wife; how does it feel to be in the money?" "Oh, Andy, I can't believe it. Twenty-five dollars a week; we'll be able to save some money now." "Yeah, it's a far cry from twelve dollars a week. Even in the weeks when I work late and make a couple of extra bucks, it's still hard to have a few cents to save or go to a movie without feeling the pinch. You know something, Ethel?" "What, Hon?" she asked. Andy said, "If I could make twenty-five dollars a week for the rest of my life, I'd be a happy man."

Suddenly Andy's expression changed. "What is it?" Ethel asked. "Oh God," he said, "How am I going to tell my brother? I've been so excited with our good fortune that I forgot about Mello." "Well, now's as good a time as any, I guess," she said. "I just heard him come in the downstairs door. You've got to give him plenty of notice, Andy. I'll go downstairs with the kids and leave you two alone." She picked up Francie and took Joey's hand, and as she walked out the door, she said, "Hi Charlie!" "Hi Ethel, how ya doing today?" "Pretty good, Charlie, and you?" "Not bad; not bad at all." He tousled Joey's hair and smiled at Francie. Ethel turned back and gave Andy a little kiss on his cheek and whispered in his ear, "Courage!" "Hey, Mello!" Andy called. "Come on in; I want to talk to you about something."

Charlie took the news pretty well, surprisingly. He was a little upset at first but he did understand that Andy needed to make more money, and this was an opportunity he couldn't pass up. He also felt that with two children, the army could possibly be calling on Andy at any time. Charlie felt pretty secure with four children.

Andy reminded him about the young fellow who came into the shop a couple of times in the past two weeks asking for a job. He had just graduated from barbering school and was eager to start working in a shop. "He certainly seems to have ambition," Charlie said, "and he lives right around the corner from the shop. I'll go over there tomorrow and see if he's still interested. If he is, I'll give him a two week trial period; if he works out, I'll hire him." "Perfect!" Andy said. "I'll stay on for the two weeks and train him in the Vitello Brothers' style of cutting hair." "I'll miss having you in the shop, Andy," Charlie said. "Me too, Mello, I'll miss going in and coming home together, too." "Well, things change, Andy; I've been waiting for the right time to tell you my news, too," Charlie said. "What news, Mello?" Andy asked. Charlie hesitated a moment, then said, "Margaret and I bought a house in Roxbury; we're going to be moving in around the end of next month." "Mello! That's wonderful! Good for you!" Andy cried. "Boy, things *are* changing fast around here." Charlie nodded. "Mello, have you told Ma and Pa yet?" "No, I figured I'd wait till the last minute. I don't think I could stand Ma crying every time she looks at me or Margaret or the kids." Andy chuckled, "Yeah, that's the way it's going to be, all right. Man, am I going to miss you guys; it's hard to imagine this house without all of you in it." "Yeah, I know," Charlie said. "But, six of us in four rooms has been murder, Andy, honestly." "I can imagine. God, Mello," Andy said, "remember when we first came to this country? How the heck did Ma and Pa do it? All five of us cramped into two rooms." "Boy, I'll never forget that," Charlie said. " And the bedbugs! Do you remember that, Andy, or were you too young?" "Oh yeah, I remember it; poor Ma, all she wanted was to go back to Sicily." "But Pa wouldn't have any part of it," Charlie said. "I'm real glad for that now." "Yeah, me too," said Andy, "at least our changes aren't as drastic as the ones Ma and Pa had to make."

"You know, Andy, Margaret's just sick over the idea of telling Ethel; she's going to miss her terribly." "Yeah, I know," Andy said, "Ethel will be heartbroken when she hears this, too; but believe me, Mello, she'll be happy for the two of you.... you're right, though, things change; nothing stays the same for long."

Ethel was filled with mixed emotions when Andy told her the news about Margaret and Charlie. She ran right upstairs and she and Margaret held each other and cried; then they laughed and talked about the new house, and then they cried some more. They both knew that things couldn't always stay the same. The families were growing, and their needs were changing. Moving to different locations was inevitable. They knew they'd always be close, but they also knew they'd never again have the same kind of relationship they'd had for the past six years. Yes, change was coming.

*****

On December 7, 1941, Ethel, like many other wives in America, heard her husband cry out, "Oh my God! No, it can't be!" Ethel ran into the living room. "What's happened? What is it Andy?" "Oh God, Ethel, the Japs have bombed Pearl Harbor in Hawaii." "What? Oh no, Andy!" Ethel cried. "Hawaii? Why? Why would the Japanese bomb us? We're not at war with them." "We are now, Hon!" Andy said. "Oh, Andy, what's going to happen? So many of our men are over in Europe now." "Yeah, I guess that's exactly what the Japs were thinking," Andy said. "They figured we're vulnerable right now. Well, let me tell you something, Ethel, they've figured wrong. You mark my words; President Roosevelt isn't going to take this lying down. He'll keep America safe. Those Japs obviously don't know who they're dealing with. They've made the biggest mistake of their lives if they think the United States of America can be bullied." "Andy, listen, they're giving early casualty reports. Oh, this is horrible!" "God help them!" Andy whispered.

WAR! That's what everyone was talking about. "What are we going to do about it?" was what the average person was asking. "Those damn Japs can't get away with this!" It was a real bad time; Asian people everywhere were suspected of being traitors. America was scared! First and second generation Japanese were being rounded up and sent to internment camps. Faithful Japanese-Americans, many who fought in the First World War, and their families, were sent to the camps and labeled as possible traitors and spies. Americans hated Hitler for what he was doing to the Jews in Europe, yet sadly, any Asian American... Chinese, Korean, Vietnamese, anyone who resembled Japanese, was insulted, abused and even beaten by so-called 'Good Americans'. "They all look the same!" was what many Americans said; "Japanese, Chinese, what's the difference?" They wanted them 'out of sight.' Most Americans were not part of this terrible ostracizing, but those who were, made the rest of America ashamed.

"I hate those damned Japs," Andy said one day, as he sat in the kitchen reading the newspaper. Ethel had just poured two cups of coffee. "They're all sneaky sons of b------; none of them are any good. I'll bet all the Japs in this country are in cahoots with the Japs back home." "Andy! I can't believe I'm hearing this from you," said Ethel. There are many good and loyal Japanese-Americans in this country; many fought in the First World War, for heavens sake. How can you forget the shame and embarrassment you felt, let alone the anger, when so many people thought that all Sicilians in this country were cutthroats… members of the Mafia? How can you, of all people think this way? I'm ashamed of you right this minute, Andy, I really am." Andy was quiet for a moment; he felt like he had just been hit with a sledgehammer. "You're right," he said. " I can't believe how easy it is to think like that. Forget what I said, Hon; it's not *really* the way I feel. It's just that I hate the Japs who did this." "I know," she said. "Believe me, I feel the same way, Andy, but we can't let ourselves be caught up in the fear and hatred that's infecting this country right now. And we mustn't ever let Joey hear this kind of talk." Andy nodded, "Mmm," he said. They sipped their coffee, and sat quietly, thinking, for some time.

*****

Life changed for most Americans; there were victory gardens sprouting up everywhere, tin cans were being flattened and saved, along with rubber and paper. Trucks would come by from time to time and collect them. War bonds were being sold everywhere, and rationing cards were issued to families. Everyone did his or her part. Men, women and children did whatever they could to help the war effort. Women everywhere were entering the work field. If their husbands, fathers, brothers and sons could go to the front lines, they would do their part on the home front. They were needed to take over many of the jobs the men held, and it was necessary to make ends meet. Grandparents became the parents, and mothers became welders, riveters, and whatever else was needed to do their part to keep America on her feet. Many did volunteer work or worked in USOs. Neighbors helped one another, and families pulled together; no one had it easy. It was an exciting time, and it was a sad, uncertain time. Pitching in helped to keep them from worrying about their loved ones who just might be giving their lives to keep America safe. They carried on. Crocifessa continued to make up baskets of food for the less fortunate families in the neighborhood, and hand out free candy to children from those families. She would always say, "It's the least we can do. We have it, and they don't; they need to eat."

Andy was working at the shipyard and making good money. He and Ethel bought war bonds and victory stamps whenever they could. When Joey started going to school, his mother gave him dimes to buy stamps in school. Andy felt good about his job, not only for the money he was making, but because he was doing civil defense work. He was glad to be doing something to help the war effort. As war-worn ships came into the yard to be repaired, he and many others were there to get them back in fighting shape.

Andy was becoming a pretty good painter, but he was also doing a lot of other jobs on the ships. He would volunteer for any job if extra pay came with it, no matter how dangerous, and he would work as much overtime as he could get. When Ethel would ask how his day was, he would tell her only what he thought she could handle and no more. She always knew there was more, but she thought it best not to pursue it. She would say to him every morning, "Please be careful, Andy; don't take chances." She prayed as she watched him walk down Parker Street to get the trolley to work, "Lord, bless him and protect him today."

One day Andy volunteered to go down into the bottom of a ship and crawl through one of the large metal cylinders that were used to fill the ballast tanks with water. Andy's job was to coat the inside of the cylinder with a rust preventative. The cylinders were almost the length of the ship. About three quarters of the cylinder had already been done, so Andy was to finish the job. Of course the pump that filled it with water was shut off. Working in a cylinder on his knees was not Andy's favorite kind of work, but he said to himself, *"It's*

91

lousy work, but somebody's got to do it, and it might as well be me; that bonus money will make it worth my while, that's for sure."

Andy got about another quarter of the cylinder done when he heard a sound that just about froze the blood in his veins. What happened next, no amount of money could have made what he went through in that cylinder worth his while. He began to realize that the sound he was hearing was rushing water, and it was getting louder and louder. *"Oh my God,"* he thought, *"It's in this cylinder."* He managed to turn himself around and began to crawl on his hands and knees as fast as he could toward the opening. He dropped the light he was carrying, as it became too difficult to crawl fast with it in his hand. His heart was racing and his head was pounding; he was becoming exhausted, but he knew he couldn't slow down. He could hear the water getting closer and closer. It was so very dark. He was beginning to feel that he wouldn't make it to the end of the cylinder before the water engulfed him. He was sweating profusely, and could hardly breathe. His lungs felt like they were ready to burst. "Lord, help me, please," he cried aloud. It seemed to be taking forever to get to the end. All of a sudden he saw a pinhole of light; he knew it was the light at the end of the cylinder. He tried to yell to the men at the end of the cylinder, but it only used up his breath, so he had to keep quiet and just 'run' on his knees. *"Please God, please, don't let me die like this."*

As Andy got closer to the end, the men working there now realized what was happening. Someone yelled, "Oh my God, that's water we're hearing." They began yelling to him, "Hurry, Andy! Hurry! Come on, you can do it!" He kept hearing them yelling, "Hurry!" It seemed to give him a final boost of energy. He could see them now; they threw a rope in for him, and someone yelled, "Andy! Wrap it around your hand!" As he grabbed it, he felt water come up over his feet and legs, and then up his back. The men pulled hard and fast, and Andy came sliding out. The moment he was out, they sealed the hatch.

Andy was exhausted and too emotionally drained to feel anger at that moment. Ordinarily, he'd have been kicking and swearing; they'd have had to hold him back from pummeling whoever was responsible for what had happened, but all he wanted was to lie down for awhile, catch his breath and go home to his wife and kids. As he was being carried to the infirmary, he heard the foreman say, "Heads are going to roll for this!" He felt some tiny bit of satisfaction in that, but he couldn't even react to it.

As he lay down in the infirmary, he thanked God for bringing him safely out of the cylinder. He began to cry, and he started shaking all over. He was embarrassed in front of the nurse but he simply could not control it. The nurse said, "You're experiencing a slight case of shock, Mr. Vitello; just let it all out." She understood what was happening to him and gave him a mild sedative to calm him. His knees and his hands were cut and bleeding, and every muscle in his body seemed to be hurting. He knew the nurse was washing his knees and bandaging them, but he barely felt it. He kept hearing Ethel's words in his head, *"Please be careful, Andy; don't take chances."* He quietly wept, as the realization of what could have happened swept over him. *"Oh, Ethel,"* he thought, *"Why am I so bull-headed?"*

That night Andy woke up screaming, reliving in his sleep what he had been through that day. Ethel had known something wasn't right when he came home; he was very quiet, and just wanted to be left alone. "Andy, what is it? What happened today?" Ethel asked, as she held him and tried to comfort him. He told her what had happened at work and she came close to tears. "I knew something was very wrong when you came home, but you wouldn't talk about it. Andy, you mustn't keep things like that to yourself; you should have told me." "I know, Hon; I didn't want to worry you," he said. "Believe me, Ethel, I've learned my lesson; I'll never volunteer for anything that dangerous again." A shiver went through Andy's whole body. "I don't think I'll ever forget the sound of that water." They held each other a long time before falling asleep. Ethel thanked God over and over for saving her husband. Andy was right; years later, every now and then, he still experienced nightmares reliving that incident in the cylinder.

*****

93

Francie began talking at a very early age, much like her brother Joey. English was spoken to them upstairs, but downstairs Crocifessa and Peter were teaching them Italian. Francie's first Italian word was "mangia", which had been Joey's first Italian word. To Crocifessa, eating together was the best thing a family could do. Every time they sat down to eat, Francie and Joey would holler, "mangia everybody, mangia." Crocifessa and Peter would laugh, and beam with pride. Andy and Ethel would laugh, too, and say, "Si, mangia." The next word they learned was "pane". It was the same with Franny, Peter, Junior and Margie. When the whole family would eat together, all six kids would yell "Mangia pane; eat your bread!" Everyone would laugh. The first sentence Francie learned to say was, "Pielya la scoopa"(spelled phonetically), which loosely translated meant, "Get me the broom." Every time she'd go downstairs, her grandmother would say, "Franzie, pielya la scoopa!" She knew Francie loved the idea of speaking Italian to them, so she would use it whenever she thought Francie would understand it. Francie would grin and say, "Si, si, Grandma." Francie loved being Italian; she always wished she had been born in Sicily.

*****

When Francie was three years old, Dr. Desimone said she needed to have her tonsils out. She had been having bouts with tonsillitis for two years. She would run a high fever and her throat would be raw and so sore she couldn't eat or drink without crying. She was kind of delicate and probably a little spoiled, and wouldn't let her mother out of her sight when she wasn't feeling good. Ethel said to the doctor, "She'll never stay in the hospital without me there." "That doesn't have to be a problem," Dr. Desimone said. "We can take them out right here at home; I can come by for a couple of days afterwards to make sure she's fine." "Can you really do that?" Ethel asked. "Sure! It's a pretty simple operation. I've done it many times in the patient's home; haven't had a problem yet, and don't expect to." "Wow! I didn't know it was that simple," Andy said. "What do you think, Ethel?" "Well, if you feel it's perfectly safe, doctor, then, I guess it's okay, but where will you do it?" "Right here on the kitchen table!" Dr. Desimone said. "Oh my word!" Ethel cried. Dr. Desimone laughed, and gave Ethel a list of what she needed to do to set things up. He gave Francie a shot of Penicillin and said, "I'll operate as soon as the inflammation and the fever are gone."

Two weeks later Francie had her tonsils out at home on the kitchen table. A few days later, after much ice cream and pampering, she was doing just fine.

*****

Francie and Joey played together constantly. At five years old, Joey was a real good big brother. He was very protective of his little sister, and felt it was his responsibility to watch over her like a mother hen. He loved to tell her stories. He couldn't read yet, but he would hold a book in his hands and make up stories and act them out. Francie thought he was the smartest and funniest brother in the world. She was a very happy little girl.

Joey started Kindergarten when he was five years old, and Francie was heartbroken. He was her playmate and now he was gone for most of the day. In the afternoon Ethel would say to her, "Joey will be coming pretty soon." She would run to the parlor window and wait for him. She could hardly contain her joy when she would see him coming down Parker Street. "Joey! Joey!" she would yell. He'd wave to her and his mother, and start running home.

After Joey had been in school for a few weeks, Francie noticed he wasn't hurrying home to play with her like he was before. She also noticed him walking with a boy who lived across the street; his name was Larry Ryan; he was a year older than Joey. Joey would run up the stairs, change his clothes and run out again. He and Larry became the best of friends. Francie liked Larry but he and Joey were always together doing the things they liked to do. Francie was always excluded; she was just too little to play the rough games they played. Her mother tried to fill in and play with her and read to her, which she loved, but she missed her big brother.

The following year the Boston School Board changed the age for children to start Kinder- garten. Francie was just under the wire, and she wanted to go to school like Joey. Ethel and Andy thought

95

she was too young, but she was a very bright child so they decided to enroll her in Kindergarten. Joey was now happily in the first grade. Ethel was pregnant again and suffering terribly with morning sickness. She hated to admit it, but she was looking forward to having some time alone in the mornings. So, everyone was happy. At four years and four months old, Francie set out holding her mother's hand for the Lucretia Crocker School where she would spend her first day in Kindergarten. The school was just up a little way on Parker Street, about two minutes from her house. She was happy and excited about going to school, but when it was time for her mother to leave, she started to cry and begged her not to go. So Ethel stayed for quite a while, fighting back nausea, and feeling horrible the whole time. After awhile Miss Sullivan, the kindergarten teacher, told her to slip out while Francie was playing a game with some other children. She did, and Francie had no idea she was gone until it was time for lunch. By that time she was beginning to like being at school, and she especially liked Miss Sullivan. Miss Sullivan told her that her mother would be there when school got out, and of course she was.

Francie was a very cute, very sweet little girl; she was also the youngest and the smallest in her kindergarten class. Miss Sullivan became very fond of her and was very kind to her. Just before the end of the school year, on Francie's fifth birthday the class sang "Happy Birthday" to her. Francie thought that was just the nicest thing; she felt very special. It didn't compare, though, to the joy she felt later when Miss Sullivan showed up at her house with a birthday present for her. It was a lovely little porcelain doll with a pretty pink dress. Francie was thrilled; she couldn't believe her teacher actually came to her house…and brought her a present. Miss Sullivan said she couldn't give it to her at school because it wouldn't seem fair to the other children, and she asked Francie not to say anything about it. Ethel insisted she stay and have coffee and birthday cake with them; so she did.

Francie was about as happy as she could be. It was a wonderful birthday and, although she didn't know it then, she would remember it fondly for the rest of her life.

*****

One day, not long after Francie started going to Kindergarten, Ethel began hemorrhaging and was in a lot of pain. She called down to Crocifessa, and after coming upstairs and seeing Ethel, she yelled down to Peter to go to Abie's and call the doctor. Dr. Desimone said he'd send an ambulance and meet them at the hospital. There was no way to get in touch with Andy, so Peter went with Ethel in the ambulance. Crocifessa stayed home to be there when Francie and Joey got home from school. When Andy came home Crocifessa was waiting for him with the news. He ran to Abie's store and called a cab; forty-five minutes later he was in the emergency room of St. Elizabeth's Hospital demanding to see his wife. Dr. Desimone came out when they called him and said to Andy, "Ethel lost the baby, Andy; I'm real sorry about that, but she's doing fine. I'd like to keep her here overnight to make sure she's okay. and then she can go home tomorrow."

Andy and Ethel both felt a deep sense of loss; they had looked so forward to having this baby. Ethel was terribly disappointed, and Andy held her close, as tears rolled down his face.

*****

Francie had a sweet girlfriend who lived three doors down from her on Parker Street. Her name was Rita McGrath, but everyone called her Riri. She was born on May 1, 1939, three days before Francie was born, and they used to pretend they were twin sisters. They didn't look anything alike as Riri was fair-skinned and had blond hair, and Francie was slightly darker with dark brown hair. But that didn't matter; they were twins and that's all there was to it.

Riri went to Blessed Sacrament Parochial School. She got out of school at 2:30 in the afternoon, and Francie got out at 2:45. Riri would get to Lucretia Crocker School at just about 2:40 every day, where she would wait for Francie to get out. They would hold hands as they walked down Parker Street to their homes. "See you in a little while," Francie would yell, and they would run up the stairs to their apartments to change their clothes. After a while they would meet outside to spend the next two hours playing hopscotch, jump rope or jacks. Sometimes they would just play with their dolls. It didn't matter what they did, as long as they could do it together.

Francie met Rosemarie Fontana and Mary Pinciaro in Kindergarten and they became fast friends. They usually got promoted into the same class together. Francie's first grade teacher was Miss Fox; Francie didn't like her at all. "She's too cranky, and she's always yelling at the kids; she's not nice like Miss Sullivan."

When Francie, Rosemarie and Mary were promoted to the second grade, so was Miss Fox. Francie wasn't too happy about that, but she always made the honor roll, and was always respectful to Miss Fox, despite the fact that she disliked her immensely. Then in third grade, Francie got Miss Ellis for her teacher. She was pretty strict but she was fair, and didn't scream at everybody like Miss Fox did.

The Lucretia Crocker School only went to the third grade, so Francie and her friends would be going to the Lowell School for fourth grade, which was located at the corner of Centre and Mozart Streets. Francie was excited about going to a new school.

When they were promoted to the fourth grade, 'the biggest catastrophe of all time' occurred.... Miss Fox began teaching the fourth grade at the Lowell School. *"No! It can't be!"* Francie thought, as she stared up at Miss Fox on the first day of school. "Hello Frances," Miss Fox said. "Hello Miss Fox," Francie said, dejectedly, feeling the weight of the world on her little shoulders. Later at home she sobbed. "It's not fair, Mom; it's just not fair." After much consoling from Ethel, Francie knew there was nothing she could do about it but 'grin and bear it.' "This is the worst thing that ever happened," she cried. It wasn't easy, but she got through the year on the honor roll and was promoted to Miss McAndrew's fifth grade class. She liked Miss McAndrew a lot, and breathed a sigh of relief that Miss Fox didn't 'get promoted' to the fifth grade also.

When they were alone Ethel said to Andy, "Good grief, Hon, I was beginning to think she was going to go through all twelve grades with Miss Fox." Andy laughed, "Yeah, talk about a lesson in humility."

*****

A little way up Centre Street, from Parker Street, was a large factory called Plant's Factory. It housed a lot of different businesses. One of them was Hanlon's Shoe Store. Ethel always took Francie and Joey there when they needed new shoes.

Hanlon's had a foot X-ray machine there. After Ethel would pick out the right shoes, then Francie or Joey would stand up and place their feet, with their new shoes on, in the bottom part of the machine. There was a place to look into at the top of the machine. Then the salesman would press a button, and all of a sudden it would light up a bright green color, and the whole outline of the shoes, *and* the feet in them, would show up. Francie always thought it was almost miraculous that she could actually see each bone in her foot.

The X-ray machines couldn't have been good for the feet, though, because about a year later Hanlon's, and other shoe stores did away with them. Mothers were disappointed because it sure did give an accurate picture of how the shoes fit; there was no guess-work involved.

*****

Plant's Factory blew a loud whistle three times every day... eight o'clock in the morning, noontime, and five o'clock in the afternoon, to let the workers know it was starting time, lunchtime, and quitting time. That whistle could be heard for miles around. Francie and Joey knew when they heard the five o'clock whistle, they had better be on their way home. When they heard it they would start running. Other kids in the neighborhood must have had the same rule, as Francie and Joey would always see kids running for home at the sound of the whistle. They knew not to push too much in that area, as Andy wouldn't listen to excuses. Supper was at 5:15, give or take a few minutes. If they weren't there shortly after the whistle blew, they'd better have a darned good excuse or they would be punished. Of course, there were times when there were extenuating circumstances, but Andy would always be the judge of that.

Andy was a strict disciplinarian, but he was not a mean man. He believed in children obeying without question, and total respect for parents and grandparents was expected. He told Ethel one day he believed strongly in what his father used to say, "If a parent has to speak to a child more than once, that child needs a good spanking." Ethel thought that might be a little rigid. "God forbid that child is ever in a fox-hole one day, facing the enemy," Andy said. "He'd better be able to do what he's told *immediately*, or he'll get his head blown off." "Well, that's a pleasant thought," Ethel said grimacing. "Well, it's true, Ethel," he said, "If a kid doesn't learn obedience at home, he'll never be able to obey those in authority anywhere." "Oh I agree completely, Andy," she said, "It's just the very vivid picture you present." "Yeah, well, it may not be pleasant but it's true," he said. Every now and then, when Joey would do something he shouldn't do, he would get a spanking from his father. Francie would beg him not to spank Joey, but her father would say, "Joey misbehaved and he has to learn." Andy had a barber strop hanging on the kitchen door, and if he felt the offense called for drastic measures, he would use 'the strap' on his children's bottoms. Ethel would never go against her husband, even if she thought he was being unreasonable. She would wait a proper time after the spanking, then go and talk to the hurting child and console him, *or her*, as the case might be. She would explain to them where they went wrong, and why the spanking was necessary. Joey, or Francie, would then go to their father, whimpering, and he would talk to them, and say the words no child ever believed, "When I spank you, it hurts me more than it hurts you."

****

Francie and Joey (circa 1944)

Francie's second grade class picture 1945
Francie: Bottom row, second from left; Rosemarie: Bottom row,
third from right; Mary: Top row, third from left.

CHAPTER FIVE
The Cottage

On the Saturday mornings that Andy didn't work, he would send Joey to Hoffman's Bakery on Centre Street for donuts. Joey would bring home warm jelly donuts, honey-dipped, and plain donuts that came right out of the oven, and just about melted in your mouth. The moment Joey would open the downstairs door, the aroma would waft up the stairs and start everyone's mouth watering. Andy always said, "Hoffman's makes the best donuts in the world." They all agreed; it was a treat they all looked forward to on the Saturdays Andy was home. No donut ever compared with Hoffman's donuts.

After breakfast, Francie and Joey would go with their father or with Peter to the North End to buy cold cuts, cheeses, vegetables, fruit and wine. They would go from pushcart to pushcart to find the freshest and best looking vegetables, and then Peter would barter and argue with the vendor. They'd raise their voices and wave their hands in 'disgust' and Peter would call the man a thief for charging so much, and on and on it would go until the vendor came down in his price. He always did, and he and Peter would say "Ciao," and wish each other "Buono fortuna" when the buying and selling was finished. There were never any hard feelings, as this kind of bartering was expected. They wouldn't admit it, but it made the shopping experience a lot more fun for the buyer *and* the seller.

Sometimes Crocifessa would go to the North End, too. It was absolutely amazing watching her in action. Andy used to laugh and say, "My mother is like "Dr. Jekyll and Mr. Hyde." All of a sudden this sweet, lovely, soft-spoken little woman would become a tough, confident shopper who would take no guff from anyone. Francie and Joey would be in stitches laughing when she would barter with the vendors. Afterward, she would go back to being her usual kind, gentle self again. She could never understand why everyone in the family got such a big kick out of her dealing with the vendors. To her it was just the most natural thing in the world. Andy always said, "Seeing Ma shopping at the pushcarts in the North End is a sight to behold."

Going to market at the North End was an experience Francie always looked forward to; the smells and sights simply delighted her. After they had shopped for a few hours, Francie and Joey would start asking, "Where's the pizza guy, Papa?" They were looking for a little bald man, wearing a white sailor's cap and a white apron stained with red sauce. He pushed a makeshift oven he had attached to the frame of a baby carriage all around the streets of the North End, calling out, "Pizza! Pizza! Get your pizza here! Only a nickel a slice." When Francie and Joey heard him yelling, they would jump up and down, all excited. "There he is, Papa! There he is! Can we get a slice, please?" Peter would always say, "No, no, you don't need any pizza today." It was a little game they played and they all understood it. Francie and Joey would 'plead' with him for some pizza, and finally he'd 'give in', saying in his broken English, "Oh all right; you kids are going to put me in the poor house." Francie would giggle, and Joey would call out, "Over here! Over here! Three pieces please!" It was always the same...and nothing in the world ever tasted as good as pizza from the pizza man. Francie cherished those trips to the North End. Sometimes they would all go, Ethel and Andy, Crocifessa and Peter, and Joey and Francie. Those were the really special times.

*****

Thursday, April 12, 1945 was a sad day for the American people; President Roosevelt passed away. Ethel and Andy felt terrible. Neighbors came out to speak to each other; they felt like they had lost a close friend. "This is no time to lose a president," Andy said, "with the war going on." Vice President, Harry S. Truman was sworn in as our thirty-second president. It *was* a crucial time in the war, and people everywhere were nervous of what the future would bring. At school, the principal came on over the intercom and said, "In honor of our beloved President, Franklin Delano Roosevelt, there will be no school for the rest of this day or tomorrow. You may all go home, and have a safe weekend." Francie knew it was a sad time, but she, and every other kid, were thrilled for the extra time off. The following day, President Truman gave Americans some hope. "The world may be sure that we will prosecute the war on both fronts, east and west, with all the vigor we possess, to a successful conclusion. In that faith and with that spirit of courage we must carry on."

Less than a month later, on May 7th, Germany surrendered, and Adolf Hitler was believed to be dead. Americans everywhere were celebrating. Andy and Ethel and Peter and Crocifessa ate dinner in Ethel and Andy's parlor that evening, listening to every news report they could find. A little later, Charlie and Margaret came over. "Isn't it wonderful?" Margaret said. Charlie said, "Thank God the world is rid of that fiend." "Now, if those damned Japs would just surrender," Andy said, "we might see the end of this war yet."

As they listened to the radio, they heard President Truman say, "The victory we have won in the west, must now be won in the east." The Vitello family, sitting in their parlor cheered, and Andy shouted, "Go to it, Harry! Give 'em hell!" They all laughed and for the first time in over five years, they felt that world peace was in the near future. President Truman also said, "I only wish that Franklin Delano Roosevelt had lived to witness this day." They fell silent, and for a moment, each one of them felt an overwhelming sense of sadness and joy.

Almost four months later, on August 6th, President Truman gave the order to drop the Atomic bomb on Hiroshima. It had never been used before. The world knew that Japan had to be stopped, but even after Hiroshima was bombed, the Japanese continued their 'onslaught of destruction' throughout the Pacific. Three days later, on August 9th, America dropped a second bomb, this time on Nagasaki. It was necessary, but it wasn't anything to celebrate.

On August 14th, 1945, Japan finally accepted terms of surrender, ending their almost four year 'reign of terror'. It was an exciting day for all Americans. People all over the world were experiencing the joy. "First Germany and now Japan," Andy yelled. "Hallelujah! Good for you Harry!" Truman hadn't actually announced V-J Day yet, but to people everywhere, the war was over, and nothing could hold back their celebrating.

Soon, ticker-tape parades were taking place in major cities all over the United States. When the parade took place in Boston, Andy took his family to see it. Andy said to Ethel, "I want these kids to remember this day for the rest of their lives." They tried to get as close to the street as possible. Soon marching bands came by, followed by our wonderful fighting men, Army, Navy, Marines and Air Force. They all came marching by; some were in army trucks and tanks. Andy pushed Joey up in front so he could see everything, then he lifted Francie up on his shoulders so she could see General Dwight David Eisenhower as he rode by in an army car, waving to the cheering crowd. The bands were playing and thousands of people were yelling and cheering, "The war is over!" "God bless America!" Confetti rained down on everyone. Francie waved to General Eisenhower as he rode past them, and she was certain he was waving back at her.

Francie looked around and was surprised to see so many people crying; her mom and dad were crying, too, and laughing at the same time. "Mommy, why is everybody crying?" she asked. "I thought this was a good thing." "Oh, Honey," Ethel said, "It is a good thing; it's a wonderful thing. Some people are crying because they're happy that the war is finally over, like we are. But some are crying because their fathers, sons or husbands were killed in the war. Others may have lost a brother or a friend." Francie saw a woman sobbing, with her face buried in her husband's chest. When the bands played the "Star Spangled Banner," and "Grand Old Flag," everyone sang the words out loud, and tears flowed down every face. Francie began to cry softly, and she buried her face in Andy's neck. She whispered, "Oh, Daddy, I feel so sad for those people." Through his tears Andy said, "Honey, none of us should ever forget this. It may not represent a pleasant memory, but it certainly is one of the most important." "You're young yet Francie," Ethel said, "but when you're older you'll understand what this war was all about, and you'll cherish the freedom that men fought for, and so many died for."

*****

Betty and Jack McDonnell moved into Margaret and Charlie's old apartment upstairs. They were a little younger than Andy and Ethel, and had no children yet. Soon Ethel and Betty became good friends. Andy was always pleasant but there was something about Jack McDonnell that he didn't like. Now and then Betty and Jack would come downstairs and have coffee and dessert with Ethel and Andy, but something about Jack gnawed at Andy; he didn't know why he felt that way, he just did.

Not long after moving in, the company that Jack worked for started failing and Jack's hours were cut almost in half. Betty was a couple of months pregnant, and they were struggling to make ends meet. Crocifessa felt badly for them, so she convinced Peter that they should lower their rent from twenty-five dollars a month to twenty dollars a month. Many months they couldn't pay anything at all, and Crocifessa would tell them not to worry about it. Finally Jack lost his job altogether. He did some bookkeeping once in a while for a couple of small businesses, but those jobs were few and far between.

At least once a month Crocifessa would fill a box with vegetables, bread, cereal, eggs and milk, and have Peter bring it up to them. If Peter started to object she would say, "We have it and they don't; they need to eat." Many nights when she was cooking supper, she would prepare enough for Betty and Jack and send it up to them. Crocifessa's kindness knew no bounds. It was a hard time for many people, and Betty and Jack were not the only people she helped over some rough times. When their daughter was born six months later, Crocifessa made certain that she had what she needed, and Ethel gave Betty some of Francie's baby clothes and toys. It was a tough time for them, but Crocifessa and Ethel did what they could to help Betty and Jack. "I don't know what's the matter with him," Andy said to Ethel one night. "There's been a few jobs Jack could have taken, but he keeps saying, 'It's not the right job for me,' or I'm going to wait for the right job.' I'll tell you the truth Ethel, I don't think there *is* a right job for him. Big deal, he does a little bookkeeping now and then; I don't think the guy *wants* to work. I mean, why should he? He's got you and my mother giving them food and clothes, and charging very little rent. He's never going to go back to work when he's got the 'life of Riley' right here in this house." "I know, Andy," Ethel said. "I've been bothered about him turning down job opportunities too; maybe he just needs a little more time." Andy shook his head, "Yeah, time… right; meanwhile, we're supporting them."

*****

May 4, 1946 was an exciting day for Francie. Not just because it was her seventh birthday, but also because she was making her First Communion. Francie was wearing a lovely white communion dress and veil, and because everyone said she resembled Shirley Temple, her mother made sure she curled her hair like Shirley's with the curling iron. "There!" Ethel said when she was finished. "Now you're ready to go." She met Riri downstairs and they walked up Parker Street and met Mary and Rosemarie. They all walked together in their beautiful dresses and veils to church. They had to be there early, to get last minute instructions from the nuns. Ethel had said, "We'll see you at the church, Honey." "Grandma and Papa are coming, aren't they, Mommie?" Francie asked, "and Nana, too?" "Yes, of course they're coming." Ethel said. "Do you think they'd miss something this important? Nana is going to meet us at the church; Uncle Ernie and his friend Lena will be there, too." "Oh, good!" Francie said. "I really like Lena, Mom, don't you?" "Yes, Honey, we all do."

"All right, now," Sister John Marie said, "Quiet down! Frances Vitello and Rita McGrath will be leading off the procession from St. Gerald's Hall to the church. All public school children will be filing behind Frances, and all Blessed Sacrament School children will be behind Rita. You'll start here, go out the front door and walk down the walkway to the sidewalk, then turn to the left and continue on to the church. You'll walk along the sidewalk until you're right in front of the center door, then turn together and walk up the steps and through the door. Sister Robert Angela will be inside to show you to your pews. Blessed Sacrament School children will be seated in the front rows, and the public school children will be in the rows behind them; boys on the left, girls on the right. Now, then, are there any questions?" No one dared ask a question, because they were supposed to know all this by now, and also, because they were scared to death of the nuns. "Good! Now remember, keep straight lines, keep your hands in a praying position, your eyes straight ahead at all times… and absolutely no talking!"

Francie and Riri began the procession, looking like angels. All the other communicants filed along behind them, girls in the front, boys pulling up the rear. As they came down the walkway, Francie was shocked at the crowd of people along the sidewalk, smiling and softly cheering them on. She and Riri felt very important in their leadership roles. Actually, they were chosen because they were the two littlest in the First Communion class, but they believed it was because they were so special. Ethel and Andy were there, beaming with pride, and Joey took advantage of the opportunity to stick his tongue out at his sister as she walked by. Francie scrunched her nose at Joey, and gave a little toss of her head as she passed him. Her three grandparents were there, smiling at her and waving. As she and Riri made the turn to go up the steps into the church, Francie spotted Ernie and Lena waving at her. She couldn't wave to them, but she gave them a big smile.

Inside the church, the ceremony started. As Francie went forward to receive her First Holy Communion, she felt a little nervous, and hoped she was good enough to receive Jesus. The Sisters had said that you had to be in 'a state of grace' to even think about taking the communion. She wanted to be in a state of grace, even though she had absolutely no idea what a state of grace was. As the priest came to her, she put out her tongue and he placed the host on it. *"I'm pretty sure I am in a state of grace,"* Francie thought, *"I'm feeling more graceful than I've ever felt."* As she came to her pew, and was about to enter it, the euphoria Francie was feeling ended abruptly when Sr. Robert Angela whispered sternly, "Don't chew!" Francie didn't know why she couldn't chew. Then a disturbing thought came into her mind, *"Oh, my goodness! Of course!"* she thought. *"Jesus feels it; oh, I'm so sorry Jesus, I hope it didn't hurt too much."* A moment later another disturbing thought entered her mind, and her eyes filled with tears... *" I don't think I'm in a state of grace, 'cause I don't feel graceful anymore"*

When the ceremony was over, the communicants all filed out of their pews into the center aisle; the boys from the left and the girls from the right. As they walked down the aisle together and filed out of the church, with hands in praying positions, they looked like angelic little brides and grooms. Outside, the communicants filed back the same way they came, and entered St. Gerald's Hall for a First Communion breakfast. They were served scrambled eggs, a slice of bacon, toast and orange juice. Francie and Riri and Rosemarie and Mary were all thrilled with the activities of the morning and they loved their new white rosary beads and scapulas. Francie especially loved the little white prayer book with the picture of Jesus' mother Mary on the cover.

Back at home everyone congratulated Francie and hugged and kissed her; the family was big on hugs and kisses. Ernie wanted to take lots of pictures with his new Kodak camera, so everyone had to go outside to have their pictures taken with Francie. Margaret and Charlie and the kids came over (they now had five), and also Sarah and Pat, and Sarah's sister, Phil. When Pat came in, he handed Francie a white rose. He said, "This is for my little princess." Francie was very pleased; Pat was always such a gentleman, and he was one of Francie's favorite people in the whole world. "Thank you, Pat," she said, "Thank you so much." She kissed him on the cheek and ran to put her beautiful flower in water.

Francie noticed that everyone came with presents for her; she couldn't wait for dinner to start, so she could open her presents afterwards. Crocifessa had made some pasta, and sausage cacciatore. Ethel had bought some nice cold cuts and cheeses and she made a huge salad, and there were rolls and fresh Italian bread. Sarah and

Phil made a lovely birthday/ First Communion cake for the occasion. Dinner was terrific, as usual.

Riri came in later for birthday cake and tonic, and brought Francie a birthday present. It was a Shirley Temple coloring book and crayons. Francie received lots of nice presents, but her favorite was a book from Sarah; it was "The Secret Garden" by Frances Hodgson Burnett. She could hardly wait to start reading it. Her mom and dad gave her the best present of all. They said, "Honey, sometime in August, you're going to have a baby brother or sister to play with." Francie decided that her seventh birthday/First Communion day was the best day of her whole life.

*****

About two weeks after Francie's birthday/First Communion, Andy bought a car, a black 1938 Packard. He pulled up to the curb right near where Francie and Riri were playing. "Hop in!" he called. "I'll take you for a ride." "Daddy, are you sure you know how to drive a car?" Francie asked. He just laughed and said, "Of course I know how to drive; come on, you two, get in." Francie and Riri got into the car, and as Andy pulled away from the curb, Francie asked, "Whose car is this, Daddy?" "It's our car," Andy said. "I just bought it; what do you think of it?" "I love it!" Francie exclaimed, clapping her hands, "I just love it!" "Well, if you love this," Andy said, "You're going to flip over my next surprise." "Ooh, what is it Daddy?" "I'll tell you when we get back to the house," he said, "Your mother and I want to tell you and Joey together." Francie gasped, "Did Mommy get the new baby?" Andy laughed. "No, no, Honey," he said. "It's not that kind of surprise."

*****

"A SUMMER COTTAGE?" Joey cried. "That's terrific! When can we go see it, Dad? "We'll go on Saturday," Andy said. "We'll leave about six o'clock in the morning. "This is the best thing that ever happened," Francie cried. "Don't expect anything beautiful," Andy said. "The place needs a lot of work. You see, what used to be the barn is now the house. The original house burnt down; the people who owned it gutted the whole inside of the barn and made rooms in it." "Oh, wow!" Joey said. "I can't wait to see it." "Me too," said Francie. She wrinkled her nose..."Ooh, does it smell like a barn?" Andy chuckled. "No, it doesn't smell like a barn at all." "Can I have my own room?" Francie asked. "Well," Ethel said, "we'll have to wait and see." Joey was real excited. "Will we be able to go swimming there, Dad?" "Swimming?" Andy said. "We'll be swimming every day; wait till you see the lake, Joey. It's called Long Sought For Pond, and it's really beautiful; you're going to love it."

"Where *is* the cottage, Dad? Is it near here, or far away?" Joey asked. Andy said, "It's in a remote little village called Westford, about forty-five miles from here. Your mother and I spent quite a few weekends there before you were born, Joey." "Yeah, I remember you and Mom talking about Westford," Joey said. "That's where Uncle Joe and Aunt Mary have a cottage, right?" "Yep, that's where we used to stay," Andy said; "only now Uncle and Auntie have a large brick house there, not a cottage. Their house used to be an inn where church groups would go for a week, or a weekend. When I was a kid, I went there a few times with a group of kids from the Methodist Church in my neighborhood. I think it was called the Epworth Society. I never forgot Westford; I wanted to go back so badly. I couldn't believe it when years later Uncle and Auntie bought the place. Westford was like another world to me; it still is."

"What has to be done to our place, Dad?" Joey asked. "Well, it needs some carpentry work and a lot of paint. It comes with over two acres of land; a lot of it is just woods, but the grounds around the house need a lot of work." "I can help you, Dad," Joey said. "I'm not a little kid anymore, I'm nine now, and I'm strong." "You're right, Joey," Andy said, "You are strong; you'll be a big help to me." "Me too, Daddy?" Francie said, "Can I help, too?" "Absolutely!" Andy said. "Your mother's going to need your help." "Francie," Ethel said, "you and I will have plenty to do, believe me." "Oh, good, Mommie, I want to help in the new cottage."

It seemed to take forever to get to Westford, but as soon as they saw the sign that said, "Westford", they all yelled, "Westford! Hurray!" Every single trip they made to Westford over the next eight years called for the same yell. When they finally made their way down Dunstable Road, and drove by the lake on their right, Francie and Joey nearly shrieked with excitement. "It's fabulous, Dad," Joey cried, "I can't wait to go swimming." Long Sought For Pond *was* probably a pond, but those who had camps in Westford always referred to it as "The Lake."

Every now and then, Francie could see a cabin set deep in the woods. Some were painted and looked nicer than others. Some of them were so old they looked like they were leaning to one side, and a good wind might blow them over. Finally Andy said, "Now look on your right; you'll see a cottage set back with a sign over the door that says, "The Peter Pan." That's Rose and Slim Giuliana's place." Slim was a good friend of Andy's. As they came to the end of the lake, Andy turned left onto a dirt road. A battered old sign said, "Long Sought For Pond Road." There seemed to be nothing on the road but woods on both sides. About a half mile up on the right, was a kind of dirt driveway. Andy turned into it, and Joey and Francie started yelling, "Is this it, Dad? Are we here?" "We're here!" Andy yelled. Ethel, Joey and Francie all yelled, "Yippee! We're here!"

At first glance, it looked kind of like a wind-battered barn, except for the porch that ran the length of the front of the house. There was a huge square hole in the front yard where the original house had stood; it was about ten feet deep. There were lots of rocks and debris thrown into it to try and fill it in. "This area is off-limits!" Andy hollered. Ethel groaned softly as she looked over the cottage and the grounds. "There really is so much to be done before we get this place in good living condition," she said. For a few moments she felt overwhelmed at the enormity of the situation. At seven months pregnant, everything seemed overwhelming to her. Andy put his arm around her and said, "Come on now, Hon, sure there's a lot to be done, but it's ours, Ethel. We don't have to do everything right away. It will take a few years, but we'll get this place just the way we want it. We'll have lots of help remember; Pat and Slim are coming over today, and Pa and Charlie are coming next weekend to help. It really is going to be wonderful for all of us, Ethel." Ethel nodded, "You're right, Andy, there isn't any big rush to get it perfect. We'll take our time and enjoy the place while we fix it up; it *will* be wonderful." Joey and Francie already thought it was wonderful; they were city kids, and they were in the country. All they could see was the woods, and the excitement and adventure of it; to them it was a kid's paradise.

Andy roped off the hole in the ground, and drilled his children on not going near there. He was right; there was a lot of work to be done. Joey and Francie set out exploring the woods around the cottage. For city kids, strangely enough, they were right at home in the woods of Westford, and loving every minute of it.

The cottage came with furniture in it, such as it was, so Ethel made up the beds, and Francie helped. "Can I have this room Mommie?" Francie asked about one of the bedrooms. "Well, you can as long as it's just us here," Ethel said. "But sometimes you'll have to sleep wherever it's convenient, when the rest of the family or friends come to stay." "Okay, but I can sleep here tonight, goodie." Ethel and Francie began sweeping and cleaning the rooms to make them a bit more livable. Andy said to Joey, "I think the first thing we should do is get that marvelous porch in shape." It was a great porch, about nine feet wide. All the screening needed to be replaced, so Andy took measurements and he and Joey went to North Chelmsford to get the screening. Slim and Pat came over and helped, and by early evening, the screening was all done. They had their supper of franks and beans out on the porch, and went to bed early. Andy, Pat and Slim worked all the next day; Andy was very pleased at all that was accomplished during their first weekend there.

Andy and Ethel and the kids arrived back home in Jamaica Plain around midnight Sunday. Andy had to go to work in the morning, and Joey and Francie had to go to school. They were all completely exhausted; Joey and Francie slept most of the way home. Ethel kept dozing, but tried to stay awake to make sure Andy stayed awake.

In a few weeks, Joey and Francie would be out of school for the summer; they couldn't wait to get back to Westford. Andy would be commuting back and forth to work everyday. Andy said to them, "You kids understand we can only stay until the middle of July, because Mommie needs to be at home as it gets closer to August." "We know, Dad; a whole month at the cottage will be great."

"School's out! We're going to Westford!" Joey shouted as he ran up the stairs, with Francie running behind him, yelling the same thing. They had gone most weekends and worked on the place, but now a whole month at the cottage was an adventure they couldn't wait to get started on. Two days later they were on their way to Westford.

Andy, Charlie and Slim had painted the entire cottage inside and out during the past few weekends, after they did a little carpentry repair work here and there. "Thank God the weather has been good," Andy said. Charlie's son Peter and other family members spent time working on the cottage, too. Everybody was excited and wanted to see the work get done. They were all city folk; a summer cottage with a lake nearby was like a dream to them.

Peter fell in love with the cottage and the grounds, and Crocifessa felt like it was the closest thing to being in Sicily that she had experienced since they first came to America. Needless to say, they both loved it.

The living conditions at the cottage in Westford could definitely be described as rustic.... very rustic. To begin with there was no electricity; kerosene lamps were used in every room. There was also no indoor plumbing, no running water and no bathroom. There was a very old outhouse, a two-seater, about twenty yards from the house. In the evening, if anyone needed to use the outhouse, he or she would take a flashlight along. No one would dare venture out of doors after dark without a flashlight, as "one's hand cannot be seen in front of one's face outside at night," as Ethel would often say. Andy made sure there were lots of flashlights, and always plenty of batteries on hand. In the middle of the night, if anyone needed to relieve himself, there were "pots" under each bed for that purpose. It was Joey and Francie's job to empty all pots in the outhouse every morning, a job both of them dreaded. It was unpleasant, but necessary. "Rinse them out and wash your hands good," was Ethel's cry every morning. She was well aware of how careless kids could be In another area of the yard, about thirty yards from the house, was a well. It was boarded over and a pump brought water to the surface. It was Joey's job to fill large milk pails with water every morning and bring them to the house for his mother. Each weekend, when they were packing to go to the cottage, Ethel would never fail to say, "Make sure we have a bottle of water with us." The water was for priming the pump; without water poured down into the pump, while it was being primed, it would not work. To the right of the house was a large shed, where Andy kept tools, ladders, lawnmowers, paint, and lots of other stuff.

The front yard was quite large, and there was another yard, even larger on a lower level. Andy and his father laid long granite slabs in place for steps going down to the lower yard. After the lower yard was cleared of rocks and weeds, and mowed clean, Peter started his garden. He planted tomatoes, cucumbers, eggplant, zucchini, lettuce, and green beans. He also planted basilicor (basil) and spearmint. He loved basil and mint in the spaghetti sauce and broken up on top of a plate full of pasta. Peter tended that garden with such love and care, it made Andy happy just to watch him. He also planted flowers around the upper yard, and he and Andy and Joey planted five pine trees, each one smaller than the other. Andy said the biggest one was his tree and the smallest was for the new baby that was coming in August. Peter and Andy built a large barbecue pit in the lower yard. Many nights they cooked the meat there, which gave Ethel and Crocifessa a little break.

On entering the cottage you stepped into a large parlor, with a pot-bellied stove against the center of the far wall. It was the only source of heat in the house. It was connected to a brick chimney that went upstairs and stayed hot for hours after the stove went out. On the right wall in the parlor was a long couch, with a window over it. Along the wall beside the front door was a kind of day bed, which was used for seating, and as a bed when needed. In two corners of the room were old, worn, easy chairs. It was a comfortable room, where the family gathered after dinner on evenings when it was too cool to sit out on the porch. They'd talk and read and play games. To the left of the parlor was a small room, which became a guest bedroom. Ethel put up a drape to close it off from the parlor. It was Crocifessa and Peter's room. When they weren't there, Ethel Sr. would sleep there. Beyond the small bedroom was a large kitchen. There was a large wood/coal stove where Ethel and Crocifessa cooked and baked. Along one wall were the kitchen table and six chairs, and along the far wall Andy had put in a soapstone sink and wooden counters for Ethel to work at. She would pour water from the milk pail into a kettle, heat it up on the wood stove, then pour it into a basin to wash dishes, etc., and then it would drain through a pipe to the outside. Over the sink was a window that looked out into deep woods.

To the right of the kitchen was a small storage room where canned and boxed foods were kept, and wood or coal was stored. Pots and pans and small tools were kept there, and coats were hung there, also. It was kind of an all-purpose room. At the far end of that room was the staircase that led up to two bedrooms. The first room upstairs was an average size room; it held a double bed, a bureau and a chair comfortably. There was a closet tucked in over the stairway. The other room was very large. It held two double beds, two bureaus, a table between the two beds, and two chairs, and still left plenty of room to walk around.

Between chores during the day, and on warm evenings, the front porch was where everyone loved to relax. At night, sitting out there with a couple of kerosene lamps glowing, listening to the crickets, was about as cozy and peaceful as anything could be. At one end Andy had taken a metal twin bed spring and attached chains to it on both ends and hung it from the beams of the porch. He put an old twin mattress on it and a pillow, and it became the most comfortable hammock ever invented. Many people took naps on it, and on hot nights it was a favorite place to sleep if you could claim it before someone else did. Near the hammock was a long, three-cushioned glider, and near the door into the main house was a large round table that easily sat eight to ten people. Most meals were eaten there, and they all agreed, it wasn't their imagination... meals eaten on that porch, whether breakfast, lunch or supper, were the best meals they had ever eaten.

Most of the cottages in Westford had signs over the doors with the name of the cottage on it. Ethel decided that their cottage should have a name that described it perfectly, so Andy carved out and painted a sign and hung it over the door..."Camp Pleasant." The cottage never failed to live up to its name.

That pretty much describes the house and the land. The cottage wasn't really beautiful; it was simply wonderful. But the land around it was just lovely. It became the joy of everyone who ever came to stay there…and many did, some for a day or a weekend, and some for weeks at a time. It was a little bit of paradise that no one wanted to leave. Charlie loved being in the 'country' so much, that a couple of years later he bought a cottage of his own in Littleton, Massachusetts.

*****

Dorothy Ann Vitello was born on August 11, 1946 at the Boston Lying-In Hospital. Ethel's doctor was concerned about the RH-negative possibility for problems. After the miscarriage three years before, he didn't want to take any chances with her and the baby. He felt that the Boston Lying-In Hospital was the best place to be if there was going to be a problem. Ethel had a difficult delivery, but no real problems. She and the baby were both fine.

Dorothy was a perfect, healthy and adorable baby. Andy was simply thrilled with her. He said to Ethel, "She's beautiful, Hon; a real knockout! I thought Francie had a lot of hair; this little doll has a full head of black curls." He looked at Ethel and smiled. "This was a tough one, wasn't it?" She nodded and smiled at him, and said, "It's over now." Then he held the wife he loved so much, and thanked God for keeping her and his baby girl safe.

"Please, Daddy, please take us with you to see Mommie and the new baby," Francie cried. "I will, kids, but you have to understand, you can't see her in the hospital." "Well, why not?" Joey asked; "we're her kids." "It doesn't matter," Andy said, "Children aren't allowed in the hospital." Joey said, "That's not fair, Dad." "Well, fair or not, that's the way it is. But I'll tell you what we can do…we can go around to the side of the hospital where your mother's room is, and you can see her and speak to her through the open window." "Oh yes, Daddy; I want to see Mommie," Francie cried. "You don't remember, Joey, but when your mother was in the hospital when Francie was born, I took you to see her that way. You made her very happy." "Okay, Dad, let's do it!" Joey said. Can we go tonight?" "I don't see why not," Andy said. "Let's hurry and eat supper, so we can get going." So, Francie and Joey visited their mother via the open window. They couldn't see their baby sister, but seeing their mom and talking with her meant so much to all of them, especially Ethel. They waited in the waiting room downstairs while Andy went to spend a few minutes with Ethel. He brought her flowers, and pictures Joey and Francie had drawn. Each day they wrote letters to their mother, and Andy would deliver them to her when he went to see her. It became a special part of Ethel's stay in the hospital, and each day she looked forward to seeing what the kids would send her.

At seven years old, because she was so little, Francie still slept in the crib in her parents' room. There was only one other bedroom and it was tiny; Joey slept there. Before baby Dottie and her mother came home from the hospital, Ethel said to Andy, "Francie should have the little room, now that the baby needs the crib; Joey can sleep in the parlor."

The next day Andy went out and bought a twin bed and put it in the parlor for Joey. He also bought a small radio that fit nicely inside one of the kitchen cabinets, so that he and Ethel could listen to their favorite radio programs in the evening without keeping Joey and Francie awake. Francie was thrilled to have the little room, but the first night she slept there she had a nightmare and woke up screaming. The streetlight outside her window had cast shadows in the room, and Francie was convinced there were monsters there. "I'm never sleeping in that room again," Francie cried. "Please Daddy, don't make me...please." "We'll figure something out, Honey," Andy said.

When Ethel and the baby were ready to come home, the crib was ready for the baby. Francie was sleeping on the twin bed in the parlor, and Joey was back in the little room. Everyone was happy; Francie finally had a real bed, and her own room, albeit the parlor. "This is the best thing that ever happened," she said, as she drifted off to sleep that night.

A few days later Andy brought Ethel and the new baby home. The whole family came out to greet her and see little Dottie Ann, as Francie decided she should be called. Ernie came over later with his mother and Lena. Crocifessa didn't make her 'famous' chicken soup this time, as it was a very hot day and no one was interested in hot soup. This time she cooked veal cutlets; they were absolutely delicious. She served them with pasta, Italian bread and salad. Crocifessa was an exceptionally good cook, and everyone oohed and aahed over everything she prepared. Every occasion revolved around her food. Ethel was becoming an excellent Italian cook also, under her mother-in-law's tutelage.

The next day Margaret and Charlie came over to see Ethel and the new baby. They brought Margie, and Bobbie, who was now four years old, with them. Francie was thrilled; she loved her cousin Margie and always looked forward to playing with her. But Margie was a bit of a tomboy, and always seemed to have more fun playing with Joey, which always left Francie disappointed and sometimes angry.

Francie's cousin Franny had just turned eighteen and was positively gorgeous. Whenever Francie was at her cousins' house, she used to love to watch Franny putting on her makeup and fixing her hair. "You're so beautiful, Franny; when I grow up I hope I look just like you." Franny would always laugh and say, "You'll be prettier than me when you grow up; you'll see." Francie admired everything about her beautiful cousin. She used to practice walking like her, and talking like her, and even laughing like her. Franny was like a glamorous movie star, and Francie was her greatest fan.

*****

Around mid-October, Andy and Ethel and the children packed up and went to Westford for a long weekend. They left Thursday as soon as Andy got home from work. Ethel took everything she needed for baby Dottie who was now two months old. Dottie was a very good baby, sleeping through the night, and was almost never cranky. She was her daddy's little angel, and Joey and Francie loved their baby sister. They all wanted to see little Dottie in the cottage. By now, she was the only one in the family who had not been there. It was a mild October and everyone was excited; they couldn't wait to get back to Westford.

Most weekends throughout the fall and early winter were spent at the cottage. That little pot-bellied stove in the living room put out a lot of heat. When it was real cold, the kitchen stove was kept going. Between the two they heated the whole house; and at night the chimney stayed hot for a few hours after the stove burned itself out. In the morning, Andy always got up before everyone else to get the fire started, as the mornings were real cold. It was a lot of fun going to the cottage in early winter. Meals were usually eaten in the kitchen, and most activities took place indoors. There was fixing up to do and cooking and cleaning, and in the evening, lots of games were played. Often times the adults played Poker or Whist, and the kids played War or Old Maid. No one minded the cold; it was warm and cozy inside. They were at the cottage, so they were happy.

****

CHAPTER SIX
Dear Santa

Thanksgiving was always a major event at 952 Parker Street. Crocifessa and Ethel cooked up a feast. Ethel always insisted on a traditional 'American' Thanksgiving…turkey and all the fixings. Ethel Sr. came over the day before and helped with the meal. Charlie and Margaret and the kids came over for dinner also. When everyone was seated and grace was said, Joey, Francie, Peter, Junior, Margie, and Bobby all yelled at the top of their lungs, "Mangia, everybody!" Franny laughed with the adults, as she was no longer interested in doing the things the 'kids' did.

No family ever enjoyed meals together more than the Vitello family. It was a time of feasting and fun, joke telling and story telling. While passing the stuffing and the gravy,

Andy or Charlie would tell stories of their early days growing up in America, and of their different jobs, and barbering together. The kids loved hearing about the time Andy held the razor to the guy's throat, and he ran out of the shop scared to death. Another of their favorite stories was about the molasses explosion, when Charlie and Andy had to 'run for their lives.'

After dinner the women cleaned up in the kitchen and the men went into the parlor to listen to the football game on the radio. The younger ones, Joey, Francie, Margie and Bobby would play cards or a board game as soon as the table was cleaned off. At the end of the day, when everyone was exhausted, Andy would say, "This was the best Thanksgiving ever." He said that every year, but every year he really meant it.

*****

One or two more trips to Westford after Thanksgiving, and then it was just too much to ask of the wood stoves to keep them warm. Besides, it was the Christmas season, and there was much to do at home. Shopping for gifts was so much fun for Francie. She had saved her birthday/First Communion money she received to buy Christmas presents. She and Joey would often pool their money and get gifts together. Every Christmas they bought the same gifts... Evening in Paris cologne for their mom and a paintbrush for their dad. After all, they knew their parents loved those things because of the excitement they showed the last couple of years, when they opened their presents Christmas morning. Most of Francie and Joey's shopping took place in the 'Five and Ten', a store way up Centre Street in the Hyde Square section. Francie wasn't allowed to go that far alone, but with Joey, who was nine and a half, her mother would let her go.

When the time came to buy the Christmas tree, Joey and Francie always went with Andy to help him pick out just the right one. Ethel often went too, but with Dottie only four months old, she decided to stay home. This particular year the price of trees was real high... two dollars. Andy practically called the man a thief, but it was too cold to try and find one cheaper somewhere else. Andy said to Ethel when they got home, "This is the last year we buy a Christmas tree." Francie and Joey were shocked. "But Daddy," Francie said, "We have to have a Christmas tree." She was close to tears. Joey said, "Dad, I'll save my money and help you pay for the tree next year." Andy laughed and said, "Nope! Nobody's buying another Christmas tree in this house.... From now on we go to Westford and cut down our own Christmas tree; what do you think of that?" "Yippee!" Joey cried. "That's terrific, Dad!" "Yeay!" Francie yelled. "You know, Andy," Ethel said, "That's a wonderful idea."

The Christmas season was a festive and wonderful time in their home, as it was in most people's homes. To Francie, Christmas was magical and enchanting. Like most children, she couldn't wait to see it come, and hated to see it leave. Every Christmas Eve, Ernie and Lena and Ethel Sr. would come over, and Crocifessa and Peter would come upstairs. Ethel would put out hors d'ouvres and Ernie would always bring the fixings for tasty mixed drinks for the adults. Francie and Joey would drink Coca-Cola or Orangeade. There would always be peanuts and Christmas candies to nibble on, and later Ethel would make coffee and bring out dessert, which was usually apple pie and ice cream, and chocolate cake that Lena brought. Francie and Joey could hardly wait to open their presents from Ernie and Lena. They thought Ernie was tremendously rich, because he always had the best cars, cameras, record players, and two-wheeled bikes. But mostly it was because he always gave them terrific gifts, and every time Ernie bought a new bike, Joey got his old one. He was thrilled because 'old' to Ernie was definitely 'new' and wonderful to Joey.

Christmas Eve was always special, and relaxing for everyone. The shopping, the wrapping, and the decorating the house and the tree were done, and now they could just sit back and enjoy, until, of course, Joey and Francie went to sleep; then Andy, with help from Ernie, would put together toys and arrange presents under the tree.

A few years ago, when Joey was six and a half, and Francie was four and a half, Santa Claus brought Joey an electric train set; it was huge and took up most of the parlor floor. He loved it, and played with it almost constantly. Santa had also brought Francie a carpet sweeper; she loved that, too, and 'cleaned house' often. Three days after Christmas, Francie was 'doing her chores', as Joey was playing with his trains. She pushed the carpet sweeper across the train tracks to get to the other side of the parlor. The carpet sweeper was made of metal, and as it went over the metal tracks, a kind of mini explosion occurred, with smoke pouring out of the train's generator. Francie screamed and Joey started yelling; "You broke my trains! Mom, she broke my trains!" Ethel came running into the parlor and pulled the plug out of the wall. Joey was ready to 'kill' Francie. He ran after her to hit her, but Ethel grabbed him and said, "Joey, she didn't mean to harm your trains; she didn't know what would happen when the carpet sweeper went over the tracks." "She did, too!" Joey yelled. "I hate you Francie!" "All right! That's enough!" Ethel cried. "I know you're upset, Joey, but I won't have that 'hate talk' in this house. Now, when your father gets home, I'm sure he'll be able to fix your trains." Francie felt terrible; she knew it was all her fault, but she never meant for that to happen. Sobbing, she said, "I'm sorry, Joey; I didn't mean it." "Go away!" Joey screamed. He was crying and very angry. "Ethel said, let's all go in the kitchen; I'll make us some hot chocolate, and when your father comes home, Joey, he'll fix everything. Come on, Francie; come in the kitchen with me; Joey, come on; it's going to be okay."

When Andy came home that evening, he examined the train set, and said, "I'm sorry, Joey; the generator is burnt out; even the tracks are burnt in places. There's no way to fix it." Joey started crying again and ran into his room and slammed the door. Andy felt real bad; there was no way he could afford to buy another train set. Francie was hurting for her brother; she knew how much he loved those trains. She wanted to make up for it somehow, but she didn't know how. Christmas joy, that year, didn't last very long; they all felt really bad.

Francie and Joey were allowed to stay up until ten o'clock, and then, exhausted but excited, they said goodnight to everyone and went to bed. Francie knew she'd never be able to sleep; It was the most exciting night of her life. Santa Claus was coming, and she wanted to stay awake and try to get a glimpse of him.

Francie had written Santa a letter about a month earlier, asking for a Cocker Spaniel puppy. When she received a letter back from him, she was about as excited as she had ever been in her life. The return address on the envelope said: "Santa Claus, North Pole." She could hardly breathe as she carefully opened it. Her heart sank, as she read: "Dear Frances, I am sorry to have to tell you this, but I cannot bring you a puppy for Christmas. You see, I can only bring things that I can make, with the help of the elves. Only God can make a puppy, so maybe you should talk to your parents about that. But, Frances, you have been such a good girl all year long, and because I know just what you want in the line of toys, I promise, you won't be disappointed on Christmas morning. Have a very merry Christmas." The letter was signed: "With all my love, Santa."

Francie was disappointed about the puppy, but what Santa wrote did make sense to her. She decided to turn her thoughts to what he would bring her on Christmas morning. She began thinking about the beautiful doll she had shown her mother in the toy department of Jordan Marsh. She thought, *"I sure hope Santa can make that one."* Even though she was disappointed, Francie cherished the letter from Santa Claus, and kept it in her 'Secret Garden' book, which was her most prized possession.

The next thing she knew, Joey was shaking her and saying, "Get up, Francie, it's Christmas; Santa Claus came last night." "Santa Claus!" Francie gasped, and jumped out of bed. "Hold on now!" Andy yelled when he heard them up. "Wait for us!" Andy got his new Kodak camera that Ernie gave him for Christmas, and took pictures of Francie and Joey coming into the parlor. Ethel banged on the floor over Crocifessa and Peter's bedroom to let them know the kids were up. They came upstairs in their nightclothes to watch their grandchildren open their presents.

Francie felt like she was in a fairyland as she came into the parlor and saw the beautiful doll that she wanted, sitting in a doll carriage under the tree. There were also games and toys, and all kinds of wonderful things. Santa was right; she wasn't disappointed at all, she was thrilled beyond words. There were more wrapped presents to be opened, and presents to exchange with each other. It was fun watching Dottie's huge eyes light up when a present was given to her. She sat in her little seat and played with the rattle Francie and Joey gave her, and a teddy bear that Santa brought. She was like a real live Christmas doll, and laughed at everything.

When all the presents were opened, Ethel went to the kitchen and made bacon, scrambled eggs, toast, and coffee and juice. Crocifessa helped get the table set, and then they ate breakfast together. Afterwards, they all got dressed and went to church...even Peter.

Usually Ethel, Sr. came on Christmas Eve and stayed overnight, and spent Christmas day with Ethel and Andy and her grandchildren. But this year Ernie wanted his mother to spend Christmas day with him and Lena and Lena's mother, so Ethel, Sr. went to the Castellano family on Christmas day. She liked Lena a lot, and was glad she and Ernie cared so much for each other.

As Ernie and his mother drove to the Castellano home, she thought, *"Mrs. Castellano seems like a real good woman. Ernie will probably marry Lena. Imagine, both my children marrying Italians. Who'd have believed it? I don't think Lena is Sicilian, though. Ah well, it's going be a nice day, and one thing I'm sure of, the meal will be terrific. Italians do seem to have a magic touch when it comes to cooking, and Mrs. Castellano is no exception."*

Christmas dinner was legendary in the Vitello household; it was eaten downstairs in Peter and Crocifessa's apartment. After grace was said, came the traditional, "Mangia, everybody!" from the kids, and then dinner would begin. It started off with Crocifessa's 'famous' chicken soup with little meatballs and escarole in it. Then came a huge antipasto salad, made by Margaret, served with the freshest Italian bread. Next came Crocifessa's 'famous' baked macaroni, which could not be rivaled, served with meatballs and sausages. Charlie would say every time, "Ma, you make the best meatballs in America, and in all of Italy and Sicily, too!" Crocifessa would blush and wave her hand at him, as if to say, "Oh no, that can't be true."

After the baked macaroni, meatballs and sausages, with a little breather in between, came Ethel's roast pork and gravy, mashed potatoes, carrots, and homemade applesauce. Steamed green beans, tossed in olive oil and garlic, were always a big hit. Wine was always served with Christmas dinner, and even the kids were allowed to have a little bit in a glass.

After dinner, when everyone felt stuffed to the point of bursting, one by one, they'd get up and move about, then sit in the parlor and relax; everyone but Ethel, Margaret and Crocifessa, who were clearing the table between courses. Peter would always fall asleep; sometimes Andy and Charlie would, too. Francie and Joey and their cousins would play with their toys, or play a game together.

A little while later dessert and coffee were served, and everyone came back to the dining room table, with their mouths watering again; this time for coffee and sweets. Cannoles, almond cookies, pies and ice cream would be put on the table, along with Coca-Cola, Ginger Ale, and Orangeade. Amoretto, a tasty liqueur, was put out for those who would like a little in their coffee, or on their ice cream.

When Crocifessa would buy the ricotta to put in the baked macaroni, it came in a metal quart-size container with waxed paper over the top and a rubber band around it to keep it secure. One year as everyone was eating the macaroni, Joey cried, "what the heck?" "What's the matter, Joey?" Ethel asked. All of a sudden he pulled a rubber band from his mouth. Crocifessa was shocked and embarrassed. "Oh Madre Deo!" She cried. "What is that?" Andy started laughing. "Ma, it's the rubber band from the ricotta container; it must have fallen into the mix without you seeing it." Poor Crocifessa was wringing her hands, almost in tears, apologizing to Joey. "That's okay, Grandma," Joey said, "I thought it seemed a little chewy." Everyone started laughing; after a moment a red-faced Crocifessa joined in. Every year after that, even when ricotta was no longer sold in metal containers, Joey would have a rubber band handy, and at some point while eating the macaroni, he would look shocked and say, "What the heck is this?" Then he would pretend to be pulling it out of his mouth. It took Crocifessa years before she recognized that it was Joey's 'macaroni joke' he would play on her. She would always look shocked first, then embarrassed, and then she would give Joey a little whack on the arm as she covered her face with her hand and giggled.

Christmas dinner was something in the Vitello household that everyone looked forward to, and relished like it was the first time they ever experienced it.

That evening, after Charlie and Margaret and the kids went home, Andy and Ethel and their three went back upstairs, feeling tired and content. Andy said to Ethel, "This was the best Christmas ever!" He said that every year, and every year he meant it more than the last.

*****

The house on Parker Street was very old, and always seemed to have something that needed fixing. One thing that constantly aggravated Andy was the downstairs back door that led out to the back yard. No matter how many times he fixed it, it would never close right. They always had cats because there was a constant mouse problem, especially living right next to an alley where rubbish barrels were kept. Ethel actually liked the fact that the downstairs door didn't close right. It kept her from having to go up and down the stairs every time the cat needed to go out, or come back in.

Francie loved the different cats that they had over the years. Blackie II was Francie's favorite, but she got hit by a car and died. There was never a shortage of cats in the neighborhood; that was for sure. In fact, a family who lived on Parker Street had a cat that had just delivered seven kittens, and they wanted to get rid of them.

One day the thirteen-year-old boy who owned the kittens came out of his house with a sack over his shoulder. Joey called out, "Hey, Billy, what's in the sack?" He said, "The kittens. I've got to get rid of them." Francie said, "We might be taking one when it's ready to leave its mother." "Well, can't wait!" Billy said. "I've got to get a rock and smash them all." Francie gasped, and Joey said, "Gee, Billy, how come you have to do that?" "'Cause my father told me to," Billy answered. "Too many cats in the house."

While Joey was talking to Billy, Francie ran in the house, "Mommy, Mommy, please don't let Billy kill the kittens." "Francie, what are you talking about?" Ethel asked. "Billy's father told him he has to kill all the kittens, because they have too many in their house. He said he's got to get a big rock and smash them all." "Oh, good Lord," Ethel said. "Come on, Francie." Ethel ran down the stairs with Francie right behind her. Joey started yelling, "Mom, Billy's going to kill the kittens." "Yes, I know, Joey; where is he?" He went down the alley to look for a big rock," Joey said. Ethel grimaced. She ran down the alley with Joey and Francie. She spotted Billy and called out to him. "Billy, wait, I want to talk to you." Billy started walking toward Ethel. "What is it, Mrs. Vitello?" "Billy," she said, "Why are you going to kill those kittens?" "My dad said I have to," Billy answered. We asked around, but nobody wants them." "How does your mother feel about this?" Ethel asked. "My mother said we don't have enough to feed ourselves, never mind a parcel of kittens, and if no one wants them, then they have to be done away with." "Do you think it would make a difference if I spoke to them?" Ethel asked. "No," Billy said. "There's no sense talking to them; their minds are made up. Look, Mrs. Vitello, if I come home with these kittens, my dad'll beat me good. I've got to do this." Ethel knew his parents, and she knew he was right. They would never listen to anyone if their minds were set on something. She felt sick to her stomach; she knew she couldn't change Billy's mind. He had to do what his parents said.

"You better leave now, Mrs. Vitello," Billy said. "You aren't going to want to see this." "All right, Billy, but I would like to have one of those kittens before I go." Francie drew a breath, and Joey just stared at his mother. "You sure?" Billy asked. "I'm sure," Ethel said. "You know they still need the nipple," he said. "I know," she said, "I'll feed it with a dropper." "Okay," he said, as he turned the sack over and seven tiny, mewing kittens dropped out. Francie started to cry. "How can you kill them, Billy?" "Hey, I got no choice; I'll get it good if I don't." "Can't you just let them go?" she asked. "No, he can't," Ethel said, before Billy could answer. "They'll be mauled and eaten by an animal, a dog or another cat, or even a rat. This will be quick, if nothing else. Francie, pick out the one you want," Ethel said, "and let's go home." With tears rolling down her cheeks, Francie picked out a kitten with tabby colors, orange, rust and white. She said, "I'm going to call him "Tiger". Not another word was said. Ethel, Joey and Francie walked silently up the alley to their house, as Billy proceeded to do what he had to do.

*****

Almost every day after school, before meeting Riri, Francie would go into her grandparents' apartment downstairs. Crocifessa was there most afternoons, unless she needed to stay a little later at the store. Francie would ask the same question every day, "Grandma, is it okay if I play the piano?" Crocifessa never refused. The piano was a large, beautiful player piano; beside it was a piano roll cabinet. There were all kinds of music rolls, but the one Francie loved the best was "Are You Lonesome Tonight?" She would carefully fit the two ends of the roll into the slots provided in the piano, then gently pull down the tab on the roll and hook it onto the empty roller just below. She would start pumping the 'pedals', and the music would begin, as the piano keys went up and down with each note. The words to the song were printed on the roll and as it went from one roll to the other, Francie would sing along. Sitting at that player piano was wonderful fun to Francie; she would pretend she was a famous entertainer, and sing and 'play' her heart out. On holidays, or anytime the whole family was together at 'Grandma and Papa Vitello's', Andy or Charlie would 'play' the piano, and the whole family would sing along. Those were the times of family fun that none of them would ever forget.

*****

On weekends Francie used to love to run downstairs early in the morning when she knew Crocifessa and Peter were up. She would go into her grandmother's bedroom, and Crocifessa would smile and hand Francie a lovely silver hairbrush. Brushing her Grandmother's hair was such a joy to Francie. She knew her cousins Franny and Margie brushed their grandmother's hair whenever they stayed overnight, but when Francie brushed her hair, it was their special time together. Crocifessa always wore her hair pulled back in a bun, and when she took it out, her hair would cascade down her back to the tops of her thighs. Her hair was so long she could actually sit on it. Francie had never seen hair so long. At night her grandmother would make two, thick, long braids at bedtime. She said it made her hair wavy.

Francie could never understand why her Grandmother wanted wavy hair when all she ever did with it was wind it and roll it into a bun. Years later, when Francie was sixteen, she asked Crocifessa, "Grandma, why do you always braid your hair at night to get wavy hair when no one ever sees your wavy hair?" Crocifessa answered, "I don't make braids for wavy hair to be seen by anyone; I do it because it makes the winding and rolling in the morning so much easier than when it's perfectly straight." Francie laughed, "Wow, Grandma!" "I always thought it was kind of strange, but that makes such perfect sense." "Si! You should braid your hair at night, too;" her Grandmother said, "then you won't have to cook your hair with that curling iron you use all the time." Francie laughed, "I just might start doing that, Grandma, and maybe I'll let my hair grow all the way down to my behind, too." Crocifessa chuckled, "And are you going to roll it into a bun every morning, too?" "Hah! No!" Francie said, "That may have been stylish when you were a girl in Sicily, but it sure isn't the style today. I want the boys to *like* me, Grandma, not drive them away." Crocifessa laughed heartily, and kissed Francie's cheek, "Face' bella! With that face, you'll never have to worry about driving the boys away; they'll never want to leave." Francie smiled and kissed her grandmother; she never failed to make Francie feel so very special.

*****

As June came around again, school got out for the summer, and Joey and Francie were ready and eager to get back to Westford. Two days before they were leaving, Ethel said to Francie, "We have a surprise for you." "For me? Ooh, what is it, Mommie?" Francie asked, all excited. "I spoke to Mr. and Mrs. McGrath today, and they've agreed to let Riri come with us to Westford for a couple of weeks." "Oh, Mommie," Francie cried, "Is she really coming with us?" "Yes dear, it's all set, she's coming." Francie ran right down to Riri's house. Riri had just gotten the news from her parents, and was on her way out her front door as Francie got there. They both screamed with delight, and hugged each other, jumping up and down. "Oh, Riri, we're going to have so much fun, you'll see," Francie said. "I can't wait to go," said Riri. "I'm so happy,"

Two days later they were on their way to Westford. Joey, Francie and Riri sat in the back seat, and Joey teased them unmercifully all the way to Westford. Riri yelled out "Westford! Hurray!" with them, as they passed the sign. When they finally drove up the driveway, Riri, who had never been out of the city, looked all around and said, "Oh, this is so beautiful; it's like we're in heaven." Andy and Ethel smiled and said, "That's just how we feel too, Riri."

Francie and Riri filled the two weeks with swimming, blueberry picking, visiting Dubinski's Farm, taking long walks, and exploring the woods around the cottage. They laughed hysterically when they used the outhouse together. "I never heard of a bathroom outside the house," Riri said, "and one with two toilet seats; this is so funny."

133

They visited Rose and Slim, and Andy's Uncle Joe and Aunt Mary. Joe and Mary had a very large red brick house that was really quite beautiful, very unusual in remote and rural Westford. It was once an inn, before they owned it. There was also a small, one-room cottage on their property and a large barn. Francie used to like to play with her cousin Charlotte (Voltero) whenever Charlotte was staying there with her grandparents. There weren't a lot of cottages nearby, but what there was, was very rustic. Joe and Mary's place stood out like a beautiful Italian villa.

When it was time for Riri to return home, Andy had Francie come with them, which helped alleviate the sadness the girls were feeling. They stayed at home on Parker Street overnight, and returned to Westford the next day. Crocifessa and Peter went with them.

Every minute spent in Westford was like being in a wonderful dream. Francie and Joey made friends with Bobby and Barbara, whose family owned Dubinski's Farm. They loved being at the farm, especially Joey; he learned to milk cows and round them up and lead them into the barn. He fed the cows and the pigs with Bobby, and cleaned out the barns. Francie and Barbara used to feed the chickens, and collect the eggs from the hen house. There were two dogs at the farm, Rex, a German shepherd, and Rusty, a reddish collie mix. Rex was a nice dog, but Rusty was an ankle nipper. He drove Francie crazy when he was around. Joey would just laugh when Rusty tormented her, and all Bobby would say was, "He won't really bite, he's a sheep dog; that's what sheep dogs do to get the sheep to move." "Well, what's the matter with him? Doesn't he know the difference between a sheep and a girl?" Francie asked. Joey and Bobby doubled over laughing. Francie thought they were both so mean.

When Bobby and Barbara's chores were finished, then the fun started. They would all go to the upper level in the barn and leap off into the huge haystack that was down on the bottom floor. They did this over and over, and then they would just lie on the hay and relax. Francie looked at Joey and Bobby lying in the hay one day, with a piece of hay between their teeth, and she started giggling. "What's so funny?" Joey asked. "You two look just like "Tom Sawyer and Huckleberry Finn"." The dogs would jump on them, lick their faces, and roll around with them in the hay. After a while they would all head for the lake to go swimming, dogs included. Many times Joey and Bobby would tell Francie and Barbara to 'beat it! scram! take off! get lost!' or whatever. Subtlety was not a part of most ten-year-old boys' natures. They didn't always want to be bothered with two silly kid sisters hanging around them. For the life of her, Francie couldn't understand why.

The best part about going to Dubinski's farm for Francie was Rex, a beautiful black, gray and white German shepherd. Rex was very friendly and gentle to Francie; she came to love him very much. Unfortunately, Andy and Ethel had made it very clear that they would never have a dog. They didn't really dislike dogs, but they didn't want one in the house, especially back home in the city.

Crocifessa had once been bitten by a dog, and still bore a small scar on her hand. Also, when Andy was a child, still living in Sicily, he had been bitten in the stomach by a dog. He didn't remember much of it, but his parents sure did. So it seemed that having a dog was definitely not in Francie's future. Well, she enjoyed Rex while she could, and that was something. She would play with him for hours, sometimes just tossing a stick or a ball that he would bring back to her. Sometimes they would run as fast as they could (well, as fast as Francie could) through the pasture together; and other times just walking and talking to him was special to her. Rex seemed to enjoy Francie's company as much as Francie enjoyed his.

One thing Andy and Ethel were adamant about was that Francie had to be home before it started to get dark. When Francie would leave the farm she would cut through the woods on a small path that Joey made, that led right to the back of their cottage. It was a kind of long and somewhat rough walk, and sometimes she and Joey would see and hear animals as they walked. It never bothered her though, because when she was alone, Rex would almost always walk with her all the way home. Ethel once said to Andy, "I swear that dog is deliberately protecting her; he seems to love her very much." "I know, I've noticed that, too," said Andy. "He's a great dog, that's for sure."

One day Francie stayed too long at the farm; she left when it was really starting to get dark. Joey and Bobby had gone with Bobby's uncle to North Chelmsford to pick up supplies. Once Francie headed into the woods everything seemed much darker. Where was Rex? He hadn't been around for most of the afternoon. She began to get a little nervous and she couldn't see the path any longer. Before she knew what was happening, she was lost, and it was getting darker. "Oh God," she prayed, "Help me to find the path again, please." She kept walking, but she knew she wasn't going the right way; nothing seemed familiar and the woods seemed to be getting thicker. She called out, "Daddy! Daddy!" hoping she was near enough to the cottage that he might hear. But she heard nothing, and it was getting darker. She was becoming very frightened, and began to cry. She heard an animal nearby and was afraid it might be a wildcat. She heard that there were wildcats in the woods. Or maybe it was a porcupine. She remembered when a porcupine stuck Joey. She could hear the animal getting closer. "Oh God, it's so dark; please, please help me; make my Daddy come, please." She heard growling, and rustling in the woods near her. She panicked and became hysterical, sobbing and calling for help. She heard the growling again; it was definitely getting closer.

She began to run, not knowing where she was going in the dark. Then she heard what sounded like a bark. She could still hear the growling, but this was different. It was definitely a bark; then she heard a lot of barking and more growling. Then the growling stopped and all she heard was loud barking, getting closer and closer. It was definitely a dog's bark. "Rex! Rex, is that you?" There he was, coming through the woods. She had to look hard to see him, but yes, it was Rex. She was sobbing as he ran up to her, jumping up and licking her face. "Oh Rex, you're here, you're really here." Francie hugged him and kissed him, and then she followed him, and he led her right to her door. Ethel came running out. As soon as Francie saw her mother, she broke down in tears again. "Francie, are you all right? Are you hurt?" "No, Mommie, I'm okay," she cried. "Where have you been?" Ethel asked. We've been so worried. Your father has been driving around trying to find you. He went to Dubinski's, but they said you had left a while ago. We didn't think you'd be coming through the woods because it was getting dark." Just then her father drove up the driveway; he had a very stern look on his face, and for a moment Francie thought she was in big trouble. Andy jumped out of the car and ran to Francie. He had planned to spank her for staying out after dark, but instead he picked her up and hugged her. "Francie, you had us scared to death; where have you been?" Andy put her down and she told them the whole story, exactly how it happened. Andy and Ethel both knelt down on the ground and hugged Rex. "Oh, you wonderful, wonderful dog!" Ethel said. Andy stroked Rex's back and said,

"I know this sounds crazy, but it's almost like God sent this dog to be Francie's guardian while she's in Westford. We've felt this before, Hon, and tonight just proves it to me." "You're right, Andy," Ethel said. "He's a wonderful four-legged angel, as far as I'm concerned." They brought Rex into the house and Ethel cut a big slice of meatloaf she had made for supper and gave it to him. Bobby's uncle dropped Joey off down the road, and when he came in the house, he was shocked to see Rex there. They all related the story to him, and all he could say was, "Wow! Unbelievable! Good boy, Rex!" It was real dark out by then, so Andy said, "Come on, Rex; you deserve a ride home tonight." Ethel, Joey, Francie and Dottie went with him, and afterwards Andy took them to Kimball's Ice Cream Farm and they enjoyed hot fudge sundaes, except Dottie, who slept the whole time. "I swear," Andy said, "Kimball's makes the best ice cream anywhere." No one disagreed. Later, Ethel and Andy prayed, and thanked God for protecting their little girl, and for sending Rex into their lives.

*****

Andy made good on his promise about going to Westford and cutting down their own Christmas tree that year, and every year after, while they owned the cottage.

*****

Living most of the year in the city had its own charm. One of the things Francie and Joey loved about the city was the arrival of the iceman a couple of times a week. He would come down Parker

Street and deliver blocks of ice to his customers. Customers would put a card in their front window. One side of the card had a large black square on it; that meant they wanted a large block of ice; the other side had a small black square on it, hence, a smaller block of ice. No card…no ice. The iceman would stop at each house, put a heavy leather cape over his shoulder, and with large ice tongs he would carry the block of ice over his shoulder into their house and put it in their icebox. As soon as the iceman entered a house, every kid on the block would come running. One kid would jump up into the back of the truck, and with the ice pick he would start chopping pieces of ice for each kid and throw them off the back of the truck. He'd keep doing this until someone yelled, "He's coming!" Then the 'thief' would jump off the truck and look as innocent as the day he was born. Each kid would hide his piece of ice behind his back. The iceman seemed so surly; he always knew what was going on, and sometimes he'd yell at the kids and they'd take off running, afraid of being caught by him. A large, disheveled man with an ice pick and tongs in his hand and a black leather cape around his shoulder was a menacing looking figure to an eight or ten year old. Sometimes the 'thief' would even ask the iceman if he could have a piece of ice. If the iceman didn't suspect that he was the one in the back of the truck chopping ice for everyone, he would chip a small piece of ice and hand it to him. "Oh, thank you, Sir," the kid would say. When the iceman would drive away, the 'thief' would start laughing and bring out his hidden piece of ice and start sucking on both pieces. It was only a piece of ice, but somehow to Joey and Francie and all the other kids in the neighborhood, sucking on that chunk of ice was a treat to be savored, especially when it was a real hot day. The kids who got ice would pat the 'thief' on the back as if he had performed some incredible feat. After all, he did put his life on the line to purloin those pieces of ice for all the kids. The 'thrill of the crime' was definitely what made it so special.

Now, the ragman was a sight to behold. He was dirty and scruffy looking, wearing old, torn, 'raggedy-looking' clothes. He came by every couple of weeks driving his horse and wagon. He'd ride up and down the streets, and with a kind of twang in his voice he'd yell,

"Rrraaags! Rrraaags! Any rags today?" He also collected paper, mostly newspapers.

Many people, including Crocifessa and Ethel would save old, worn-out clothing, curtains, sheets, towels, anything made of cloth that was no longer usable. When the ragman would come down Parker Street, Ethel and Crocifessa would bring out their bags of rags for the ragman. He would hang the bag on a hook on a scale, and pay them about a dime for a bag full. "I know he cheats something awful," Ethel would say every time she'd sell him a bag of rags, "I can't prove it but I know he pulls up on that scale a little as he's weighing the bag." Crocifessa said, "He's a thief and he's good at it, that's for sure."

Every evening, after Andy and Ethel read the newspaper, and Joey and Francie read the 'funnies', it was put out in the back hall until there was a week's worth of them. Joey would then tie up a bundle or two, and when the ragman came by, Joey would bring his bundles of newspapers out to him. He'd hang them on the hook and weigh them, tell Joey it comes to one pound, and pay him a dime. Every single time, Joey would come back in the house, mad as a hornet, saying, "That guy's a crook; there was a lot more than one pound of newspapers in that bundle; all he gave me for them was one measly dime."

When Andy came home, and they told him how they felt about the ragman, he said, "I've got a good idea; we should take the bundles of rags, and the stacks of newspapers over to the store and have Pa weigh them on his scale. Then when the ragman comes, we'll see what his scale says, and catch him red-handed trying to cheat us." "Dad!" Joey said, "That's a great idea! I think we should stick some rocks in the middle of the bag of rags, too, to weigh it down." "Wait a minute!" Ethel called out from the other room. "What are you saying? That makes you worse than him." "Mom's right, Joey," Andy said. "I know how you feel.

That guy's been cheating people for years, but we can't stoop to his level, although I'd like to give him a taste of his own medicine. Besides, I know people who have tried that. He always knows; he feels all around the bags before weighing them." "Okay then, we'll just have Papa weigh them on his scale from now on," said Joey. "Good decision!" Ethel yelled.

A few weeks later, they weighed the bundles on Peter's scale at the store. When the ragman weighed them, his scale said a lot less. Ethel nervously asked him to weigh them again. She told him she had weighed them at her father-in-law's store and they weighed three and a half pounds, not one and a quarter pounds, as he had said. He was furious; "I'll give you twenty-five cents, and no more," he bellowed; "take it or leave it!" Ethel said, as calmly as she could, "That will be fine; I'll take it."

Later, when Andy came home and she and Joey related the story to him, he laughed. "Boy, I wish I had been there." "Mom was great, Dad!" Joey said. "You should have seen her." "Yeah, great," Ethel said, "I was so nervous, but I knew I was right. My voice must have been shaking real bad; honestly Andy, I was scared to death." "Well, it didn't show, Mom," Joey said, "honest." "You did good, Hon," Andy said, "I'm proud of you." Ethel knew the ragman still cheated them when he came around, but at least now she knew it was just a little.

Whenever the ragman came down the street, the kids in the neighborhood would all gather around his horse, and pat him and give him little pieces of stale bread or whatever their parents would give them for the horse. The poor old horse always looked like he should have been retired and put out to pasture years ago. Andy used to say, "That old nag was ready for the glue factory a long time ago, but that guy will work him 'til he drops in the street." After a while the ragman would come back waving his arms like a madman and yelling, "Get away from my horse, you little hoodlums." Not one kid would even *think* of hurting his horse, but it was obvious he just wanted to be nasty.

Francie wondered what he did with all those rags; she couldn't imagine a single use for them. Joey said, "I think he stuffs his mattress with them." Francie giggled. "Yeah, Joey, I'll bet he does." The ragman was a strange one; that's for sure. Francie never found out what he did with the rags. Someone said that paper was made from them; that made no sense to Francie.

Now and then a horse and wagon would come down Parker Street selling fresh fruits and vegetables. Everyone, men and women alike, would come out to buy tomatoes, peppers, apples, peaches, and more, because the prices were a lot less than the store prices. The kids loved patting the horse; the fruit and vegetable man never seemed to mind. Sometimes he'd even give the kids pieces of broken apples to give to the horse.

Once in a while a wagon would come around and the vendor would yell out, "Fish! Fresh fish here! His wagon would be loaded with crushed ice and all kinds of fish. He had a huge black leather tarp over everything, similar to the smaller one the iceman used to put over his shoulder. Crocifessa and Ethel would run out to buy haddock, mackerel, trout, or whatever the 'fish man' was selling that day. Ethel never failed to ask, "Is this fish absolutely fresh?" She knew it was, or her nose would tell her for sure. 'Course, the 'fish man' always responded, "Caught it all myself this morning." Whether he caught it himself of not, really didn't matter; it *was* always fresh.

Every now and then the 'fish man' would have eel on his truck. He knew Crocifessa would want that, as Peter loved it. "Oh God, Ma," Ethel would say, "How can he eat that?" Crocifessa would answer, "God only knows; I only cook it… he eats it. Everyone in the family groaned every time Crocifessa placed a plate of eel, cooked in tomato sauce, in front of Peter. He would laugh and proceed to devour his 'feast.' Eventually, everyone would leave the room and let him enjoy himself. Andy said, "I'll try anything at least once, but once was too much for eel."

It was always exciting hearing the horses' hoofbeats and hearing the vendors calling out their wares. Horses were a rare sight in the city. Francie and Joey loved it when they came around.

*****

Daddy, lift us up!" Fran called to her father as he finished supper. "Hey, you guys are a little big for that now, don't you think?" Andy said. "Aw, come on Dad," Joey said, "Lift us up." They ran to their father, and he said, "All right, grab on!" Francie wrapped her two

141

hands around Andy's muscular left bicep, and Joey did the same on Andy's right arm. Then Andy let out an exaggerated grunt and lifted the two of them up off the floor, hanging from his upper arms. "You know, you kids shouldn't do that anymore," Ethel said, "you're getting too big, especially you, Joey. You're going to hurt your father." "Ah, they're okay," Andy said, "I guess they're not too big yet." "Maybe so," Ethel said, "but you're getting too old for these games." "*Old?*" Andy cried, "I'm thirty-six; I'll show you who's too old." He ran toward Ethel, and swooped her up in his arms and swung her around, as she screamed and laughed. "Put me down, you crazy *old* man, you," she giggled. Joey laughed, and Francie squealed with delight. Andy was laughing, too. Finally he put his giggling wife down and, with a silly smirk on his face, said, "You talk to her Joey, no decent person would."

One day, many years later, during a family discussion, Andy jokingly said to Francie, "Honey, you talk to Joey, no decent person would." All of a sudden it was like a light bulb went on in her head, and she said, "Hey, it just dawned on me... that's a shot at the two of us, isn't it?" Andy looked surprised, and Ethel, too. "Oh come on, Francie," Andy said, "you're kidding, right?" "No," she said, "I'm serious." Joey started laughing, "You mean to tell me, after all these years hearing Dad say that, you never understood it?" "No," she said. "I never paid much attention to the words; it was just a silly thing Dad always said." She smiled and said, "Wow! A double whammy! I can't believe I never realized that." Andy and Ethel were laughing. "You talk to her, Dad, no decent person would," Joey said. Andy let out a howl; by this time they were all laughing.

****

Cottage in Westford (circa 1948)

Joey, Francie and Dottie at cottage 1948

**Francie and Dottie (Ethel in background)
at cottage in Westford 1948**

CHAPTER SEVEN
B.B.s And Farmer Burke

Tiger became Francie's favorite cat of all time. It turns out that she was a female, much to Ethel's chagrin. Tiger was a pleasant well-behaved cat with a sweet disposition. She turned out to be the best mouse-catcher they ever had.

One day Ethel announced to her children that Tiger was going to have kittens. Francie was thrilled; she could hardly wait for the day to come. Ethel thought it was somewhere around sixty days gestation period, so she counted out on the calendar about how long it would be before the kittens would arrive. She added a few days, because she knew if they didn't arrive when she thought they would, the kids, especially Francie, would grow impatient.

About a month and a half later, when Joey and Francie got home from school, Ethel said, "Guess what arrived today." She had a big smile on her face, and Francie knew immediately what it was. "The kittens!" Francie yelled. She and Joey ran to the back hall where the box was set up for Tiger and her kittens. There they were, six of the tiniest kittens Francie had ever seen. They were even smaller than Tiger's brothers and sisters that were killed. Francie wanted desperately to pat them, but she held back, and said, "Don't you worry, little kitties, no one will ever hurt you in this family." "Wow, they're cute." Joey said, "and so little." "Okay," Ethel said. "Listen up! There's got to be some rules here; so here goes…. No touching the kittens when they're being fed by their mother; no touching them when she's cleaning them, and no picking them up until I think it's safe to

145

do so. We don't want to see happen to these kittens what happened to Blackie's kittens, do we?" "No, Mom," Joey said sadly. "We'll be careful, we promise; right, Francie?" "Right! I promise, Mom; I'll do whatever you say." "After what happened with Blackie," Ethel said, "I never wanted another cat or kittens in this house; but we definitely need a cat to keep the mice away, and Tiger's done an excellent job at that. But here we are again with kittens so, as long as we've learned a lesson from our past mistakes, and as long as we adhere to the rules I've set down, then we'll be fine, and her kittens will be fine; okay?" "Okay," Francie and Joey said together.

Two years earlier, Blackie had three kittens, and she was very protective of them. The children picked up the kittens and played with them so much that Blackie decided to hide them. She thought she was just putting them in a little nook to protect them. What she didn't realize was that it was a hole in the wall in the bathroom, where a drainpipe went through. Two of the kittens dropped way down in the wall. Andy was able to save only one of them. They could all hear the kittens mewing, but no matter how Andy tried, he couldn't reach them. They went from the wall in the second floor to somewhere in the wall in the cellar. Andy broke through the wall in the cellar, but still couldn't reach them.... Eventually the mewing stopped. Andy repaired and sealed up the openings; it was all he could do.

Not long after that, Blackie got hit by a car and died instantly. Everyone in the house at 952 Parker Street knew they would never forget what happened to Blackie and her kittens. Ethel swore then that she would never have another cat in the house.

Joey and Francie obeyed the rules about the kittens faithfully. As difficult as it was to stay away, they wouldn't go out in the back hall often, and when they did, they would look but not touch. Tiger seemed to be content with her kittens; she was a very good mother and fussed over her babies all the time. Francie and Joey couldn't wait for the day when their mother would tell them it was all right to hold them and play with them.

One Sunday afternoon, Andy and Ethel took the kids over to Ethel's mom's house in Medford. They had a nice dinner there and afterward Francie and Joey begged their Nana to let them explore the attic. They did this every time they went there. They loved their grandmother's attic; it was full of very old chests and beautiful old-fashioned dresses on life-size dress forms. There were also hats, some men's and some women's. Francie loved trying on the women's hats, with all the ribbons and bows and beautiful veils. There was a large, elegant baby pram up there, and old-fashioned baby clothes inside it. There were lovely old dolls with long dresses, and a large beautifully painted rocking horse. The attic was a child's delight, with very old toys and games, and if one had a great imagination, you could become a princess or a king, or just a beautiful mommy and a handsome daddy. In Nana Dalton's attic, Joey and Francie entered a fantasy world that nothing could compare with. They loved going to their Nana's house, especially to the beautiful, land of wonder upstairs.

When Andy and Ethel and the kids got home after a nice day at their Nana's house, they heard a strange sound coming from the back hall. It sounded like a baby crying or a kind of wailing. Andy said, "Ethel, keep the kids here," and he went out into the back hall. A moment later Andy let out a cry, "Oh, God, no! Come here Tiger, come here girl." Ethel told the kids to stay where they were, and she went out into the back hall. Francie was frightened and close to tears. A moment later Ethel came back into the house, looking pale as a ghost. "Mommy, what is it?" Francie and Joey asked in unison. "What's happened? Tiger didn't try to hide the kittens, did she?" "Come sit down in the kitchen; I need to talk to you," Ethel said. "Oh Mommy, what is it?" Francie was crying by this time, and Joey was having trouble holding back tears. They both knew it was bad, whatever it was.

Ethel began, "Something got into the back hall and..." Her voice broke. "Mom," Joey said, his voice shaky, "Are the kittens hurt?" Ethel continued, "Whatever got into the back hall attacked Tiger and her kittens." "Oh no!" Francie screamed; no, Mommy, no, please!" "I know, Honey," Ethel said as she hugged Francie. "We're all upset, but we've got to be brave; there's nothing we can do about it, except to just love and nurture Tiger." "Mommy," Francie cried, "Are they dead? Are they all dead?" "I'm afraid so, Francie. We think Tiger will be okay, but she put up an awful fight for her babies; she's hurting pretty bad." Francie was sobbing by now.

Joey and Francie were crying as Andy came back into the house; he was ashen. "I'm sorry, kids," he said. "Oh Daddy, how did this happen?" Francie cried. "I know how it happened," Joey said angrily. "It was that rotten tomcat that lives in the back alley. I caught him in the yard the other day sniffing at the back door and trying to nudge it open. I took a stick and hit him with it and shooed him out of the yard, but he must have gotten in again somehow." Andy said, "I think you're right, Joey; that rotten son-of…" "Andy!" Ethel quickly broke in. "Yeah, I know, I know," Andy said. "You kids stay here with your mother; I've got to get a box from the cellar and take care of this." "I'll help you Dad," Joey said. "No, Son," Andy said, "You don't need to see this; you and Francie help your mother tend to Tiger; make sure her wounds are not deep." "Daddy, can we please bury the kittens in the backyard?" Francie asked, whimpering. "Sure, Honey, I think we can do that."

Andy brought Tiger in the house and Joey, Francie and Ethel gently took care of her, as Andy went back out in the hall to pick up the poor little dead kittens and bring them out to the backyard for burial. All of a sudden, Andy yelled, "Ethel, come here! Hurry!" Ethel left Tiger with Joey and Francie and ran out into the back hall. "Oh Andy! Thank God!" she cried, as she looked at Andy holding a kitten, very much alive, and unhurt, in his hands. "I heard him mewing, and found him inside the hole in one of the stair risers," Andy said. "Tiger must have put him there to protect him from the carnage that was happening to her other babies." "Oh Andy, I'm so glad at least one of them survived. That will take some of the pain away for Francie, and Joey, too," Ethel said. "Yeah," Andy said, "That miserable son of a b---- tomcat didn't get this one; at least Tiger will have one of her kittens." Ethel brought the trembling kitten into the house and Francie and Joey both screamed with delight when they saw it. Ethel put the kitten down in front of Tiger, and she began licking it all over, and then she lay down and nursed her precious little baby.

Tiger healed nicely from her wounds, but she never seemed quite the same after that horrible day. She did what she had to do for her kitten, but something was gone in her.

One day, about a month later, Francie was sitting at the kitchen window that looked out over the backyard and the alley. She saw Tiger walking down the alley toward Bromley Street, which was not an unusual occurrence; she did that every day. She always came home when she was hungry, usually at suppertime. All of a sudden Francie felt an overwhelming sadness come over her, as she watched Tiger come to the end of the alley and turn onto Bromley Street. It was a feeling like she was seeing Tiger for the last time, and the thought made her feel sick to her stomach.

Tiger didn't come home that day. She didn't come home the next day, either. They looked everywhere for her, but she was nowhere to be found.... They never saw her again.

*****

Sometime the following year, Andy and Charlie bought a grocery store in Watertown. The owner had made it sound like a gold mine; well, 'fool's gold' was more like it. They had put all their savings into it to modernize it a little and make it more attractive. But nothing they did brought in business; they were losing money 'hand over fist'. After a few months they decided to sell the store. "Maybe someone else can make a go of it; we certainly can't," Charlie said. "How are we ever going to convince anyone to buy this store?" Andy asked. They discussed it with Peter and they came up with a plan. Whenever a potential buyer came to look over the store, they would have every member of the family, and even close friends, coming in and 'buying' large amounts of groceries. They would also have someone at home calling the store every few minutes and 'placing large orders to be delivered'. They kept this up for weeks until they finally sold it. "Never again!" Charlie said. "You can say that again!" Andy responded.

Andy and Charlie were able to recoup most of their losses in the sale of the store. They felt a little guilty about deceiving the man who bought it, but they heard he pulled the same trick on another buyer three months later. This last buyer turned the store into a thriving business.

*****

The following June they headed for Westford. This time Larry came with them and stayed for almost a month. Joey took him all over and showed him everything. Joey got a Daisy B.B. rifle from Andy and Ethel at Christmas, to be used only for target practice in Westford. Andy made it clear… "No birds, no squirrels, no chipmunks, or any other animal, unless your life is at stake," which probably would never be the case. Joey and Larry really enjoyed shooting that rifle at every tree and every rock, and often at a target they placed on the outhouse. Many times it scared the bejeebers out of someone who was using it at the time.

Across the road from the cottage was a large pasture. There was a farm at the other end of it belonging to Farmer Burke; his cows would always be grazing in the pasture. There was a short wall of rocks around the pasture. Some of the cows would come right up over the rocks, and many a morning Ethel came out onto the porch to find a cow looking in the screen door. Others were grazing on the lawn. Joey or Andy would have to come out and kind of guide them back across the road and into the pasture. It always gave them a good laugh to see the cows on the lawn, grazing comfortably, as if this was their home.

One day a man, in his late fifties, came knocking at the door of the cottage. He introduced himself as Mr. Burke, the owner of the cows in the pasture. Francie overheard Joey say to Larry, "Oh, oh! I think we're in for it." Mr. Burke explained to Andy that he had found B.B.s stuck in the hide of many of his cows. He wanted to know if Andy's son owned a B.B. rifle. Andy was furious; he apologized to Mr. Burke and told him he could be assured that it would never happen again. Andy called Joey and told him he owed Mr. Burke an apology. Joey didn't deny shooting at the cows; he knew it was useless. He apologized to Mr. Burke, and asked him if there was some way he could make it up to him. Mr. Burke told him that if his cows get out of the pasture, he'd like Joey to round them up and get them back into the pasture, and then set up the rocks the cows might have knocked over. Joey told him that he already does that, but that he would keep watching out for them. Mr. Burke was quiet for a moment, and then said, "I came over here mad as a hornet, expecting an argument. Instead I find a good family who've been taking good care of my cows... for the most part." He half-smiled as he glanced over at Joey. I also find an honest young man here. I doubt there'll be any more problems." He said goodbye and left. Andy told Joey to bring him the B.B. rifle. "You're not allowed to have the gun for two weeks," Andy said. "I think you've learned a lesson here today, Joey, and two weeks won't kill you. I'm sure you and Larry can find other things to keep you busy." "Okay, Dad," Joey said softly. "I know you're disappointed, Son," Andy said, "but this is your own fault, you know that. It's a good thing you told the truth, Joey; for that, I'm proud of you. If you hadn't, you would have gotten the strap." When Joey got his rifle back two weeks later, he confined his shooting to trees and targets, and, of course, terrorizing people in the outhouse.

A few days later, a pickup truck pulled up the driveway, and a man got out. He said his name was Bob and he was delivering something to the Vitello family. Andy and Ethel came out, and Bob brought two large boxes, and one smaller one onto the porch. Two of them were filled with corn; at least four dozen ears. The smaller box contained about three dozen large eggs. He said that Mr. Burke sent them over. Ethel was thrilled with the corn and the eggs. Andy said to Bob, "Please give our thanks to Mr. Burke, and tell him if he ever needs anything, we'd be glad to help. "I'll do that," said Bob, "and you folks have a nice day." He drove off, and they never saw him again; in fact they never saw Mr. Burke again, either. He was a simple man, and he and his wife kept pretty much to themselves.

Being at the cottage was wonderful, but there was an unfinished problem that was 'a thorn in Andy's side.' It was the large hole in the front yard, and to him it was an eyesore, let alone dangerous. No matter how many branches and rocks and all kinds of debris Andy threw in it, each year it seemed to settle, and he felt like he was fighting a losing battle. He laid wide, heavy boards across it and made a kind of fence around it to make sure no one would fall into it. He also didn't relish the thought of trying to get one of Farmer Burke's cows out of the hole if one ever fell in.

One day Joey yelled to his Dad, who was in the lower yard, "Hey, Dad, Slim and Pat are pushing an old car up the road. Wow! Wait 'til you see it, Dad...it must be a hundred years old." "Umm, I don't think it's quite that old, Joey." "Yeah, well, it's pretty old; why do you think they're bringing it here?" "You got me Joey," Andy said. "Well, let's go give them a hand and find out." As they ran out to the road, Andy could see Slim's brother in the car steering. "Hey there Andy," Slim called out. "Hi ya Guys," Andy said, "Whatcha got there?" "This," Slim said, "is the answer to your problem, so come on, and give us a hand here." "Wait a minute!" Andy said, "What am I supposed to do with that old wreck?" Pat started laughing and said, "Joey, go pull down the side of the fence around the pit that faces the driveway, and pull the boards out of the way." "Oh, I get it!" Joey said, and ran back up the driveway. "Hold on," Andy said, "I'm not taking the fence down." Slim chuckled, "Well how the hell are we going to get this car in the hole?" Andy looked shocked for a moment and then started laughing. "I don't believe it!" he cried, and ran over and joined Pat and Slim in pushing the car up the driveway. "Mom! Mom!" Joey yelled as he pushed and pulled until he finally got the fence out of the ground. Ethel came out the door and said, "Joey, what's going on?" "Look, Mom, it's fill for the hole." "Oh my Lord!" was all Ethel could say as she saw the old broken down wreck being pushed up onto the lawn. Still laughing, she helped Joey pull the boards away from the hole.

"Hey, you guys," Slim's brother yelled out, "Don't forget to stop before you get to the hole!"

*****

When Joey was twelve years old he told his father he wanted to swim the length of the lake. Joey was a strong swimmer, so Andy said he could do it, but he and Pat would have to be close by in the rowboat, the whole way. "Great! Dad," Joey said, "How about tomorrow?" "It's fine with me," Andy said, "but don't expect your mother to be happy about this." "What?" Ethel cried, "Have you both lost your minds? Andy, he's just a boy; that lake is much too long for a child to swim." "But Mom, I can do it," Joey cried, "honest I can; I'm not a little kid, I'm twelve now." "I know how old you are; that's why I'm upset... Andy!" Ethel said in frustration, "Say something!" "Ethel, I think he can do it. He's a real good swimmer, and strong; and Pat and I will be in the boat right beside him. I'll have a swimmer's tube in the boat to throw to him if he gets tired, and he can get in the boat anytime he wants, or if I decide he has to. Don't worry! I'm not going to let anything happen to him." Andy and Pat were both excellent swimmers; that alleviated some of Ethel's fears. When Ethel left the room, Andy said to Joey, "Listen Pal, if I say, 'get in the boat', no arguments, you got that?" "Okay, Dad, whatever you say, but you won't have to." Joey started at the beach, and swam the entire lake without needing to stop and rest. Pat had a boat horn with him, and when Joey walked out of the water at the other end of the lake, Pat sounded the horn so Ethel, who was waiting on the beach, knew Joey had made it safely. She was so excited; she and Sarah and Francie started clapping and jumping and laughing. Dottie was clapping, too, although she may not have understood exactly what all the excitement was about. Other people who were there on the beach started clapping and whistling. Ethel was actually very proud of Joey at that moment. Joey wanted to swim back to the beach after he rested for a while, but Andy said, "Are you kidding? Your mother will have my head.... get in the boat!" Joey and Pat laughed, and Joey knew he'd best get in the boat. When they got back to the beach, everyone on shore cheered for Joey, and Ethel hugged and congratulated him. Andy smiled at her, and raised one eyebrow, as if to say, "See...I told you he could do it." She humbly smiled back.

A couple of days after Joey swam the lake, Francie said to her father, "I want to swim to the 'Rock', Daddy." The Rock was where swimmers swam to, when they were testing their ability to swim further than usual. Ethel said, "Oh, I don't know; she's kind of young, Andy, and it's very deep out there." "Ethel, these kids are excellent swimmers, you know they are," Andy responded. "You're being too protective of them. Francie can do it, and I'll be right beside her all the way." "Well, I don't like it, I really don't like it, Andy," Ethel said. "It's not that I don't appreciate your feelings, Hon," Andy said, "but I think you're going to have to accept the fact that our kids are not just city kids anymore. They're very countrified now, and swimming is a way of life to them when they're here. Francie's ten years old, and she's going to swim to the Rock tomorrow, and I guarantee you in three years, when Dottie is six, she'll be swimming to the Rock, too." "Oh Andy, how can you say that?" Ethel cried. "She's just a baby." "She's just a baby who has been swimming like a fish since she was a year old," Andy said. "She started way before Francie and Joey. You mark my words, Ethel, she'll be swimming to the Rock in two years, maybe even next year." "Well," Ethel said, "You can bully me into letting Francie swim to the Rock, Andy, but believe me, if you even think of having Dottie swim to the rock before she's at least eight years old, there's going to be a battle-royal in this family." Andy realized he had gone too far. "I'm sorry, Hon," he said. "I never meant to bully you, and I promise I'll listen to you, and I won't force the issue when it comes to Dottie, for the next few years. Okay?" "At least five years," Ethel said. "All right," he responded. "I'm really going to hold you to that promise, Andy." "That's fine," Andy said, "but Ethel, you need to trust my judgment, too. Do you think I would ever suggest anything that might harm our children?" "No, of course not, Andy, but you also need to trust my judgment." "Well," Andy said, "between the two of us, we should be able to come up with some sensible decisions. I mean, two good brains are better than one, right?" Ethel just smiled, and said, "Well…. one good brain, anyway." "Oh! Ha ha! Very funny!" Andy said. "Pardon me if I don't laugh." Despite themselves, they both started laughing.

Francie swam to the Rock the next day with her dad. She swam it quickly and easily, and she and Andy spent time climbing up and diving off the Rock. Ethel could see her from the beach, and waved to Francie a number of times. Finally, Andy said, "What do you think? Are you ready to swim back?" She answered, "I guess so; I wish we could stay out here all day, Daddy." "Well, it's time to go back; we don't want your mother getting upset at us now, do we?" "No; okay, let's go," Francie said, as she dove off the Rock. Andy had to hurry to catch up with her. "That was fun, wasn't it

Daddy?" "It sure was, Honey," Andy said. "Could we do it again soon?" Francie asked. "Absolutely," Andy answered. "How does once a week sound?" "Oh, that would be terrific," she replied. "I could swim out to the Rock by myself some times, if you didn't feel like it Daddy." "Look, Honey, let's get one thing straight right now. You are never, and I do mean never, to swim to the Rock alone," Andy said, "at least not until you're over fifty, Okay? Do we have a deal?" "No! Oh Daddy, you're so silly," Francie said. "All right," he said, " but you understand what I'm saying, right?" "I understand, Daddy; I won't go alone."

Francie and her dad swam to the Rock many times after that first time; a lot more often than once a week. She cherished those special times with her dad. Sometimes her mom and Joey would swim along with them; those times were real special, too. Everything they did in Westford had its own special charm; everything was fun, no matter who joined in.

*****

The following year Margie and Bobby stayed for the whole month of July and part of August. Francie and Margie were very close. Margie was beginning to lose some of her tomboyishness, and she and Francie were really enjoying the summer together. Joey and Bobby, and Margie and Francie loved exploring some of the dense woods of Westford. At the end of Long Sought For Road was a very large 'cave' in the woods. Inside the cave were huge boulders and thick vines hanging from high above. It was always kind of dark inside, as the trees and vines blotted out most of the sun; but that made it all the more exciting and mysterious for the foursome. They simply loved that cave. They would climb up on the largest boulder, grab hold of a vine and swing from one boulder to another. Joey and Bobby would yell out a "Tarzan" call as they swung through the air, and Margie and Francie both imagined they were "Jane." Other than swimming, vine swinging in the cave was the best part of their days.

One day Joey and Bobby challenged Francie and Margie to a treasure hunt. Margie and Francie would go off in one direction, and

Joey and Bobby would go off in another. Each couple was to find the best treasure they could before four o'clock in the afternoon. Francie said to Joey, "Margie and I will go toward the pasture, and up the road this way, okay?" "Okay," Joey said. "Bobby and I will go in the woods beyond the pump. When we find a treasure, we'll come back to the house. If you don't find a treasure before four o'clock, you lose. "Don't worry about us," Margie said, "we'll find a great treasure." "All right, it's now almost one o'clock, so we have three hours," Joey said. "Come on, Bobby, we'll show these girls what a treasure is all about." Ethel reluctantly, but kindly, agreed to be the judge.

When Francie and Margie had been gone most of the afternoon, they climbed up on a rock under a huge apple tree in the pasture; it was nice and shady there. It was three forty-five and they hadn't found a treasure worthy of the challenge. As they sat there feeling sorry for themselves, Margie stood up on the rock and picked an apple off the tree and began eating it. After a moment she shrieked, "Francie, taste this!" Francie took a bite and could not believe the sweetness and deliciousness of that apple. She stood up and picked one for herself. They sat there moaning in ecstasy as they ate their 'treasure'.

When they finished, they ran back to the house as fast as they could to get there before four o'clock. "It's about time," Joey said. "Me and Bobby have been here for an hour and a half, and we've definitely won the contest. Wait until you see what we found; it's going to put anything you two found to shame." "Oh, yeah?" Francie retorted, "Margie and I have found a "magical" treasure." "Hah! A magical treasure," Joey said. "That's a good one! This I gotta see." "Okay," Bobby said, "Aunt Ethel, you're going to judge the treasures, right?" "Right!" Ethel said. "Okay, Bobby, you and Joey were first, so, lead the way."

Joey and Bobby led Ethel and Margie and Francie into the woods behind the pump.... way into the woods. They came upon a very old, rusted automobile. What a strange sight it was, just sitting there, all by itself, with branches and dirt and leaves inside it. Ethel said, "My goodness! I think this is an old Model T. I think it's older than the one in the hole out in the front yard." Well, it was something like that anyway. *"Wow!"* Francie thought, *"This is really a great find*; it looks like *Margie and I have lost the challenge."* Joey finally said, "Okay, so where is this great 'magical' treasure of yours?" Francie and Margie took Ethel, Joey and Bobby to the pasture to their wonderful apple tree. They weren't quite as excited and vocal about it as they were a little while ago. Somehow, their treasure didn't seem quite so wonderful and magical as it had before they saw the old car. Joey and Bobby laughed and said, "You think a tree is as great a find as an old Model T car?" "Taste an apple, Aunt Ethel," Margie said. "Yes Mom, taste it," Francie said. Ethel said nothing; she just reached up and picked an apple off the tree and took a bite. Suddenly she had the same wide-eyed look on her face that both Margie and Francie had when they tasted the apples. "I've never tasted an apple like this," she said. "This is the most delicious fruit I've ever eaten. Boys," she said, "Come and taste these." Joey and Bobby reluctantly tasted the apples; they both agreed they had never tasted apples so delicious. Ethel finally said, "As good a treasure as Joey and Bobby's car is, this tree is truly a 'magical' tree made by God." THEY HAD WON! Francie and Margie couldn't believe it. Margie cried, "We won, Francie…we won!" She grabbed Francie and started dancing around with her. Joey and Bobby were not happy at all, but the agreement was that Ethel would choose, and that would be the end of it. The apples were completely ripened, so Ethel said for everyone to go back to the house and get baskets, bags, pots and pans and pick all the apples we could. Even Crocifessa and Peter helped. During the following two weeks, Ethel and Crocifessa made lots of pies, tarts, applesauce, and apple crisp. They sent some over to Andy's Uncle Joe and Aunt Mary, and some to Rose and Slim. Everyone agreed they were the best they'd ever tasted. Margie and Francie were thrilled.

Francie and Margie always believed that it really was a magical tree; it certainly was a treasure to all of them. Also special to Francie that day was what a good sport her mom was, traipsing through the thick woods, with all she had to do, for a silly challenge the kids made. That summer was one of Francie's favorite summers, because Margie was with her.

*****

The war ended, and the work in the Shipyard tapered off. In 1948 Andy joined the Painters' Union. He had become an excellent painter and knew he could get jobs and make good money by joining the Union. The Union sent him to all kinds of jobs, working for different contractors, and working for the city. One memorable job was when he was assigned to a crew that was painting the Mystic River Bridge. He was strapped into a type of boson's chair, and lowered over the side of the bridge by a pulley; it was not always perfectly safe. Sometimes the wind would take him and send him far to one side and then to the other. "If I don't hold on for dear life," Andy said, "I could very easily fall out. I dread windy days; they're scary as all hell." There were days when the pulley got stuck, and one time it let go and sent Andy and the chair plummeting down toward the river. Andy thanked God for the swift actions of the men up on the bridge, or this story might have had an altogether different ending.

While he was painting the bridge, Andy met a man named Frank Spano, and they became close friends. Frankie was a real good worker, but the thing Andy liked most about him was his disposition. Andy once said, "I don't think I've ever seen him without a smile on his face." When the work on the bridge was finished, Andy and Frankie were sent on a lot of the same jobs; they were a team and worked well together.

Before long, many contractors put requests in to the union for Vitello and Spano. One of those painting and contracting companies was John W. Graham & Son, an old respected, Boston company, established in 1871. Andy and Frankie were on quite a few Graham jobs together.

After a few years Frankie began working full time for a painting company. For a long time Jim and Al Graham kept Andy busy on their jobs because they knew the union would send him somewhere else the minute a Graham job was finished, and they didn't want to lose him. They knew that workers like Andy don't come along every day, and if they didn't do something soon, some other contractor would grab him up.

By this time Andy was tired of moving around, not knowing what contractor he'd be working for each day; he was ready to settle into one company. He liked the Graham company; it was a very professionally run business, so when the Grahams offered him a permanent full-time job, he accepted. Ethel was thrilled. There wasn't a day that went by that she didn't worry about his safety. She had been praying that one day Andy would have a permanent position in a good company, and she secretly hoped it would be the Graham Company. To her they were the best. Now she'd know where he was working and what he was doing. She thought of a verse her father had taught her when she was a child...Psalm 37:4,5, *"Delight yourself in the Lord, and He will give you the desires of your heart. Commit your way to the Lord; trust in Him and He will do it."* Ethel felt a peace come over her she hadn't felt in a long time.

That evening Andy and Ethel thanked God for His faithfulness, and celebrated their good fortune by going to a nice restaurant for dinner, and enjoying a glass of champagne. "Are you happy, Andy?" Ethel asked, as they were finishing their dinner. "Very," he said. "I'm very happy, Hon. You know, Ethel, I'm pretty sure I made the right decision, but if, for some reason, it doesn't work out, I'll always be able to get work. I can always go back and work on different jobs for the Union; or even to barbering, if I absolutely had to. I have two solid trades I can work at, if for any reason this doesn't work out." "It's going to work out," said Ethel. "I've prayed so hard for this, Andy." Andy had no idea then, the magnitude of his decision.

*****

Early in 1949, a notice was sent to all the families on Parker St. and all the streets in the surrounding area, announcing that the entire area was going to be torn down and a housing project built in its place. It would simply merge with the Heath Street Project. The city would pay fair market value prices for the homes if people sold within eighteen months. Some families said they would fight it, but there really wasn't much anyone could do about it. Andy and Ethel had felt for quite a while that it was time to start thinking about moving to a better neighborhood, so this gave them the impetus to start looking. Crocifessa and Peter would be going with them, which meant they would have to sell the store, too.

*****

Riri's family was one of the first to leave Parker Street. They were moving to an apartment in East Boston. The day the movers came to move them, Francie and Riri hid in Francie's backyard, in the little shed that held the trash barrels. They huddled together crying and holding onto each other, whispering so no one would hear them. After awhile they heard Riri's mother and father and her brothers and sister calling for her. They remained very quiet, barely moving. "Don't let them take me, Francie," Riri whispered.

All of a sudden the doors to the shed opened and Joey and Riri's brother Bobbie both yelled, "Hey, here they are! We found them! Over here!" Riri and Francie clung to each other and they both cried. Francie hated Joey at that moment; he actually seemed to be gloating. "You're mean, Joey!" Francie cried. "You're nothing but a dirty rat." Joey just laughed. She and Riri were sobbing when her older brother Johnny came, and he and Bobby literally pulled them apart. "Please don't make her go," Francie pleaded with Mr. and Mrs. McGrath. "She could stay with us; my parents won't mind." "She has to come with us, Francie," Riri's mom said. "You can come and visit us anytime you like." Francie and Riri hugged each other one more time, still crying… then Riri and her family drove away.

"I hate you, Joey! I hate you!" Francie yelled as she ran into her house and up the stairs and into her mother's arms. She sobbed for a very long time; she felt sick in her stomach. To live without Riri being three doors away was totally inconceivable to her. To Francie, she and Riri were 'twins' who were now being separated. She couldn't explain it, but somehow she felt disconnected from everything. She didn't think she could ever love another friend as much as she loved Riri. Francie's heart was breaking.

A little while later Joey came in the house. Francie wouldn't look at him, never mind talk to him. "Don't be such a big baby," Joey said. "Did you really think you could keep Riri here when her family is moving away?" "Don't you talk to me, Joey," Francie screamed at him; "I mean it! I really hate you!" "All right! That's enough!" Ethel said. "I understand how badly you're feeling, Francie, but I don't want to hear that "hate" talk anymore. Do you understand?" "But he was laughing when we...." "I know what he was doing, and Joey and I are going to have a little talk about it, but no more of that "hate" talk; Is that clear?" "Yes," Francie said, pouting. Later, Joey came to Francie and said he was sorry for the way he acted, and for being insensitive to her feelings. She knew those were her mom's words, but that was okay. Joey apologized, and she didn't hate him anymore. Joey was just a brother, and sometimes kind of mean to her, but somehow at that moment, Francie felt a powerful need for his friendship.

Three weeks later, on Saturday morning, Andy drove Francie to Riri's house. It was all planned; Francie would stay for the day, and Andy would pick her up at eight o'clock in the evening. She and Riri had the most perfect day together. When eight o'clock came, they could hear Andy coming up the stairs. Riri said, "Come on Francie, hide in here." She opened a large chest that was in the back hall, and Francie climbed in. Andy came in the house and sat down to have a cup of coffee with Rita and John McGrath. Rita called, "Francie, your dad is here." No response. "Riri, come here," her mother called. Riri came into the kitchen and her mother said, "All right, where's Francie?" "I don't know," Riri responded. "Oh, no!" Andy laughed. "Not again!" Andy and Riri's parents walked around the house calling Francie. No response. Finally, John McGrath pointed to the chest in the hall. Andy said, "Okay Francie, if you don't come out right now, you will never be allowed to come to Riri's house again; I mean it." The lid to the chest opened and Francie stepped out. "You two!" Rita McGrath said. "I swear, you're going to drive us all crazy with your antics." Riri and Francie looked at each other, and instead of crying, they both started laughing. Francie hugged and thanked Mr. and Mrs. McGrath for everything, and then she and Riri hugged, both now struggling to hold back tears.

"I'm proud of you, Francie," Andy said, when they were in the car. "You handled that like a mature young lady, except of course, for the trunk incident." Francie and her dad laughed about it. She felt better about leaving Riri this time; she and Riri had made plans for Riri to come to her house in three weeks. They got together about once every couple of months for the next year, and then their visits became less frequent as time went on.

Francie and Rosemarie seemed to grow much closer; and Mary's friendship became very dear to her. She still missed Riri, but...not quite so much anymore.

*****

One day Francie came running in the house, yelling, "Guess what? Rosemarie's father bought a television set. You should see it, Joey, it's terrific." "When are we going to get a television set, Dad?" Joey asked. "When we can afford one," Andy said. Francie said, "I'll bet Mr. Fontana doesn't make more money than you do, Daddy." "Oh, great!" Andy said. "What do you kids think, I'm made of money? Just because Rosemarie's father, or anyone else can afford to buy something, doesn't mean that we can do the same." "Oh, but Daddy," Francie cried, "It would be so wonderful; it's like having the movies right in your parlor." "Well," Andy said, "I'm afraid we can't afford a television set right now." "Daddy," Francie said, "I promise, if we get a television set, I'll never go to the movies again." "Yeah, Dad," Joey said, "You won't have to give us money for the movies if we have a television set; we won't need to go to the movies anymore." "I said we can't afford it right now," said Andy. "Joey mumbled under his breath, "we're always the last ones to get things." "That's enough out of you, Joey," Andy said. "If we ever get a television set, it will only be when we can afford one, and I don't want to hear another word about it from either of you; is that clear?" "Yes," Francie and Joey said dejectedly.

About four months later, Andy came home one day and called up the stairs to Joey, "Come on down here and help me bring this heavy damn television set up the stairs." "Wha..? A television set?" Joey just about screamed, as he ran down the stairs as fast as his legs would carry him. They managed to get the television set up the stairs and set it in place in the parlor. It was a 16" RCA console. Francie came running into the parlor, literally jumping for joy. "Oh, Daddy, it's just beautiful." "Boy!" Joey said, "sixteen inches; that's huge, Dad. Most of the televisions in Alpert's Furniture store are only nine and twelve inches. I'll bet we've got the best television set in Jamaica Plain." Ethel laughed, "Considering what it cost, I think you might be right Joey."

"Okay, now, I just have to get the antenna set up, and then we'll be able to watch it," said Andy. "Do you have to go up on the roof, Dad?" Joey asked. "Nope," Andy said, "With this baby you just connect the 'rabbit ears' to the back of the set." "Wow! Dad, this really is the best television set in Jamaica Plain." "Oh," Francie said, "This is the best thing that ever happened." "You say that about everything, Joey said, "but you're right this time."

Watching television was a major project in the Vitello home, as it was in almost every home with a television set. Andy would turn it on and the picture would inevitably be snowy, or it would flip over and over. He would then turn the rabbit ears one way and then another, slowly pulling the antennas up or down. Finally, when the picture was somewhat viewable, he would carefully let go of the antennas. "Oh shoot!" Someone would yell. "The picture's gone again." Andy would always get angry and say, "Well, I'm not standing here all night holding these damned rabbit ears." Eventually they'd get a halfway decent picture, and when their favorite show, "The Texaco Star Theatre" came on, starring Milton Berle, Andy would finally settle in with the rest of the family and enjoy an hour or so of some of the best entertainment they had ever seen. Peter and Crocifessa usually came upstairs to watch television with the family. Of course, they didn't understand much of the dialogue, but when 'Uncle Miltie' got going, words weren't necessarily important. He was hilarious, and the whole family would be doubled over with laughter at his antics.

One day, about two months later, Francie and Joey came home from school to find a shiny black telephone sitting on top of the television set. "Mom!" Francie yelled, "Is it really ours? Does it actually work?" "Yes," Ethel said, "It's ours." "But, does it work?" Francie asked. "Well, why don't you call Rosemarie or Mary, and find out for yourself." "I'll call Mary; Rosemarie doesn't have a telephone yet." "Oh?" Ethel said, "You mean we're not the *last ones* to get a telephone, *Joey*?" Joey didn't say a word. Ethel just smiled and pinched Joey's cheek. Francie squealed with glee as she called Riri. Riri was thrilled to hear from her. "Mom," she called, "Riri wants to know our telephone number; do you know what it is?" "Yes, Dear, it's Ruggles 2-1-3-8." Charlie and Margaret had just gotten a telephone about a week earlier, so she called Margie next.

"I can't believe we have our very own telephone," said Francie, after she finished her calls. "Yes," said Ethel, "Now we don't have to run down to Abie's whenever we need to make a call. There are a few rules that apply when using the telephone though." "Rules? What kind of rules, Mom?" Joey asked. "Well, most importantly, you need to understand that we share the telephone with another family." "Another family?" Francie cried, "What are you talking about Mom?" "It's called a two-party line." "Yeah, I've heard about that," said Joey. "Some kids in school were talking about it." "We're actually very lucky," Ethel said. "Some people have a four-party line, or even a six." "But what does it mean, Mom?" Francie asked. Ethel said, "It's hard to explain, but basically it means that there is one telephone line for every two, or more, families." "Who is the other family who shares our line, Mom?" Francie asked. "Well, we're not told who they are," Ethel said. "It doesn't really matter who they are." "So, what are the rules Mom? Joey asked again. "Okay, this is most important," Ethel said. "When you pick up the telephone, you must make certain that no one is talking on it before you start to make a call. If there are people on the line, you never, ever listen in on their conversation. Do I make myself perfectly clear?" "Yes, I guess so," Francie said, somewhat confused. "But what do we do if we hear someone talking when we pick up the telephone?" "You simply say, 'Sorry,' and hang up the telephone immediately, and then wait a little while and try again. We need to be considerate of the other party if we want them to be considerate of us, right?" Francie and Joey both responded, "Right!" Of course, they didn't always obey that order; it was much too tempting to stay on the line and listen for a few moments when a conversation on the other line sounded interesting. But for the most part they were considerate of the other party.

Between the television and the telephone, life had changed dramatically for the Vitello family. A whole new and exciting world had opened up for them.

*****

"I'm getting fat!" Francie cried, as she tried on a skirt and sweater for school at Gilchrist's. "You are not!" her mother responded. "You're just a little chubby.... pleasingly plump." *"Chubby,"* Francie thought, *"What an awful word...and 'pleasingly plump' is even worse."* "Mom, old ladies are pleasingly plump. There's nothing pleasing about being eleven and a half and being plump." "You're a very pretty girl, Francie; you shouldn't even think about that," Ethel said. "You'll outgrow it and become a beautiful young lady in a couple of years, you'll see. And besides, there's nothing wrong with having a little meat on your bones; it shows you're healthy." *"Healthy!"* Francie thought, *"Who cares about being healthy?"*

*****

When Joey was in the sixth grade he was a high honors student. The teachers and the principal convinced Ethel and Andy that he was Boston Latin School material, and he should start seventh grade there. *"Latin School material; what a stupid thing to say,"* Joey thought. He hated that expression. *"Material...What am I, a piece of fabric or something?"* Joey didn't want to go to Latin School; he knew it was going to be very difficult, and anyway, he didn't believe he was 'Latin School material'. He told his teachers and his parents how he felt, but it made no difference. "We know what's best for you," the principal had said.

Joey didn't do well at Latin School as it turned out; he ended up failing for the year. Needless to say, he was real upset. It just didn't make sense; he was an honor student a year ago, but now he would have to repeat the year. He didn't blame his parents; they only did what they thought was best for him. Andy and Ethel took him out of Latin School.

165

In two weeks school would be starting again. Joey and Francie would both be going into seventh grade at the Mary E. Curley Junior High School on Centre Street. Joey wasn't happy about being in the same grade and some of the same classes with his kid sister. But, of course, Francie could hardly wait to be going to Junior High School.

Seventh grade turned out to be harder than the earlier years for Francie. She didn't make the honor roll at all that year. She did well, but now her grades were mostly A's, and B's, and one or two C's. She wasn't pleased at all about that. On the other hand, Joey breezed right through the seventh grade at the Curley School, and was back on the honor roll. Ethel and Andy realized that Joey had been right when he said, "I'm not Latin School material." They felt badly about that, but what was done was done.

*****

Andy and Ethel found a very nice three-family house at 40 Parkton Road, which was in a much nicer section of Jamaica Plain. Parkton Road was off Perkins Street and the Jamaicaway, and close to Jamaica Pond, which was a large, beautiful pond with walking paths all the way around it. Ethel and Margaret used to walk from Parker Street to Jamaica Pond on nice days. They'd walk around the pond, pushing their baby carriages and/or strollers. They'd pack a lunch and have a picnic sitting on benches or under a tree. It was a lovely place to walk, and Ethel said many times, "It's so nice up here; I'd love to live in this area, so close to the pond." She was excited when they were going to look at a house on Parkton Road; and when they saw it, Andy, Ethel, Crocifessa and Peter all fell in love with it. So did Joey and Francie, especially since Jamaica Pond, the Curley School and the Jamaica Theatre were practically around the corner.

When the city bought the house on Parker Street, Peter and Crocifessa gave the money to Andy and Ethel for the down payment on the new house. All three apartments were identical, and since the third floor apartment was available, Peter and Crocifessa wanted that one; they felt the exercise, going up and down the stairs, would be good for them. A nice older couple lived on the second floor, and Andy and Ethel and the kids looked forward to moving into the first floor apartment.

There was a lot that the family would miss when they left Parker Street. One thing was the Madison Theatre, which was just up a little way on Centre Street, not five minutes from the house. Joey and Francie loved going to the movies. Almost every Saturday afternoon, when they would get home from the North End, they would go to the movies. For twelve cents they got to see two full-length motion pictures, between five and seven cartoons, and a weekly serial. They would stop at Abie's or Saul's store and buy a huge dill pickle for a nickel. If they really loved the first movie, they would stay and watch it all over again. Some days Francie and Joey would be in the theatre for four or five hours. If they weren't home at five o'clock Ethel would say, "Must be a good movie." They didn't stay much after five, as they knew they'd be in trouble with their dad if they were late for supper.

The Jamaica Theatre was nothing like the Madison (the "Madhouse", to all the kids in the neighborhood). The Jamaica was always clean, and smelled clean. It had red 'velvet' carpeting all throughout. It even had ushers in uniform. The cost to get in was twenty cents, which seemed outrageous to Joey and Francie. The few times they had been there with their parents were special birthday treats.

The Madison, on the other hand, was definitely not clean, with gum stuck on the floor and on, or under, the seats. There was no carpeting; there was old, worn out linoleum on the floor. When one walked into the theatre the smell of urine was the first thing you noticed, combined with the wonderful smell of popcorn. The Men's room was to the left and the Ladies' Room was to the right. They were downstairs, and with each step down, of course, the smell got stronger. Most people avoided walking by the Men's room if at all possible. Actually, the Ladies' room wasn't a whole lot better. Ethel insisted that Francie and Joey not use the bathrooms in the theatre, as she was afraid they'd come home with some horrible disease. Also, there was always someone who said he had seen a rat downstairs, so Francie wouldn't go down there if she were bursting. The owner was a man whom everyone called 'Dutchy'. He was grouchy some times, and tough on the kids who didn't behave themselves, but for the most part he was pretty fair.

Many times, the theatre had "dish" night. With the price of a ticket you could get a plate or bowl or cup and saucer. Many women, like Ethel, acquired a full set of dishes that way, and all the serving pieces, too. It took a long time, but no one was in a big hurry. There was much about the Madison that wasn't pleasant, but to every kid who lived in the neighborhood, when the lights dimmed and the movie started, it was just the greatest place in the world to be. Many adults felt the same, like Andy and Ethel, whose first date was at the Madison Theatre.

Another thing they would all miss was the player piano; it was just too big and too heavy to try to move. After much discussion there was only one solution… Andy, with the help of Charlie, took an axe to the piano, and chopped it up for the trash. No one they knew wanted it, and even if they did, no one could afford to hire piano movers to transport it. "Isn't there any way we can take the piano with us, Daddy?" Francie asked. "No, Honey, there really isn't; this is the only way." Everyone went back into the house to keep from watching 'an old friend' be done away with. That piano provided wonderful memories for the whole family, and Francie knew she'd miss it a lot.

*****

June 15, 1951 was moving day; it was a day of mixed emotions. They were looking forward to moving into their nice new home, but they were all feeling rather sad, knowing that their house at 952 Parker Street and every other house in the neighborhood would soon be torn down. Ethel and Andy said "good bye" to those neighbors who hadn't left yet. Francie and Joey said "good bye" to their friends who were still there. They all, with Crocifessa and Peter, made one last visit to the store they had loved so much. That wonderful store that had provided such a good living for Peter and Crocifessa, and had helped so many people through some rough times, had been sold it to a very nice Jewish man. It was a very sad moment.

*****

The first floor apartment in the new house had so much more room than the house on Parker Street. It had a large reception hall, which they made into a kind of TV/family room. It held a small sofa and easy chair, the television, and a 'gossip bench' and telephone. To the left of the reception hall was a good-sized dining room. Andy took out the built-in china cabinet and made a closet in its place. That room became Francie and Dottie's bedroom. Beyond the dining room was a large eat-in kitchen; off the kitchen was a large pantry. From the kitchen, the back door led out into the back hall and also onto a large porch. All three apartments had front and back porches, to Ethel's delight. To the right of the reception room were a good-sized living room, and two bedrooms. Straight ahead, leading out of the reception room, was a kind of short hall with the bathroom at the end of it. The bathroom was the most thrilling part of the new apartment; it actually had a sink in it and a bathtub with a shower attachment. The best part was the toilet; there was no overhead water box and no pull chain. It was all so very 'modern'. There was nice white tile halfway up the walls, and wallpaper with water lilies in a pond on the upper half of the walls. Another thing they all loved about the bathroom was that it had a window in it. A lot of jokes went around about that, mostly at Andy's expense; he just chuckled. "You talk to them Ethel; no decent person would." Ethel just smirked and shook her head while Joey and Francie laughed.

Everyone was thrilled with the new house; they felt like they were now living in the 'ritzy' section of Jamaica Plain. Francie was so glad her close friends stayed in Jamaica Plain. Rosemarie moved to Walden Street, and Mary moved to Preising Street. Another friend, Rose moved to Centre Street.

Right across the street from Francie and Joey lived two brothers, Warren McManus and his brother Bobby, whom everyone called Mickie. Joey became friends with them very quickly. He also got to know some of the other kids in the neighborhood. Francie wasn't really interested in meeting any of Joey's new friends; she would ride her bike to Rosemarie's house, or Mary's house, or they would come to her's. She was getting to know some of the kids in

Rosemarie's neighborhood, and was hanging around with them. She always enjoyed Mary's company, too. Mary was funny, and kept Francie laughing; and because Francie was little, Mary always felt it her duty to protect her if anyone picked on her.

*****

They didn't get to Westford until the middle of July that summer. No one minded very much; they were all enjoying the new home, fixing it up and getting settled. Larry came with them for most of the summer, and Rosemarie came for a couple of weeks.

One day near the end of the summer, when everyone was getting ready to go down to the beach, Francie came out of the cottage with Dottie, and they sat in the lawn chairs and waited for the others. Larry came out first, wearing his swim trunks, carrying a towel. It was in that moment that life, as Francie knew it, had suddenly changed.

For over nine years Joey and Larry spent most of their free time together. Larry shared many a meal with Joe's family, and he spent much of the summers at Westford with them. He picked on Francie and teased her all the time, just like she was his own kid sister. Francie liked Larry for the most part, but there were times when he would tease her so unmercifully, she would scream at him, "You're just a big jerk, Larry!" Francie had never thought of Larry any differently than she did Joey. He was like a brother to her, with all the good and the bad that comes with it.... but, somehow Larry seemed different to Francie this day; he had become... handsome... and positively 'hunky'. *"When did that happen?"* she thought. For the first time since she first met Larry, she saw him in a different way. She felt kind of embarrassed, even blushing at times when he was around. *"Why do I feel so strange?"* she thought. *"It's Larry, for Pete's sake."*

Francie was also surprised at how many cute boys there were in the new neighborhood. It just amazed her that there hadn't been a single cute boy in the old neighborhood, or even in the Lowell School. Warren was the first one she took real notice of since he lived right across the street. He was fourteen, and very nice looking.

Whenever he was around, Francie would fix her hair and make herself look pretty. Joey knew what she was doing; he'd laugh at her, and in his usual 'sensitive' way, he'd say, "Don't be a jerk! He's not interested in you!"

Somehow, life didn't seem as simple as it used to be. Something was changing, and Francie was puzzled by it. She didn't feel happy about it; in fact she felt rather sad. She didn't want anything to change, but she knew it was.

****

CHAPTER EIGHT
You Judas!

When Francie and Joey were going into the eighth grade, Dottie was starting Kindergarten. Ethel and Andy had decided to send Dottie to Blessed Sacrament School. They wanted her to get a parochial school education. Unfortunately, Blessed Sacrament School had no Kindergarten. As it turned out, the Mary E. Curley Junior High School offered Kindergarten classes to neighboring families, so Ethel enrolled Dottie in Kindergarten there. It would work out perfectly; Francie was assigned the task of seeing to it that Dottie got to Kindergarten at 8:45, which gave Francie less than a minute to get to her homeroom. The only problem was that the Kindergarten class got out at 2:30, and the Junior High school got out at 2:45. For the sake of fifteen minutes, Ethel asked the principal if Dottie could go into Francie's room and wait the fifteen minutes there. She promised that Dottie would be quiet and no trouble at all. The principal said it would be fine. A few minutes after 2:30 every day, Dottie would show up at Francie's room. She would walk into the room with a big smile on her face and run to Francie and hug her.

Ethel was right, Dottie was quiet and no trouble at all, but the one thing Ethel didn't count on was that Dottie would be a great distraction to the girls in the class. They all thought she was adorable, and would talk to her and play with her when the teacher wasn't looking. Actually, Miss O'Connor, Francie's teacher came to like Dottie, too; she would have a lollipop waiting for her every day.

Francie was very proud of her little sister; she was as cute as can be, and very sweet. At 2:45 all the kids would say, "Bye, Dottie; see you tomorrow." Dottie would respond, "'Bye Carol, 'bye Patty, 'bye…." She got to know them all. Dottie was the little princess, and she loved every minute spent in Francie's class. Francie loved it too.

*****

At twelve and a half Francie decided that "Francie" was a little girl's name, and she wished to be called "Fran" from now on. She told everyone that she would no longer respond to the name 'Francie'. "Oh, is that so?" her mother said. "Well," Francie said, "I'll only respond to my parents and grandparents. I mean, most people are calling Joey, 'Joe' now, so won't you at least *try* to stop calling me 'Francie,' Mom? Dad?" "I'll try, Honey," Andy said, " but I can't promise you anything." "Mom!!" "All right, we'll try," Ethel said, "but don't expect us to stop overnight calling you what we've called you since the day you were born." "Okay, Mom and Dad, that's fair," Francie said. "But try real hard, Okay?" Everyone made an effort to call Francie, 'Fran'. It took a while but eventually most people began calling her 'Fran'. Most people, that is, except her grandparents, Margaret and Charlie, and her cousins. They had the most trouble of all. Her cousin Franny had made the switch to 'Fran' quite a few years earlier, so it seemed Francie was destined to stay 'Francie', at least within the family.

*****

Betty and Jack McDonnell came to visit Ethel and Andy one afternoon. They raved about the house, exclaiming as they walked through each room. They went upstairs to say hello to Crocifessa and Peter. It was a nice visit, and Ethel invited them to stay for supper.

Fran had liked Betty a lot. She was fun and youthful, and some evenings when her husband was out she used to yell down to Fran, "Come on upstairs, we'll make some penuche." Fran had never heard of penuche, but she soon discovered that it was similar to fudge, but not made with chocolate. It was the most delicious candy Fran had ever tasted; it would almost melt in her mouth. It had always been fun chatting with Betty about school and so many things while they made the penuche. Fran missed Betty when they moved; she missed her penuche too. Years later Fran was still trying to find a penuche like the kind Betty made; they all paled in comparison.

About a month after Betty and Jack's visit, Crocifessa and Peter were served legal papers. They were very confused, so they went downstairs to show the letter to Andy. "What the…?" Andy was totally shocked at what he was reading. "What does this mean, Angelo?" Peter asked. "Good Lord!" he exclaimed, "I don't believe this." "Andy, what's going on? What's happened?" Ethel asked, as he handed her the summons to read. "They're suing Ma and Pa." "Angelo, what is it?" Crocifessa pressed. Andy did his best to explain it to his parents, but they simply couldn't understand why Jack and Betty would be suing them. "Those miserable sons of b----s," Andy said. "They were just here; they ate our food and laughed and chatted with us, as friendly as can be. I knew there was something about him that wasn't right; that lazy, good-for-nothing leach. They took all my mother was willing to give, even to paying a low rent, and this is how they repay them." Peter was angry; he said to his wife, "How many times have I told you, 'when you give people an inch, they'll take a yard from you.'" Crocifessa was crying; she couldn't believe that people could be that greedy and selfish. Peter headed back upstairs. When he was out in the hall they heard him mumbling, "Miserabela bastardos! They're no good! No good!"

Jack and Betty McDonnell had gone to court and filed a complaint against the Vitellos, claiming they had paid them too much rent during the years they lived in their house at 952 Parker Street. Of course it wasn't true, but what *was* true, was that of the twenty dollars a month that the McDonnells paid them, Crocifessa and Peter only claimed fifteen of it on their taxes. The reality of it was that most months they didn't even take twenty dollars from them, only fifteen, and *only* when Betty and Jack could pay it at all. There were many months when Crocifessa would slip upstairs, unbeknownst to Peter, and give them back part of their money; she was afraid the children would go without. Unfortunately, she never thought to change the rent receipt. Crocifessa and Peter didn't think it was so wrong to hold back five dollars on their taxes. They gave back to Betty and Jack so much more than that. They were able to give them boxes of food and clothing for the kids whenever they needed it, which was most of the time, because Jack worked so little. Some months they paid no rent at all, and of course, they never made it up.

"How could they do this to Ma and Pa, after all they did for them?" Andy asked. " What kind of people are they?" "Greedy, jealous people, Andy," Ethel said. "Most people wouldn't 'bite the hand that fed them', but they're not most people." "Oh my word," she said, as she read on. "They're claiming your parents owe them three hundred dollars." Andy was mad, and getting madder by the moment. "For God's sake, they hardly ever *paid* their rent!" he yelled. He paced the floor, angrily punching his hand. "Oh, Andy," Ethel said, "how *can* they do this to people that were so good to them?" "Well," Andy said, "they're not going to get away with this. Ma and Pa may not be able to fight them in court, but I am, and I'll fight this with everything in me. They're not getting another cent from my parents, those greedy sons of b-----s."

The judge decided, because Crocifessa and Peter charged the McDonnells twenty dollars a month for rent during the time they lived there, but only claimed fifteen dollars a month on their taxes... they had overcharged the McDonnells five dollars each month. The judge ordered them to pay the McDonnells two hundred and fifty dollars. Andy explained to the judge how good his parents were to them, but he said, "I'm sorry, but they have all their rent receipts." "But half the time they didn't even *pay* their rent," Andy said, "and when they did, many times my parents gave money back to them; doesn't that mean anything?" "That was an oral agreement Mr. Vitello, that Mr. and Mrs. McDonnell deny ever having with your parents," the judge responded. "There's no proof that Mr. and Mrs. McDonnell did not pay their full rent those months; they have their receipts. I'm sorry, but my decision stands." And that was the end of it.

Andy turned around and looked straight at Jack McDonnell. Neither Jack nor Betty would look at him. Andy pointed his finger at him and said, "You Judas! You miserable Judas! You'll burn in hell one day, you ungrateful, greedy leach!" Andy started toward Jack. Ethel very quickly was at Andy's side; she slipped her arm through his and said softly, "No, Andy; please stop." His wife's voice caused him to hesitate. The judge reprimanded him, and said, "Mr. Vitello, sit down right now. I understand how you feel, but you *will* be held in contempt of this court if you continue this outburst." He looked over at his parents and could see they were frightened; Crocifessa was weeping softly. Andy turned slowly toward the judge. "I apologize, Your Honor," was all he could say. He was so angry he was trembling, and he could feel tears welling up in his eyes, and *that*, he did not want them to see. He wanted to hit Jack McDonnell so badly; he wanted to punch him right in the mouth, but of course, Ethel would never have let that happen, and the judge would have charged him with contempt of court anyway, so... right or wrong, fair or not, it was over.

Jack and Betty McDonnell left the courthouse as quickly as they could, and were never heard from again. They had their two hundred and forty dollars, and as Crocifessa said, "They'll never have a peaceful moment with that money." Andy responded with, "Those miserable, greedy Judases; if there's any justice in this life, they'll burn in hell one day." He was angry over what they did to his parents.... very angry. He knew he would never ever forget it.

*****

One day as Fran was riding her bike down Parkton Road, she heard someone call, "Hey, Joe Vitello's sister!" She pulled over and a girl came over to her; her name was Maryellen Hemmer. She said, "Hi," and introduced herself. She and Fran started hanging around together. Through Maryellen, Fran met all the kids who lived on Parkton Road and nearby. They included Warren and Mickie McManus, Jackie Capen, Donald Noseworthy, Sandy Paterson, Ronny Foo, Richie Shong, and Maryellen's brother, Alfred, whom everyone called Buzzy. She introduced Fran to Mary Manning, who lived around the corner on Parkwood Terrace. Fran and Mary became very good friends.

Parkton Road was what was called a horseshoe street. To a person driving by on Perkins Street, it looked like there were two Parkton Roads. It was only one road, which was a very steep hill, but when you came to the bottom of one side you could just stay on the curve, and go right up the other side. Warren and Mickey, and Sandy lived on the side where Joe and Fran lived, and Maryellen and Buzzy, and Jackie and Donald lived on the other side. At the bottom of the two roads where they met, was Parkwood Terrace, where Mary lived, a short street with only three houses on it that led out to the Jamaicaway, where Ronny and Richie lived. Across the Jamaicaway, opposite Parkwood Terrace, was Daisy Field, a large field where kids played baseball and all kinds of games. Almost every day after school the kids would meet at Daisy Field and decide what they were going to play that day. Often it was dodge ball or billy-billy-buck. They also loved thinking of places they might explore.

One of their favorite places to explore was the 'haunted house' on the corner of Perkins Street and the Jamaicaway. It was a large old place that was obviously once a very beautiful manor house. Andy and Ethel thought that it might have belonged to the Perkins Manor, a lovely apartment complex nearby. The house was all boarded up, and the grass had grown up tall all around it.

One day they found a basement window with very few boards on it. They climbed down into the basement and made their way to the first and second floors. It was fabulous! It was also kind of spooky; floorboards creaked, and on windy days the wind seemed to howl throughout the house. There was no electricity so many areas were quite dark, especially the basement. There were fireplaces every-where; some were made of brick, and some of stone. Most of them were very large and some were very ornate. Large rooms had two of them on opposite walls. The kitchen had a large stone hearth with an oven built into it, and there was a very large icebox made of wood and stone built into a wall There was even a type of bowling alley in the basement. Fran was fascinated by everything in the house. She said to Maryellen, "Very rich and grand people must have once lived in this house." "Well, I don't know how grand they were, but they sure must have been rich," she responded.

Some days there was a caretaker around the place. He didn't like kids hanging around, and he and his dog would chase them off if he saw them. But that never deterred Fran and her friends; if they were chased away, they'd go back later or the next day. It was just too great an adventure to pass up.

Joe came to the "haunted house" a few times, but he usually had work to do on Saturdays and after school. "You better watch your step in there, Fran," he once said to her. "That house looks like it might be condemned, or it will be soon enough. You could fall through a floorboard or a broken stair; just be careful. And watch out for that caretaker; he doesn't seem too friendly, never mind that dog of his."

Whenever Fran and her friends went to the "haunted house", they brought candles, *lots* of candles, and matches. They also brought cigarettes that a few of the kids swiped from their parents. Andy and Ethel never smoked, so cigarettes were not available to Fran. Sometimes someone would tell a horror story which scared the bejeebers out of the girls. Other times, they would bring a portable radio, which they played softly. With potato chips, Cokes and cigarettes, they would have a "party" in the house. Now and then, someone would yell, "the caretaker!" Then they would hurry and blow out the candles, and scurry out a basement window and run like crazy. They knew they shouldn't be there, but it was so exciting being in a grand old manor, and using their imaginations to bring it to life again. It was so much fun. It *was* dangerous though, Joe was right; there *were* loose floorboards, and steps missing from the staircases. And, of course, a bunch of foolhardy kids lighting candles and smoking all through the house wasn't too safe either.

About a year later, the "haunted house" was torn down. Fran and her friends were terribly disappointed; it held some really nice memories for them. Later, the Jamaica Towers, a huge apartment building, was built on the site. It was very high and seemed to loom up into the sky. Fran always hated going by the corner of Perkins Street and Jamaicaway after that. They had torn down something old and wonderful, and put up something new and monstrous, as far as Fran was concerned. *"Whatever were they thinking?"*

*****

When Charlie and Margaret were coming to Jamaica Plain to visit Crocifessa and Peter, Margie would usually come with them. Fran and Margie spent a lot of time together during their teen years. The family was very close, even though Charlie and Andy didn't always see eye to eye; they would sometimes argue over the littlest things. But the love they shared was always evident. Charlie would walk into Andy and Ethel's apartment and Andy would stop whatever he was doing, and yell, "Mello! Margaret! Come on in; come in." Hugs and kisses were the norm when they all got together. They were always happy to see each other and spend a few hours together. They'd have coffee or a glass of wine, and often they'd all have lunch or supper together, either upstairs or down. If it were a Saturday, Margie would often stay overnight with Fran. They would talk and laugh, listen to records, and talk and laugh some more. Andy used to say, "There's no two people alive who can giggle as much as those two." Fran and Margie always had fun together, but being two years older, Margie would often 'introduce' Fran to things neither of their fathers would permit; nothing bad, but certainly not anything their parents would appreciate. For instance, Fran smoked her first cigarette with Margie, and bleached the front of her hair with Margie, which was the fad of the day. They both panicked when they saw how orange and yellow their hair looked. They kept the front of their hair set in pin curls whenever they were at home around their fathers.

One day Charlie said to Margie, "You know, I'm getting mighty tired of seeing you with bobby pins in the front of your hair, or in that kerchief wrapped around your head like a turban. What are you hiding anyway?" "Nothing, Dad," Margie responded. Charlie pulled the kerchief off her head and said, "Remove those pin curls right now." Margie tried to object but she knew she was caught and there was nothing she could do about it. "Holy mother of God!" Charlie screamed. "What in the hell did you do to yourself?" Margie felt like crying, but she was so nervous that she started laughing. "Oh, you think this is funny?" Charlie said. "You're being punished, young lady!" "I didn't mean to laugh, Dad," Margie said. "I just got so nervous when you started yelling at me." A strange look came over Charlie's face, and he said, "Francie keeps her hair in pin curls lately, too." He was red in the face and yelling quite loudly. "You should be ashamed of yourself; did you do this to Francie's hair?" "Well," Margie said, "we kind of did it together." "You should know better, Marguerite," you're two years older than her." "I know," Margie said, "I'm really sorry, Dad." "Well, you're grounded for two weeks, and no argument about it; you hear?" "She hears!" her mother said. "The whole neighborhood hears."

Fran was in her room when the telephone rang. She heard Joe say, "Dad, it's uncle Charlie, and he sounds mad." "He always sounds mad," Andy said jokingly. "No, he *really* sounds mad, Dad." A few minutes later Andy was banging on Fran's door, and yelling, "Come out here, young lady; you're in big trouble." Fran was grounded for two weeks also.

Two weeks later, when Margaret and Charlie came over to visit, Margie came with them. As soon as Ethel opened the door, Fran and Margie looked at each other and started laughing hysterically. It wasn't just their hair; they weren't sure themselves what they were laughing at, but it was hilarious, whatever it was.

*****

Margie's sister Fran had secretly married Harold Wight in a ceremony performed by a Justice of the Peace. Margie and Hal's brother stood up as witnesses for them. Fran and Hal had been going together for quite a while and wanted to get married. Hal was in his third year at Massachusetts Maritime Academy, and the cadets were not allowed to be married while still in school, hence the elopement. The whole family liked Hal a lot. He was handsome, intelligent, outspoken, and funny as can be. The thing everyone liked the most about Hal was that he was crazy about Fran. Later, after graduation, Hal and Fran were married at the Episcopal Church his family belonged to in Brookline, Massachusetts. They moved into a nice apartment nearby. They were very happy. Soon their daughter Carol was born, and a few years later their son Dana was born.

*****

The war in Korea was going on, and in 1950 the United States forces entered combat over there. So many young men had to go. People everywhere prayed that the war would end soon. The pain and loss of World War II still affected people everywhere. Andy and Ethel knew quite a few families who had sons sent to Korea to fight. They thanked God that their son, Joe was too young to be called up. They hoped and prayed that the war would be over before he was of age to be drafted.

Communism was everyone's great fear. There was a kind of witch-hunt going on for anyone who had any ties to communism. Many celebrities and other important people were hauled in to answer questions. Sadly, that time was being dubbed "McCarthyism." Ethel heard someone say on the radio, "We must do everything humanly possible to keep the "Red Menace" from infecting our country." It filled her with great concern. *"Please protect us, Lord, from the Communists,"* she prayed. She really didn't know much about communism, but she had heard that it was something to dread, and she did.

*****

Fran always had little jobs here and there; she baby-sat whenever she could, she worked after school when she was fourteen at a nursing home, and she worked for a couple of months before and after Christmas at the Five and Ten in Hyde Square. Joe had different jobs after school too. When he was fourteen he worked at Millikin's Market in Roxbury, delivering orders in a pushcart. Andy saw him one bitter cold day; he was struggling with the pushcart in a snowstorm. It was loaded with orders to be delivered, and he looked like he was freezing. Andy was heartsick; he said to Ethel, "We're not poor that we have to have our kid working like that." When Joe came home that day, Andy told him to quit the job right away. He got no argument from Joe. Joe had a few other part time jobs after Millikin's. His cousin Junior worked at Drury's Drug Store on Dudley Street, and he was leaving to start a new job. Joe had just turned sixteen, so Junior asked him if he was interested in working there. "Heck, yeah!" Joe said, so Junior put in a good word for him to the owner. Joe got the job and started working there after school and Saturdays; he liked working there a lot.

*****

About this time Dottie got very sick; she seemed to have just a bad cold, but again Crocifessa insisted it was Pneumonia. "Ma," Andy said, "every bad cold is not necessarily Pneumonia." He was a lot more worried than he was showing. "I don't know, Andy," Ethel said, "Maybe we should listen to her; she was right with Fran when she was a baby; I'm calling Dr. Desimone." "I'll be there first thing in the morning," he said. "I guess we'll all feel better once he examines her," said Andy.

Dr. Desimone came bright and early, just like he said he would. He walked in the door and went right to the pantry. He took a small pan off the hook, put a little water in it and put it on the stove to boil. He did this whenever anyone had what sounded to him like the flu or a bronchial infection, etc. He would then place a hypodermic needle in the water. While it was being sterilized, he would examine the patient to see what was wrong, and if they needed a shot of Penicillin, he was saving time by having the needle already sterilized.

After examining Dottie, he said, "Well, she has Pneumonia!" "Crocifessa began crying, and Dr. Desimone assured her and everyone else that "a shot of Penicillin today and another one tomorrow would heal Dottie very quickly." He always spoke Italian to Crocifessa and Peter, and they really appreciated that so much. He came back the next day and gave Dottie another shot of Penicillin. Dottie seemed a little better after the first shot of Penicillin, but after the second shot she seemed to get awfully sick again. The next morning she had broken out in a rash on different parts of her body. It was Tuesday and Ethel was glad that her mother was coming over. By the time Ethel Sr. got there, which was about nine thirty in the morning, Dottie was worse. The rash had spread all over her body, and she was becoming all swollen; her face was puffed up to twice its size.

Ethel called Dr. Desimone, and told him she was bringing Dottie to the hospital. "It sounds like a reaction to the Penicillin," he said. " I'll call the hospital Ethel and tell them you're coming, and I'll meet you there." Ethel called a cab and it arrived in less than ten minutes. She wrapped Dottie in a blanket and tried to carry her out, but Dottie was so sick, she just hung in Ethel's arms. Ethel asked the cab driver if he would please carry Dottie out to the cab. He took one look at Dottie and said, "Look Lady, I've got kids of my own at home; are you sure she has nothing 'catching'? Ethel assured him that the doctor was convinced it was a bad reaction to the Penicillin. "Okay, little girl," he said, as he took her from Ethel, "Let's get you to the hospital so you can get better." He carried her gently in his arms down the stairs, and when Ethel was seated in the cab, he placed Dottie on her lap. His name was Tom, and he was a very kind man.

When they left, Ethel Sr. sat down at the kitchen table, took off her glasses and covered her face with her hands and wept. Fran had never seen her Nana cry; it shocked her and she began to cry also.

As they were getting closer to the hospital Dottie began gasping and choking. Ethel cried out to the cab driver, "Hurry! Please hurry! She's not breathing right." The cab driver stepped on the gas, went through red lights leaning on the horn and sped to the hospital. He stopped right in front of the Emergency entrance, picked up Dottie, and ran into the hospital with Ethel running right behind. He yelled loudly, "We have a child here who's not breathing; we need help right away." Nurses, interns, orderlies seemed to come out of the woodwork. They called for Dr. Desimone and he came quickly. He gave Dottie a needle in her bottom, and then a nurse inserted an I.V. into her arm and started a powerful antihistamine going. They put her on oxygen, too. They worked quickly together and soon she was breathing easier. "It's going to take some time but she's going to be fine, Ethel," Dr. Desimone said. "Who would have thought she'd be allergic to Penicillin?"

Soon a nurse came into the room and said, "Mrs. Vitello, there's a cab driver out in the waiting room who asked how your daughter was. I told him I'd find out for him, but maybe you might want to speak to him yourself." "Oh my word!" Ethel said as she hurried out of the room. She went up to Tom, the cab driver and shook his hand. She said, "I can't believe you waited all this time." He said, "I just couldn't leave 'til I found out how your little girl was; I got kids of my own." "Oh, I can't begin to tell you how much you've done for us today," Ethel said. "My daughter is very sick, but the doctor assured me she is going to be fine, thanks to you and your quickness in getting us here. I can't thank you enough for your help, and for your concern. You're a good man, Tom; your children are blessed to have you." "Well, thank you," he said, looking embarrassed. "I'm just very glad your little girl is going to be okay. Do you need me to hang around? I mean are you going to need a ride home?" "No, my husband will be coming over soon," Ethel said, "thank you anyway." "Well," he said, "good luck to you and your little girl, and God bless you both." After he left Ethel thought of a scripture in the book of Hebrews, which speaks of being kind to strangers; "*…For by this some have entertained angels without knowing it.*" *"Tom the angel!"* she said under her breath. *"Hmm… I wouldn't be at all surprised."*

Dottie stayed in the hospital for almost three weeks. Her class made their First Communion while she was there. Ethel had asked the priest if he would consider coming to the hospital and hearing Dottie's first confession and administering her First Communion. It was kind of unorthodox, but he said he would be very happy to do it. "But my beautiful dress and veil," Dottie said, with tears in her eyes. Ethel said, "No problem!"

The day the priest came, Ethel had fixed Dottie's hair, and dressed her in her lovely white dress and veil. "Oh Mommy," Dottie cried, "thank you, thank you so much." She was very weak and couldn't stand alone, so she sat up, propped with pillows, looking like a little doll, all dressed in white. The nurses at the hospital were very kind and waived the hospital rule about visitors. Joe and Fran were there with Andy and Ethel. A few of the nurses came in; they brought Dottie a beautiful red rose, and had cake and soft drinks for everyone. Later Dottie said to her parents, "This was a super First Communion."

*****

When summer came, and school was out, they went to Westford. Andy commuted back and forth every day. Once in a while, when he had to work a little later, he would stay the night in Jamaica Plain.

Things were changing… Joe didn't want to leave for the whole summer as he had a job, and also because he didn't want to leave his friends for that long. Fran also didn't want to go for that length of time. She didn't want to leave her friends, and she wanted to get a full-time job for the summer. They still loved the cottage, but they were growing up, and had friends, and activities at home that they didn't want to miss out on. Andy and Ethel let them stay with their grandparents for a few weeks, but they knew that Crocifessa would be too lenient with them, and they'd 'get away with murder', so to speak. Fran and Joe were 'forced' to spend most of the summer at the cottage. They had such mixed emotions. They loved Westford, and the cottage and the lake, and the cave and the farm and the woods and the people, but they missed their friends and activities in the city. They griped and complained a lot and Andy and Ethel got tired of hearing that they didn't want to be there. "They're just ungrateful!" Andy said. "No, Andy," Ethel said, "They love this place as much as we do; they're just at an in-between stage in their lives. They're not children any more, but they're not quite adults." "Yeah, well, they're a long way from being adults, especially Fran," Andy said with some bitterness.

By the end of the summer Andy was fed up. "That's it! I'm selling the place," he said. "Oh, Andy, do you really think that's necessary?" Ethel said. "In a few years they'll both want this place again." "I don't care," he said. "Next year they'll want to stay home for the entire summer. They'll have jobs and they'll never want to be here. I'm not leaving them in the city with my parents; Ma and Pa don't really know what Joe and Fran are doing. They're just too young, and Fran's a little wild; they're not old enough to be on their own. No! I think we should sell." They were both confused and disappointed, and unsure of what the future held.

Andy and Ethel sold the cottage in Westford. Everyone was heart-broken over it, especially Joe and Fran; they knew it was because of them. A feeling of heaviness and emptiness came over them all that they couldn't seem to shake. Somehow, they sensed that they would regret this for the rest of their lives.

*****

About a year later, Joe started working at Herman's Health & Beauty Aids. It was located on the ground floor of Plant's Factory on Centre Street. He was packing orders and some days delivering them in the truck.

After a while Fran applied for a part time job there, too. She got the job and started working as a marker. The job entailed marking the price on each product and keeping the shelves stocked for the order pickers. She started at seventy cents an hour, which was more than she had made at any other part time job. She really liked working at Herman's; it was different from anything she was used to. She liked most of the people there, although some of them used bad language, which she wasn't used to. Her dad swore a little when he was angry or excited, but he was never crude. Joe had said, "I'll put in a good word for you, Fran, but you know you're going to be hearing a lot of swearing. No one's going to change the way they do things just because you're there." "I know," she had said. I can take it."

Joe wasn't at all sure Fran should be working there. At fifteen she was real cute, and he knew the guys there would be making passes at her. He just hoped they wouldn't get too bold, because he knew he would have to stand up for her if it came to that.

Fran was a little flirtatious and enjoyed the attention she got from boys. Andy could see it in her and he did not like it; neither did Joe. Fran was finding out that having a big brother like Joe was kind of like having two fathers. Joe knew that six months ago, when she was about fourteen and a half she had been 'dating' a fellow named George, and he didn't like him at all.

Fran had recently seen a movie called "The Wild One", starring Marlon Brando. It was about a motorcycle gang, and one good-looking guy who wore tight jeans, boots and a black leather jacket. His hair was slicked back in a D.A. (a hairstyle crudely referred to as a duck's ass). He had a smoldering, almost brooding personality, and Fran thought he was the coolest. Well, when she met George with his black leather jacket, boots and tight jeans a week after seeing the movie, all she saw was Brando. Even his hair was the same as Marlon's. She played it cool, and George pursued her, and did everything in his power to get her to go with him. He had no idea that she wanted to go with him in the worst way. 'Going together' meant having Cokes at Ollie's, a kind of ice cream/coffee shop with a jukebox and a couple of booths. Kids would come in, order a coke, play their favorite records and start dancing. Ollie was pretty good about it most of the time. For a nickel Coke, and a quarter, you could pick out six songs and sit and listen, or dance for an hour or so. If all the booths were taken up with teenagers, and 'paying customers' came in to have a hot dog or hamburger, Ollie would say to the kids, "Either buy something to eat or you'll have to leave." Most kids didn't have enough money for Cokes, music, *and* food, so they'd leave and wait around until the paying customers left. Then everyone would pile back in, fill up the booths, and order cokes and play the jukebox again.

It was a great place for teenagers, but it was located on Heath Street, and Andy (and Joe) didn't like her going there. "I moved my family out of that area for a nicer, safer place to live," Andy said, "and what do you do? You go right back there to hang out with kids we've never met. I don't like it Fran; I don't like it one bit." "Dad," Fran said, "they're real good kids, honest." "Ah, famous last words!" Ethel cried. Of course, her parents knew nothing about her 'going with' George. Andy would have taken one look at him and thrown him out bodily. *They* saw "The Wild One" too, much to their chagrin. "A waste of money," Andy said.

One Sunday afternoon Larry came over. Andy and Ethel had gone out somewhere and taken Dottie with them. Fran was in her room listening to records, and Joe was in his room getting dressed. Larry pounded on Fran's door and said, "I want to talk to you, Fran." Fran opened her door and said, "What is it? What's the matter?" "I'll tell you what's the matter," Larry said. "You need to break up with that loser, George." "What are you talking about?" Fran demanded. "And he's not a loser, Larry." "He's no good, I'm telling you! He's a bum and a hoodlum; that's what he is." "Who are you to call him a hoodlum?" Fran asked. "You don't even know him." "Oh, I know him all right," Larry said. "He was at Dispy with me." "Ha!" Fran laughed. "He was at Disciplinary School when *you* were there, and *he's* a hoodlum, but you're not?" "No, I'm not, and you know it, Fran. You know the only reason I was there was because I hooked school too many times." "Well, maybe that's why George was there," Fran said, "you don't know." "But I do know," Larry said. "And it wasn't for hooking school. Tell me, did he ever tell you he was at Dispy?" "No," she said, "but that doesn't make him a hoodlum." "No, that doesn't," Larry said, "but other things do." "Well, what did he do?" she asked. "You get him to tell you." "I will!" she said, "and you'll see how wrong you are, Larry."

Larry knew she was real angry, so he tried to smooth things over in his usual 'big brother' obnoxious way. Fran had pictures and posters all over her room of actors Tony Curtis, who was her favorite, and Tab Hunter. Larry, slyly, looked in her room and, with a grin on his face asked, "So tell me, how are 'Phony' Curtis and 'Scab' Hunter these days?" "Get out of here, Larry! Joe!" she called. "Will you get him out of here, please?" Joe heard everything that was said, and he was laughing. "Come on, Larry, let's get going. And you better listen to him, Fran, or I'm gonna tell Mom and Dad about George the Loser." All Joe heard was something hitting the bedroom door.

Fran did break up with George, although he kept calling her. He denied being at Dispy, and she knew he had lied about other things, too. She was seeing things about him that she didn't like, and lying was the worst. At first she felt bad; George was her first 'sort of' boyfriend, and of course, at fourteen and a half, she thought it was going to last forever.

She knew Larry had told her the truth. She didn't think Joe would squeal on her ordinarily, but if he thought it was for her own good, he might. When George kept calling, Joe and Larry went down to Heath Street and scared the life out of him. They didn't hurt him, they just threatened him and bullied him enough so that he stopped calling Fran, and by this time she was darned glad. Joe was not a 'tough' guy, but Larry could be when he needed to be. *Sometimes having an older brother, and a good friend who acts like he's your older brother, isn't so bad after all,"* Fran thought. *"Comes in darned handy sometimes."*

*****

Barry Gillespie worked at his aunt and uncle's store, which was directly across the street from Ollie's. He was real nice, and nice looking, too. He was so completely different from George that Fran started liking him more and more. Barry liked her a lot too, and started calling her on the phone; they would sometimes talk for hours. Joe was usually out for the evening, so she would bring the phone into his room, close the door and settle in for a marathon call. Eventually Andy would yell, "You've been on the phone long enough; someone might be trying to get us." That 'someone' was usually Mr. Graham, and Andy did not want to miss his call. Mr. Graham had already complained quite a few times that their phone was always busy when he tried to get hold of Andy. But, unfortunately, talking on the phone was Fran's favorite pastime.

Finally, Andy put a 'lock' on the telephone. It was a metal device that was inserted into the number one hole on the dial, and then locked with a key, which kept anyone from dialing. When he, or anyone in the family needed to make a phone call, Andy would unlock the lock, and when their call was over, he would lock it up again. Of course he put a ten-minute time limit on Fran's calls. But after much experimenting, Fran found if she simply pressed down on the receiver buttons ten times real fast she would get the operator, and would simply ask the operator to connect her to whatever number she wanted to call. Of course Andy never knew of her little trick, and whenever Mr. Graham or anyone else told Andy and Ethel they couldn't get through to them, Fran would say her friends had called her. It wasn't the truth, but what on earth was a teenage girl to do?

*****

Eventually Barry asked Fran to go out on a real date. She had never been on a real date, certainly not with George; all they did was sit in Ollie's, and then he'd walk her halfway home. Andy had always said she couldn't date until she was sixteen. She had just turned fifteen two months earlier and she was certain her dad would refuse, but she didn't want to sneak out on her first real date. She wanted her parents and Joe to meet Barry and to give her their permission.

"A date? Certainly not!" Andy bellowed. "Who's this Barry?" Joe asked. "How old is he, and where did you meet him?" "Well, he's seventeen and he lives in Medford," Fran said, "but he works in his aunt and uncle's store across the street from Ollie's." "Ollie's again!" Andy cried. "I've told you I don't want you going down there!" "Dad, I never go down there anymore," she said, which was the truth. She glanced over at Joe; he said nothing.

After a lot of discussion, Andy finally said, "I'll tell you what; I'll allow you to go out with this fella on one condition." Fran couldn't believe her ears. "What condition, Dad?" "That someone else goes with you on the date." "Good grief, Dad, are you talking about a chaperone? This is 1954, nobody has chaperones on dates; even you and Mom didn't have a chaperone, and she wasn't much older than I am." "Don't get excited; I'm not talking about an actual chaperone," Andy said. "I'd just like for Joe to go with you." "What?" Joe cried. "I'm not going on anybody else's date." "Now, hold on," Andy said. "You could ask Rosemarie or Mary to go with you." "Dad, they're our friends," Joe replied. "I'm not going out with them." "Rosemarie has a boyfriend, Dad," Fran said, "How about if they go with Barry and me?" "No! You don't understand," he said. "It has to be a family member, or not at all; and that's the end of it! And what kind of a name is Barry, anyway? I mean, Larry is short for Lawrence, Harry is short for Harold, but what the hell is Barry short for...Barold?" Joe laughed, and Ethel said, "Oh, Andy, leave her alone." "I'm serious," he said. "It's not short for anything," Fran said. "His name is just Barry."

Fran told Barry about her conversation with her father. He thought about it for a moment, and then said, "What about your cousin Margie? Is she going with anyone?" "No," Fran said. "Well, she's your family; would your father let you go if Margie and a date came with us?" "Gee... Margie; I think he might go along with that," Fran said. "I don't know if she would ask a guy out though. "Well," Barry said, I could get her a date." "First I'll have to see if she'll go along with it," Fran said, "but I think she will; she went through this when she went out on her first date. But who will you fix her up with? He has to be a real good guy." "He is;" Barry said, "he's my cousin, Gene, a terrific guy. But, before I call him, tell me, what does Margie look like? I mean is she okay looking?" "Oh, yes, she's real cute; I'm sure your cousin won't be disappointed," Fran said, sarcastically. "And what about Gene?" she asked, smiling, "Tab Hunter or Andy Devine?" "Oh, definitely Tab Hunter," Barry said, "He's what you girls would call a 'hunk'." "Hmm, maybe I should go out with him myself," she said chuckling. "Oh, very funny."

The big day finally arrived for Fran's date with Barry; Charlie drove Margie over to Fran's house late in the afternoon. Margie's brother Junior came with them. After visiting Crocifessa and Peter for a while, they came downstairs to talk with Andy and Ethel. Ethel made coffee, and she and Andy and Charlie sat in the living room. Junior and Joe went in the kitchen, and Margie and Fran went into her room to get ready for their date.

"Honestly Francie," Margie said, "the men in this family are all alike; can you believe my brother had to come along to check out my date? I mean I'm not a kid anymore; I'm seventeen. It's embarrassing; Gene and Barry are going to think we just came over on the boat." Fran laughed, "Boy, I'm glad it's not just me." "Don't expect it to change either," Margie said, "They'll be like this 'til we walk down the aisle. In fact, they'll probably come on our honeymoons with us to make sure our husbands do it right." Fran laughed out loud, "Margie, you're terrible!" "Terrible? Picture this...the four Vitello men, Charlie, Andy, Junior and Joe, all sitting around the marriage bed giving instructions." Fran was doubled over at the thought of it. She and Margie were in hysterics; their laughing could be heard all over the house.

When Barry and Gene arrived, they were both wearing suits and ties. Margie and Fran looked out the window as they heard them coming up the front stairs. Margie said, "Wow! They sure are good looking; which one is Gene?" "He's the one in the dark suit," Fran said. Margie said, "a suit and tie; I like this guy already." "Yeah, let's just hope they pass inspection with the board of approval out there." Andy and Charlie were duly impressed by Barry and Gene. Fran knew Barry would make a good appearance, but, of course, she didn't know Gene.

Margie and Gene liked each other right off, which pleased Fran and Barry. They took the train into Boston and walked to Chinatown. They ate at The Good Earth Restaurant, which Fran found exotic and delightful. She had no idea the variety of Chinese food there was; chop suey and rice was all she was familiar with. She decided that she loved Chinese food, especially chicken wings in oyster sauce. She couldn't believe something in 'oyster sauce' could be so delicious.

Afterwards, they walked around the Public Garden, holding hands, and then took a cab home. It was a wonderful evening, one Fran knew she would never forget; to her it was a perfect first date. She and Margie stayed up half the night talking about Barry and Gene, and the nice time they had. "Barry kissed you goodnight, didn't he?" Margie said, smiling. "Yes," Fran said, "Did Gene kiss you goodnight?" "Oh, yes; I really kind of like him," Margie said. "He seems very thoughtful." "Mmm," Fran said, "Barry is, too."

*****

One day in late summer Andy was doing a job at the Connelly Branch Public Library on Centre Street, when an unexpected hurricane started; at least it was unexpected to Andy, as he hadn't heard any forecast of it. He decided to keep on working, as he didn't think it would amount to much. But then branches began falling and debris was flying all over the place. He called Ethel and said, "Where are the kids? Is everybody home?" "Yes, we're all here," she said. "Ma and Pa just came downstairs. What are you going to do, Andy?" she asked. "I think I'd better stay here 'til it dies down," he said. "Good idea, Hon," Ethel said. "It's getting pretty bad out." "Well, stay away from windows, all of you," Andy said, "and if it gets worse, go down into the cellar." "We will," said Ethel. "Right now, we're all in the reception room; there's no windows here in the center of the house so I think we'll be okay." "Good thinking," Andy said. "If the lines go down, I won't be able to call you, but I'll be safe here 'til this blows over. I love you, Ethel." "I love you too, Hon," she responded. "Take care of yourself." "You, too!"

Andy continued to work in the library as long as he could, but it became so dark that he couldn't continue to paint, and there were no lights as the electricity went off. He started cleaning things up when he heard a window breaking; someone in the library yelled, "Stay away from the windows." Soon, a loud, dreadful cracking sound shocked everyone in the library. All of a sudden they heard a terrible noise like an explosion, and some people ran to the windows on the parking lot side of the library where the sound came from. Soon someone yelled out, "Who owns the gray '42 Buick in the parking lot?" "I do!" called Andy, "Why?" "Well, you better come here and take a look." Andy ran over to the window and couldn't believe what he was seeing. A huge tree uprooted, and fell over onto his car, caving in the roof. "Oh, no!" Andy cried. "Son of a b----! The only car left in the parking lot and that tree had to land on it. Damn!" "Too bad!" A man said. "That's rotten luck; sorry, fella." Someone else said, "You make sure you take some pictures of that for your insurance company." "Yeah, that's right," Andy said. "Thanks, I'll do that."

Andy kept hearing sirens, and wondered if police cars, fire engines and ambulances could get where they needed to go with all the debris on the streets. He tried to call home a few times, but, of course, all the lines were down.

When the hurricane was pretty much over, Andy walked home. "Mom!" Joey cried, "It's Dad, and he's walking." They all ran out onto the front porch to meet him. Ethel hugged him and said, "Andy, where's the car?" Andy came into the house; "You're not going to believe it," he said. "What do you say we all take a little walk up to the library?" "Yeah, let's go," Joey cried. "I want to see the damage along the way." "Alright," Ethel said, "but let your father have his supper first." "Okay," Andy said, "A quick supper and we'll go." "Fran," Ethel said, "hurry and set the table; you too, Dottie, you can help." "Fran," Andy said, "do you have film in that little Brownie camera of yours?" "Yes, I have film, Dad," Fran answered. "Good!" He said, "I want to take some pictures." "Oh! Oh!" Joe said, "this doesn't sound good." "Pictures of what?" Ethel asked. "You'll see," he replied.

All along the way, they saw trees uprooted or broken off, windows broken in businesses, homes, and automobiles. They saw a couple of overturned cars, and trucks piled with debris, some with trees on top of them. They saw barrels, bicycles, and all sorts of debris everywhere. "Be careful where you walk," Andy said. "Dottie, give me your hand." They were stepping over all kinds of things all along the way. As they got closer to the library, Andy waited for their reaction. Sure enough, they all gasped as they saw the car nearly buried by the tree. It had crushed in the roof and looked like it was resting on the tops of the seats. "Oh my Gosh," Joey cried; "that's our car; look at the size of that tree!" "Oh Andy, what a shame," Ethel said. "Daddy, our car is ruined," said Dottie; "how are you going to get to work?" Andy replied, "The same way I always got to work before we had a car…the good old MTA." "Dad, can the car be saved?" Fran asked. "I don't know, Honey, it doesn't look too promising. Hopefully, the insurance company will reimburse us for the damage; tomorrow we'll make a few calls, if the phones are working." "Dad, let's look around some more," Joe said. Andy said, "Okay; Fran, you stay and take some more pictures from every angle. I want some good pictures for the insurance company." "Okay, Dad, I'll get some good ones," she answered.

After they left, Fran started taking pictures of the car. A few minutes later a man carrying a large camera on his shoulder came over to her. "Do you know who owns this car?" he asked. "Yes," Fran replied; "my father does." "Oh, I'm sorry," the man said. He handed her a card and said, "My name is Bill Forsythe; I work for the Boston Globe. Would you mind if I took a couple of pictures of your father's car? "I guess not," said Fran. "You mean, it's going to be in the newspaper?" "That's right," he said. Why don't you stand beside the car?" Fran said, "Sure!" and ran over to the car, quickly fluffed up her hair, and smiled for the camera. "Well, thanks a lot;" the man said. "Make sure you get the Globe tomorrow." "The picture's going to be in the paper tomorrow?" Fran asked. "Yep!" he said. "Good luck to your dad." "Thank you. Oh, by the way," Fran said, "my uncle works for the Globe. His name is Ernie Dalton; do you know him?" "Sure, I know him," he answered, "I mean, not personally, but I see him all the time, and I read his column every day. He's terrific! So Ernie Dalton's your uncle, huh?" "Yes, he is," said Fran proudly.

When Andy brought the paper home the next day, he said, "Guess who's become an overnight celebrity." "Ooh, let me see it, Dad," Fran cried. Andy opened the paper and they all looked at Fran, grinning from ear to ear, standing beside the car with the tree on top of it. "Oh God, I look like a goof ball!" she cried. "You sure do!" laughed Joe. "Fran," Ethel said, "You look adorable; Joe, knock it off!" Andy read the article to them and when he got to the part about who was standing by the car, it read: "Standing beside her father's car is Frances Vitt Vitello." "What?" Fran cried. "That dummy! Couldn't even get my name straight." "Hah! Now everyone's going to think your middle name is Vitt," Joe laughed, "What a riot!" "Oh, be quiet, Joe," Fran said. "The only time you'll get your picture in the paper is if they're looking for the ugliest guy in town." "Oh, she stabbed me deep!" Joe chuckled. "You two!" Ethel said, as she waved her hand in mock disgust. "You talk to them Andy, no decent person would." Andy laughed heartily.

The city finally got around to Andy's car and removed the tree from on top of it. "Dad," Joe said, "let's see if it starts." "I doubt it will," Andy said, "but, yeah, let's give it a try." Joe squeezed part way into the front seat and put the key in the ignition. "Hear goes nothing!" he cried, as he turned the key. Vrroom! It started right up. "Hallelujah!" Andy cried. "Unbelievable! Boy, they don't make cars like these old Buicks anymore; that's for sure!" "Dad, I'm going to get the guys; we'll use mallets and whatever else we need, and see if we can get this roof up enough to get in the car and drive it home." "Go to it!" Andy said. "See what you can do." The 'guys' were Joe's friends, Larry, Ernie Weinacker and Billy Dugan. Joe knew they would love a challenge like this, and they did. Little by little they were able to hammer the roof up enough to get into the car. They were all hunched over and squeezed in, but they managed to drive it home.

Fran came home and saw the car in front of the house. When she looked inside the car, there was Joe, Larry, Billy and Ernie lying on their backs with their feet up on the roof of the car, grunting and groaning as they pushed upwards with their feet. Fran started laughing. "What a sight!" she cried. "Do any of you know what you're doing?" "Get lost!" Joey grunted. "Can't you see we're busy?" "Oh, pardon me!" she said, "I didn't mean to bother you four geniuses." She went in the house laughing.

Joe and his friends did get the roof up but the damage had been too great and the frame of the car was digging into the tires, and the steering was all off. The guys had a few days of fooling around with the car, but it really was dangerous to drive, never mind the eyesore it was. Andy said, "I guess it's had it, guys; it'll cost too much money to try to get it fixed, even if we could find a mechanic who would do it." Eventually they drove (and pushed) it to a junkyard.

Ernie had owned the car first, and after five years he was going to trade it in for a new car. Since the Packard, at the time, was on its last legs, so to speak, Andy had bought the Buick from Ernie. Timing is everything in life. As it turned out, Ernie was getting ready again to trade in his 1950 Buick for a new car. The '55s were coming out soon, and he really wanted one of them. So Andy bought Ernie's old car from him again, at a lot less than he would have paid a stranger. Ethel and the rest of the family were thrilled with the "new" car. It was a rich shade of green, and so much more modern and 'streamlined' than the older 'boxier' types. To Andy it was a new car, and he loved it. He felt like he was coming up in the world, and he thanked God for all His blessings.

*****

Fran saw Barry from time to time over the next year. She started seeing other guys, also. One day Barry told her he had enlisted in the army. He said he didn't want to wait until he got drafted; he wanted to make his own choices. He wanted to get a good education and felt this was the best way to do it, and at the same time fulfill his obligation to his country. Fran felt bad; Barry was a good friend, and she knew she would miss him. After Barry left, he and Fran wrote now and then for about six months, then it tapered off, and eventually they stopped writing.

Ethel Dalton (circa 1954)

**Ethel Dalton, Ethel, Andy and Dottie
(circa 1955)**

CHAPTER NINE
Whistling Girls And Crowing Hens

J.W. Graham & Son Painting & Contracting Company had been established in 1871. Al Graham was Jim Graham's younger brother, and the two brothers owned and operated the business since their father died. Andy became more and more important to Jim Graham. Mr. Graham relied on him for so many things having to do with the business. He also looked to Andy to take care of a lot of things that had nothing to do with the business. He was a lonely old man in need of help and companionship now and then. He would call Andy at any time and ask him to do some shopping for him or to come over and fix something that wasn't working properly. Sometimes he'd ask Andy to take him to a certain restaurant that he wanted to go to, or to visit an old friend. He even had Andy give up a couple of weekends a year to take him to New Hampshire or Vermont. Ethel didn't mind a lot of the extra things Andy did for him, considering Mr. Graham's age and all, but asking him to leave his family for a weekend really bothered her. The last thing Andy wanted to do was leave his wife and kids to spend a weekend in the White Mountains of New Hampshire with an old man, but he would always be gracious about it and agree to do it. "He's my boss," Andy would say; "we have food on the table and a roof over our heads because of him." Andy was from the 'old school', so to speak, and truly believed you did whatever your boss asked you to do, as long as it was legal. "These young people today," he would say, "have no gratitude whatsoever. 'That's not my job', is all they say, as if they should argue with the man who signs their paycheck; it's disgraceful. They should have lived through the Depression, when you'd give your 'eye teeth' just to *have* a job."

Now and then Ethel would have Mr. Graham over for supper; he was always very thankful. He liked Ethel, and Joe, Fran and Dottie, too. Andy would always insist that the kids be there for dinner, and on their best behavior when Mr. Graham came. He used to aggravate Fran and Joe something awful though. Mr. Graham was very hard of hearing, and no matter what anyone said to him, it would have to be repeated two or three times; each time louder than the last. "He's my boss," Andy would say, "and if I can put up with him, *and respect* him, *every* day, then you can certainly do it for two hours, three or four times a year.... right?" "Right Dad."

Once in a while Mr. Graham would invite Ethel and Andy out to a nice restaurant for dinner. He would insist that they order whatever they would like from appetizers to dessert. "Huh!" Fran once said, "he never asks me and Joe or Dottie to come." "Now, are you going to stand there and tell me you would *want* to go?" Andy asked "God no!" Fran said, "I just thought it would be nice to be asked." Joe laughed, and Andy smiled. "You're a pip, Fran," he said, chuckling. "You talk to her Joe, no decent person would." Fran just laughed.

*****

Margaret Mary Kenny worked at Herman's, and from the moment Joe set eyes on her he was smitten. 'Mae' was very pretty and had a nice personality. She was also twenty and Joe was only eighteen. This bothered Joe a lot because he was afraid that Mae saw him as just a kid.

Each day he would go into work and see Mae working or talking with someone. He wanted to ask her out so badly, but he was afraid she'd turn him down. Fran knew how much he liked Mae and told him he was crazy not to ask her out. "She's two years older than me," he said, "and besides, I think she's interested in Charlie." Charlie Doyle worked at Herman's, too, and it was obvious that he liked Mae a lot. "She's not interested in him," Fran said. "Oh, and you know that, do you?" Joe asked. "Well, I can tell when a girl really likes a guy, and I just don't think she feels that way about Charlie." "Well," Joe said, "that still doesn't mean she'd be interested in me."

Each day got worse for Joe; every time he saw Mae and Charlie talking and laughing together, it bothered him a lot. One day Joe got angry with Charlie and came close to hitting him; Mae was shocked at Joe's behavior and didn't know what to think. Fran asked Mae to meet her in the lady's room, and proceeded to explain to Mae the reason for Joe's actions. She told Mae how the two-year age difference bothered him, and how it kept him from asking her out. "Would you go out with him, Mae, if he asks you?" Fran asked. "Well," Mae said, "I don't know; when he finds the courage to ask me himself, then I'll decide." She wasn't saying she would, and she wasn't saying she wouldn't. What she *was* saying was that she wasn't going to give Fran that answer. Fran knew she had stepped over a line with Mae, and she hoped she hadn't ruined Joe's chances altogether. She liked Mae, but Fran was young and outspoken, and a little too impetuous. Mae was a bit confused, but not really upset. Fran had started the ball rolling, and it was up to Joe now. Joe realized that his actions needed an explanation to Mae. He asked her to go for a walk with him the next day after lunch. He told her of his feelings for her and finally asked her if she would go out with him. She said, "Yes." Needless to say, Joe was thrilled.

Mae was born and raised in Nova Scotia. She was living in Braintree with the family who sponsored her to come to the United States almost two years earlier. Joe borrowed his father's car and picked Mae up at the house in Braintree. He was terribly nervous and wondered how Mae would feel about him that night. They went for a nice long ride and stopped at a Howard Johnson's for something to eat. They talked about everything, and the age difference didn't seem to matter at all. They began seeing each other outside of work at least once a week, whenever Joe could get his dad's car. When Andy and Ethel had plans on the weekend, Joe would take the train to Braintree. They saw each other every day at Herman's during the summer while Joe was on school vacation, and would spend their lunchtime together. Eventually Charlie stopped hanging around Mae; it was becoming obvious that Joe and Mae were beginning to be a 'couple'.

Soon Joe bought an old 1941 Chevrolet Coupe. It was a beauty; it was the prettiest shade of light green, and had been well taken care of. Joe absolutely loved it, especially since he didn't have to rely on his dad's car anymore. Andy was happy about that, too.

Fran met a very nice guy through a friend she worked with at Herman's; his name was Ken Gerten. She and Ken started going steady and after a while they were certain they were in love. They wanted to get engaged, so they decided to talk to her parents about it. Andy and Ethel liked Ken a lot, as did Joe and Mae and Dottie. Ken was the kind most people liked. He came over one evening and spoke to Andy and Ethel. "Fran and I love each other," he said, "and we want to get engaged." "What?" Andy bellowed; (he had bellowing down to a science when he wanted to make a point). "She's only sixteen years old!" "Sixteen and a half," Fran said. "I know that Sir," Ken said. "We thought we'd get engaged now, but wait until she turns eighteen to get married." "Ken," Ethel said, "You're barely nineteen; becoming engaged isn't something to take lightly." "I know that, Mrs. Vitello, and we're not taking it lightly. I guess what I'm asking is, would you have any objections to Fran marrying me when she turns eighteen?" "No, Ken," Ethel said, "we have no objections to the two of you marrying one day in the future, do we Andy?" Andy just shook his head; he was still in a state of shock, but managed to say, "No… in the future…way in the future."

A few months later, Ken bought Fran a diamond engagement ring from E. B. Horn Jewelers in Boston. It cost one hundred dollars. Ken put twenty dollars down and promised to pay the balance within one year. Needless to say, Fran was ecstatic…. Andy and Ethel were not.

Fran and Ken often double-dated with Joe and Mae. One Sunday afternoon they all took a ride to Plymouth and walked around. It was nice seeing Plymouth Rock and the Mayflower. It was a lovely day until it started raining; very quickly it began pouring hard. Joe and Mae, and Fran and Ken started running for the car. All of a sudden Ken decided to play the gallant 'knight in shining armor' and swooped Fran up in his arms and started running toward the car. As he stepped off the curb into the street, his foot slipped and down they both went. Ken tried to shield Fran, but the back of her head hit the pavement hard. She was knocked out for a few moments, and Ken picked her up and put her in the car. She woke up sobbing hysterically, with her head against Ken's chest. She didn't know what was happening, or why her brother was speeding like a madman down the road. She kept falling asleep and waking, and felt a little sick to her stomach. They finally arrived at the Jordan Hospital in Plymouth. Joe ran in and came back out with an orderly and a gurney. They lifted Fran onto the gurney and rushed her into the hospital. After examining her and taking an X-ray of her head, the doctor said she had a mild concussion. He wanted her to stay there overnight, but Fran just wanted to go home. She promised she would do whatever the doctor told her to do.

Poor Ken was miserable; he felt like a fool and kept apologizing over and over. "I'm so sorry, Fran; can you ever forgive me?" Finally Fran said, "Of course I forgive you, Sir Galahad; why wouldn't I forgive you? You have the secret to showing a girl a good time; you drop her on her head." She smiled sheepishly at Ken who groaned. They all laughed; each one had been so tense, they needed a good laugh. "Hey guys, what do you say we go home?" Joe finally said. Mae, Ken and Fran responded in unison, "Oh, yes, let's go home."

Ken liked Fran's family a lot, and they all liked him. One of his favorite people in the family was Fran's grandmother, Ethel Dalton. She liked Ken very much, too. "He's a fine young man," she said, when she got to know him. She didn't say that about everybody. "I love your grandmother," Ken said. "She's such a hot ticket."

When Ethel, Sr. would come over on Tuesdays, either Andy or Joe would drive her home. Many times Mae, and Fran and Ken would go along for the ride. She would have them in stitches, as she would give a running commentary on every family she knew, and every business and restaurant they would pass in Medford before arriving at her house. They'd go up the stairs with her and she would take Ken and Mae all over the house, showing them her favorite things. One time Fran took Ken up into the attic. "Wow!" he said, "This sure is a step back in time, isn't it?" "Yes, it's one of my favorite places in the whole world," Fran said.

Her 'Nana Dalton' was one of Fran's favorite people, also. She wasn't a tall woman, but she was a very round woman. They say that overweight people are jolly; well, she certainly could be that. She was a lot of fun, and loved doing things with Joe and Fran.

When they were young, Ernie would get tickets to baseball and basketball games. They would meet their 'Nana' at South Station and go together to Fenway Park or to Boston Garden to see the Red Sox or the Celtics play. The best part of the games for Fran was waving to her Uncle Ernie, and him waving back from the Reporters' box where he sat covering the game.

Fran had heard so much about Ted Williams, and couldn't wait to see him hit one of his famous home runs. In all the games they went to, she never saw Ted do anything special, except make numerous adjustments to what she assumed was an ill-fitting undergarment. She knew he usually did do great things in a game, but unfortunately, it wasn't when she and Joe were there.

When she saw Bob Cousy play basketball, that was a different story altogether; he lived up to his fame. Fran couldn't get over how he would weave in and out and around the players, leap for the basket and make the shot. And he seemed so much smaller than his team members; she thought he was fantastic. Ethel, Sr. would get so excited at the games she would leap out of her seat, yelling and cheering. She loved Bob Cousy, and loved watching him. When the Celtics or the Red Sox didn't win, she would say a little rhyme she always said whenever something didn't turn out the way she hoped … "Oh me, oh my…come see, come sigh." Fran never quite understood why her Nana always said that.

Ethel, Sr. was full of life, and could be so much fun. Fran always enjoyed being with her.

On the other hand, as Fran got a little older, there was a side to Ethel, Sr. that always rubbed her the wrong way. She could be very critical at times, and it seemed to Fran she was always picking on her. She would criticize the way she washed dishes, the way she wore her hair, her clothes, or the way she would sweep the floor. If there were music playing, Fran would sometimes forget her Nana was there, and dance around the kitchen with the broom as her partner. Ethel, Sr. thought that was foolish and scatter-brained, and didn't hesitate to say so.

Fran loved to whistle, and was good at it. She could whistle an entire song straight through and never miss a note. One of the things that aggravated Fran a lot was when her Nana would criticize her for whistling. Ethel, Sr. would never fail to say, "Whistling girls and crowing hens always come to some bad end." That just about drove Fran crazy every time she would say it. Fran loved her grandmother very much and she tried not to let the things she would say bother her. "Mom," she would plead, "Please speak to her; she's driving me crazy."

Ethel knew what her mother was like and she knew how Fran felt. She did speak to her mother, nicely of course.... many times. Ethel, Sr. would be better for a while, but she'd slip right back into criticizing when she noticed something she thought should be corrected. Andy did not take kindly to his mother-in-law finding fault so much, and poor Ethel was put in the middle so many times.

The thing that bothered Fran the most was her Nana's lack of understanding when 'that time' would come around for Fran. She suffered greatly every month with nausea, and terrible cramping in her stomach and lower back. She used to hope that it wouldn't happen on a Tuesday, because if she were in school, or later in work, she would have to come home and go straight to bed; and, of course, Ethel, Sr. would be there.

Her mother was always very kind and sympathetic. As soon as Ethel looked at her, she knew what was happening. She would say to Fran, "Go right to bed, Honey; you're white as a sheet. I'll bring you in the hot water bottle and a hot cup of tea and two aspirins." If it was a Tuesday, Fran would always hear her Nana saying, "Ethel, you pamper her too much; she needs to toughen up. Maybe she wouldn't be a big baby about such a natural thing if you didn't coddle her so much."

One day Fran heard her mother say, "Stop it Mom! You don't know what you're talking about; you said yourself you never had a cramp in your life. She's not a big baby Mom; she's suffering, but you can't seem to understand that." When Ethel brought in the hot water bottle to Fran, with the tea and aspirin, Fran hugged her mother and whispered, "Thanks, Mom.... I mean for everything."

205

As Ethel was leaving the room, she smiled and simply replied, "You're welcome."

One Tuesday, when Ethel Sr. was at the house, she said to Fran, "You're a good girl, Fran; I'm very proud of you." Fran was shocked; when she was little, her Nana said nice things to her, but as a teenager, she mostly criticized her. Fran looked over at her mother, and she just smiled at her.

Later Fran said, "Mom, Nana is such an enigma; one minute she acts like I'm stupid, and the next minute she's proud of me." "She loves you very much, Honey," Ethel said, "you know that. She's just bristly and outspoken; always has been, and I don't think she's ever going to change, but she does have her kind side, too. Whether you realize it or not, you have a bit of her in you." "Oh gosh," Fran said, "what do you mean?" "Well, you can be a bit bristly at times, and you *are* outspoken." "Mmm, I know, Mom," Fran said. "I really love Nana so much but she does drive me coo-coo sometimes." Her mother smiled, "I know, Fran, I know... believe me, **I know**." They both laughed.

Joe and Fran graduated from Jamaica Plain High School in 1956. Joe took Mae to the senior prom. Joe in his tux, and Mae in her gown were a beautiful couple; they had a wonderful time the whole evening. Fran didn't go to the prom, as she and Ken had broken off their engagement three weeks earlier. Fran was feeling down, and wanted no part of going to the prom with someone else. Later they got back together, but it only lasted for another two months when they realized it was definitely over. They didn't break up on good terms, and Fran always regretted that. They were both so young; Fran, especially, had a lot of growing up to do.

*****

Joe and Fran both started working full-time at Herman's, while keeping their eyes open for better jobs. Neither of them wanted to be working in a dusty factory forever.

*****

206

When Joe was nineteen and Fran was seventeen, Ethel, Sr. got sick and was under a doctor's care. She was suffering from serious Edema and was taking a very strong diuretic, which forced her to stay home and close to the bathroom. "What a lot of nonsense; now I can't even leave the house," she said begrudgingly. "Now Mom," her daughter said. "Just be a good patient, and do everything the doctor tells you to do. You've taken care of other people all your life, family and strangers; now it's your turn to be taken care of." "Stuff and nonsense!" was her mother's reply. "I never needed anyone to take care of me before, and I certainly don't need anyone now. This is a big waste of time and money; there's nothing wrong with me." Ethel knew her mother would be a terrible patient. "That doctor's a quack," Ethel, Sr. said, "he doesn't know anything." "None the less, Mom," Ethel said, "he's the doctor, so please do what he says. I'd like you to stick around another twenty years." With tears in her eyes that she was trying to hide, her mother said, "What would I do without you, Ethel?" Ethel was shocked at her mother's show of emotion, as her mother never seemed to need anyone or anything. She was moved close to tears herself, as she responded, "What would I do without *you*, Mom?" She hugged her mother, and her mother kissed her, and as quickly as Ethel, Sr. moved into a show of emotion, she moved out of it. "Go on now; go home and take care of that husband and those kids; they need it more than I do." "Okay Mom," Ethel said, "I'll call you later." "It's not necessary, Honey; you mustn't worry about me; really, I'm just fine." "Well, I'll call you anyway," Ethel said. "Fine; now be careful going home," her mother said. "I will; Andy's going to pick me up at Dudley station." As Ethel went toward the door, she turned and said, "Mom?" "Yes, Dear?" "I love you." "I love you, too, Dear," her mother responded.

A week later Ethel, Sr. suffered a stroke, and died two days later in the hospital. Fran felt a tremendous sense of loss, and cried for a long time. She knew her mother was suffering terribly; she could see the pain in her eyes. She tried to understand what her mom was going through, but when she tried to imagine her wonderful mother dying, the thought of losing her was too awful to even imagine. *"I love you so much, Mom,"* Fran thought. *"Please don't die for a very long time; I couldn't stand it if you weren't here."*

Ethel Dalton was a very unique person who had made a huge impression on her family. She had her faults, for sure, but she was greatly loved. Fran knew she would never forget all the good times her Nana had created for her; Joe felt the same way. Dottie was only ten years old, but she felt the loss of her grandmother in her own way.

Andy was always very kind and supportive of Ethel; when she suffered, he suffered with her. It was no secret that he was never crazy about Ethel Dalton, but she was his wife's mother and he respected her for that reason. Strangely, there were things about her he knew he'd miss a lot.

*****

For the next year and a half Fran dated a lot of guys. In fact, she and Larry dated a few times, but they both began to realize that 'good friends,' and nothing more, was what they wanted to remain. Joe never dated anyone else but Mae. He was a lot like his father that way; when he met the woman who took his breath away, there was no need to look elsewhere. Mae was everything Joe wanted, and he loved her dearly.

*****

Fran and her dad had their problems during her dating years. Andy was very strict, and Fran had, what she believed, an unreasonable curfew imposed upon her. She enjoyed being out and having fun, whether on a date or just hanging out with Rosemarie or Mary. At seventeen she had to be home at night by ten o'clock, including weekends, dates or no dates. Andy was stubborn as a mule, and Fran loved her freedom…. not a good mix. It's amazing she had the time to date as much as she did, as she was always being punished for coming in late. 'Late' to Andy was any time after ten o'clock. When she turned eighteen, Andy said she could stay out 'til eleven o'clock. It really didn't change a heck of a lot; she always seemed to come in close to that time anyway. Of course, she was still being punished because now she was coming in at 11:30, and sometimes closer to twelve. It wasn't that she meant to be disobedient; it was just that an eleven o'clock curfew was a little unreasonable, especially when she was out on a date. The hardest part of all was that Joe also had a curfew, an hour later than Fran's, and he always seemed to be home on time. *"I can't understand it,"* Fran thought. *"Doesn't he have any fun?"*

Soon Fran and Joe found better jobs. Joe started working for Goodyear Tire Company, and Fran started working at O'Brion, Russell Insurance Agency on Water Street in Boston.

*****

It was the middle of November 1957, and Fran was eighteen and a half. One day while on her lunch break, she met a young man at the coffee shop across the road from her office. When she walked into the coffee shop, he asked the woman behind the counter who she was. Since there were other girls in there at the time, she asked which one he was referring to. Fran heard him say, "the one with the white collar." Fran felt her face flush because she knew he was talking about her. When the woman asked her what her name was, she answered, "It's Fran, but don't tell him that." A few days later she saw him in the coffee shop again. This time he came up to her as she was getting ready to leave and asked what her name was. Fran said, "It's Zelda." He just looked at her and smiled and said, "I don't really think that's your name; come on, tell me your name." As she was leaving, she turned and said, "My name is Fran." She started to walk out of the coffee shop when he called to her and said, "Don't you want to know my name?" "Not really," she answered. He just laughed, and she smiled at him as she walked out the door.

Later, Fran asked the woman in the coffee shop if she knew who he was. "I don't know his name," she said, "but he works at Maryland Casualty Insurance Company around the corner. I know Louie Quatrucchi, his boss; they come in together sometimes."

When Fran went back to the office, she asked her boss, Billy Moretti, if he knew Louie Quatrucchi from Maryland Casualty. He said, "I've met him a few times; seems like a real nice guy; why do you ask?" "Well," she said, "I ran into a fellow who works for him, and I was just wondering what his name was." "Oh, I get you," Billy said, with a wry smile. "Okay, so what does he look like?" "He's about six feet tall, slim, with light brown hair," Fran said. "Any distinguishing features?" Billy asked. "Well," she said, "he has kind of large front teeth...I mean, not buck teeth, or anything like that." "Okay," he said, "I'll see what I can find out." "Billy," Fran said, "Make sure he doesn't know I was asking about him." "Don't worry," he said. "I'll be the height of discretion."

The next day, when Fran came into work, there was a note on her desk from her boss...

"His name is John Charles Roche, and he's a junior underwriter at Maryland Casualty." "ROCHE?" Fran cried; "that's a horrible name!" Billy, whose desk was right in front of hers, turned around laughing. "ROCHE isn't so bad," he said. It just sounds a little buggy." "Hmm," Fran said, "You can say that again."

A few days later Fran went into the coffee shop, secretly hoping John Roche would be there; he wasn't. She had a cup of coffee, and as she was paying the check, he walked in. He came right over to where she was sitting and pulled up a chair. "Why don't you want to know my name?" He asked. Before she could say anything, he continued. "I was hoping we could go out some night; you know, maybe take in a movie and a pizza, but if you don't even care to know who I am, I guess that's not a very good idea." Fran enjoyed his boldness at first, but she was beginning to feel a little embarrassed. She got up and put on her jacket. As she did, he got up and said, "Well, nice knowing you, Fran," and started walking away. Fran said, "Your name is John Charles Roche, and you work for Maryland Casualty Insurance Company." He turned around and smiled and said, "How did you know that?" Fran said, "I have my sources." He chuckled and said, "So, does this mean you'll go out with me?" "I guess it does," she said. "Good! How about Saturday night?" "All right, John," she said, and wrote her address and telephone number on a napkin. "What's your last name?" He asked, as he looked at the napkin. "Oh, it's Vitello," she answered. "Italian, huh?" he said. "Half Italian and half English," she said. "Nice combination," he responded with a grin. "By the way.... call me Jack."

The following Saturday evening Jack arrived at Fran's house at 6:30 sharp. Fran had told him to come early because her parents would want to talk with him before she and he went out. He was dressed in a nice gray suit, white shirt and tie. His shoes were polished, and his hair combed perfectly; he looked terrific. Fran introduced him to her parents and her brother Joe. Her parents were very impressed with Jack after giving him what Fran called "the third degree." Her father felt that Jack was a young man with a fine future. Joe liked him, but reserved his opinion until he got to know him better. Joe was like that with everyone.... except Mae; with her it was love at first sight.

So, where would you like to go?" Jack asked Fran, when they were outside. "How about a movie in Boston and pizza afterwards?" Jack didn't have a car, so they would catch a train into Boston. "That sounds good to me," Fran said. Do you know what's playing?" He had the movie section of the Boston Globe in his pocket, and he started to read off all the movies that were playing, and their times. "Pal Joey", with Frank Sinatra sounds good," he said. After reading the whole list of movies, Fran decided on "Rodan," a large prehistoric bird that was terrorizing Japan. She loved scary horror movies.... Jack didn't. He hated the movie and just couldn't hide his feelings. "It was just so corny," Jack said. "Well, you should have said something," Fran laughed. "It didn't have to be 'Rodan'; we could have seen something else." "I *did* mention 'Pal Joey,'" Jack said. She laughed again. "Next time you pick the movie," she said, still laughing at the look on Jack's face. "Oh?" he said, "does that mean there's going to be a next time?" "It depends," Fran said. "On what?" he asked. "On your choice of pizza," she chuckled. "I like mushroom and onion on pizza," Jack said, "but if you don't like that, we can get them on one half, and whatever you like on the other half." *"Mushroom and onion?"* Fran thought, *"Oh, this guy is definitely a keeper!"*

Fran and Jack went out the following Saturday night; they went bowling at a very popular bowling alley in Boston. It was very crowded so they had to wait for a lane to be available. While they waited a man came over to them and asked if they would like to make it a foursome when a lane opened up, or they'd be there all night waiting for individual lanes. Jack looked surprised and stood up when the man started talking. "You're Satch Sanders, aren't you?" He said. "Ah, yeah," the man said. They shook hands and Jack introduced him to Fran, "This is Satch Sanders, Fran; he plays for the Boston Celtics." Fran hadn't heard of him, but she wasn't surprised, as he was the tallest man she had ever met. Being only 4'11", to her Satch Sanders looked like a giant. He introduced Fran and Jack to his girlfriend, and they ended up bowling four strings together. Jack was a good bowler, and Fran did okay, but they were no match for Satch and his friend. When it was over, Satch said, "This was fun; I'm glad we met you guys." "Sure it was fun," Jack said joking, "You guys beat the pants off us." Fran and Satch's girl-friend laughed, and went up to the snack bar and ordered Cokes for the four of them. It was a real nice time, bowling with Satch Sanders and his friend. They were both very nice.

Fran and Jack started meeting a few days a week for lunch, and now and then he would meet her after work and go back to her house for supper. They'd watch TV or take a walk, or just sit in the kitchen and talk and talk and talk. "What do they find to talk about after so many hours?" Ethel said many times. They talked about every-thing … families, high school, friends, work, movies, books, sports, anything and everything that came into their minds. Andy and Ethel liked Jack a lot; he had more liveliness and energy than anyone they had ever known. Joe and Mae liked him, too. Dottie thought he was terrific, and lots of fun. He *was* fun; he kept Fran laughing, and everyone else too.

Jack grew up in Hyde Park, and was second oldest of eight chil-dren. His dad was a custodian at a school not far from where they lived. They were not poor, but they certainly didn't have a lot, not with eight kids to feed. Jack had made up his mind years before that he would one day make a lot of money, and never want for anything. He was a no-nonsense person, and a hard worker with a lot of ambi-tion, and he knew exactly what he wanted out of life. He worked Thursday and Friday evenings and all day Saturdays at Roche Bros. market on River Street in Hyde Park (no relation). "I'm going to be a millionaire before I'm twenty five," he once told Fran. In 1957 millionaires were hard to come by, but Jack truly believed that he would do it. Fran thought it would probably never happen, but she admired his ambition, and, even more, his zest for life.

*****

Maryland Casualty had a basketball team; they would play against other insurance companies. Jack loved basketball, and played all through high school, so he jumped (no pun intended) at the chance to play for Maryland Casualty, and would never miss a game. He had invited Fran to come to one of his games at a local gym, and on a cold night in January, she was there, cheering him on.

Jack was good at the game, and Fran was impressed. At one point during the game he ran toward the net, dodging players, and leapt for the basket. The ball went in, and everyone, including Fran jumped up and cheered. A moment later Jack was rolling on the floor, grimacing in pain, and holding his leg. The coach and Louie, his boss, carried him over to the benches. His ankle started swelling almost immediately, and began turning black and blue. "I don't think it's broken," Louie said, "but it's a real bad sprain." Someone got a basin with water and ice in it and Jack soaked his foot for about a half hour. He didn't say much at first; he was in too much pain to talk. Finally, he looked at Fran and forced a grin. He said, "Some good time, huh?" "You're not worried about *me*, I hope," Fran said. "I enjoyed the game immensely; I'm just so sorry you got hurt. You're a real good player, Jack." "Yeah, I'm okay, when I can stay on my feet," he quipped. Louie wrapped Jack's ankle in an ACE bandage and drove Fran home first, and then Jack. Fran liked Louie a lot, and he seemed to like her. He had a great sense of humor and loved teasing Fran about her height (or lack of it). Louie and Jack got along real well; he was a good boss, and Jack was a good worker. It was a good combination.

The next week, after Jack had sprained his ankle, he played basketball again. Fran thought it was too soon to play, but he said his ankle felt fine, a little tender, but he'd be careful.

Fran was watching and cheering for the team, when Jack came running down the court, in and around the other players, dribbling the ball, and heading for the basket. He leapt up.... and everyone cheered as Jack made the basket; then history decided to repeat itself. In the blink of an eye, he was down on the floor, grimacing with the pain, and holding his leg.... the *other* leg. Fran felt terrible as Louie and another player carried Jack over to the benches where she was sitting. He was in a lot of pain, and again the ankle swelled right up and started turning black and blue. Someone got ice and water in a basin and Jack soaked his foot for a while. "Gee, Jack, maybe I'd better not come to any more of your games," Fran said. "I may be jinxing you." "Nah, if anything, you bring me good luck," Jack said. "This would have happened whether you were here or not." For the second time in a week, Louie wrapped Jack's ankle with an ACE bandage, and drove him and Fran home.

The next day was Saturday, and it was snowing out. Fran and her mother were having a cup of tea with Ethel's friend, Eleanor Kramer, who lived across the street. The doorbell rang and Fran went to answer it. She was shocked and happy to see Barry Gillespie standing there. They hugged, and Fran cried, "Come in! Come in, Barry!" It had been almost three years since they had seen each other. "Mom! You remember Barry," Fran said, as they came into the kitchen. "Of course I remember Barry," Ethel responded. "How have you been?" "I've been fine, Mrs. Vitello, and you?" Barry answered. "Oh, we're all well here, thank God," Ethel said. "I took a chance that you'd be home, Fran," Barry said, I hope this isn't a bad time." They all assured him that it was not. Ethel asked, "Are you still in the army, Barry?" "No," he said. "I got out about a month ago." Fran introduced him to Mrs. Kramer, and then poured Barry a cup of tea. Ethel and Eleanor went into the living room and left Fran and Barry to talk in the kitchen. "It's so good to see you, Fran," Barry said. "You look wonderful!" "Thank you, Barry," she said, "It's good to see you, too; and *you* should talk; you look great! Oh, we have so much to catch up on, Barry." They talked for about an hour, and Fran made Barry a sandwich and another cup of tea. They were enjoying their reunion immensely.

All of a sudden Fran heard her mother say, "Oh my Lord, I don't believe it!" Fran called out, "What is it, Mom?" "Umm," she said, " Fran, Jack is coming down the hill on crutches." "Oh my gosh!" Fran said. "I can't believe it; it's snowing out; he'll kill himself on this hill." "Ah, Fran?" Barry asked. "Who's Jack?" "Oh… well, he's a fellow I've been seeing," Fran answered, uncomfortably. "Oh," was all Barry said.

Andy had been upstairs talking with his parents when he saw Jack from the window, slowly making his way down Parkton Road. He came downstairs and went outside to help Jack up the front steps. "What are you doing, coming out on a day like this, and on crutches?" Andy said. "Well, It wasn't this bad out when I left the house," Jack replied. "And if it had been?" Andy asked. "I would have come anyway," Jack said. "Mmm, that's what I thought; crazy kids!" Jack laughed, "Come on, Mr. V.," he said. "You'd have done the same thing when you were going with Mrs. V." "Yeah, you're right, I would have." Andy chuckled.

Ethel and Eleanor were just about having silent fits, trying to get Fran's attention to get Barry to leave. By this time everyone was crazy about Jack, and they were afraid he might be upset over another guy visiting Fran. But Fran knew that Jack would not be jealous over a simple visit with an old friend. When Jack came into the house, Ethel filled a basin with warm water for him to soak his foot. Andy pulled a chair up for him and Fran asked him if he'd like a nice hot cup of tea. "Hi!" Jack said, when he saw Barry sitting there. "Oh! Jack," Fran said, "this is Barry Gillespie, an old friend of mine; Barry this is Jack Roche…. my…. boyfriend. They shook hands, and said, "Nice to meet you," and, "How're you doing?" A minute or two passed and Barry said, "Well, I guess I'll be running along now." Fran said, "Barry, you don't have to leave." It was a very awkward moment, and Barry said softly, "Yeah, I think I do; I think *now* it's a bad time." He said "goodbye" to everyone, and "nice to meet you, Jack," and Fran walked him to the door. "I'm sorry, Barry," she said. "I've really enjoyed seeing you again." "Me, too, Fran; It's been great seeing you," he said. "Will you call me?" Fran asked. Barry hesitated a moment, then looked toward the kitchen; " Umm, I don't think so…. You hang on to that guy, Fran," he said. "I think he *really* loves you." Fran was speechless. "I wish you all the happiness in the world, Fran." "Me, too, Barry," she said. They hugged and said, "goodbye," and he left.

Fran felt bad about Barry; she had strangely mixed emotions at that moment, but almost three years was a long time. She knew she'd never forget him, because he was one of the nicest guys she had ever known; and because he was the one who took her out on her first real date. She came back into the kitchen. As she looked at Jack sitting with his foot in the basin of water, she thought, *"Barry's right; I don't know if Jack is really in love with me, but he sure must like me a lot. Anyone who would come out in a snowstorm, hobbling on crutches, just to be with me, is someone I don't want to lose."*

*****

Jack asked Fran to go steady with him a few weeks later, and she said, "Yes," even though she hadn't gone out with anyone else since she first met him. They had a lot of fun getting to know each other better. They talked and talked, and went to movies, and watched TV. They walked around Jamaica Pond, and often double-dated with Joe and Mae, or with Rosemarie and her boyfriend, Bill Buckley. They were falling in love, and loving every minute of it.

Fran had always loved to dance; she especially loved dancing with her father. Andy was an excellent dancer, and he had taught her how to waltz and fox trot and polka when she was very young. If a polka came on the radio, Andy would grab his daughter and they would dance all through the house. Ethel would laugh and pretend frustration, and say, "Oh, you two; I can't get anything done when you two are home and that radio is on." At weddings or other functions, Fran and her dad would dance most of the dances together, which made Ethel happy, as she didn't care to dance more than one or two dances.

Fran and Jack used to go to a nightspot near Canton called "The White Dove". They had a lot of fun there; they would order pizza and Cokes, and spend a few hours listening to the jukebox and dancing. Fran had taught Jack to 'Jitterbug', and he was getting pretty good at it. They usually went there with friends, as Jack didn't have a car, and it was kind of a long walk after taking the MTA. They even took her parents there once or twice; they liked it a lot, too. Fran and Jack loved The White Dove; it was just a real nice place to go to have a good time on a Saturday night without spending a lot of money.

*****

One night Fran and Jack went to Blinstrub's, a famous night-club in South Boston. Frankie Laine was performing there, and both Fran and Jack loved Frankie Laine. He was one of the most popular singer/entertainers at the time.

Fran never really drank, and Jack wasn't really a drinker, but they were all dressed up, and Jack said, "Let's order a drink." Jack was twenty, but Fran was only eighteen, and the drinking age was twenty-one. "Oh, I don't know, Jack," she said, "they'll never believe I'm over twenty-one; what if the waitress asks for some identification?" "She probably won't," Jack said. "She might ask you what year you were born, and if she does, don't hesitate; you just say, 1936, okay?" "Okay," Fran said, "that's not too bad." Fran lit up a cigarette as the waitress was coming towards them. When the wait-ress asked what she could get them, Jack answered, "We'll have two Seven & Sevens." The waitress looked at Fran, and Fran felt her face flush. The waitress smiled and said, "Look, Honey, I don't care one way or the other, but I know the bartender is going to question your age, so why don't you tell me what year you were born." Fran was terribly nervous but she knew she shouldn't hesitate, so she blurted out, "1926." She saw Jack's face drop, and the waitress just grinned and said, "How about a Coke, Honey?" Fran was so embarrassed; all she could do was nod. "**1926**?" Jack said, with a confused look on his face; whatever made you say 1926, Fran?" "Jack, I'm embar-rassed enough; I just panicked, I guess." "1926!" he said again; that would make you thirty-one." He started laughing, and finally, Fran started laughing, too. "I can't believe I said that; what a dummy." "No, you just got nervous," he said. "Come on, the show's going to start soon; this is going to be great!"

It *was* great; it was better than great. Frankie outdid himself; what a performer! At one point, near the end of his show, Frankie asked the audience what they might like to hear. That's all Jack needed; he stood up, whipped off his belt, and threw it up on the stage. Frankie

217

laughed and picked up Jack's belt, and, cracking it like a whip, the music started, and he began singing his hit song, "Rawhide." It was so exciting; it was one of those times that Fran knew she and Jack would never forget. Frankie Laine returned Jack's belt, and shook his hand when the song was over.

*****

Jack asked Fran to marry him; actually he said, "What do you think Fran? You think we ought to get married?" She said, "yes," and on April twenty-third they became officially engaged. Jack bought Fran a beautiful diamond solitaire ring set in a platinum band. They wanted a September wedding, but Ethel and Andy talked them into getting married in November, as they would have known each other a full year by then. Fran and Jack were on 'cloud nine' and they, and Ethel and Andy began making plans for the big day.

They went and talked with Fr. Mulcahy at the church; he was very nice and accommodating. He said he would speak to the organist, and take care of a few other details. He seemed genuinely happy for Fran and Jack; he said he wanted to talk to them again in a few months.

Jack and Fran decided, rather than going out, they would spend most of their time at Fran's house, so they could save money for the things they really needed.

Fran started running Popular Clubs in her office, and with her family and friends. She would show them the catalog, which contained everything from clothing to furniture to household items. Her customers would place an order and pay one dollar a week for every ten dollars of their order. If their order came to thirty dollars, they would pay her three dollars a week, and so on. They would go on a list, and each week she would send in the next order on the list. Each 'club' lasted ten weeks; sometimes she had two and three clubs going at one time. She got quite a few orders, and with the commission she made, she was able to get a George Washington bedspread, curtains, draperies, lamps, tablecloths, pillows, and many other items she knew she would need.

Jack and Fran had a lot of fun with her parents, making plans for the wedding. They made out the guest list and picked out invitations. It seemed like they went over the seating arrangements a hundred times. They spoke to Fr. Mulcahy again and looked at halls for the wedding reception.

Fran asked Rosemarie to be her maid-of-honor, and Mary, Mae, and Mary Manning to be bridesmaids. Margie was busy planning her own October wedding to Bob Lang. Dottie was thrilled when Fran asked her to be a junior bridesmaid. Fran and the girls had a ball looking for gowns. There was so much to do, and she was enjoying every moment of it.

Eleanor's husband Frank owned Kramer's Furniture store on Centre Street in Jamaica Plain. He gave Fran and Jack a good discount on their bedroom and kitchen sets. They bought a turquoise sectional sofa from Jordan Marsh Co., and a walnut kidney-shaped coffee table and end tables to go with it from Frank.

Fran and Jack started looking for apartments, but for the rent they could afford, the apartments weren't very nice. Frank Kramer put their furniture on lay-away, as did Jordan Marsh, but November was coming on fast, and as of September they still hadn't secured an apartment.

A few years earlier Andy bought a house across the street at 47 Parkton Road as a financial investment. It proved to be a very wise move. The apartments were identical to their home at number 40, and Andy was getting good rents for them. One day in mid September, when Jack and Fran arrived at her home after work, Andy said, "I've got a surprise for you two." "Ooh, what is it Dad?" Fran asked. "The people in the second floor across the street have given me their notice. They're moving out October 15th; you guys can have the apartment if you want it." Fran screamed with delight, and hugged her father. "If we want it? Oh yes, Dad, of course we want that apartment." "That would be great, Mr. V.," Jack said, "but, to be honest with you, I don't think we can afford the rent." " I've got a deal for you," said Andy. "Oh, what's that?" Jack asked. "Well, how does fifty dollars a month for two years sound? That way you'll be able to put some money away for the future." "That sounds great," Jack said, "but what happens after two years?" "Then the rent goes up to seventy five dollars a month; by then, hopefully, you'll be making more money," Andy said. "Oh, I will be, for sure, Mr. V." Jack responded. "You can bet on it." Fran was ecstatic; she ran to her mother and hugged her. Ethel laughed. "I knew you'd be happy over that, and after some of the apartments we've looked at, we're just glad that you'll have a decent place to live, and it's right across the street from us." "I'm so happy that we won't have to move away from you and Dad," Fran said.

Jack gave his notice at Roche Bros. market, and two weeks later started working at Meatland, a market on Centre Street. He figured it would be more convenient working at a part time job in Jamaica Plain, after he and Fran were married, than going out to Hyde Park. He was able to get the same hours he had at Roche Bros. He'd work Thursday and Friday evenings from six to nine, and Saturdays from eight a.m. to six p.m. Jack was taking home fifty dollars a week at Maryland Casualty, and Fran was taking home forty-three dollars a week at O'Brion Russell. The extra money helped a lot.

Fran happened to be thinking one day, *"Jack will turn twenty-one on November 24th, "How is he going to make that million dollars he said he'd make before he turns twenty-five?* She smiled to herself, *"Ah, well, it's a real nice dream, anyway."*

****

220

Crocifessa and Peter (circa 1957)

CHAPTER TEN
Fried Chicken Every Night?

"SURPRISE!" Over fifty women yelled, as Fran and Jack entered the Doyle Post in Hyde Park. Jack's dad, Jim, had asked them to come by and see the new paint job on the place. Fran was shocked seeing all the women in her family, and so many of her friends there. She was numb, but quickly realized that this was a bridal shower for her. She started laughing, and jumping up and down and hugging Jack; and although she was laughing, the shock and the excitement brought her close to tears. Her mom was smiling and clapping, and Dottie was jumping up and down. Jack's mom, Phyllis, and his sister Jane, were laughing and clapping. Margaret, Fran and Margie were there, and Lena. Of course, Crocifessa was there, with her 'famous' baked macaroni, and Sarah and Phil came and brought a gorgeous bridal shower cake that they had made, and some marvelous homemade pastries. Eleanor Kramer and her daughters, Marie and Elaine, were there also. It seemed like every woman that Fran loved was in that room, and was so happy for her.

Rosemarie, Mary, Mae, Mary Manning and Dottie planned the shower, and decorated the hall. They bought food, flowers, lovely favors, and all the extras that make a shower wonderful; and it truly was wonderful; the girls outdid themselves. Fran received lots of great gifts, and money gifts, also. She was becoming well equipped for running a home.

Two weeks later, Sarah and Phil invited Fran and Jack over for dinner. When they got there, much to Fran's surprise, Sarah and Phil had planned another shower for her. There were about twenty-five people there, and as many gifts. Mostly, it was the Westford crowd, and a few family friends who hadn't come to the first shower. Ethel, Andy and Dottie were there, and Crocifessa and Peter also. It was a wonderful evening.

Later, as she lay in bed going over the two bridal showers in her mind, all Fran could think was, *"I am so overwhelmed at all the love my wonderful family and friends have shown to me. I'll never forget this as long as I live."*

A week before the wedding, all the girls in Fran's office took her out for dinner to the Top of the Hub Restaurant at the Prudential Building in Boston. There were eleven girls, counting Fran that went. When they got there, her boss, Billy Moretti, was waiting for them. Fran laughed; "I didn't expect to see you here," she said. Bill gave her a hug and said, "Are you kidding? I'm the rose among the thorns." She laughed again, and said, "I'm glad you're here, Billy." "Me too," he said. "I wouldn't have missed it."

After a wonderful dinner, they had a lovely shower cake for her; the restaurant sliced it and served it with ice cream. Then the girls and Billy gave her two beautifully wrapped gifts; one was a Hamilton Beach mixer, and the other a Hamilton Beach electric fry pan. Fran was positively thrilled; she had wanted both of those real bad, although she really couldn't understand why; hopefully it was a sign of things to come...not what actually was. As strange as it seems, with Crocifessa and her mom living in the same house all those years, the only thing Fran knew how to cook was fried chicken. *"I'm going to have to pay more attention to Grandma and Mom cooking things from now on,"* she thought. *I can't believe I never took the time to learn how to cook. They kept after me all these years to learn, but I guess I just thought Mom and Grandma would always be there to do the cooking. Oh, well, I've got one thing I can cook, and I can open a can of peas; but fried chicken every night? Mom...help!"*

*****

Jack's friends all took Jack out on the town two nights before the wedding. By the time they brought him home he was 'three sheets to the wind,' so to speak. Jack's mom called Fran in the morning, "I don't think he's able to make your lunch date, Fran; he can hardly get out of bed." "You mean he's sick from being drunk?" Fran asked, shocked. She had never seen a single member of her family, or even her friends, drunk. "That's about the size of it!" Phyllis said. "How sick is he?" Fran asked. "Well," Phyllis said, "He's spent most of the night and morning in the bathroom, if that's any indication." "Well, good!" Fran said; "glad to hear it!" There was silence for a few seconds, then Phyllis started laughing, and so did Fran. "Now here's a woman after my own heart," said Phyllis. "It doesn't make sense to me," Fran said, "What's the big deal about getting so drunk that you're sick as a dog? How can that possibly be enjoyable?" "I'll be darned if I know," Phyllis said, "Ask your future father-in-law." They both started laughing again.

*****

Fran and Jack were married at three o'clock on Sunday afternoon, November 16th, 1958 at Blessed Sacrament Church. Fr. Mulcahy performed the ceremony. Fran looked and felt beautiful. Her gown was stunning, with a satin beaded and lace bodice, scalloped neck-line, long satin and lace sleeves, and a very full, floor length skirt. When her father saw her, he got so choked up he had to leave the room. He said to Ethel later, "I never thought any bride could be as beautiful as you were, but Fran runs a very close second." Jack's friend, Hank was the best man, and Fran's brother Joe, and three of Jack's friends were ushers; all the men wore black tuxedos.

Rosemarie and Dottie wore rose-colored dresses and matching shoes, and carried pink bouquets. Mary, Mary and Mae wore the same dresses and shoes, but in a lighter pink; they carried deep rose-colored bouquets. It was a beautiful wedding party. Ethel was a very pretty woman, and looked elegant in a royal blue velvet dress and matching shoes. She wore the mink stole Andy had bought her on her last birthday. Andy was positively handsome, himself, in his new black suit. He was so very proud of his wife, his two daughters, and his son this day. Crocifessa looked very nice, too, in a black crepe dress. The fabric was different, but the color was always the same; she never wore anything but black during autumn, winter and spring. In summer she would wear a lighter colored housedress. Peter looked and felt like a politician in his new black suit. "Papa," Fran said, before they left for the church, "You look like the President of the United States, only handsomer." He grinned and kissed her hand and said, "Et tu, Franzie, la princepessa." He always said she looked like a princess, but he never meant it more than he did this day.

Frank Kramer had offered his new Cadillac, and his services for the wedding. The car was solid black, and shone like glass; it was a real beauty. Fran was very pleased, as only real well-to-do people could afford to hire a limousine. Frank picked up Fran, Andy and Rosemarie at 2:40, and drove slowly to the church, which was only about five minutes away.

When Fran walked down the aisle on her father's arm, she felt like a princess; she knew she looked beautiful, and that all eyes were on her. It was her special day, and she would make it last as long as possible. As she came near to the altar, Jack's face lit up, and he beamed with pride as her dad lifted her veil and kissed her cheek. She took Jack's hand and the ceremony began. Jack whispered to her, "You look so beautiful!"

During an emotional moment in the ceremony, Mary (Pinciaro) began to cry. She knew she would, so before they had left Fran's house, she ran around trying to find some Kleenex tissues. When she couldn't find any, she grabbed the end of the toilet paper and pulled a long strand of it out, and tucked it down inside the front of her dress. During the ceremony, when Fran said, "I do", Mary became emotional, and started to cry. She reached down the front of her dress, took hold of the toilet paper, and pulled; out came a string of toilet paper about three feet long. "Oh my Gosh," she whispered to Mae, "it didn't break." She started stuffing it all back in her dress, but by then quite a few people had seen what was happening. The muffled laughter could be heard all over the church. Mary was embarrassed, but couldn't stop giggling, Mae was trying to stifle a laugh, and Andy was 'killing himself laughing,' with Ethel nudging him to be quiet. He said later, "Mary can look like a duchess coming into a room, but you can be 'sure as shootin', she'll trip over her gown and fall flat on her face. She's lovely, but she sure is clumsy." Fran and Jack never saw any of it, which probably was a very good thing. Had Fran known what was going on, she'd have been in hysterics laughing.

Fr. Mulcahy made it a lovely ceremony, with his gracious and dignified manner. When he introduced Jack and Fran as Mr. and Mrs. John Roche, all Jack and Fran's friends stood up and clapped and whistled. Fran was shocked, but enjoyed the moment. She wasn't too sure Fr. Mulcahy would, though, but he just smiled and clapped with everyone else.

The wedding reception took place at Liederkranz Hall in West Roxbury, and Eddie Castle and his band provided the music. It was a wonderful time; the meal was terrific, and when Fran and Jack danced their first dance as husband and wife, they were about as happy as two people could be.

Shortly after their dance, the emcee told Fran to take her father onto the dance floor. They started playing "Daddy's Little Girl." As they danced, Andy said to Fran, "Other than your mother, you're the most beautiful bride I've ever seen; and I really mean that. I love you so much, Honey." As soon as he said it, Fran was filled with emotion; she put her head down on his chest and started to cry. "Oh, Daddy, I love you so much, too," she said. That was all Andy needed; he could not control his emotions any longer; so father and daughter simply held each other and cried, as they slowly danced around the floor.

Everyone had a terrific time at the reception, especially Fran and Jack. They hated to see it come to an end, but it was getting late. Joe and Mae drove them back to the house to change, and then drove them into Boston. Neither of them had ever been in a real nice hotel, or any kind of hotel for that matter. They looked forward to spending their wedding night in the honeymoon suite of the Statler Hotel.

The next morning, Fran and Jack took the train to New York City for their honeymoon; they stayed at the Prince George Hotel. They had a wonderful week in New York; they saw the Empire State Building, and the Statue of Liberty. They rode around Central Park in a cab, and went to Rockefeller Center. They ate at the Automat, and at Mama Leone's, two totally different types of restaurants. They had never eaten at a restaurant like Mama Leone's; the food and the service were so fabulous, they felt like celebrities. They went shopping at Macy's and at Gimbals, and went to a couple of shows. Fran wanted to do everything her parents did on their honeymoon, but they were told that Coney Island was nothing like it used to be, so they decided against going there. She was disappointed, as she wanted to have their picture taken on the "honey-moon", but Jack was probably right when he said, "It's probably not even there anymore Fran." She never did find out, but it didn't matter; they had a wonderful time anyway.

When it was time to go home, Fran and Jack weren't sure what time they would arrive at South Station, so they took a cab from there to the house. Ethel and Andy and Dottie ran out on the porch to greet them. Joe was there, too, and hugged and kissed his sister, and shook Jack's hand. Crocifessa and Peter came downstairs. Crocifessa started hugging and kissing them. Jack and Fran had souvenirs for everyone. It was so much fun talking to the family about their trip. After bringing them up to date, Ethel called from the kitchen, "Dinner's ready; come to the table while it's hot." Everyone was hungry, and something smelled real good. "Oh, Grandma," Fran cried, before she even saw it, "you made your baked maca- roni; you're so sweet." "Justa for you, Franzie," she said. "Come... mangia, mangia." She was gently pushing Jack to sit and have some of her macaroni. "Oh my gosh!" he cried. "I've never tasted anything this good." "Grandma," he said, "you could put Mama Leone's out of business." Andy translated, and Crocifessa beamed with pleasure. Jack continued to rave about it; he just couldn't believe that, even to the last mouthful, it was still delicious. They all felt that way; it was always wonderful. Fran was certain it was all the love and caring that went into it. Crocifessa said to Andy in Italian, "He's an Irishman, but he knows good food.... he's all right."

After dinner, Fran and Jack opened wedding presents and enve- lopes. They received some lovely gifts and quite a bit of money. "Oh, Mom," Fran cried, "Look what Ernie and Lena gave us," as she showed her mother the one hundred dollar bill that was in the card. "Oh, my word, that's extremely generous of them," her mother said.

Most of the cards held checks of ten or fifteen dollars; now and then, a twenty. Jack was very excited, rubbing his hands together as each card was opened and its contents revealed. "This is great," he said. "We should put all this in the bank." "Well," Fran said, "Maybe we could keep a *little* aside, Jack, for things we might need right away; what do you think?" "I guess so," he said, but I'd sure rather see it all go into the bank...but I guess we could keep out a few dollars." "Ooh," Fran said, laughing, "The last of the big spenders." "Well, that's the difference between you and me, Honey," Jack said, "you want to buy things with it, and I'd rather save it." "Oh, I get it," Fran said, "towards that million you're going to have in the next four years." "Well, you have to start somewhere, right Mr. V.?" "Right, Jack," Andy replied, "but you have to find a happy medium, too." Jack paused for a moment. "Right!" he said..."I guess."

"Mom and Dad," let's go across the street to our apartment. I want to see how all our furniture and things look," said Fran. "I'll make a pot of coffee, okay?" "Well, Fran," her mother said, "maybe Jack's tired, and would rather just go home." "No, no, I'm fine," he said. "It's only four o'clock." "Come on, let's go over," Fran said. "Okay," Ethel said, "I'll bring the dessert over,". Crocifessa and Peter were tired, and had already gone back upstairs. "You, too, Dottie and Joe," Fran called. "I can't make it, Fran," Joe said. "Mae and I are going out with Helen and Chet tonight; we'll come over tomorrow." "Okay, Joe, say hi to them for me," Fran called, as she headed for the front door. "I will," Joe yelled after her. "See you tomorrow."

*****

Mae's sister Helen had come to the states from Nova Scotia about a year before, and she and Mae had got an apartment together in Braintree. Helen met Chet Kertanis a little while later, and they started dating. Joe liked Helen a lot, and felt the same about Chet. The four of them became very close. Fran and Jack triple-dated with them a few times. Fran liked Helen; she was a hot ticket, with a wacky sense of humor. Chet was a real gentleman, a very funny guy, and as nice as could be.

*****

When dessert and coffee were finished in their new apartment, Fran and Jack rearranged some furniture, put some knick-knacks around, and hung some pictures. Fran was having so much fun fixing up her very own apartment. She loved having her mom there to share her happiness with, and also for Ethel to add her own special touches. Andy and Jack were needed to move and lift the heavy stuff, and help hang the pictures, but they left the knick-knacks to Fran and Ethel.

The next day Fran made Jack the *only* thing she knew how, fried chicken, baked potatoes and peas. She added cranberry sauce for a special touch. The chicken turned out great, and Jack loved it, and ate quite a bit of it. The following day was Saturday, and Jack had to work at Meatland, so first thing in the morning, Fran called her mother, and said, "Mom, can you teach me how to make the sauce today? And, maybe meatballs, too? Please? I'll run to the A&P and get what we need; you make a list, Mom, okay? Please?" Ethel laughed, "Okay, but I have everything we need here. Come over as soon as you can, and we'll get started right away. I'm defrosting hamburg right now; I was going to make a meatloaf for dinner, but meatballs it is. Do you want me to ask Grandma to come downstairs and help, too?" Absolutely!" Fran answered; "It'll be fun, Mom, you'll see. "Yes it will," Ethel answered. "It's about time!" Crocifessa said. "Buono!"

Fran paid close attention to everything her mother and grandmother did. Every Saturday she would go across the street and watch Ethel and Crocifessa put together a marvelous meal. Andy said one day, "I can't believe we're having Ma's baked macaroni and veal cutlets, and it's not even a holiday." Peter was thrilled; he was having his favorite dishes every Saturday night and Sunday. Jack simply couldn't believe his good fortune to marry into a family where all the women were such great cooks. The cooking lessons paid off; Fran became a good cook very quickly. She found, much to her surprise, that she absolutely loved cooking. "Hey, Grandma and Mom, how come you never wanted to teach me to cook before I was married?" Fran asked, with a grin on her face. Ethel and Crocifessa looked shocked for a moment, and then shook their heads laughing. Her mom snapped a towel at Fran's behind, and said, "Ooh, you... you take the cake!"

*****

Fran and Jack had a lot to be thankful for that first Thanksgiving they were together; they were so very happy. They had a wonderful dinner with Andy and Ethel, Joe and Dottie, and Peter and Crocifessa. After dinner Charlie and Margaret came over with Junior, Bobby and Richard. Fran and Hal came over, too, with their little daughter, Carol, and Margie and her husband, Bob Lang. Peter, and his wife Dolly dropped by, too. Everyone had dessert and coffee, and Crocifessa brought out Vermouth, and poured a little in liqueur glasses. Peter was very thankful that his family was still close, and saw each other often.

When Charlie and the family went home, Andy said to Ethel, "This is the best Thanksgiving ever." He said that every year; and every year he really meant it.

Later, Joe left to spend the rest of the day with Mae and Helen and Chet. Fran and Jack went to Hyde Park to visit Jack's parents and his brothers and sisters. They had more coffee and dessert there. "Jack said, "If this is the way we're going to eat every holiday, we better have a good supply of Alka-Seltzer in the house; my stomach is bursting." Fran laughed; "Brioschi!" she said. "Brioschi? What's that?" Jack asked.

*****

Christmas Eve was real nice; Ernie and Lena came over, and Joe brought Mae over. Jack gave Fran a Longines-Wittenauer watch. She was thrilled; "I've never had such a nice watch," she said. She bought Jack a nice desk; he had mentioned that he could use one. It wasn't big, but it was just what he needed. After Ernie and Lena went home, Andy and Ethel, Peter and Crocifessa, Fran and Jack, and Dottie all went to midnight mass at Blessed Sacrament Church.

Christmas day was wonderful, as it always was, but to Fran this Christmas was better than ever because Jack was part of the family now. Jack was positively overwhelmed at the food that had been prepared. He had Crocifessa's 'famous' chicken soup, and the antipasto salad and Italian bread; he had her 'famous' baked macaroni and meatballs. Then he had Ethel's roast pork with stuffing and gravy, and her mashed potatoes and carrots. "We'll take a breather," Ethel said, "and have dessert and coffee in a little while." "Oh, my Gosh," Jack said, "dessert! Grandma, where's the Brioschi?" They all laughed, and Crocifessa ran to get Jack the Brioschi, which he didn't really need, but knew Crocifessa loved getting it for him.

Later, when Andy and Ethel were alone, Andy said, "This was the best Christmas ever." He said that every year, and every year he meant it more than the last.

*****

By the end of January, Fran was pretty sure she was pregnant. Jack was thrilled, but held his excitement back until she had seen the doctor. Eleanor Kramer had had Dr. Weiss deliver her two daughters; his office was on the corner of Perkins Street and South Huntington Avenue. She called Dr. Weiss, and made an appointment for Fran to see him. Fran and Ethel went to see him a week later. After examining Fran, and asking her many questions, he confirmed that she was indeed pregnant. She was ecstatic! She secretly hoped it would be a girl. Since she was about ten years old she had dreamed of one day having a little girl; she would name her Teresa Marie, but call her Terry.

Dr. Weiss said, "Your due date is August ninth, Fran." "What? Oh, no!" Fran exclaimed. "It can't be August ninth!" "Well, why not, for heaven's sake?" Dr. Weiss asked. "Because Jack and I were married on November sixteenth; this baby can't be born before August sixteenth." "Well, I'm sorry, Fran, but your due date is August ninth." "Oh, Lord," she said, "August ninth is too early; it won't be a full nine months; people might talk." "Fran," Dr. Weiss said, "Is that what you're worried about? Well, anyone who would start counting for a matter of a couple of days isn't worth worrying about." He was very kind to Fran; he could see that, at nineteen years old, she needed a lot of reassurance. Andy and Ethel had hoped that Fran and Jack would wait a few years before having children, just so they could spend time just being husband and wife before becoming Mommy and Daddy. They both seemed so very young. But, Fran was pregnant, and it was wonderful.

Fran didn't have morning sickness, and she never felt better in her life; she absolutely loved being pregnant. The only time she actually felt kind of sick, was one day when she walked into her mother's house. She and Jack didn't have a washer or dryer yet, so Fran did her laundry at her mother's. That day Ethel was frying peppers, to make peppers and eggs. All of a sudden Fran felt her stomach turn, and she ran into the bathroom. She didn't get sick, but as soon as she opened the bathroom door to come out, the smell of frying peppers assaulted her nostrils; she felt nauseous again. "I don't understand it, Mom," she said, "I've always loved the smell of peppers cooking." Her mother said, "Oh, Honey, It's got to be the pregnan ..." "Oh, God, Mom!" Fran felt her stomach turn again. She literally ran out of the house. "I'll be back later to do the clothes," she yelled. As she walked back across the street, she gulped the fresh air, and soon the nausea left. Ethel came over later to see how Fran was feeling, bringing Fran's clean laundry with her. "Oh, I feel much better, Mom, and thank you so much for doing my laundry. You know something Mom?" "What's that?" Ethel asked. "Well, every time I even *think* about the smell of the peppers frying, I feel nauseous all over again." "There's a good solution to that," her mother said. Fran chuckled, "Yeah, just don't *think* about the peppers, right?" "Right!" Ethel said with a grin. "Oh Mom," Fran said, "Poor Rosemarie; now I have some small idea of what she's been going through."

Rosemarie and Bill had gotten got married soon after Fran and Jack; she too got pregnant right away. She was due in October, and she had been suffering terribly with morning sickness. Fran would call her and they'd chat for a while; then, all of a sudden Rosemarie would say, "Oh, oh, be right back!" and she would run for the bathroom; she'd return to the phone, and say, "Okay; I'm okay for a while."

*****

One day, while visiting Jack's parents, his mother said to them, "Well, guess what, Fran; it looks like you and I are going to have babies not too far apart." "What?" Jack cried.

What do you mean, Ma...you're pregnant?" "Yep, I'm three months along." "Oh my word," Fran said, "Are you feeling okay, Ma? When's the baby due?" "I feel great!" Phyllis said. The baby is due in October." "Well, that's great, Ma," Fran said. "I'm really happy for you." "Well," Phyllis said, "Some things are not planned, but you make the best of them anyway. I never planned on nine kids, that's for sure." Jack wasn't saying anything; he was still in shock.

*****

August ninth came, and no baby yet; Fran was taking it nice and easy. One day her mother came over and asked her if she'd like to take a walk. "It's such a nice day today; it's not hot out like it has been." "No thanks, Mom," she said. "I'm not going anywhere." "What's wrong, Fran?" Ethel asked. "Do you think something's starting?" "Oh no," Fran said, " I'm just going to do all I can to help this baby stay right where it is." Ethel laughed, "You hot ticket," she said. "All right, I'm going to walk up to the A&P. I'll bring us back some cold cuts and some Italian bread, and we'll have a nice lunch right here; how does that sound?" "It sounds great, Mom; thanks." "I'll be back soon;" Ethel said. "Put some coffee on."

August sixteenth came, and no baby yet; Fran was relieved. Jack couldn't have cared less what people might think about the baby coming a few days earlier than nine months, but Ethel admitted she was kind of glad the baby waited 'til after the sixteenth.

Joe belonged to the National Guard, and he was gone for two weeks every summer. So, those two weeks Fran and Jack spent at her parents' house, and stayed in Joe's room. It was only across the street, but Fran felt better being that much closer to her parents. She and Jack couldn't afford a car yet, so Andy would be driving them to the hospital when the time came.

234

On the seventeenth, it was so hot that Fran kept dousing herself with cold water. She and Jack went to an air-conditioned movie after an early supper, just to feel cool for a while. They got home about seven-thirty. Her cousin Fran was there; she was going to go over to the opening of the new Orbit department store, and she thought that Fran and Ethel might like to go. "Oh, yes, I'd love to go," Fran said. "It's air-conditioned, right?" "Oh, sure," her cousin said, "they're all air-conditioned now." Ethel said, "Okay, let's go; I'd like to see what it's like." Andy said, "Hey Jack, there's a fight on TV tonight; Ethel hates them, but we can watch it while they're gone." "Great!" Jack said, "who's fighting?" "I don't know," Andy said, "but who cares? It's a boxing match." Ethel just shook her head. "Fran, you talk to them; no decent person would." Fran and her cousin Fran laughed; so did Andy and Jack. "Mom and Fran, I'm just going to run in the bathroom," Fran said. "I'll be right with you." "Lately it seems like I have to go every five minutes." "Oh God, I remember that," her cousin said.

When Fran came out of the bathroom, she said, "Jack… Mom… my water just broke." "Oh my!" Ethel said. "Okay, I'll call Dr. Weiss, and, Fran, sit down, for God's sake before you slip and fall." Dr. Weiss said, "It could be a while before her pains start, but you should go now to the hospital. A little while later they were in the hospital and Fran's pains had started.

"Say goodbye to your husband, Mrs. Roche," the nurse said. As soon as they had arrived at the hospital, Fran was put in a wheel-chair, and wheeled to the Labor Room. Jack kissed her goodbye and went back out to the lobby where Andy and Ethel were waiting.

Fran was very nervous; she had never spent any time in a hospital; she even had her tonsils out at home on the kitchen table. They brought her into the Labor Room, got her undressed and into a johnnie, then into a bed, and left her there, all alone. She was very frightened. A nurse came in about every fifteen minutes to check on her progress. Soon Dr. Weiss arrived; he examined Fran, and then went to tell Andy, Ethel and Jack that they should go home. "First deliveries are usually long," he said. "Don't worry; I'll call you as soon as the baby is born."

They went home, and Andy paced the kitchen floor, Ethel tried to concentrate on a magazine article in the living room, and Jack went to bed and slept. Ethel was angry with him for not 'worrying', but his attitude was, "There's nothing anyone can do until Dr. Weiss calls, so no sense losing sleep in the meantime." Later Andy said to Ethel, "What an insensitive s.o.b!" "Andy," Ethel said, "just forget about it; there's no sense in getting upset over it." "Yeah, forget about it...right! How am I supposed to do that? My poor daughter is in labor, probably in agony right now, and he's in bed sleeping away, without a care in the world. Yeah, I can forget that...sure I can!"

Fran was terribly scared; she kept thinking, *"Who are all these people who keep coming in and examining me? Oh God, I don't want to be here; I just want to go home."* Her pains were coming closer and closer. She hadn't seen Dr. Weiss for a little while. She began to cry softly with each pain; she had never felt so lonely. *"Oh God, where is he? Has he forgotten about me?"* She thought of the only thing she knew in the Bible, the 23rd Psalm: *"The Lord is my shepherd, I shall not want, He maketh me to lie down in green pastures, He leadeth me beside the still waters, He restoreth my soul."* Her mind went blank; *"Oh what's the rest of it? Something, something, something;"* all she could remember was, *"Yea, though I walk through the valley of the shadow of death, I will fear no evil, for Thou art with me."* "Yes," she thought, *"That's the part I wanted."* She said it over and over; she tried very hard not to be afraid, but she was hurting so much, and she was all alone.

"Fran...Fran, can you hear me?" Dr. Weiss was there, speaking to her; she could hardly make out what he was saying. A nurse had come in and given her a needle; she said it would help the pain. Fran knew it was making her groggy, but the pain was so bad she was glad for it. *"Did Dr. Weiss say, 'Delivery Room? It sounded like Delivery Room."* The next thing she knew her bed was being wheeled down the corridor. "Where are we going?" Fran asked whoever was pushing the bed. "We're going to the Delivery Room," a very pleasant voice responded. "You're going to have your baby soon." "Where's Dr. Weiss?" Fran asked. "He's waiting for you in the Delivery Room, Dear," the pleasant voice answered. She was wheeled into a very bright room, and Dr. Weiss stood over her, about to tie on his facemask. He smiled at her, and said, "Fran, your baby is coming; we're going to roll you onto your side, so we can give you the spinal. You'll feel a pinch at the base of your spine, but soon you'll feel no pain at all. As they rolled her onto her side, a very hard contraction started; Fran muffled a scream as the pain intensified. Soon she felt nothing.

At one point during the delivery, Fran realized she couldn't feel her legs when a nurse moved them. She tried to move her big toe; she tried real hard, but nothing would move. *"My God, what if there was a fire? I couldn't get off this table. No...no, I won't think about that now."*

Dr. Weiss was saying to her, "We're almost there, Fran, just a couple more good pushes and your baby will be here. Come on, Fran, I know you're tired, but here comes another contraction; I'll tell you when to push." He didn't need to tell her; she couldn't have stopped the pushing even if he told her to. "Your baby's head is almost out, Fran, one more good push and your baby will be here." "I can't," she said. Her voice was weak from exhaustion; "I just can't." But no matter how exhausted she was, she seemed to have no control over the pushing; her body was doing what was natural, whether she had the strength to do it or not. "Come on, Fran; you can do it. That's it! Here it comes!"

*****

Teresa Marie Roche was born at 6:23 a.m. on Tuesday, August 18, 1959. She weighed eight pounds, two ounces, and was twenty one inches long. Other than her 'baby' sister Dottie, she was the most beautiful baby Fran had ever seen. A nurse laid her lengthwise down Fran's body for a few moments, then wrapped her in a blanket and brought her back for Fran to get a good look at her. "Aren't you going to count her fingers and toes?" the nurse said. "Why? Aren't they all there?" Fran asked nervously. "Oh yes, Honey, of course they are; it's just that a lot of mothers like to count their baby's fingers and toes, just to make sure." *"Of course they're all there,"* she thought. *"If they weren't, you never would have asked me if I was going to count them."* Fran thought it was silly, but she started counting her baby's fingers, and then, exhausted, she said, "I'll take your word for it."

The telephone rang about quarter to seven in the morning; Andy and Ethel both ran to answer it. "Ethel," Dr. Weiss said, "You have a beautiful granddaughter, and your daughter is fine." "Oh, thank God," Ethel said, "how wonderful!" "Is Jack there?" Dr. Weiss asked. "I called his house but there was no answer, so I assume he's still at your house." Ethel knocked on the bedroom door; she knocked again and Jack jumped up and opened the door. "Any news?"

A few hours later, Fran was brought to a four-bed ward. Before the nurse left she said, "You need to stay lying flat on your back Mrs. Roche for about seven more hours because of the spinal. You also had stitches, so you might feel better lying down anyway, okay?" "Okay," Fran said, "I don't really feel much like sitting up yet. Jack came in to see her soon after she was settled in the room; he brought her a lovely bouquet of flowers. They kissed and held each other for a few moments, and Jack asked, "How are you feeling, Honey? Was it bad?" "No, it wasn't too bad," she replied, "It was more scary than anything, but Dr. Weiss was with me and he was awfully nice." "Have you seen the baby, yet?" Fran asked. "No," he said, "I'll go down to the nursery in a few minutes, but I wanted to see you first." "She's really beautiful, Jack; wait 'til you see her. Ooh, Jack," Fran said, "you wouldn't believe what a spinal is like; you're so completely numb from the waist down that you can't even move your big toe." "Are you serious?" Jack asked. "Yes," she said, "it's amazing. Boy, I hope you never have to have one of those." "Ah… yeah, me too," he said.

About fifteen minutes passed, and Andy and Ethel came into the room; they had waited to give Jack a few minutes alone with Fran. "I'll be back in a few minutes," he said, as he headed for the nursery. "Oh Mom," Fran said, "I'm so glad you're here." Her mother bent over her and kissed her cheek. Andy came up beside Ethel, and kissed Fran; his eyes were filled with tears. "Are you feeling okay, Honey?" He asked. "Oh yes," she said, "I'm a little sore, but I'm just glad it's over. I can't wait for you to see your granddaughter."

After a little while, Jack came back, grinning from ear to ear. "Wow! Fran," he said, "she's a little doll, and she's so tiny." "Actually,

Jack," Fran said, "eight pounds, two ounces isn't tiny for a newborn; she's really a pretty good size, and," Fran said, grimacing, "I've got the stitches to prove it." Jack groaned. Fran laughed and so did Ethel. "Go now, Mom," Fran said; "you and Dad go see her." They didn't need any coaxing; "We'll be back shortly," Ethel said, as she and Andy hurried out the door. They had just been waiting for Jack to return, so Fran wouldn't be alone.

Fran was so pleased that Jack was excited over the baby; he seemed really happy. "Tell me the truth, Jack," she said, "Are you disappointed that she's not a boy?" "No way!" he said. "We have plenty of time to have a little Jack, Jr." "Are you happy?" she asked. "Yes, Hon, I'm very happy," he said. "Me too, Jack; I hope nothing ever changes that."

A little while later her parents returned, smiling and talking, and Andy had tears in his eyes again. "Oh, Fran, she's adorable," Ethel said. "She's beautiful." "She's just perfect!" Andy said, wiping a tear away. "Andy, you're such an old softy," Ethel said smiling.

The next day was a record-breaking day for heat. The temperature climbed to one hundred and six degrees. Of course there was no air-conditioning in hospitals, and they wouldn't allow the family to bring in an electric fan because they were afraid the patient would catch a chill. "A chill!" Fran said. "Do you believe that? It's about two hundred degrees and they're afraid I'll get a chill. Passing out, I think, would be more the problem." She and every other lady in the room lay in their beds, a mass of perspiration, fanning themselves with magazines, trying to get a breath of air.

Three times a day, a nun would come into the room and say, "All right, ladies, over on your tummies." All four girls groaned every time the nun gave that 'command.' "Twenty minutes!" she'd say. Sure enough, twenty minutes later she'd be back. "All right, ladies, you can turn over now." One of the women in the room with Fran asked the nun why they had to go through this ritual three times a day. "It is to bring your uterus back into shape," the nun answered. When Ethel and Andy came in, Fran asked her mother if she had to do that when she had her babies. "Four times a day!" Ethel said, "and remember, I was in the hospital for two weeks each time. At least you'll only be here a week." Fran had a lot of visitors, which helped the time pass quicker.

*****

Fran and her baby daughter came home from the hospital a couple of days later. At ten o'clock in the morning Andy and Jack went to get them, while Ethel and Crocifessa prepared Fran's favorite foods in Fran and Jack's apartment. Fran could smell the food cooking as soon as she got out of the car. Ethel and Crocifessa were there as she walked in the door. "Grandma's baked macaroni and veal cutlets," Fran cried. "Oh Mom, you and Grandma cooked all this food in this heat? You're both wonderful! Thank you so much." "Well, we're getting it done early before it gets too hot to cook," Ethel said. "This is for supper, because two homecomings in the same day call for an excellent dinner. Fran thought she meant her and the baby. "Joe called," Ethel said, "and he's coming home today; he said he'd be here around five o'clock. He can't wait to see you and the baby." "Oh I'm so glad," Fran said, "I've really missed him, Mom; I'm dying for him to see her." "I know, but I think you should go to bed now Fran," Ethel said. "I will, Mom, right after I give 'Terry' her bottle and change her diaper." "All right," Ethel said, with a pretend pout, "but I'm just dying to feed and change and wash that beautiful baby." Fran laughed. "Whatever was I thinking? Okay, Mom, I am tired, so you feed her and do her diaper." "Terrific!" Ethel said, "and while you nap, I'll sterilize the bottles and make a batch of formula." "Are you familiar with Enfamil, Mom?" "No, but I can read directions," her mother said, "so you just get changed and take a nice nap, and Terry and I will be fine." "Okay, Mom," Fran said, "Thanks a lot." "Believe me, Dear, it's my pleasure." Crocifessa smiled at Fran, and said, "Buono, Franzie, you sleep."

A little while later Dottie came running up the stairs, all excited. "Where's Fran?" She asked her mother. "She's taking a nap," Ethel said, "but the baby's over here in the living room with Grandma." "Ooh, can I hold her?" Dottie pleaded. Crocifessa handed the baby over to Dottie. Dottie took the baby in her arms and sat down in the rocking chair. She lifted the baby to her face, and placed the soft, tiny cheek against her own, and in that moment, a wonderful bond began to form between baby Terry and her Auntie Dottie.

Fran had been asleep for about forty-five minutes, when she heard a knock on the door and her mother talking to someone. A minute later, Ethel said, "Fran, are you asleep?" "No, Mom, just resting; who was at the door?" "Why don't you sit up, Honey; Mrs. Hallahan is here to see you." Mrs. Hallahan, Fran's downstairs neighbor, came into her room and placed a bed tray on her lap. "Oh, Mrs. Hallahan," Fran said, "What is that marvelous smell?" "It's my Irish bread, Dearie," she said in her charming Irish brogue, "and a pot of tea for you and Jack, and your mom." Fran couldn't believe it; on the tray was a round loaf of Irish bread, which Fran had never had before. It had obviously just come out of the oven. There was also a stick of butter on a lovely crystal butter dish, a china teapot filled with very hot tea, and a pretty china teacup and saucer. "Oh, this is so nice of you, Mrs. Hallahan," Fran said, "and it couldn't have come at a better time; I woke up hungry as can be." Well, you enjoy it, Dearie," she said. "And now, I want to see that darling baby." "Come with me," Ethel said.

As Ethel and Mrs. Hallahan were leaving the room, Fran was already cutting into the Irish bread; the aroma was driving her crazy. "Thank you so much, Mrs. Hallahan," Fran called. "You're very welcome, Dearie," she called back. When Ethel came back into the room, Fran was on her second piece of bread. "Mom, this is the most delicious bread I've ever tasted," she said. "Have you ever had Irish bread?" "Yes I have, and let me at that thing before your father and Jack come back and polish it off." Fran and Ethel sat there eating Irish bread slathered in butter, and moaning in ecstasy over its wonderful flavor.

*****

Terry was an exceptionally good baby; she ate well, very seldom cried, and slept through the night at two and a half weeks old. Fran was shocked out of a sound sleep when the doorbell rang one morning, and it was the telephone repairman. "What are you doing here so early?" she asked him," thinking it was about seven o'clock.

"They said you'd be here around nine." "Um, Mrs. Roche," he said, 'it's almost nine-thirty." "Nine-thirty?" she cried. "Oh no! It can't be!" A feeling of panic came over her as she ran into Terry's room. She had given Terry her last bottle at 11:30; she expected her to wake up by 4:00 or 5:00. She had been sleeping about five hours between bottles the last couple of days. When Fran looked in the crib, Terry was lying there wide-awake, just 'looking' around. Fran picked her up and she seemed to be fine. Fran couldn't get over it; she didn't know an awful lot about babies, but this seemed 'out of the ordinary,' to say the least. She called her mom and she said she would come right over.

Fran heard a voice saying, "Maam, is the baby all right?" The repairman was still standing in the doorway. "Oh my word," Fran cried, "Yes, I believe she's fine; I just can't get over the fact that at two and a half weeks old, she slept for ten hours." "Wow! That *is* something!" He said. "Please come in," she said, "the phone's over there; I need to get this baby her bottle." Ethel came in and looked at Terry gulping down her bottle. "I'm sure she's fine, Fran, but it wouldn't hurt to call Dr. Desimone and have him take a look at her." Fran called him, and he said he was going to be in Jamaica Plain later that day, and he would drop in to see her.

Fran called Jack at the office, and he said, "I'm sure it's nothing, Fran; I really don't think you needed to call Dr. D., but call me after he sees her." Dr. Desimone came about three-thirty, examined Terry and said, "She's a fine, healthy baby, Fran; you're just one of the lucky ones whose baby is very contented." "But, ten hours contented, at only two weeks old?" Fran asked. "It happens; what can I say?" the doctor said. "Stop worrying about it, and enjoy your beautiful, contented baby. You'll find that she'll be taking more formula at each feeding from now on, and that's good." Jack called as Dr. Desimone was leaving. "See, I told you she was fine," he said. "Jack, how could you be so definite? You know less about babies than I do. I'm not going to take it for granted that she's fine just because you say so, when you're not even here." "No, I'm not there," Jack said, " but I think I know a little more about babies than you do." "Oh? And why would that be?" Fran asked, feeling a flush of anger rising. "Well, there's been a lot of babies in my house over the years." She couldn't argue with that, but she didn't agree. She was seven years old when Dottie was born and Ethel had nursed her. Fran was too young to change or bathe her, so she didn't learn much about babies from Dottie. She found it hard to believe that a young boy, whose mother nursed all her babies, would have learned much from his baby brothers and sisters either. "Maybe," was all she replied. Dr. Desimone was right; Terry was a very healthy, happy and contented baby. She became the joy of the whole family.

*****

On October third, Rosemarie gave birth to a baby boy, and they named him William Robert Buckley, Jr. Little Billy was a beautiful, healthy baby, and Rosemarie and Bill were pleased as could be with him.

*****

Terry was four months and a week old at Christmas. Fran and Jack had so much fun buying little toys and things for her. She was mesmerized by the lights on the Christmas tree, and was reaching for everything. Andy and Ethel had already made it their life's quest to spoil Terry as best they could, and they were certainly putting all they had into it. But Terry was too good to be spoiled; she had the sweetest and gentlest way about her. She smiled at anything and everything, and would laugh out loud at the 'drop of a hat.'

It was a wonderful Christmas; the family did things the same way they'd done them for many years, but this Christmas so very special because of Terry. She had brought a new joy to Christmas that they hadn't felt since Dottie was a baby.

"This was the best Christmas ever," Andy said. He said that every year, and each year he meant it more than the last.

*****

Terry continued to grow and thrive, and was getting smarter every day. She said, "Da-da" at six and a half months old, and "Mama" at seven months; words just seem to flow out of her so naturally. With every day she brought new delights to her family.

Fran had left her job at O'Brion, Russell Insurance Agency three months before Terry was born, and she was enjoying motherhood more than she ever dreamed possible.

*****

The following April, when Terry was eight months old, she was sitting in the living room one day with her toys around her. Terry was a quiet, happy baby, who needed very little to keep her occupied. She would sit sometimes for hours looking at her baby books and playing with her dolls. Fran sat with her for a while and played a little game, and then went back to her housework. Ethel and Andy had gone away for a couple of days, and Jack was working. It was a beautiful day and Fran opened the back door to let in some fresh air. She started washing dishes at the kitchen sink, and listening to the radio.

Fran never saw Terry crawl from the living room into the kitchen, and she never heard her as she crawled right behind Fran towards the open back door. What Fran did hear was a thud, and then another thud. Panic hit her like a sledgehammer as she realized Terry was no longer in the living room. More thuds, and then she heard her scream, and then another thud, and another. Fran was running toward the back door, her mind racing…. *"Terry! Oh God, no!* "Terry! Terry!" she screamed as she flew out into the back hall. She prayed as she ran down the back stairs, *"Please God, please don't let her be badly hurt."* Just as Fran was getting to Terry, the downstairs back door opened and Mrs. Hallahan stood there shocked. "Oh dear God," she cried. "Oh God! Oh God! Oh God!" Fran kept saying over and over as she carefully picked up Terry who was screaming something awful. She clung to her mother as Fran tried to calm her. She brought her into Mrs. Hallahan's apartment and laid her on the kitchen table. Terry continued to cry as Fran gently felt all over her body; she slowly bent her legs, her arms, her neck and her back. She felt all over her head; Terry didn't react differently to any of it. Her crying let up and Mrs. Hallahan offered her a cookie, and she took it and smiled at her. When Fran saw her smile, Fran just seemed to come apart; she started crying and trembling all over. Mrs. Hallahan said, "Oh you poor dear; what an awful fright you've had. Let me make you a nice cup of tea." "I wish my mother was home," Fran sobbed. "Oh, I know Dearie; there's nothing like having your mother nearby when something goes wrong." She poured the tea, and as Fran sipped it, Mrs. Hallahan said, "I think she's all right, Fran; she seems to be fine now." "Yes she does," Fran said, feeling more relaxed, "but I think I'll have our doctor look at her anyway." Mrs. Hallahan said, "That would probably be best, Dearie; better to be safe than sorry."

After the tea, Fran thanked Mrs. Hallahan and went back upstairs with Terry. She closed the back door. She called Jack and then she called Dr. Desimone. He said, "Bring her over tonight; I'll be here after six o'clock."

Jack got home and went right in to see Terry. "Look at her," he laughed. "If we fell down a flight of stairs, we'd probably have broken bones, but she's crawling and playing and laughing; what a little trooper." " I think you'd better keep the back door closed from now on," he said. "You really needed to tell me that, Jack?" Fran said. She felt a sharp twinge of disappointment in him, and a little resentment too.

They waited for Joe to get home, and he took them over to the doctor's office. After examining her Dr. Desimone said, "She doesn't have any broken bones, and she's not in any pain, even when I examine her. Babies are a lot tougher than we think," he said. "Just keep a close watch on her, Fran for the next few days; if anything seems unusual, call me right away, but I honestly believe she's fine."

As they left Dr. Desimone's office, Jack said, "There, you feel better now?" "Yes Jack," Fran said, "I feel a lot better now." She kept feeling twinges of guilt, but she would never let Jack know that; she was just so very thankful that her little girl was okay. Joe carried Terry to the car. "Come on, Beautiful, let's go home," he said. Terry smiled at her Uncle Joe. She was sound asleep two minutes later on her mother's lap.

****

Fran's bridal party, 1958; (left to right) Mae, Mary Pinciaro, Fran, Mary Manning, Dottie and Rosemarie (kneeling).

CHAPTER ELEVEN
Amazing What You Can Get For A Dollar

Joe and Mae were married in a double wedding ceremony with Mae's sister Helen and Chet on September 24th, 1960. Fr. Fahey officiated at the nuptial mass at St. Francis of Assisi church in Braintree. It was a lovely wedding, and Mae and Helen looked beautiful. They had a nice reception at the Hollow Restaurant in Quincy. The two couples went on their honeymoon, first to Quebec, and then to Nova Scotia to visit with Mae and Helen's parents.

Unbeknownst to anyone, Joe had lost his job at Goodyear Tire Company one week before the wedding. He told Mae, but he didn't want anyone else to know about it yet. He was upset and didn't know what he was going to do. Mae was worried, too, but she was not one to feel overwhelmed by setbacks. She was working at Sigma Instruments at the time, and reassured Joe that they would be fine until he found another job. "You'll get a better job when we get back home, Joe," Mae said. "This is all going to turn out for the good, you'll see." She was scared, but she was a positive thinker, and wouldn't let Joe get down on himself. Joe wouldn't have let losing his job bother him so much if it wasn't for the fact that he and Mae had just bought a nice little house on Allen Street in Abington. It took all of their savings just to raise the down payment.

When Joe and Mae got back from their trip, Joe told his parents about losing his job. They were terribly upset knowing that he now had a mortgage to pay. "You could come and work for the Grahams, Joe; they'd take you on." Andy really didn't want Joe to become a painter, but it would be a steady paycheck coming in. "No thanks, Dad," Joe said, "I hate painting." "Hey, so did I when I first started," Andy said. "It takes time, but once you get used to it, it becomes like second nature to you." "I appreciate it Dad," Joe said, "but I'm going to try my hand at selling." "Selling? Selling what?" Andy asked. "Well, I applied for a job as a Fuller Brush man, and I was accepted," Joe said. "I start on Wednesday." "Door-to-door selling?" Andy said, "there's no security in that, Joe; one day you do well, and the next day you sell nothing. Are you sure that's what you want to do?" "I'm not sure of anything right now, Dad," Joe answered, "but I'm going to give it my best shot. If it doesn't work out, I'll try something else."

*****

It was mid 1960 and Andy got the call that Mr. Graham had passed away. Mr. Graham had been bed-ridden for a while, and Andy knew it was coming. He felt real bad; as difficult as Mr. Graham could be at times, he was a good old guy. Six months later, his brother Al died also. Al's wife asked Andy if he would like to buy the J. W. Graham Company. She always liked Andy, and knew what a faithful employee he had been to both brothers. She wanted to give him first chance to purchase the business. Andy discussed it with Ethel, and she told him it was his decision to make, and whatever he decided, she would support him one hundred percent. She knew Andy was an excellent painter, but owning and running a business was an entirely different thing. She wanted him to be sure that he wouldn't be taking on more than he could handle. They talked with Ernie about it, and he said, "This is a great opportunity, Andy; why would you hesitate? You know that business inside and out; you practically run it now." Andy and Ethel prayed that God would help Andy to make the right decision.

*****

In November of 1960, the senator from Massachusetts, John Fitzgerald Kennedy was elected to the Presidency of the United

States. Most people in New England were thrilled, especially those in Massachusetts, as Kennedy was born in Brookline. The Kennedy family was very well known; they were ambitious and vibrant and very active in politics. The last three Presidents had all been much older. First there was Franklin Delano Roosevelt, who was in a wheelchair; next there was Harry S. Truman, and then an old retired army general, Dwight David Eisenhower. Fran liked President Eisenhower during his time in office; she always remembered how he had waved to her when he rode by in the parade when she was a very little girl. Then came Jack. President Kennedy was a breath of fresh air to people for many reasons. He was charming; he had a way of speaking that attracted men with his humor and his sincerity, and fascinated women with his boyish good looks and broad, toothy smile. He was the first Catholic to be elected President, and he was the second youngest man elected to that office. Teddy Roosevelt held that record by less than a year.

In 1961 Jack Kennedy established the Peace Corps, and young people all over the country, with a heart for the underdog, rushed to sign up. He appointed his brother Robert to the position of Attorney General. A major 'thorn in brother Bobby's side' was organized crime, and he was determined to find Jimmy Hoffa and bring him, and others like him, to justice.

Bobby looked like a sweet, mild-mannered husband and father, but deep down inside he was a tough adversary to those who were involved in organized crime. He also worked very hard toward equal rights for black people everywhere. He had a deep respect and admiration for Martin Luther King, Jr., as did his brother, the President.

Then there were the family touch football games on the White House Lawn. The President and his brothers and sisters acting like normal people; whoever heard of such a thing? To top it all off, Jack had a beautiful young wife, a little girl, and a baby boy. Babies in the White House! Who could even imagine it? It was all so refreshing and delightful. "Camelot", was what everyone was calling it.

Women everywhere admired Jackie, the Presidents wife. Jacqueline Bouvier Kennedy made fashion history with her charm and grace and impeccable taste. She was lovely in every way, and the world fell in love with her.

Washington truly became 'Camelot', and everyone, especially New Englanders, were enchanted by it.

*****

It was February, and Mae was three months pregnant; everyone was thrilled, especially Joe. The baby was due in August, and Mae was suffering terribly with morning sickness. Joe was working as a Fuller Brush Man, and Mae was still working at Sigma Instruments. They were barely making ends meet, but they were thrilled about the baby coming; they knew that 'God would provide.' Joe did some painting with his father on a Saturday every now and then, and that helped a lot.

*****

In 1961 Andy became the owner of J. W. Graham & Sons Painting & Contracting Company. Mrs. Graham made him an offer he couldn't refuse. She sold him the entire business, 'lock, stock, and barrel' for one dollar. Andy was shocked. "Really? One dollar?" "Yes, Andy" she said. "One dollar." It was her way of thanking him for his loyalty to her husband and his brother all those years. Andy was very pleased about it, but also scared to death. He had no idea what the future would hold, but he was going to forge ahead with all the excitement, and anxiety he was feeling. *"One dollar,"* he thought. *"It's like a miracle."*

Ethel was pleased with his decision, but nervous, too. She didn't welcome major changes in their life, and she really didn't like taking chances. She would always feel a lot more trepidation than Andy would about change, unless she was certain it was for the best. *"Imagine, buying a successful, established business for a dollar,"* she thought. *"Who could even imagine such a thing?"* She decided she would look forward to, and trust God for whatever He had in store for them.

*****

Two and a half months before her due date Mae went into labor. The doctors did everything they could to keep the baby from being born so prematurely, but a determined Shaun Roger Vitello decided that June 8th, 1961 would be a good time to be born. He weighed less than four pounds, and was sixteen inches long. He was placed immediately into a new, special type of incubator. Each day he lost a little more weight; it didn't look promising for him. His weight went down to three pounds, three ounces.

After days of waiting, baby Shaun very slowly began to gain weight. After two months in the incubator Shaun was ready to come home. The day he came home from the hospital, Joe left early that morning for his two weeks with the National Guard. He hated leaving Mae to fend for herself with a tiny new baby, but there wasn't a thing he could do about it. He felt a lot better when Ethel said she would stay with Mae as long as she needed help with the baby.

After a few weeks Mae realized that baby Shaun couldn't take regular formula, so he was put on a soybean formula. "Good grief!" Joe would say every time he fed the baby, "this formula smells like dog food." But Shaun began to thrive on it, and to grow stronger every day.

When Joe and Mae celebrated their first wedding anniversary, they thanked God for their beautiful, healthy little son, and for bringing them through a very difficult and worrisome first year of marriage.

*****

Fran was pregnant again, and due in November, and again she was feeling at her very best. Rosemarie was also expecting, and again she was feeling terrible. Rosemarie always amazed Fran; when the first three months of her pregnancy were over, she would start to feel terrific. She would call Fran around nine o'clock in the morning and say, "Are you going to be home today?" If Fran were, she'd say, "Yes, are you coming over?" Rosemarie would almost always answer, "Yeah, I'll be there in less than an hour; I'll bring some donuts." "Great!" Fran would say, "I'll put on some coffee.

251

"Rosemarie would arrive with a dozen donuts under one arm and Billy, Jr. under the other.

Rosemarie was not quite 5'2" tall, and never weighed more than 105 pounds (except when she was pregnant). She was real cute with an adorable figure (except when she was pregnant). She and Fran would sit down at Fran's kitchen table to have their coffee and donuts, and smoke their cigarettes while Billy and Terry would eat their donuts in Terry's playpen. That way, they'd keep the mess confined. The amazing thing about Rosemarie was that she could sit down and eat six or seven donuts at one sitting with absolutely no ill effects (even when she was pregnant).

Ethel came over one day and had a cup of coffee and a donut with them. She couldn't believe how many donuts Rosemarie ate. Ethel was strangely impressed, and said to her, "I am absolutely flabbergasted, Rosemarie, that you are not terribly distressed." "Nope," Rosemarie said, "In fact I think I might have another." Ethel and Fran just looked at each other and started laughing, and then Rosemarie joined in. "I don't know where she puts it," Ethel said laughing. "Me neither, Mom, I'll probably gain five pounds just being in the same room with those donuts." "You're both just jealous!" Rosemarie said giggling, as she reached for another donut. "You bet we are!" Fran and her mother said in unison.

*****

One day, when Fran was seven months along, she confided a fear she had to her mother. "Mom," she said, "I'm terribly afraid I won't be able to love this baby." "Why, what makes you say that, Fran?" Ethel asked. "Because I can't even imagine loving another baby as much as I love Terry," she said. " I'm really worried about it, Mom." "Honey," Ethel said, "Lots of women feel what you're feeling right now." "They do?" Fran said. "Yes; it's because this baby isn't here yet," Ethel said. "When you see your baby and hold it in your arms, you will feel exactly the same way you felt about Terry." "Oh, Mom, I hope you're right; you seem so sure of that," Fran said. "I am sure," her mom said. "I'm one hundred percent positive; you'll see, Hon."

On November 27th, 1961 Fran gave birth to a beautiful, healthy baby boy. He weighed seven pounds, ten ounces, was 20 ¾ inches long, and had lovely blond hair. "Look at that baby," her father said. "Fair skin, blond hair, and blue eyes; he's an Irishman if ever I saw one." Ethel laughed and said, "Well, there *is* only one quarter Italian blood in him, Andy; what did you expect?" He just chuckled. Fran and Jack were thrilled; Jack had his son, and Fran had a baby she fell in love with the moment he was placed in her arms.

When Fran came home from the hospital with her baby boy, Mrs. Hallahan came upstairs carrying a bed tray with Irish bread, butter, a pot of steaming tea, and a china cup and saucer. The aroma quickly filled the apartment. "Oh, Mrs. Hallahan, you're a doll," Fran said. "You make my homecoming so much more special; thank you so much." "You're welcome, Dearie," she said. "You just enjoy it." "Oh, that I will," Fran said, already slicing into it.

Three weeks later, Jack took the baby to Blessed Sacrament Church to be baptized. Ethel and Andy went also, as they were to be the godparents. Fran stayed at home again, very reluctantly. The baby was christened John Charles Roche, Jr.

Jack had gotten his insurance broker's license, and was selling insurance on his own, and doing very well at it. Jack was the type who did well at everything he endeavored. He had ambition, but more than that, he had drive; and he had the personality and the courage to take chances that a lot of people would never take. Somehow he just knew that things would work out the way he wanted them to. He was cocky, there's no doubt about it, but he wasn't foolhardy; he just had all kinds of confidence. For instance, one day Jack walked into an insurance broker's office and said to the owner, "Mr. Burke, I think you should hire me to work here with you." The man looked at Jack and smiled and said, "Now why do you suppose I should do that?" Jack, very seriously, said to him, "Because I'll make you a millionaire in just a few years." Mr. Burke laughed and said, "Look young fella, I've got a small business here; I do all right at it, and I'm not looking to set the world on fire. I'm fine just the way I am." "You know, Mr. Burke, you're making a big mistake not hiring me," Jack said with a sly grin on his face. "You'll wish you had one day." Mr. Burke just smiled and said, "Well, then it'll be my loss, I guess;

I can live with that. Good luck to you, son." He shook Jack's hand and Jack said goodbye, and left.

*****

Ethel and Andy were becoming very worried about Fran. They noticed that she seemed very distant and sad at times; they couldn't put their finger on it, but something was wrong and they knew it. She was happy with Terry and Jackie, but she and Jack were not getting along, and were arguing a lot. When Ethel asked Fran if everything was alright, she simply said, "It's just that he's working so much, Mom; he's hardly ever home anymore." Ethel sensed something else was very wrong; Fran wasn't just acting like a disgruntled housewife, it was more than that; she was different. She could be exuberantly happy one moment, and then fly off the handle the next; and in and around those moments, there were times of quiet sadness. Ethel and Andy were very, very concerned about her.

*****

From time to time, Andy would buy a three family house that needed work. He'd fix it up, then sell it and make a nice little profit. Jack was doing the same, only more so. He was buying property every chance he got, fixing it up, and selling it for a big profit. Andy once said, "It seems like everything he touches turns to gold; the guy's got the 'Midas touch,' I swear."

One day Jack said to Joe, "What are you doing selling brushes Joe? I mean, I can't afford to hire J. W. Graham painters to spruce up the houses that I buy, but you know how to paint. I can keep you busy for quite a while, and pay you good money. You should think about it Joe and get back to me before I hire some cheap painter to do the work. I'd rather give you the money and know the work will be done right." Joe thought about it and talked about it with Mae, and decided to take Jack up on his offer. He wasn't making enough money selling brushes anyway.

*****

'Jackie' was a real good baby; of course he didn't sleep through the night at two weeks old, but he did at six weeks old. Fran became a little concerned about him though; he didn't take his bottle the way Terry did. She knew she shouldn't compare everything about him to her, but Terry was all she had to go by.

When Dr. Desimone came to the house one day to treat an ear infection Terry had, Fran explained to him the problem Jackie was having taking his bottle. Dr. Desimone examined Jackie's mouth and said, "He's tongue-tied." "Tongue-tied?" Fran said, "What exactly does that mean Doctor, and can anything be done about it?" "Oh, sure; it's a very simple procedure," the doctor said. "I have to snip the cord a little under his tongue; it's actually quite common." "Oh, Gosh," Fran said. "Will it be very painful?" "No, he'll feel a little sting, but that's about all," he said. "I can take care of it right now." "What? Oh no; I'm not too crazy about this; Dr. D., shouldn't this be done in a hospital?" "Nah!" he said. "This is nothing; you can help, Fran." "Oh, oh!" she said nervously. "What do I have to do?" "You just hold him perfectly still, that's all," the doctor said. "It'll only take a minute."

Dr. Desimone snipped the cord under Jackie's tongue, held the gauze there for a few moments, and it was over. Jackie cried when it was first done, but he calmed down very quickly. The doctor was right; almost immediately Jackie began taking his bottle normally. Fran was very much relieved. After that, Jackie thrived and began growing like a weed.

*****

Fran and Jack seemed to be arguing more and more; they had nice times in between, but Fran was becoming more and more depressed. It took very little for her to fly off the handle and start yelling at Jack. He was working late every night and Saturdays, and he was working quite a few Sundays too. She was angry with him, and very hurt that he wanted to be working so much, rather than spending more time at home with her and the kids. It wasn't that Jack didn't love Fran, because she knew he did, and he loved Terry and Jackie too. But he was determined to make his million while he was still young, and that takes working all hours. Sarcasm, snide remarks and disrespect for each other seemed to be the normal way in their home of late. Fran had bad headaches a lot, and Ethel noticed she cried easily.

"All I want...all I've ever wanted was to have a marriage like you and Dad have," Fran sobbed to her mother one day. "I always thought that if two people love each other, then they automatically have a good marriage. I just assumed that bad marriages, and marriages that end in divorce, happen to people who don't really love each other. I've never, in all my life, seen you and Dad fight. I mean, I've seen Dad upset about bills, or angry with us kids, or work, or something, but I've never seen him angry and hateful to you. And you, Mom... I've never heard you yell at Dad, or be nasty to him. Why, Mom? Why are Jack and I so different from you and Dad? I just don't understand; I'll never understand." Fran buried her face in her hands. Ethel's heart was breaking for her daughter. "Fran," she said, "whenever Dad and I didn't agree on something, we never wanted you kids to know about it. I realize now that we didn't do you any favors by not letting you see our disagreements once in a while. It's true, we don't fight; we learned early on how to deal with those times when we don't see eye to eye. You've got to understand, though, that every marriage is different, every couple is different; no two couples deal with things in the same way." "Fran, marriage takes a lot of work, and..." "Oh Mom, I know all that," Fran said, "It just simply doesn't work for me and Jack." "Oh Honey," Ethel said, "I don't know what I can say to make you feel better." "I don't think there's anything anyone can say, Mom," Fran said. " I'm a mess; I feel all twisted up inside, like the world is coming to an end, and I'm the only one who knows about it. I drink too much coffee, I smoke too much, and I can't sleep. I lie in bed staring at the ceiling most of the night. I'm exhausted, but I feel like my mind doesn't know enough to shut down for the night. I have bad headaches, and sometimes I feel sick all day long, when there's nothing wrong with me. Some days I feel happy, and even though nothing has really changed in between, other days I'm so sad I could just die. I don't know what's wrong with me, Mom." Ethel held her daughter for a long time, and Fran clung to her mother and cried.

*****

Jack had met a real estate broker named Rita Caulfield. She was very impressed with Jack and thought he would fit in nicely in her business. She owned the Caulfield Real Estate on Centre Street in Jamaica Plain. Jack got his real estate license, left Maryland Casualty altogether, and started working with Rita Caulfield. After awhile it became the Caulfield Realty and Roche Insurance Agency. Jack was selling insurance and selling homes also. He was working very long hours and Fran was becoming more and more depressed.

*****

On November 5th, 1962 Mae gave birth to a baby boy two months premature. He weighed four pounds, one ounce when he was born, and was placed immediately in an incubator. He was baptized right away in the hospital, and once again Mae and Joe kept up a vigil every day and evening. One month later they took their baby home; Joe and Mae were very relieved, and very happy. A short while later he was christened Paul Joseph Vitello at St. Bridget's Church in Abington.

*****

Fran had started seeing Dr. Sullivan, a psychiatrist, at the suggestion of Dr. Desimone. He prescribed tranquilizers for her, which helped her to feel calmer, and get her through each day. Because she couldn't sleep at night he prescribed sleeping pills also. Eventually, she started taking more tranquilizers than the doctor had prescribed.

"How come you're taking so many tranquilizers?" Jack asked her one day. "It looks to me like you're taking more than you're supposed to." "How would you know how many tranquilizers I take, when you're never around?" was Fran's response. "I'm around enough to know you're taking too many," he said. "Well, they make me feel good, which is more than you do," she said, as she walked away from him.

Jack spoke to Andy and Ethel about Fran and the tranquilizers. "I thought she might be taking too many," Ethel said. "She seems groggy much of the time." "She seems to be taking care of the kids all right," Andy said. "Ethel goes over every day to make sure she's okay, and she and the kids have supper here most nights."

"Jack," Ethel said, "you're going to have to start staying at home more. We don't want to tell you what you should be doing, but we're not blind to what's going on. She's not well right now, Jack. You can't leave it up to us to watch over her and the kids every day." "Yeah, I know; I've got a few big deals going on right now," Jack said. "Once I get them squared away, I'll have more time to spend at home." "Don't take too long, Jack, please," Ethel said. "We're terribly worried about her."

*****

Fran was feeling absolutely miserable. She had spent the morning in and out of her bedroom and the bathroom so Terry and Jackie wouldn't see her crying and wringing her hands. She felt agitated and frightened. She had awakened at almost 8:00 in the morning; she didn't want to get out of bed, but she could hear Terry playing in the living room, and Jackie was fussing in his crib. There were times when she resented them so. *"Why don't they just let me sleep?"* She thought. She forced herself to get up, and gave them both some cereal. She changed Jackie and put him in his playpen with his toys, and then she turned the TV on to a kid's program that Terry liked. She had a cup of coffee and smoked a cigarette. The feeling that she was going to jump out of her skin seemed to get worse and worse as the day went on. She tried praying, but she didn't believe that God listened to her anymore. "Oh God, what's wrong with me?" she cried, not really talking to Him. She took two more tranquilizers…. "Do something, for God's sake!" she cried. "Do something!"

The familiar sadness and dark, oppressive feeling was all about her, and she knew she couldn't shake it. At one o'clock she gave Terry and Jackie their lunch, and then put them to bed for a nap. She took two more tranquilizers because the ones she had taken two hours earlier hadn't done a thing. She waited another half hour and took a couple more; nothing was helping.

Fran didn't know what time it was, but it seemed like hours had passed. *"That's the good kids,"* she thought, *"you sleep a little longer 'til Mommy feels better. I'll make you both some hot chocolate when you wake up."* She was starting to feel a little easier, a little calmer, *"But,"* she thought, *"it won't last long; I know it won't."* She decided to take a couple more tranquilizers to make sure that what she was feeling was real, and that it would last for a while. She had lost count of the amount of tranquilizers she had taken, *"but,"* she reasoned, *"they don't do much anyway."*

Fran began to feel different, kind of warm and tingly, like she had had a little too much to drink. "Oh, this is great," she thought. "I knew I needed those extra tranquilizers; everything's okay now. I think I'll take a little nap while the kids are asleep." When she stood up she realized she was very shaky, and could hardly walk; she had to hold onto furniture as she made her way into the bedroom. *"Oh, wow!"* she thought, *"Maybe I took one too many pills."* She lay down on the bed, and after a few minutes she felt tingly all over. A few minutes later she couldn't seem to focus on anything, and she couldn't lift her arms or her head. She tried to stand up, and realized she couldn't. She couldn't think straight. One part of her was loving this strange euphoria; she wanted to just let go and let it take her wherever…. All of a sudden it was as though something was tugging at her senses. She somehow knew that this wasn't right; it wasn't the way she wanted to feel. She tried again to get up, but she could hardly move. She looked down at her feet and was shocked to see her toenails were purple. "What's happening? Oh, God, help me, please help me; something's wrong."

Somehow, Fran managed to drag herself off the bed and crawl to the phone in the reception hall. She pulled the whole telephone off the table, and struggled to dial Jack's office. It was all she could do to keep her mind focused on what she was trying to do. He yelled through the phone, "What did you do? What did you do?" She could hardly speak; all she could mumble was, "Jack, help me." The next thing she knew her mother was standing over her; she looked like she had been crying, *"but she hardly ever cries,"* Fran thought. She could hear Jack coming up the front stairs and yelling. Before she realized what was happening she was being carried on a stretcher down the stairs. She could hear Jack talking to her, but she didn't know what he was saying. She was put in an ambulance and taken to St. Elizabeth Hospital. A doctor put some tubes down her nose and started pumping out her stomach. A nurse was telling her to stay awake, but she just couldn't. She felt herself drifting...and drifting.

Fran woke up to a nurse taking her blood pressure. "Well, hello," the nurse said. "Where am I?" Fran asked. She felt terribly weak, and her voice was shaky. "You're at St. Elizabeth Hospital, Mrs. Roche," the nurse responded. "You were brought in yesterday afternoon." "Am I all right?" Fran asked. "You had a bad experience, Hon," the nurse said, "but yes, you're okay now. Your doctor is here, and he'll be coming in to see you shortly."

Dr. Sullivan came in the room and sat down in a chair by Fran's bed. "How are you feeling?" He asked. "Horrible," Fran responded through half-opened eyes. "My head is killing me, and my throat is sore, and I feel kind of like I've been beaten up." Dr. Sullivan said, "You're a very lucky girl, Fran. Do you remember everything from yesterday?" "I think so," she answered. "Look, Doctor, I just want you to know, I didn't try to...you know; I just wanted to go into a kind of temporary stupor until the kids woke up. I just couldn't stand the way I was feeling for another minute. It was stupid, I know; next time I'll try booze; the only problem is I don't like the taste of liquor." "There's not going to be a next time," Dr. Sullivan said, "not if I can help it. I'd like you to go to a special hospital for a little while, Fran." "What kind of hospital?" Fran asked. "It's called Bournewood; it's an excellent psychiatric hospital in Brookline. You wouldn't be there long, but I can treat you and take care of you a lot better there than once a week in my office. I think this would be the best thing, Fran, at least for now." "Well, maybe you're right; maybe I do need to be in a nut-house," Fran said. "Bournewood is not a nut-house Fran; most of the people who go there simply can't cope. To use a cliché, they can't seem to 'play the hand that's been dealt them'. I really think that's where you're at right now. I'd like you to go there right from here, and not go home first. Will you do what I suggest?" "I don't really care anymore, Doctor," she said. "

I'll do whatever you want me to do." "All right, good; I'll make the arrangements."

After a moment Fran asked, "How long will I have to stay at that hospital?" Dr. Sullivan raised an eyebrow. "Fran, just the fact that you want to know how long you'll be there," he said, "shows me that you do care. What about Terry and Jackie? You care about them, I know you do." "Of course I care about them," she said, "they're the only reason I called Jack for help." "And your parents?" the doctor said. "I know how much you love them Fran, and how much they love you." "Yes, we love each other," she said, "but all I seem to do lately is hurt them." "And what about Jack? Can we talk about him for a minute?" "No!" Fran said emphatically, "I don't want to talk about him." "All right, we don't have to talk about anything else right now," he said. "You rest; I'll come in to see you before I leave."

"I want to see Terry and Jackie before I go anywhere," Fran said. "Terry must have been scared to death; I just want her to see that I'm okay." "All right," he said. "I'll have your mother bring them in to see you tomorrow, when you're feeling a little better, and she can bring your clothes and whatever else you'll need at the same time." "Tell me something, Doctor," Fran said, "has Jack even asked about me?" "Yes, he called me this morning," Dr. Sullivan said. "I thought you didn't want to talk about him." "I don't...just curious."

It was decided that Terry and Jackie would be staying with Ethel and Andy while Fran was away, and Jack would be there in the evenings. Saying goodbye to her children was difficult; trying to assure a three and a half year old that she'd be back soon wasn't easy for Fran. Jackie was just a little over a year old, so he was just happy to see Mama. Fran held him and kissed him and played with him. She talked with Terry and told her how much she loved her. "Mommy is sick, so I have to get better, right?" She asked Terry. "I want you to get better, Mommy, but I don't want you to go away," said Terry, with tears in her eyes. "I know, Honey," Fran said, "but I have to; I'll be back real soon though, you'll see."

Ethel was close to tears when they all said goodbye. She very rarely cried, at least not in front of anyone; Andy was the sensitive, emotional one. He always called his wife 'Stonewall Jackson', whenever anything sad or touching was going on, even a 'tearjerker' movie. She was always the stoic one, while he would be blubbering into his handkerchief every time. He hated that part of himself, but no matter how he tried, he couldn't seem to change.

The next day Andy came and picked Fran up and drove her to Bournewood Hospital. He cried his heart out all the way home. Jack didn't go with him because Dr. Sullivan had made it very clear that she needed to be away from him for a while, and if Jack wanted his wife to get better, he should listen to and trust the doctor. "Why doesn't she want to see me?" he had asked. "I don't know, Jack," the doctor said, "but it needs to be this way for a little while. When she asks to see you, I'll let you know."

Bournewood Hospital didn't seem too bad. Fran was in a room with another young woman about her own age, named Mary, and a young girl of sixteen, named Rachel. Fran liked Mary; she and Mary got on nicely right from the start. Mary's husband had left her for someone else, after only a year of marriage, and she had tried to commit suicide. She had been at Bournewood for four weeks.

Rachel was quiet; she didn't say much, but when she did, sparks usually flew. She was admitted to Bournewood a week before Mary, and had the attitude that Mary, and now Fran, were imposing upon her privacy. In her mind it was her room and that was all there was to it. Fran tried to befriend her, but she wanted no part of anyone. When Fran and Mary tried to talk with her, she would always be very rude to them. They simply did their best to keep out of her way.

After her first week at Bournewood, Dr. Sullivan told Fran that he believed electric shock treatments would help her a great deal. "Electric shock treatments?" Fran said. "Aren't they dangerous?" "No, they're not dangerous," he said. "They help to remove some bad memories. Fran wondered how the shock treatments could differentiate between the bad and the good memories. She told Dr. Sullivan she'd do it if he truly thought it right for her. He said he did.

The morning of her first scheduled shock treatment Fran was very nervous; she wasn't sure about this at all. She wanted to tell Dr. Sullivan that she didn't want to go through with the treatment, but he believed it was the right course of action for her, so she decided to trust his judgment. After all, he must know best; he's the doctor.

"You cannot have anything to eat before a shock treatment," the nurse said, "and no water at all either, not even one drop." She was given a shot in her arm that seemed to dry her up. "I feel like I have cotton in my mouth," she said to Mary. "Yup, that's exactly how it makes you feel," Mary said. "Tell me the truth, Mary," Fran said, "Does the shock treatment hurt?" "No, you won't feel anything," she said, "you'll be asleep, but you'll wake up with a beaut of a headache."

"What's that?" Fran asked, as a nurse put an I.V. in her arm. "It's Sodium Pentathol, Fran; I want you to count back from one hundred. Fran began counting… one hundred…ninety-nine…ninety-eight…nine…ty…sev."

Fran awoke in her bed some time after the treatment. "*Mary was right; I've never felt a headache like this,*" Fran thought. "*Oh gosh, I can't even open my eyes, it hurts so bad. This is for the birds; I'm not going to put myself through this twice a week.*" "Mrs. Roche? Are you awake?" She could hear someone calling her, but she didn't really want to come to full awareness yet. "Mmm," was about all she could manage. "I have a cup of coffee and some toast for you," the voice said. She opened her eyes and it was an aide from the kitchen. "I'm not supposed to let you have this unless you're fully awake and sitting up," she said. "I'm awake," Fran groaned, as she tried to sit up. When the aide was sure she was awake, she left the coffee and toast on the table and left. Fran sipped the hot coffee; it felt good going down. She didn't feel like eating anything, but she figured if she ate the toast and drank the coffee it might help ease the headache a bit. A little while later a nurse came in and gave her two aspirin. "This will help, Fran; I wanted to make sure you had something in your stomach before you took the aspirin." "Oh, thanks so much," Fran said. "You'll feel better in a little while," the nurse said, "you'll see."

Two weeks later Fran had had four shock treatments. She had been at Bournewood for three weeks and she was missing Terry and Jackie something awful. She missed Jack, too, and told Dr. Sullivan that she wanted to see him. Two days later Dr. Sullivan made arrangements for Jack to come to see Fran. When he came, they talked about Terry and Jackie mostly, and he made her laugh a few times. She had forgotten how nice it was to just sit and talk and laugh with Jack. She had forgotten how funny he could be; he had seemed so serious and business-like for the past year or so. He deliberately didn't mention real estate or insurance, or his office or anything related to it. Dr. Sullivan had told him it would be best not to talk about his work. She felt a little nervous while he was there, but all in all, it was a nice visit. He hugged her and kissed her goodbye when he was leaving, and for a brief moment she clung to him, and then quickly let him go.

"I want to go home," Fran told Dr. Sullivan a couple of days after Jack's visit. "I want to see my children, and I know they need to see me. Please, Doctor, let me go home this weekend. "All right," he said. "I'll make arrangements for you to go for the weekend, Fran, but you need to come back here Sunday evening. Do we have a deal?" "Yes, I'll come back," she said. "I know I'm not ready to go home for good; every time I think of it, I break out in a sweat, and feel sick to my stomach. I must be a horrible person, not wanting to be home with my children." "You're not a horrible person, Fran," Dr. Sullivan said, "and don't be thinking like that; you're a good person who knows she needs some help at this point in her life. You need to concentrate on getting well; that's what's important right now."

Jack picked Fran up at five thirty Friday afternoon. Ethel had a roast beef dinner with all the fixings ready when they got home. When Fran walked into her parents' home, everyone ran up to her and hugged her. Terry ran up to her mother and started crying, "Mommy, Mommy." Fran sat down on the floor and held Terry a very long time. They were both crying, and so was everyone who was watching them. Andy could not control his emotions; he kept wiping his eyes with his handkerchief, and blowing his nose. Dottie was sobbing, and Ethel's eyes were moist with tears.

Crocifessa and Peter came downstairs to greet Fran. Crocifessa hugged and kissed her granddaughter; "Franzie, Franzie," she cried, "Mia bambina." She was crying and drying her tears with her apron. Peter hugged Fran; he wasn't good in situations like this. In his broken English he just kept saying, "You be ahright, Franzie; you be ahright." No one noticed him slip out the door a moment later and walk down Parkton Road. It was how he handled things; it was his way.

Sunday evening came too quickly. Fran had enjoyed Terry and Jackie so much; they climbed into bed with her both mornings; (Jackie needed a little help from his father). They all played and snuggled together. Jack had been especially attentive to Fran the whole weekend, and she hated to see it end. *"Oh Jack,* she thought, *"why can't it always be like this? This is how it was when we first got married."* She knew she had to go back to Bournewood, not just because Dr. Sullivan said so, but because she knew every day would not be like this weekend, and she wasn't ready to face it when it changed.

****

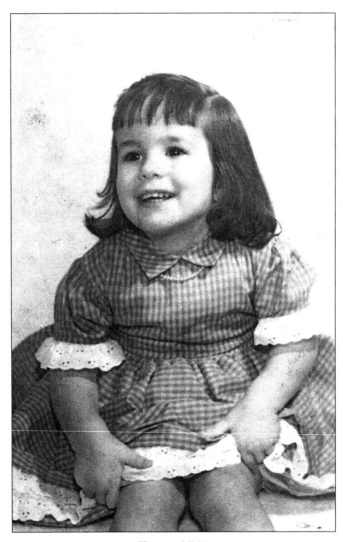

Terry 1961

CHAPTER TWELVE
Which Came First, The Chicken Or The Egg?

One evening as Fran and Mary lay in their beds in their room at Bournewood, they began talking softly. They talked about their parents and their childhoods. Mary's parents seemed real nice and not so very different from Fran's.

Rachel spoke up, rudely as usual, "Will you two shut up? I want to get some sleep." Fran said, "It's only eight fifteen, Rachel; you never go to sleep this early." "Well, tonight I feel like sleeping early," "Oh Rachel," Mary said, "We're talking very softly; I really don't think we're bothering you." "Well, you are!" she said. "Well," Fran said, "we'll talk softer." "No!" said Rachel; "You won't talk at all!" "That's not very fair, Rachel," Mary said. "Too bad!" she responded. Fran said, "Oh, forget it, Mary, she's just being a brat as usual." Like a flash, Rachel was out of her bed and across the room before Fran realized what was happening. She started punching Fran and pulling her hair. Rachel was a big girl and she had Fran pinned down on her back on the bed. Fran tried to push her off so she could get out of bed, but it was impossible. Mary tried as hard as she could to pull Rachel off of Fran but she couldn't do it, so she ran out in the hall and screamed for help. Two nurses came running into the room and grabbed Rachel and somehow managed to get her away from Fran. Another nurse, Miss Elliott, came in with a very large orderly, and they managed to subdue Rachel, and get her out of the room.

"Are you hurt, Fran?" Nurse Elliott asked. "I...I don't think so," Fran said. "My head hurts a little." "Oh dear," the nurse said, "you're bleeding; Rachel must have scratched your forehead; I'll be right back, Fran." She hurried out of the room and came back a couple of minutes later with bandages and Mercurochrome. Here, let me clean that and bandage it for you; it's a nasty scratch. Rachel has a very short fuse as you know, but I never thought she'd go this far."

Fran was shaking uncontrollably and all of a sudden she started sobbing hysterically. "Oh you poor thing," Nurse Elliott said. "I'm so sorry this happened, Fran. She put her arms around Fran and held her for a moment, and then she said, "Mary, take over for a minute, I'll be right back." She left the room, and Mary sat down and held Fran's hand. "That little wildcat has been nothing but a problem ever since I've been here," she said. "She should be in a padded cell, that one." Fran was still shaking, and couldn't seem to stop sobbing. Mary was rubbing Fran's hand and her arm, not knowing what else to do.

After a couple of minutes the nurse came back. "Here Dear, take this; it's just a mild sedative, but it will help you to relax. I called your doctor, and left a message for him to call me." "Thank you, Miss Elliott," Fran said, "You're very kind." "It's the least I can do, Hon." "What's going to happen to Rachel?" Fran asked. "She's being taken to another building," Nurse Elliott said. "She can't stay here any longer." "Thank God!" Mary called from across the room. "Good riddance!" "God, I need a cigarette!" Fran cried, as she reached for the pack. "Got an extra one?" Mary asked. "I ran out." Fran flipped her a cigarette, and then her lighter.

After a few more shock treatments Fran noticed that she didn't remember a lot of things right away. She and Mary would talk, and Mary would remind her of something Fran already knew but had obviously forgotten. Most things Fran would remember after a short while, but sometimes when Jack or her parents were there, they would mention something she just had no memory of. Fran wasn't sure if that was good or bad. *"I really don't have any horrible memories I need to forget. I just want to feel normal; I want to feel like I used to,"* she thought. *"God, I hope I'm not forgetting things I might want to remember."*

*****

One evening when Jack came in to visit Fran, he said, "I've got a surprise for you." "A surprise? What is it?" Fran asked. "I bought a house for us on Pond Street," he said. "What? You bought a house for us; why did you do that, Jack?" "What's wrong?" He asked. "I thought you'd be happy to have your own home." "Well, I don't even know what it looks like," Fran said. "Believe me, Fran," Jack said, "you're going to love this house. When you come home next weekend, I'll take you over to see it; how would you like that?" "Uh, okay," she said, still shocked. "I guess so." "Really Fran, you're going to love this house," Jack said again. The following weekend he took her to see the house on Pond Street; she agreed it was great, but wished she had had something to say about the decision to buy it.

*****

Fran broke down crying one day when her mother was visiting her. "Oh Mom, all I want is to feel like I did when I was a kid. I was happy; you and Dad, and Joe and me, and Dottie, and Grandma and Papa. Everything felt right; I felt right, the way a person *should* feel. I felt safe and protected." "Fran, you said it yourself," Ethel said... "'When you were a kid'." "Honey, you're not a kid anymore; things change, and we need to change with them." "Mom," Fran said, "I don't want to change; I want to feel like I did back then; I want to feel like I did in Westford. I just want to feel right again." "I know, Dear," Ethel said, as she stroked Fran's hand, "I know." "I'm beginning to feel very uncomfortable about these shock treatments, Mom," Fran said. "I don't like not remembering certain things, things that I must have enjoyed. I mean, sometimes when you or Jack mention something, I may not remember it right away, but I'll remember it about twenty minutes or a half hour later if I concentrate real hard, but some things never come back to me at all. Dr. Sullivan said that they would take away bad memories, but Mom, I don't have any really bad memories. I loved my childhood, my family, Westford, Christmases, etc., etc. How do I know that the treatments aren't causing me to forget some of those times?" "I don't know, Fran," Ethel said. "I never wanted you to have them; I just don't like the whole idea of them."

Fran had her tenth electric shock treatment, and Dr. Sullivan had her scheduled for another series of ten. This particular morning, Fran woke up after the treatment to the aide bringing her coffee and toast. "Oh, thank you," she groaned. Her head was pounding and she was still groggy. She sat up and sipped the hot coffee; it tasted and felt so good. Mary came over and sat on the edge of Fran's bed. "How are you feeling, or need I ask?" Fran said, "You needn't ask." "Uh huh, that's what I thought," Mary said. Mary's shock treatments were always on the days between Fran's treatments. She and Mary were both glad for that; this way they were able to help each other.

As they sat there sipping coffee, Fran happened to look over at the bureau. "Oh, aren't they cute," she said, as she looked at the picture of a little girl and a baby boy. "Are they yours?" "What?" Mary said. "Fran, that's Terry and Jackie!" "Who?" Fran asked. Somehow, somewhere inside her the names sounded vaguely familiar. "Fran, for God's sake," Mary said, "look at the picture!" She got up and brought the picture to Fran and said, "Look at them, Fran; study the picture." Fran felt panic rising. "Why are you acting like this Mary?" she asked. "Fran, these are *your* children," Mary said. Fran knew Mary wouldn't joke about such a thing. She became hysterical; "No! They can't be!" She screamed. "I don't know them; don't say that to me! Oh, God, they can't be my children! I don't know them!"

Mary called the nurse and told her what had just transpired. Fran was sobbing uncontrollably. "Oh God, what's happening to me?" She cried. "How can they be my children when I don't know them?" The nurse came in and sat and talked with her. "Listen to me Fran," she said. "You *do* know these children; you need to concentrate. It took about twenty minutes before the picture began to look familiar, and about forty-five minutes before Fran recognized fully the two beautiful children in it. "I want to talk to Dr. Sullivan right away," Fran said, trembling. The nurse agreed to get in touch with him.

"I will never, *ever*, have another shock treatment," Fran told Dr. Sullivan. "Never!" "I have you scheduled for one on Wednesday, Fran," he said. "I think you should…." "Well, cancel it!" Fran said.

270

"I won't be here for it anyway. I'm going home Doctor; I can't stay here any longer. I need to be with my family." "Fran, I'm not sure you're ready to go home," he said. "I didn't know my children," Fran said. "What?" he asked, confused. "Do you understand what I'm saying, Doctor? I looked at a picture of Terry and Jackie, and I had never seen them before." "Fran, that's just the…." "Dr. Sullivan," Fran interrupted, "If I have to live with emotional problems for the rest of my life, I will, but at least I'll know my children. I've been here for over six weeks; it may take time, but I honestly believe I'll never be any more ready to go home than I am now. Please believe me, Doctor, it's time for me to go home, and with or without your permission, I'm going." "All right, Fran," Dr. Sullivan said. "I'll make arrangements for you to leave tomorrow, but I want to see you in my office every week, okay?" "Okay," she said. A feeling of blessed relief swept over her.

Everyone was happy Fran was coming home. It had been hard on everyone, mostly Ethel. She had two children thrust on her the whole time Fran was gone. She loved Terry and Jackie very much, but taking care of two little ones and worrying about her daughter at the same time took its toll on her. In the six and a half weeks that Fran was in the hospital, Ethel had lost fourteen pounds, and she looked exhausted.

Terry was very excited that her mother was coming home for good. Dottie was glad Fran was coming home, too, and probably glad to have her room back to herself. It had been hard on her, too. She loved her big sister, and although they argued from time to time, Dottie always looked up to Fran, and wanted to be like her. The next day Fran said goodbye to the nurses, and they hugged her and wished her all the best. "Don't come back!" They quipped. "I won't," she said smiling. *"Please God,"* she thought, *" don't ever let me have to come back here."* She wondered if God heard her.

Mary walked her to the front lobby and waited with her until Jack came. "I'm going to miss you, Fran," she said. "How the heck am I going to stay here now without you?" "Mary," Fran said, "You seem so much better now than when I first came here. Your parents want you to come home with them; don't you think you could now?" "I've been thinking a lot about it lately, " Mary said. "I think maybe

I *should* give it a try." "Oh Mary, I'm so glad to hear you say that," Fran said.

Just then Jack walked in; he hugged Fran and said, "Are you ready to go?" "Yes Jack, I'm ready." She turned to Mary and they hugged each other, and wished the best for each other. They were close to tears as they said their goodbyes. They exchanged addresses and telephone numbers and promised to keep in touch, but they both kind of knew that they probably wouldn't, although they truly meant it when they said it.

Bournewood was a good hospital; Fran knew that, but it would always hold some awful memories for her. As she and Jack walked out the main door of the hospital, she determined in her mind and heart never to let this happen to her again. She said a silent prayer for protection to a God she wasn't even sure was there. They drove away, and she never looked back.

*****

The house on Pond Street was in the Moss Hill Section of Jamaica Plain, a lovely, kind of exclusive, area. That didn't mean much to Fran, but to Jack it meant prestige and success. Appearances were very important to him. "Let's go over to the house on our way home," Jack said. "I want you to see it." As they drove up to the house, Fran was impressed with the way it looked; she liked the house a lot, but she wasn't prepared for what she found when the front door was opened. All their furniture was already in the house. "Surprise!" Jack said, as he picked her up and carried her over the threshold. "I don't understand," she said. "You mean we're all moved in here?" She was a little shocked and confused; she didn't know this house, only the things that were in it. "Yep, I had it all done this past weekend," Jack said. "Rosemarie and Bill helped, and Mary Lou and Jack, too." Mary Lou and Jack Roth were Fran and Jack's new friends. They had a little girl Karen, a year older than Terry. "You might want to change things around to the way you like them," Jack said. "You mean we're not staying at our apartment, Jack?" Fran asked. "No more," he said. "This is our home now." She wasn't sure how she felt about that. She started to say something to Jack when a wonderful aroma wafted into the living room, immediately followed by Ethel and Andy, Crocifessa and Peter, and Dottie, who had all been in the kitchen. "Welcome home!" they all yelled. Terry ran up to her mother and hugged her legs. Fran picked her up and hugged and kissed her. Dottie was carrying Jackie and she placed him in Fran's arms. Fran forgot her confusion about the house and just hugged and kissed Terry and Jackie, and roughly nuzzled her face in Jackie's neck, while he laughed almost hysterically. Between bouts of laughter, he kept saying, "Mama," and just kept hugging her.

"Dinner's ready!" Ethel called. They all sat down in the dining room and Crocifessa brought in her 'famous' baked macaroni. "Oh, Grandma, thank you so much." There were other smells familiar to Fran, too; they were roast beef and gravy that Ethel had made, mashed potatoes and broccoli. "This is like Christmas dinner," Jack said. "This is great, isn't it Fran?" "Yes," Fran said. "It's....great."

They were all stuffed after dinner, and decided to wait a while before having coffee and cannoles for dessert. "Oh Gosh, Grandma," Jack said, "Where's the Brioschi?" He knew that Crocifessa got a kick out of him asking for the Brioschi, so he would never let a meal like this one go by without saying it. "Mom and Grandma," Fran said, "this was wonderful; thank you both so much." "Well," Andy said, "Your mother and Grandma figured this house needed to be christened with the Vitello culinary talents." It was a warm welcome home to Fran, even though 'home' wasn't home anymore.

Fran soon got caught up with fixing up the new house, and began enjoying it more and more. She missed living right across the street from her parents, but things change, and, as her mother once said to her, "we need to change with them." She hoped that she could.

Fran was trying hard; she was determined to make everything right again. Jack was trying, too, but his drive to reach the goals he had set for himself was causing arguments between them. She wanted a simpler life, with a husband who was home on Sundays, and at least as many nights as he worked, but that wasn't enough for Jack; he wanted more, much more. She began to believe that he would never change, and she didn't think she could either.

Fran had a quick temper and a sharp tongue; not a good combination when you're upset, and she was upset with Jack a lot. She would try so hard to not blow up at him, but she was terribly disappointed at the way life was turning out. She began to resent him more and more, and more and more he seemed not to care. There were some good times in between the fighting, but just not enough of them.

After only five weeks in the house on Pond Street, they decided, (with the aid of some very strong arguments), to separate for a while. Fran and Terry and Jackie moved back in with Ethel and Andy and Dottie. It was difficult for everyone. Fran felt bad for her parents, having to have three more people living there. "I'm so sorry to have to involve you again," she said. "I really am." "Don't you be concerned about us, Fran," Andy said. "To be honest with you, your mother and I hoped for the best, but suspected that it would come to this." "Really Dad?" Fran said, with tears in her eyes. "We've been worried about you ever since you came home from Bournewood," Ethel said,. "We were against you going right into that house, but Jack felt it was the best thing for you. We're truly sorry for the way things turned out Fran, but we're glad you're here, you and the kids." "Oh, thank you Mom," Fran said, very much relieved, as she hugged them both.

It was pretty crowded at her parents' home, and no matter how kind they were, in her heart she always felt that she was imposing on them. The days were fine, but the evenings and the sleeping arrangements were difficult. Ethel had started working for Andy at the Graham shop on Newbury Street in Boston. She took care of the books, paid the bills, and made out the payroll for the painters. She and Andy would leave together in the morning and return home around five-thirty in the afternoon. Dottie was a sophomore at Blessed Sacrament High School, so she would be gone 'til after three. Fran had the house to herself and the kids for most of the day. She was glad for the much needed time alone. She would have supper ready when they all got home.

Fran had bought a Rambler American automobile when she and Jack separated. It was a totally stripped model; standard shift, no chrome, no extras at all. It didn't even have a radio. "Gee, thank God it at least has a heater in it" Andy said. Fran loved that car and so did Terry and Jackie.

*****

One day Jack came over to see 'the kids'. He told Fran that he had just purchased a little town house on Goldsmith Street in Jamaica Plain. "It only has four rooms, but it's brand new, and it has a nice, large fenced-in back yard. I think it would be perfect for you and Terry and Jackie. I'd really like for you to move into it, Fran, as soon as possible." Fran knew that Jack wanted her away from her parents. He cared a lot for Andy and Ethel but he was going to try to get his family back, and he knew that would be very difficult while Fran was in their home. "I suppose I could take a look at it," she said. "Great, come on, let's go now," Jack said, enthusiastically.

Fran liked the house on Goldsmith Street; it had a nice eat-in kitchen, and living room on the first floor. Upstairs were two bedrooms and a full bath. Jack was right about the backyard; it was large and all fenced in. She agreed to move in there, as long as it was just her and the kids. "That's fine," Jack said, "for now, anyway." "I mean it, Jack," Fran said. "I know, I know," said Jack, "but I'm thinking that one day that could change." "I can't think about that now," she said. Fran and the kids had been living with her parents for three months when they moved into the house on Goldsmith Street. They were very comfortable there, and the kids loved the back yard. Fran felt a peace within her that she hadn't felt for a long time. She missed Jack, but he came to the house often to see them. "I think we see him more now, living apart, than we did when we were together," she told her mother one day.

*****

Joe was working evenings selling Fuller brushes, and days painting Jack's houses. He didn't want to rely on Jack any longer for work. He felt he was getting nowhere, and knew he had to make a decision on what to do with the rest of his life. He had never wanted to become a painter, or to make it his life's work, but with two children and a mortgage to pay, he decided to take his father up on his offer to work for him. It was 1963 when Joe began painting for J. W. Graham Painting Company. Joe had no idea then the magnitude of his decision.

*****

Three months after Fran and the children moved into the house, Jack moved in with them. Right away he started looking for another house, a little larger than the house they were in. He found one on Prince Street, just off the Jamaicaway. It was a lovely old brick home with three bedrooms upstairs and a full bath. Downstairs, on the first floor, were the kitchen, dining room, fireplaced living room and half-bath. Fran loved the house and couldn't wait to move into it. It needed some painting and wallpapering, but other than that they figured, with the help of Ethel and Andy and Joe, the house would be ready in about two weeks. Fran was there almost every day, and the rest of the family were there most evenings.

One afternoon Jack came home early, about three thirty, and told Fran that he had just sold the house on Prince Street, and he had bought six acres of virgin land in Milton, on Blue Hill Avenue. "What?" Fran cried. "You sold our house on Prince Street? Are you crazy? We've almost got the house ready to move in." "Yeah, I know," Jack said, "but this is going to be great; we'll get the land cleared and build our own home just the way we want it." "But, we've *got* a house just the way we want it," Fran said. "Why on earth would you sell it?" "Why? Because this is a great opportunity, that's why!" he said. "I love that house, Jack," Fran said. "I want to live there, not in Milton. I can't believe you did this!" she said, disgustedly. "You're such a jerk sometimes, honestly Jack; who do you think you are, anyway? And what makes you feel you can do anything you want without even mentioning it to me? Don't you ever think about what I might want?" she asked, tears burning her eyes. "I'm so sick of this Jack, I really am; I'm sick and tired of you just deciding how everything is going to be without a word to me first." She turned away so he wouldn't see the tears rolling down her cheeks. "Why do you get so upset when I'm doing this for you?" Jack asked. "Oh, Bull! If you were thinking of me at all," Fran said, "you wouldn't have sold that beautiful house on Prince Street, at least not without asking me how I might feel about it. You knew when you sold it how much I loved it. No, Jack, you don't do anything unless it benefits *you*, regardless of who you hurt, and it's usually me." "For God's sake, Fran, this is going to be fabulous," Jack said. "Why do you have to put the kibosh on all my plans?" "That's it exactly Jack," she said. "They're *your* plans, not *ours*; they're very rarely *our* plans." "Oh, come on, Fran, just think about it, will you, six acres of land to do with what we want." "I don't want to hear about it, Jack; do any damn thing you want; it doesn't matter anymore."

Later, when Jack had gone back to work, Fran thought, *"Am I being unreasonable? Most people would give their right arm to have six acres of Milton land to build a home on... But, it's not the land or the house, it's how totally unimportant I am to him. I feel like a boarder, not a partner in this marriage."* She began to cry; she had been feeling very emotional lately, and right at this moment she felt extremely vulnerable. It had been seven weeks since Jack moved back in, and what should have shown up by now hadn't, and she was beginning to believe she was pregnant. She didn't want to even *think* about having another child at this time. She and Jack had problems, and she felt that their marriage was in serious trouble, but she knew she *had* to think about it. *"Okay, I probably am pregnant.... so I'm just going to concentrate on this baby, and not on Jack's arrogance. I'm not going to let myself get sick again, that's for sure. A baby will be great, and what the heck; I can design a house; that is if his majesty allows me to have some say in it. Maybe he really is doing it for us; I don't know anymore. God, if you're listening, I could use a little help down here."*

*****

Jack hired a crew to cut down trees and clear the land. He was about as excited as Fran had ever seen him. She didn't think it possible, but it was definitely rubbing off on her. The more he talked about the land and the beautiful new home they would build on it, the more excited she became. Jack had a gift that was for sure; he had a zest for life, and a smile that drew people into his sphere of excitement. That, with the enormous confidence that he had, was a definite ticket to success. As Andy once said of him, "Jack has the Midas touch; every thing he touches seems to turn to gold." Fran wished their marriage were one of those things.

Fran was indeed pregnant, and feeling physically great. She knew her mom and dad were not thrilled about this pregnancy at all. They worried about Fran; they could see things were not the way they should be with her and Jack. They hoped and prayed that their marriage would get better, but they never really believed that it would.

Ethel and Andy were upset with Jack for selling the house on Prince Street. They knew how much Fran loved it, and how upset she was that he had sold it. Jack had made a nice profit on the house, and although Ethel didn't want to be cynical, she kind of thought that a profit was all that was important to him. She also felt that buying six acres of virgin land in Milton was sheer folly. But, as Andy reminded her, "He'll make it work, Ethel; you should know that by now," he said. "Folly" is not a word in Jack's dictionary.

*****

Rosemarie was pregnant again, and sick with morning sickness. During all three pregnancies, at one time or another, she said to Fran, "You don't know how lucky you are!" "Gosh, Rosemarie, I suppose I don't," Fran said. "I've never experienced it, and I sure don't want to, after seeing what you go through." After a couple of months, Rosemarie was back to feeling fine, and visiting Fran with Billy and little Christina in tow. Of course she always brought a dozen donuts with her. Jack once asked, "How come whenever Rosemarie comes over and brings a dozen donuts, there's never a single donut left over?" Fran laughed and said, "You wouldn't believe it, Jack; you have to *see* it to believe it." She told Rosemarie what Jack had said, and she just laughed. The next time Rosemarie came over with donuts, she brought two extras, one to leave for Jack, and one more in case she or Fran wanted it. Jack laughed when he saw the donut, and said, "How many did she eat today?" Fran said, "she had eight; I had three, and Terry and Billy each had one." Jack just grinned, "Please tell me she doesn't eat them all at one sitting." "No, of course not," Fran said laughing. "She had five for breakfast, one after lunch, and two in between." "That girl's going to be written up in "Ripley's Believe it or Not," Jack said, "as 'the most donuts ever eaten by a small pregnant woman.'" They both laughed. "And she never gains an extra ounce," Fran said. "I think I'll kill her."

*****

Jack decided to just have three acres of the land cleared, as it would take forever to clear six. Whenever he had a spare hour, he would join the crew and cut down a few smaller trees. He said it was to help speed up the work, but Fran knew he just had to be involved in the physical end of the work. Fran loved that side of Jack, the down-to-earth, out-doorsy side. He was having a wonderful time being part of the action, and loving every second of it.

Jack hired a contractor to build the house when the land was all ready. His name was Mario Corsi, and he had an excellent reputation. Fran was amazed that Jack let her have so much to say about the design of the house. She was in her glory talking to Mario about the style and configuration of the house, the amount of bedrooms and bathrooms, and fireplaces, etc., etc. She had gotten caught up in Jack's excitement, and there was no turning back.

Despite the fun and excitement of planning the house, Fran and Jack were arguing a lot. She tried pushing it out of her mind and pretending that everything was just fine, but deep down she knew it wasn't. *"Maybe, when the house is finished and this baby is born things will be better,"* she thought. But as nice as that seemed, somehow she knew things were not going to get better because of a new house and the birth of a new baby. If anything, it would probably put more stress on their marriage. *"Well, I'm not going to think about that now,"* she thought. *"I'll deal with that when I have to."*

*****

279

Dottie was wracking her brain trying to decide what she would do for the annual Science Fair. She was a junior at Blessed Sacrament High School, and she and every other student was expected to prepare an exhibit that would honor the school. Every student taking a science course in every school, private and public, in the greater Boston area, was involved in it. Dottie decided to do "The Living Growth of a Chick Embryo". Ethel and Andy thought that she might be taking on more than she could handle, but Dottie was determined to see it through from the fertilized egg to the hatching of a live baby chick.

Andy took Dottie to a chicken farm and she bought a dozen fertilized eggs. She was told exactly what she would need…light bulbs, thermometers, mason jars, formaldehyde, and more. To create a type of incubator she put some straw in a box, set the thermometers in it, a light for heat, and a small bowl of water for humidity. The wattage of the bulb had to be just perfect or the chicks would not develop in the eggs, or worse, they could end up roasted. Unfortunately, there were a few disasters, and Dottie had to buy more fertilized eggs. Eventually she got a perfect environment for hatching chicks. The 'incubator' was placed up high on the shelf in the reception hall closet. The incubation period for the chicks was twenty-one days.

Dottie had no idea when she started this project how distressing it would become when every other day she had to carefully crack open an egg and put the embryo in a jar containing the formaldehyde. Then she would mark the date and time on the top of the jar. At first it wasn't too bad, but after the fifteenth day she opened an egg every day. The embryos were not just embryos any longer; they were underdeveloped chickens. Dottie nearly gave up on the project a number of times; it was very upsetting to her to have to deliberately stop the life-growth of the little chicks.

Near the end, she just couldn't stand doing it any longer. She pleaded with others in the family to do it for her, but no one else could stand to do it either. She had come this far, and had reached a point of no return. She knew she had to do this by herself; she would simply have to see it to the bitter end.

Each day the embryos were getting to look more and more like baby chicks. On the eighteenth and nineteenth days of the incubation period, when she cracked open an egg, it was a living, moving baby chick, which died moments later. Dottie was beside herself. She ended up being sick in the bathroom, crying her heart out. "I hate this! I can't do this any more!" She sobbed. "I never should have started this; I feel like a murderer." "But, Dottie," Ethel said, "you did start it, and as disturbing as it is, I know you'll see it through. There's only one more day for you to open an egg, and then, hopefully, the next day, you'll have a few chicks that will break out of the eggs themselves, alive and kicking." "I know you're right, Mom," Dottie said, "I just don't think I can do it again tomorrow; It's just so awful." "I know, dear, we're all feeling badly about it, but it will be worth it in the end, and you'll have a science project you can be proud of."

On the twentieth day it took Dottie quite a while before she could crack the egg. She had to keep telling herself that this was for science, but she still couldn't seem to do it. Finally, Andy helped her; they carefully cracked it open, and a live chick tumbled out. He tried to stand, but couldn't; he died about a minute later. Dottie was close to hysteria; it was all she could do to hold herself together. She cried and cried as she carefully picked up the little dead chick and placed him in the jar of formaldehyde. She put the cover on the jar, and labeled it, then went to her room sobbing. Fran came over to see how the science project was coming along. When she looked at the last two jars, all she could say was, "Oh my word! Oh Gosh, Mom, that's awful; how did she ever do it?" "Not too easily, that's for sure; she's feeling very sad and guilty about all of this," Ethel said. "She's really very upset, Fran; why don't you talk to her?" "I will; is she in her room?" "Yes."

Dottie looked terrible when Fran saw her; her face was red and her eyes were swollen. As Fran walked into the room Dottie said, "I never should have done this Fran; honestly, I feel like a murderer." "I know, Dottie." Fran said. She put her arm around her kid sister, and Dottie started crying again. "Dottie, try to imagine how scientists must feel when they have to do experiments on large animals like dogs and cats, or cattle," Fran said. "They do it though, because it's to benefit mankind in some way." "Well I'm not benefiting mankind," Dottie said. "All I'm doing is killing baby chickens." "But that's not why you're doing it,"

Fran said. "You wouldn't hurt a little chick for anything, I know that. You're doing it for mankind in a much smaller way than scientists do it." "Oh right!" Dottie scoffed. "Dottie, I've learned so much since you started this project," Fran said. "Just seeing what occurs inside the egg is so wonderful; I had no idea. Believe me, Dottie, just giving people the opportunity to see.... what's it called....'The Living Growth of a Chick Embryo"?" Dottie nodded. "They'll be fascinated by the contents of those jars. I'm really very proud of you; I know how difficult the last few days must have been." "Really, Fran? I'm so afraid people will be disgusted looking at it." "Disgusted? Oh no, Dottie," Fran said. "They'll marvel at it, believe me." Fran hugged her sister, and Dottie said, "I don't even know if tomorrow any of the rest of the eggs will produce live chicks, and if I have no live chicks, I have no science project." "Well, don't think about that anymore today," Fran said. "You'll find out one way or the other tomorrow, and there's not much you can do about it until then. If you have to, you'll go to the chicken farm and get a couple of newly hatched chicks." "Yes, but I would always know that my project actually failed."

Fran went to her parents' house around two o'clock the next day; no one was home, so she used her key and let herself in. Terry and Jackie were with her. She gave them some cookies and a glass of milk, and while they were eating she got up on the stool Dottie had put in the reception hall closet to check on the eggs in the 'incubator'. Nothing was happening at the moment, and Fran got down. She felt a little anxious. *"What if nothing happens?"* Fran thought. *What if there are no live chicks? Oh gosh, I really hope some of them hatch, I mean, at least one; and I really hope it lives, at least 'til after the Science Fair."* She didn't want Terry to know yet that today was the day the chicks were supposed to hatch. She felt that she was too young to understand if nothing happened, or if one hatched and died moments after. Terry didn't need to know all the gory details.

At three o'clock Dottie called. "I knew you'd be there," she said. "Nothing's happening yet, is it?" "No, not yet Dottie; where are you?" Fran asked. "I'm at Gerry's house; I'll be home in a little while." Gerry Pilato was Dottie's best friend and soul mate. *"Poor Dottie,"* Fran thought. *"She just can't hang around watching and waiting for something that might not happen."*

About a half hour later, Fran went back into the closet and stood on the stool. She looked into the 'incubator' and gasped at what she saw. Three eggs were moving, and two of them had cracks in one end. As she watched she saw a tiny beak trying to peck through the shell. She quickly got down off the stool and called Gerry's house. When Dottie came to the phone Fran cried, "Dottie, come home right away! You're about to become a mother!" "What?" Dottie said. "Is something happening?" "It sure is, Dottie…hurry!" Dottie dropped the phone and headed out the door, with Gerry yelling, "Wait for me!" Dottie wasn't waiting; she ran all the way home, with Gerry fast on her heels. She ran up the stairs, and into the house; she ran into the closet and jumped up on the stool. "Oh, they're doing it!" She cried. "They're pecking their way out of the shells. Oh Fran, isn't this wonderful?" "Yes, it is, Dottie; it is wonderful." Dottie very carefully brought the box down for Terry and Jackie to see. Fran was a little apprehensive about that, but she said nothing. They all watched as the little chicks pecked and pecked until they made a good size opening, and then they kind of pulled themselves out of the shells altogether. They were all wet and funny looking, with pieces of egg shell sticking to them, but they seemed okay. Terry was just squealing with delight, and Fran had to hold Jackie to keep him from grabbing one of them. Fran was sure he thought they were toys for him to play with. Dottie was absolutely thrilled. "Oh, please God," Dottie said, "keep them alive for the Science Fair in two days."

The day before the Science Fair one of the chicks died. Dottie was so afraid the others might die too, but they didn't. She took good care of them, and the morning of the Fair they looked healthy and adorable. Andy helped her bring everything and get it set up in St. Gerald's Hall, right next to the high school. Fran left Jackie with a friend, and took Terry with her to the Fair. Ethel and Andy were already there. Dottie's 'incubator', and the jars lined up containing the embryos and underdeveloped chicks from day one to day twenty, looked very impressive, but of course, the "piece de resistance" was the two live chicks.

Two of the school nuns and a priest were the judges. They walked around studying every exhibit inside and out, from one end to the other, and writing notes on their clipboards. Some of the exhibits looked like rocket scientists had created them. "Boy," Andy said, as he looked at one exhibit, "this is the work of high-school students? These kids are brilliant."

The judges' decisions were about to be announced. Fran and the rest of the family watched as the judges conferred among themselves. Finally the priest stepped up onto the stage. He tapped the microphone, cleared his throat, and said, "Students, faculty, families and friends, thank you all for being here and showing your interest and support in this year's Science Fair. Before we announce the winners, I would like to say to all of you students, you have done extremely well. You have thoughtfully and imaginatively prepared your exhibits. You have done your school proud." He then announced the Third Place Winner; another judge went to the student and congratulated her and pinned the Third Place ribbon on her and on her exhibit. Everyone clapped and cheered. Dottie said, "She's the one I thought would win *first* prize." She clapped hard for her.

When the clapping and cheering calmed down, the priest announced the Second Place Winner. Again, another judge went to her and pinned the Second Place ribbon on her as the crowd clapped and cheered. Then, the judge spoke into the microphone very emphatically, "FIRST PRIZE GOES TO JUNIOR, DOROTHY ANN VITELLO, FOR HER EXHIBIT OF "THE LIVING GROWTH OF A CHICK EMBRYO." Fran screamed, Andy and Ethel were jumping up and down, clapping and hugging Dottie, and Joe was whistling and clapping. Dottie was stunned! She never gave it a thought of actually winning anything in the Science Fair; she just wanted to get it done and over with. Everyone was patting her on the back and cheering her. Another judge came to her and congratulated her and pinned FIRST PLACE ribbons on her and on her exhibit. Dottie said, "thank you," but she was still stunned. She simply couldn't believe it. All her tears and frustration and guilt melted away under all this attention and excitement. It was all so wonderful...Dottie had won first place in the Science Fair! The whole family was very excited and proud of her. She was positively thrilled, though she still could hardly believe it. Later that afternoon, when they arrived home and Crocifessa heard the good news, she immediately started making her 'famous' baked macaroni for a celebration for Dottie.

Two weeks later the First Place winners from all the different schools in and around Boston met at Brandeis University in Waltham, to compete for First, Second and Third place. By now the two chicks were a lot bigger, so Dottie went to the chicken farm again the day before, and bought two newly hatched baby chicks. Again, Andy took Dottie to Brandeis and helped her to set up her exhibit. This time she had the two much grown original chicks, and two brand new baby chicks, which made her exhibit look even better than the first time. "I know I'm not going to win anything this time," Dottie said. "It's just so exciting to think I'm actually here, in the company of all these future scientists. Look at all these marvelous exhibits, Dad." "It's unbelievable," Andy said. "I thought the exhibits at your school were terrific, but these are incredible." Well, that's because these are all the winners, Dad," Dottie said. "Boy, they really are incredible. How I ever got this far, I'll never understand, but I'm loving every minute of it." "What do you mean, you don't understand it?" Andy said "Why, your exhibit is terrific, Dottie; you worked damned hard on it." "Well, yeah, for Blessed Sacrament, I guess, but certainly not for Brandeis. I feel a little silly here with my exhibit compared to the rest of these." "Well, don't you feel silly; you did real good," Andy said. "You made it here, and that's what's important." "Thanks, Dad," Dottie said, "I appreciate that." "Well," Andy said, "the rest of the family will be over around noon, so I'm going to grab a couple of those chairs against the wall for us. It looks like it's going to be a long day."

The judges were from the Massachusetts Science Fair Association. After much time was spent examining every exhibit, it was finally time to announce the winners. The voice came loudly through the speakers...."THIRD PLACE GOES TO JUNIOR, DOROTHY ANN VITELLO, OF BLESSED SACRAMENT HIGH SCHOOL IN JAMAICA PLAIN, FOR HER EXHIBIT OF "THE LIVING GROWTH OF A CHICK EMBRYO." The judge said the words but Dottie couldn't believe it; she felt like she was in a dream.

"This can't be real," she thought. *"Oh, God, if this is a dream, I definitely don't want to wake up."*

Andy shouted, Fran screamed, and Joe whistled. They clapped, they laughed, they cheered, as the judge pinned the ribbon on Dottie and her exhibit. They all hugged Dottie and jumped up and down with excitement and pride, enjoying every second of the moment. After the Second and First Place winners were announced, the three winners had their pictures taken together, and then individually with their exhibits. After that, refreshments were served for everyone. Dottie was feeling like a celebrity, which of course, she was.

"What an accomplishment," Ethel said to her, as she touched the ribbon on Dottie. "I'm so proud of you, Honey." "Who knows?" Andy said, "Maybe one day you'll become a great scientist. "Either that or a chicken farmer," Joe chuckled, as he hugged his little sister. Dottie was still in a daze. "Uh uh, not a scientist, and not a chicken farmer either," Fran said. "She's going to become a famous playwright, or at least a Broadway actress, after all the plays she's produced, directed, and starred in." They all laughed, remembering how Dottie would get all the kids in the neighborhood involved in a play she would put on. "I don't think a week ever went by," Ethel said, "without a Dorothy Vitello production taking place on the front porch or in the backyard." They all laughed again, and nodded in agreement. "Oh, Lord," Dottie said, "was I corny or what? And everyone had to do things my way, or they couldn't be in the play. Mom, you were great, though; you always helped me with makeshift costumes and scenery. "Hah," Ethel laughed, "such as they were." They were all enjoying the celebration. It was an exciting and happy time.

Andy took Dottie and the four chicks back to the chicken farm the next day, and Dottie gave them to the owner. She had had enough of chickens, and as far as eggs go, it took her a very long time before she could eat one again.

The following day the pictures appeared in a few different news-papers. Neighbors and friends were calling to congratulate Dottie when they saw the article and her picture in the newspaper.

Well, Dottie had accomplished something she never dreamed possible; not only winning First Place in her own school, but winning Third Place among all the winners of the Greater Boston Science

Fair. It was the most exciting time of her young life. It was the most exciting time of the whole family's life, too. The Vitello family had always been an average, ordinary, simple family, no great winners or champions of anything, no trophies, no ribbons, just a hard working, loving family. What Dottie had achieved was extraordinary to them, and they all reveled in her glory.

****

CHAPTER THIRTEEN
The Death Of Camelot

On October 12, 1963 Joe and Mae and the boys moved into their new home at 24 Oakden Ave. in South Weymouth. It was a much bigger house than the house in Abington, and with another child coming, they needed a lot more room. Oakden Ave. was a lovely, quiet street, and with the large backyard that came with the house, they knew it would be a perfect place to raise their family. Life was good and getting better all the time. Joe and Mae thanked God for His blessings and His provision.

*****

On Fran and Jack's fifth anniversary, Jack called her about nine-thirty in the morning from work. "What would you like to do tonight?" He asked. "I don't know," Fran said. We could go out for dinner and maybe a movie." "Nah, that's not good enough," he said. "Not good enough?" Fran asked. "Well, do you have something better in mind?" "I sure do," he said. "Guess what I'm holding in my hand." "I don't know, Jack, what is it?" she said. "Are you sitting down?" He asked. Fran could feel the excitement mounting in her. "Ooh, Jack, what are you getting at?" she asked. "Come on, guess," he said. "Oh Jack, I can't; I have no idea, tell me." He said, very mysteriously, "I am holding in my hand…. TWO TICKETS TO MONTICELLO'S," he yelled through the phone. "Monticello's!" Fran gasped. Jack continued, "TO SEEEEE ……" "Jack, I'm going to murder you if you don't tell me right now," she said. Fran heard him chuckle. "To see…. PHYLLIS DILLER," he yelled again. Fran screamed, "Phyllis Diller? Oh Jack, are you serious?" "I sure am," he said. "The show starts at eight o'clock, so we'll go early and have…what do you think…a lobster dinner maybe?" "Oh Jack, this is so wonderful," Fran said. "Phyllis Diller! I just love her! Oh, I can't wait." "Okay," he said, "I'll be home early; we should leave the house by six o'clock, 'cause it takes a while to get to Framingham. Your mother's going to take the kids tonight, right?" "Yes," Fran said. "We'll just drop them off on our way." "Good!" Then, I'll see you about five o'clock."

Fran was so excited, she ran upstairs to figure out what she was going to wear to a place like Monticello's. At six and a half months pregnant, Dr. Weiss told her she was either carrying twins or one very good size baby. Nothing fit her right. *"I feel like Two-Ton Tony Galento,"* she said, as she tried things on in front of the mirror. Andy always said that about anyone who was unusually large. There was a fighter or a wrestler who had that moniker, and right now she felt like she fit the name. She decided to go to a little maternity shop in Mattapan Square and buy something special that fit her right. She picked out a lovely white brocade two-piece maternity dress with a mandarin collar and frog closings. "We can do the alterations for you right now, seeing as you need it for tonight." "That would be fine, thank you," Fran said. They shortened the skirt and top for her while she waited. *"I should hope they'd shorten it for me right away at these prices,"* Fran thought. *"Oh well, who cares what it cost; I look good enough for Monticello's, that's all I care about right now."*

Jack was home at five-thirty and Fran was all dressed and ready to go. "Happy Anniversary" he said, and handed her a bouquet of flowers. "You look gorgeous!" He said. He kissed her warmly on the lips and she just held him for a few extra seconds. Jack was not always the most thoughtful person, and she wanted to hold onto the moment. She knew he was trying to please her, and it meant the world to her. "Really," he said, "you look fabulous; that's a beautiful dress." "Thank you, Jack, I needed that, and thanks for these beautiful flowers." "Okay, I'm going to take a quick shower," he said, "and I'll be ready to go in twenty minutes."

Monticello's was magnificent. Fran and Jack had been to Blinstrub's a couple of times, and they thought that was beautiful, but Monticello's was like nothing they had ever seen before. The whole place looked like gold, with immense crystal chandeliers and thick, plush, red carpeting. The tables were set with gold colored tablecloths and white linen napkins. The dinnerware was white with gold trim. Fran and Jack were so impressed and excited as they were brought to their table.

They ordered baked stuffed lobster and all the extras. It was a delicious dinner, and they were both stuffed when they were finished. When the waiter asked if they would like dessert, Fran declined, as she was beginning to feel a little queasy. "I guess I ate too much," she said. "Not me," said Jack, "I'll have the apple pie a la mode." He had a terrific appetite, and he wasn't sparing any expense on this evening. Fran felt like she was about to burst with excitement and happiness…. and too much lobster.

All of a sudden Fran felt like her legs went numb, and she couldn't move them. She told Jack that she didn't feel right, but she couldn't get up to go to the Ladies' Room. Jack had worn new shoes, which were bothering his feet, so he had taken them off during dinner. As he struggled to get them on, Fran passed right out of the picture, with her beautifully coiffed head nestled in what was left of her mashed potatoes. Jack jumped up without his shoes and lifted Fran's head out of her mashed potatoes. A woman who was at a nearby table came over and helped him. She dipped Fran's napkin in water and wiped Fran's face, then held the napkin to her forehead. After a few moments Fran came to, and was horribly embarrassed. People were staring and she just wanted to crawl under the table. "Can you get up now, Fran?" Jack asked. "No; I don't know what's wrong, but I just can't move my legs."

If what had already happened wasn't bad enough, what happened next definitely was. Fran felt her dinner on the rise. "Oh no!" she cried. "Jack, I'm going to…." Up came the lobster, up came the mashed potatoes, up came the green beans almondine, and not necessarily in that order. Fran just leaned to the side and let it all come, not that she could have stopped it. Poor Jack; he had to leap out of the way before it all hit his new socks. It just kept coming out…all over the beautiful red carpet. When it was over, the feeling slowly came back to Fran's legs. She watched Jack, as he ran to look for a wheelchair without his shoes on. If she hadn't felt so dreadful and humiliated, she might have been laughing.

When Jack returned, he helped Fran into the wheelchair. He was very angry that after all that had happened, no one stopped to help them; not a waiter, a busboy, the maitre de, no one. Waiters were going by constantly, but no one even asked if they could help. Jack made a mental note to call the manager the next day. He brought Fran to the Ladies Room, and without thinking, wheeled her right in. Fran said, "I'm okay now, Jack; I think you better leave before you cause a riot." She smiled a weak smile at him, and he left. When Fran came out of the Ladies Room, Jack was standing there waiting for her. "Are you okay to wait here by yourself while I get the car?" He asked. "Car, Nothing!" Fran said. "We're not missing Phyllis Diller. I feel much better Jack, but I don't want to go back to where we were; it's too embarrassing. Let's find a table on the other side and watch the show from there." They found a table closer to the stage than the one they had before, and where no one would recognize the up-chucking pregnant lady with the shoeless husband. Phyllis Diller put on a show they would never forget; she was absolutely hilarious. They were so glad they stayed.

On the way home Fran and Jack 'killed themselves laughing,' about him in his socks, and her with her head in the mashed potatoes, and ruining the carpet at Monticello's. "They're not going to want to see us back there any too soon, that's for sure," Jack said laughing.

Although it could have been a complete disaster, Fran knew that she would never forget this evening, and she would always cherish it. She stared at Jack as they drove home. *"This was the man I fell in love with,"* she thought. *"We always laughed and enjoyed each other when we were going together, and when we were first married he seemed to care so deeply for me. Oh God, why did he change? Why did I change?"*

The next day Fran called Dr. Weiss, and two hours later, she was in his office. Ethel went with her while Crocifessa watched Terry and Jackie. After examining her he said, "What I believe happened was that the baby was pressing on a nerve that caused the numbness in your legs. It's not that uncommon in the last few months of pregnancy. Just be very careful from now on, Fran; the baby is large, and you're a very small woman. It just hasn't got a lot of room to move around."

*****

One day Fran's friend Mary Lou called her and asked if she'd like to meet her at Zayre's department store. They could do a little Christmas shopping and then go to the Pewter Pot for lunch. Fran was glad to get out for a while. She left Terry and Jackie with Ethel who was home that day, and headed for Zayre's. She was listening to her favorite Rock station, when it was interrupted with a special announcement. Fran thought she was hearing things when she heard the newscaster say that President Kennedy had been shot during his motorcade in Dallas. "He was rushed to the hospital only moments ago." The newscaster was crying as he gave the announcement. Fran gasped when she heard the news. "Oh no! Oh God, please let President Kennedy be all right," she prayed aloud.

When she got to Zayre's, people were standing around looking absolutely shocked and confused; many were crying and wiping their eyes. Fran spotted Mary Lou, who was sitting on a bench crying. She looked up and saw Fran pulling into a parking space. She ran up to her as she was getting out of the car. "Fran, have you heard the news?" "Yes," Fran said, crying, I simply can't believe it. Let's go inside and see if there's anything on the television sets about it." They stood watching the news on TV for what seemed like a very long time. They soon learned that President Kennedy had been shot in the head. Fran and Mary Lou couldn't believe what they were hearing. "The nation is praying for its' President," one announcer said. Another newscaster said, "Our leader needs your prayers at this time." Another asked for the prayers of the people for the President. All of them were filled with emotion as they spoke.

A little while later, a newscaster spoke. His eyes were red and his voice was shaking and he kept swallowing hard. When he spoke, the tears ran down his face as he said, "The President is dead." He broke down and couldn't say much more. Fran started sobbing, and Mary Lou was doing the same. All over Zayre's people were crying; men and women unashamedly wiping their eyes and exclaiming things like, "Oh no! Oh God, no!" "It can't be!" " I can't believe it! I can't believe it!" "How could this happen?" People were numb with the stark reality of what had happened to their President.

Fran drove home in a daze; she wanted desperately to just erase the last few hours, to have it never have taken place. She cried as she drove home; she couldn't seem to stop. She loved Jack Kennedy; she loved Jackie and she loved the whole 'Camelot' era in the White House. She felt like her heart was breaking.

When she got home the phone was ringing. She picked it up and she heard Jack say, "Fran, have you heard the news?" She started sobbing and couldn't speak for a minute; then she said, "I can't believe it, Jack; I just don't want to." "Jack's voice cracked as he said, "I know, I feel the same way. I'll be home in a little while; nobody can work here now anyway." "Jack, the kids are at my mother's house; would you please pick them up?" "Okay." As he got to their house, Andy was just pulling up. His eyes were brimming with tears, and he could hardly speak. When they went in the house, Dottie was sobbing and ran up to her father and hugged him. "Oh, Dad, isn't it awful? Poor President Kennedy; she couldn't stop crying. Ethel's eyes were moist with tears. "This is so terrible," she said. "I cannot believe this has happened." Terry was sad, too, although she really didn't understand what had happened, but the sadness Dottie was feeling, and the people crying on TV made her feel sad also.

Jack loved Jack Kennedy; Fran knew he was hurting a lot over this. When he came home with Terry and Jackie, they ate their supper in the living room as they watched TV. They felt numb as they watched the videotape of the shooting. Jackie Kennedy looked positively horrified; everyone's heart broke as they saw what she went through sitting right beside her husband in the car in the motorcade. Later that same day she stood beside Vice President Lyndon B.

Johnson as he was sworn in as President of the United States on the plane back to the White House. Jackie's beautiful pink Chanel suit was stained with her husband's blood.

For the next few days, every channel carried the story, showing videotapes and interviews with people who were there, and saw it firsthand. No one was watching regular TV fare; there seemed to be a need to know every detail of what was happening, as sad as it might be.

Lee Harvey Oswald had been arrested for the crime. As they were taking him out of the Dallas jail to transport him to another facility, Jack Ruby shot and killed him in front of millions of Americans who happened to be watching TV at that moment. Fran was one of them, and she sat horrified as Jack Ruby rushed though the crowd that was there and shot Oswald before anyone realized what was happening. It was all so unbelievable.

The day of the funeral was an agonizing day for most Americans. Fran and her family watched the funeral procession as the flag-draped casket containing the body of President Kennedy made its way down Pennsylvania Avenue. A very sad sight in the procession was seeing the boots turned backwards on the sides of a riderless horse, symbolizing a fallen leader. Jackie, dressed in black, wore a veil over her face, undoubtedly to hide from the public the stress and sadness she was feeling. She walked serenely behind the casket, holding her brother-in-law Bobby's hand. There was a slight slope to her shoulders that no one ever saw before; her head wasn't held quite as high as it always was. Though the veil hid much, the TV cameras didn't, and one could see the lovely face of our nation's First Lady strained with sadness and tears. As the cameras scanned the Kennedy family, young Ted's face showed the grief he was feeling. To Fran, the saddest moment of the entire day was seeing Jackie, holding her children's hands as they approached the casket. Jackie knelt, and for a brief moment, kissed the flag-draped casket, and then all America was moved to tears as two and a half year old John-John saluted the casket that held his father. Fran sobbed as she watched that heart-wrenching sight. She felt like many Americans did, like a member of her own family had died. The assassination of President John F. Kennedy was a tragedy that was felt by everyone, whether they loved him or not. The death of a country's leader is always tragic.

Fran heard someone on TV say, "I truly believe that the heart-breaking events of the past few days will forever live in the hearts of the people of this country and beyond, but especially New Englanders." *"Oh, I thoroughly agree,"* she thought.

*****

It was a crisp cool day this particular Saturday, and Jack was doing his Paul Bunyon thing. He loved being at the land in Milton and chopping down trees with the crew that was there. He had just sharpened his axe on the wheel stone sharpener and was half way through a medium-size tree when somehow the axe missed the tree and went deep into Jack's knee. The men in the crew ran to him and laid him down on the ground. His leg was bleeding profusely. One of the men took off his belt and made a kind of tourniquet above the knee. Someone ran to call an ambulance, and another put his jacket around Jack as he was obviously going into shock. The ambulance came and took him to Milton Hospital.

Eleanor Kramer and her daughter Marie were visiting Fran when the phone call came telling her what had happened to Jack. "Oh my God," Fran said, "Is he all right? I mean, is it serious?" The nurse said, "I really don't know; he'll be going into surgery soon, that's all I know." "Surgery! Oh God," Fran said, "I'm coming right over." She was beginning to tremble, so Marie drove her to the hospital, while Eleanor watched Terry and Jackie.

When Fran got to the hospital, Jack was being given a spinal and had been sedated. The nurse told the doctor that Jack's wife was waiting to talk to him. Dr. Wallace came out and told Fran not to worry. "I'll do everything I can to save his leg," he said. "Save his leg?" Fran said, shocked. "You're telling me he could lose his leg?" "Well, not if I can help it," the doctor said, and then he was gone. Fran prayed silently and hoped that God would hear her. *"He can't lose his leg, God; he's such an active and energetic person. He just can't."*

Jack was in surgery for what seemed like an eternity to Fran. Dr. Wallace finally came out to talk with her. When Fran saw him coming toward her, her heart started pounding in her chest. "Well, it went well," he said, "he'll keep his leg, but he will very likely walk with a limp." "Oh, thank God," Fran said. "You know, Mrs. Roche," the doctor said, "that axe went two-thirds of the way through his knee; he came dangerously close to losing his leg."

When Fran was finally able to see Jack, the nurse was trying to make him lie flat on his back. "I feel okay," he said," I want to sit up." "Mr. Roche," the nurse said, "I know you're not feeling much pain right now because of the morphine you're getting, but you must lie flat; you've had a spinal. "But like I said, I'm okay," he responded, "I'm not going to lie down if I feel fine; I'm going to sit up." "Jack," Fran said, as she walked into the room, "Why don't you do what the nurse tells you to do? There's a good reason why she's insisting that you lie down; am I right?" she asked, looking at the nurse. "Yes," the nurse said, exasperated. "When a person has had a spinal they need to lie flat for eight to ten hours or they could get what's called a 'spinal headache'. "And believe me," she continued, "you don't want to have one of those." "Jack," Fran said, "I had a spinal with each baby, and they insisted that I stay lying down for that length of time. There must be something to it; maybe you ought to listen to the nurse." "I know how I feel," he said, "and besides, I never get headaches." "Okay," the nurse said, "Do what you want; I've done my job." Jack sat up to talk with Fran. "It must be wonderful to know more than the experts," Fran said sarcastically. Jack just grinned.

A few days later Fran and Andy picked Jack up at the hospital. He was doing great; he had to use crutches, but of course that was to be expected only days after surgery. Jack got in the back seat of the car so he could keep his leg outstretched on the seat. When they were almost home Fran heard soft moaning in the back. She turned around and Jack was holding his head. "Are you all right, Jack?" She asked. "Yeah, I've just got a little headache," he said. Fran knew if it was just a 'little' headache he would not be moaning. Soon, he began moaning loudly, and a few minutes later he was almost screaming with the pain. Fran had never seen him like that; she was very frightened. "We're almost home Jack," she said.

Andy pulled up in front of the house on Goldsmith Street and jumped out of the car and opened the back door. Fran got out and together they managed to get Jack out of the car and into the house. Ethel was watching the children; she came to the door and was shocked when she saw the condition Jack was in. He just wanted to go to bed, so Andy and Ethel helped him up the stairs, and into bed. Fran was already calling Dr. Wallace's office. She explained to his nurse what was happening, and the nurse said she'd page the doctor and have him call her right away. What seemed like hours was actually less than ten minutes, and then the phone rang. Fran explained everything to Dr. Wallace, and he said he would phone in a prescription to the drug store for pain medication for Jack. Andy went to pick it up a few minutes later.

Jack was in terrible pain; he just rocked back and forth on the bed, holding his head and moaning. When Andy got back, Fran gave Jack a pill and some of Crocifessa's 'famous' chicken soup. He didn't really want anything to eat, but she told him what the doctor said, that if he took the pills on an empty stomach he would be suffering with more than just his head. Jack ate the soup. A few hours later Fran gave Jack another pill with some tea and toast. A little while later Jack was feeling somewhat better. He still had a bad headache but the excruciating pain was letting up. He was able to sleep for a while. He awoke after a few hours and before anyone knew what was happening he had hobbled one step at a time down the stairs. "Why didn't you call me?" Andy said. "You shouldn't come down the stairs by yourself yet, Jack." "I wanted to see if I could do it," he responded. "Honestly, Jack," Fran said, "You're incorrigible." "So, when did the doctor say I could go back to work?" Jack asked Fran. "Do you really care what the doctor says?" She asked. "I mean, you're going to do exactly what you want anyway, right?" "Well, I'll see how I feel," he said. "Jack," Fran said, "Dr. Wallace said that you should stay off your feet for at least a week, then take it very slowly." "Well, we'll see," he said. Fran just shook her head; she didn't tell him all that Dr. Wallace said. He had said, "That horse's ass; I thought *he* had all the answers. I should let him suffer a while;

it would serve him right. You can tell him I said so if you wish." Fran felt it wasn't quite the right time to tell him that while he was still in so much pain, but she would definitely enjoy telling him when he was feeling better.

The doctor told Jack to use a cane for at least three weeks; Jack used it for three days, and he *never* walked with a limp. Andy said, "He's the luckiest guy I've ever known; he could fall in you know what, and come up smelling like a rose."

Work on the land in Milton came to an abrupt halt with the cold weather and lots of snow. There was much to be done with Christmas coming on fast. Thanksgiving was just a blur, with all the things that seemed to be going on all around it.

*****

Terry was close to four and a half, Jackie had just turned two, and Fran was enormous with her third child. Dr. Weiss was becoming concerned about the weight she was gaining. At seven months pregnant she had gained about fifty-five pounds, and she still had two months to go. He put her on a strict but nourishing diet. "I want hot-fudge sundaes," she said, as she told Jack what the doctor said. "Well, he knows best," Jack said. "Oh, I see," Fran said. "When it's about me, the doctor knows best, but when it's you, you do any darn thing you please." "Yeah, but this is different, Fran, and you know it." "I know, but it's not fair," she said. "I never had a problem when I was pregnant with Terry and Jackie. I only gained about twenty pounds with both of them. What the heck am I going to weigh by the time this baby is born?" "If you follow the diet Dr. Weiss gave you, you'll be okay," Jack said. "That's easy for you to say," Fran said, "You can eat anything and everything and never gain an ounce." "Well, I don't have a problem, you do, so just do what the doctor says and you'll be fine." Fran felt like screaming at Jack; everything was black or white with him. He had no idea what it was like to have to give up the foods you love. The only problem he ever had was that he would eat enough for three men and then need a little Brioschi. *"Oh well,"* Fran thought, *"I guess I have no choice."* She may have felt like screaming at Jack, but deep down she knew that if *he* had to do it, he would do it. He would make his mind up to lose twenty pounds, and he would lose twenty pounds, no more and no less. Fran really resented his strong constitution at that moment. *"Oh hell, if he can do it, so can I."* It was just wishful thinking on her part; she couldn't understand it, but she kept putting on weight.

*****

Christmas Eve was lovely at Andy and Ethel's; Crocifessa and Peter came downstairs and Ernie and Lena came over, and Joe and Mae came with two and a half year old Shaun and one year old Paul. They all came in carrying beautifully wrapped presents. It was a real nice evening. Christmas day was delightful; Terry and Jackie were so much fun when they came into the living room in the morning. Jack and Fran just watched and laughed. Sometimes Fran cried a little; she was very emotional lately.

Terry was so excited and happy to see the beautiful doll and carriage Santa brought her, plus all the other toys and games. She was quiet in her excitement; her eyes opened wide and her mouth dropped open and she just squealed sweetly. Jackie, on the other hand, was much more loud and verbal in his excitement. He was so cute as he ran at the toys and presents, screaming with excitement. He spotted a large teddy bear, and then a red and yellow dump truck, and a colorful little chair, and a toy box. He went from one toy to another, loudly exclaiming about each one as he grabbed them in his hands and hugged and kissed them. He was nothing like Terry; he was a cute and funny little roughneck. Fran was crazy about them both; she had a sweet and dainty little daughter, and a funny, adorable son who was all boy. Ethel laughed watching Jackie one day. "He's just like his uncle Joe was at his age...a bundle of energy and loud as can be."

They had a nice time opening presents and having breakfast, and then they got dressed and went to the eleven-thirty mass at St. Thomas Aquinas Church on Centre Street. After mass they went to Andy and Ethel's for Christmas dinner. Of course Crocifessa made her 'famous' chicken soup, and her 'famous' baked macaroni and meatballs. Ethel cooked a fabulous roast pork and gravy, and made mashed potatoes and carrots. The Italian bread was real fresh and the wine was delicious. Even Terry had a little bit. It was a wonderful dinner and later Jack said, "Oh my poor stomach; Grandma, where's the Brioschi?" She laughed as she went to get it for him.

Fran noticed that lately when her grandparents came down the stairs they came down much slower than they used to. Of course Peter made sure everyone heard him groaning as he made his way down. "Stamortena! Stamortena!" he'd cry, with heavy emphasis on the "te", so that it came across as "stamor_teee_na!" which translated was his way of saying, "I'm dying, I'm dying." "You don't think it's going to be today, do you Pa?" Andy would ask him. Everyone else would say, "Aw, Papa, come on, have some dinner; you'll feel better." "Oh no," he'd say every time, "No, no mangia, I can't eat.... stamortena." Of course, each and every time, he would sit down at the dinner table and say, "Well, maybe just a little bit.... pica, pica," he would say." and Ethel would load up his plate with food, and he'd eat every last mouthful, and fill up his plate again. It wasn't that no one cared about his feelings; it was that Peter had been saying, "stamortena" for the last forty years. He was healthy as a horse and almost as strong, but as Dr. Desimone said, "He just wants everyone to know that he's an old Italian man now, and it's almost his duty to moan and groan." Andy said, "What about forty years ago, Doctor, he wasn't an old man then." The doctor would laugh. Every time he examined him, Dr. Desimone would say, "Peter, you'll outlive your kids and probably your grandchildren too. You've got a heart like a bull; stop moaning and enjoy your life." Peter's response was always the same..."Stamortena."

Peter would one minute be moaning, "stamortena," and the next he'd be opening a coke bottle with his teeth. Ever since Fran could remember, instead of using a bottle opener, he would actually use his teeth to pry the cap off a bottle. He had all his own teeth, and had never been to a dentist. Only once in his life did he have a toothache; it was a very loose bottom molar, and both Andy and Charlie had told him they would take him to the dentist to have it taken out. Peter would have nothing to do with that, so he took a pair of pliers and pulled it out himself. When he came downstairs with the pliers and his tooth in his hand, everyone groaned. "Pa, what the hell...? You pulled it out yourself?" Andy cried. "Sure, it was loose," he said. "You think I'm going to pay some rich dentist to pull my tooth when I can do it myself?" "Ooh, Papa, that's awful! Fran said. "Good grief!" Ethel said. "That man is impossible, and he says he's dying." All the kids were "grossed out," to say the least, which was exactly the reaction Peter had hoped for. He chuckled to himself as he went back up the stairs.

It was almost 1964, and Peter was in his mid-eighties. He would still walk up Parkton Road, go to Hyde Square, do some shopping, and carry the bundles home in his two leather shopping bags. Then he would climb the stairs to his third floor apartment and he and Crocifessa would put the groceries away. Of course, for the rest of the day he'd be moaning, "stamortena, stamortena." Andy and Ethel would always tell him to wait until they got home and they would take him shopping, but Peter actually loved walking to the stores and shopping, even carrying the bundles home, but, of course, he couldn't let anyone think he could do all that, and not be 'dying' afterwards. He didn't go to the North End anymore unless Andy or Charlie took him, and they worked most Saturdays, so walking up to the stores at Hyde Square became a pleasant shopping experience for him. There was a small variety store, owned by an Italian man that sold the Italian newspaper and Italian bread that he loved, and a few other Italian goodies. He would stop a while and chat with the owner, then move on to the A&P for the rest of his groceries. He found out very quickly that it did no good to try to barter with the store clerks like he would do at the North End. That was something he sorely missed.

Crocifessa was eighty-one in 1963 and did all her own cleaning, vacuuming, sweeping and floor washing. She did laundry, sewing, crocheting, and of course cooking. Like Peter, she had always kept busy; her home and her family were all she lived for. She still went to church every Sunday, and still brought chicken soup to sick relatives and neighbors. If they lived a little distance away, Andy would take her after work. She was a tireless worker, with a kind and generous heart. She was no pushover, though; if she thought something was wrong, she would always speak up and try to do something to right it in her own simple way. To all who knew her, she was the sweetest woman who ever lived.

Fran was thankful that her grandparents were in such good health, and still physically active.

*****

It was cold! Fran felt it so much more this year on the few occasions she went out. In the house she was always hot, but the moment she stepped outside, the cold would go right through her. The baby was due March 1st, and she was retaining fluid so much that her feet and ankles were terribly swollen. Not a single pair of her shoes fit her; she had to wear slippers all the time. Her hands and fingers were awfully swollen also. She tried to get her wedding ring off because she was afraid it would cut off the circulation in that finger, but she couldn't. *"Oh Lord, I'm a complete mess,"* she thought, *"4'11" and weighing over 180 pounds, and I've still got three weeks to go."*

Fran could hardly walk those last few weeks, and couldn't sleep at all at night. She felt like her rib cage was up in her throat, and her bladder was deliberately tormenting her. She had enjoyed every minute of her other two pregnancies, but this one had become almost unbearable. She was certain she'd never make it to March 1st.

Dr. Weiss was certain she'd go early, but February 15th came and went, and still no baby. Dr. Weiss was very concerned about all the weight she had gained. He told her he wouldn't let her go too much longer. He knew the baby was big, and he was expecting a tough delivery, possibly Caesarean. Fran was absolutely miserable, on the verge of tears every moment.

Then on the evening of February 20th, Fran felt the pains starting, and a little while later her water broke. When Jack called Dr. Weiss, he said, "Get her to the hospital right away; I'm a little concerned about this one." Jack called Ethel to watch Terry and Jackie. He told her what the doctor had said. "We'll be right over," Ethel said.

After about twelve hours of painful labor, Fran asked Dr. Weiss, "Is the baby all right?" "Yes Fran, it seems fine, but it is a big baby, and he or she is having a tough time getting born. It's too late to take it Caesarean, so you're really going to have to help me with this one. I can't give you anything yet, because I need you and the baby to work with me. She didn't think she could stand the pain much longer. She muffled moans that were close to screams, and she prayed real hard.

Just before the baby's head crowned, Fran began screaming with the pain. She couldn't believe she was doing this, screaming at the top of her lungs. There was no way to hold it back; it just kept coming out of her. She didn't care any more if anyone heard her outside of the delivery room; she couldn't stop if she tried. She had heard other women scream during delivery, but she never dreamed that she ever would. She just kept screaming. "I'm dying, aren't I?" she said. "Please don't let me die Doctor." "I'm not going to let you die, Fran," he said. "You're going to get through this."

At 10:30 on the evening of February 21, 1964, after twenty-three of the most agonizing hours Fran had ever thought possible to live through, she finally gave birth to a ten pound, one ounce baby boy. He was twenty-two inches long and positively beautiful, with a full head of dark brown hair. Ten-pound newborns weren't that common in 1964, and everyone in the delivery room was exclaiming about it. "He looks two months old," one nurse said, as the doctor laid him along Fran's body. "Look at this," Dr. Weiss said, "He's almost as tall as she is." Fran smiled weakly, and the nurse laughed. "That's a beautiful baby you've got there," the nurse said. Fran was exhausted and could hardly talk; all she wanted to do was go to sleep, but the doctor and the nurses worked on her for what seemed like a very long time.

When Fran woke up, Jack and her parents were sitting by her bed. Dottie was taking care of Terry and Jackie at home. Andy looked like he had been crying, and Ethel looked worried. Jack stood up and kissed her and said, "It was pretty bad, huh?" "Yeah, it was pretty bad," she said, "but thank God, it's all over, and.... have you seen him?" "Yes," they all said together. "Oh, Fran, he's just beautiful." "I can't believe the size of him," Andy said. "When we were down at the nursery, there were people there talking about the ten pound baby." "We just laughed," Jack said, "we knew they were talking about our baby." "How do you feel right now," Ethel asked. "I'm awfully sore," Fran said. "I feel like I've been hit by a truck; everything hurts. I...I thought I was dying, Mom... I'm so glad I didn't." "Me too," Ethel said. "Yeah, me too," Jack said. Andy couldn't say anything.

The very next day Fran asked a nurse if she could weigh herself. "Sure, Honey," she said. "Come on, I'll take you." When Fran got on the scale, she couldn't believe her eyes. She had weighed herself only hours before she had gone to the hospital, and she had weighed over 188 pounds; now, about thirty-six hours later, she weighed 166 pounds. "Oh, my Lord," Fran said, "I lost twenty-two pounds on the delivery table; how fabulous." Three days later she had lost another seven pounds. Each day, even when she was at home, she kept losing weight until it finally tapered off. The last twenty pounds were a lot harder to get off.

Four weeks later, their beautiful baby boy was christened Steven Michael Roche at St. Thomas Aquinas Church. Jack's mom and dad were the Godparents, and this time Fran went also. The priest seemed a little perturbed. When it came time to name the baby, the priest was insistent that Steven, with a V, was not a saint's name. "It has to be Stephen, with a PH," he said. "Well, we want his name to be to be Steven, with a V." Fran was just as insistent; after all, it was their baby, not his. "I really don't think that St. Stephen would mind if we spell it with a V instead of a PH," she said. The priest, Fran was certain, thought she was impudent, but she didn't care; Steven, with a V was what she and Jack wanted. Very reluctantly the priest wrote down Steven Michael Roche.... with a V. Fran was very glad that she had been there, not just to make sure of the spelling of the name, but because she enjoyed watching her baby be baptized. *"Why on earth would they keep mothers from being a part of this?"* She thought. *"They need to smarten up, and change this rule real soon. I cannot abide rules that make no sense, especially when those in control can't give a sensible reason for them."*

Steven was a pleasant, contented baby right from the start. Jackie was absolutely fascinated with his little brother, and Terry just automatically became his second mother. She was very helpful to Fran; in fact there were times when Fran relied a lot on her. Terry was very responsible for a four and a half year old. Jack wasn't home that much, so Terry became Fran's helpmate. Jackie, on the other hand, really *was* just like his uncle Joe at his age, as Ethel said. He was into everything, and screamed and carried on when he didn't get his way. He would take temper tantrums and lie down on the floor and kick and yell. Finally Fran would pick him up, take him to his room and put him down on the floor, and say, "When you can act like a nice little boy you can come out and be with the rest of the family." Of course he'd yell all the more, kick things around, and all in all be very disagreeable until he realized that his mother meant business. When he got it all out of his system, Jackie would come back into the room where Fran was, look up into her face with those big blue eyes, and smile and say, "I be good now, Mommy." He could melt Fran's heart and bring her close to tears, especially if she felt she had been harsh with him. When Jackie wasn't misbehaving, he was very affectionate and loveable. He'd climb up onto Fran's lap, especially when he was tired, and just snuggle with her. He'd say, "I love you, Mommy," and kiss her cheek and her hand. Granted, often times it was shortly after he had been 'banished' to his room for misbehaving. When he wanted to, he could wrap her around his tiny little finger. Jackie was a precious little boy, with almost platinum blond hair, pink and white skin, and the bluest eyes Fran had ever seen. She loved him so much, but he sure did try her patience something awful, *"He's only two and a half and he's into everything. If this is what the "terrible twos" are all about,"* thought Fran, *"I can't even imagine what the "horrible threes" are like. Lord, give me patience!"*

Fran wished so much that Jack would take an interest in helping out with the kids. It wasn't that he didn't love them, she knew he did, but just as with her, his first love was not in the home. She used to think, *"Maybe if we moved into his office he'd pay more attention to us."*

*****

It was early spring and the work on the house in Milton was almost finished. It was a beautiful antique brick house with nine rooms and two and a half baths. It had three fireplaces, and a lovely patio with a flagstone floor. The family room was quite large, with one wall of glass, which opened out to the patio. The large finished basement had a fireplace in the center of the room. The house was set back from the street three hundred and sixty five feet. It was a lovely, private setting, with no other homes to be seen.... only woods.

Fran, Jack, Terry, Jackie and Baby Stevie moved into their new home in early May. They were absolutely thrilled with the house. Terry had her own lovely 'pink' room, and Jackie and Steven shared a nice large 'blue' room. The master bedroom was large and bright, with it's own bathroom. There was also a very nice guest room. Fran thought, *"We must be rich, to have a house as big and as beautiful as this."* She was very pleased with the house, but she couldn't help thinking of all the nights she would probably be alone there with the kids. "I'll be home a lot more from now on, you'll see," Jack said to her one day when she voiced her concern about it. She was sure Jack meant it when he said it, and while the newness was still there, he did spend a little more time at home. Fran couldn't help but feel that his driving ambition, and his desire to get further and further ahead, would soon keep him working at the office as much as he possibly could. But she kept hoping.

Fran fixed the house up beautifully, with nice curtains and draperies, and pictures on the walls, and all the little extras that make a house a home. Everyone raved about the house, especially Jack; he called it the Roche Estate. He was the king of his castle; he had his beautiful, expensive home, his attractive wife, and his three lovely children. He had it all; at least that's the way it looked to outsiders.

Fran's fears became reality; Jack was hardly ever home. He would come home late, and he and Fran would fight about him working so late, and many nights he would sleep in the guest room. Fran didn't really think he was doing anything but working, but the fact remained he was rarely home, and it never seemed to bother him. She was beginning to resent Jack more and more, and disliked everything to do with his work. She knew that his greatest love in life was money, and his own self-importance, not his family. To add to the problem, Fran was becoming very nervous, spending so many nights alone in that beautiful home, in that beautiful, six-acre *private* setting. Every strange noise bothered her, and the terrible darkness outside every window was nerve-wracking. Not another house could be seen, or a light coming from anywhere. "Don't be such a big baby," Jack said to her one night when he came home. "A big baby?" Fran said. "How dare you say that to me? You leave the kids and me alone out here night after night and you have the nerve to call me a baby. You have no idea how I feel, do you Jack? No, of course you don't; how could you? You're not the one alone way back in this isolated place with three babies to care for." Fran knew she was talking to the wall; the bored, 'I'm not interested' look on Jack's face told her so. When he walked into the family room and turned on the eleven o'clock news, she knew it was his way of saying, "Discussion ended!"

The fights between Fran and Jack were happening more and more often, and becoming more and more serious. Fran knew that the children were seeing and hearing too much. She was miserable, and so was Jack, and she knew that Terry must be too. Jack would never change; she knew that now. She didn't know what to do, but it was obvious she had to do something soon. None of them could go on like this for much longer.

*****

On May 10th, 1964 Mae gave birth to a beautiful, healthy, full term baby boy, who weighed seven pounds, eleven ounces. His mother was thrilled, and relieved to be bringing him home from the hospital with her. A few weeks later, he was christened Mark Ernest Vitello, in honor of his great-uncle Ernie Dalton.

Things were getting much worse with Fran and Jack; arguing and hurt feelings were getting to be commonplace. The nasty remarks, the sarcasm, and the shouting were the norm; and disrespect for each other was at an all-time high. Finally, on October 15th Fran and Jack reached a point of no return. That night a lot of things were said and done that convinced Fran that they could not continue in this marriage any longer. For everyone's sake, especially the kids, it was best to separate. Jack had what he had always wanted; he had become a millionaire in five years. Fran knew in her heart he had traded her and the children for that status.

Fran bundled up the kids, took what she needed for the time being for each of them, and called her parents to tell them that she and the kids were coming. Jack tried to stop her; it was a bad scene, but she managed to get the kids into her car. She drove to Ethel and Andy's house, sobbing all the way. She still loved Jack; she hated him, but she still loved him. Terry was frightened and whimpering, and Jackie just kept saying, "Mommy, why are you crying? What's wrong, Mommy? Don't cry, Mommy." Fran could hardly speak to comfort and reassure them. Terry told Jackie to be quiet because Mommy was sad. Fran's heart was breaking, and she didn't know what she could say to help her children. *"My poor babies,"* Fran thought, as she drove, *" I feel like all I do is bring them pain; first the fighting and then my breakdown, and my stay at Bournewood. Then the fighting, and the separation from Jack for five months; and tonight the fighting, and now this. Oh, God, if you're really there, please take care of my kids; help us all to get through this."*

When Fran and the kids arrived at her parents' house, they ran out to the car to help them. Ethel got Steven out of his car seat and carried him into the house, and Andy carried Jackie in, and Terry held her mother's hand. "Are you okay, Mommy?" she asked. "Yes, dear, I'm okay now," Fran said. "Are you okay, Terry?" "Yes, Mommy, I'm okay, too."

The next day Andy and Joe took Fran back to the house in Milton to get some things she needed for her and the children. Fran knew that Jack would not like Andy and Joe coming in with her, but there was nothing she could do about it; she needed their help. Steven was just seven and a half months old, and he needed his crib, diapers, clothes, etc.

"Don't think you can come in here and take anything you want," Jack shouted. "Don't you take anything that belongs to me!" "We don't intend to take anything of yours, Jack," Joe said. "We're just here to get a bed, the baby's crib, some clothes, and some of their toys, that's all." Jack was seething; Fran could see that. She told him that all she wanted was what she and the children needed. She knew he was angry and confused, just like she was, but this had to be done. She just wanted it done peacefully, and as quickly as possible. Jack did everything to stand in their way and make things difficult.

Fran took the guest room furniture and let Jack have their lovely bedroom set; she didn't really want it. She gathered up clothes and toys for the kids. When Joe went downstairs to get the things out of the dryer like Fran asked him to, he took only the kids clothes and a few of Fran's. "What have you got there?" Jack asked Joe. "Nothing of yours Jack," Joe said. "Let me see that!" Jack cried, as he grabbed the laundry basket out of Joe's hands. Everything in the basket went all over the floor. Joe could feel himself getting more and more agitated as he picked up the clothes from the floor. "Jack, why don't you just go do something else, and let us do what we have to do. This isn't pleasant for any of us, but it has to be done. We're *not* going to take anything of yours."

As Joe picked up the laundry basket again, Jack shoved him, almost knocking him over. Joe just saw red, and before he could stop himself, he swung and punched Jack right in the mouth, and knocked him to the floor. Andy came in and said to Jack, "Be smart Jack, and stay down, because if he doesn't knock you down again, I will." Jack swore. Joe was almost hoping that Jack would get up. "You're a real tough guy, aren't you Jack?" Joe said. "Real tough with my sister; come on, get up and let's see how tough you are with someone your own size." Fran came into the room and couldn't believe what she was seeing. "No, stop this," she cried, "please!" She left the room crying. Andy said again, "Just stay down Jack, and we'll be out of here in no time."

When they got back to the house, Andy and Joe unloaded the truck; Fran and Dottie carried in the light things. Fran felt terrible watching Joe and Andy take apart Andy and Ethel's beautiful new dining room set to make the room into a bedroom for her and the kids.

That night, and every night for the next six months, Fran and Terry slept in the double bed, Jackie slept on an army cot, and Steven slept in the crib. There was just room enough left for a chest of drawers. It was very crowded, and Fran had not one minute of privacy, but she was grateful for a place to live under the circumstances. She was grateful for the love and kindness of her parents, for she had no idea what she would have done without them.

CHAPTER FOURTEEN
A Boy From Canton

Fran went to see a lawyer in Boston about getting child support from Jack, as he wasn't sending her any money for the children. She called him several times asking him to do his part for them, but it always ended in an argument. She felt that it wasn't fair that the children's support should fall to *her* father when *their* father was a wealthy man. She had hoped for a peaceful and amiable separation, but it didn't look like that was going to happen.

Her lawyer told her that she and Jack had to be legally separated for six months before filing for divorce. Fran wasn't sure she actually wanted a divorce, but after six months of constant battling with Jack in and out of court for child support, Fran had Jack served with divorce papers. Her lawyer told her that once the court grants a divorce, there's a six-month waiting period for the divorce to be final. Then, and only then, will they be legally divorced.

During this time, Fran's lawyer had a lien put on an apartment complex that Jack was building. Jack was awfully angry, but Fran's lawyer assured her that this was common practice in these types of cases. She told him she wasn't out to destroy Jack; all she wanted was child support. He said, "Now Fran, you need to trust me; I know what I'm doing, and I've got your best interest at heart." Not fully understanding it all, she believed him. It wasn't until a few years later that Fran *really* understood what putting a lien on property entailed. It meant work on the property came to an abrupt halt, and Jack probably lost a good deal of money because of it. She had put her trust in a lawyer who didn't really care about what happened to her, and couldn't care even less for what might happen to Jack. She realized that all he was interested in was getting all *he* could get of Jack's money for his fee.

Fran was sorry he had done that to Jack, but it was long past, and Jack would never have believed that she didn't understand all the repercussions of it when it was going on, and he would never have believed that she felt badly about it. How could he? They argued every time they spoke. Sadly, sarcasm and hatefulness was all they showed to each other.

Shortly after the divorce became final Jack married a girl from Jamaica Plain named Betty, and had two children with her. Their marriage lasted longer than Fran and Jack's did, but eventually they divorced. A few years later Jack had gotten himself in a lot of trouble for overcharging his customers for their insurance. He was arrested, and charged with insurance fraud. The judge sentenced him to three years at Alanwood Prison in Pennsylvania, and ordered him to pay back to his clients what he owed them, which was a large amount of money. Jack served two years of his sentence, and was released on good behavior. Terry and Jackie were very sad hearing about their father on television, and reading about him in the newspaper. Steven was young, and never got to know Jack to feel much about it one way or the other. Fran was also sad over what was going on in Jack's life; she never wanted anything bad to happen to him, though he would probably not have believed that.

Jack did not come to see Terry, Jackie and Steven very often. After he started his second family he would call about once a year or so, and come to see them, usually at Christmas time. Eventually he stopped coming altogether.

*****

When Steven was sixteen months old, Fran noticed a large lump on his groin when she was changing his diaper. She took him to see Dr. Desimone who told her it was a hernia. "A hernia?" Fran said, "but he's only a baby; my *father* has a hernia." "I know," Dr. Desimone said, "but it often happens to babies; it probably developed during his long and difficult birth. "Well, what do we do about it, Dr. D.?" Fran asked, "and is it serious?" "No, not necessarily; often times these types of hernias in babies will just dissolve and go away by themselves," he said, "but for now, you'll have to make a type of truss for him to wear." "You're kidding, right?" asked Fran. "No," he said, "this is what you do; you take a silver dollar and wrap it in a piece of cloth. Wrap it real good to give it some padding; then stitch it securely, and sew on two strips of cloth to tie around him. What you need to do is maintain pressure on the hernia." "Good Lord, Doctor," Fran said, "he's a baby; he wets and poops; the truss will be a mess within a couple of hours of him wearing it." "Hmm, you're right," Dr. Desimone said, "then I suggest you make two or three of them." He smiled, and Fran started laughing. "This is going to be a fiasco," she said. "I just know it."

A week later, even wearing the trusses, the hernia became as big as a golf ball. Fran took Steven to see Dr. Desimone again. "Let's give it a little longer," he said. "Try to keep him from crying too much, as crying pushes the hernia out. I don't like operating on a little one unless it's absolutely necessary."

Fran did everything the doctor told her, but one evening, about two weeks later, Steven was crying in his crib. Not wanting him to cry for long, she picked him up and he continued to cry, which was unusual for him. She laid him down and took his pajamas off and then the diaper. She gasped at what she saw; the lump at his groin was as large as a baseball. Fran thought she was seeing things. She called Dr. Desimone and described the lump to him. "All right, get him to the hospital right away," he said. "I'll meet you there." "Is he going to be operated on?" Fran asked. "It looks that way, Fran," he said. "I'll see you shortly."

Fran was frightened and terribly worried. She knew that many babies have much more serious operations than a hernia, but she also knew that when something happens to *your own* baby, it's the worse thing in the world.

Steven was operated on the next morning; Fran and Ethel waited in the waiting room. She tried not to think about what could happen, but she found herself weeping whenever she would picture Steven on the operating table. She forced herself not to think that way.

Finally the doctor came in. "Everything went well," he said, "and he did great!" A rush of relief came over Fran, and tears burned in her eyes as she felt her mother's arm go around her shoulder. "He'll be in the recovery room for a while," the doctor said, "but he really shouldn't see you when he comes out, Fran." "What? Why not?" Fran asked. "I'm his mother." "Exactly," said the doctor. "We don't want him to get excited or cry. As long as he's still sleeping you can see him when he comes out, but please, if he starts to wake, don't let him see you. It's for his own good, Fran, okay?" "Okay, I guess I understand," she said reluctantly.

When Steven was wheeled into his room in the Nursery, he was still sound asleep. Fran cried when she saw his little, chubby body lying there in the crib; there was some dried blood on his side. "My poor little Stevie," she cried, as she carefully and gently held his hand so he wouldn't wake up. "Oh, Mom," she said, "Why do babies have to go through such awful things? I've never broken a bone, or even had stitches, and here's my sweet little baby boy having been through major surgery." "I know Dear," her mother said. "It's very sad when it's little children. But thank God he's okay Fran; can you imagine what your two grandmothers had to endure?" "Oh Mom," she said, "how did they ever get through those tragedies?" "Their faith in God is what got them through," Ethel said. "Well, I know Grandma always had a strong faith," Fran said, " but I thought Nana wasn't at all religious." "She wasn't really," Ethel said, "but my father certainly was. I believe *his* faith is what got them through those times."

Fran and Ethel stayed with Steven a long time until he started to stir. Then Fran very gently kissed his little forehead, and she and her mother slipped out the door, just as a nurse was coming in to check on him. She smiled at Fran and said, "He'll be fine, Mrs. Roche." Fran thanked her, and felt a little better about leaving.

"Isn't it strange Mom," Fran said, as they drove home, "Grandma has always had such a strong faith in God, and Papa hasn't, and Grandfather Dalton had such a strong faith in God and Nana didn't." "Yes," Ethel said, "but God honors those who are faithful to Him, and others benefit from that." "Yeah, I guess so," Fran said. "Boy, It must be comforting to have that kind of faith." "Well," Ethel said,

"Grandma's been praying for you for many years to know the Lord the way she does; I don't doubt that you will one day."

On the third day after the operation, when Fran went in to see Steven in the morning, there was, what was called, a 'croup tent' all around his crib with a vaporizer pumping medicated steam into the tent. Fran was familiar with it, as Steven had had bronchial problems before, but it frightened her nonetheless. Steven had already had a couple of bad colds in his young life, and they quickly settled in his chest, and he had a terrible time trying to breathe. Dr. Desimone called it asthmatic bronchitis.

The first time it happened Dr. D. came to the house, examined Steven and called the local drug store and ordered a vaporizer and a small bottle of Tincture of Benzoine Compound. Andy went to the drug store to pick them up. Dr. Desimone filled the vaporizer with water, put a little of the TBC in the place provided and turned the vaporizer on. He put it on a chair beside the crib, away from Steven's reach, and wrapped a bedspread around the chair and the crib, tying the four corners of the spread to the chair and the corners of the crib, making a kind of tent. It looked ridiculous, but the next morning his breathing was much better.

Steven ended up being in the hospital longer than expected because of an infection that set in. That, and the croup kept him there for twelve days. Fran had been terribly worried; first the surgery, then the croup, and then an infection. She just wanted him home with her.

When it was time to take him home, the nurses all came in his room to say good-bye. Most of them kissed him and hugged him, and all of them said he was, without a doubt, the most pleasant baby who ever stayed there. "He has the sweetest disposition of any baby I've ever seen," one of the nurses said. "No matter what you're doing to him, he never gets upset, and very rarely cries. He's a happy little boy, always smiling; we're going to miss him."

The whole family and all their friends had been very concerned about Steven the whole time he was in the hospital. Crocifessa had been lighting candles and praying constantly for him. Margaret and Charlie, and Margie and cousin Fran called many times to see how he was doing. Ernie and Lena were very concerned, too, as was Sarah and Pat.

Terry and Jackie were so happy to see Steven when Fran brought him home; Jackie kept kissing him on the cheek, and Terry kept picking him up and hugging him. Dottie kept hugging and kissing him, too. Crocifessa and Peter were relieved to see their little great-grandson home and well again. Steven smiled at everyone and hugged them, and immediately started running and playing with Jackie as if nothing had changed.

Crocifessa hugged Fran and kissed her cheeks; there were tears in her eyes, and she said, "mia bella bambin(a),"*(or was it 'o')?* Fran wasn't sure if her grandmother was referring to her or to Steven. She hugged Crocifessa and kissed her. "I love you so much, Grandma," she said. "Thank you for praying for Steven." "I pray for you, too, Franzie," she said, "every day." "I know, Grandma," Fran said. She felt an overwhelming need to hug her grandmother again, so she did. Crocifessa was the only adult Fran knew who was shorter than she was, and it felt good to hold her. Fran wanted to protect her grandmother always, as Crocifessa had always protected her.

*****

Terry was enrolled in Blessed Sacrament School, and loving every minute of it. Fran knew she'd be an excellent student; she was eager to know everything, and quick to learn. When Terry wasn't at school she was a big help to Fran at home; she was the epitome of 'mother's little helper'. She was very good with Jackie and 'Stevie'...a bit bossy, which caused her and Jackie to come to blows occasionally, but nonetheless, a terrific little helper. Fran was very proud of her, and enjoyed her company.

Jackie was an adorable child, but into everything. Fran got the feeling that her friends groaned when they found out that she'd be visiting with the kids. They knew it was time to rearrange the furni ture, put up barricades, and put away everything that was near and dear to them.

When Jackie entered a friend's house, his head would be jerking left and right; his eyes practically jumping out of his head as he looked around to see what might be fun to wreck. Of course he never *meant* to wreck anything, but he usually managed to. Fran couldn't take her eyes off him for more than a second. When Terry was with them, she would watch over Jackie like a mother hen with her chick. She was only two years and three months older than him, but those two years and three months made a world of difference; that and the fact that Terry believed she was put here to be Jackie's mentor...whether he liked it or not. "No! Put that down! No, no!" was all Fran would hear from the other room. "Don't touch! STOP!" Jackie would reluctantly obey Terry for the moment, but he'd be off straight away in another direction with Terry in hot pursuit. She was a gem to Fran when Fran wanted to have a cup of coffee and a few peaceful moments to chat with a friend. Her cousin Fran always had such beautiful things in her lovely home in Wellesley Hills. She soon learned that to have her younger cousin's company meant dashing about, making things disappear before Fran arrived with the kids. Poor Jackie; he really was a sweet little house wrecker.

Jackie's 'saving grace' was that he was a very affectionate child. He could just sweep a person off his or her feet when he'd look up at them with those beautiful blue eyes and reach up with both arms, and say, "I wanna hug you." He wasn't looking for anything; he really did just want to hug them. Fran felt that she was one minute hugging and kissing Jackie, and the next minute scolding and/or spanking him. He wouldn't be over a punishment for more than five minutes (unless he was asleep) before Fran was scolding him again. Well, thank goodness for those five minutes; at least they got a few hugs and kisses and laughing in during that small reprieve. Jackie was a bundle of energy and when he wasn't being scolded, he and his mother had a lot of fun together. Jackie *loved* the times alone with his mother, when Terry was at school, and Steven was napping... and Fran *cherished* them.

*****

On July 1st, 1966 Mae gave birth to a beautiful, full term, healthy baby boy. A few weeks later he was christened Neil Robert Vitello.

On August 29th the unthinkable happened....baby Neil died in his sleep. The doctors called it Sudden Infant Death Syndrome (SIDS). Needless to say, Joe and Mae were devastated. The whole family hurt for them, but there was little anyone could do. Besides the God they loved so much, their greatest source of help and comfort came from Mae's sister Helen who was Mae's dearest and closest friend. Her strength and her love did so much to help Mae and Joe through this terrible time.

*****

Fran and the children moved into the first floor apartment at 32 Parkton Road, right next door to her parents. It became available, so Fran took it. She wasn't sure how it would work out, because Jack never sent the child support when he was supposed to, and he never sent the amount he was supposed to. But it was time to give her parents, and Dottie a break. As much as they loved her and the kids, it had been difficult for everyone.

Fran was pleased with the apartment; it was identical to her parents'. Andy did some painting, and Ethel and Dottie, and even Crocifessa helped her clean and decorate it the way she wanted it. What a thrill! She had her own bedroom, Terry had her own room, which was designed to be a dining room, and Jackie and Steven shared a room. Everyone was excited.

During the fourteen months that Fran and the kids lived at 32 Parkton Road, Fran had some real bad setbacks. A few things happened that caused Fran to believe that she might end up back in Bournewood Hospital. Now and then she would feel herself slipping into depression, and it scared her terribly. Rather than staying in bed and blotting out the world, she would get up, turn on happy-sounding music, or tear into some household chore she'd been putting off. Sometimes she'd hop in the car and go shopping, or call a friend and meet her for lunch. She would do anything she could to get through those days. *"I'm not going to get sick again, and that's all there is to it!"* Somehow she got through them, and although she didn't realize it then, she was, little by little, becoming stronger and stronger. She tried praying, but she began to believe that God simply wasn't listening. She decided that she needed to be tough, as *she* was the *only one* she could rely on. She became absolutely determined that no one would ever hurt her again.

Fran decided she needed friends who laughed easily; she didn't want to be around people who were depressed or always feeling sorry for themselves. Rosemarie and Mary P. were always quick to laugh; she enjoyed both of them so much. Mary was still single, so she came over to see Fran often. She'd come right after work on evenings when she didn't have a date, and stay for supper, and on weekends many times she'd stay over. She'd sleep in Terry's bed and Terry would sleep with her mother.

Fran gave Mary a key to the apartment, and many nights when Mary had a date, rather than letting her father know how late she was getting home, she'd use her key at one or two o'clock in the morning, at Fran's house. Fran would wake up in the morning and see Mary in Terry's bed, sleeping like a baby, and Terry sound asleep too, completely unaware that she was there.

Mary was so much fun to Fran and the kids. She was a good friend, and was always right there if Fran needed her. She was a very attractive girl, albeit a rugged one. She never lost the thought that it was her job to protect Fran. She loved Terry, Jackie and Steven, but she would speak up if she saw any one of them misbehaving, or not moving right away when Fran spoke to them. Fran always said that Mary was just like her father in that respect. Somehow the kids knew her bark was stronger than her bite, but boy, did they move when she spoke. They were crazy about Mary; she always made them laugh.

Mary worked at Stride-Rite Shoes and got Terry, Jackie and Steven's shoes there. She'd outline their feet on a piece of cardboard and pick out the shoes right for them. Fran knew Mary was only charging her half of what she should be paying, so Fran tried to make up for it by making meals Mary loved, or a special dessert when she knew she was coming over. She was a good friend to all of them.

The whole family loved Mary, and Mary loved them like they were her own family. "You're so lucky, Fran," Mary said many times, "to have grandparents living with you. I never knew my grandparents;

319

they died in Italy before I was even born." Mary shared many meals with the family, and Fran ate many a meal at the Pinciaro house, too. Mrs. Pinciaro was a fabulous cook, and loved to cook for others. Fran believed that it was a strong Italian trait, loving to cook, and sharing what you cooked with other people. Her grandmother taught her that.

Fran and Mary both had a popular hairstyle in the fifties and sixties called a DA (crudely referred to as a 'Duck's Ass'), so Andy would cut their hair. No hairdresser could have done a better job; Andy had the style down to a tee. Mary would occasionally come over and say to Andy, "Hey Mr. V., any chance of getting a haircut tonight? I've got a big date tomorrow night with a real cute guy, and I want to look my best." Andy was always good about it; he'd usually say something like, "Oh Geez, Mary's got a heavy date tomorrow night. Fran, go get my tools; you never know, this could be the one." Mary would laugh and say, "Boy, I hope you're right, Mr. V." She appreciated the haircuts, and would always tell him so.

*****

Marilyn Antosca lived with her parents on Parker Street before moving to 28 Parkton Road. She married John Molino and they moved into the third floor apartment in her parents' house. She was three years older than Fran, so they never hung around together when they were kids on Parker Street, but now that they were both mothers of three children, they realized they had a lot in common. Marilyn's parents were very similar to Fran's parents, and their children's ages were almost the same. Little Johnny and Terry were in the same class together at school.

Many nights Fran would be reading until very late, or she'd be watching Johnny Carson on the Tonight Show. She would never miss the Tonight Show if she could help it. Johnny Carson was her all-time, absolute, favorite television personality. Marilyn would look out her window, see Fran's light on and call her on the phone. "You got any coffee on the stove?" She'd ask. "As a matter of fact I do," Fran would usually say. "Good, I'll be right there." Marilyn would show up at the door in her bathrobe and slippers, and she and

Fran would watch Johnny, drink coffee and talk for hours. She was a lot of fun, and Fran enjoyed her company immensely.

*****

An odd, but very nice man in his fifties lived on the second floor, just above Fran. His name was Frank Daley; he was a quiet man and minded his own business. Fran met him outside one day, and said, "Hello Mr. Daley," to him; he was polite and pleasant, but it was obvious he didn't care to chit-chat. He nervously said, "Hello, nice to see you," and he was on his way up the stairs. He was not a well man, Fran came to find out; he had a bad heart, and was very hard of hearing, which was probably a blessing with Jackie Roche living under him. Jackie could be extremely loud when he wanted to be. Frank wore two hearing aids, and even at that could barely make out what someone was saying. He wanted his privacy, and that was fine with Fran, as she coveted her own. He once patted Jackie on the head, and smiled very briefly at him, and then he was gone. Jackie was surprised because Frank barely looked at him or Terry when he saw them outside. Fran thought, *"Hmm, maybe he can hear better than I think he can, and what he'd really like to do is pound Jackie's head, not pat it."*

One day Fran was next door in her parents' apartment. Her washing machine was not working, so she was doing her wash in her mother's machine. All of a sudden Marilyn came running in. "Wait 'til you see the dress I bought for my cousin's wedding. You've got to tell me the truth about how it looks." "Okay," Fran said, "I will; let's see it." Marilyn pulled a hot pink cocktail dress out of the bag and quickly pulled off her shirt over her head and slipped out of her jeans. She was standing in the kitchen, right in front of the windows, in only her bra and panties. "Marilyn!" Fran cried, "Frank Daley can see you!" Marilyn looked at the window, grabbed her shirt to cover herself, then threw it down and simply said, "Oh that's okay, he's deaf!" As she tried on the dress Fran was killing herself laughing. "Yeah, he may be deaf," she said, "but he's also got a bad heart; you probably just pushed the poor man over the edge." They both laughed. Fran liked the dress, and told Marilyn so.

321

The day of the wedding Marilyn flew into Fran's apartment...
"Tell me the truth, do I look all right?" Marilyn was attractive, but
with three kids and a home to take care of, she was usually in jeans
and a sweatshirt; she rarely wore makeup or changed her hairstyle.
Fran was actually stunned; Marilyn was positively radiant. She had
an olive complexion and very dark hair and dark eyes; her makeup
and her jewelry were perfect. She had a nice figure, which sweat-
shirts didn't show off. The hot pink dress, with her coloring was
breathtaking. Fran said, "Johnny *is* going to this wedding with you,
isn't he?" Marilyn said, "Yeah, of course; why?" "Because he's
going to have his hands full fighting off the guys that are going
to come on to you," Fran said. "Oh, get out; no one is going to
make a pass at me," Marilyn said. "Take my word for it, Marilyn,
you look beautiful." "Wow!" Marilyn said, "You have just made my
day! Thanks, Fran." "You're welcome," Fran said. "If I get home
early enough," Marilyn said, "I'll come over for coffee." "Okay,"
Fran said, "have fun!" She *did* come over later, in her bathrobe and
slippers. They drank coffee and talked for hours about the wedding,
and many other things too. And they laughed; they laughed a lot.
Marilyn was 'just what the doctor ordered'; she was fun and interesting, and filled a void in Fran's life. Between Mary and Marilyn,
Fran spent a good deal of time laughing. It was just what she needed,
at a time when she needed it the most.

*****

Fran dated very little at this time in her life, but once in a while
she'd go out to a nightclub, or to a party with Mary. Mary had some
interesting and fun friends. One night, a couple of days before
Halloween, Fran went with Mary to a costume party that was being
held at a function hall in Boston. Fran went as a vampire, and Mary
was dressed as a sexy nurse.

At the party people were dressed in all kinds of costumes from
Superman to a giant pumpkin. "Wait 'til you meet Yogi," Mary said.
"Who's Yogi?" Fran asked. "He's just about the wackiest, craziest,
funniest guy you'll ever meet," she said. "I heard he was going to be
at this party; I hope he comes."

Fran was enjoying herself; she danced with a few guys, and talked with Mary and her friends. As they were having some refreshments, Fran heard a noise, and someone yelled, "Oh my gosh, look at that!" Fran looked up, and at the top of the staircase stood a large 'gorilla', banging his chest and roaring loudly. All of a sudden he leaped over the railing, grabbed onto the very large chandelier that hung from the ceiling, and swung down onto the stage where the musicians were. He started hugging the musicians, banged on the drums for a moment, and then leaped off the stage onto the floor. Fran assumed he had been hired as part of the entertainment. Everyone was laughing and clapping, including herself. The gorilla bowed to all four corners of the room and then jumped over to where Fran and Mary and her friends were. "Say hello to Yogi, Fran," Mary said. "Hello Yogi," Fran said, laughing and still somewhat shocked. "That was a great entrance for a party." Yogi pretended surprise. "Party? What party? Is this a party?" "*Wow!*" Fran thought. "*These things are only supposed to happen in the movies, not in real life. How did he know that chandelier would hold him? I can't believe the management hasn't shown up by now to throw him out, but man, that was great!*" Yogi was outrageous, to say the least, but Mary was right; he *was* the wackiest, craziest, funniest man Fran had ever met.

Fran and Mary went to a club one night to listen to a local band play. Mary and her friend Ann knew two of the guys in the band. While they were there, in walked Yogi. Everyone seemed to know him, and he said hi to everyone. Yogi was the kind of guy who, in or out of a costume, drew all eyes to himself. He was not especially good looking, but there was a presence about him, which was hard to ignore. "Hey there, Francie girl," he said as he came over to their table; nice to see you again." "You too, Yogi," Fran said. "*I wonder how he knew I used to be called Francie,*" she thought. But when he called Ann 'Annie', and Frank 'Frankie', she figured he probably adds an 'ie' to *everyone's* name.

After the show they called a cab to drive them all home. Mary, Frank and Ann sat in the back seat and Fran and Yogi were in the front seat with the driver. Yogi had his arm on the back of the seat behind Fran's head, and at just the right moment he reached over and started massaging the cab driver's neck and playing with his ear. Fran, Mary, Ann and Frank were laughing so hard that the cab driver finally realized that Yogi was just a real character, and not someone he needed to deal with. He grinned, and in the next moment, whether he wanted to or not, he was laughing. "Oh Yogi, leave the poor guy alone," everyone in the back seat was saying. Yogi stopped his antics and said to the driver, "Hey, You're all right, man; you're a good sport."

Yogi said that he needed to get some cigarettes, and would the cab driver stop somewhere so he could get them. The cab driver said he didn't think anything was open at midnight, but he could stop at the Hayes and Bickford restaurant up the street. Yogi said that was fine, and when the cab driver pulled over in front of Hayes and Bickford's, Yogi got out and went inside. While they waited for Yogi to get his cigarettes, Fran and the others chatted with the cab driver, who proved to be a real nice man, working a second job driving a cab nights to support his wife and three kids. Lovingly, and with pride he showed them a picture of his family.

After a while they were all saying, "What's taking Yogi so long to get a pack of cigarettes? Doesn't he know the meter's running?" A couple of minutes more went by when all of a sudden the cab driver started chuckling. "Look at your friend," he said. They all looked over, and sitting at a table right in front of the window of Hayes and Bickford's was Yogi, eating scrambled eggs, bacon, home fries and toast, drinking a cup of coffee and reading a newspaper. Fran, Mary, Ann, Frank, and the cab driver were doubled over with laughter. "Where'd you find this guy?" the cab driver said, as he shook his head laughing. "I'll tell you the truth, this is the best night I've ever had driving this cab, and *that guy* is the funniest guy I've ever seen; he should be on television."

Yogi finally came out, carrying his toast and his newspaper and got in the cab like nothing was out of the ordinary. "Okay," he said, "you guys ready to go?" They all burst out laughing again, and told Yogi, "You're paying for the extra time on the meter." "Oh fine, if you want to be that way about it," he said, and continued eating his toast. They couldn't stop laughing. The cab driver needed to compose himself before taking off again. Yogi just looked at them, shrugged his shoulders and continued eating his toast, which of course, made them laugh all the more.

It was a fun night; the cab driver said he had never met anyone who could get away with the things Yogi could. He was outrageous, all right, and Mary was right...he was *definitely* the wackiest, funniest, craziest guy Fran had ever met. She never saw Yogi again, but whenever she thought about those two nights, she would laugh all over again.

*****

Mr. and Mrs. Norton, who lived in the second floor apartment in Andy and Ethel's house, gave their notice to Andy. They were moving in with their son and his family. Andy asked Fran if she and the kids would like to have the Norton's apartment. "Are you kidding?" Fran said. "I can't think of anything that would make me happier than to live between Grandma and Papa and you and Mom. Oh, thanks Dad, I can hardly wait." Fran was thrilled.

When Mr. and Mrs. Norton moved out, Fran and Ethel, and Dottie and Crocifessa looked over the apartment to see what needed to be done to make it right for Fran and the kids. Andy did some painting and Fran and the ladies hung curtains and pictures, and did all the 'cute' things that make a house a home. Crocifessa and Ethel cooked a lovely dinner to celebrate move-in day. Crocifessa was getting old and she was tired when they were finished. But to her, it was worth it, as cooking a nice meal for her family was the thing she loved most to do. She and Peter, and Ethel and Andy and Dottie sat in Fran's 'new' kitchen with her and Terry, Jackie and Steven, and enjoyed their wonderful meal of pasta, sausages, salad, and Italian bread. After dinner they relaxed with a cup of coffee. Fran was very happy; she felt safe, <u>really</u> safe, for the first time in a long time.

One night, Alfred Hitchcock's movie "The Birds" was going to be shown on television. Fran made popcorn and had Cokes for her and Dottie upstairs, and Ethel and Andy would be watching it downstairs. During commercials Fran or Dottie would call downstairs to see if their Mom and Dad were as frightened as *they* were. A couple of times they ran downstairs. "Did you see that? Wasn't that horrible? they would ask Andy and Ethel. It was a scary movie; that was for sure. Andy knew that the moment the movie ended, Fran and Dottie would come running downstairs, exclaiming over the scariness and the goriness of the movie, so the very second it ended Andy ran upstairs, and started scratching hard on Fran's door with his fingernails, and making weird kinds of 'bird' sounds. Fran and Dottie started laughing, knowing what he was doing. Fran opened the door, and immediately Andy tossed a frozen chicken into the room, all the while making a loud kind of 'caw...caw...caw' sound. Fran and Dottie were doubled over with laughter. "A frozen chicken?" Fran asked, almost choking. Andy was trying not to laugh. "It was the closest thing to a bird I could find," he said. They could hear Ethel in the hall downstairs. "And you think Fran and I are weird?" Dottie said. "Hey, Mom!" Fran called. "Yes?" she answered. "You talk to him, Mom, no decent person would." Andy was guffawing. They were all laughing by this time. Fran loved her father's humor. Andy was not what one would call a real funny guy, but he could be positively hilarious when he wanted to be. Ethel, on the other hand, truly appreciated good, clean humor, and laughed often, but she was not a 'funny' person, per se. Unlike Andy, she would never *try* to make people laugh. She was simple, quiet, and sweet, and everyone loved her that way.

*****

Dottie graduated from Blessed Sacrament High School in 1965, and attended Chandler School for Women for a year. She started working at Boston University in the George Sherman Union in 1966 at the height of the Vietnam War, when all one saw around college campuses were signs saying, 'MAKE LOVE NOT WAR', and 'HELL NO, WE WON'T GO'! There was even a sit-in in Dottie's office a few times, with students sitting all over the floor. Not much work got done on those days, that's for sure.

*****

Joe and Mae carried on with three little boys at home to care for. Then on August 21st, 1967 Mae gave birth to another beautiful baby boy; he weighed eight pounds, nine ounces. Two weeks later he was christened Peter Vincent Vitello.

*****

Dottie came to like her job a lot; she loved being in a college atmosphere, and seeing the students every day. She also kind of liked the guy who worked in the bookstore there.

"He's cute, and seems real nice," she told Fran one day. "Have you spoken to him much?" Fran asked. "No," Dottie said. "He's always busy, and I'm not good at starting up a conversation with a guy I don't know." "Do you know his name Dottie?" "Well, I heard one of the other clerks call him John," she said, "but that's all I know about him." "Well, I'm sure that one of these days you'll find a reason to speak to him," Fran said. "Courage! My dear sister... Courage!"

One Saturday Fran asked Dottie if she wanted to come to the library with her, as she wanted to see if she could find a book on the African Bushmen. Fran had read a little about the Bushmen, and found them intriguing. She had always thought that she would go to college and one day become an anthropologist; different peoples and cultures fascinated her. But in 1956 it was kind of understood that if anyone was going to go to college it would be Joe. Also, by the time high school was over, Fran's mind was more on guys and dating, and not on college or anthropology. Soon marriage and children drove the thought of it far, far away, but the interest in other cultures was always there.

"I've got a good idea," Dottie said. "Let's go over to the bookstore at B.U. Maybe we'll see that fellow John there. I'll bet there's all kinds of books on the African Bushmen there, too." "Okay," Fran said, "let's do it; I've been wanting to see that bookstore ever since you started working at B.U. I'll ask Mom if she minds watching the kids for a few hours."

When Fran and Dottie walked into the bookstore at Boston University Dottie said, "That's John over there." She kind of cocked her head in his direction. Fran looked over and saw a young man in a blue smock waiting on a customer. When he was finished Fran walked over to him and said, "Excuse me; could you give me some help?" "Sure," he said, "What can I help you with?" Fran told him what she was looking for, and he took her and Dottie over to the section on primitive cultures. Fran started talking to him about the African Bushmen and other peoples. After awhile she introduced herself and Dottie to him, and he told them his name was John Murphy. He said he was born and brought up in Canton, and he was taking courses nights at B.U. and working at the bookstore. Soon the three of them were talking like they had known each other for years.

It didn't take long to see that John had a terrific sense of humor; he had Fran and Dottie in stitches most of the time that they were there. Humor seemed to come so natural to him, "*This guy is great,*" Fran thought. "*Dottie's so shy, and even though John is funny, I can tell he's kind of shy, too. I've got to do something to get these two together, or I can tell it's going to end here.*"

After a while John said that his shift was over, and he hated to say goodbye, but he had to catch the train back to Canton. Before Fran could think about it, she said, "We'll give you a ride home." He kind of laughed and said, "No, that's okay, it's way out of your way; thanks anyway." "No, I'm serious," Fran said. "Our mother is taking care of my kids, and I'm enjoying my time off. Dottie and I were just going to go for a ride when we left here and get an ice cream somewhere, so we'd be very happy to drive you back to Canton, wouldn't we Dottie?" Poor Dottie was stunned. "Uh, yes, sure, that would be fun," was all she could say. John kind of laughed again and said, "Okay, let's go; the ice cream's on me."

While John got his jacket, Fran paid for the books she got. She bought "The Flame Trees of Thika," and two books on the African Bushmen. She was very pleased with her purchases.

John bought them ice cream at the Neponset Valley Farm Restaurant in Norwood, and gave them a grand tour of Canton. Fran invited him to dinner the following week on Sunday, and she and Dottie were both shocked when he said he would come. Dottie was pleased that the ice was broken, and Fran had high hopes for John and her sister.

After a nice dinner on Sunday, Fran pretended to have forgotten to get ice cream to go with the apple pie for dessert. "John, why don't you and Dottie run up to the store and get some ice cream while I clean up a little and make some coffee, okay?" "Sure," John said, "Dottie, you'll have to show me where we're going; I don't know Jamaica Plain very well." Fran hoped that he would ask Dottie out on a date while they were out, but when they came back, Fran gave Dottie a questioning look and Dottie just shook her head, no.

When they were having dessert Fran asked him what made him accept their invitation to dinner. "Well," he said, "when you and Dottie drove me home from B.U. last week, I thought I was being abducted by a couple of crazy sisters from Jamaica Plain." Fran and Dottie laughed, and Fran said, "Okay, so then what?" "Well, I had a blast with the two of you that day so I thought, "What the heck, I've got no plans for Sunday; this could be a lot of laughs. 'Course, I had no idea what a good cook you were, so this was a bonus." "Thank you," Fran said, "we certainly *have* had a lot of laughs; I'm glad you came, John." Dottie nodded. "You've had us in stitches all afternoon, John," she said. "You're a riot."

Fran thought about all the guys with great senses of humor she had known, and there were many, Larry, Barry, Ken and Jack, to name just a few. There was also Yogi, but he was in a weird category all his own. *"I think John is the funniest guy I have ever known,"* she thought. *"He's just perfect for Dottie."*

John came over to the house to see Dottie and Fran a couple of times more after that Sunday. Fran couldn't understand why he hadn't asked Dottie out yet; they got along so well and seemed to have so much fun together. They laughed all the time and had pillow fights with Fran's throw pillows on the sofa. Fran was certain that he was just shy, and that soon he and Dottie would be dating. "Just be patient," she told Dottie. "I know he likes you, so he's definitely going to ask you out soon." "You know something, Fran?" Dottie said. "What's that?" Fran asked. "I think you want this more than I do. I mean, I'm not sure I really like John that way; I mean I just think he's the funniest guy in the world, and I do enjoy his company, but I honestly don't think I'd be horribly disappointed if we never actually dated. "Really, Dottie?" Fran asked. "I just think he's terrific, and I'd love to see you two get together." "I know you would," Dottie said, "but, seriously, Fran, I think it would be even better if we could just be friends. I really don't want you to try to get us together anymore. I appreciate what you've been doing, but let's just leave it the way it is, okay?" "Okay, I guess so," Fran said. "I am a little disappointed, though." "I know," Dottie said.

John's visits became less frequent, and soon stopped altogether. Fran and Dottie missed him at first, but not long afterward, Mae asked Dottie if she would like to write to a fellow in the Air Force who was stationed in Vietnam. His name was Chet Malcolm, and Mae knew his mother. Dottie thought it might be interesting to write to someone in Vietnam, so Mae gave her his APO address and Dottie wrote to him.

"Dottie, have you heard from that fellow in Vietnam?" Fran asked one day. "Oh no," she answered. "I never expected him to write to me; I just did it because Mae said he might appreciate letters from people back home. "He probably thinks I'm weird, writing to someone I don't even know." "Oh, I doubt that," Fran said, "I read that people all over the country are writing to our soldiers in Vietnam; they love getting letters from people in the states. You're going to write to him again, aren't you?" "Why? I did my part for the war effort," Dottie said chuckling; I'm a very patriotic person." Fran laughed, "You're impossible, honestly."

"Thank God it's Friday," Dottie said as she walked in the house after work. "Rough day?" Andy asked. "There was another sit-in in my office today Dad; there must have been sixty or sixty five kids sitting all over the floor. The first sit-in was kind of exciting, but now it's getting to be a real pain. We can't get anything done."

The phone rang and Ethel answered it. "May I please speak with Dottie Vitello?" the voice on the other end said. "Yes, who is this calling?" Ethel asked. "My name is Chet Malcolm," he answered. "Just a minute," Ethel said. "Dottie, it's for you." Dottie was surprised, to say the least. Chet asked if they could meet, and have dinner together some evening, so they decided on Monday after work. She gave him directions to the George Sherman Union, and they made plans to meet at five o'clock. She went upstairs and told Fran that Chet Malcolm had called and they were going to go out Monday after work. "Oh, that's nice Dottie," Fran said. "Well, Little Sis, I hope he turns out to be a really great guy, and the two of you fall madly in love, get married, have lots of little Malcolms, and live happily ever after." "Well, the perfect fairy tale," Dottie said, "but a bit unrealistic, wouldn't you say?"

It was about three thirty Monday afternoon when Dottie noticed someone peering in the window of her office. She got up from her desk and opened the door, and asked the young fellow if she could help him. She assumed he was just another student needing some assistance. "I'm looking for Dottie Vitello," he said. "I'm Dottie," she said. Suddenly he thrust out his hand, smiled a big toothy smile, and said, "Hi! I'm Chet Malcolm."

Dottie liked Chet right from the start, and it was obvious that he felt the same about her. They dated for about three months when he asked her to marry him. They were crazy about each other, and she accepted. He bought her a lovely diamond engagement ring, and they decided on an October wedding. Dottie asked Fran to be her matron-of-honor, and her friend Gerry to be her maid-of-honor. She asked another friend, Ellen Sullivan to be a bridesmaid, and Terry to be a junior bridesmaid. Needless to say, Terry, at nine years old, was positively thrilled.

****

Terry, Steven and Jackie 1966

CHAPTER FIFTEEN
Heaven Is All The More Wonderful Now

"Franzie, come uppa stairs," Crocifessa called down, "I want you to see how nice Joey painted my pantry." "Okay, Grandma," Fran yelled, "I'll be right up." Terry and Jackie were in school, so Fran took Steven's hand and said, "Come on, Honey, let's go upstairs to see Grandma and Papa." "Yeay! Let's go upstairs, Mommy." He loved going upstairs, because he knew his Grandma would have something good for him to eat. She always kept candy on hand for the children. Fran would smile when she'd offer candy to the kids; it always brought back pleasant memories of the store they owned when she was young, where she could always be sure her Grandma would give her a piece of candy, with the ever present warning, "No tolla Papa."

Fran and Steven went upstairs, and Crocifessa rushed them right in to see her pantry that Joe had painted the day before. "It looks beautiful, Grandma," Fran said. Crocifessa smiled as Steven said the same thing. She bent down and kissed Steven on the forehead as he was enjoying the Hershey's Kisses she gave him.

As Fran and her grandmother were leaving the pantry, Crocifessa didn't notice Steven in her path. Suddenly, before Fran realized what was happening, Crocifessa stumbled over Steven and fell. She screamed as she hit the floor, and Fran knew she was really hurt. She rushed to Crocifessa as Peter came running into the kitchen. He panicked when he saw his wife of sixty-five years on the floor. He kept trying to pick her up but Crocifessa was making a kind of wringing motion with her hands, and crying. In Italian she was trying to tell him that she thought she had broken her hip. "No! No, Papa!" Fran cried. "Don't touch her; her hip may be broken." Fran ran to the phone and called the police for an ambulance. She then called Andy and Ethel at the Graham shop. Steven was terribly scared, crying hysterically. He ran out of the house and ran downstairs. He kept calling to Fran, "Mommy, come down here! Please come down here." He didn't understand what was happening. Fran felt bad that she couldn't go downstairs and comfort her little boy, but of course she couldn't leave her grandmother. She didn't realize that Steven thought it was his fault that his Grandma fell. All the while Peter was crying and Crocifessa was moaning in pain.

Andy and Ethel arrived home just as Crocifessa was being carried down the stairs on a stretcher. Andy was very close to tears, and Ethel was trying to calm Peter. "Fran, call Charlie, will you?" Andy called as they were leaving. "Okay Dad, I will," she answered. Peter went with them to the hospital, while Fran waited at home for news of her grandmother's condition, as she tried to comfort and reassure Steven.

"It's broken!" Fran heard her mother say on the other end of the phone. "Oh Mom, how awful; poor Grandma," Fran said. "Is she still in a lot of pain?" "Not as bad now," Ethel said. They X-rayed her hip, and put her right on a strong pain medication. They're going to operate tomorrow; they think they'll have to put some kind of pin in her hip." "Oh Mom, do you think she'll be able to walk again?" "Well, we just have to pray that God will let the operation be a complete success, and that she'll be able to walk okay. She *is* eighty six years old, Fran; she may not recover perfectly from this." "Well, we'll just take real good care of her when she comes home Mom," Fran said. "It's about time *she* was taken care of; she's been taking care of everyone else all these years." "That's right, Fran, it's her turn now," Ethel said. "We'll stay here at the hospital until she's asleep; they're giving her a strong sedative with the pain medication. If there's any change we'll call you. Did you call Joe?" "Yes, I did," Fran said. "He's waiting to hear from me again; I'll call him back right now." "Okay," Ethel said, "How's Dottie taking this?" "She's real upset, Mom," Fran said, "but she's okay." "Good!" Ethel said.

"We'll see you soon... be praying." *"Be praying,"* Fran thought; *"does God really want to hear from me?"* She decided to try. *"I know You don't hear from me often Lord, and I'm not even sure You'll listen to me now,"* Fran prayed, *"but I would really appreciate it if You would help my grandmother. Please let her be okay... not because I'm asking, but because she has always loved You so much. Thank You; Amen."*

Crocifessa was operated on, and pins were put in her hip. The doctor said that the bone was shattered, and because of her age, it didn't look like she'd ever walk again. Everyone in the family was devastated. She had been healthy and active, still doing her own housework and cooking, and going up and down the stairs like she was twenty years younger.

Crocifessa was in an awful lot of pain. A few weeks after the operation, a bad infection set in. The doctors and nurses were watching it carefully, but she didn't seem to be getting any better. Everyone was terribly worried. Peter tried to be brave, but he cried every time he saw her. Charlie and Margaret and their family, and Andy and Ethel and their family took turns staying with Crocifessa every day and into the nights until a nurse would tell them they had to leave. The nurses were pretty good about letting them stay late, but rules were rules.

After about a week, the infection seemed to be getting better, which of course was a relief to the family. She was developing a bad cough, though, which was a little disconcerting. About a week later the phone rang at Andy's house. "She has pneumonia," the doctor said. "It happens a lot to patients who can't get out of bed. We're doing all we can for her, but maybe you should alert the family to her condition." "Will she be alright?" Ethel asked. "It doesn't look good," the doctor said. "I'll tell Andy as soon as he gets home," she said.

"Pneumonia. Mom?" Fran cried. "Oh God, is she going to get better?" "I think it's pretty bad, Fran," her mother said. "But who knows? She's a 'tough old bird', God love her."

Crocifessa's hip was paining her terribly and she was wheezing badly. She had developed a couple of bedsores that gave her a great amount of discomfort also. The doctors were doing all they could for her, but she was just miserable. She took Fran's hand one evening and said, half in Italian and half in broken English, "Please Franzie, *please,* ask God to take me; please pray that I die and go to Jesus." Tears were rolling down her cheeks. Fran felt horrible; she started crying, and all she could say was, "Grandma, I can't, I just can't pray for that; please don't ask me."

Each day Crocifessa seemed to get steadily worse. One evening she was whimpering almost silently, and Fran thought, *"God, if you care for my grandmother at all, please help her; please take away her pain." She's loved you all her life, and has always been faithful to you. Please don't let her suffer any longer."*

Crocifessa Bellanti Vitello passed away on July 11, 1968, at St. Elizabeth Hospital. She and Peter had *'celebrated'* their 65th wedding anniversary while she was in the hospital. Every member of the Vitello family felt the sharp pain of losing someone so completely wonderful. Her death especially affected Fran's cousin Fran, as her grandmother died on her birthday. Crocifessa was finally where she wanted to be…at home with Jesus. Friends and relatives from all over poured into the funeral home to mourn her passing. "She was the finest person I've ever know," Ethel said. "She never thought of herself; it was other people who were important to her." Fran felt that an enormous amount of goodness had left the world, and it would never again be the same. *"But heaven,"* she thought, *"is all the more wonderful now."*

Two weeks after the funeral Dottie and Chet approached Andy and Ethel. "I think we should postpone the wedding," Dottie said. "We feel it might be too soon after Grandma died to have a celebration, but both Andy and Ethel said, "No, Grandma would not want that." "But Dad, what about Papa?" Dottie said. "How is he going to feel about it?" "I'll talk to him," Andy said. "I think he'll say that Grandma would want you to go ahead with your wedding plans." "Okay Dad, I just don't want to hurt or slight him in any way." "I know that, Dottie, and he will too." Andy said.

*****

A few weeks after Crocifessa died, Fran heard from John Murphy. He called one day and she invited him over. When she opened the door she didn't recognize him right away; he had grown a moustache and goatee. "It looks great," she said. "I think a moustache and beard are very masculine; it makes you look older and distinguished." "Well, that's good," he said, "'cause I think it's here to stay."

Dottie came upstairs when John arrived. They were all glad to see each other. John was dating a girl from Seekonk, and he was very pleased to hear of Dottie's engagement. Fran invited him to stay for supper, and Dottie insisted on it. Chet was coming over later, and she wanted John to meet him.

Chet and John got along great; they liked each other right away. Chet had a good sense of humor, and John just seemed to be energized by it. They kept Fran and Dottie in stitches the whole evening. After John left, Chet said, "You know something? I believe he's the funniest guy I've ever met; I like him. Fran, you should be dating him." "What? Oh no," Fran said. "He's too young for me." "Well, you look so much younger than you are, and he certainly seems older than he is," Chet said. "Believe me, the age difference doesn't show."

John would drop in every now and then, for coffee and conversation. One evening he came over, and he and Fran sat at the kitchen table and talked 'til two o'clock in the morning. John and the girl he was dating had broken up; he said it was for the best because they definitely were not right for each other. John was intelligent and very funny, and nice to talk with, and Fran enjoyed his company a lot. "I can't believe the time," Fran said. "Where did this evening go?" "Wow! I can't believe it's actually two o'clock," John said. "You're about the easiest person I've ever known to talk to Fran; honestly." "Well, you'd better get going," Fran said, "you must be exhausted. You have to drive back to Canton; I don't want to read about your tragic demise in the paper tomorrow, and more important than that... ha-ha... I've got to get some sleep; those kids will be awake pretty soon."

John started going over to see Fran about once a week. They were very fond of each other; they talked, they laughed and they watched Johnny Carson together. Sometimes they'd hop in the car and go to a Dairy Queen and get an ice cream. One day Ethel said, "He stays awfully late sometimes, Fran; don't you think that might look bad to the neighbors?" "Oh, hang the neighbors Ma; we're just friends, honestly. I enjoy his company and he enjoys mine; that's all there is to it." "Well," Ethel said, "that's how serious relationships start, don't they?" "Mom, he's a lot younger than I," Fran said. "This isn't going to develop into a romance, believe me."

*****

In late 1968 Fran read an article in the newspaper about foster parents. *"That's what I want to do,"* she thought. *"I want to use my home to give babies a safe place to live while waiting to be adopted."* She asked Terry, Jackie and Steven how they felt about it. They were all thrilled and excited over the idea. When she told her parents what she was planning to do, they thought it might be too much for her, with her own children to care for. But she was determined to do this. "Mom, I want to do something worthwhile, something that will make a difference in a child's life. Terry's nine years old, Jackie's seven, and Steven will be five in a few months. Terry and Jackie are in school all day, and Steven goes half days to pre-kindergarten. I don't know why, but I just really feel this is something I need to do."

Fran contacted the Child Guardianship in Boston. They came to the house and interviewed her and her children. They looked in every room to make sure the house was suitable for a foster child. Fran had two more meetings with them and then she was accepted as a foster mother. She told them that she just loved caring for babies, and would prefer to get them right from the hospital when they were just days old. The people from the Child Guardianship were glad to hear that, as most foster parents preferred children a little older.

The first baby she took in was seven days old, and he weighed nine pounds, four ounces. His name was David, and he was a chubby, beautiful, little Puerto Rican baby, with the most pleasant disposition. Terry, Jackie and Steven just loved him; everyone in the family was crazy about him. David was such an easy baby, and as he grew he became one of the happiest, smilingest babies they had ever seen. He was a joy to everyone, especially Fran.

David stayed with Fran and the kids for three and a half months, and then he was adopted. Fran felt very sad the day he left; she had grown extremely fond of him. A couple of days later the social worker, Elissa called and said, "Are you interested in taking another baby right away?" Fran didn't hesitate in responding, "Yes, definitely." "Well, a baby girl was born two days ago. Her mother is white and her father is black. They're not married yet; they're trying to work out some problems, but the mother wants to take her baby as soon as possible. You don't have a problem taking a racially mixed baby, do you?" "Oh gosh, no," Fran said. "And your children? Will they be fine with this?" "Absolutely," Fran said, "they'll be very pleased." "Okay," Elissa said, "then I'll bring her to you on Friday." Fran told Terry, Jackie and Steven that they would be taking another baby, a little girl, and that she was half black and half white, and she was coming on Friday.

When Friday arrived, so did Elissa with baby Jennifer. She was only five days old, a tiny little thing, weighing six and a half pounds. She was not very dark, but she had a full head of black hair. She was a sweet and dainty little girl, and Fran liked her right away.

When the kids got out of school they raced home to see the new baby. Fran heard them running up the front stairs. She met them at the door, and Jackie said, "Did the baby come?" "Yes," she said, "but you must be quiet because she's sleeping, okay?" "Okay, Mommy, we'll just tiptoe in to see her."

Terry thought she was adorable; Jackie said, "she's so little," and Steven said, "Oh, she's so cute, Mommy.... turn her over so we can see the black side." Fran stood there speechless for a moment; Jackie just smiled, and Terry started giggling. "I guess I've got some explaining to do," Fran said to Terry, as they both muffled their laughter.

Later Fran told Ethel and Andy what Steven had said; they burst out laughing. "Oh Fran, you should write that down so you never forget it," Ethel said. "That's absolutely precious." "It *is* precious, isn't it Mom?" Fran said, "I was thinking about it afterwards, and I wondered; how many times do we say things to children, and just simply take it for granted that they understand? When I told Steven that Jennifer was half black and half white, I never dreamed that he would picture her as having a white side and a black side to her body, like there's a line right down the middle." "Yes, it's true," Ethel said. "Kids must spend a lot of time being confused because they don't see things the way we do." Andy said, "that child said the sweetest, most innocent thing Fran. It really *is* precious, and, like your mother said, it's something to remember forever; I know I sure will." As Andy walked out of the kitchen, Fran and Ethel heard him chuckling, and mumbling, "turn him over so we can see the black side.... what a riot." Fran and Ethel both laughed. "He's right," Fran said. "It really *is* a riot. I don't think I could ever forget it, but I'm definitely going to write this in Steven's baby book."

Jennifer's parents came to visit her about once a week. They both seemed like real nice people. Her mother told Fran that her family was completely against her marrying a black man. "Even now when there's a baby in the picture?" Fran asked. "They want me to put the baby up for adoption," she said, "but Jennifer's father and I really want to get married. I'm not sure what I should do, but I need to make a decision soon. I'm glad she's here with you in the meantime."

Jennifer was with Fran and the kids for about three months; then one day she got a call from Elissa. "Jennifer's parents have gotten married," she said, "and they'll be taking her home with them in about a week." "Oh, that's good news," Fran said. "I know that's what they truly wanted. I'll miss Jennifer; she's been a delight to all of us." "Well," Elissa said, "I'll be bringing you another baby when Jennifer leaves. His name is Timothy and he was born four days ago.

Timothy was with Fran and the kids for two and a half months when he was adopted.

About a month after Timothy was adopted, Fran got a call from Elissa. "Fran, would you be willing to take a little black boy eleven months old?" "Well, I really didn't want to take anything but a newborn," Fran said. "I'm not sure, Elissa, I'll have to think about it."

"Fran, I'm in a real pickle," Elissa said. "I have to find a foster home for him...today!" "Why is it so urgent that you place him in a home today?" Fran asked. "Because I have this child with me right now at the office. He was *in* a foster home, but a twelve-year-old boy in that home beat him, and he was taken to the hospital. He's all right, but we have no home for him to go into at this moment. To be perfectly honest with you, Fran, if you can't take him, he'll have to come home with me tonight. I have no crib or anything else for a baby. If you could just take him for a week or two, until we can find a suitable and safe home for him, it would be so greatly appreciated. Please, Fran, please don't say no."

His name was Tony, and when Elissa brought him, he clung to her and wouldn't let go. He was very frightened and was trembling. Elissa explained to Fran that Tony was born to a fourteen year old girl. "Fourteen?" Fran asked, shocked. "She's just a child herself." "Well, the truth is, Tony is her second child," Elissa said. "She had a baby girl when she was twelve years old; she too is in a foster home." "Oh, my word," Fran exclaimed. "That is so awful, Elissa; isn't anyone caring for this fourteen year old girl?" "Well, she lives with her mother and her twenty year old brother, and her mother's latest boyfriend." Elissa went on to explain that Tony's mother had had Gonorrhea, and that Tony was born with it. He stayed in the hospital for six weeks before he was completely healed of it. She also explained that the three foster families he had been with had not fed him properly. At birth he weighed eight pounds, eleven ounces, and at almost eleven months old he weighed less than fifteen pounds. *"No wonder he clings to Elissa,"* Fran thought. *"Why would he trust me or anyone else?"*

"Will he come to me?" Fran asked. "He won't like it right away," Elissa said, "but he was the same way with me at first. Just take him from me, Fran; he'll cry for a while but soon you'll be the one he clings to. Give him time, he's really a very sweet child; I know he's going to love you and your children." Elissa had stayed a long time and Fran knew she had to leave, so with much difficulty she managed to pry Tony from Elissa's arms. He cried, and kept reaching for Elissa, but after only a few moments he calmed down and held onto Fran. "Only a week or two, right?" Fran said. "Three at the most," Elissa said, as she hurried to leave for her next appointment.

Elissa was right, Tony was a *very* sweet child; he took to Fran very quickly, and soon he realized that Terry, Jackie and Steven were his friends, and not to be feared. Terry was a big help to Fran, and Jackie and Steven were wonderful with him. Tony had a voracious appetite, and no matter how much food he was given, he always seemed to want more, so Fran would give him as much as he wanted. She noticed that he would eat as much as he could get, which was always too much, and then he would be distressed and throw it all up. She soon realized that because he wasn't fed enough in the last foster home he was in, his little mind thought he'd better eat all he could get at a meal, 'cause there may not be any more coming. *"Poor little boy,"* Fran thought, *"they must have practically starved you."*

A week turned into three weeks, and three weeks turned into three years. Tony became a son to Fran and a little brother to the kids. They loved him like he was born into their family, and he loved them the same way. Fran's parents and everyone else came to care deeply for Tony. John too, grew very fond of him. Tony was a very affectionate child, hugging and kissing everyone. He was no longer afraid of people; he was a happy, contented little boy.

*****

Chet came over to see Dottie as often as he could. When he would walk down Parkton Road in his uniform, all the kids in the neighborhood would come out to see the 'soldier' who had fought in Vietnam. He was real tall and to the kids he was bigger than life. Jackie and Steven were fascinated with Chet, and would stare in awe at him when he was in uniform. He would absolutely thrill the neighborhood kids when he'd salute them, or when he would call out, "Atten-tion!" They would stand as stiff as boards, waiting for him to say, "At Ease!" He was a real-life hero to them, that's for sure.

Dottie and Chet were married on October 20th, 1968 at Blessed Sacrament Church. Dottie was a beautiful bride, in her gorgeous gown and veil, and Chet, at 6'2" was dashing in his black tuxedo.

Fran and the other girls wore emerald green and peacock blue gowns; Terry looked adorable. Ethel and Andy looked terrific, too. Jackie, with his very blond hair and blue eyes, and Steven, with his very dark hair and brown eyes, both looked positively handsome. They were dressed alike in navy blue pants, white shirts, and blue Nehru jackets. Tony stayed at home with a friend of Fran's. Peter didn't go to the wedding, as he wasn't feeling well. A neighbor offered to stay with him. The reception was held at Longwood Towers in Brookline. It was a beautiful and elegant reception. Dottie and Chet went to Bermuda on their honeymoon, and had a great time until Dottie had an accident while driving a moped. She came home all bruised; Chet took a lot of ribbing about that. Because Chet was stationed at Westover Air Force Base in Chicopee, Massachusetts, he and Dottie got an apartment nearby in Ludlow.

*****

Peter missed Crocifessa terribly. As time went on he became more and more depressed; he cried often. "Stamortina," was what the family heard from him most of the time; "I'm dying," now seemed not just a statement for attention, but his heart's desire. Strangely, when he wasn't crying, he was singing the old Italian songs he always loved to sing. His health was failing, and Dr. Desimone started coming to the house once a week to check on him. His unhappiness was felt deeply by everyone in the family. Everyone helped out, but being in the same house, it was Ethel who did most everything for him.

Andy stared at his father one day, as he ate his dinner. He thought about the many times he heard Peter say, "You shouldn't measure a man from the neck down, but from the neck up." It always meant a lot to Andy, being barely 5'4" himself. *"You're right, Pa,"* he thought. *"You've always been a very big man in my eyes."*

Peter suffered a mild stroke in mid 1969. He couldn't do much for himself and was incontinent. The tests showed that he also had the beginning of prostate cancer. Dr. Desimone said, "he's almost 94 and he's got problems that you can't really help him with by your-selves. He really needs to be somewhere where his particular needs can be cared for." "Are you talking about a nursing home, Doctor?" Andy asked. "The Holy Ghost Hospital in Cambridge is a hospital and also a type of convalescent home," Dr. Desimone said. "I know it well; it's an excellent hospital and home. I see patients there at least once a week. I think it's the perfect place for him, Andy; he'd be well taken care of and the burden would be off of you and Ethel. I know you love him and want to keep him with you, but you have to face the fact that he's not going to get any better; he's only going to get worse." "Oh God, I don't know; we need to think about this, Doctor," Andy said. "We've never thought of him living anywhere but with us."

About a week later, Peter slipped and fell in the kitchen. He wasn't hurt bad, but Ethel couldn't lift him up from the floor. Fran heard the thud and ran upstairs. She and her mother together managed to pick him up. Ethel called Dr. Desimone and he came over that evening. "Andy, have you thought any more about what we talked about last week?" He asked. "I thought about it, and Ethel and I, and Charlie talked about it, but until now we hadn't been able to make that decision," Andy said. He looked at Ethel, and said, "But I think we have to make it now. "Ethel," he said, "I think we should do what Dr. D. feels is best for Pa." "I think so, too, Andy," Ethel said. They called Charlie and he agreed.

Dr. Desimone made a couple of phone calls and two weeks later Peter was settled in his room at the Holy Ghost Hospital. Andy and Ethel went to see him almost every night, unless they had something they had to do that couldn't wait. Margaret and Charlie and their kids went to see him as often as they could. The whole family did their part taking turns to make sure someone was there every night and most days.

One day, about three weeks later, Peter was moved to a different room. Fran went in that evening to see him. She brought him some pasta and Italian bread; she knew he'd like that. She asked at the front desk what room Peter Vitello had been moved to. The woman grinned and said, "You take the elevator to the second floor; when you get off, just follow the singing; if you don't hear it, then just ask the nurse at the desk." Fran chuckled and thanked her. She laughed right out loud when she stepped off the elevator and heard a rousing chorus of O Sole Mio coming from down the hall. She glanced at a nurse who had turned to look at her, and with great pride, said, "That's my grandfather."

*****

Andy decided it was time to go through Crocifessa and Peter's things and decide what to keep and what to get rid of. It wasn't going to be easy, as they had accumulated a lot of things over the years. He called Charlie and he came over the following Saturday. Between the two of them they decided who got what in the family. They went through linens and curtains, small appliances, dishes, and all kinds of miscellaneous things. After awhile Ethel came upstairs and helped. Charlie and Andy discussed the furniture, and many other things.

When the day came to finally disperse all of Peter and Crocifessa's belongings to different members of the family who could use them, they started taking things apart, boxing and crating items and deciding what goes where. Most families go through this at some time or another. It's very sad, but it can also be a charming and uplifting experience, as it was this day. As Andy and Charlie were taking down the dining room furniture, Ethel and Margaret were packing up smaller items in boxes in the living room. All of a sudden they heard Andy cry out, "I don't believe it! Mello, look at this! They heard Charlie laugh loudly, and say, "God love Ma!" The women ran into the dining room, saying, "What's going on?" "Come here, you guys; look at this," Andy said. He and Charlie were on their knees under the table. Ethel said, "what on earth are you doing?" Ethel and Margaret knelt down to look; they both started laughing. There, hanging from between the leaves of the table, was a black sock. Ethel reached up and pulled the sock down. "Oh my gosh, there's something in this sock." Margaret said, "No; don't tell me…" "How much is there?" Andy asked." Ethel reached inside and smiled; there in the sock was four hundred and sixty two dollars. The four of them sat there on the floor laughing. "Poor Ma," Charlie said. "She never could bring herself to trust banks." "Yeah," Andy said. "I'll bet Pa had no idea it was even there." "That 'sock' money helped me get my own barber shop," said Charlie, "and put a down payment on our house." "Right," Andy said, "It helped me out a lot too, and helped us buy *this* house. Ma was always there when we needed help, that's for sure." They all sat there silently on the floor for a few moments, then Ethel counted out two hundred and thirty one dollars and gave it to Charlie and Margaret. "Thanks Ma," Ethel said. "Yeah, thanks Ma," they all said…."for everything."

*****

On December 26, 1969 Mae gave birth to a six pound, seven ounce baby girl. She was a precious little 'bundle of joy', and unlike her brothers, who were fairer-skinned and light haired, she had a slightly olive complexion and dark hair. She was beautiful, and Joe and Mae were so pleased to finally have a little girl added to their family. She was christened Claire Margaret Vitello. Her cousin Terry was thrilled; after ten years, she was no longer the only girl in the family.

Andy and Ethel bought a lovely single home at 23 Coolidge Road in Norwell, and moved into it on a cold day in January 1970. This was something they had wanted for many years, but there was always Peter and Crocifessa living upstairs, and then Fran and the kids, too. After years of taking care of everyone else, Fran was thrilled for her parents. It was a beautiful ranch style home, with a good amount of land, and she knew they were going to love it. All week long Fran and Joe were helping to bring things over to the new house and do clean-up work also. Dottie and Chet lived too far away to be able to help much, and Dottie was also six months pregnant.

That Saturday, Andy and Ethel said goodbye to Fran and the children. They were all in tears; they wouldn't be there to see the kids every day, and they knew they would miss them terribly. As Andy and Ethel pulled away from the curb, with the moving van following, Andy looked up at the window and saw Fran and the three kids waving to them. He could tell that they were crying. Andy broke down in tears, and said, "I'm not going to leave them here for long; I'm going to start looking for a house right away, somewhere on the South Shore, so they can be closer to us. I don't like leaving

Fran alone with the kids with no one to help her." "I'm so glad to hear you say that, Andy," Ethel said. "I've been thinking the same thing. I hate that Dottie is so far away too, and pregnant now, but at least she has Chet." "Everything is changing, Ethel," Andy said. "Dottie's out in Ludlow, and now we're moving. I love our new home, but there's a real sadness that I feel leaving this house; just so many memories." "I know what you mean, Hon," Ethel said. "I feel it too."

As they drove away from Parkton Road, Ethel said, "Remember how we felt so many years ago on Parker Street when Charlie told us that he and Margaret bought a house and were moving?" "Yeah," he said, "and when Ma and Pa sold the store, and we moved out of the house and came to live on Parkton Road." "And Andy, remember how sad we all were when we sold the cottage? We thought life would never be that good again, but it was, and it is. We'll adjust to this change, Andy; Dottie will have her baby, Fran and the kids will move closer to us, and life will go on."

*****

On April 8, 1970 Dottie gave birth to an eight pound, six ounce baby girl. She was an adorable, sweet baby, with blond hair and blue eyes. It was a difficult delivery but when it was over Dottie and the baby were fine. Andy and Ethel went to Ludlow right away to see Dottie and their new little granddaughter. Ethel was planning to stay for a few days to help Dottie.

Not long after the baby was born, Fran called Dottie. A nurse brought the phone over to her. Dottie was still feeling the effects of the anesthesia, and was talking 'ragtime' to Fran. Fran laughed at some of the things Dottie was saying. She kept insisting to the nurses that someone should answer the phone. Of course there was no phone ringing, but Dottie kept yelling, "Will someone please answer that damn phone." Fran made a mental note to remember that, and all the other strange things Dottie was saying, so she could tell her about them later. Dottie had a good laugh over it the next day.

Fran was very excited, and couldn't wait to see her little niece. A few days later she drove up to Ludlow. She took the kids with her, and let Jackie, Steven and Tony stay at Dottie's with Ethel while she and Terry went to the hospital. Dottie was so happy to see them. Fran fell instantly in love with her little niece, and Terry was just thrilled with her. A short while later, little Cynthia Angela Malcolm was christened. Fran was her very proud godmother.

*****

Andy bought a two-family house on the corner of Oak and Main Streets in Quincy, and on August 27, 1970 Fran and the children moved into the first floor apartment. Fran couldn't understand why it was called Main Street. *"Perhaps,"* she thought, *"many years ago it was a main street, but certainly not today."*

Fran hated leaving her large, lovely apartment on Parkton Road, but was happy to be living so much closer to her mom and dad, and Joe and Mae, too. It was nowhere as big as the other apartment. The living room was small, and a bedroom off the living room was small, which became Fran's room. One bedroom off the kitchen was tiny; that became Terry's room. The other bedroom off the kitchen was a good size, and that became Jackie, Steven and Tony's room. Jackie and Steven slept in bunk beds and Tony slept in a crib. The bathroom was off the kitchen also, and it, too was very small; there was barely enough room to turn around. The thing that saved the apartment was the large, bright, eat-in kitchen. Fran loved the kitchen; it wasn't modern, but it was big and airy and it looked like it belonged in a country farmhouse. Another thing Fran loved about the house was that it had a nice back and side yard. In Jamaica Plain the back yard was tiny; there was no room to plant a garden or to do much of anything. The kids loved the new yard. The first thing Jackie did was climb the huge oak tree that was near the driveway, and soon after moving in, he proceeded to build a tree house high up in the tree. The entire house and yard were completely fenced in, with a double gate at the driveway, which was on Oak Street, a very small, quiet street, with only three houses on it. Fran was absolutely thrilled having her own driveway. Parkton Road was such a narrow, steep hill, with very little place to park, especially on snow days; having a driveway was a major luxury to Fran. It took some getting used to, but 59 Main Street soon became home to all of them.

*****

Earlier, when John was twenty years old, he had applied for the Criminal Justice School at Northeastern University, but wasn't accepted. He had good marks, but unfortunately not great marks. He had planned to go on the Co-Op plan, which meant he would go to school three months and work three months, and then repeat the process. It was the long way to get a degree, but he couldn't afford to do it any other way and neither could his parents.

Fran couldn't believe that he hadn't gotten in, so she decided to write a letter to Senator Edward Brooks. She had never met Senator Brooks, but she liked him and felt that he was a decent, honest man. She knew he was a lawyer, so she asked him in the letter to remember when he was young, and eager to attend the college of his choice. She had praised John and his attributes to the hilt, and had asked Senator Brooks if there was anything he could do to get John into Northeastern University. About three weeks later John had received a letter from Northeastern, accepting him to the university. There was a P.S. at the end of the letter stating that Senator Edward Brooks had personally called Northeastern University requesting that John M. Murphy be accepted there. John couldn't believe it, and Fran was ecstatic. "Do you *always* get what you want?" John had asked her. "No, not always," Fran had said, "but I don't believe in 'leaving any stone unturned' if there's even a remote chance." Needless to say, John was very pleased; he laughed, and grabbed Fran and hugged her. "I can't get over your 'chutzpa,'" he had said.

About a year later, John made plans to go to Canada to visit his Uncle Claude and his Aunt Alice, who lived in New Brunswick. John's Dad grew up in New Brunswick, and John decided he wanted to spend some time there. "I need to get my head together," is what he had said. "What's wrong with your head?" Fran asked. "Is something bothering you?" "Well, yeah, sort of," he said. "I really just want to get away for a while...you know, do some thinking."

"Oh," Fran said. "Will you be gone long?" "I'll be there for close to two months," he said. "I'm planning to be home by Thanksgiving though." "Wow," she had said, " Are you all right John?" "Oh, yeah, I'm fine, Fran; I just have some things I have to figure out. I'm leaving on Friday with my dad, but he's only staying for a week. I'll be working with my uncle while I'm there." "Well," Fran said. I'm certainly going to miss you; I hope you'll write to me." "I'll write," he had said. She hugged him and wished him well, and then he left.

Three weeks after John had left for New Brunswick, Fran realized that she was missing him a lot more than she thought she would. It was a bit disconcerting. *"This is crazy; he's just a friend, no more than that,"* she had thought, *"and I'm darned sure John sees me the same way. "Besides, he's much too young for me. But, it's been three weeks since he left, and I haven't heard a word from him; what if he's not planning to come back? Why the heck am I thinking about him like this? Knock it off, Fran; this is not a good idea."*

John wrote to Fran and she wrote back to him. He was working hard for his uncle, cutting down trees and making pulpwood. They were long, exhausting days, especially for a college student who wasn't used to doing that kind of work. In one of his letters he told Fran, "They sure don't eat like we do back home. Supper usually consists of homemade bread, cheese and some fruit.... SEND HELP! I think they're trying to starve me!" Fran had chuckled when she read it. "*Sure,*" she thought. "*Nobody eats like we do here in America; I'm sure they're all real slim, too.*"

The day before Thanksgiving Fran got a call from John. "Where are you?" "I'm in Quincy," he replied. "Quincy? No kidding! How did you get here?" She asked. "I hitchhiked," he said. "Hitchhiked?" Fran was shocked. "All the way from Canada?" "Yeah, it was actually kind of fun," he said. "So, can you pick me up?" "Sure," she said. "Tell me where you are." "I'm on the Southeast Expressway over by Howard Johnson's Restaurant," he said. "I'm not sure how to get there," Fran said. "You'll have to give me directions." "Directions? Fran, I'm not even ten minutes from your house; you know how to get here. You've driven this road a hundred times." "No, honestly John, I really can't picture where you are," she said. "You'll have to explain to me how to get there." John tried to explain to Fran exactly where he was and how to get there, but she still couldn't 'picture it'. "All right, Fran, never mind; I'll call my dad to pick me up." Fran could hear the exasperation in his voice. "No, that's okay John," she said. "I'm pretty sure I know where it is; I'll be there in a few minutes." "Are you sure, Fran, 'cause I can call my father?" "No, I can do it; I'll be there shortly," she said. "No problem."

What John didn't understand was that Fran was one of those people who can drive on a road or go to a place many times and still not be able to 'see it' in her mind when she needed to. She would come close to panicking when she had to go somewhere she wasn't 100% sure of. She would try so hard to picture the road or the place in her mind, but usually it was to no avail. The fact that she had been there many times didn't necessarily help. It was like her mind would draw a complete blank; she might just as well have been in downtown Hong Kong. She always hated this about herself; she didn't know what made her like that. She was an intelligent woman, but no matter how hard she would concentrate, nothing ever changed. What most people, including John, could never understand was that she truly couldn't help it.

As Fran backed out of her driveway, she started to break out in a sweat. After a few mistakes and a few wrong turns, things began to seem more familiar. She finally found herself on the Expressway and after a few minutes she caught sight of the Howard Johnson's in the distance. As she got closer she could see John leaning against a post with a duffel bag on the ground beside him. She breathed a sigh of relief; "I made it."

It was good to see John, and he seemed just as pleased to see her. They hugged and then John threw his duffel bag in the back seat. "You look beautiful!" He said. "I can never get over how much you look like Elizabeth Taylor." "Thanks," she said. "You look pretty good yourself; none the worse for wear, I see. Starvation agrees with you." He chuckled. He looked like he had been taking a bodybuilding course. He had lost some weight and was very muscular; he looked terrific. "It was all that hard work," he said. They talked non-stop on the way back to Fran's house. Fran made some pasta and cooked up some sausages, and they talked during and after supper. John oohed and aahed with every mouthful. "I'm telling you, they were trying to starve me," he said. "Uh huh," Fran said. "Funny, you never looked healthier." He just smiled.

After supper Jackie and Steven wanted to wrestle, so they jumped on John and tried their darnedest to pull him down to the floor, but they just couldn't do it. John wrestled with them for a while. They loved wrestling with him; he would flip them and get them into the weirdest positions, and then he'd tickle them unmercifully. They would screech with delight, laughing hysterically. Tony kept trying to join in, but he would end up getting hurt and crying, and Fran would have to explain to him that he was just too little for that kind of rough playing. Later, Fran drove John home to Canton.

The next day was Thanksgiving. Fran and the kids went to her parents' house in Norwell, and Ethel prepared a feast for her family. Before dinner Ethel always served cut celery filled with cream cheese, with black olives on top and sprinkled lightly with paprika. Then Thanksgiving dinner always began with chicken or turkey soup, then roast turkey, with Ethel's delicious stuffing and gravy, mashed potatoes, butternut squash, a green vegetable, and cranberry sauce. Fran and Mae and Dottie brought different pies and desserts. Everyone missed Crocifessa and Peter; it just wasn't the same without them, but Ethel and Andy did their best to make Thanksgiving wonderful… and it was. Andy and Ethel went to the Holy Ghost Hospital in the evening to see Peter; Dottie and Chet went with them.

Later, when Fran and the kids got home, John came over and enjoyed some of the left over desserts that Fran brought home with her. He wrestled with the boys until it was time for them to go to bed, and then he and Fran sat and talked some more about his trip to Canada.

When John was leaving, Fran hugged him. "It's nice to have you home again," she said. He held her close for a moment and kissed her cheek. She sensed that their relationship had gone to a slightly higher level, and she wasn't sure how she felt about that, or how John was feeling about it. *"I don't want to get serious with anyone right now,"* she thought, *"let alone someone so much younger than I. Oh well, I'm not going to think about that now; I'll worry about it later. Good grief, I sound like 'Scarlett O'Hara'."*

*****

Peg Kenny came to the United States from Nova Scotia and stayed with her daughter Helen and her husband Chet, who had bought the house right next door to Joe and Mae. Mae and Helen were thrilled to finally have their mother living here in the states with them. Their father had passed away the year before, and they wanted Peg to be nearby. After a time Peg took a position as house-keeper at the rectory of St. Albert the Great Church in Weymouth, and made her permanent residence there. She was perfect for the job, and the job was perfect for her. She spent most of her free time with Joe and Mae, and Helen and Chet. Peg was a quiet, simple, and lovely woman, and everyone who came to know her loved her.

****

CHAPTER SIXTEEN
"Who Are We?"….. "GIANTS!"

Fran and John's relationship escalated fairly quickly. They both knew they loved each other, and both were very concerned about that. Fran was ten years older than John, and had been married and divorced, with three children, four counting Tony. John cared a great deal for Terry, Jackie and Steven, and he was crazy about Tony too, but wasn't sure he could handle the responsibility. Fran was very leery of getting involved with another 'young' fellow; John wasn't much older than Jack was when she and Jack got married.

There were times when Fran was alone that she thought about ending their relationship. She felt it wasn't fair to John to keep it going. Three, or four children that weren't even his own to care for was more than she could ask of him. She loved her children more than anything in the world, but she had longed for the love and attention of a good man; and John *was* a good man, a truly good man, albeit a young one.

John enjoyed playing with the kids, especially Jackie and Steven. He was an avid ball player. When he was a kid he played little league baseball, and went on to play in a Babe Ruth League. As an adult he was in a men's softball league. He played shortstop, and was one of the best hitters and fielders on the team. Most years he'd win the "Most Valuable Player" award. He loved baseball, so in 1971, when Jackie was nine and a half, and Fran signed him up for St. John's Little League, John was at every practice helping out. Jackie was assigned to the "Giants". The coaches, Paul Beatrice and

Tom Turynowicz, asked John if he would like to help coach the team. John jumped at it; he became an excellent coach. He was not as mild-mannered as Tom, but a lot easier going than Paul; he was a good combination of both, and the coaches and the kids liked and respected him.

Jackie loved little league; at nine and a half he already showed signs of being a pretty good baseball player. Fran went to every practice, and discovered that she loved it, too. Jackie was left-handed, so the coaches decided to try him at first base. It was a good choice; he became an excellent first-baseman.

At every practice and at different crucial times during the games, the coaches and the boys would get into a huddle. They'd put one hand in and the coaches would yell, "WHO ARE WE?" All the boys would yell their answer as loud as they could…. "GIANTS!" It was inspiring, and would get the boys all pumped up. They all came to love that ritual.

Jackie's first real game for the Giants was very exciting, as was his first time up at bat. He got a hit and was safe at first base. Fran found that she loved everything about little league baseball. She loved the ball field, the bleachers, and the excitement. She loved the other parents, the coaches, and she especially loved all the boys on the team. They ranged in age from nine to twelve; twelve being the last year a boy could play in little league. The rest of that first season was so much fun. Jackie was a pleasure to watch on the ball field; he was becoming a terrific little ball player. Fran loved watching him, and he loved her being there.

One mother who came to the ball games had an older boy who was stationed in Vietnam. So many times Fran would think about her and other mothers whose sons were fighting in Vietnam, and she would try to imagine what they must be going through. She'd look at Jackie and thank God in her own way that he was young, and that she wasn't one of those mothers who wondered every day if her son would be coming home alive. The way the war was dragging on, she just hoped it would be over before Jackie became of age to go. *"Oh well, I'm not going to think about that now,"* she thought. *"I'll think about it if and when I have to."*

*****

Jackie and Steven grew to love John very much, and Tony did too. But Terry withdrew and wanted no part of him. There were times when she would be downright rude to him. John had no idea how to handle the situation, and many times, unknowingly, he made it worse. Fran understood that Terry was jealous of John; she knew Terry felt that he was stealing her mother from her. Fran tried to be patient, but one day Terry went too far. "Oh, shut up, John," she yelled. "You're a jerk." "That's just about enough, young lady," Fran said. "We need to have a talk." John, Jackie and Steven had been wrestling in the kitchen, so Fran said, "John, would you and the boys go wrestle in the yard for awhile?" "Sure; come on guys," he said, as they tumbled out into the backyard. Terry was not, by nature, a disrespectful girl, but Fran knew things were getting out of hand. When they were alone, Fran grabbed Terry by the arm and pushed her down into a chair. "You listen to me, Terry," Fran said. "You will *never* again insult anyone in this house; do you understand?" "Well, he's always here, Mom," Terry said. "*That* is not a good enough reason to tell John to shut up, and to call him a jerk," Fran said. "I'm ashamed of you, Terry, and I'm mad, I'm real mad. How dare *you*, an eleven-year-old girl, insult an adult? This is our home, and he's my friend, and you *will* respect him, whether you want to or not." "Well, why does he have to be here all the time?" Terry asked. "Because I like him being here," Fran said, "and your brothers like him being here, so you'd just better get used to seeing him here. Terry stood there pouting. "You're my daughter, Terry, and I love you very much," Fran said. "No one is going to take your place in my life, but I've been very lonely, and kind of sad. I don't expect you to understand, but John simply makes me feel good. I wish you would try to join in more when we're doing things. You have to admit John is a funny guy; why can't you just enjoy him instead of resenting him so much?" Terry said nothing; she just folded her arms and looked down at the floor. "Terry," Fran said, "there is no excuse for the way you acted, and if it ever happens again you'll be grounded for a very long time; do you understand?" Terry nodded. "Oh, and by the way," Fran said, "when John comes back in, you *will* apologize to him; am I right?" Terry hesitated for a moment, and then said, "yes."

Terry apologized to John, but not much changed; she still resented him but she never again spoke to him in a disrespectful way.

*****

Chet had finished his time in the service and he and Dottie left Chicopee and moved back to the South Shore. They stayed with Ethel and Andy for about four months. Chet started working at Reliable Fence Company in Norwell. Andy bought a nice little house on Manatee Road in Weymouth, and Dottie and Chet moved into it and paid Andy an affordable rent. Cindy was about five months old when they moved into the house in Weymouth.

John had left Northeastern University after two years. He couldn't seem to get the courses he would sign up for, and he had decided that criminal justice was not the career he wanted. He didn't know what he wanted to do with his life, but in the meantime Chet helped him to get a job working in the yard at Reliable Fence Company. He started in February, an absolutely bitter cold day. He had to grasp heavy rolls of chain link fencing when trucks delivered them to the yard. He would lift them and throw them into neat stacks. He also would load them into Reliable trucks that would take them to different jobs. He did this for eight freezing hours.

When John got home that night, he had frost in his beard and mustache, and he couldn't open his hands all the way. He was shivering badly and was close to tears, he was so cold and in so much pain. Fran took one look at him and then ran into the bathroom and started running the hot water into the tub. She helped him remove his jacket and hat and his work boots. "I can't remember ever being this cold," John said. "I don't think I can go through this again tomorrow, Fran." "Well, if you can't, then don't," she said. "Wait and see how you feel later before you make that decision, and whatever it is, I know it will be the right one." After his bath and a cup of hot coffee John said, "I'll see how I feel in the morning."

The next morning John decided to try it again, especially since he and Fran had gone out after supper and bought a heavy, heavy-duty pair of insulated gloves that would not only protect his hands but keep them a lot warmer, too. He made it through the day much better than the day before, although he had to keep taking the gloves off to get his fingers through the rolled up chain link. Soon it became second nature to him.

One day about two and a half years later John was standing on the blades of a forklift, which was raised up about twelve feet to reach a pallet of pickets that was not balanced properly. While he was straightening out the problem, the hydraulic power of the fork-lift let go. The blades, which were made of heavy steel, seven feet long and four inches thick, made a rapid descent, with John falling in mid-air. When the blades hit the ground they bounced upward and caught John on the left thigh as he fell to the ground. His leg was badly hurt, with a deep groove made by the impact of the forklift blade. His pants were ripped and after a minute or two he could see his thigh swelling, and already beginning to change color. His thigh muscle was twitching badly and he could barely stand. He was shaking something awful and felt sick to his stomach.

The foreman on the job told him to sit down for a few minutes and then get back to work. John couldn't even think straight, but he knew he couldn't continue to work. Fran picked him up and drove him home. She wanted to take him up to the hospital, or at least to the doctor's office, but he said he just needed to lie down for a while. He was in a lot of pain and spent a very uncomfortable night; he couldn't stop the twitching in his leg. The next day he went to see the doctor. He told John it was a massive hematoma, and gave him a prescription to relax the muscle. John stayed home for a couple of days, and then returned to work, limping. He never did lose the groove in his thigh. John worked at Reliable Fence Company for three years.

*****

It was mid-1972, and Tony had been with Fran and the kids for almost three and a half years. During that time a few couples had come with the social worker to meet him. Fran always knew the ones who were looking to adopt a black child as just some kind of status symbol. They would come in and see Tony and talk to him for a few moments and leave. He was obviously not the picture-perfect black child they had in mind. Tony was not a 'beautiful' child; neither was he an outgoing, personable child. He was simply an adorable, sweet, precious, and loveable child, who was also very shy around strangers. His most beautiful feature was his eyes; they were very large with the longest lashes Fran had ever seen. Most couples that came to see him were obviously looking for a little Sidney Poitier or Harry Belafonte, two very handsome black actors at the time.

Elissa had moved to a different city and a Mrs. Moses was now the social worker in Tony's case. She kept bringing couples to see him; she kept trying to get him legally adopted. Fran would have adopted him in a second, but at that time, she was told, the agency would not let a child be adopted by an unmarried woman. Fran argued that for over three years she had been the only mother Tony had ever really known, and that he should stay with her and her family. That meant nothing to Mrs. Moses as she didn't really know Fran or the home life that was now Tony's.

One day Mrs. Moses brought a couple to see Tony. When Fran opened the door something in her went cold. A lovely young woman shook Fran's hand, and then crouched down to talk with Tony. Her name was Celeste, and Fran could tell right away that she and her husband Bob liked Tony a lot. Fran was surprised when Tony smiled at them and shook their hands. "Look at those eyes, Bob." Celeste said. "What a sweet, adorable little boy." Bob agreed. *"Oh no, God,"* Fran silently prayed. *"Please don't let them like Tony."*

Fran served Celeste and Bob and Mrs. Moses tea and cookies. Celeste held Tony on her lap and talked with him and played with him. Bob took him out into the backyard and walked with him, and Tony showed him everything in the yard. Fran could see them through the kitchen window and her heart ached.

The next day Bob and Celeste brought their little girl Arden with them; she was eight years old, and she took right to Tony. John was there and he too sensed what Fran already knew. Celeste asked if they could take Tony out to McDonald's for lunch. Fran wanted so badly to say, "no", but instead she said, "If Tony wants to go, it's fine with me. Tony wanted to go; Fran couldn't believe it. He would never go anywhere with anyone he didn't know very well.

Later, when they brought Tony back home, Celeste said, "Fran, we want to adopt Tony. Fran felt sick to her stomach. *"Why Lord?"* She thought. *"Why can't he just stay with us forever?"* "Fran, it's obvious how much you and your family love Tony," Celeste said, "and we sure don't want to hurt any of you, but we've been looking to adopt for a few years now. Bob and I both believe that Tony is the child we are meant to adopt. We already love him, and we have so much more love to give him." Fran could feel her eyes burning and she knew her lip was starting to quiver. John moved his chair closer to Fran and held her hand. Fran forced herself not to show her feelings, and Celeste continued. "Fran, "I truly hope that you and John and the children approve of Bob and I; I know it would make me feel a lot better if I thought that you liked us." "Please Fran," Celeste said, "tell me how you feel." It was all Fran could do to keep her composure. She said, "Celeste, you don't want to know how I feel, but I will tell you this, I do approve of you and Bob, and I like you very much. I just can't believe that this is really happening. I never really thought that Tony would be adopted. Others came to see him and he was simply not right for them." Fran had to pause to gain her composure again. "I honestly believed that he would always be with us."

Terry had gone into her room and Fran knew she was crying. Soon Jackie and Steven came in the house and Steven said, "Mom, you can't let Tony go with them; he belongs here with us." He was trying not to cry. "Steven, we'll talk about it later." Steven went into his room in a huff. Jackie looked like he didn't know what to do; Fran knew he was hurting too. John followed them into their room to talk with them.

Celeste and Bob left to go back to the motel where they were staying and about two hours later Mrs. Moses called. "Well, it's all set; Bob and Celeste will be adopting Tony. They're taking him home to Vermont with them tomorrow." "Tomorrow!" Fran cried. "Isn't that kind of soon?" "No, I don't think so," Mrs. Moses said. "It's best to get these things over with as quickly as possible, for the child's sake." "But, Friday to Sunday," Fran said. "Mrs. Moses, I don't know how Tony is going to be with all of this; it's all happening so fast." "He'll be fine," she said. "Children adjust to change a lot better than adults do." "I don't agree with that, Mrs. Moses," Fran said. "I don't agree with that at all. And what about *my* children's feelings?" "They'll be fine," was all Mrs. Moses would say.

Sunday morning, Fran had Tony dressed in his best clothes and his things all packed. She spent the morning hugging and kissing him. She didn't know how she was going to let him go; her heart was breaking. Terry was fighting tears, Jackie was too, and Steven was sobbing. "Please don't let him go, Mommy; please," Steven said more than once. They were all confused and hurting. "Mrs. Moses is wrong," Fran said to John. "This is all happening too fast for Tony, and Tony isn't the only one to think about here. What about Terry, Jackie and Steven? John, they love that little boy; he's their brother now." "Yes," John said, "I know, and he's your son, just as sure as if you gave birth to him. I know how you're feeling Fran; I love Tony too. Three and a half years is a long time to have a child, and then lose him. We'll get through this, Fran, and we'll help the kids to get through it, too."

At eleven o'clock Celeste and Bob arrived. Terry, Jackie and Steven hugged and kissed him, fighting back tears the whole time. John picked him up and hugged him. Tony hugged and kissed them all, but when Fran went to pick him up, he wouldn't let her. "Tony," Fran said, "aren't you going to kiss Mommy goodbye?" "No," he said. John and Terry were trying to get him to kiss Fran, but he wouldn't. Celeste asked Tony to kiss Fran, but he didn't budge. Finally, they had to get going. When Tony climbed into the back seat of their car, Fran thought her heart would burst. Celeste asked him once more to give Fran a kiss, but he wouldn't. As the car pulled away from the curb John put his arm around Fran to support her. Just then they heard Tony screaming, and the car stopped and backed up to them. Celeste opened the window and held Tony as he reached both arms out the window. "Mommy, Mommy," he was calling, "I want to kiss you." Fran ran over to the car and reached in and held Tony. He clung to her for a long moment and kissed her and said, "I love you, Mommy." Fran was sobbing by this time. She told him one last time that she loved him, and then let him go.

As they drove away, Fran ran into the house with Terry and John right behind her. Fran didn't know what to do to ease the pain she was feeling. She wanted to run; she wanted to break dishes; she wanted to scream, but she knew nothing would make her feel better, and nothing was going to bring Tony back. She felt as if one of her children had died.

Around nine o'clock in the evening the telephone rang. John answered it and said, "Fran, it's Celeste." Fran said, "Hello," and Celeste said, "Fran, I just wanted to call you to tell you that I'm hurting for you; I wouldn't want to be you right now for anything in the world. I have such mixed emotions Fran; your loss is our gain, and I know you must be heartbroken." "Thank you so much Celeste," Fran said. "I am heartbroken; we all are, but if Tony had to be adopted, I'm glad it's by you. I know you'll be a good mother to him, and I know deep in my heart that he'll be happy with you. You're a good person, Celeste." As sad as Fran was, she deeply appreciated the call from Celeste.

The next day Terry, Jackie and Steven very reluctantly went to school, but John took the day off to stay with Fran. They talked about Tony, Fran cried, and then they talked about Tony some more. At about ten o'clock Fran yelled to John in the living room. "John, let's get a dog!" "What? Are you serious?" He asked. "I'm dead serious," she said. "I don't expect a dog to take Tony's place, but I think it would give the kids something to think about besides Tony. What do you think?" "I think it's a great idea," he said. "Let's check the newspaper." John found a Winchester Kennels ad, saying they had some dogs for sale. "Let's go!" Fran said.

They drove out to Winchester and found the kennels. The woman who owned the kennel showed them around. They looked at a few dogs; they liked a beautiful Husky, but he seemed a little too rough. Then they saw a lovely fawn colored mixed breed. Fran went over to her and patted her through the chain link fence. She licked Fran's hand. "She's a lovely dog," the woman said. "She's playful, but she's very gentle." "Does she have a name?" Fran asked. "Yes, it's Samantha; she's a year and a half old. We think she has some Shepherd in her, but whatever else is anybody's guess. She's spayed, and she's had all her shots." "How much does she cost?" Fran asked.

"Fifteen dollars is the usual price for a spayed female mongrel." The woman opened the pen and let Samantha out. She put a leash on her and handed the leash to John, and said, "Run with her, play with her and see how you like her." After a little while Fran said, "We'll take her." John was thrilled; he was crazy about her.

When the kids came home from school they went wild for Samantha. "Great idea, Fran," John said. "This was just what the doctor ordered. Fran, you're the strongest person I know; you're going to be fine, too." "Yes, I know I will, John," Fran said. "It just hurts so bad." John put his arms around her; "I know Hon, he said…"I know."

*****

Fran was working part-time in the Graham shop, which had moved to Weymouth on Washington Street. Andy was getting ready to retire and Joe was more and more taking on the duties and responsibilities of running the shop. They now had the South Shore Paint and Wallpaper Company also, so Fran worked in the J. W. Graham office, and waited on customers when they came in the store.

*****

A few years earlier Andy had gotten a call from an old friend from Westford telling him the sad news that their wonderful cottage, Camp Pleasant, had burned to the ground. Andy and Ethel, and Joe, Fran and Dottie felt so very sad, like an old friend had died. Andy and Ethel drove to Westford that night; what they saw was heartbreaking. All that was left were bricks from the chimney that had stood behind the pot-bellied stove in the center of the house. Fran and John took a ride to Westford the following Sunday; John climbed over all the rubble, and managed to get a brick for Fran. When she looked at it the word PRAY was compressed into it. "That's strange," Fran said. "I wonder where this brick *was* in the chimney; I never noticed that before."

*****

One November day in 1972, Fran was at her desk in the office. It was a quiet day, not much business. She sat down to have a cup of coffee and read the newspaper. She happened to look through the classifieds and saw an ad that read: "HUNTERS…Log cabin on a beautiful pond in Maine, surrounded by hills and woods…very rustic… good hunting and fishing… Weekly rates." Fran noticed that a Weymouth telephone number was listed. She decided to call the number to find out more about the log cabin set on the beautiful pond. For some time she had been wanting to take her children to a 'rustic cottage' somewhere to enjoy a more natural way of life, if only for a week or even just a weekend. She knew neither she nor John could afford to pay very much, so just maybe this 'rustic cabin' would be in their price range. Fran had always longed to find a country cottage set in the woods somewhere where she could feel again those wonderful feelings she had as a child in Westford. She hoped that this cabin in Maine was what she had been longing for.

When Fran talked with Tim Taylor, the owner of the cabin, he described the cabin and the pond and the surrounding area to her. He told her it was in Rome, Maine, about twenty miles west of Augusta. He suggested that she and John come over to his house in North Weymouth to look at pictures he had of the cabin. She and John went over that night. They liked Tim and his wife Jean almost immediately. Jean served coffee while Tim talked about the cabin and showed them the pictures. There was one large room, which made up the kitchen area, the dining area and a kind of sitting area. One corner of the room was partitioned off and had a bed and a small bureau in it. There was a large, sturdy ladder that led up to an open loft where there were four twin beds. Tim explained that there was no indoor plumbing, just a small homemade sink and a hand pump. A hose that was in the pond had to be hooked up to a filter attached to a hose under the cabin that lead to the sink and the hand pump. The outhouse was just outside the cabin. The only heat in the cabin came from a large pot-bellied stove, but there was a small propane gas stove for cooking. Fran knew that Tim was trying to prepare her for things she might find difficult, but the more he talked the more she couldn't wait to go. Tim gave them the keys and the directions, and a list of things they would need to know. John gave him payment for two nights stay.

Fran and John made plans to go the day after Thanksgiving. They decided to go without the kids in case it turned out to be a disaster. Jackie and Steven were disappointed, but Fran promised them that if the cabin were all she hoped it would be, then they would all go in the spring. Terry didn't seem too interested, especially when she heard the word 'outhouse'.

It took over four hours to get to Rome. John and Fran had left at four o'clock in the afternoon, and found the cabin at about eight-thirty. It was pitch black at the cabin; no lights anywhere. Tim had said to bring a flashlight, and they did. They could hear the water nearby, but couldn't see the pond. They entered the cabin and groped the wall to find the light switch. Fran was *so* glad that there was electricity in the cabin. John turned the outside lights on in the front and in the back while he groped under the cabin to find the two ends of the hoses for hooking up the water. They brought some water with them to drink, and also to prime the pump. Finally they had 'running' water. The next thing they needed to do was get a fire going in the pot-bellied stove. They threw in kindling and newspapers and got the fire started. They put in logs that were stored right beside the stove. Before long they had delicious warmth in the cabin, but they also had *smoke*... lots of smoke. It was filling up the cabin. They soon realized that the flue was closed. Once opened, the smoke cleared out. They made the beds and Fran made some coffee.

Fran was feeling a little nervous; they could hear a loud eerie screeching sound every now and then coming from out back, in *or* around the pond. Other than the sound of water lapping at the shore, that eerie sound was the *only* sound they could hear. Tim had said they might hear a loon, but of course they didn't know what a loon sounded like, and what they were hearing was scaring the bejeebers out of Fran. She felt isolated, and outside was so dark that she was afraid to fall sleep, expecting something terrible to happen. She decided that she wanted to go home first thing in the morning, and she would certainly never bring her precious children to this awful place. *"Gosh, Tim and Jean Taylor seemed so nice; how could they let us come to this God-forsaken place?"*

The following morning John was shaking Fran. "Wake up," he said. "You've got to see this." Fran came out of the bedroom; John was standing out on the screened-in porch. As she stepped out into the porch she gasped. "Oh my gosh," she exclaimed. "It's beautiful!" Fran couldn't believe what she was looking at. Right in front of her was one of the prettiest ponds she had ever seen. It was quite large, and on the other side of the pond was nothing but woods. She and John stood there for quite a while admiring the beautiful scenery. A little while later they untied the canoe and rode around the pond. The pond was surrounded by mostly woods; every now and then they'd see a cabin similar to the Taylor's. It was so lovely and so peaccful…and so very cold. It was the end of November and by the time they got back to the cabin they were shivering. The fire in the stove felt real good as they entered the cabin. "Oh John," Fran said, "I can't wait to bring the kids here. I just hope they like it." "They're going to love it," he said. "I guarantee it."

The following April, 1973 John, Fran, Jackie, Steven, and Samantha went to the cabin in Maine. Terry stayed with Ethel and Andy. John was right; Jackie and Steven fell in love with the place, and Samantha was in her glory. They explored the woods, and fished off the pier. It was much too cool to swim but later they all rode around the lake in the boat and fished out in the middle of the pond. At night, Jackie and Steven climbed up to the loft to their beds and slept like logs. Samantha slept contentedly on a mat in front of the stove.

The next day they drove around Rome and the neighboring towns. They found "Blueberry Hill" and walked all around it and looked out at the beautiful view. Fran took a picture of John standing in front of a tree with Jackie on his shoulders, and Steven, standing on a limb just above Jackie, looking like he was on his shoulders. When Fran saw the picture she called it 'her loveable totem pole'.

While they were driving around they came upon an old antiques and collectables store. The old battered sign across the top of the house read: POLLY PETERS USED ITEMS. It had been closed up for years, but all over the ground in front of the place were things that, Fran assumed, there was no room for inside. There was an old sink, and the bottom of an old sewing machine. There were milk bottles and many other glass items, plates and cups of every type. There were chairs, small tables, rusted old pots and pans, an old sharpening wheel, and boxes and boxes of books, magazines and newspapers. Jackie found a newspaper dated November something, 1938, and Steven found a fascinating old toy, probably from the twenties or the thirties.

Fran and John and the boys spent at least two hours just poring through all the old, interesting things there. Fran said, "It's too bad Terry didn't want to come; she would have loved this place." The boys wanted to take a few things that they liked, and John found an old, worn, leather case that fascinated him. Fran found *many* things she was tempted to take, but she knew she and John had to set a good example. Fran said, "It's not right for us to take any of these things; they belong to someone." "Oh, come on Mom," Jackie said. "Just look at this stuff; no one cares about it. You can tell it's been here for a *long* time." "Well, that doesn't make it automatically ours," Fran said. "But I will let you take one thing; you can take that old news-paper. It's musty and getting slightly mildewy. Even though it's been in that box, the weather is definitely getting to it, so you can take the newspaper, just so we can preserve it, but nothing else." Jackie and Steven were a little disappointed. John had really wanted that case, but he knew she was right.

Later, John said, "You're an honest person Fran, and I know you'd cut off your hand before you'd steal anything, but all that fascinating old stuff just sitting there? Tell me the truth, if Jackie and Steven hadn't been with us would you have taken anything from there besides the newspaper?" "Of course not!" she said indignantly. "But then on the other hand, you never know; some of that old glass-ware might have found its way into my pockets." "Hah! You big phony!" John said grinning. "Well, maybe," Fran said. "But, you know, I think Jackie's right; I really don't think anyone cares about that stuff anymore. I think the owners just left it all there hoping people like us would come by and clear it out. But to Jackie and Steven, I can't simply justify taking anything they want just because it *looks* like nobody wants it." "It's a good lesson for them, that's for sure," John said. "But you're still a big phony; if they weren't around, you'd have loaded up the car, wouldn't you?" Fran smiled deviously at John and raised one eyebrow, "You've got *that* right."

The most charming feature about the log cabin was the walls inside. There was no paint or wallpaper; it was just logs, and all over the logs people over the years had carved initials or remarks, and dates of their stay there. One read: "It took fourteen hours to get here, but we finally made it...It was worth the trip...Bill & Joan & the kids...8/14/39." Another one read: "Back again this year...Joe & Annie...1934." They were all similar; people writing down for posterity their time at the cabin. The one Fran and John liked the best read: "It's been five years since we've been here...the war is over...Glad to get back...Pete & Mary... 1947. Jackie and Steven let out a holler when they saw written on the wall: "Love it here...John & Fran...Nov. 1972." "Can we do it, Mom?" Steven pleaded. "Can we put our names in the wall too?" Jackie had already started.

Sunday afternoon, they were all feeling bad about leaving to go home. Jackie and Steven and Samantha walked in the woods for a little while, and then took the boat out once more with John. As they were packing up the car, they extracted a promise from their mother and John that they would all come back to the cabin at the soonest possible opportunity. Fran and John promised. John smiled at Fran. "Did I tell you they'd love it?" He whispered.

By this time Fran and John and Tim and Jean Taylor had become good friends. They visited each other often, and ate dinner at each other's homes. Tim introduced Fran and John to some nice restaurants he and Jean enjoyed, and Terry, Jackie and Steven got along great with Timmy, Kathy, Debbie, Pauline and Tommy. They had great fun in Tim and Jean's swimming pool. Fran and Jean became the very best of friends. Fran soon found out that Jean was a born-again Christian. She would talk about the Bible and Jesus to Fran now and then, but she didn't 'force-feed' it to her. Fran was crazy about Jean, despite the fact that she was one of those strange 'born-agains'.

*****

The second year of little league was even better than the first. Jackie was becoming a terrific ballplayer, and watching him was so much fun. Fran loved watching the kids, and cheering them on. "Come on Mikey! (or whoever on the team was up at bat). Watch the ball all the way! You can do it!" She'd yell. Fran became the team mother to all the kids on the Giants.

One of the parents that came to the games was Bob Hall; his son David was on the team. Bob was a born-again Christian, and a very zealous one at that. He would corner Fran in the parking area of whatever park the game was at, and talk to her about Jesus Christ and how He died for her sins. He was so much more gregarious than Jean; Fran thought Bob was a religious fanatic, so she would try to be down on the field before Bob got there.

One evening Bob Hall cornered Fran, and was telling her how she was a sinner who needed a Savior. She didn't want to hear about it this night; she was late and she simply wanted to watch the game, which was already going on. She could hear the coaches yell, "WHO ARE WE?" Then the response from the boys, "GIANTS!" Bob just kept talking. *"Maybe he doesn't care about the game, but I do,"* she thought. She would never be rude to him; he was a really nice man, who obviously loved the Lord more than anything else in this world, but she loved her son and wanted to watch him play ball. From where she stood she could see that there was a 'man' on second and a 'man' on third. When Jackie didn't see her at the start of the game, he kept looking for her; he kept asking John, "Where's Mom? Where is she?" It was important to Jackie that she be there.

As Bob kept 'preaching' to her she could tell it was Jackie's turn up at bat and there were two outs. She was feeling angry with Bob for keeping her there. She wanted to be down on the field cheering Jackie on; after all, it was a crucial moment in the game. As she turned to say something to Bob, she heard a loud 'crack'. She turned around just in time to see Jackie hit the ball out of the park. "That's enough about me going to hell, Bob," she said, as she dashed down onto the field, screaming and clapping and jumping up and down. It wasn't Jackie's first home run, but it sure was the most exciting one. John came running over to her; he lifted her up and spun her around, all the while yelling, "He did it! He did it! He hit a home run!" They were laughing and calling out to Jackie, and cheering for him, and for the two other boys who ran 'home'. After a minute John said, "Where have you been? I thought you'd be here a half hour ago." Fran answered him with one word, "Guess!" He said, "Bob Hall, right?" "Right! That's it, John! I mean it. I'm going to have to be rude to him, I guess. I come here to see the games, not to get bombarded with the Bible." From then on Fran made sure she left the house *with* John and Jackie every time there was a game.

Jackie hit quite a few home runs in his four years on the Giants. He was not only a good fielder, but he was also one of the best hitters on the team. He was a bundle of energy, and real exciting to watch. Fran was so proud of him.... except during one game......

There were two outs when Jackie got up to bat. He hit a line drive right out to right field; he was out at first base. Jackie was mad, at himself more than anyone else. He slumped down onto the bench with his head in his hands, feeling angry, and sorry for himself. It was the Giants turn to take the field, and all the boys ran out to their positions.... except Jackie. He just sat there pouting. John and Paul and Tom kept calling to him, "Jackie, get out there; take your position." Jackie didn't move. They kept yelling to him. The umpire finally said to Paul, "Get your man on first base or get someone else to relieve him." Paul yelled to Jackie again. Nothing. Fran said to Jackie, "What's wrong with you? You know you have to take the good with the bad in baseball. It's not all home runs and glory. I know you're disappointed, but get over it, and take your position." He didn't budge. Fran finally stood up, and said to him, "I'm ashamed of you, Jackie; I mean it, and if you don't get up right this minute and act like a man, and get out to first base, I'm walking off this field and I will never come back. I will never again be here for one of your games." She waited a moment and then started to walk. Jackie jumped up and said, "I'm going, Mom; don't leave, please." He ran out to first base and Fran sat back down. She heard someone say, "That kid could use a good beating." She was embarrassed; she knew what the other parents were thinking. It was what she would have been thinking, had it been one of the other boys.

When the inning was over, Fran told Jackie he needed to apologize to John, and to Paul and Tom. He did, and apologized to Fran too, and he never acted like that again on the ball field. He knew his mother was disappointed in him, and he also knew she meant what she said about never coming back to another game. Fran breathed a sigh of relief when he finally did the right thing. She knew she would have had to live up to her word and she'd be heartbroken if she were no longer a part of the Giants, and not seeing Jackie play baseball would have been a major disappointment to her.

At the end of every little league season Fran and John held a cookout for the boys on the team, and their parents. Fran would have trophies made for the boys, with plaques on them. The plaques always read the same:

"WHO ARE WE?"
"GIANTS!"
Jackie Roche
1972

Every boy got the same "GIANTS" trophy with his name and the year on it, whether he was a good ball player or a not-so-good ball player. John said, "Each boy is important to the team in some way, no matter what kind of ball player he is."

Every now and then a boy would join the team who was a bit of a wise guy. John always told the boys, "We don't allow bad language on this team for any reason." Inevitably some wise guy would chuckle and say, "Does that mean the coaches, too?" The answer was always the same, whether it came from Paul or John or Tom. "When you hear one of *us* using language, then you can, too." John never used bad language, on or off the field; it was just never a part of him. He figured if he could get angry and not swear, then certainly the boys should be able to, also. They never had a problem.

During Jackie's last two years in little league he was picked as an all-star with two other boys to represent the Giants in the All-Star Game at the end of each season. At the end of each All-Star game, balls were given out to the best players in the game. The first year Jackie won the ball for best fielder in the All-Star game. The second year he won the ball for best hitter in the All-Star game.

Jackie ended his four years on the Giants by hitting a home run his last time up at bat. The ball soared right over the fence. The umpire said, "I've never seen anyone in *this* field hit a ball over that fence." Fran was yelling and cheering, and John was whistling; they were very proud of him. Jackie ran those bases with a huge grin on his face.

*****

One evening around nine o'clock Ethel and Andy got a call from Holy Ghost Hospital. They had spent the afternoon with Peter, and they were very tired and about to go to bed. Peter had Pneumonia and wasn't doing well at all. In the past few hours he seemed to have taken a real bad turn for the worse. The hospital felt that maybe they might want to come back as they didn't believe Peter would make it through the night. Andy called his brother, and he and Ethel met Charlie and Margaret at the hospital. It was obvious Peter was much worse than he had been a few hours earlier. They stayed by his side through the night.

At four-thirty, the morning of February 15, 1973 Pietro Vitello died at Holy Ghost Hospital. He was almost 97years old. He was buried at St. Michael's Cemetery beside his wife Crocifessa, whom he had loved so dearly, and had spent over 65years with.

Peter never learned much English, but he and Crocifessa had become American citizens many years earlier. He returned only once to his beloved Sicily with his brother Giuseppe, when their mother was dying. [Giuseppe had opened a somewhat exclusive clothing store, which later became a chain of stores known as Tello's]. When Peter left Sicily, somehow he knew he would never go back there again. That part of his life was over. He knew he would always love Sicily, especially Riesi where he grew up, and where his children were born, but home was wherever Crocifessa was…. home was here in America.

The family mourned his passing, and the passing of an era they would never, ever see again.

*****

Steven started playing on the Giants in 1974 when he was ten. It was Jackie's last year on the team, and Steven was thrilled to be on the Giants with his big brother. Steven was small for his age, and wasn't quite the ball player that Jackie was, but he tried hard, and that was all that John asked of him. Steven was never jealous of Jackie; if anything, he was Jackie's greatest admirer. He was very proud of his All-Star brother.

Steven loved being a part of the team. He didn't love baseball the way John and Jackie did, but he loved the fun part and the social part, and especially the team spirit. He played right field, and most times while he was out on the field he was picking dandelions or buttercups for his mother. When a ball was hit to right field John and Paul, Fran, and everyone else would scream, "Steven…heads up!" At the last second he'd drop the flowers and go for the ball; sometimes he caught it and sometimes he didn't. Later, when the pressure was off, Fran and John would kill themselves laughing over their little dandelion picker out in right field.

Steven played on the Giants for three years and loved every minute of it, as did Fran and John. Tom moved away, and Paul couldn't coach any longer. John continued to coach the Giants for fourteen years, and Fran was there at most practices and every game. Hearing John yell, "WHO ARE WE?" And all the kids yell at the top of their lungs, "GIANTS!" never failed to bring a smile to Fran's face.

Steven became an assistant coach with John during the last few years. He may not have been the greatest baseball player, but he became a real good coach under John's tutelage. Fran continued to have the cookout each year with trophies for every boy. Those years with the Giants were happy times for all of them, even Terry, who came once in a while to watch the games, but mostly it was to see a particularly handsome boy on the team named Al Pasquale.

*****

Fran and John became good friends with Paul and Debbie Beatrice. They enjoyed each other's company immensely. They would get together one week at Fran's house and the next week at Paul and Debbie's in Holbrook. They'd order Chinese food and play 'Oh Hell', a card game that they loved. They would go to flea markets on Sunday afternoons in good weather. They had a lot of good times with Paul and Debbie; they were a terrific couple.

Another couple that Fran and John liked a lot was Bill and Cheri Robinson who lived nearby in Quincy. Bill was a good friend, and always willing to help Fran and John if they needed it. He and John worked together at Reliable Fence. Fran and John would get together with them also and play 'Oh Hell'. They were a real nice couple.

Fran and John got together often with Dottie and Chet too; they'd order pizza and watch a hockey game on TV. They were crazy about the Boston Bruins, and in particular, Bobby Orr and Phil Esposito. The four of them always had fun together; John and Chet would keep Fran and Dottie laughing almost non-stop.

One evening at Dottie and Chet's, Fran and Dottie decided to make a cheese fondue to have while they watched the hockey game. They made it according to the directions but it just didn't taste very good. They tried to doctor it up a little but it still wasn't good. Finally Fran opened Dottie's cabinet and took down the Nestlé's Quick powdered chocolate. Dottie started laughing. "You're *not* going to put that in the fondue." "Hey, Dottie, it's a waste now anyway," Fran said, as she scooped out three heaping spoonfuls and stirred them into the fondue mix. "Let's have some fun with the guys." "All right!" Dottie said. "Let's see what else we've got here." She began to produce all kinds of things, from Gravy Master to spices like oregano, rosemary and garlic powder. Fran opened the refrigerator and found a jar of horseradish and some mustard; a few tablespoons of each went into the cheese fondue.

When the 'fondue' was good and hot, Dottie said, "Should we taste it?" "Sure, why not?" Fran said. "It's all good food. Just because none of it should ever go together, doesn't mean it can't be eaten." They both tasted it and immediately spit it out into the sink laughing. "Oh God," Fran said, "they're going to kill us." Dottie was trying to muffle all-out guffaws while cutting up the French bread for the 'fondue'.

When it was all ready, they brought the 'fondue' into the living room and set it on the coffee table with napkins and the fondue forks. "Mmmm," Chet said, "that smells good!" Fran looked at Dottie and they both turned and ran back into the kitchen. "Oops!

Forgot something!" Fran yelled, as the two of them broke out into gales of laughter. When Dottie and Fran went back into the living room after composing themselves, Chet and John had already started eating the 'fondue'. "What do you think of it?" Fran asked. "Well, it's not bad," John said, "but there seems to be a kind of *undertaste* to it. To be honest with you, I can't say I'm crazy about it." Fran bit her lip trying to look serious. It was all she could do to keep from bursting out laughing. *"Undertaste?"* she thought, *"that's the 'under-<u>statement</u> of the year."* "I don't mean to hurt your feelings," John went on, "I know you two went to a lot of trouble, but this just isn't my 'cup of tea'." Chet said, "Gee, I don't know, I think it's pretty good," and he kept eating. Was he serious? They couldn't tell. Finally Fran and Dottie couldn't hold it in any longer. "Oh God, Chet," Dottie said, "Don't eat any more of that!" "Why not?" He asked. "It's good." Fran and Dottie could hardly stop laughing long enough to tell him exactly what was in it. "Well," he said, as he took another mouthful, "I think you guys are on to something here." Fran, Dottie, and even John were laughing out loud at that point, but Chet just shrugged his shoulders and ate some more. "Meet my husband," Dottie said, "Mr. Cast Iron Stomach." Dottie took the fondue away and told Chet it was for his own good. He gave John a wink as Dottie left the room. John just shook his head and laughed Dottie brought out potato chips and onion dip. "Now you're talking!" John said, as he reached for a large chip.

Years later, any time anyone mentioned cheese fondue, Dottie and Chet and Fran and John simply groaned. John would always add, "Fran and Dottie have a terrific recipe for cheese fondue; you should try theirs some time."

*****

The first weekend in November 1973 Fran and John and Dottie and Chet headed up to the cabin in Maine. Ethel and Andy took Terry, Jackie, Steven, and Cindy for the weekend. They left Thursday right after work and arrived at the cabin around nine-thirty. It was very dark and Dottie felt a little like Fran did the first time she was there. They hooked up the water, and got a fire going in the stove. Fran made coffee right away and before long the cabin was warm and cozy. They sat up talking for a while, but soon realized how very tired they were, and went to bed. In the morning Dottie was just as amazed as Fran had been looking out over the pond. "You were right Fran; this is just beautiful," she said. Chet and John were already out in the canoe fishing. Dottie and Fran made coffee, bacon and eggs and toast, and called the guys in for breakfast. Later they went to Blueberry Hill, and then to POLLY PETERS USED ITEMS. Dottie always loved antiques and Fran knew she would love Polly Peters. Dottie couldn't believe her eyes as they drove up to the old antiques and collectables store. Nothing had changed. They had great fun rummaging through all the items outside Polly's. "What a step back in time this is," Dottie said. "Boy, would I love to own this place." Fran said, "Who knows? One day you might have your own shop." "Mmm, wouldn't that be nice?" Dottie said, smiling.

The whole weekend was such fun for the four of them. Fran and Dottie rowed around the pond in the boat, and John and Chet spent a lot of time in the canoe fishing. After supper, they played cards one night, and Monopoly the next. They spent the whole weekend laughing, as John's antics had them all in stitches; Chet did his part too.

Fran had brought a little cassette recorder with her, and Dottie had brought a cassette of Seals and Crofts singing, "*We May Never Pass This Way Again.*" They played it almost constantly when they were inside the cabin; it became the perfect song for that weekend.

Unfortunately things change, and Fran, John, Dottie and Chet never *did* pass that way again. But in years to come that song never failed to bring to mind the sweetest memories.

Chet was getting edgy; he wanted more than what Reliable Fence Company could ever offer him. He missed the Air Force and started talking about reenlisting. There was no fear of him being sent to Vietnam again, as the war was over in Vietnam, and the last remaining troops stationed in Saigon had been sent home.

Chet wasn't making enough money at Reliable to support a family, and if he signed up before three years was up, he'd be able to go right back in without losing anything; it would be like he had never left. Dottie wasn't happy about it, but she had always wanted to travel, and this looked like the only way she'd be able to afford to do it. And, if nothing else, the service did offer security…so they decided on the Air Force again.

Everyone in the family was disappointed, especially Ethel. She took it very hard. "God only knows where they'll send them," she said. "I thought we'd be watching Cindy grow up like we have with Fran's children." Ethel was kind of angry with Chet; she felt he was taking her family away from her. She knew Dottie and Cindy were *his* family now, but she was just so very disappointed.

Chet received his orders and he and Dottie and Cindy were sent to Biloxi, Mississippi. Andy said, "Well, Ethel, we can thank God that the war is over, and that they're not being sent out of the states; at least we can get to see them once in a while." Ethel *was* grateful for that, and *very* thankful that the war in Vietnam was ended…. everyone was.

****

Terry and Jackie with Tony at two years old.

Giant's coaches: John, Paul and Tom

St. John's Giants 1974
(Steven sitting, first on left, Jackie standing, first on left)

CHAPTER SEVENTEEN
A Torture Rack

On July 4, 1974 Fran was getting her macaroni salad ready to take to her parents' for a cookout. John was outside mowing the grass, and Jackie and Steven were in their room changing their clothes; Terry had been at Andy and Ethel's for a couple of days.

As Fran was rushing to get things ready, she slipped on some spilled water on her kitchen floor. As she fell she reached out to grab onto the cabinet that was right beside her at the time. Her right hand went through the glass door of the cabinet, tearing her wrist open. She knew an artery had been severed because blood was spurting forcefully from the wound, and actually hitting the refrigerator and wall on the other side of the kitchen. Fran knew this was bad; she screamed for John. When he came in he couldn't believe what he was seeing. There was blood everywhere, and Fran was standing in a pool of it. She held her left hand over the cut to apply pressure, but blood was still spurting out between her fingers.

"Oh my God! Oh my God!" John kept saying as he looked at Fran. She said to him, "John, get me a large towel to wrap around my wrist. You've got to take me to the hospital; it looks like I'm going to need stitches." John looked like he was in shock. Fran said it again. "Hurry John," she said. He ran for the towel, wrapped it around her wrist, and hurried her out the back door. "The boys!" Fran yelled. Just then Jackie and Steven came out of their room. "Mom! Oh Mom!" Jackie was nearly hysterical, and Steven started screaming. "Your mother's had an accident," John said. "I'm taking her to the hospital." "I'll call you from there." "John, is she okay? What happened?" Jackie yelled. Steven kept crying, "Mom! Mom!" "She'll be okay," John cried, as he was getting Fran into the car. "I don't have time to explain; I'll call you as soon as I can. Don't touch anything; I'll clean up when I get home. Just sit tight; say a prayer for her!"

John was terribly frightened. By the time they pulled out of the driveway the towel around Fran's wrist was completely saturated, and Fran's lap was a puddle of blood. *"Oh God, this is not good,"* John was thinking. As they neared Quincy Center Fran noticed that the buildings seemed to be wavy and floating. *"Please God, don't let me pass out before we get to the hospital,"* she prayed. When they came up to the light at Hancock Street it was red. John started to slow down as there was quite a bit of traffic. "John," Fran said, "Put your hand on the horn and go straight through the light." He kept his hand on the horn all the way to the hospital. John was so nervous that he pulled up at the emergency room door, jumped out to help Fran, and forgot to put the car in PARK. A man yelled, and John jumped back in the car, and set the car right. "As he and Fran got out of the car, Fran said, "It's okay, John; I'll be all right." He helped her through the door, and as they walked into the emergency room Fran felt herself passing out. "John... I can't..." John grabbed her and held her up as an orderly rushed to her; then John lifted her onto a gurney. Nurses, doctors, and orderlies seemed to just come out of the woodwork to help her. John made a mental note to thank them all later.

A little while later, although Fran had no idea how long, she opened her eyes and realized she was in an operating room. A nurse was doing something to her wrist. "What are you doing?" Fran asked. "I'm irrigating your wound to make sure we get all the glass out before the operation," she said. "The surgeon should be here soon." "Operation?" Fran asked. "A surgeon? Is a surgeon necessary just to put a few stitches in my wrist, and send me home?" "Oh, well, don't you worry about anything, dear," she said. "Dr. DiTullio is the best surgeon in this hospital. He'll get you all fixed up." *"I wasn't worried,"* she thought. "Funny, I can't feel you doing that to my wrist," Fran said. "It doesn't hurt at all." "Well, that's a blessing,

Hon, isn't it?" The nurse said. Fran was very confused but too groggy to really think it through. She turned her head to look at her wrist and she came close to screaming. "Oh my God!" she cried. "That can't be my hand!" Her wrist and hand were completely opened up and flapped over. It looked like an open book to her. She became almost hysterical. "Oh no! No!" she cried. "How can this be?" Just then someone came into the room. "Frances, my name is Dr. DiTullio," he said. "I'm going to be operating on your hand. I need you to try to relax." She kept repeating, "Oh God! Oh God!" " I'm going to do everything I can to get you to be able to use your hand again. *"Use my hand again?"* Fran was shocked and confused.

Dr. DiTullio had asked John if Fran had eaten anything in the last few hours. John couldn't remember, so the doctor gave Fran a local anesthetic, five shots administered in her armpit. The first two were very painful; the rest she hardly felt. Despite all that was happening, a crazy thought came into Fran's mind, *"Oh, I'm so glad I shaved under my arms this morning."* Later she laughed about that and thought about a Bible verse her mother had quoted a couple of times from Ecclesiastes, *"Vanity of vanities; all is vanity!"* She had no idea who, where or what Ecclesiastes was in the Bible. Dr. DiTullio told the nurse he wanted a screen put over Fran's arm and upper body. He didn't want her seeing all he was doing.

That evening, Dr. DiTullio came into her room. She had been sleeping since the operation. She awoke with a start as he was examining her fingers, which were grossly swollen. "How are you feeling Frances?" he asked. "Very tired," she said. "Are you in much pain?" "No, not much," she answered, "Only when you call me Frances." He smiled; what do you like to be called?" "Fran," she said. She was glad to see him as she had a lot of questions for him. "What exactly happened to my hand and wrist?" She asked. "Well, Fran, when your hand went *through* the glass not a lot of damage was done," he said. "It was when you pulled your hand *out* of the glass window that all the damage occurred. As you know an artery was severed; tendons, ligaments and nerves also. The *really* bad part happened when the median nerve was severed." "What is the median nerve?" Fran asked. "Putting it very simply, it's what gives your hand movement," he said. "Oh great!" Fran said. "Tell me the truth, Doctor;

am I going to have the full use of my hand?" "Well, I don't think you'll have the *full* use of your hand, but I do believe that most of it will come back in time." *"Most of it,"* Fran thought. *"Oh God, what does that mean?"* Fran felt like she was slurring her words when she talked. "Am I talking funny?" she asked the doctor. "I feel like I'm talking funny." "It's the medication," he said. "It's making you groggy. Fran, your arm and hand are bandaged and in a removable cast for now," he said. "I'll be keeping a close watch on you while you're here in the hospital. Afterwards I'll see you at my office." Fran asked, "How long will I have to stay here?" "You'll be here for about five days; we'll see how you do," he said. "You lost a lot of blood, Fran. Also, you may be feeling a lot more pain tomorrow. When you do, I've left instructions for pain medication at the nurses' station for you. "Later, when your wrist is healed, you're going to need a lot of physical therapy. It's going to be a long grind, Fran," Dr. DiTullio said. "It's going to take between nine months and a year for the median nerve to grow back." "It *will* grow back though?" Fran asked. "It's like a tight rubber band," he said. "And it's been cut, so it needs to heal and kind of stretch out again. It should 'grow' back approximately an inch a month." Fran barely heard the last things he said to her, as she drifted off to sleep.

Dr. DiTullio had understated the amount of pain Fran would be feeling. She spent the next day moaning, and close to tears with the pain. At times it seemed unbearable.

It was eight weeks later when Dr. DiTullio told Fran she didn't need the 'cast' any longer. After being in the cast for so long her hand had formed itself into what he called, a "claw." Fran couldn't straighten out her fingers; she couldn't move them at all. She had no feeling whatsoever in the entire hand. "Is the feeling going to come back?" she asked. "I'm right-handed, Doctor; I can't do anything with my left hand." "It's going to take time," he said, "but I believe you'll get back most of the use of your hand. And Fran, you will be very surprised at how much you'll actually be able to do with your other hand. It's amazing what we can do when we have to, you'll see."

It *was* a long grind. The physical therapy was very painful. The therapist worked on one joint at a time with each finger. Fran learned to comb her hair, put on her makeup, eat, and even write, although not very well, with her left hand. She couldn't cut up her meat at dinner, but she had John and three helpers to do it for her. The kids were terrific during that time, especially Terry. She did everything, from helping with the housework, to helping Fran get dressed. They were all very helpful, and John, well, he couldn't do enough for her. When the therapist had done all she could do, it was up to John to continue the therapy on Fran's hand at home. He did it faithfully with Fran, one joint at a time. He was her strength during that most difficult time.

As the months passed, more and more feeling came into her fingers; not all of them, but the thumb, forefinger and middle finger seemed to be coming back. Fran was pleased with the progress she was making. There was still no feeling at all in the ring finger, little finger, and the heel of her hand. "I told you not to expect a hundred percent, Fran," Dr. DiTullio said. "Getting back the thumb and two fingers is really terrific. You'll be able to do most things with just those three fingers."

A few years later Fran realized that she had some feeling on one side of her ring finger, not the side next to the little finger. She never got the feeling back in the little finger, and the heel of her hand always felt like there was a shot of Novocain in it. She got used to it, and eventually did everything she used to do before the accident. There were a few embarrassing times though, although sometimes laughable, when Fran would put out her hand to receive change back from a clerk and it would all fall between her fingers without her feeling it. There were real aggravating times also, like when her little finger would get caught on loose threads in her pocket, and she couldn't understand why she couldn't get her hand out of her pocket. Or when she'd be writing and her hand would cramp up badly around the pen, or the needle, if she were trying her hand at sewing. There were lots of other funny or embarrassing things that occurred because of the lack of feeling in the fingers. A little more serious were the many times she would burn her fingers on hot pans and not even know it. It took a lot of adjustments but she learned how to live with a hand that didn't always respond the way it used to. But one of many good things was, that even only using three fingers on her right hand, she was able to type pretty well again. Her hand *did* work, and that's all that really mattered; she was very, very thankful for that. Considering what many other people have had to live with, she felt very lucky.

*****

John left Reliable Fence Company, and on his last day there, Fran came to pick him up. As he walked up the ramp to punch his card in the time clock, he could see her sitting in the car. There were other people waiting there to pick someone up also. John waved to Fran and she waved back as he approached the time clock, which was housed in a wooden enclosure. As he pushed his card down into the slot he let out a yell. He continued yelling, as the clock *appeared* to be sucking him in; he seemed to be disappearing into the clock enclosure. Fran almost screamed with laughter, as John's legs were sticking straight out of the time clock. He was putting up a 'good fight' but it looked like the clock was winning. His legs were kicking and his arms were flailing. A woman in one of the other cars was laughing hysterically, as was Fran. When John finally extricated himself from the clock, he jumped back with both fists in the air like he was daring the clock to try that again. Fran had tears rolling down her face as John approached the car. "You are, without a doubt, the weirdest person I've ever known." She couldn't stop laughing, and he started laughing with her. She laughed all the way home, and every time she thought about it she laughed, even years later.

Andy offered John a job painting, and in September of 1974 John started working for J. W. Graham Painting Company. He didn't know much about painting, but until he decided what he wanted to do for the rest of his life, painting would do. Andy put him on easy jobs to gain some experience. The very first job John did was with Andy, painting the bleachers at a ballpark in Hingham. At first John seemed to have more paint on himself than on whatever he was painting, but after a while, with experience, he started becoming a pretty good painter. Meanwhile, Joe was being primed to take over more and more of the responsibilities of running J. W. Graham Co.

Andy planned to retire in a few years and the company would pass to Joe.

*****

Andy and Ethel rented a cottage in Westford a few years in a row, right beside Slim and Rose Giuliana's cottage. Like Rose and Slim's place, the cottage was right on the edge of the lake. Terry, Jackie and Steven spent a lot of time there with their grandparents, and Fran and John came up on the weekend. Joe and Mae rented the same cottage at other times; Shaun, Paul, Mark, Peter and Claire loved the place, too. Joe and Fran were thrilled to see their children coming to know their beloved Westford and enjoying their wonderful Long Sought For Pond.

When Steven was ten years old Fran noticed that he had a slight hump over his right shoulder blade. It wasn't noticeable until he bent way over at the waist. It concerned her and she brought it to the pediatrician's attention, who in turn made an appointment for Steven to see Dr. Richard Kilfoyle, an orthopedist whose office was in Weymouth. Fran took Steven to see Dr. Kilfoyle; he examined Steven and had x-rays taken of his back. He said that Steven had a somewhat severe case of Scoliosis, with a thirty-eight degree curvature of the spine. He wanted him measured and fitted for a Milwaukee brace right away. Dr. Kilfoyle asked Fran if anyone in the family had Scoliosis. "Well, I have always had a curve in my spine," Fran said, but I don't know if it's Scoliosis." Dr. Kilfoyle examined Fran and said, "You have Scoliosis, and a somewhat prominent curvature of the spine. When you were a kid, they didn't know much about it, but today Steven is able to have the benefit of proper treatment for Scoliosis that you never had.

Fran hated that Milwaukee brace; she always felt badly for Steven. He was a handsome boy, with his huge brown eyes and thick dark brown hair, but no matter what he wore, his clothes never looked right with that brace on underneath. Steven had to wear it 23 hours a day; he could take it off to do his exercises and take a shower. He had to wear it to bed, which took a lot of getting used to. Fran let him take it off to play baseball but it would go right back on before they left the ball field. Steven didn't mind the brace as much as his mother did; he got so used to it that after awhile it became like a part of him.

Dr. Kilfoyle started seeing Steven at the Massachusetts Hospital School in Canton for his appointments, which were every other month. The curvature held to thirty-eight degrees for over three years. There was always the understanding that Steven would probably have to have surgery on his back, but Dr. Kilfoyle wanted to wait until after he had a growth spurt. At almost fourteen Steven was only 4'9" tall. The doctor explained that a metal rod about a foot long would be put in his back, fusing it to the upper and lower part of his spine. He would grow very little after that, as the fusion stops growth in the spine. Dr. Kilfoyle was relying on the brace to keep the curvature from getting worse until Steven grew taller.

*****

Fran and John, Jackie and Steven went to the cabin in Maine in August of 1974. That time, besides fishing, and going to POLLY PETERS USED ITEMS, they spent a lot of time swimming and diving off the raft. Again they had a wonderful time.

In June of 1975 Fran and John decided to go to the cabin in Maine again. This time Fran insisted on Terry coming with them. "You'll never understand how beautiful and natural the place is unless you at least spend one weekend there," Fran said. "And I'm always the only female with three sweaty, smelly guys." "Oh joy! I can hardly wait," Terry said. Fran laughed, and Jackie said, "That's right Terry; we don't wash, use deodorant, or shave. We live like the early settlers lived, no TV, and no telephone. We cut down trees for the wood stove, we fish for our dinner, we pump cold water in the sink, and we use the outhouse when nature calls. Oh yeah, Terry, you're going to love the outhouse. It smells like a bed of roses, and the spiders keep you company while you go." "Oh God," Terry said, "What did I ever do to deserve this?" "Oh Jackie, don't be mean," John said. "It's not like that Terry." "So there *is* a TV, there's *no* wood stove, there *is* hot water, and there's no outhouse, John, right?" John and Jackie just smiled. "Mmm, that's what I thought," Terry said.

"Mom, do I *really* have to go?" "Yes, you're going!" Fran said. "If you hate it, I'll never make you go again. If I can put up with those inconveniences whenever we go, you can certainly do it for one weekend. You're going to love it."

Terry hated it! She agreed the pond was beautiful, "But how can anyone put up with that outhouse and no hot running water?" Fran had asked her to go for a cruise around the pond, or to go for a walk in the woods; she went for a walk but that's all she wanted to do. John asked Fran, "Are all fifteen year old girls this moody?" "Usually, yes," Fran said. "But she's almost sixteen; let's hope it gets better soon."

Terry sat, most of the time, on the porch listening to her radio. Finally Fran said, "Come on Terry, you and I are taking the boat out; we'll row around the pond and see if any of the cabins have people staying at them." "Oh Ma, who cares?" "I do," Fran said. "I like knowing if anyone is nearby or if we're up here alone." Terry knew her mother was getting perturbed at her for just sitting around, so she figured she'd go and maybe Fran would leave her to herself afterwards.

Fran and Terry were actually enjoying the time together in the boat. The sun was warm and comfortable out on the pond, although it was a fairly cool day. After rowing around the pond, they decided to head back and dock at the raft and just relax on the raft and take in the sun. John and the boys were fishing off the pier; every now and then they'd yell something out to Fran and Terry like, "Hello the boat!" Fran would yell back, "Hello the pier!" Terry thought it was all very corny, and that her family had become a bunch of mountain hillbillies overnight.

Fran and Terry arrived at the raft and Fran told Terry to grab a corner post and loop the boat rope over it. Without thinking, Terry moved all the way to the side of the boat and reached for the post. Fran said, "Don't go so close to the edge Terry; the boat will tip over." Before Fran had the sentence out of her mouth the boat started tipping over. Terry tried to get back into the center, but it was too late; over it went dropping Fran and Terry into the water. They were shocked at first, but after a few seconds Fran started laughing. Terry couldn't hold back; she started laughing too. John was yelling to them, "Are you okay? Do you need help?" Fran yelled to him that they were fine. She tied the boat to the raft, and she and Terry decided to swim back to the pier. They just wanted to get into some dry clothes, as Fran was in shorts and a shirt, and Terry was in jeans and a shirt.

As Terry and Fran were swimming, Fran noticed that Terry was getting further and further behind her. She called back to her, "Terry, are you all right?" "Yeah, I'm okay," she answered. After another minute or so, Terry was quite a way behind Fran, and she wasn't swimming as high in the water as she started out doing. Fran called back again, "Terry, are you sure you're all right?" "Yeah, I'm... okay," she responded. She didn't sound too sure of herself, and when Fran looked back a third time, the water was up to Terry's nose, and she was struggling to raise herself up higher. Fran yelled, "John, Terry's in trouble!" Jackie immediately grabbed the inner tube that was on the pier and dove into the water. As he was swimming toward Terry she was close to going under. "Terry," he yelled. "Grab the tube," as he threw the tube as hard as he could in her direction. It was a good toss. Terry grabbed onto the tube and a few seconds later Jackie reached her. "Just relax and hold on, Terry," he said, and I'll just pull you.. She was exhausted trying to stay above water, so she just held on and let him bring her to the pier. As she reached the pier John grabbed her hand and started pulling her onto it. "What the heck?" He cried. "Terry, did you gain about fifty pounds out there on the pond?" Fran was still in the water waiting for Terry to get up onto the pier. When she looked up she started laughing. "Terry, you're losing your pants!" she cried. "I know," Terry said. "I can hardly move. My jeans are completely soaked; they're pulling me down. John pulled her up onto the pier, while Terry did her best to keep her jeans from winning the battle and ending up around her knees. They were all laughing, even Terry, as she hobbled up the steps into the cabin. They laughed about that incident many times after that. Terry had fun that day, but she never really wanted to go back to the cabin again, and she never did.

*****

Jackie was playing basketball for Quincy Point Junior High School. He loved basketball, and he was one of the best players on the team. He and his friend Paul Bandera got more than three quarters of the baskets in every game. Fran and John went to a few of the games, and Fran couldn't get over the fact that Jackie was just as exciting to watch playing basketball as he was playing baseball. So often throughout the game the kids seated on the benches all around the gymnasium were calling out, "Ro-chie, Ro-chie, Ro-chie." Fran felt proud, and very pleased for him.

*****

Steven had just come out of the shower when Fran noticed that the hump on his back seemed more pronounced. She had him bend way over at the waist. She was shocked at what she saw. Not only was the back hump more pronounced, but now there seemed to be a hump protruding from his left hip. Fran called Dr. Kilfoyle right away, and the next day they went to see him. Jackie was home from school that day, so he came with them. Jackie was not always the most sensitive older brother, but Fran could see he was worried.

After examining Steven and taking more x-rays, Dr. Kilfoyle wanted to speak to Fran alone. "He needs the spinal fusion immediately," he said. "What? I don't understand," Fran said. "I thought we were going to wait until he was at least seventeen, 'til he had a growth spurt." "That's what we hoped for," Dr. Kilfoyle said, "but things have changed drastically. The curvature is pushing his ribs out, and pushing on his kidneys." "We were just here two months ago, and the curve was holding its own," she said. "How could so much have changed in that short time?" Dr. Kilfoyle knew that Fran was frightened.

"Fran, I've performed this operation many times," he said. "I'm confident that Steven will come through this with flying colors." "But his *spine*," she groaned. "He's only 4'9", and he hasn't had a growth spurt yet." "Well," he said, "on the operating table, as we straighten the spine as much as we can, he'll gain a few inches. Think of his spine like a piece of cooked spaghetti that's bent." He said. "When you straighten it out it becomes longer; the same will happen to his spine. Let's just hope we can get him over five feet. He's going to be fine, Fran; try not to worry." "Oh, right!" she said.

When Dr. Kilfoyle told Steven that he had to be operated on as soon as possible, he got kind of upset. He was trying not to cry, but it was obvious he was very scared. Steven said he wanted to go for a walk around the grounds; Jackie went with him, giving him moral support.

Ethel and Andy were quite upset when they heard the news. They came right over to see Steven and to talk with Fran about the surgery and what it entailed. After hearing the gory details, they left feeling worse than when they came. They loved their grandchildren so much, and they hurt when any one of them hurt. They especially hurt for Steven, who had to wear that darned brace for three years, only to end up needing the spinal surgery.

Monday morning, Fran brought Steven over to the Mass. Hospital School for pre-op testing. His surgery was scheduled for Tuesday morning. He wasn't nervous at all; he had resigned himself to the fact that he had to have the operation, and that was not going to change. Fran stayed with him all day and John, Jackie and Terry came over in the early evening. Ethel and Andy came over, too. Fran hated to leave Steven that night, but he knew she'd be back first thing in the morning.

John took the day off Tuesday, and he and Fran got to the hospital about nine o'clock in the morning; Steven's surgery was scheduled for ten-thirty. He was so glad to see them walk in the room. They talked for a while, and John had Steven laughing.

Dr. Kilfoyle and Dr. Aprin came in to talk with them and explain more about the surgery and to reassure Steven that he would be fine. Steven began to get a little nervous after they left. A couple of nurses came in at different times; they were as nice as could be to him.

At about ten o'clock Steven started getting *very* nervous, and soon he began to panic. "I don't want to do this, Mom," he said. Fran could hear the panic rising in his voice. "Steven, you know you need to have this operation," she said. "Please try to relax Honey." "No! I want to go home!" he cried. "Mom, just take me home, please." "Steven, don't do this," John said, as he put his hand on Steven's shoulder; you have to have this surgery, you know that." Steven brushed John's hand from him, and started to climb out of the bed. "No! I'm going home!" he yelled. Fran was close to tears by this time, pleading with Steven to calm down. A nurse came into the room and grabbed Steven to keep him from getting out of bed. She said, "Steven, I'm going to give you a shot; it will relax you and you'll feel terrific." "No!" Steven said. "I'm not staying here; I'm not going to have the operation; I'm going home!" The nurse signaled to John to hold him down and John did just that. Fran's heart was breaking for her son, but she knew this was the only way. Steven kept yelling for a few moments after the shot was administered in his right buttocks, but soon he calmed down and was about as mellow as mellow could be. He was no longer frightened and panicky. He wanted to hug his mother; he told her he loved her and through her tears Fran smiled and kissed him and said, "I love you so much Steven; John and I will be right here when you come out of surgery." He hugged John and told him he loved him, too. John returned the love to Steven. Just then an orderly came in with the nurse to take Steven to the operating room. Fran kissed him again and said, "Remember, we'll be right here when you come out." "Okay," Steven said, and he was wheeled out of the room.

Fran nearly collapsed after he left. The emotion that had filled that room was more than she could handle at that moment. She broke down crying; deep sobs came pouring out of her. John held her for a long time while she cried. "He's going to be fine, Fran," he said.

"You've got to believe that." "He's only thirteen, John; why does he have to go through this? We've all been so lucky in this family. Except for the accident with my wrist, I've never been operated on; I've never had stitches except after giving birth, and I've never broken a bone. It's the same with Terry and Jackie, and Jackie's the wild one.

After a minute or so Fran said, "I know it's not my fault, John, but I passed Scoliosis on to him; I just feel so badly about that." "I know, Fran, I know," was all John could say. He knew there was nothing he could say that would make her feel better. They waited and paced the floor, got coffee, and paced some more. Fran felt at times like she was coming out of her skin. She felt sick to her stomach every time she thought about what the doctors were doing to her boy.

The operation took about six hours, and then Steven was in the recovery room for quite a while after that. By the time he came out Ethel and Andy were there, and Joe and Mae also. John's sister Mary, who lived close to the hospital, came over too.

Steven was put on a Stryker frame right away. The doctor explained that he couldn't be moved or turned over. The Stryker frame was a metal frame with straps that made up the part the patient lay on. There was no mattress, just the straps. When Steven had lain on his stomach for three hours, then the nurse put another frame on top of Steven, screwed it onto the head and foot part of the bottom frame, and with a wheel at the foot, turned Steven *and* the frame right over, so that he was then on his back. It was a marvelous invention for sure, but to Fran it looked like a torture rack.

Two nights after the surgery, someone carelessly removed some of the straps in one of the frames. Steven had been turned over onto his stomach and was complaining that he was in a lot of pain. Fran went and told the nurse, Ellen, how he was feeling, and all she said was, "Well, he just had his shot an hour ago; he's not due for another two hours." "Well," Fran said, "he seems to feel that something's wrong." "He's just being a big baby," the nurse said. "I beg your pardon," Fran said, "Steven is not a big baby; he rarely complains, and you ought to have a little compassion for a kid that's just been through this kind of surgery." Fran was mad; real mad. She had liked every single nurse at the hospital school right from the start, except this particular one. She was cold and unfriendly, and now Fran could see that she had very little kindness and compassion in her. When Fran returned to Steven's room John said, "He's really in a lot of pain, Fran. I mean, the kid never complains, so when he does, it seems that someone ought to listen to him."

After a few minutes Steven started moaning and crying. "Something's wrong, Mom," he kept saying, "something's not right; I feel like I'm falling, like my back is sinking down." Fran didn't know what to do, so she pulled the blanket off of him, and to her his back *did* look like it was dipping down in the middle. She got down on her knees and crawled under the Stryker frame. Fran could not believe what she was seeing. There were straps missing from the frame and Steven was hanging down between the straps. Fran was almost hysterical; she ran out to the nurse and told her what was happening to Steven. "You've got to turn him back over onto his back," Fran cried. "You've got to get him off of that broken frame." "Oh no," the nurse said to her. "The frame is certainly not broken, and he was just turned less than an hour ago. He can't be turned for another two hours." "Come in his room and see the frame for yourself," Fran said. "I am much too busy right now for this," Nurse Ellen said. "You need to calm down, Mrs. Roche." "How dare you tell me to calm down?" Fran said. "My son is suffering in there and you couldn't care less. Are you going to turn him over or not?" "No I am not!" the nurse said. "Fine, I'll do it myself," Fran said, as she stormed away from the nurse's station. "Don't you even think about it, Mrs. Roche!" the nurse called after her.

"It really is a torture rack," Fran thought, as she ran back into Steven's room. John was coming out from under the frame. "They've got to turn him back over," he said. "You're right, Fran, his whole midsection is hanging down through the straps." "Well, the nurse refuses to do it," Fran said, "so you and I are going to turn him over." Steven was really crying; he was suffering terribly. Tina, one of the other nurses came into the room just as Fran and John were tightening the top frame onto the bottom one. "What do you think you're doing?" She cried. "You can't do that!" "Then you do it!" Fran yelled. "First crawl underneath and take a look at that 'torture rack' Steven's lying on." Tina got down on the floor just as Nurse Ellen came storming into the room. As Tina looked up under the frame, she cried, "Oh, my Lord! Ellen, help me turn Steven over!" "He doesn't get turned over for another two hours," Ellen said indignantly. "We're turning him over!" Tina shouted. Tina checked the top and bottom where Fran and John had tightened the bolts, and then spun the wheel, and over Steven went. He was moaning in pain. She went and got another shot of pain medication and gave it to Steven. "I'm sure he's okay, Mrs. Roche," she said. "I'll inform Dr. Kilfoyle and Dr. Aprin about this in the morning." "Thank you for your help, Tina." Fran was shaking badly. "Something should be done about Nurse Ellen," she said. "She shouldn't be working in

this hospital; she's not at all like the rest of you." "Well," Tina said, "I don't have the power to do anything about it, Mrs. Roche, but I promise you those who do will hear about this."

Tina had to go to another section of the hospital. Fran decided to ask Nurse Ellen for Dr. Aprin's home telephone number. If any harm had come to Steven she wasn't going to let it wait until the next day. The nurse was cold and would not accommodate Fran. One of the other nurses came into Steven's room. She said to Fran, "I can't tell you his telephone number but he lives in Weymouth; but you didn't hear that from me." Fran thanked her and went right away to the public telephone down the hall. She looked in the phone book for Dr. Aprin's number. Nothing was listed for a doctor Aprin, so she looked through the few Aprins that were listed. She didn't know his first name but she did find an Aprin listed in Weymouth. She dialed the number and waited. *"Oh, please be him, and please don't be asleep."*

A man answered the phone and Fran said, "I'm sorry to bother you at this time, but would you be Dr. Aprin from the Mass. Hospital School?" "Yes, this is Dr. Aprin," he said, "And who are you? Fran told him who she was, and then proceeded to tell him everything that took place earlier that evening. Dr. Aprin's response was exactly what she hoped for. He was upset and concerned. "Mrs. Roche," he said, "I will go over to the hospital to see Steven at 7:00 in the morning, and I'll have x-rays taken right away. Please don't be worried; the rod that we put in his back is firmly in place; it will take a lot more than what happened this evening to do any real harm." She felt a little better but was still very worried.

Fran and John stayed with Steven for another half hour. The shot Tina had given him had put him into a deep sleep. They left the hospital at just about 9:30, both of them exhausted. She was so very thankful that Steven was sleeping soundly and didn't seem to be in any distress. Also, the straps were back in the frame where they belonged.

At a little after midnight the telephone rang; it was Dr. Aprin. "I'm sorry to wake you, but I wanted you to know that I've been to the hospital to see your son." "Oh, thank God," Fran said. "And no, I wasn't asleep." "When I got there," Dr. Aprin went on, "the nurse told me I had just missed you. I examined Steven thoroughly, and we brought an x-ray machine into his room and took x-rays of him on his back and over on his stomach. I've seen the x-rays and they look perfect. I compared them with his x-rays immediately after the surgery, and nothing has changed; I'm confident that he's fine, Mrs. Roche." "Oh, thank you, Dr. Aprin," Fran said with much emotion. Thank you so very much for not waiting 'til morning to see him." Dr. Aprin added, "About Nurse Ellen, I have written up a complaint against her. In the morning I will speak with the two other nurses who were there. Now you try to get some sleep, Mrs. Roche, and I'm going to do the same. I'll see you in the morning."

Steven seemed okay when Fran went in the next day. Joe stopped by to see him about 2:00 in the afternoon. It was getting near the time for Steven's pain medication; he was in a lot of pain when Joe walked into the room. After a little while the nurse gave Steven his shot, and turned the Stryker frame over. Joe hadn't seen him turned over in that 'torture rack' until this day; it bothered him a lot. Finally the medication took hold and Steven fell asleep.

"How long have you been here?" Joe asked. "Since about quarter of nine." Fran said. "I came as soon as Terry and Jackie left for school." "You look exhausted, Fran," Joe said. Fran told him everything that had happened the night before. "Oh, good God," Joe said. "You poor kid. Look, why don't you let me drive you home, and then you can come back with John later." "Oh, no Joe, I don't want to leave Steven," she said. "If he wakes up and is in pain, and I'm not here, he might feel bad." Just then Tina walked into the room. "Mrs. Roche, I think your brother is right. Why don't you leave your jacket on the chair by Steven's bed so he sees it when he wakes up; he'll think you're getting a cup of coffee or talking to one of the nurses." "That's a good idea Fran," Joe said. "Come on, it's 3:00 now; you'll be back in a couple of hours." Finally Fran said, "I really would like to go home for a while; all right Joe, let's go right now." Tina smiled, "If he wakes up while I'm here, I'll tell him you'll be back shortly." "Thanks, Tina," Fran said, and she and Joe left.

Out in the parking lot Joe put his arm around Fran, and that little show of tenderness opened the floodgates, and she started sobbing. He held her in his arms while she cried, and she could feel his body shaking; he was crying also. It was an intimate, tender moment between brother and sister that Fran knew she would never forget. It reminded her of how much she loved Joe. He had always been her protector, and she felt it so very strongly at that moment.

Steven began to feel much better after about a week. He was still on the Stryker frame, and would be for another week.

One day Fran walked into his room and he was not there; the Stryker frame was gone also. In its place was a freshly made bed. She went to the nurse's station and asked about it, and the nurse smiled and said, "Look down the hall and see who's coming to meet you." Fran nearly burst into tears as she saw Steven, all 'trussed up' in a body cast that went from way up under his chin all the way down to the top of his thighs. He was grinning from ear to ear as he walked the hall to meet her. He was walking with another boy who had been put into a cast also. Steven walked up to his mother and kissed her, and Fran, with tears blinding her eyes, kissed him back. "I thought you weren't going to be put in the cast for another week," she said, "Dr. Kilfoyle and Dr. Aprin examined me this morning and took x-rays, and said I'm doing great, and that I was ready for the cast." "Oh Steven, that's wonderful," Fran said. "Hey, you look taller; I think you're as tall as me." "I'm actually a little taller, Mom," Steven said with a grin. They just measured me in the cast room; I'm 4'11 ½". "Well, that's great," Fran said. "Yeah, It's good, I guess," Steven said, "but I was hoping I'd be over five feet." "Well, you will grow a little more," Fran said. *"Please God, for his sake, let him grow a little more."* She was so relieved that he would no longer be on the Stryker frame.

"There you are, Mrs. Roche." She turned as she heard Dr. Kilfoyle's voice. "I've been trying to call you," he said, with a big grin on his face. "Our boy here is doing great."

Steven came home on Thanksgiving Day, 1977, much to everyone's delight. They went right from the hospital to Ethel and Andy's house for dinner with the family. He wasn't scheduled to come home for two more days, but Dr. Kilfoyle was there and he said he was ready to go home, and what better day than Thanksgiving. Ethel was almost in tears at the sight of Steven walking through the doorway. When Ethel brought the turkey and all the fixings to the table, Andy thanked God for the food, and for keeping His hand on Steven, and bringing him safely home to all of them. Later he said, "This was the best Thanksgiving ever." He said that every year, but this year he meant it more than ever.

Steven spent nine months in the full-body cast, and then he went into a half-body cast for another five months. That was a lot more comfortable. It was a difficult time for him; it was difficult for all of them. The full cast came way up the back of his neck, and high in the front. It came up around his jaw and his chin, preventing him from turning his head to either side or from looking down. He would have to turn his whole body to see to the side, and he wouldn't be able to go up and own stairs safely in school without help. The Daniel Webster School provided a home tutor for him, which worked out fine, but he did miss out on a lot of the social aspects of the eighth grade.

During the year that Steven was in his cast he spent some very lonely and uncomfortable hours. He had gotten very friendly with a boy in school just before he had the operation. His name was Doug D'Olimpio. He was a dear, sweet boy who became Steven's closest friend. Many nights he went with Fran and John to the hospital to visit Steven, and when Steven came home from the hospital Doug would always stop in after school and spend a little time with him, playing games or watching TV. Many evenings Fran would call his mother and ask if Doug could stay for supper. Amy D'Olimpio was a kind and understanding woman, who was always agreeable to Doug doing whatever he could to help Steven get through that difficult time. To Fran, Doug was an angel sent from heaven to keep Steven busy and to keep his spirits up. He stayed overnight almost every weekend. Jackie gave up his bed and slept on the sofa those nights because he knew it meant a lot to Steven.

Doug became like a third son to Fran; she loved him dearly. He was a part of the family, loved by all of them, and Fran knew deep in her heart she'd feel this way about Doug the rest of her life.

Fran always tried to find things that she and Steven could do to keep him from getting bored. On the days the tutor didn't come Fran would take Steven out to lunch to break up the day, and now and then they would go to the North Shore Music Circus to see plays and other performances. They saw "Oklahoma," "Showboat," "Hello Dolly," "Man of La Mancha," and many others. She also took him to see Liberace, the famous pianist, at the South Shore Music Circus. Steven really wasn't interested in seeing Liberace, but Fran talked him into it. "You're going to love the show, I promise you." She was right; Steven couldn't believe how very talented Liberace was, *and* how utterly 'outrageous' and fun he was. It turned out to be a terrific evening, and despite Steven's earlier misgivings, he loved the show.

*****

Terry had always been an excellent student; she received high honors most of the time. Even as a little girl she was so quick to learn that she used to shock Fran and everyone else with her knowledge. She also had phenomenal retention; she could remember, almost word for word, things she would read, and she had a memory for details that was hard to believe. She could remember details from something that happened years earlier as if it were just yesterday.

One day Fran was talking about something that happened just before Terry was born. John teased her and said, "You must remember that, Terry." Terry knew he was teasing her and she said, "John, I wasn't even born yet." "I know," John said, "but you were probably in your mother's womb; you can remember back to the womb, can't you?" Terry grinned and responded, "No... back to the delivery room, but not much before that." John guffawed. "Hey Terry," he said. "That was a good one; I'm proud of you." Terry grinned and bowed at the waist. She was more serious than Jackie and Steven; then again, most people were. They were both following in John's footsteps in the humor department, that's for sure. Terry wasn't a joker, but she appreciated good humor and laughed a lot at other people's antics. Jackie and Steven were always cracking her up; even John, now that she had matured a lot and was accepting him as part of the family. "John's the funniest guy I've ever known, Mom," she told Fran one day. "He'd make a fortune in television; he's funnier than any comedian *I've* ever seen on TV."

When Terry attended Quincy Point Junior High School she had gone from a cute little girl to an awkward teenager. During her high school years she went through some difficult times, and her marks suffered somewhat during her junior year. Fran was beginning to see that Terry, like herself, tended toward depression. She went to counseling during that time and after a while seemed to get back on track. By the start of her senior year, Terry had developed into a very pretty girl, and boys were beginning to play a much more important role in her life.

By the time Terry graduated from Quincy High School in 1977 she had become a beautiful young woman. She went to her senior prom with a handsome young man named Andy. Terry was positively radiant.

****

**Jackie, Steven and Samantha in front of Polly Peter's Used
Items in Maine 1977**

CHAPTER EIGHTEEN
We Just Walked Right Over A Car!

John's father, Vernon Ellison Murphy was born December 28, 1901, and raised in New Brunswick, Canada. He came to the United States when he was a young man, and married Doris Montgomery. They had a daughter Elsie, a son Christy, a daughter Naomi (who died of Leukemia at a very young age), and a son Bruce. Sadly, Doris died from complications immediately following Bruce's birth.

Vern worked as a milkman during the depression years, and when the war started, he got a job working at the Charlestown Navy Yard. After his wife died, he struggled desperately, trying to work and raise three children. He had to hire a woman to care for the baby, Bruce.

Two years later he married Mary Margaret McKenna from Canton. She was 13 years his junior, and worked in the office at the Navy Yard. They had four children of their own: James, John, Maureen and Mary. 'Margie' McKenna Murphy cared for all seven children as if she had borne them all.

In 1945, at 44 years old, Vern started working for Shaughnessy and Ahern Rigging Company. He needed to work 25 years for a company before he could retire with a pension. He hoped he could do it with Shaughnessy and Ahern.

At age 19, Christie went off to Korea to fight in the war. The base he was on was shelled many times. Ironically, while he was on leave, he was killed in a motorcycle accident. Many years later, when Elsie was 42, she was killed in an automobile accident; she had three daughters and one son. Sadly, Vern had already lost a wife and three of his children.

Bruce married Ann Landon, and they settled in Canton. They had two children, Stephen and Lisa. Jim married Carol Covany, and they settled in Canton also. They had three children, Lauren, Erin and Brian. Maureen married Dennis Dickson; they divorced a couple of years later. Maureen had a son, Sean. Mary lived at home with her parents.

In 1970, when Vern was sixty-nine years old, he suffered a massive coronary and had to retire from work. He had worked for Shaughnessy and Ahern exactly 25 years, and he retired with his pension. At seventy years old he taught himself to play golf and became an excellent golfer.

*****

For years Margie Murphy disliked Fran; she would ignore her when she and John would come to the house to visit. Fran understood that it wasn't her personally. It would have been *any* older woman her son was seeing who was divorced, with three children. To Mrs. Murphy, Fran was the 'gay divorcee' from Jamaica Plain who seduced her son.

When Fran and John would visit his family, Mrs. Murphy would leave and go upstairs. She would stay there throughout the entire visit. It was embarrassing for Fran, and it made her angry also. John's father was very different; he liked Fran right from the start. He was always nice to her and treated her respectfully. He knew she liked coffee, so he would always offer her a cup when they arrived. The only problem was, it was coffee he had boiled on the stove at seven o'clock in the morning, and had reheated it many times. "Dad," Fran would say, grimacing, "your coffee is poison, I swear. I'm going to die if I drink this." Mr. Murphy never failed to laugh at Fran's reaction. He would drink the coffee and love every mouthful, no matter how many times it had boiled and reboiled.

Vern Murphy would always walk out to the driveway with John and Fran when they were leaving to go home. Fran always appreciated it, after the cold shoulder she would get from his wife. Fran would hug him just before getting in the car, and to John's surprise, he always hugged her back. The Murphys weren't used to a lot of hugging, like Fran was. Slowly but surely, she got John's dad and Mary and Maureen hugging them whenever she and John came to visit; of course John's mother was a different story.

Fran finally told John, "I'm not going to your parents' house anymore, John. It's been quite a while, and your mother still hates me. I've only kept going for your sake, but I'm sorry, I just can't do it any longer. I love your Dad and your sisters, and Jimmy and Bruce are great, but enough is enough. You can go, but I'm through subjecting myself to Margie Murphy's shunning." "I understand Fran; I'm not going to go there either, not for a while anyway. My mother is going to have to understand that you're here to stay, whether she approves or not, and that's all there is to it."

Four months went by, and Fran said to John one day, "I've been thinking Hon; I think we've been handling your mother all wrong. I think *not* going there is defeating our purpose. I think we *should* go." "You know how she's going to act when we get there, Fran; just because we haven't been there in four months doesn't mean she'll be any different." "I know that John, but this is no good; you need to see your family and they need to see you. I've decided to try a little different tack with your mother." "Oh yeah?" John said, "like what?" "I'm going to *make* her like me. After all, I'm a nice person, lots of people like me. Instead of backing away, from now on I'm going to keep her downstairs as long as I can before she disappears to the second floor." "I don't know how you're going to manage it," John said, " but go to it, girl; if anyone can do it, you can." "I'm serious, John; I haven't really tried with your mother, but I'm going to give it my all, and I'm going to make that woman like me if it kills me."

A few days later Fran and John went to Canton to visit the Murphys. Fran took a deep breath and readied herself as they entered the house. Mary and Maureen were happy to see them, and Mr. Murphy seemed just as pleased. Mrs. Murphy said hello to John and headed toward the stairs; Fran deftly cut in front of her. "Mrs. Murphy," she said, "I wonder if you could help me out with something." Before she could respond, Fran continued. "I've been trying my hand at making casseroles lately, and failing miserably. I just can't seem to make a good casserole. John tells me that you are the best at making casseroles, and I was wondering if you could give me some tips or advice on how to make a decent one." Fran stood her ground and held her breath. Mr. Murphy, Mary and Maureen were dumbfounded, and Mrs. Murphy looked stunned. There was, what seemed to Fran, an endless silence. Finally Mrs. Murphy said, "I haven't made casseroles in quite a while; I doubt if I can help you." With that, she went upstairs.

Every couple of weeks, when Fran and John visited, Fran would have some excuse to talk to Mrs. Murphy, but of course, her responses were always the same. Fran was determined not to give up. One week she complimented her on her plants, and asked how she keeps them thriving. Other weeks it would be something else. Mrs. Murphy would respond with as few words as possible. Fran felt like she was getting nowhere, but she refused to give up. "Ooh, she's infuriating," Fran said one evening as they left the Murphys. "Your mother is going to like me, or I'm going to throttle her." "Oh yeah," John said, "That'll do it; she just loves a good throttling." They both started laughing.

One Sunday afternoon Fran and John stopped in to visit the Murphys. Fran was ready for the cold shoulder, and she had her plan of action all prepared. As they entered the house Fran noticed that Mrs. Murphy wasn't heading for the stairs right away. She said hello, and even looked at Fran for a second. Then she did something that surprised everyone there. She handed Fran some cards and said, "These are some recipes for casseroles." Fran was speechless for a moment, and then said, "Thank you, Mrs. Murphy; I appreciate that." Mrs. Murphy busied herself in the kitchen for a few minutes and then went upstairs.

The next time John and Fran went there to visit, Mrs. Murphy had cut out an article from the newspaper on taking care of house-plants, and she gave it to Fran. No one said anything, but Fran knew they were all just as surprised as she was. Each time she and John visited, Mrs. Murphy stayed downstairs a little longer, and even talked a little, not necessarily to Fran, but at least she was talking. Fran felt that she was making headway with her, and she was glad for John's sake. A few more weeks and Mrs. Murphy was talking to Fran directly; it was always kind of matter-of-fact and to the point, but she was warming up to Fran, and that was all Fran wanted. She knew that John loved every moment of this, and she was happy about that.

On one of their visits to Canton Mrs. Murphy came downstairs with a box in her hand, and she said to Fran, "Come to the dining room table, I want to show you something." As the contents of that box spilled out onto the dining room table, Fran knew in that moment that she was finally accepted, even liked, by Mrs. Murphy. There on the table lay pictures, lots of them, of John when he was a baby and older. Some were alone and others were with his parents and brothers and sisters. Fran was thrilled as she and Mrs. Murphy pored over the pictures, sometimes laughing at the silly faces John put on in most of the pictures. "Boy," Fran said, "some things never change." Fran had never heard Mrs. Murphy laugh before that time, and it pleased her. Eventually Mr. Murphy, John, Maureen and Mary came over to look at the pictures. Jimmy walked in the house a few minutes later and joined them. He was a little surprised, to say the least. It was a special time that would always be precious to Fran and John.

Mrs. Murphy became warm and friendly to Fran. On their way home after visiting the Murphys one evening, John said, "You did it, Fran... you really did it! My mother really likes you. Believe me, I know how hard this was on you." "Well, it was worth it, I guess," Fran said. "I think the whole family feels better about it now." "Oh, there's no doubt about it," John replied. "Thank you Fran; you can't imagine what this means to me." "I think I know, Hon," she said. "It means a great deal to me too. I don't believe anyone ever finds true peace in life, if there's no real peace in his own family." "Boy, that's for sure," he said. "Well John," Fran said, "one good thing came out of all of this ....at least now I get a fresh cup of coffee when we visit." John chuckled. "Yeah."

A few months later John had an opportunity to have an extremely rare heart-to-heart talk with his mother. They sat on the front porch and John said, "Ma, there's something I've wanted to say to you for quite some time now." "Oh? What's that John?" "Well," he said, "I can't remember ever telling you that I love you." Margie Murphy looked shocked and uncomfortable. "Well John, we're not a mushy family; we're not the types to say those things to each other." "Well Ma, I *am* the type now; and I think we *should* say those things to each other. Love shouldn't just be silently understood, it should be spoken also. I just wanted you to know how much I've always loved you." His mother *really* looked uncomfortable now. "Ma, I also want you to know that since I've been with Fran and her three children, I have a greater understanding and appreciation of the love and patience you had raising all of us. Mary and Maureen weren't so bad, but Bruce, Jimmy and I gave you a lot of headaches, and disrespect at times, and I'm realizing it more and more. I'm sorry Ma for those times when I was disrespectful; you deserved better."

Margie Murphy sat there with tears in her eyes listening to her youngest son pour his heart out to her. She was uncomfortable, but she loved hearing it. "John hugged his mother and she said, "I love you too John, I may not always say it, but I do. And, thank You Son, for the other things you said; it *is* nice to hear, and I appreciate it."

It was a rare and precious moment for both of them, something John would cherish forever. He would always be thankful that he took advantage of that moment when he spoke his mind, and shared his heart, with his mother.

*****

Near the end of January, 1978 a blizzard hit New England. Fran was amazed at all the snow that was falling. "No school!" was all Jackie and Steven and every other kid in Quincy heard. John was working a half hours ride away, but it took him three hours to get home.

Fran and John had recently bought a four-wheel drive International Scout. John was dying to give it a good test. He and Jackie set out to help people whose cars were stuck in the snow. They shoveled out quite a few cars, and were able to get places where a regular car couldn't. John felt great helping people out, but he learned something that day about four-wheel drive vehicles; they can still only get as far as the car stuck in the snow in front of them. They ended up shoveling themselves out of a huge snowdrift John was certain he could overtake. They came home exhausted, but gratified.

It was an exciting time, and the kids were having a ball with all that snow. Fran kept yelling at Steven to be careful. He kept climbing large piles of snow and Fran was worried that he could hurt himself, or that the cast would get soaked. But no matter how much she yelled, he just couldn't look at all that snow without having some good old-fashioned fun. Jackie was helping him build a snow fort. Jackie called to his mother, "Aw, come on Mom, it's great out here; let him have some fun. I'll watch out for him." Now Jackie watching out for Steven didn't exactly allay Fran's fears. Jackie was a 'wild man' who'd try anything, and nothing seemed to hurt him. Well, Steven had been through too much to blow it all for a snow fort.

She finally gave up yelling and brought Steven in the house and tied and taped large trash bags all around his body to cover the cast. She helped him get dressed again, making sure the bags stayed in place. She knew he felt frustrated at having to be 'trussed up' the way he was. She had a lot to do in the house, but as she watched him make his way outside, she said, "Ah, the heck with it!" She put on her jacket, boots, and gloves, and went outside. "Okay guys, let me at that fort." Jackie started laughing as she trudged through the snow to where they were. "You're going to help us build the fort?" he asked. "Sure," she said. "I know all about building forts." Jackie laughed again. "I know you Mom, you're out here 'cause you think I'll let Steven do anything he wants, right?" He teased. "You got that right, Kiddo!" She said chuckling. "You're having much too much fun out here."

*****

One day John got a call from his brother Bruce. "John, Ma is in the hospital; she's had a stroke." "Oh God, no!" John cried. "When did it happen, Bruce?" The doctor thinks it happened around eight o'clock this morning; Mary found her when she got home from work about five thirty. It doesn't look good, John; she's in pretty bad shape." "I'll go right over," John said. "Do you want me to come with you, Hon?" Fran asked him. "Yes, I do," he said.

It was obvious that the stroke was a bad one. The doctor in charge didn't seem hopeful. The family kept up a vigil. On February 2, 1978 Margie Murphy passed away peacefully in her sleep; she was only 63 years old. Because of the frigid weather and the amount of snow on the ground, her interment would take place in the spring. John thought back to that day on the porch with his mother, when he told her of his love and appreciation for her. He remembered her words, *"I love you too John; I may not always say it, but I do."* With tears in his eyes he silently thanked God for that precious time with his mother.

John was very concerned about his father. Vernon Murphy had had so many tragedies in his life. He had lost his own mother when he was only fifteen. He was the oldest of ten siblings, and he outlived them all. He had lost two wives, one child to an illness, and two children to violent deaths. Vern was a rugged old guy, of good, tough Canadian stock, but he had suffered and survived two major heart attacks. John was so glad that Maureen and Mary lived at home with him; at least he wouldn't be alone.

*****

On February 6th another blizzard hit New England, only this time it was the 'mother' of New England blizzards. "I've never seen so much snow," Fran said. She had called John a couple of times at the telephone company in Revere where he was working. He was in the basement and had no idea how much snow was falling. "John, you have to leave right away," Fran said. "The newscaster on TV said that no cars are to be on the roads after three o'clock. The police are already starting to pull people over." "Don't worry, Hon, I'll be fine," John said. "No John, you won't be fine; you need to go upstairs and look outside." John was a dedicated worker, and couldn't see leaving the job because of "a little snow." "Oh all right, I'll go take a look; hang on. "Good grief! Where'd all that snow come from?" He cried, as he picked up the phone. "John," Fran said, "didn't anyone come downstairs to tell you to go home? Didn't my brother call you?" "Yeah, Joe called a couple of hours ago; he said to leave if it got real bad. The only problem is I can't see outside from down here. There's only a few people still working upstairs; they thought I had already left. It's a good thing there's a phone down here." "Well Honey," Fran said, "if you don't leave right now, I really don't think you're going to make it home." Four and a half hours had passed since their last phone call. Fran was very worried. Twenty minutes later John pulled into the driveway that she and Jackie and Steven had shoveled for him; it was covered over again with snow. It was 7:30 and he was tired and hungry. "Thank God I used the bathroom before I left," he said, as he ran through the kitchen, unbuckling his belt. "Out of my way!" He yelled to Steven as he came out of his room. Jackie yelled to John, "Hey John, mention my name and you'll get a good seat." "Ha, ha, very funny!" John said as he disappeared into the bathroom. Jackie, Steven and Fran let out a howl as they heard a deep sigh from John in the bathroom. "Feel better?" Fran asked as he came out of the bathroom. "Yeah, I heard you guys chuckling out here." Jackie and Steven were still laughing.

Fran set John's supper on the table and a hot cup of coffee. "I'm just glad I had a full tank of gas; a few cars ran out of gas on the road, and the owners had to push them off to the side as best they could, but mostly they were just left right there in the middle of the street. Can you believe that? Right in the middle of the street." Jackie and Steven were fascinated listening to John talk about his very long drive home. "Remind me to listen to you the next time something like this happens," he said to Fran. "Yeah! Right!" Fran responded with a smirk.

The plows simply couldn't keep up with the snow; there was no place to push it. The snow was falling on top of all the snow from the blizzard of ten days earlier. It snowed all night and in the morning the snowdrifts were close to twenty feet high, in some places thirty feet high. Fran and John and the boys couldn't believe their eyes; it looked like a fantasyland outside. It was positively beautiful. Fran and John's four-wheel drive Scout was no match for the snow this time.

For the first time in years people were outside sharing their experiences and just chatting with neighbors they never knew existed.

Fran and John took Steven's sled and walked down to the Stop & Shop to buy a few things. Every day they saw people doing the same thing, and on the way, they would stop to talk with total strangers who didn't seem like strangers anymore.

On one of their walks, Fran and John realized they had just walked right over an automobile and didn't know it. The snow was so high it just seemed like the road had a slight incline to it. It wasn't until John happened to look back and could see an antenna sticking up through the snow. He laughed and said, "No way! It can't be!" "Can't be what?" Fran asked. "Look!" He said, as he cleared some snow away from what was obviously the roof of a car. "Oh my word!" Fran exclaimed. "We just walked right over a car and didn't even know it?" "I think we walked over a few of them," he said laughing.

It was an exciting and happy time. Fran and John were enjoying their walks in the snow. Later, they learned that almost thirty inches of snow fell, in and around Boston. They heard on the news tragic stories of people who were lost in the snow, and there were quite a few deaths. The flooding was disastrous. People's homes were destroyed, especially those who lived on the Cape and on coastal areas, all throughout New England. Public shelters were filled up with the homeless, and people who had nowhere else to go.

It was a terribly sad time for many people, but for others, like Fran and John and the boys, it was also a fun time. Kids everywhere were having the time of their lives jumping off of roofs into the snow, sledding down 'mountains' of snow, and building the best snow forts imaginable.

*****

The day Steven got out of the *full* body cast was a day to celebrate. He then went into a half body removable cast. This was a lot more comfortable and allowed him to sit for longer periods of time. They went out to eat, and then went to the Braintree Twin Drive-In Theatre to see "Rocky", which was showing again. Jackie and Steven hadn't seen it yet . Terry came out to eat with them, but she passed on the movie as she was going out with her boyfriend Tom later. Fran and John had already seen the movie at a regular indoor theatre, and they couldn't wait for Jackie and Steven to see it.

The movie was a big hit with the boys. Afterwards Fran felt like *she* had been in the ring with Rocky. All Jackie and Steven did throughout the entire movie was punch and pound 'Apollo Creed'... on the back of her seat. Her ears were still ringing from the ear-piercing shouts and cheers that exploded out of them during the exciting boxing scenes. She and John were laughing at Jackie and Steven's reactions to the movie. It was a real fun night; one they knew they'd remember fondly, especially since it was the first evening Steven had spent in almost fourteen months without a big, bulky cast covering his body.

*****

Terry went to Quincy College for a year, and worked part-time at different jobs. Ashmont Discount in Braintree was one of her jobs, and Paperama in Weymouth was another. She then decided she wanted to go to the University of Massachusetts at Amherst.

The day Terry moved out, Steven moved into her room, lock, stock, and barrel. He and Jackie were thrilled to be having their own rooms. Terry laughed as she was leaving. "Good grief!" she said, "I'm not even out the door and Steven's moving his stuff into my room." She hugged Steven; "Gee, we hate to see you go Terry," she mimicked him, "but here's your hat, what's your hurry?" They all laughed and kissed her goodbye.

Terry came to love the western part of the state; it was no longer the 'boonies' to her. Later she got a small inexpensive apartment and started working as an assistant manager at Tempo Fashions in Greenfield. She was content with what she was doing.

*****

Fran quit smoking in January 1979, after smoking for 25 years. She had a bad case of bronchitis, and the doctor feared, because of her smoking, that it could be something worse. He ordered x-rays taken of her lungs. On the way home she decided to ask God

413

for help. She didn't talk to Him much, and she wasn't even sure if He'd bother with her, but she decided to ask Him for help anyway. She told Him that if He would let her x-rays show that nothing was wrong, she would never smoke another cigarette as long as she lived. Right after she said those words out loud, she felt a wave of panic come over her. *"Oh Gosh, how am I going to get by without my cigarettes?"* she thought. *"But, I'll have to keep my promise; I can't very well break a promise to God. I'll really be going to hell if I do that."*

Three days later the doctor called. Fran was half way through a cigarette when she answered the phone. "Your lungs are clear, Fran," he said. "Just keep taking the antibiotic and you should be over the bronchitis in a few days." Talk about mixed emotions. She was very relieved that her lungs were okay; she knew that smoking for twenty-five years had really been pushing her luck. She hung up the phone and snuffed out the cigarette. "Stop smoking?" She said aloud, "I just know, Lord, that I can't do this." She started to break out in a sweat. "I never should have promised You I'd stop smoking. Oh God, what am I going to do?" She cried. She sat for a few moments with her head in her hands. Finally she said, "Well, when I set my mind on something Lord, I usually see it through, and if nothing else, I keep my promises…at least I try." Fran sat there thinking; she was scared, but she was becoming more and more determined to see this through. Finally she said, "If You're still listening, Lord, You have *got* to get me through this. I'll do all I can on my end, but I just know I can't do it without supernatural help; that's where You come in." She knew, no matter what, she'd do all she could to keep her promise to God, but she figured she would have to go through hell and back to do it. She waited for the withdrawals she knew would come, but they never came.

Strangely, from that moment on, she never had the slightest desire for a cigarette, not ever. Fran never *did* have another cigarette. She thought about it many times, and she had to admit that the God she wasn't sure would bother with her, had to have done it, although she couldn't understand why. At the end of each day she thanked Him; she wasn't sure what He was all about, or if He was even listening, but if He was, she wanted Him to know that she was grateful, and she wanted Him to know that *she knew* it was *all* His doing.

*****

One day in May 1979 John walked into the kitchen where Fran was cleaning up after dinner. "I want to talk to you, Fran," he said. "The boys are out, and this is as good a time as any, I guess." "Oh my goodness," Fran said. "You sound so serious." "I am serious Fran; can we sit down please?" Fran dried her hands and sat at the kitchen table. *"Oh Lord,"* Fran thought, *"We've been together for almost nine years; is he breaking up with me? No, it can't be that; he loves me, and he loves the kids and he loves the life we have. No, it's something else; it must be something else…I hope it's something else. Gosh, I wish I still smoked."*

"Fran, I'm putting my foot down," John said. "What do you mean?" Fran asked. "I think we should get married," he said. "Now, before you say anything, let me just get this out, all right?" "Okay," she said, relieved that it wasn't her first thought. John went on, "I know you're older than I am, and years ago you said you wouldn't marry me because I was so young. But I'm not that young anymore; I'm about to turn thirty. We've been together for nine years. I love you, and I know you love me, and I want us to be married before the kids get any older. I've taken care of you and the kids these past nine years. It's time Fran; I think I've proven my devotion to you. If you don't know by now that this marriage will work, then we might as well call it quits right now. In fact, if you say no… then I'm leaving." Fran was pretty sure that John would not leave, but she knew he was right; the years were flying by. Terry was going on twenty, Jackie was seventeen and a half, and Steven was fifteen. She owed John so much. He had done so much for her and her family.

"Hmm, a proposal with an ultimatum; you're so romantic, Darling," she answered with a grin. "Well Honey, if you had wanted a romantic proposal, you would have gotten one years ago," John said, "but marriage was the last thing you wanted." "Our life is so good John," Fran said. "I just don't want to rock the boat; I need to think about this for a while." "No Fran," John said. "You don't need to think about it; you've had nine years to think about it. I know you were hurt in your first marriage, but you and I have been together almost three years longer than you and Jack were married. And you just said it yourself…"Our life is so good." You must know that I would never deliberately do anything to change that. No Fran, you don't need any more time to think about it; you need to make a decision right now. Fran was quiet for a few moments. She was surprised and kind of pleased at John's forcefulness; she had never seen him like that. A wave of emotion welled up in her for this sweet, gentle man. She smiled and said, "You're right John, it *is* time we got married." "Are you serious?" John asked. "Yes," Fran said. "I do love you John, and you're the best friend I've ever known. You're also the best father I could ever have hoped for for my children." "This better be a definite yes," John said smiling. "I mean, you're not going to change your mind and back out of this, are you?" "No; you can't get rid of me now," she chuckled. John laughed. He picked her up and swung her around and cried, "All right! Let's do it! When do you want to get married?" "As soon as possible," Fran said. "You're absolutely right, we've waited long enough; how does September sound?" "September's great!" John said. "Yeah, this is great! I can't wait to tell the kids."

Terry, Jackie and Steven were thrilled with the news. Steven said, "So now we'll really be your kids, right John?" "Well," he said, "as far as I'm concerned you will be." John wanted desperately to adopt the kids, but while two of them were still under eighteen, he knew they'd need their biological father's consent. Terry was older and although she now accepted John, and got along pretty well with him, John knew that he would always be just a stepfather to her. None of them had seen or heard from Jack Roche in many years, and Jackie and Steven really wanted John to adopt them, but as much as Fran would have loved to see that happen, she was definitely not ready to deal with Jack on that issue. "When they're a little older they'll be able to make that decision themselves," was all Fran had to say about it.

Ethel and Andy were ecstatic. They hugged and kissed Fran, and hugged John and shook his hand. "Good for you," Andy said. "It's about time. " I've been praying a long time for this," Ethel said. "The kids must be thrilled, huh?" "I'll say," Fran said. They're making all kinds of plans for the wedding."

Fran and John stopped in to see Joe and Mae on their way home from Andy and Ethel's. Their reaction was surprise and sheer joy. She knew they loved John, but when they heard the news, Mae actually screamed and ran over to Fran and hugged her, as Joe was pumping John's hand and hugging him. Then Joe hugged his sister, and said, "This is the greatest news Fran; I'm so very happy for you." "Let's go in the living room and tell the kids," Mae said. Shaun, Paul, Mark and Peter were hugging Fran and jumping all over John. They were genuinely pleased with the news. Claire was a bit confused; "I thought they *were* married," she whispered to Shaun. Claire turned to Fran and with a sheepish look on her face said, " Kids probably aren't coming to the wedding.... are they?" When Fran told her that they would all be coming to the wedding, she got very excited. It pleased Fran and John to see how happy everyone was that they were finally getting married.

Fran called Dottie in Florida to tell her the news; Chet picked up the extension. "Where's Cindy?" Fran asked. "She's right here," Dottie said. "What's up?" "We're getting married!" Fran yelled into the phone. She had to pull the phone away from her ear with the screaming, whistling, laughing and crying that was coming through the phone. They were all thrilled.

A friend told Fran she should speak to Fr. Dan Graham at St. John's Church. "Why?" Fran asked. "I can't be married in the church; I'm divorced." "Well, you should talk to him anyway," her friend said. "Lots of people are getting annulments in the church these days; who knows? Maybe you could, too." Fran thought it was ridiculous, but for the sake of the two families, if there was a chance that they could be married in the church, she would look into it. She always liked Fr. Graham, so she called and made an appointment to see him.

"How old were you when you got married, Fran?" Fr. Graham asked her. "I was nineteen," she said. "How long after you got married was your daughter born?" "Exactly nine months and two days," she answered. They talked for a long time, and Fr. Graham asked her a lot of other questions. Finally he asked her about her breakdown; he seemed very interested in that. "All right, Fran," he said. "I'm going to set up a meeting for you at the Chancellery in Brighton, and I'll do everything I can to help you." Fran couldn't even imagine what he would say to them. He knew Jackie and Steven from church and from their participation in the 'Son-Seekers', a group he started for young people in the parish. The kids loved Fr. Graham; he was very good to them. But he knew Fran only went to church on Christmas and Easter, and once in a while in between, but he seemed glad that she had made her children go to church, nonetheless. You'll be hearing from them shortly." She thanked him and left.

Two weeks later Fran was sitting in front of three priests at the Chancellery in Brighton, answering a myriad of questions. She had to bring letters with her from three different people who knew her well. The priests at the Chancellery said they would notify her of their decision. As she drove home from her meeting with the priests, her mind was racing, *"This is ridiculous; what am I doing seeking an annulment? I have no right to an annulment; I wasn't a child bride and I wasn't forced into marriage. I don't even go to church, and I certainly can't deny my three kids. I just wish I knew what the Chancellery is looking for. I'm certain I'm not going to get the annulment. Oh well, I tried. I don't care if a Justice of the Peace marries us; what difference does it make anyway?"*

Three weeks later Fran got a letter from the Chancellery. She took a deep breath and opened it. Inside was a letter, and an official form stating that her marriage to John C. Roche had been annulled. It explained that her marriage to him was now considered only a 'legal' marriage, which had ended in divorce, but the '*sacrament*' of marriage was what was annulled. It also explained that she was free to be married in the Catholic Church.

Fran was glad that she and John could be married in the church, not so much for her sake, but for John's and for both of their families. John was not a strong Catholic at all, and Fran knew that he would have married her, no matter who performed the ceremony, but having a church wedding was certainly nicer than being married by a judge or a Justice of the Peace.

Fran began making plans for the wedding. She and John wanted it small and intimate. It seemed strange though; she always thought that the wedding she would plan would be Terry's, not her own. It was all very exciting though; she was having fun, and loving it.

One day, while Fran and John were driving to Canton to visit John's brother Jim and his wife Carol, a song came on the radio that they had never heard before. It was an instrumental, and it was the most beautiful song Fran had ever heard. They arrived at Jim and Carol's just as the song was ending. They waited to catch the name of the song but it was never mentioned. Fran asked Carol if she could use her phone and she called the radio station and asked for the name of the song that just ended. They said it was called 'Verdi', not to be confused with the composer by the same name, and it was by the M&G orchestra. Fran wrote it down and decided that she would try to find it at a music store.

The next day Fran went to two music stores and two department stores but nobody ever heard of the M&G orchestra. At home she called a few other stores on the phone but to no avail. She heard the song four more times over the next week, always on the same radio station. The more Fran heard it the more she loved it. She was determined to walk down the aisle on her wedding day to 'Verdi'. She called the station again and told them how much she loved the song and wanted it for her wedding song. This time she was told that the owner of the radio station heard the song while he was in Italy, and brought it back to the states to play on his station. The woman she spoke to told her that it was very unlikely that she would be able to get it in this country. Fran gave the woman her telephone number and asked her if she found out anything more about the song, would she please call her. The woman agreed.

*****

Charlene Josephs lived upstairs in Fran's house with her two children, Jennifer and Robbie. Fran and Charlene had become good friends and Robbie had played on the Giants for a few years. When Fran went upstairs to tell Charlene and the kids that she and John were getting married, Charlene couldn't have been happier. She laughed and cried with Fran, and Jennifer and Robbie hugged her. They were even happier when Fran told them that they were all invited to the wedding. While she was there talking with Charlene, Fran told her about the song she had heard and how beautiful it was. Charlene had a piano, and played it a lot. She couldn't read sheet music; she could only play by ear. "Fran, I just thought of something," Charlene said, "If we only knew exactly when they were going to play that song, maybe we could tape it on your cassette recorder." "Oh Charlene, that's a marvelous idea," Fran said, "and then you could play it on the organ in church at my wedding." "Oh, no," Charlene said. "That's not what I meant." "I know it's not," Fran said, "but you *could* do it, couldn't you?" "Well, I don't know; I'd have to hear the song and practice it on my piano many times," Charlene said. "I'm not promising anything Fran, honestly."

Fran spoke again to the woman at the radio station, and then waited for her call. She called a couple of days later and said, "We'll be playing 'Verdi' around six-thirty this evening Fran, so have your tape recorder ready to go. It will come on right after 'Moonlight Serenade'; are you familiar with that song?" "Yes," Fran said, "and thank you so much." "You're welcome," she said, "and good luck."

At six-fifteen Fran and John and Charlene had the recorder right in front of the radio waiting for 'Verdi' to start. Fran took the phone off the hook and closed all the windows and doors. When 'Moonlight Serenade' ended, Fran turned on the recorder and waited as it recorded the song she had fallen in love with. When it was over Fran pressed rewind, and brought the tape to the beginning. When she pressed play, her heart sank; they could barely hear the song, and what they *could* hear was very scratchy. "Oh no!" Fran cried. "It's terrible!" John was very disappointed too. Charlene said, "Let me take it upstairs and listen to it on my recorder."An hour and a half later Charlene called Fran and John upstairs. As they started up the stairs John said, "Listen." Floating down the stairs were the familiar notes of 'Verdi'. Fran and John flew up the stairs and there was Charlene sitting at the piano, smiling at them as she played that beautiful song so perfectly. She agreed; it was one of the prettiest songs she had ever heard, and yes, she would play it at their wedding. "Charlene," John said, "You're an angel." Fran hugged Charlene and thanked her. "This is just so perfect!" Fran said.

"Oh, yes Mom! I'd love it!" Terry cried, pleased and excited to be her mother's maid-of-honor. Fran knew that Dottie would be upset if she weren't involved in the wedding, so Fran called her sister in Florida and asked her to be her matron-of-honor. Dottie screamed with delight. "Oh Fran, I'm so happy you asked me; I'm so excited." "Well, you *should* be my matron-of-honor," Fran said. "If it wasn't for you, John and I would never have met."

John asked Jackie and Steven if they would both be his best men. They were very excited; especially Jackie, because Fran asked him to walk her down the aisle and 'give her away'. "Oh, sure Mom," Jackie said, "I'd be happy to give you away; in fact there have been many times over the years when I would have liked to…." He chuckled and grinned at Fran as she chased him through the house. "Nice talk!" She said. "Come over here so I can give you a smack." Jackie let her 'smack' him and then he hugged and kissed her, and she kissed him back. "Remember," she said to Jackie, as his 5'11" frame stood looking down at her, "you're never too big to get whacked." "Yes Mother," he said laughing. She hugged him again.

Fran and John loved anything rustic, that's why they chose the Adams Room at the Hollow Restaurant for their reception. It was a lovely room with a rustic décor. It had a beamed ceiling, and lots of natural wood, a large stone fireplace and hearth, and old iron decorations everywhere. It was a beautiful room and tastefully decorated; it was just perfect for them.

Fran and Terry were at the South Shore Plaza one day, and as they passed the Steinway Piano store they saw a young fellow playing the piano. They stopped to listen as he played all kinds of different songs, some classical, some rock, some show tunes, and others. Then he switched and started playing a keyboard. It sounded like a full orchestra with many different instruments. As they stood there watching and listening to him play, Terry said, "Mom, he's very good; you ought to speak to him about playing at your wedding."

Fran and John couldn't afford to have a band play at their wedding, and Charlene absolutely refused to play at the reception. She was very nervous about playing at the church, but she knew how much Fran wanted it, and that she was the only one who could play the song. They weren't sure what they were going to do about music for the reception. "Oh Terry," Fran said. "He may not even do that, and if he does, he probably charges more than we can afford." "Well, you'll never know unless you ask," Terry said. "Okay," Fran said, "let's go speak to him."

Richie Famularo was a real nice young man and very talented. "Yes, I do weddings now and then," he said. They talked for quite a while and Fran was pleased to discover that Richie didn't charge as much as she thought he would. He agreed to play at the wedding.

Fran and John were married on September 9, 1979 by Father Graham in the lower chapel at St. John's Church in Quincy. The lower chapel was Fran's choice because they were having a small, intimate wedding, but John always joked that they had to be married in the cellar of the church. Fran wore a lovely turquoise gown and carried a bouquet of pink, white and turquoise flowers. Terry and Dottie wore very simple dresses of soft burgundy and carried similar bouquets. They looked beautiful, and so did the guys. Ethel was radiant in a navy blue silk dress, and Andy was his usual handsome self in his black pinstriped suit.

Jackie walked Fran proudly down the aisle as Charlene played 'Verdi' on the organ. As they reached the altar, Jackie took his place beside John and Steven. "You look gorgeous," John said, as he took her hand. As Fran stood beside John, Fr. Graham smiled and said to John, "I told you she'd look just like Liz Taylor. Fran, you look absolutely stunning." Fran was a little nervous walking down the aisle, with everyone looking at her, but after the glowing compliments from John and Fr. Graham, she felt completely at ease.

The reception was wonderful; sixty people were invited and sixty people attended. They had tried to keep the number under fifty, but it wasn't possible. There were others they would like to have invited, but they needed to draw the line at sixty. The music was great, thanks to Richie, and the food was fabulous. Fran and John had chosen the Chicago roast beef. It looked great hanging from a hook over the carving table. The chef, wearing a white coat and white chef's hat stood behind the table ready to slice the roast for each person. Salad, rolls, mashed potatoes, and green beans almondine were served family-style on each table. It was an 'all you can eat' feast, and everything was delicious. Jackie, Steven, Shaun, Paul,

Mark and Peter were having a ball; they must have made five trips each to the carving table.

The wedding party sat at a long table facing their guests, and as everyone was enjoying their meal, John turned to Fran and said, "Isn't it great, Fran? Every one here in this room are people that we love dearly." There was no one invited because they *had* to be invited; all the people in that room were those that meant a great deal to Fran and John.

Jackie gave a beautiful toast, speaking openly of his affection for John. Everyone seemed to have a wonderful time, and Fran said later, "This was the best wedding I've ever been to, not because I was the bride, but because it was just *so* nice, and the music wasn't so loud that people couldn't talk. Everyone was talking and enjoying each other's company. Fran and John were happy with the way it all turned out; they loved every second of it.

The next day Fran and John drove to Pennsylvania to Amish country. They stayed one night at the Strasburg Inn in Strasburg, which was beautiful and elegant...and a little too expensive for them. They stayed the rest of the week at the Amish Lantern Motel in Lancaster. They loved the Amish people and their simple way of life. They also loved their food, and the family-style dining that was so prevalent throughout Amish country. They fell in love with Shoo-Fly-Pie and brought home about ten of them to give and enjoy with their family. They took dozens and dozens of pictures. They had an absolutely wonderful time.

They loved Amish country so much that they went back the following year, and Steven went with them; he loved it too. They stayed at the Cherry Lane Motel, and Hershey Farms in Lancaster.

*****

Jackie graduated from Quincy High School in 1980. He was a bright kid albeit a sometimes foolish one, and he could have spent his time a little more wisely. He was voted class artist, and also class clown. He was handsome, talented, and a good athlete; he was also one of the most popular guys in school. Girls and guys alike were crazy about him. He had a terrific personality, and an outstanding sense of humor; at parties and family gatherings, Jackie kept everyone, friends and family alike, in stitches. He could be outrageous at times in the things he would say and do, but he would never deliberately slight or insult anyone. There were two things that Fran always admired in Jackie. One was that he only saw the good in people; he could never see the bad in them, even when everyone else did. The other was that he *never* held a grudge against anyone, no matter what they might have done. There were times when his trust in others got him into some trouble, and Fran always wished that he would choose his companions more wisely.

Jackie had a kind and compassionate heart. For instance, whenever he and Steve, and Fran and John went out to dinner, if an older person were sitting alone at a table, Jackie would plead with his parents to let him invite that person to come and eat with them. He hated to see people eating alone and looking lonely.

One year, when Jackie was driving a cab part time, he invited a ninety-one year old widow to come and have Thanksgiving dinner with his family…and she did. Jackie picked her up at her home in Braintree and brought her home to meet his family. With Fran and John, Terry, Jackie and Steven, Ethel and Andy, Joe and Mae and their kids, Mae's mom Peg, Dottie, Chet and Cindy, and John's two sisters, Maureen and Mary, and Maureen's son Sean, and a few assorted friends, counting Jackie's widow friend, 'Mary', there were twenty-seven in all for Thanksgiving dinner. It was tight, but it was also fun, and Jackie's soft heart for the elderly and lonely gave a dear old lady a family to spend Thanksgiving with. He just hated for anyone to eat alone.

Later, with a full stomach, and a heart filled with warmth and love for his family, Andy hugged Ethel and said, "This was the best Thanksgiving ever." She smiled and said, "Yes, it was." He said that every year, and every year he meant it more than the last.

*****

Jackie liked just about everyone, and he loved women, all types and ages of them, and they all seemed to love him. He was charming and flirtatious with young women, and kind and respectful to older women. He had a lot of girlfriends; many of them were nice girls, but there were a few his mother did not approve of at all. She was also very concerned that Jackie and his friends might be drinking, and smoking pot, although Jackie would never admit it of course, and she and John could never *really* prove it. Fran spent more than a few sleepless nights worrying about him.

"I just don't understand why people like to drink so much," Fran said to John one day. "Alcohol tastes terrible, and if they drink too much they get woozy, or worse, drunk. Then they get sick, and the next day they feel terrible. It makes absolutely no sense." Fran wasn't used to people drinking; the only drinking that took place in her family was a glass of wine occasionally with a good meal. Now and then Andy and Joe might have a cold beer on a hot day, but usually only one.

John wasn't much of a drinker either. Like her father, he enjoyed a cold beer on a hot day, **but**.... *there was that one time,* early in their relationship when John went out with the guys for drinks and Chinese food after a softball game. He came over to Fran's house just before midnight, 'three sheets to the wind.' Fran was furious. "How dare you come to my house in this condition, and at this hour?" John was beginning to feel poorly. "Ooh, my stomach feels awful," he said. "Of course it feels awful; you had too much to drink." "Oh Fran, don't be mad;" John said. "I don't feel so good; do you have any Alka-Seltzer or Pepto-Bismol?" "Umm, yeah," Fran said. "I have something even better for your stomach." She went into the bathroom and came out with a small bottle, and then went and got a spoon from the kitchen. "Here, take this," she said, as she poured the liquid into the spoon. "This will do the trick." "What is it?" John asked, as he swallowed two spoonfuls. "It's called Ipecac," Fran said smiling. "It's just what you need right now; yep, this'll fix you right up." About ten minutes later John was in the bathroom throwing up the booze, the Chinese food, and from the sound of it, his breakfast and lunch that day. It went on for quite a while, so long that Fran began to get very nervous. *"Oh my Lord,"* she thought. *"What have I done? I must have given him too much Ipecac."* When John finally came out of the bathroom he lay down on the floor in the living room; he was moaning and holding his stomach.

After a few minutes he stopped moaning, and he just lay as still as can be on the floor. Fran went over to him and called his name; there was no response. She called him again, and still no response. "Oh my God, I've killed him," she exclaimed. She knelt down beside John on the floor and shook him gently. He groaned and said, "Oh, just let me die, please." Fran was afraid he just might. She got a pillow and put it under his head and covered him with a blanket. She sat on the sofa with a blanket around her all night. She dozed off and on, and woke each time with a start. Each time she woke, she shook John gently, and when she heard him groan she let him be.

John woke up around seven in the morning with a splitting headache and very sore stomach muscles. Fran made coffee and scrambled eggs and toast. John ate gingerly, but he seemed all right. "Boy, I had no idea how sick you can get from drinking too much," John said. "My head is splitting," Then, after apologizing to Fran he said, "Boy, I'll never drink like that again." Fran gave him two aspirins. She didn't tell him right then what *really* made him sick. It wasn't until eight years later that she told him the truth about that night. After the shock wore off, John said, "You little devil, you!" Then he started laughing. Fran said, "I wanted to teach you a lesson, but honest to God John, I thought I had killed you." He started laughing again, and so did Fran. They laughed 'til tears ran down their cheeks. Fran said, "I'm glad you didn't die, by the way." "Oh, thanks a lot," he said, still laughing. John drank very little after that.

Fran's uncle Ernie had a mixed drink almost every night, but she never saw him drink to excess. He was a refined and dignified man, and respected by everyone. She figured all reporters drank a little; the movies always seemed to show them with a drink and a cigarette, and Ernie did like both.

Fran missed Ernie; he had passed away eight months after retiring from the Boston Globe. An aneurysm in his stomach had burst and he collapsed on his living room floor. Ernie died at South Shore Hospital on May 1st, 1971, and was buried on Fran's birthday. Ernie had started working part time for the Globe at fifteen, as a copy boy and 'go-fer'. After he graduated from high school he began working full time, and in a few years he became a schoolboy sports reporter, covering high school and college games. Many years later he was

426

made editor of schoolboy and college sports. After Ernie died, the "Dalton trophy" was started in his honor, and awarded each year to the school with the best athletic record. For a few years Ethel and Ernie's wife Lena represented him at the presentation.

The whole family was pleased for Ernie, especially Joe, Fran and Dottie. He was their uncle, and they were proud of him. Ernie was quite a guy.

****

Fran and John's wedding day, September 9th, 1979

CHAPTER NINETEEN
A Tool Bag And A Bible

A couple of months after graduation, Jackie, his friend Dave Rodberg, and another guy hitchhiked cross-country to California. Fran and John were nervous about the trip, but Jackie was going on nineteen, so they gave him their blessing and just hoped that he'd be careful and use wise judgment. Jackie and his friends had a wonderful time, and, for the most part, used wise judgment, except for a really bad experience they had in Denver, Colorado, where they all landed in the hospital for a couple of days. Jackie called Fran from the hospital, and she did everything she could to get him to come home at that point, but he insisted they were fine, and they just wanted to continue their trek to California. They made it all the way, and Fran was so glad when they were finally on the way home. They arrived safe and sound, with a plethora of stories to tell. Fran knew that there were other stories that she and John never heard about, but that was okay; she figured what she didn't know couldn't hurt her. He was home and well, and she was glad. In her own way she thanked God for bringing him home none the worse for wear. She simply hoped he had learned some valuable lessons on his trip.

*****

Steven was a junior at Quincy Vocation Technical High School, and a 'very satisfactory student'. Like Jackie, he could have done better things with his time…like studying, but again like Jackie, it was more important to have fun than to get good marks. It became a joke with Fran and John; because Steven always got 'S's for Satisfactory, or 'B's and 'C's on his report cards, he became the "satisfactory student". He was a good kid, but again, like Jackie, at times a foolish one. "Why do you have to take after Jackie in everything?" Fran asked him. "Can't you take after Terry when it comes to studying and getting good marks?" "Well, Terry's just smarter than we are," Steven said. "No!" Fran said. "I don't buy that; Terry's 'smarter' than you because she studies, and puts time into her school work and her homework. Taking information into your brain makes you smart," Fran said. "No studying… no information…no smarts. Case closed!" She felt like she was talking to a brick wall sometimes.

Jackie at one point, decided to go to art school because he thought it was what he *should* do, so Fran and John enrolled him in Butera School of Art in Boston, a school founded by Sarah's brother. When it was time to start classes Jackie changed his mind and never went.

It used to make Fran angry to think that both Jackie *and* Steven had real art talent, but neither one of them had any desire to pursue an art career.

Jackie thought he'd like to try his hand at acting, so his parents helped him to get into the Actors' Workshop in Boston. Jackie was good looking, well built, personable and funny. Fran said to John, "If Richard Gere could do it, why not Jackie? He's better looking than Gere." Jackie attended the Workshop for a couple of months and then decided that acting wasn't for him either. He worked at a few jobs including driving a cab, but was very restless and unsure of what he wanted to do with his life.

*****

One day in the spring of 1981, John was painting a church in Walpole with two other Graham painters. Joe's red truck pulled up, and Joe got out, and John noticed another car pulling up right behind Joe's. A guy dressed in painter's clothes got out, and they walked up to where John was working. As John got a better look at him, he thought, *"Wow! This guy looks just like the actor Caesar Romero."* "John, this is Joe Hopkins," Joe said.

When John got home that day he said to Fran, "Your brother hired a new painter today." "Oh?" Fran said. "He's the strangest guy I've ever met," he said. "What do you mean, strange?" Fran asked. "Well," he said, "he looks like Caesar Romero." "No kidding," Fran said. "So how does that make him strange?" "He came to work with his tool bag in one hand and a Bible in the other," he said. "Oh, no John; don't tell me he's another one of those born-again Christians like Bob Hall. For Pete's sake, Hon, keep away from him." John kind of laughed and said, "You know, he seems like a real nice guy." "Well sure he's a nice guy," Fran said, "they're all *nice,* but they all seem to have this weird love affair with Jesus. I mean it John, try to keep your distance from him." "Well, that might be kind of difficult, as he's going to be working with me, at least on this job."

Each day John would come home and tell Fran what Joe Hopkins was talking about while they were working. At first Fran didn't want to hear any of it, but after a while it became more and more interesting. Finally she met Joe Hopkins, whom the crew nicknamed 'Hoppy'. He seemed like a nice enough guy, but later Fran said to John, "He's just like Bob Hall, overzealous for his faith and the Bible." But for reasons Fran could not discern, she was drawn to him, and actually enjoyed most of what he talked about. Hoppy told Fran his 'testimony', and how he had not lived a good life. Fran was shocked that God would have anything to do with a man like him. She questioned whether God could ever really forgive sinners like him, or even if Hoppy was actually genuine and honest about his testimony.

But there were two things Fran couldn't deny; one was the deep love that Joe Hopkins had for Jesus Christ; it was real, there was no doubt about it. The other was the undeniable fact that he was no longer the same man he told her about. Fran was confused, and becoming more and more curious about the man Jesus, and what he had accomplished for sinners like Joe Hopkins….and herself, when he willingly went to the cross.

One day John came home from work and told Fran that Hoppy had invited them to join him and his wife for Labor Day weekend at Word of Life, a Christian camp at Schroon Lake, New York. "Oh no," Fran said. "I don't even *know* his wife; there's no way I'm spending an entire weekend with people we don't know." "Well, we know Hoppy," John said. "He's a good guy; I'm sure his wife is nice." "Oh, you're sure of that, are you?" Fran said. "She's liable to be more of a Jesus freak than he is; maybe you can put up with him all day long but I'm not sure I can take a whole weekend with the two of them. Maybe she *is* a nice person but I don't *know* her, John; I really don't want to go." "All right, we don't have to go if you're really against it," John said, "but I would really *like* to go, Fran." Fran thought about it and after a while decided that if John really wanted to go, then she would go, and just make an effort to enjoy the weekend. Two days later Fran asked, "How long does it take to get to Schroon Lake, Hon?" "About five hours," he said. Fran groaned. *"Five hours in the car with people I don't know,"* she thought, *"and then a holy-rollers weekend… super; I can hardly wait."*

"It's so good to finally meet you Fran; I've heard so much about you. We're going to have a wonderful weekend." Joe's wife Betty was nothing like Fran thought she would be. She was an attractive woman, who seemed totally unaware of it. Her love for Jesus soon became obvious, but she didn't overwhelm Fran with talk of sinners, blood and sacrifice. She was warm and friendly, and a perfect lady; she also laughed easily. Fran liked her right away.

The ride to New York was pleasant. Joe read things from the Bible that Fran and John had never really understood. He talked to them about Jesus, and strangely, Fran was not turned off at all by what he was saying. She realized that she wanted to know more about Jesus.

The weekend was a wonderful experience for John and Fran, and on the way home Joe asked both of them if they believed that with true repentance Jesus had taken all of their sins, *everything* that they had ever done wrong, and wiped the slate clean. Fran and John both knew that for the first time in their lives, they truly believed that. "So, if we were in an accident right now, and we all died, what would happen to you?" Joe asked. Fran said, "Well, I never believed in Purgatory, and I truly believe now that Jesus paid for my sins with His life, so I guess I'm going to Heaven." "Yep, I'm going to Heaven when I die," John said, "whether it's today or when I'm old and gray. I understand now that the *only* sin that can keep us out of Heaven is the sin of unbelief; *that's* the 'unpardonable' or 'unforgivable' sin the Bible talks about." "Of course," Joe said, "being saved doesn't give us a license to sin; As Paul said, "May it never be!"" Fran and John agreed. "Whether you guys realize it or not, you're both saved; you're born-again Christians." Fran said, "Boy, that's something I never wanted any part of, but now I think it's wonderful; but does this mean we're no longer Catholics?" "No, not at all," Joe said. "Where you go to church doesn't matter, as long as they open up the Bible to you, and they preach salvation through Jesus Christ, and Him alone." "I understand that Joe," Fran said. "I feel so different now; I feel like I'm on the right side for the first time in my life, and I don't ever want to be on the wrong side again." Fran and John both felt a love they had never ever known, and a kind of peace that was totally alien to them.

Fran and John started going to St. John's Church faithfully every Sunday morning, but they wanted to really *study* the Bible so they started going to Christian Life Center in Walpole on Sunday evenings. The Bible was preached and taught by Spirit-filled pastors there, and Fran and John learned more in five months about the word of God than they had ever known in all their lives. They continued going to St. John's on Sunday mornings, and C.L.C. Sunday evenings for two years. They finally realized that C.L.C. was where they wanted to worship. Joe Hopkins was right; it didn't matter where they went to church as long as they were being taught from the Bible, and encouraged to study it. They felt, for the first time, at home in church.

Ethel and Andy, and Joe and Mae were upset at Fran and John's decision to leave the Catholic church; they simply couldn't understand why. Every time Fran tried to explain to her parents or to Joe how she and John felt, they ended up in an argument. Joe and Mae were strong Catholics, and felt that Fran and John were wrong in their decision, but Fran and John were absolutely *certain* that they were right. They had never really known the Lord like they knew Him now, and they had never been happier. They knew they could never go back to the way they were. Fran and John were totally committed to their new Christian life, and had found a love for Jesus they never knew possible.

Fran and John, and Betty and Joe became very close friends. They went on weekends together to Word of Life, and on retreats to Rumney Christian Conference in Rumney, New Hampshire. One year they went for a whole week to Hershey, Pennsylvania for an intensive Christian seminar, run by Bill Gothett. They always had fun with the Hopkins; they spent so much of the time laughing at John, and listening to Joe's corny jokes. Fran and John thanked God every night for sending Joe and Betty into their lives, and for the precious salvation that Jesus bought for them with His life.

After six and a half years at Christian Life Center John and Fran realized that C.L.C. was far from perfect, but for the years they were there it was perfect for them. They left Christian Life Center and started going to a Baptist Church. Years later they became members of Community Baptist Church in Weymouth.

*****

One day Fran got a call from her cousin Fran. She could hardly speak the words she was about to say. "Francie, I've got some terrible news." "Oh no, what is it?" Fran asked. Her cousin Fran hesitated, then said, "Francie, Margie passed away last night." "What? Oh God, No!" Fran said. She couldn't believe what she was hearing; it just wouldn't register in Fran's mind. It was like a terrible dream. *"Cousin Margie gone? No...she can't be dead; dead is forever,"* she thought. *"God how could you let this happen? It just can't be true; not Margie."* But it *was* true, and the entire family was shocked by it. Somehow they all got through the wake and the funeral. Margie's sister Fran and her children were heartbroken. Peter and his wife Dolly, Charlie Jr., Bobby, Richard, and their families were all devastated. It was a horrible tragedy that stunned and saddened everyone.

Margie had suffered from serious depression for many years, and was always searching for God. She would cut religious articles and poems out of magazines and newspapers, and tape them on her

434

refrigerator and on mirrors. She saw psychiatrists and took medication for her depression; she spent a lot of time in hospitals and rest homes. She would go to different churches and talk to priests, but she never seemed to find any lasting comfort or inner peace. Now and then she would go to St. Francis Friary in Brookline and talk with a friar there. He was kind to her and she felt comforted for a short while. Nothing ever helped for long.

Margie had lived in Roslindale with her husband Bob. She and Fran used to have long conversations on the phone and they usually were able to laugh about something. There were other days when Margie couldn't laugh at all. But when Fran would visit her, Margie would open the door, and despite all her problems, she and Fran would burst out laughing, even before saying hello. "Why do you think it is, that we start laughing as soon as we see each other?" Margie asked one day. "I think it's because of all the crazy things we did together as kids," Fran said, "and all the wild secrets we've shared over the years." "Yeah, I think you're right," Margie said. "Well, thank God for crazy things, and wild secrets."

Fran had always loved Margie, and was terribly saddened by the fact that she'd never see her again. "Lord, why couldn't I have come to know You a few years ago?" she prayed. I truly hope Margie has found You now, and that wonderful 'peace' that Your Word says, "surpasses all human understanding.'" Fran knew she would miss Margie a lot.

*****

Terry met Jim McClelland in May 1981 at a college hangout in Amherst. They dated for a few months, and then Terry wanted her parents to meet him. "You're going to like him Mom," she said. "He's a real nice guy." "Does he live in Amherst?" Fran asked. "No, he lives in Greenfield, a few towns over." "You must really like this guy," Fran said. "You haven't brought anyone home to meet us since Tom." "I do like him, Mom," she said. "I like him a lot."

They decided to meet one Sunday in late August at the North River House Restaurant in Hanover. Fran and John were seated at a table waiting for Terry and her new beau to arrive. After a couple of minutes Fran looked up and saw Terry walking in, and right behind her was a very large black man. Fran was shocked. "Oh, I'm going to murder her for not telling us he's black," she said to John. "Nothing like taking us by surprise," John said. "She knows we'd accept whoever she was going with as long as he was a good and decent man," Fran said. "But it's so unlike her not to at least prepare us a little."

John waved to Terry and she waved back and started walking towards her parents. Just then Fran saw a young, nice looking blond man come up right beside Terry, and at the same time the black fellow walked in another direction. Fran and John started laughing. "Oops," John said. They were still laughing as Terry introduced Jim to them. "What's so funny?" Terry asked, grinning at her parents' jocularity. "Well," John said, "Let's just say, we're *very* pleased to meet you Jim." They giggled again and told Terry and Jim about the 'new beau' they thought Terry was bringing to meet them. They all laughed.

Terry was right; Jim was a nice guy. He was quiet and respectful, and Fran and John liked him right away. He told them he grew up in Greenfield. He had attended Deerfield Academy, and graduated from Trinity-Pawling Prep School. In a few weeks he would be starting his last year at Ringling School of Art in Sarasota, Florida. They learned that his father was a surgeon in Greenfield and his mother was a retired nurse. He told them that his sister Jean was a nurse also, and his brother Alan was in medical school. It was obvious that Jim was a little nervous meeting Terry's parents.

The following week Terry and Jim came down from Greenfield to visit Fran and John again. They chatted for a while over coffee and then Terry said, "Mom and John, we want to talk to you about something." "Oh? What is it?" Fran asked. Terry looked uneasy. "Well, when Jim goes back to school in Florida in a couple of weeks," she said, "I'm going with him." "What?" Fran asked, incredulously. "I was going to call you on the phone," Terry said, "but I knew you wouldn't have liked that, so we decided to come down and talk to you in person. I don't want you to be upset." "Upset? Of course I'm upset!" Fran said. "You two have only known each other for a couple of months, and now you're going off to Florida with him?"

Jim was looking more and more uncomfortable, and Fran simply didn't care.

Something was needling at Fran and she had to get it off her chest. "So your mind is made up Terry?" "Yes," she said. "Please don't be upset, Mom; this is something Jim and I have talked about and decided to do." Jim wasn't saying anything, and John was just as quiet. John knew there was nothing he could say; he knew that Fran would handle this in her own direct way. "Okay," Fran said. "One thing bothers me a whole lot. I have not heard either of you mention the word 'love' in this conversation. Fran was agitated, and she didn't care that they knew it. "Jim, I don't mean to be crude, but there's just something I need to know. "Do you love my daughter, or are you just planning to shack up together?" She took them both by surprise. Finally Jim spoke and it was obvious that he was very nervous. "Mrs. Murphy, I love Terry; I don't know why I hadn't said it up to now, but I want you to know that I love her very much." "Well, that's kind of nice to know Jim," Fran said. "It would have been helpful if you had mentioned that before now." "Mom," Terry said, "I really love Jim. I know how you think now, and why you're upset; it was definitely something we should have made clear to you before we started this conversation." The agitation Fran had felt began to lessen a little. They talked for some time, and when they were finished, each felt they had a little clearer understanding of the other.

As Fran was putting dinner on the table Jim said, "Boy, that smells good Mrs. Murphy; I've heard what a good cook you are." "Well, thank you Jim; I hope you enjoy it," she said. "This is her grandmother's 'famous' baked macaroni," John said. "You'll love it, and if you don't, you can't sit at this table with the family." Jim looked surprised. "Just kidding," John said smiling. "But I guarantee you'll love it; everybody does." Jim loved the macaroni, and he and Terry, and Fran and John enjoyed the rest of the day together.

Terry and Jim decided to visit her grandparents in Norwell before heading back to Greenfield. Fran hugged Jim and said, "You take good care of her Jim." "Don't worry, Mrs. Murphy," he said. "I will." Terry said, "I'll call you next week, Mom." As they pulled out of the driveway Fran said, "Now that I know Jesus, I feel differently about two people living together John." "Yeah, I do too, Fran," he responded. "She knows how we feel about that now; we can tell them how wrong we feel it is, but she's not going to listen to us." "I know," Fran said. "Why would she listen to two people who lived together for nine years, got married, found God, and now say it's wrong? If I were her, I'd think they were hypocrites too." John nodded. "No one could tell *us* it was wrong Hon; we loved each other and that was that." "Yep, it's true," Fran said. "Well, I do like him John; he really does seem to be a good man, doesn't he?" "Yes he does," he said, "We just need to rely on God now to show them His way." John hugged Fran tightly. "He did love your pasta, didn't he?" "Yes he did," she said. "Which, of course makes you like him even more, right?" "Well," Fran said smiling, "it certainly helps."

When Jim left for school two weeks later, Terry went with him. She was able to transfer to the Tempo Fashions store in Sarasota. Fran and John were still not pleased with the arrangement but Terry was twenty-two and Jim was twenty-four; they were both pretty sensible adults. It was obvious that they loved each other very much and did not want to be separated. There wasn't much Fran and John could do, except put them in God's hands.

When Terry and Jim came home for Christmas, Terry was happily flashing a lovely diamond engagement ring on her left hand. Needless to say, Fran and John were very happy. Terry and Jim decided on an April 1983 wedding. It was a delightful Christmas. Ethel and Andy were happy for Terry and Jim; Jackie and Steven liked Jim a lot and thought it was great.

Jackie also made an announcement to the family. "I've enlisted in the Air Force," he said. I'm leaving next month for basic training at Lackland Air Force Base in Texas, and then right after that I leave for tech school at Lowry Air Force Base in Colorado." Fran and John and Steven knew all about it, but it came as a shock to everyone else. Jackie had wanted to tell the rest of the family himself. Ethel and Andy hugged Jackie, and Ethel said, "I can't believe you'll be leaving us too." Jackie smiled and hugged her tightly and said, "you can't get rid of me that easily Nana." "Will you be gone long Jackie?" Andy asked. "About six months, and then I'll be home for a month before I go to wherever the Air Force is going to send me."

Fran kept staring at Jackie as he talked about going into the Air Force. He had just turned twenty a month ago, and to her he was still her little boy. She and Jackie were so different in so many ways, and they 'butted heads' all too often, but they also enjoyed each other, and she knew she was going to miss him a lot. She had mixed feelings about him going into the service; he was a little wild and could be kind of reckless at times, and he had a bit of a problem with authority, which could prove to be a big problem for him in the service. "But, then again," as John had said, "maybe the service is just what he needs." "He has so many wonderful qualities, John," she said, "and he has so much going for him. I really hope you're right; *something* has to get him on the right track." "Don't worry, Hon," John said. "He'll be fine." Fran knew she'd be doing a lot of praying for this wild and wonderful son of hers.

*****

Steven started dating a girl from Edwards Street, which was one street over from Main Street. Her name was Theresa King, and Fran and John liked her a lot. Steven was seventeen and a half, and she was about to turn sixteen, and they seemed so right together. Theresa was a genuinely lovely girl, well bred, and pretty as a picture. Fran and John became quite friendly with Marie and Don, her parents. Fran especially came to love Marie; she was warm and friendly, and funny, also. John was crazy about her too; her sense of humor went so well with his. Marie was Italian and, true to her nationality, she was a phenomenal cook. Fran and John enjoyed many a delicious meal at the King household. In every way the Roche/Murphy family and the King family seemed like a perfect match.

*****

Jackie left for Lackland A.F.B. in January 1982 for basic training. Three months later he was in Colorado at Lowry A.F.B. for his tech training. When he finished tech school he called his mother from Colorado to tell her that he had received his orders. "Where are they sending you, Jackie?" She asked. "You are staying in the states,

439

right?" "No, Mom, I'm being sent to Clark Air Force Base in the Philippines." "The Philippines? Oh no, Jackie. " Fran was shocked and disappointed. John came into the kitchen. "Did I hear right? Did you say the Philippines?" "Yes." "Hmm," he said. He had a strange look on his face; he shook his head and left the kitchen.

Later Fran asked John why he reacted so strangely when he heard that Jackie was going to the Philippines. "Fran, anyone who's been to Clark A.F.B. will tell you that there's an awful lot of unsavory things going on in and around it. "What do you mean, unsavory?" Fran asked. John told her a few things, but he left out the worse things. He knew she'd be terribly upset if he told her what he had just read in the newspaper about Clark A.F.B. He also knew she wouldn't have a peaceful moment the whole time Jackie was there.

*****

Steven worked two summers as a counselor for the Y.M.C.A. at Camp Burgess boys' camp, in Sandwich, Mass., a town in Cape Cod. Steven loved working at the camp with the kids, but he missed his family and Theresa a lot. Fran and John would drive down to the Cape every other weekend to spend a few hours with him; many times Theresa and her mother went with them. Steven was able to come home every other Sunday for the day. Of course, when he was home, he spent most of the time with Theresa. Fran didn't mind; she just wanted him to be happy.

Steven graduated from Quincy Voc-Tech High School in 1982, a 'very satisfactory student', as John called him, because Steven always got B's and C's and 'Satisfactory' on his report cards. He took Theresa to his senior prom and they had a ball; Theresa looked beautiful and Steven looked handsome. Steven's looks were very different than Jackie's. Jackie was 5'11" and slim, with fair complexion, blond hair and blue eyes. He was more 'Roche' in appearance. Steven had grown to 5'6", which Fran believed was an answer to prayer, after having the spinal fusion. He had a stockier build than Jackie, and was a handsome young man with a little darker complexion, dark brown hair and brown eyes. Steven was definitely more 'Vitello'. Terry was a combination of both, although she had dark brown hair and brown eyes. There were times when Fran looked at Steven and could clearly see her father in him. When she mentioned it to Andy, he said, "Funny you should say that, because for the past year or so I've thought the same thing. I think I looked a lot like Steven when I was his age."

*****

Jackie spent a year and a half at Clark A.F.B., on Luzon Island, Angeles City, in the Philippines. Jim had asked him and Steven to be ushers in the wedding party, so Jackie planned his leave around Terry and Jim's wedding. The whole family was excited about Jackie coming home. Ethel and Andy couldn't wait to see him. Fran screamed with delight when she saw him, and leaped in his arms. "Wow!" Fran said, "You're handsomer now than when you left. You're so blond and tanned; you look like a California surfer." He hugged her tightly, and said, "It's good to be home Mom." He hugged John and Steven, and they brought in his bags. Fran thought he seemed a little distant and somewhat confused. "Just give him a little time, Hon," John said. "It was a horribly long trip home; he just needs some of your good cooking, and a good night's sleep." "You're right, John; I guess I just wanted him to be his usual excitable, wacky self; I've missed that." "I know, Hon; I think you'll see a big difference in him tomorrow."

As Jackie entered his room, he laughed out loud. "Wow! Will you look at this room! It hasn't been this clean since the day we moved here. Where's all the junk Steven?" Steven laughed. "I cleaned it all up yesterday, with Mom's help, of course. I got rid of a lot of stuff." "It looks great," Jackie said. He looked around and said, "Hey, where's Sammy? I hope she hasn't forgotten me." At the sound of her name Samantha came out of the living room and hurried into the bedroom. "Gosh," Jackie said, "she's really aged in the past year." She couldn't jump up on him like she used to, but she came right up to him, licking his hand. Fran could see the sad expression on Jackie's face as he looked at the dog he loved so much. "Come here, girl," he said as he bent down to hug her. She kept licking his face, and her constantly wagging tail showed she hadn't forgotten, and was very glad to see him.

Jackie ate very little, and after dinner he went right to bed. The next morning he apologized to Fran and John for his strange behavior the night before. "It's hard to explain, but the life I've been living in the Philippines is so totally different than life here. To be honest, when I first went to the Philippines I felt like I was on some alien planet, but, whether I wanted to or not, I got used to it. When I saw you and entered this house, I felt the same way I did when I first went to the Philippines...like I was on an alien planet." "Oh God, Jackie," Fran said, "But this is your home, not the Philippines; that's just a temporary stopover in life." "I know that Mom; I'm feeling a lot better this morning; it's like I just need to get my bearings again. That afternoon they drove out to Norwell to see Ethel and Andy. Later Jackie said, "Being with them is a real dose of reality; it's just not home until I see Nana and Papa." "So, does this mean you're back?" Fran asked. "Oh yeah, I'm back!" Jackie said smiling. He hugged his mother and she clung to him. "I love you Jackie." "I love you too, Mom."

Terry and Jim were married on April 10, 1983 at St. John's Church in Quincy. Fr. Dan Graham performed the ceremony. Terry wore a gorgeous antique white satin gown and a matching wide-brimmed bridal hat with veil. She carried calla lilies in the crook of her arm, as her grandmother Ethel did when she married Andy. *"She's the most beautiful bride I've ever seen,"* Fran thought, as Terry walked down the aisle on John's arm...."*On John's arm... hmm."* Fran thought back on the years when Terry was filled with so much anger and resentment towards John. Her eyes filled with tears. *"I knew if you just gave him a chance, Terry, you'd learn to care for him,"* she thought. *"One day I know you'll love him, too. I'm really proud of you, Terry. "You've come a long way, baby".*

It was a beautiful ceremony; Terry's friend, Jean Svizzero was her maid-of-honor, and two other friends were bridesmaids. Terry's cousins Cindy and Claire looked adorable as junior bridesmaids. Fran wore a lovely plum-colored crepe gown. "It's fabulous on you Mom," Terry said. "I never spent so much on a dress in my life," Fran said, "not even my wedding gown." "Well, it was worth it, Mom;

you look beautiful." "Thank you Terry, but beautiful is what *you* are today; I've never seen a more beautiful bride." "Thanks Mom."

As they were entering the church John said to Fran, "Have I told you how gorgeous you look today?" "Yes, you told me at home," Fran said, "but thank you; I never tire of hearing it. You know, you look pretty good yourself there, Handsome."

Afterward they drove to Whitman to The Toll House Restaurant for the reception. It was pouring so hard that they needed to pull over a couple of times on the way. Fran felt bad for Terry; The Toll House had the most beautiful grounds, and brides loved having their pictures taken in the garden. It never stopped raining the entire day.

Fran and Terry had decided on The Toll House's specialty for the wedding dinner: Chicken Kiev. Dinner began with salad, ziti in sauce, and rolls and butter. Then the main entrée was served with baked potato and carrots and mushrooms. The dinner was delicious.

After dinner a dessert table was wheeled out with a huge bowl filled with scoops of vanilla ice cream sitting on a tray of ice. In front of the ice cream were smaller bowls of hot fudge sauce, straw-berries, and whipped cream. The wedding cake had been sliced, and there were trays piled high with their famous tollhouse cookies. It was a delightful dinner from beginning to end that everyone seemed to enjoy, and the dessert table was a big hit, especially with the kids. The music was great, too, thanks again to Richie Famularo. The entire wedding, from beginning to end, was lovely.

Terry and Jim left the next day for Captiva Island in Florida for their honeymoon. They had a nice apartment waiting for them at 42 Franklin Street in Greenfield. Jim was working at Yearbook Associates and Terry was working at Tempo Fashions, both in Greenfield. They were very happy.

*****

The day Jackie was leaving to go back to the Philippines was a very sad day for Fran. She hated to see him go back there, but she knew nothing could be done about it. Before they left the house to drive him to the airport, Jackie got down on his knees and hugged Samantha. He had tears in his eyes, and his lip was quivering when he said, "I'm never going to see her again, am I Mom?" "I don't know, Jackie, I guess that's a possibility," she said. "She's almost thirteen years old, and she has a lot of physical problems. When her time comes, Jackie, we need to let her go with dignity." "Are you going to have her put to sleep, Mom?" "Well, I'm not thinking about it now, but, that day may come." "Do me a favor Mom," Jackie said. "When that day comes, don't write to me and tell me about it, okay?" "Okay, Jackie," Fran said, "I won't."

Over the next couple of months Samantha grew much worse. She had cancer and many other problems. She had begun taking seizures, and could barely walk, and she couldn't eat without losing it a few minutes later. She was suffering, and Fran and John had been to the vets with her many times recently. They all knew it was time, but it was so very hard to make that decision. Two and a half months after Jackie left for the Philippines, Samantha died peacefully on the table at the vet's office.

Steven cried openly as they drove home. John was feeling emotions he hadn't felt in many years. He was nineteen, the same age as Steven, when he had taken his dog Bullet to the vets for the same purpose. He remembered the pain he felt at that time; he reached over and put his arm around Steven. Fran had stayed home; she knew this time would come, but it would have to take place without her. Samantha was a very sweet and loveable dog; she had filled a great gap in their lives, when Tony was adopted. She'd be greatly missed by all of them.

Jackie called many times, and Fran wrote to him, but she never mentioned Samantha. Then one day about three months later, Jackie called, and during the conversation he said, "Mom, Samantha's gone, isn't she?" "Yes Jackie," Fran said. "Yeah, I knew she was gone," he said. "When did she die?" "About four months ago," she said. "Did she die peacefully?" Jackie asked. "You know what I mean Mom." "Yes, she died very peacefully Jackie; John and Steven were there." "Not you, Mom?" He asked. "No," she responded. "Are you okay with this now Jackie?" She asked. "Yeah," he said. "I'm fine; boy, I'll miss her though."

*****

One day Fran got a call from Terry. "Mom, guess what?" "What, Terry?" Fran asked. "I'm pretty sure I'm pregnant." "Pregnant?" Fran was a little surprised. "Oh Terry, that's wonderful!" "I figure I'm about five weeks along; I've been feeling kind of sicky for the past two weeks." "Yeah, that's a pretty good sign," Fran said. "I was really hoping I'd be like you when I got pregnant," Terry said, "you know, feeling terrific right from day one." "Well," Fran said, "I think I was the exception to the rule, Terry; every other woman I know was sick during her pregnancies, at least for the first three months. Have you seen a doctor yet?" "No, not yet. Now, I don't want you to get all crazy on me, Mom, but Jim and I have decided to have a midwife deliver our baby, and if possible, at home." "A midwife? At home? Terry, do you think that's wise?" "Yes Mom, I do; I've done a lot of research on the subject, and I really feel it's the best way to go. Midwives *only* deliver babies; that's all they do, Mom. They're experts at delivering babies." "But at home, Terry?" "Well, actually I'm not sure they're allowed to do it at home, but if they can, that's what I want. I've made an appointment to see one next week; would you like to come with me?" "Oh, absolutely!" Fran said. "Absolutely!"

Terry wasn't able to keep that appointment; two days later she had a miscarriage. "She was close to tears on the phone as she told her mother about it. "I'll be there in two hours," Fran said. It's nine o'clock now; I'll be there about eleven." "You don't have to come up Mom," Terry said. "I'm okay, and I'm sure you have other things to do today." "Nothing more important than this," she said.

Fran knew she was driving too fast, but she wanted to get there as quickly as possible. As she was driving through Gardner on Route 2, she saw the lights of a police car flashing behind her. "Oh shoot!" she cried as she slowly pulled over. "License and registration Maam," he said as he was writing out a ticket. "Do you know why I've stopped you?" "Yes, Officer, I was driving too fast," she said. "Couldn't you just give me a warning? I never drive over the speed limit." *"What am I saying?"* She thought. *"That's a bold-faced lie; I always drive over the speed limit. Maybe not as fast as I'm going today, but...oh shoot! Who am I kidding? You're in the wrong Fran, so shut up and take your medicine."* The officer gave her a speeding ticket in the amount of one hundred dollars. She couldn't believe it. "A hundred dollars?" she said out loud. "Yes Maam, you were driving pretty fast." "But, a hundred dollars?" "Yes, Maam; drive safely, and have a nice day." "Have a nice day?" She cried, as she drove away. "Have a nice day? How am I supposed to do that now? You just picked my pocket for a hundred dollars!" She knew he couldn't hear her so she just ranted on as she drove. "Have a nice day...Hah! Right!" She could have kicked herself, right then and there. Terry always told them to be careful driving through Gardner; there were always speed traps. After a couple of minutes Fran calmed down. "A*h well, he did seem like a nice young fellow,"* she thought. *"He was just doing his job....* but a hundred dollars!"

Terry was fine, just disappointed. She called the midwife and had an appointment to see her the next day. She and her mother sat and talked for a couple of hours until they were both quite hungry. "Come on Terry," Fran said. "I'm taking you out to lunch; let's go somewhere cute and adorable." "Are you sure you can afford this?" Terry teased. "I mean after your hundred dollar ticket." Fran groaned. "Don't remind me. Let's go."

*****

Not long after the miscarriage, Fran noticed that Terry was showing an interest in hearing about the Bible and Jesus. She started asking more and more questions. At that time Joe Hopkins was leading a Bible study in Fran and John's home on Thursday evenings.

There were about fifteen people in the Bible study, and Joe was teaching from the gospel of John. One Thursday evening in late July Terry showed up for the Bible study. Fran and John were shocked that she drove the two-hour ride from Greenfield to Quincy after work. She arrived at just about 7:30. She listened quietly, but there was a lot she didn't understand or agree with. She had a lot of questions and what Fran and John couldn't answer, Joe could. "She reminds me so much of you Fran," Joe said. "You had so many questions, and you would get a little frustrated if I didn't have an immediate answer for you." "I remember, Joe; you were so patient with me too," Fran said. "I was calling you every other night with questions." "I think, Fran, the Lord is working on Terry, just like He worked on you."

Terry started coming to the Bible study every Thursday night, which didn't please Jim at all. He called Fran one day, very concerned. "I don't like what's happening to Terry," he said. "She's changing, and I'm very worried about it. She's not going to join a cult or anything, is she?" "Oh gosh no," Jim," Fran said. "Do you think John and I are in a cult?" "No, I've never thought that," he said. "I just don't want her to change, Fran; I love Terry the way she is." "Jim, please don't be worried," Fran said. "Terry simply wants to know more about God, and she's trying to understand where she fits in with Him." "I'm really worried, Fran," Jim said. I'm afraid our marriage won't be the same." "Jim, please be patient with Terry," Fran said, "and I promise you, the change will definitely be for the better." Fran knew how Jim felt; she had the same fears in the beginning, when John was listening to everything Joe Hopkins was telling him. *"Please Lord,"* Fran prayed. *"I know You're calling Terry; won't you please call Jim at the same time?"*

On September 24, 1983 Terry and Jim both went forward in a little church in Greenfield, when the pastor gave an invitation to accept Jesus as their Lord and Savior. Not long after, Fran, John, Terry and Jim were all baptized at Christian Life Center in Walpole where Fran and John worshipped. That evening Fran said to John, "I can't remember a time in my life when I felt happier." "I feel it too, Hon," he said. They praised God for His lovingkindness.

*****

It had been two years since Fran and John accepted Jesus as their Savior. As time passed, Fran noticed that she felt an inner peace she had never known before. When Joe Hopkins asked her one day if she felt any change in herself since she started living for the Lord, her answer came quickly. "I feel a *'peaceful* happiness' I have never had in my entire life," she said. "A peaceful happiness," Joe said. "That's nice, Fran." "I have always had fun things and happy times in my life, and I've always laughed a lot," Fran said. "When

I was a child, I felt happy and secure, but from the time I became a teenager until two years ago, I more often than not felt a kind of depression in and around happy times. It was like there was a cloud always hanging over me. I went through a time when the depression was serious; I told you that I had a nervous breakdown years ago." "Yes," he said. Fran continued. "It was just a kind of 'flat' feeling that was always there. So, to answer your question, Joe, the Lord has given me '*peaceful*' happiness. The cloud isn't there any more. It may sound corny, but I feel an inner joy I had never known before. I mean life is not always 'peaches and cream', and I have my hurts, worries and disappointments like everyone else, but that's the only way I can explain it; it's joy that's coming from *inside*, not from outside. It's '*peaceful* happiness', Joe." "Praise the Lord, Fran," he said. "I do, Joe, all the time."

*****

About a year later Fran called Terry to tell her that The Toll House Restaurant had burned to the ground in a terrible fire. They were all very disappointed; not just because it was where Terry and Jim had their wedding reception, but it was Fran and John's favorite restaurant. They could never seem to find another restaurant that made Chicken Kiev, and they missed it a lot. "We'll just have to take a trip to Russia one day," John said. "Ooh yeah, wouldn't it be great to be able to do things like that?" Fran said. "You know, just fly off to Italy for pasta, and China for chow mein, and France for a glass of fine wine? What a life that would be." "Hmm, I'll settle for 'Grandma's famous baked macaroni', and a glass of Riunite any day," John said. Fran smiled. "Yeah, me, too."

*****

Terry had two more miscarriages; she was beginning to feel that she and Jim would never have children. "I never really was crazy about the thought of having kids, Mom," Terry said one day, "until I knew there was one growing inside me; then I wanted it real bad." "Terry," Fran said, "God's timing is perfect, not ours. Ecclesiastes

3:1 says, *"There is an appointed time for everything..."* Verse 2 says, *"...a time to give birth..."* I think you'll have children, Terry, but I know it will be when God decides." Terry and Jim prayed that would be the case; they knew now they wanted children, lots of them. They couldn't imagine their lives without them anymore.

*****

Steven and Theresa decided to start dating other people. They would always be friends, but they were both so young when they started dating, and they realized they were beginning to head in different directions. Fran and John, and Theresa's parents were disappointed; they had truly wanted them to one day get married, but they had seen the signs of change in both of them for quite a while. Fran and John missed Theresa a lot at first, but things were changing, and like everything else, life goes on.

Years later Theresa married a nice young man and had a beautiful daughter. Sadly, Theresa got cancer and it spread throughout her body. She died at 38 years old. Steven felt very sad; Theresa was one of the loveliest young women he had ever known.

****

CHAPTER TWENTY
Ride A Cock Horse To Banbury Cross

Dottie and Chet had been living in England for quite a few years. Ethel and Andy were upset at first, especially Ethel, who had always dreaded the time when Chet might be stationed outside the U.S.A. Dottie missed her family terribly, but she came to have a deep love affair with England. While there, she was able to travel all over England, and other countries, too. Ethel and Andy made a few trips there, once with Sarah and Pat. Dottie, Chet and Cindy came home to the states a few times too.

Dottie kept after Fran and John to come to England. "Think about it," she said, "How many places in the world can you go where you have family living there? You won't have to pay for hotel rooms or meals, and you'll have your own personal guides to show you the best of England." Finally, in April 1984, Fran and John landed at Heathrow Airport. Dottie, Chet and Cindy were there to meet them, yelling and screaming their names as they walked from the plane into the waiting area. It was wonderful to see them all again. Fran couldn't help but notice what a beautiful young woman Cindy was becoming, and it was not just outer beauty. She was lovely in every way. She was very special to Fran.

"Wow!" John and Fran exclaimed, as Chet put their luggage in the trunk of a car they never expected to be picked up in. "Wow!" John said again. "How on earth did you come by this car?" Chet laughed as he opened the doors. "Isn't it fabulous?" Dottie said. "I'll say," Fran said. "Have they made you a five-star general we don't know about?" Chet and Dottie laughed again. Chet had gotten a terrific deal on a beautiful 1966 green Jaguar with leather upholstery and a shiny wood dashboard. John fell in love with it. "You *are* going to let me drive it, I hope," he said. "Sure" Chet said, "but not yet; tomorrow you can drive it on the base for a while to get used to driving on the left side of the road, before you take it out on the main roads." "Okay, great!" John said. "I can't wait to get behind the wheel of a Jaguar."

Dottie and Chet lived in base housing and their place was much nicer than Fran expected base housing to be. Dottie had Cindy's room all ready for them with flowers and a welcome card on the nightstand. Cindy would sleep on the sofa for the duration of their visit. Fran and John were very comfortable, and just thrilled to be there.

The next day Dottie had planned a 'proper English tea' for Fran and John, and invited her friends over to meet them. Everything was great, and so beautifully presented on white linen and lace table-cloths with matching napkins. Lovely china, crystal, and silverware completed the effect. Fran and John fell madly in love with scones, clotted cream and strawberry preserves. Every time they ate out after that day, they looked for them on the menu.

Like Chet and Dottie, their friends were servicemen and their wives. They were all real nice, and Fran and John liked them a lot; they made them feel welcome and special, especially Donna Kinzie, who was Dottie's closest friend.

The next day John got to drive the Jaguar around the base at ten and fifteen miles an hour. Finally Chet said, "You drive on the left like a regular Limey; you and Fran can take the car any time you want when Dottie and I are at work." Chet and Dottie still had jobs they had to go to, but they took time off to go to places with Fran and John.

One day Chet took them to a 'fish and chips' place. The fish and chips came on a type of waxed paper and then wrapped up in newspaper. "They wrap it in newspaper?" Fran said. "Sure," Chet said. "How do we eat it?" she asked. "You just break it apart and eat it with your fingers." As odd as it seemed to Fran, in less than a moment she was hooked on fish and chips. "Oh my word!" she exclaimed at the first mouthful, "this is like no fish I've ever eaten; it's absolutely delicious." John couldn't agree more. "It just melts in your mouth; what kind of fish is this?" he asked. "It's called plaice," Dottie said. After that, whenever Dottie or Chet asked Fran and John what they'd like for dinner, the answer came swiftly from both of them, "Fish and chips!"

One weekend they all went to London; they stayed at the Waldorf Hotel, and dined in their beautiful Palm Room. They went to a couple of plays there, both nights. One was called "No Sex Please, We're British." It was silly, but fun. The other was the "Aspen Papers" with Christopher Reeve and Vanessa Redgrave. They enjoyed them a lot.

Something happened while in London that nearly devastated Fran. They took a cab to Madame Toussaud's Wax Museum. They paid the cab driver, and as they were running across the street Fran remembered she left her tote bag in the cab. The cab was long gone in just a few seconds. Fran looked like she was about to faint. "Fran, what's the matter?" John asked. "You have your purse; whatever was in the bag we'll pick up somewhere." "Oh God John," she said, "My grandmother's gold chain was in that bag." "Oh no!" was all he could say. "I took it off when my hair got caught in the clasp," she said. "I put it in the bag without thinking." Dottie, Chet and Cindy came over to them. "What's wrong, Auntie Fran?" Cindy asked. "What is it, Fran?" Dottie said. "Oh Dottie, I left my tote bag in the cab.... Grandma's gold chain was in it." "What? Oh no, Fran," Dottie said, "not your chain." "Yes, it's in that darned cab racing away from here." "Okay, let's not panic," Chet said. "He's probably going back to the hotel where he starts out; we'll just call ahead and alert the concierge." "Really Chet?" Fran asked. "Do you think that's what he'll do?" "Definitely!" He said. "They always head back to the hotel. He hesitated for a moment, and then said, "Unless... he picks up a fare on the way." "Mmm," Dottie said. "London or Boston, it's the same everywhere; not everybody's honest. Well, let's go call the hotel; all we can do is hope for the best." They called the hotel, and the concierge said, "Don't you worry; I'll personally search every cab that shows up." They knew he would, and Fran relaxed a little. They went through the wax museum and headed back to the hotel.

The bag was nowhere to be found. The cab driver remembered dropping them off at Madame Toussaud's, but he said he had picked up a fare on the way back and dropped them off at the bus station. Dottie called the police, and the Tourist Lost and Found Department. "We'll call you if anything turns up," is all they said. Four days later they still hadn't heard anything. The chain was gone; it was, by that time, draped around some other woman's neck. Fran was heartbroken. "I was sixteen when Grandma Vitello gave me that chain," she said to Cindy. "It was twenty four carat gold and was given to her by her mother. It was quite long originally. Grandma had it cut in half, and one half went to cousin Fran, and the other half went to me." "Gosh, Fran," Dottie said, "I can't believe I'll never see it on you again; you wear it all the time." John put his arm around Fran. "I know it's not the same, but we'll start now, here and at home; we'll look for a chain as much like that one as possible. And I don't care what it costs, we'll buy it." "Thank you John," she said. "You're very sweet." *"But,"* she thought, *"I just know I'll never find one like it."* "Well, I have to let it go," Fran said. "I'll be miserable if I dwell on it. The Bible says, "Where your treasure is, that's where your heart is." It won't be easy, but I'm trying not to love anything that would devastate me to lose it." "I'm proud of you Hon," John said. "Well, good luck!" Dottie said. "I'd be pulling my hair out if it were me."

Besides London, it seemed like Fran and John went all over England in the three weeks they spent there. Sometimes they traveled with Dottie, Chet and Cindy, and other times, when Dottie and Chet were working, they went off in the Jaguar alone. Chet was always nervous that they wouldn't get back onto the base in time. They cut it pretty close a few times.

They went to Glastonbury Abbey, St. Paul's Cathedral, Westminster Abbey, and the Tower of London, where the Crown Jewels are kept, and they watched the Changing of the Guard at Buckingham Palace. They went to different restaurants and shopped in adorable little gift shops. They had a 'plowman's lunch' at a pub one afternoon which John thought would be a huge lunch. Instead it was very meager. "I can't believe this," John said to Fran after the waitress left. "It's a wonder those plowmen get any work done trying to exist on a lunch like this." Another time they went to what Dottie called a 'Potato Pub.' As they looked over the menu, John said, "What do they serve *with* the potato?" "Believe me," Dottie said, "you won't need anything else." They ordered a pitcher of ale, and a potato that was at least nine inches long and stuffed to over-flowing with chicken, shrimp, broccoli, carrots, onions and cheese. "Now, that's what I call a potato," John said laughing.

One day they all went to Blenheim Palace, which was the ancestral home of Winston Churchill. Dottie jokingly called Fran, "The Ugly American", when Fran got into an argument at the front gate with a slightly pompous ticket seller, who just seemed to rub Fran the wrong way.

"We don't take Traveler's Checks," he said. "What do you mean, you don't take Travelers Checks?" John asked. "They're as good as cash money everywhere." "Well, we don't take them here," the man repeated. "That's absolutely ridiculous," Fran said. "This is a tourist attraction, and we're tourists, here from the United States." "Like I said, we don't take Travelers Checks here," he said again. "You will have to change them into *English money* at a bank." At that point John called to Chet who had gone through the gate before them. "Fran, don't bother," John said. "You're not going to get anywhere with him." It was probably just the way the ticket seller said, "*English money*", and the pompous look on his face that bothered Fran, and she wasn't going to let him get away with being so rude to them. "Well, I would be happy to do that," Fran said, "but today is Monday, you know, the day you people call a "bank holiday"? And what might my problem be?" she said sarcastically. "The banks are not *open* on Mondays." John finally said, "Forget it, Fran; it doesn't make sense, but there doesn't seem to be anything we can do about it." Dottie and Chet came back to the ticket booth. "What's going on?" Chet asked. "They won't accept our Travelers Checks," John said. "They won't? Why not?" Chet asked. "Blenheim Palace does not accept Travelers Checks," the ticket seller said again. By this time Fran was about to scream. Chet said, "Well, I'll pay for your tickets, and you can pay me back tomorrow when you get to the bank." As they all passed through the gate, Fran turned and said to the man, "Don't you find it just a bit ironic, that mostly '*travelers*' come to Blenheim

Palace, of which I am one, and Travelers Checks are good just about anywhere in the known world, but they're not good at Blenheim Palace?" The ticket seller was no longer listening.

"Did you have to carry it that far, Fran?" John said. "I mean, I was with you all the way with this guy, but you went too far. Sometimes you make me crazy with that outspokenness of yours." "Maybe I did go a little too far," she said, "but he was so rude. I had to speak my mind John, but...I guess maybe I said too much, huh?" "Too much? I'll say you said too much. You could have gotten us thrown off the grounds before we even got in. I really wish you wouldn't do that, Fran." "Well," Fran said, "I can't help it...I'M ITALIAN!" "Yeah," John said, "You're Italian! You're also like a gumball machine; a thought comes into your mind, it drops down onto your tongue and comes straight out of your mouth before you have time to think about it." Fran was shocked that John remembered that line from the movie, "The Four Seasons". She burst out laughing; John did, too. "You two are hilarious," Dottie said. John put his arm around Fran's waist. "Come on, Little Caesar," he said. "Let's go see Winnie's ancestral home, and try not to fight with anyone, okay?" "Oh, you're a riot," Fran said. "Pardon me if I don't laugh." Chet chuckled. "Little Caesar; oh, I love *that* one." John squeezed Fran's waist again and grinned at her. Fran couldn't help but laugh. "I'm sorry I embarrassed you," she said sheepishly. John just shook his head and said, "I *do* love that spice though; I *do love* that spice."

Fran and John went to Stonehenge, and the next day they went with Dotty and Chet to Banbury Cross, where Dottie and Chet had lived for a while. Fran and Dottie recited the jingle their mother and Nana Dalton used to say to them when they were children:

> *"Ride a cock horse to Banbury Cross,*
> *to see a fine lady upon a white horse;*
> *She'll have rings on her fingers and bells on her toes,*
> *And she will have music wherever she goes."*

As children, Fran and Dottie never knew there actually *was* a Banbury Cross.

They all went another day to Bath. "This is so fascinating," Fran said, as they went under ground and walked around the old Roman baths. "Those Romans sure knew how to live, didn't they?" John said. "Sure," Dottie said. "Everywhere they occupied, they built their famous baths; they were very good to themselves."

England was wonderful! Fran and John bought some lovely things to take home with them, and on their last day there, on the way to the airport, they stopped and Fran bought a dozen scones. "I hope we can find clotted cream somewhere back home," she said. As they went through customs, the inspector asked, "Do you have anything to declare?" Fran jokingly said, "just a few scones." All of a sudden hc yelled, "Agriculture!" at the top of his lungs. Fran and John were shocked, and thought he was kidding, but another man came running over. He opened the bag and was about to inspect its contents when Fran said, "Please don't touch my scones; I don't know where your hands have been." He looked at Fran and thought she was making a joke. He started laughing and said to the other inspector, "This is fine, they can go." It was all John could do to keep from laughing out loud. Later, at home, every time John would take a scone out of the bag, he'd yell, "Agriculture!" It never failed to make Fran laugh. She usually responded with, "Hey, don't touch my scones; I don't know where your hands have been."

*****

One day late in 1984, Andy and Ethel called Joe, Fran and Dottie to their home. "We called you here because we have something we want to say to you," Andy said. "What is it Dad?" Joe asked. "Now, your mother didn't think we should say anything, but I want to, so here goes. We know that the three of you are going to plan a golden anniversary party for us next June, and we just want to be able to have some input in the plans, and we want to help with the cost of it." It was all Joe, Fran and Dottie could do to keep from laughing. "Well!" Fran said, as she turned and looked at Joe. "Aren't they the pushiest two people?" "Yeah," Joe said, "and are they ever presumptuous." "Where did you ever get the idea that we would be planning a golden anniversary party for you?" Dottie said. "Yeah, yeah,

yeah," Andy said, paying no attention to what they were saying. "Now listen," he went on. "When your mother and I got married, times were tough on everyone. The best that Grandma and Papa, and Nana Dalton, could do for us was sandwiches and cookies and coffee, which was fine with us. What the heck, nobody had much back then. But during the ceremony in the church, poor people in the neighborhood went into the hall and ate all the food." Ethel interrupted at that point. "You see, kids, the reason your father wants us to have a part in the planning is because he wants this to be the wedding reception we didn't have."

"Mom and Dad," Fran said, "We remember the story of your wedding, and, yes, we have been planning a party for you. We were hoping it would be a surprise, but of course that's not going to happen now." She smiled and winked at her mother. "Mom and Dad," Dottie said, "It's going to be a wonderful time, you'll see." "That's right Dad," Joe said. "It'll be everything you want it to be." "And, Dad," Fran said, "Of course you and Mom can be in on the planning, but after all you have done for this family, you're not going to help with the cost; it's the least we can do for you." "See, I told you they'd be okay," Andy said, as he hugged Ethel. "Wonderful! This is wonderful! Thank you, guys."

*****

Steve (which he now preferred to be called) taught CCD at St. John's Church. He also helped out at the St. Anthony's Festival every year. Steve met a girl who was also a CCD teacher at St. John's and helped out at the festival. Her name was Kellie Ann Glennon, and she was 'cute as a button'. She was half Italian, which pleased Steve, and she had the largest, most beautiful eyes he had ever seen. Steve asked her out in February 1985, and soon they were dating only each other.

*****

On June 16, 1985 Ethel and Andy celebrated their fiftieth wedding anniversary in the Jessica Room at Lombardo's in Randolph. Ethel looked positively radiant in a blue silk and lace dress and Andy looked handsome in his new dark suit. Neither of them looked their age. They were happy; everything was exactly the way they hoped it would be. The room was elegant, and a hundred and fifty three guests were there to celebrate with Andy and Ethel.

The meal had been carefully thought out. Hot and cold hors d'ouvres, and fruit and cheese and crackers were served as guests arrived. After the blessing was said and the champagne toasts were ended, the meal began with escarole soup with mini meatballs, followed by a simply fabulous antipasto salad, and hot rolls and butter. Wine was on every table. Then came raviolis and sauce, followed by a little sherbet to cleanse the pallet. Then the most delicious and tender prime rib au jus was served, with potatoes au gratin and green beans almondine with sautéed mushrooms. A dish of vanilla ice cream and strawberries was served after dinner, along with coffee, and fresh fruit and Italian cookies. It was a meal to be proud of, and Andy and Ethel certainly were; they were pleased with everything, which, of course, pleased Joe, Fran and Dottie, and their spouses.

They had decided that as long as the band focused on the old songs and band music, they would go with Lombardo's own band. They were all very pleased; the music was great. There were tears in almost everyone's eyes as Ethel and Andy danced the first dance to "I Love You Truly". They danced to the old songs that they loved, and a few newer ones. Everyone was dancing, including Fran and John. Fran and Joe Hopkins danced a couple of jitterbugs together. She danced a jitterbug with her brother Joe also, but he had forgotten a lot of it. "You're such an old fogy Joe; how could you forget something as wonderful as the jitterbug?" she teased. "Well," he said, "It never meant as much to me as it did to you; I prefer to slow dance." He smiled at Fran, "that's where I shine." She laughed as he twirled her around, then they slow danced to the next song. Fran and her dad danced quite a bit, too. He was seventy-six, but you'd never know it on the dance floor; he still loved to dance. After a particularly active polka, Fran said, "I don't know how you do it, Dad; I'm worn out, and these new shoes are killing my feet." He laughed out loud. "Worn out? You're just a kid; you should still be able to dance the night away." "Well, I think we should both sit this one out," she said. "Despite what you think, we're not Fred Astaire and Ginger Rogers. And by the way, maybe you haven't noticed lately, but I'm a long way from being a kid, so come on, *Fred*, let's join Mom and John and have a cold drink." Andy laughed heartily as they walked to the table where Ethel and John were sitting. "You *are* just a kid," Andy said, as he pinched her cheek. "You're only forty-six, but you look thirty-six, and you're just as beautiful as you were when you were twenty-six." "Yeah, yeah," Fran said, as she slipped her shoes off her aching feet. "Everything is relative, I guess," she said. He laughed again.

At one point during the party Joe's son Shaun asked the drummer if he would mind if his kid brother Peter played a piece on the drums with the band. "Can he really play?" was all the drummer wanted to know. "Oh yes," Shaun said. "He's been playing for a few years and he's pretty good too. The drummer said it would be okay. When Peter was introduced the place went wild; yelling, clapping and whistling was all that could be heard. Peter started playing with the band, and as they came near the end of the song, the bandleader told Peter to solo for a minute. Peter was terrific; he played like a seasoned professional drummer, and as he came to the end he let loose on the drums all that he had. Everyone went wild with applause and whistling, even the members of the band. It was great; Peter played so well that the bandleader said to him, "Kid, if you ever want to play with a band, you let me know, and I'll see what I can do." Peter wasn't even eighteen years old yet; it was the greatest compliment he could have received. His father stood there beaming with pride.

Ethel and Andy's golden anniversary party was a huge success. Later, with tears in his eyes, Andy hugged his wife and said to his kids, "You guys did a fabulous job; *this* was the wedding reception we had always wanted; it was perfect." "Oh, yes it was," Ethel said. "It couldn't have been better; we can't thank you enough." "That's all the thanks we need," Joe said. "That's right," Fran said. "Just knowing that you both loved it, means everything to us." "I hate seeing the evening end," Dottie said. "It's been so wonderful."

*****

Not long after the anniversary party Dottie and Chet separated. It wasn't exactly a shock to the family, as they knew they were having serious problems, but everyone in the family missed Chet, especially John and Fran. They knew they'd never forget the wonderful times in England, and the fun at each other's homes, and at the cabin in Maine.

Dottie and fifteen year old Cindy left Rome, New York, where they were living with Chet, and came back to stay temporarily with Ethel and Andy. It was a decision that Dottie and Chet felt was probably for the best. She hired a U-Haul and took what she and Cindy needed; Chet helped them load it up. It was a very sad day, especially for Cindy. Dottie was always thankful that Chet continued to maintain a close relationship with Cindy.

Dottie and Cindy lived with Ethel and Andy for about eight months, and then moved into a first floor apartment in a lovely four-family house Andy owned on West Street in Braintree. "Thank God for Mom and Dad," Fran said to Dottie one day after she and Cindy moved into the apartment. What would we *both* have done without them?" "I don't even want to think about it," Dottie said. "At least you had their nice finished basement to live in," Fran said. "Twenty years ago I had to turn their lovely dining room into a bedroom for me and the kids." "Oh Fran, that must have been awful for you," Dottie said. "You and two little kids and a baby all in the same room. I don't know how you stood it. I was just young enough not to fully understand what you were going through." "Oh well," Fran said. "No sense 'crying over spilled milk'. God has given me a good life today Dottie, and He'll do the same for you if you let Him." "Well, I hope so Fran; I sure hope so."

*****

Steve was always good with his hands; there wasn't anything he wouldn't at least *try* to repair if it was broken. All the kids in the neighborhood came to him to fix their bikes, or toys that needed mending. He enjoyed taking things apart, like toasters, or radios, and seeing what made them 'tick'. So, Fran and John were not surprised when he applied for, and got, a job at ADT Security Systems. After a training period, he began installing and repairing home alarms. He really liked the work, most of it, anyway. He wasn't too crazy about the bugs and mice he met in crawl spaces, but after a while, he knew that installing and repairing alarms was what he wanted to do. It was a good career move for Steve.

Jackie was happy when his time in the Air Force was over; he never really felt that he was cut out for service life. He had a love of photography, so Terry told him that Yearbook Associates was looking for people who didn't mind traveling, to go to different colleges and take pictures of students for their yearbooks. It sounded great to Jackie, even though it wouldn't be a full-time job. To be able to go from state to state to different universities appealed to his sense of variety and adventure. He applied for the job and got it, and his first appointment was at Orel Roberts University in Oklahoma.

Jackie loved the work, and the excitement of going to different cities and meeting young people his own age. He called home often and gave a running account of where he had been and where he was going, to whoever answered the phone. He was enjoying his job and loved sharing with his mother or John or Steve where his activities took him. Now and then Fran and John knew, that while talking to Steve, judging by Steve's laughter, there were a few things Jackie was sharing with his brother that he was not sharing with his parents. "Oh well," Fran said. "What I don't know can't bother me." "Amen," John said smiling.

*****

Terry was pregnant for the fourth time. She and Jim, and Fran and John waited and prayed, and she passed the first trimester. Fran and John started hoping again for their first grand-child, and Ethel and Andy were ecstatic as it looked like their first great-grandchild was really going to be born.

When Terry was five months along, she and Jim came down to Fran and John's for the weekend. After dinner, as they were having their coffee and dessert, Terry said, "Mom, how would you like to be in the birthing room when the baby comes?" "What?" Fran was shocked, and couldn't hide the thrill that was rising in her. She jumped up and cried, "are you serious, Terry?" Terry laughed at her mother's obvious excitement. "Of course I'm serious," she said. "I really want you there, Mom; so, what do you think?" "What do I think?" Fran exclaimed. "I think it's the greatest thing that could happen. Oh, Terry, I would *love* to be there to see your baby come into this world." "John," Fran cried. "Isn't this wonderful?" "It sure is, Hon," he said. "Terry, that's the greatest gift you could ever give your mother." "Okay! Great!" Terry said, as she rubbed her tummy. "It's all settled then; you and Jim will be in the birthing room." "But how does Jim feel about this?" Fran said, as she turned toward him. "Are you okay with this? I mean I don't want to steal some of *your* joy." "Oh no, Mom," he said. "I think it's a great idea; you *should* be there." "Oh Jim, thank you so much," Fran cried, as she hugged him and Terry. "There's just one thing," Terry said. "What's that?" Fran asked. "You live two hours away." "Ooh, you're right; well, Jim, you'll have to call us at the *very first* sign of something starting." "I will," he said. "Don't you worry, Mom, I'll get you here on time if I have anything to say about it, which of course I don't, but I'll do my part anyway." Jim usually called her Fran, but every now and then he called her 'Mom', which he did a couple of times during their conversation. Fran liked it; it made him seem more of a son than a son-in-law. She cared a great deal for Jim; he was a fine young man and a very good son-in-law. She knew he'd be an excellent father.

*****

Every time Fran and John visited his father, his dad would ask, "You still painting?" John would always answer, "Oh yeah; I'm still painting." One day his dad asked him the same question, and John realized, that after twelve years of painting, his father still thought it was just a temporary thing. "Dad, I've been painting for twelve years," he said. "Oh, yeah? Has it been that long?" John knew his father had no understanding of what he was actually doing in his job, so he invited his dad to take a ride with him the following Sunday. "I'd like to show you, Dad, what my job is all about."

On Sunday John picked up his father and took him to see a couple of churches that the Graham Company had painted. One was St.

Peter's Episcopal Church in Weston, a large church they had done inside and out. His dad was quite impressed with the kind of work John was doing. He began to realize that his son wasn't just painting houses; he and the rest of the company were literally repairing and restoring great art decoration in large churches. Then John took his father into Boston, to a very large Catholic church he had worked at. John could only show him the work on the lower part of the church, but his father was greatly impressed. John pointed to the upper part of the church, the ornate walls and ceiling and explained and described what he had done. His father was stunned, and stood there staring in unbelief. "I can't get over this," he said. "You did all this?" "Well, some great artists many years ago did all the original artwork, of course," John said, "but we did a good deal of the restoration of it." "Wow!" His father said. "This is huge; it must have taken a long time to do." "Yeah, this was one of the longest job we ever did," John said. "It took months to complete." His father was studying the wall where they were standing. "You can be very proud of this kind of work John; it's all exceptional." "Well, thanks Dad," John said. ""Course it was a joint effort, but It's nice to hear you say that." "Well, I mean it," he said. "I had no idea this was the kind of work you do. You must get a great feeling of satisfaction doing a job like this." "I do, Dad; I love it," he said. "Well, most of it anyway." His dad smiled, and looked around again. "Excellent!"

From that day on, John's dad never again asked him if he was still painting. Instead he would ask, "What church are you painting now John?" When John talked about his work, he had his dad's undivided attention.

On November 10, 1986, at about two o'clock in the morning the phone rang. "Mom, Terry's had a lot of cramping in her lower back for the past hour or so," Jim said "Didn't want to call you too soon, but Joanne, the midwife said for us to get to the hospital because you never know what the first one's going to do. "Oh yes, she's right Jim," Fran said. "We'd better get going then." "Okay," he said. "We'll meet you at the hospital."

By the time they arrived at the hospital Terry was well into labor. Fran went right into the birthing room and John sat in the waiting room. He was asleep when Fran came out to give him the first of many updates.

It hurt Fran to see her daughter in so much pain, but to be there with her during this time meant so much to Fran. At one point just before the birth, when Terry was in excruciating pain, she grabbed her mother's hand and said softly, "Am I dying Mom?" Fran felt like her heart was being ripped from her chest. She remembered so clearly her own labor with Steven, and how she asked a similar question. "Oh no, Honey," she said through burning tears; it just feels that way right now, but you're right where you should be. Your baby's head is almost out; it will be over in a couple of moments." Just then Joanne said firmly, "This is it, Terry! Just one more good push!" Terry pushed as hard as her waning strength would allow. That baby came sliding out so fast Fran gasped as Joanne deftly held it in her hands. Fran and Jim hugged each other and jumped up and down as that precious little life made his entrance into the world.

"Terry," Jim said, "It's a boy!" "A boy," she repeated softly. She smiled at Jim and he kissed her. Then Joanne let Jim cut the umbilical cord, and she placed the baby lengthwise on Terry's body. Terry was exhausted and excited at the same time. "Mom, you have a grandson," she said. "I see him dear, and he's perfect, praise God."

It was eight thirty in the morning when Andrew Jonathan McClelland was born. He weighed seven pounds, ten ounces, and was truly the most beautiful newborn Fran had ever seen. Fran had nothing but praise for Joanne; she was wonderful to Terry, and very professional. Terry was right; midwives truly are experts at delivering babies.

When Terry came home from the hospital four days later, Fran was there to help her with the baby. She stayed for a week; John called every night and came up the following weekend to bring her home. They left on Sunday afternoon. As they were saying goodbye to Terry and Jim, Terry clung to her mother and began to cry. "What is it Terry?" Fran asked. "I wish you could stay," she sobbed. "I don't know what I would have done without you here this past week, Mom. I just don't feel ready to take care of him alone." "Oh Honey," her mother said, "you *are* ready; you need to believe it, and just do it. When you're alone with your little son, you'll see…it will be so natural being his mommy, and besides, you're not alone; Jim will be here in the evenings, and you have a mother-in-law and a sister-in-law nearby who are both nurses, who I'm sure would love to be able to help. You're going to be fine Terry. Call me anytime day or night, in the middle of the night even; I'll always be here for you; you know that, right?" "Yes," Terry said. They kissed goodbye, and when Fran looked back up the stairs at Terry, still in tears, she knew she would never, as long as she lived, forget that moment. Terry was a very capable and independent person and she didn't cry easily. It had been a long time since Fran had felt that Terry needed her, and Fran was moved and warmed by this show of emotion from her daughter. A few months later Terry and Jim moved to 54 Silver Street in Greenfield.

*****

October 18, 1987 was a sad day; it was the day John's dad, Vernon Ellison Murphy, passed away. He was a strong and rugged man, but for the past two years he had suffered with heart problems. John's sister Mary gave up her job to stay home and take care of him.

That night Fran and John had their friends, Joe and Betty Hopkins and Fran and Jack Roberts over for dinner. After dinner they sat around the table talking. Joe read a few passages from the Bible, and they discussed them. And in between talking and discussing, John had them all in stitches laughing. It was a nice evening, as it always was with Joe and Betty and Fran and Jack.

At about 10:45 the phone rang. Betty and Fran Roberts jumped up to get the coats as Fran answered the phone. They knew the call could come at any time, and at 10:45 at night, chances were it was about John's dad.

"Fran?" Mary said. "I think you and John should come over right now. The visiting nurse is here, and it looks like Dad's going fast." "We'll be right there," Fran said. Joe and Betty, and Jack and Fran said goodbye and were out the door in less than a minute. Fran and John raced to Canton hoping to see his dad once more before he died.

They drove in the driveway at 19 Eliot Street less than twenty minutes after Mary's call, but they were about five minutes too late. Mary was right; when the end came it came very quickly. Jim was there, and Bruce and Ann, and of course Mary and Maureen. John and Fran had been there the day before, but John was disappointed he didn't get to see his dad alive just one more time. John prayed over his father, and Fran and his brothers and sisters held hands and prayed with John.

Dad Murphy, as everyone called him, was a quiet, simple man. He loved his family, and never interfered in their lives, but they always knew they could count on him if they needed him. He was a nice man, a *very* nice man. It would be hard to imagine anyone not liking him. The night he died John said, "I never in all my life heard him say a bad word about anyone." Jim, Bruce, Mary and Maureen all agreed. Fran was thinking how Dad Murphy, right from the start, gave her the benefit of the doubt, and welcomed her into his home. Choking back tears Jim said, "He'll be missed, that's for sure."

Steve and Kellie dated for over two and a half years, and on September 12, 1987 they were married at St. John's Church. Fr. Graham had been transferred to St. Joseph's Church so Fr. Joe Connolly performed the ceremony. As Kellie walked down the aisle on her father's arm, she looked beautiful in a gown that was spectacular. Kellie had beautiful dark brown hair with natural streaks of premature silver. It looked deliberate, like it had been frosted or streaked that way. With her big brown eyes and long black lashes, she was an absolute doll. Steve looked great too, in his black tuxedo. With his dark brown hair and mustache and goatee, he was positively handsome. They were an adorable couple.

Steve and Kellie had a large wedding party. Jackie was Steve's best man, along with five ushers, and Donna Mayo was Kellie's maid-of-honor, along with five other bridesmaids, including Steve's cousins Cindy and Claire. Fran wore an emerald green gown, which John said made her green eyes look greener. The reception was held at Lombardo's in Randolph; it was a lovely affair. The next day Steve and Kellie flew to Venice, Florida to spend their honeymoon at a lovely condo Fran's brother Joe owned. When they returned a week later, they moved into a second floor apartment at 18 West Street, right above Dottie.

*****

On October 6, 1988, at three o'clock in the morning, Philip Benjamin McClelland was born. He weighed eight pounds, one ounce, and was twenty-one inches long. It was still dark when Fran and John raced up to Greenfield in the wee hours of the morning. This delivery was different than the first; it was very quick. As Fran and John ran down the hallway in the hospital they heard a baby cry. Fran said, "Oh Lord, I hope that's not Terry's baby." "I doubt it," John said. "It's only a little over two hours since Jim called us." As Fran rushed into the room, there was Jim holding the baby in his arms. The look of disappointment that came over Fran's face couldn't be denied. She wanted so badly to be there for the birth. Terry said, "Oh Mom, I'm so sorry, there was nothing I could do; I couldn't stop him from coming." "Oh gosh Terry, of course you couldn't," Fran said, as she kissed her daughter. "Never mind me; how are you doing?" "Good, Mom," Terry said. "I feel real good." "Thank God," Fran said. "So, we have another boy?" "Yes, Mom." "Oh let me see my grandson," Fran said, as she walked toward Jim and the baby. Jim smiled and placed baby Philip in her arms. By this time John knocked on the door. "Okay to come in?" he asked. He knew by the sound of the conversation that the baby was here. "Oh John," Terry cried. "Yes, come in! Come in!" John kissed Terry and hugged Jim, and came over to Fran, holding the baby. "We broke all speed records getting here, Hon," he said. "We couldn't have made it any sooner."

"I know," Fran said. "Are you terribly disappointed?" he asked. "No, not really; I was at first, but Terry having a quick delivery, takes all the disappointment away." "Good," he said. "Now let me see this little guy who was in such a hurry to be born."

Terry felt great, so great in fact, that she went home from the hospital with her baby boy at three o'clock that same afternoon. "I don't think this is a good idea, Terry," Fran had said. "You need your rest." "I can rest at home Mom, the same as in the hospital,"

Terry said, "and you're going to be with me for a few days. Really Mom, I'll be fine." Terry *was* fine, and she did take it easy at home. Every few hours Fran would bring baby Philip to Terry to be nursed. It just amazed Fran how her daughter had taken to motherhood so smoothly. Fran had to watch two-year old Andrew like a hawk. He was a very active and often difficult toddler, and was into everything. Later Fran said to her mother, "Boy, Jackie was an angel compared to him; Andrew would try the patience of a saint." He *was* adorable though.

*****

In March 1989 Terry and Jim and the boys moved into their new home at 390 Log Plain Road in Greenfield. It was a lovely ranch-style home with three bedrooms and a large finished basement, and huge back yard. Terry and Jim were thrilled to have their own home. Jim was working as a die-cutter for Lunt Silversmiths.

"The day they moved in Jim said, "God has blessed us so much, Terry. I've got a decent job, we have two healthy sons, and now we have a home of our own; what more could we want?" They held hands and thanked Him for all His blessings.

*****

In 1989 John had been working for J. W. Graham Company for fifteen years. He was becoming more and more valuable to the company, and Joe appreciated his hard work and dedication. The company had become almost exclusively church painters. They did other jobs also, but mostly they did churches, inside and out. John ran many of those jobs, and he started doing more and more actual decorating. Catholic churches had a lot of ornate painting to be done, so stagings would be set up, sometimes thirty and forty feet high inside the church. John didn't mind heights, as long as the staging felt good and solid. He loved that kind of detail work; it wasn't easy work, but to John it was the most gratifying. As Joe watched John one day from down on the church floor, he yelled up to him, "Hey John." "Yeah, Joe," John called down. Joe said, "I think you've become "the Michelangelo of J. W. Graham Company." John laughed. "Yeah, that's me; just call me Mike. But I'll tell you right now Joe, I refuse to do any painting on my back." Joe just laughed.

A couple of years later Jackie started painting for J. W. Graham Company; he became an excellent painter. He liked working in the family business, and enjoyed working on a lot of jobs with John. After a few years though, he decided to go into business with Frank Salvaggio, a friend of his, who had started his own painting business. "I love going into a home and making it beautiful again," Jackie said. "It's a great feeling of satisfaction."

*****

One warm July day Andy and Ethel decided to go to the Hanover Mall, which was in the next town. As they walked around the mall, Andy noticed a couple of young guys behind them. He was sure they were following them. He didn't say anything to Ethel, but he decided to test them. Whenever he and Ethel stopped to look in a window, the two men stopped also. When he and Ethel turned a different way, so did the men. Andy was eighty-one years old, but if he felt threatened he quickly turned into a twenty-one year old. He turned sharply and went right up to the two guys and said, "I know you're following us, and I know you've got your eyes on my wife's pocketbook. You figure because we're old, we're easy marks. Well, let me tell you something; you make one move toward my wife or me and I'll bust you right in the mouth, you miserable sons of b------." The two guys never said a word; they just took off running. Ethel was close to tears with fright. She said, "Andy, are you crazy? You're an old man now, for God's sake, and you're not a *big* old man." What's big got to do with it?" Andy said. "I knew I had to get to them first, before they made their move." "You could have been killed," Ethel said. Wouldn't it be better for them to have my pocketbook, than your life?" "Well, now they haven't got either," he said. A few people came up to them asking if they were all right. He thanked them and assured them that they were fine. As they walked away, he put his arm around his wife, and Ethel noticed he was trembling slightly. "Tell me the truth," she said. "You were scared, weren't you?" He smiled and said, "One more minute and I'd have had to go home and change my pants; if that's any indication, yeah, I was scared. But Ethel, I learned long ago, because of my size, if I don't strike first I'm liable to get my head kicked in. Some things you just have to face head on. Besides, I wanted to make a scene so we'd be noticed." "Oh, no fear of that, we were noticed, all right," Ethel said. Andy held her hand tightly as they walked.

Later when Ethel told Joe what had happened at the mall, he was very upset. Joe gently chastised his dad, and Ethel said, "That's right, you talk to him Joe… no decent person would." Andy laughed and said, "You're stealing my line again." Ethel just giggled.

Later in the car, Joe laughed all the way home. "He's still a tiger, God bless him."

****

**Dottie, Fran, Chet and John at Royal Shakespeare Company
Theatre, April 1984**

John and Fran at Stonehenge, April 1984

Andy and Ethel's **50th anniversary party 1985; (left to right: Mae, Mark, Peter, Claire, Cindy, Paul, Steve, Jim, Shaun, Terry, Fran, Jackie, Ethel, Andy, John, Chet, Joe and Dottie).**

CHAPTER TWENTY-ONE
Nah…Nannie's not funny

August 1,1990 was a terribly sad day. Mae's sister Helen suffered a ruptured aneurysm and died instantly. Helen had survived breast cancer and a mastectomy a few years earlier, and until her death, was a relatively healthy woman. It was a terrible shock to her husband and her sons Michael and Barry, and to everyone who knew her. Needless to say, it was a nightmare for Mae. She was a strong woman, but she had suddenly lost the dearest and closest friend she had ever known. Joe tried to be strong for Mae, but it was difficult for him; Helen had been *his* dearest friend also. Everyone knew they'd miss Helen; her presence was bigger than life. Holidays and family gatherings would never be the same without her unique and wonderful sense of humor.

Joe had been chosen for the deaconate program of the Catholic church, an intense five-year study course. It was a long, hard journey, and finally on September 15, 1990 he was ordained a permanent deacon. It was an exciting time for Joe and Mae and the family, but it had only been about six weeks since Helen passed away, and that sadness hung over them. Joe was in full dress, and Ethel and Andy were filled with pride as they watched their son take his vows with the other deaconates. Fran had never been happier for her big brother, or prouder.

*****

On August 20, 1991 Nathanael William McClelland was born. He weighed nine pounds, six ounces, and was twenty-two inches long. This time Fran and John got there in plenty of time. Terry was in a different type of birthing room this time. It was like being in a very large bedroom, with a queen-size bed, chest of drawers, and two nightstands with lamps. In one corner of the room there was a small, round dinette table and two chairs. Terry told John he could sit there and read, and when things were really progressing, there was a screen they would pull across to separate the dining area from the sleeping area. As Terry got closer to giving birth, Fran pulled the screen over. John could hear everything, and could follow the delivery from the other side of the screen. Finally Jim poked his head around the screen and said, "John, we have another boy!" "Another boy!" John said. "Wow! Three boys, imagine that! How are you doing, Terry?" John called. "I'm doing good now, John; just glad it's over," Terry said. "Yeah, I'm sure you are, Terry; you're a real trooper."

Terry decided to stay a couple of days in the hospital this time. With two toddlers running around, one close to five years old, and another close to three, she felt that a couple of days of quiet might be a good thing. "Good thinking Terry," Jim said. "Your mother and I can take care of things at home; you just rest."

Nathanael was a darling baby, and Andrew and Philip were wonderful, but one evening when Fran felt particularly tired, she said to John on the phone, "You know, Hon, one thing's for certain, women have babies at the right time in life...when they're young." He laughed. "Exhausted, huh?" "Well, Jim's been great," she said. "And I'm having fun with the kids and the baby, but let me put it this way, I think I'm going to need about a month to recuperate." "How about a week?" John said. "When you come home, I'll wait on you hand and foot." "Oh, you're a doll," she said, "but actually just one day will do the trick."

When Nathanael was a year and a half, he and his brothers spent a couple of days with Fran and John while Terry and Jim went on a couple's retreat with their church. Terry was again pregnant, and due in August. It was about one o'clock in the afternoon when the ADT van pulled into the driveway. Steve opened the back door and came into the kitchen. "Hi Mom," he said, "I could smell your coffee before I stepped out of the van." Fran laughed. "I swear you'd smell the coffee if you were five miles away; you always seem to come when I've just made it. If I ever need you for something, I just have to put a pot of coffee on, and sure as can be, you'll walk through the door." He chuckled. "True enough," he said. Thought I'd stop by and have my lunch with you and the kids." "That's nice, Steve; I'm glad you did. Well, if you can drag them away from the TV, it'll be a minor miracle," Fran said. Terry and Jim had decided a couple of years earlier not to have a TV in the house; they felt there was too much on television that they didn't want their children (or themselves) exposed to. They didn't mind them watching a children's video when they were at Nannie and Papa's though. When they did, they were mesmerized, and transfixed like glue in front of the TV. At that time they were watching a Bible video of Daniel in the lion's den.

Fran poured coffee for her and Steve, and sat down with him at the kitchen table. Little Nathanael was sitting on the kitchen floor eating a cookie, and Steve was going over his paper work. Fran went into the living room to check on the boys, when all of a sudden she heard Steve scream, "No Nathanael!" She turned and ran back into the kitchen just in time to see her cup of just-poured coffee spilling all down Nathanael's arm. He had grabbed the cup before Steve could get to him. Nathanael screamed with shock. Steve grabbed him and stood him on the table while Fran pulled off his shirt. "Run the cold water Steve," Fran cried. She put Nathanael right into the sink and let the cold water gently pour over his arm. "Do you think he's alright?" Steve asked. "No, I don't Steve; call 911...hurry!"

As the water poured over Nathanael's arm, Fran kept holding him close to her; he was frightened and trembling, but he wasn't crying in pain. "It's okay, Honey," she kept saying. She was very worried about his arm. "Mom, the ambulance is here!" Steve called to her. Three EMTs came running into the kitchen. "Okay Maam, we'll handle it from here," one of them said. He asked her a few questions and poured bottles of sterile water over Nathanael's little arm. "You did the right thing, Maam, running cold water on his arm, but now we need to get him to the hospital; I don't know how bad this burn is." Steve called his office and explained that he'd be out for the rest of the day. He stayed with Andrew and Philip while Fran went in the ambulance with Nathanael. She held her brave little grandson on her lap and cuddled him and talked to him so that he wouldn't be too frightened.

At the hospital a doctor examined his arm and said, "It looks like most of the arm is just a first-degree burn, which will heal fine, but there is one small area that is more like a second or even a third-degree burn. We'll keep bathing his arm in sterile water, then we'll loosely bandage it, and you can take him home. When did you say his mother was coming back?" "Tomorrow," Fran said, "but I'm going to call her when I get home. She'll want to know about this right away." "Good," the doctor said. "Nathanael needs to see his pediatrician as soon as he gets home. Don't worry though, he's going to be fine." Fran thanked him, and as a nurse was getting a basin ready for bathing Nathanael's arm, Fran picked him up and held him, and he put his good arm around her neck and clung to her. He wasn't crying at all, but Fran felt like *she* was ready to burst with tears that were fighting to come out. She didn't want her little grandson to sense that she was upset or frightened, but she was ready to cry her heart out. Except for the initial scream when the coffee came down onto him, Nathanael never really cried. He whimpered a little at first, but he seemed fine after that.

Later, when they were back home, John was there. After she explained to him and Steve what went on at the hospital, she said, "I knew it wasn't just a mild burn John; I actually saw his precious skin moving and kind of crinkling in one area. That's when I told Steve to call 911." "Oh Gosh, Fran, that must have been awful," John said. "It was. I was so scared; I just prayed that his arm wouldn't be scarred. He was so brave, John and so very sweet; he is such a precious little boy. I felt so guilty at first John, like I knew I never should have walked away from that table, not even for a moment." "Mom," Steve said, "I felt the same way; if only I hadn't been reading my work order, and if only I had seen him come up to the table, and if only I had gotten to him faster." "You could both beat yourselves up over this," John said, "but that really wouldn't make any sense, would it? It happened and it's over, and he's going to be fine, and no one's to blame. We just need to thank God that it wasn't worse, right?" "Right," Steve said. "Right," said Fran, as tears that were just aching for the right moment to burst forth, came streaming down her face. She gave up trying to hold them back.

Nathanael's arm healed nicely, except for one small area that left a barely noticeable scar.

*****

One breezy day in November, Fran and John took seven-year-old Andrew and five-year-old Philip for a ride to the Cape. They had been staying with their 'Nannie and Papa' for the weekend. They went to a lovely pond in Sandwich, and had a picnic, and fed the swans and ducks there. Fran watched the kids like a hawk, but as John was breaking up some bread for the swans, Philip went unnoticed down the stone steps that led down into the water. The steps were slippery and he fell into the pond. Fran yelled to John, who was closer to him. John went down the steps and tried to grab him, but Philip's jacket had billowed up so quickly in the breeze that it acted like a life jacket, and started taking him further away from them. John couldn't reach him so he jumped in, and half walked, half swam to him and grabbed a frightened Philip and brought him back. Fran and John got the boys up to the car, and John started the car right away and got the heat going. Fran then pulled off Philip's clothes and wrapped him in a blanket that was in the car. She kept rubbing him down until the car was warm. There was a small blanket in the trunk so she folded it for John to sit on. Philip was very quiet for a while, and John kept trying to make him laugh. Soon he was talking, and finding the whole "almost drowning" incident very exciting. "John, be real careful driving," Fran said. "We have a naked child here; we'll really have some explaining to do if we're stopped for speeding." John laughed. "Yeah, I'll say." "Papa," Philip said, "Are you dry yet?" John turned and glanced in the back seat, "Well, I'll tell you," he said. "The upper half is drying faster than the bottom half, and every time I hit a bump my bum squishes." Andrew and Philip started laughing. John knew that every red-blooded boy in America, under the age of twelve would start laughing if the word "bum" was mentioned. "Papa, you're so funny," Andrew said. "Yeah? Well, I love to see you guys laugh." he said. "Hey, Nannie's funny too; isn't Nannie funny?" There was total silence from the boys. Then, as if on cue, they both said, "No… Nannie's not funny." John said, "What do you mean Nannie's not funny? Nannie's *real* funny." Silence again… then, as serious as could be, they both said, "Mmm… nah, Nannie's not funny." Fran and John cracked up laughing. "I can be funny," Fran said, still laughing. …Silence again… Then, "Mmm…. no." "Can't compete with you, Murphy," Fran said. She and John were doubled over laughing.

*****

On August 10, 1993 Fran and John raced up to Greenfield to be there at the birth of their fourth grandchild. They didn't make it in time as this baby came in about an hour and a half. "Oh Mom, I'm sorry," Terry said. "She just came so fast." "She?" Fran cried. "Yes, Mom, it's a girl." "Oh, how wonderful!" Fran said "A little girl, after three boys. I'm so happy for you both." She hugged and kissed Terry and Jim, and then Jim placed little Johannah Ruth McClelland in her grandmother's arms. John was hugging Terry and Jim, and congratulating them, as Fran was enjoying her first grand-daughter. "Boy, she's a beauty!" John said, as he sat down beside Fran. "She sure is," Fran said. "Johannah, meet your Papa; you're going to spend a lot of time laughing when he's around." "I'm so proud of you Terry," Fran said. "You're an old pro now handling and nursing your babies." "Thanks Mom, Terry said. "Remember what you said to me, the day you were going home after Andrew was born?" "Umm, refresh my memory," Fran said. "You said, "It will be so natural being his mommy." You were right, Mom, it is so natural; I was definitely meant to be a mother." "Well, you're doing it right, that's all I can say," Fran said. "Well, Jim and I believe that we're called to raise these children for the Lord, not for ourselves," Terry said, "and that's what we're trying to do." "I know, Terry, and I think it's wonderful; I only wish I had known the Lord the way I know Him now, when I was raising you kids." "Well," Terry said, "He must have known you, Mom, 'cause you didn't do such a bad job. I'm married today with four children, Steve's married and working for ADT, and Jackie seems to be calming down, he's working steady, and he's met a nice girl." "Yes," Fran said. "Sue is an answer to prayer, she really is. I would really like to see them stay together and get married some day." "Well, I wouldn't look too far ahead," Terry said. "Jackie always said he'd never get married…that he wouldn't wish himself on any girl permanently." Fran smiled. "That's true," she said, "but I have a feeling that Susan Arendacs is different from all the girls Jackie has dated. You're right though Terry, we shouldn't look too far ahead; Jackie is definitely not your typical thirty-two year old guy. I'm not sure he'll ever be ready to settle down." "Oh well, who knows?" Terry said. "Stranger things have happened."

*****

On March 19, 1994, when Nathanael was three and a half his mother and father took him to see his doctor because of a stomach ache he had for a couple of days. He wasn't complaining about it; he would just mention it from time to time, but it seemed that it was getting worse. The doctor wanted some tests taken so they took him up to the hospital. By the time they got there Nathanael seemed to be in a little more pain. Jim's brother Alan was a surgeon at the hospital, and he came in the room to see what was wrong. He spoke to another surgeon and said, "I think it could be his appendix." After a blood test showed that it *was* his appendix, Nathanael was taken to the operating room. His uncle Alan would assist in the surgery.

When the surgeon began the operation, he found that the appendix had ruptured, and the poison had spread throughout Nathanael's body. "I can't believe this," he said. "This child should have been in excruciating pain, but he acted like he just had a tummy ache." Later, Alan came back to speak to Terry and Jim. "Nathanael must have an extremely high tolerance for pain," he said, "because his appendix had ruptured." "What? Ruptured?" Terry and Jim were aghast. "He didn't seem like he was in that much pain," Jim said. "Oh my poor little boy," Terry said. "Alan, is he going to be all right?" "Well, we've got him on antibiotics and we're draining the poison from his system; we'll know better tomorrow," he said. "Try not to worry; he's in good hands here. The nurses will fall in love with that little guy; they'll be watching him like a mother hen. I'll tell you Jim, he's the bravest kid I've ever seen." Alan left, and Terry was crying softly by this time, and Jim was doing his best to keep from joining her. He held her in his arms and prayed for God's mercy and protection for their little boy.

Fran and John drove up the following day to see Nathanael. Fran was shocked when she saw her little grandson lying in the bed with tubes connected to him. Some tubes carried antibiotics into him, and other tubes carried poison out of him. He could barely speak; he just lay there, so very, very sick. "I just can't believe this," Fran said to Terry. "That poor, darling little boy."

Fran and John went again to see Nathanael a couple of days later. Ethel and Andy went with them. "Oh my goodness!" Ethel said. She was very emotional as she looked at her little great-grandson. She didn't cry easily but Fran noticed her eyes filled with tears. She put her arm around her mother, and said, "He's going to be okay, Mom."

Ethel seemed almost fragile lately; Fran noticed that her balance was poor, and her hands were kind of shaky, and getting in and out of the car was painful. Ethel tried not to show what she was feeling, but there was no hiding it. She had fallen in her living room recently, but thanks to the thick carpet on the floor, she was okay. Ethel turned toward Fran and said softly, "Nathanael looks so pale and tiny in that bed." Fran noticed she was trembling slightly. Andy had to leave the room as tears flowed down his cheeks. *"Gosh, I'm glad they didn't see him a couple of days ago,"* Fran thought.

Fran brought Nathanael a book that she knew he would love. He was propped up in the bed, and was a little more alert, and aware of what was going on in the room. "Would you like me to read this story to you Nathanael?" Fran asked, not really expecting him to respond. He looked at her and nodded, and Fran thought her heart would break for him. She read him the story and his eyes told her that he was enjoying it. "He seems better Terry," she said. "What are the doctors saying?" "Alan said he's doing much better," she said. "I guess the worst is over, thank God. The surgeon said as long as he keeps improving, he'll be here a few more days, and then he can go home." Nathanael spent over a week in the hospital. He looked so thin and so pale when Terry and Jim brought him home. "He reminds me of Steve, Mom," Terry said, "in the sense that he's the one that everything seems to happen to… and he's still only three and a half."

Little by little Nathanael's strength returned; soon he was running all around the house again, and asking everyone, "Wanna see my 'scar'?"

*****

Ethel had taken a few falls, and a bone density test showed that she had severe Osteoporosis. X-rays also showed several compression fractures in her spine. "She has seemed so frail lately," Fran said to the doctor. "It's no wonder she's been in so much pain." The doctor prescribed Fosamax, but it didn't agree with Ethel, and she had to stop taking it. "At eighty-one years old there really isn't a lot we can do about it," the doctor said, "except to help her to be as safe and as comfortable as possible. I know she doesn't want to use her cane, but her balance is bad, and she *will* fall again if she doesn't use it. Every time she gets up out of a chair, or especially out of bed, she shouldn't take a single step without her cane."

After the last fall, the hospital arranged with the Norwell Visiting Nurses Association to have an aide come to the house three times a week to help Ethel with showering, dressing, laundry and lunches. It took a lot of the pressure off of Fran, and helped Andy tremendously. The aide who came most often was Ella. The whole family fell in love with her, and she came to love the family, especially Ethel and Andy. They looked forward to her coming like she was a family member; Ella was so very kind to them. The N.V.N.A. also had a nurse come to see Ethel once a week. Fran couldn't say enough about the N.V.N.A. She and Joe and Dottie were so thankful for their help.

*****

483

Fran and John had the brightest, cutest, most talented grandchildren that ever lived. Well, at least, that's how Fran and John saw them. They just adored their grandchildren, like all grandparents do. They became the joy of their lives.

Andrew was excitable and fun; he loved to tell a story and act out every role, and he didn't have a shy bone in his body. Fran once said, "He'd have no qualms performing for the queen of England if she asked him to." He was a great kid, and 'smart as a whip'. He loved being with his Papa, and John loved spending time with him. After a few hours with Andrew, John would chuckle and say, "That kid's a riot, an absolute riot."

Philip was great, and a lot of fun too; it was so easy to make him laugh. He had a little more serious side to him than his brothers. But there was a sweetness about Philip that was precious. Terry used to refer to him as her little 'servant', in the Biblical sense. If Terry asked for a particular chore to be done, she could always be certain that Philip would be the first to do it. He was the same way with his Nannie and Papa, and they appreciated that in him. Philip was fun, and a pleasure to be around.

Nathanael was a terrific kid; he was sweet and helpful, and he had a great sense of humor. He was a little comedian, and loved to be in the middle of anything funny. He was a 'performer' like his brothers, and loved making people laugh. Nathanael was very bright and quick to learn. He was also a very affectionate child, which, of course his Nannie loved. She always said, "Nathanael, you give the best hugs," and he'd never disappoint her.

As Johannah grew, it was obvious she was going to be tiny like her Nannie. She was a sweet and adorable little girl, but with three older brothers, she was fast becoming a little tomboy. She was also developing a kind of joking sense of humor, which John got a big kick out of. Johannah may have been a bit of a tomboy, but she loved doing 'girlie' things with her Nannie, like going shopping at the mall, or going to a movie and out to a nice restaurant for lunch. Johannah also loved planning "king's night", when she and Fran would cook and prepare a meal for John, 'fit for a king'. She was a doll and Fran was just crazy about her.

John loved telling the boys stories, especially "Black Bart" stories, and they couldn't get enough of them. John would just make them up as he went along. Black Bart was a dreadful evil-doer, and it would always take the keen senses and powerful strength of Andrew, Philip, and Nathanael McClelland (who were always the heroes in the stories) to thwart Bart's evil-doing. As John always said in the story, "The McClelland boys had 'savvy', and could always outwit Black Bart." One day Andrew and Philip said, "We McClelland boys have 'scurvy', huh Papa?" John couldn't stop laughing.

Fran loved to tell her four grandchildren stories of kings and castles, and good knights and bad knights. In every story Sir Andrew, Sir Philip and Sir Nathanael would end up rescuing the beautiful princess Johannah from the clutches of the black knight, Sir (whatever name the kids chose), and restoring her to her parents, King James and Queen Teresa. Then of course, they all lived happily ever after in the castle.

As they got a little older, Black Bart definitely became their story of choice. The last Fran heard was, while chasing after Bart, they were marooned on a huge iceberg the size of three football fields somewhere in Antarctica, with a vicious polar bear stalking them, determined to make them his lunch.

Fran and John lived near Faxon Park, a large area made up of acres of woods and paths and picnic areas, even a baseball field. Whenever the kids were spending the weekend with them, John would take the boys up to Faxon Park. They would then get into battle mode and 'drive out all the Nazis' who were hiding there, just waiting to pounce on innocent people. "Look out behind that rock Philip! There's a Nazi hiding there." "In those trees, Papa, watch out! There's three Nazis ready to shoot!" After they made Quincy free of all Nazis, Nathanael or Andrew would say, "Are we going to Prevites market Papa, for hot dogs and rolls?" "Well, of course we are," John would say. "We have to have our victory lunch, don't we?" "Yeah!" The three boys would intone. It was always the same, extra long hot dogs and fresh mini sub rolls. The *'four'* boys loved that wonderful ritual… first the battle and then lunch. They would always buy enough for Fran and Johannah too. If Terry and Jim were there, Jim wouldn't miss the chance to clear the Nazis out of Faxon Park, and of course, share in a terrific victory lunch.

"I know they're getting older, Hon," John said to Fran after one such battle, "but I never want to see these times end; they're so special." "I know," she answered. "I feel the same way." "I just hope these times are special to the kids, too," John said. "Oh, I'm sure they feel the same way, John," she said. "You're making wonderful memories for them." "I hope so," he said, "'cause they're sure making wonderful memories for me."

*****

Fran was on the phone talking to a friend. She was expecting Terry and Jim and the kids to arrive any minute. Andy and Ethel had just called and said they were on their way. Fran had made 'Grandma's baked macaroni' and meatballs for dinner. She was making an antipasto salad while she talked to her friend. She had bought some nice Italian bread and a birthday cake at Shaw's market. "July 30th is a very special day to me," she told her friend. "Today is my mother's, my husband's, and my son-in-law's birthday." "No kidding!" Her friend said. "All three of them born on July 30th?" "Yep," Fran said. "We can't always celebrate it together, but this year it falls on a weekend so Jim will be here." "Well, happy birthday to all of them," her friend said. They said goodbye just as Fran heard the front door open. "Hi, we're here!"

*****

Joe stopped by to see Fran one day and said, "We need to talk." "What is it Joe?" She asked. "I think we need to decide what we're going to do about Ma," he said. "The health aides are great, but she really needs someone with her all the time now, and it's too much on Dad." "Mom's failing, that's for sure," Fran said. "She's taken so many falls lately; I just thank God that she hasn't broken her hip." "I'd like to know what you think we should do, Fran," Joe said. "Well, you and I have been running back and forth to Norwell to help her, and it's been difficult," Fran said. "The way I see it Joe, someone is going to have to move in with Mom and Dad, and it looks like it will have to be John and me. Dottie works full time, and she's only one person. Mom and Dad need a man *and* a woman living with them. You and Mae can't do it; it would be too much on Mae, so like I said Joe, it looks like it will be John and me."

"I'm so glad you're thinking that way, Fran; it's a load off my mind." "I know, Joe, but I'm wondering how we can do this. Mom and Dad's house isn't set up for another couple, especially with one bathroom. There's no way John and I could live downstairs in their basement. That's all right for a temporary stay, but not as our permanent home." "I know; the only thing I can think of," Joe said, "is for Dad to sell this house, and their house in Norwell, and either buy a house with an in-law set-up, or build one. I think we should talk to Mom and Dad as soon as possible."

As much as Ethel and Andy loved their home in Norwell, they could see that a change had to be made. "Neither of you will ever go to a nursing home," Fran said. "The house that we buy or build will be your nursing home, and John and I will take care of you, with Joe and Dottie's help, for the rest of your lives." Andy and Ethel felt the security their children were offering them. Andy said, "My father was wrong when he said, "Years ago families took care of each other, but today one parent can take care of twelve children, but twelve children can't seem to take care of one parent." "I wonder why he said that Dad," Fran said. "You and Charlie took such good care of Grandma and Papa." "I don't know," Andy said. "I think he meant 'people today' in general. Or, maybe he was laying guilt on us, so that when his time came, we'd be there for him; who knows?"

"Dad," Fran said, "Joe and I know how much you and Mom cherish your privacy, and John and I feel the same way, so that's what we're going to concentrate on as we house hunt. If we see something promising, we'll take you and Mom to see it; we all have to agree, right?" "Right!" Andy and Ethel said.

Fran and John, and Joe and Mae looked at many homes for sale, especially those with an in-law apartment, but none of them were right. Those that had promise, they brought Ethel and Andy to see. Nothing fit their needs.

The phone rang early one morning, and Fran answered it. "Fran, are you awfully busy right now?" Joe asked. "Not right this minute," she said, "Why? What's up?" "I just found out that right up the street from me on Pond Street there's a one and a quarter acre lot of land for sale," Joe said. "I went to see it, and Fran, it's fabulous. It needs to be cleared, but wait 'til you see the potential there. I spoke to the builder who bought the land, and I told him I wanted you to see it, so he's going to hang around until you get there. Can you come right now?" "I'm walking out the door," Fran said. "Great!" he said. "Meet me at my house and we'll go together."

Fran fell in love with the land; it was private and secluded. Later, John and Fran went over to see it, and Joe picked up Ethel and Andy and met them there. "This is fabulous Fran," John said. "I love it," said Andy, but Ethel thought it was too secluded. "We'd be isolated from everything here," she said. "Mom, you need to trust us," Joe said. "When this is all cleared, you'll see that it's not isolated at all; it'll give you all kinds of privacy, just what you like. "And we can build a house perfect for the four of us, Mom." Ethel had misgivings, but she finally agreed.

Jeff Collins, the builder, worked with them on the plans for the house, making lots of helpful suggestions like, "I really think you'll be happier with gas fireplaces instead of messy wood burning ones." Another thing Fran appreciated in Jeff was his love of the land and the trees on it. When he started clearing the land he made certain that only the trees that absolutely *had* to go were cut down. It was amazing and exciting watching the land cleared and a temporary driveway made. When the foundation was poured and the building actually begun, Fran was there almost every day at some point. Jeff was a real nice guy; the whole family liked him a lot. When Fran was concerned one day about the house, Jeff said to her, "I don't want you to worry about anything Fran; I know what you and your parents want. I'm going to build your home as if I were building it for my own family." Fran appreciated that; for some reason she trusted Jeff, and knew that he would do right by them, and he did.

The house Jeff built for them was a cream-colored colonial with hunter-green shutters. The entire first floor was wheelchair accessible, with large doorways. He built a ramp that ran alongside her parents' entrance, in the front of the house, that was hidden by bushes and hedges. The deck on the back of the house, led down into the large back yard that was completely outlined with huge trees. The house and grounds were lovely, set back from the street almost three hundred feet. Andy loved the house and the land; he called it the Vitello Homestead, and on June 1,1996 they all moved in.

The main front door led into Fran and John's fireplaced living room. Beyond that was the dining room. To the left of the dining room was the kitchen and a small bathroom. Most of the rooms were not huge, but with the open floor plan Jeff had designed, the house was light and airy and seemingly more spacious than it actually was. Near the front door were the stairs that led to the master bedroom, two other bedrooms, and a large bathroom.

The far end of the kitchen had a large doorway that opened into Ethel and Andy's kitchen. Beyond their kitchen was a nice size dining area, and to the left of that was a good size fireplaced living room. The master bedroom was off of one end of the living room with a large bathroom beside it. There was a guest room off the other end of the living room, which Andy had paneled and made into an office. The house was perfect for all their needs; Andy loved it right from the start. Ethel never wanted to move from their home in Norwell, but she came to love the house, and soon 411 Pond Street became home to her. Fran and John were very happy with the house; they could keep the kitchen door closed to give each couple their privacy, but they could just walk into the other side when they needed to, and Andy and Ethel could do the same.

On their first morning in the new house, Steve woke them up at 6:45. He let himself in, and called up the stairs, "Hey you guys, rise and shine; it's a beautiful morning, and I've got coffee and donuts. Come on down." Fran and John, Ethel and Andy and Steve sat out back on the deck having coffee and donuts. "I don't know if I'll ever get used to this backyard," Fran said. "It's so beautiful and peaceful out here." "Yeah," Andy said, "and I love the privacy we have. We can sit out here in our bathrobes and slippers, and no one can see us." "Mmm, I love that, too," Fran said.

As they sat and drank their coffee and chatted, suddenly a beautiful doe loped across the yard. Fran was breathless at the sight. The five of them sat there speechless as they watched the doe disappear into the woods. "Well, that's certainly something you never see in the city," Steve said. "I think it's a sign of good things to come," John said. They all agreed.

"Oh, I just love this house," Dottie said every time she came over. "Every window in the entire house looks out onto beautiful trees and greenery. And you have so much privacy down here; I just love it." Joe too, was thrilled with the way it all worked out. He and Mae lived a couple of streets away, so if he was needed, he could be there in three minutes.

If Fran and John were home in the evening, they would play a game of Whist with Ethel and Andy, or Fran would rent a video she knew they would like, and they'd watch it together. Sometimes John would go down to the Venetian Restaurant, and pick up two orders of tripe, cooked Italian style, and two orders of veal parmesan. "Oh, Andy, how can you eat that?" Ethel would say every time. John would never fail to say, "It's like eating rubber bands with sauce on them," "You two Anglos go ahead and eat your parmesan," Andy would say, "and leave us Italians in peace to enjoy our tripe. You talk to them Fran; no decent person would." Fran would laugh, and Ethel and John would just shake their heads. No matter how many times Ethel and John tried a taste of the tripe, they would always groan. That was fine with Andy and Fran; that just meant there was always plenty for them.

Andy could be a lot of fun, even in his old age. He and John would always be thinking up ways to get a rise out of Ethel and Fran. John used to tease Ethel all the time and she'd pretend to be angry with him. The four of them enjoyed each other, no matter what they were doing. When Fran and John went out for the evening they would always alert Joe, and he'd call his parents a few times, and more often than not, he'd drop in to see them.

Andy loved the deck and the back yard. He'd sit out and read the newspaper or just take a nap. Ethel would often sit out with him, but when he'd fall asleep she'd come back in the house. Andy would sit on the deck for a while, and then walk around the yard. He'd sit on the stone bench and admire the flowers, and then walk around some more. He'd usually pick a few flowers. Many times he thought, *"Wouldn't my father have loved this yard?"* "Those are nice flowers, Dad," John said to him one warm, sunny day." "Yes," Andy answered, "They're for my darling wife." He always referred to Ethel as 'his darling wife'.

One evening Andy shocked Fran when he said, "Fran, my heart feels like it's racing, and I can't seem to take a deep breath." Fran called an ambulance, and then called Joe. He came right over, and the ambulance came soon after. Joe went to the hospital with Andy, and Fran called Dottie.

"They said he's having an Angina attack," Joe said, when he called from the hospital. "They gave him nitroglycerin, and in moments he felt better." "Angina?" Fran said. "Wow, he's been healthy as a horse all his life; is it real serious Joe?" "The doctor said it can be controlled, but they're going to keep him for a couple of days to make sure he's okay." "Is he frightened, Joe?" Fran asked. "He was quite nervous, but he's doing better now. They gave him a mild sedative so he keeps falling asleep. He told me to go on home, but I'll stay with him 'til he's moved into a room." "Mom is real anxious," Fran said. "She wants to talk with you, Joe. Would you come back here and talk to her before you go home?" "I was planning to do that," he said. See you in a little while."

Andy came home after a couple of days, and it was quite a while before he had another attack. At eighty-six years old, he was still physically active and mentally sharp.

*****

Steve and Kellie had moved from 18 West Street in Braintree to her parents' house at 203 Kendrick Ave. in Quincy. It was a duplex home, and until she had recently passed away, Kellie's ninety-five year old grandmother lived there. Kellie's parents, Tom and Anna offered the apartment to Steve and Kellie. It would give them more room than they had, so they moved. It wasn't long after the move that they realized they were going to need the extra room.

One day in March 1997 Steve and Kellie came to Fran and John's for dinner. Just before dinner Steve said, "Mom and Dad, we have something to tell you." "Oh? What is it?" Fran asked. Steve looked at Kellie, and she said, "I'm pregnant." Fran screamed, and hugged Kellie. "Oh my word, how wonderful!" She cried. John was hugging Steve, and congratulating him. Fran and John were both shocked; they had given up hope of ever hearing that news. "When are you due, Kellie?" Fran asked. "September," she said. "Oh, Steve," Fran said, as she hugged him, "I'm so happy for you both." "Well, it took ten years but we're finally having a baby; honest to God Mom, I can hardly wait."

*****

Fran had put a monitor in her parents' bedroom, and the receiver just outside hers and John's room upstairs. She could hear them in the middle of the night if anything was wrong. Ethel was failing, and becoming weaker; she could hardly walk without help. She ate very little and drank even less. Fran was constantly trying to get her to drink water and juice. Ethel had been hospitalized for dehydration, and the visiting nurse was coming to the house three times a week to check on her.

It was early in June; they had been in the house one full year when Fran and John were awakened about two o'clock one morning by Andy's voice coming through the receiver. "Fran! Fran! John! We need help! Mama fell; she's on the floor. Please come quick!" Fran and John raced down the stairs. Their hearts were pounding in their chests, as they ran over to their parents' side of the house. Ethel was lying on the floor in the bedroom doorway and Andy was kneeling over her, sobbing. "I think she's hurt bad Fran," he said. "She got up from bed to go to the bathroom. I just finished saying, 'Be careful, Hon,' when she lost her balance and fell." Ethel was moving, and Fran said, "Mom, can you hear me? Are you in pain?" "I can hear you, Dear," she said. "I think I'm all right, Andy, really; I just can't get up." Fran felt her mother's arms and legs; she seemed okay. "John, would you pick her up and put her on her bed?" Fran said. John crouched down and gently lifted his mother-in-law up off the floor.

"Okay, Mom, here we go," he said. "You know, we're going to have to stop meeting like this; Fran and Dad are getting suspicious."

She smiled at John and pinched his arm. "Ouch!" he said. "You sure haven't lost any strength in those fingers." She smiled again. She had lost a lot of weight in the past year, and John said later it was like lifting a child. As he placed Ethel on her bed she winced for a moment. When Fran asked what was wrong, she said, "I fell right on my hip; I'm sure it's not broken, but it's a little sore." "Okay, I think we'd better call an ambulance Mom," Fran said, "just to be safe." Ethel wanted no part of going to the hospital, but in a very short time the ambulance was there. "I love the fact that we're only five minutes from South Shore Hospital," John said. Fran went with Ethel to the hospital, and John called Joe to let him know what had happened, and then he called Dottie.

"Nothing's broken!" Fran said into the phone, but they want to watch her for a couple of hours just to make sure she's okay." "Ah, Thank God!" John said. "Here, your dad wants to talk to you." Andy started crying with relief when he heard the welcome news. "Thank God! Thank you, God!" he cried. "Gratsia Deo!" When Andy was frightened or overwhelmed by something, he often slipped into his original language, the language he spoke to his parents. Since Peter and Crocifessa died, he rarely spoke Italian anymore. Charlie and Margaret had both passed away a few years earlier, but every now and then, Andy, and Sarah and Pat would speak in the Sicilian dialect just to keep the language alive in them.

Fran brought Ethel home from the hospital around noontime. Andy was so happy to see her; he just kept kissing her. Fran made a cup of tea for her mother and made her comfortable, and then went over to her side of the house. Steve stopped in to see his grandmother, and had a cup of coffee with Fran. Andy said to Fran, "I'm going to pick some lilacs for your mother." "Oh, that's nice Dad, she'll like that." She watched her father go down the steps from the deck into the yard and walk toward the back of the yard where the lilac bushes were. She said to Steve, "They're getting so old." "Well Mom, he *is* eighty seven." "I know," Fran said, "but he's never seemed old to me until just recently." "Yeah," he said, "I know what you mean."

Fran and Steve drank their coffee and chatted. After a while, Fran realized that she hadn't seen Andy out in the yard for about fifteen minutes. She knew he hadn't come back in the house yet, so she said, "Steve, would you go out and see what Papa is doing? I haven't seen him for a while." "Yeah, you're right Mom," he said. "I haven't seen him since he went out." Steve went out the back door and down into the yard. Fran looked at a magazine that came in the mail. All of a sudden Fran heard Steve yelling. "Mom! Mom!" She ran out onto the deck. "Mom, Papa fell!" "Oh God, no," Fran said, as she ran down the stairs and over to where Steve was. Steve had propped Andy against a large rock in the garden. "I couldn't get him up," he said. "Dad, what happened? Are you all right?" "Fran, I think my arm is broken," he said. "Oh no, Dad. All right, don't move, I'm calling an ambulance. Steve, stay with him; I'll be right back." Fran ran into the house and called the ambulance and then called Joe at the shop. "You're never going to believe this, Joe!" she said. She was right; Joe couldn't believe it. "He was picking flowers for Mom," she said. "Unbelievable!" Joe said. "You just brought *Mom* home from the hospital." "Well," Fran said, "the ambulance will be here any minute." "I'll be right there," he said.

"His arm *is* broken," Joe said on the phone. "Good Lord!" Fran said. "What next? Poor Dad." Andy and Joe were back home a few hours later. Dottie was there, and John had just got home from work. Mae came over and brought a pan of spaghetti sauce, and she and Fran made ziti and sausages for supper.

When Joe and Andy came back home, Fran said jokingly, "Okay, Mom and Dad, here's the deal; I can take one of you falling and being rushed to the hospital, but both of you in a twenty-four hour period is too much." Andy chuckled and Ethel was smiling. "I swear you two had this all planned just to drive us crazy," Fran went on. "Well, I'm off to Afghanistan on the next cattle train if this happens again." "Afghanistan? Why Afghanistan?" Andy asked. "I don't know," Fran said. "It's just far away." "A cattle train?" John said, grinning. "Don't expect me to make sense right now," she answered. "So, that's the deal; no more plots between the two of you, okay?" Ethel and Andy both started chuckling. "Hey Joe," Andy said. "You talk to her; no decent person would." They all started laughing. Then Andy said, "Seriously Fran, I know what you guys must have gone through, but please don't worry Honey; it's not going to happen again." Fran looked at her mother and said, "Canc!" Ethel said,

494

sweetly, "I promise!" "And no more gymnastics in the garden, right?" Andy, still laughing, said, "Right!" Fran grinned and hugged her parents. "I can't stand it when you guys get hurt; it just kills me." "We know, Honey," Ethel said. "We'll take extra precautions, from now on." "I just love you two so much," Fran said, with tears in her eyes. After a moment John said, "Okay, let's eat!"

"Boy Mae, you make sauce like a natural-born Sicilian," Andy said. Mae smiled. "I guess it comes from years of watching your mother and your wife cooking." "Oh?" John teased, "then Dottie, what happened to you?" "I can cook! A little!" Dottie said grinning. "It's just that cooking is not my strong point; my talents lie in more important things." She cocked her head and waved her hand in Queen Elizabeth fashion. "Oh, pardon us, your majesty!" John said. "It wouldn't be beneath your station to pass the sausages, now would it?" They all laughed.

The next day brought a lot of the grandchildren to see Ethel and Andy.

****

**3 generations of Vitellos, (left to right) Peter,
Joe, Andy and Shaun.
'Circa 1990'**

John painting a ceiling in Braintree 1996

Jackie, Terry and Steve 1991

**Nathanael, Philip, Andrew, Terry,
Jim and Johannah 1998.**

CHAPTER TWENTY-TWO
Adopt An Adult Program

Joe's son Paul graduated from Massachusetts Maritime Academy in 1984. He was the first of Joe's children to get married. On September 20, 1986 he married Kathleen Quinn from Weymouth. Paul and Kathy have four children, Nicholas Dalton, Danielle, Leah and Jacob. They live in Tolland, Connecticut.

Shaun graduated from Bridgewater State College in 1985. On April 23, 1988 he married Maura Considine from Harwinton, Connecticut. Shaun and Maura have two sons, Sean and Neil. They live in Weymouth, Massachusetts.

Mark graduated from Westfield College in 1987. On June 15, 1990 he married Renee Poulin from Weymouth. Mark and Renee have three children, Mark Angelo, Rachel and Thomas. They live in Weymouth, Massachusetts.

Peter attended Massassoit College. In September 1992 he married Jacqueline Goyette from Cohasset. Joe happily performed the wedding ceremony for his son and his bride. Pete and Jacqui have two children, Amanda and Peter. They live in Cohasset, Massachusetts.

Claire attended Massassoit College. Her desire was to be a baker, but she found she was allergic to flour, not eating it, just working with it. She decided to change careers and went to school and became an esthetician, and worked for Elizabeth Grady Salons. She still bakes, but not for a living.

Dottie's daughter Cindy graduated from Wheaton College in 1991, and also from Gordon-Conwell College in 1995 with a masters degree in family therapy. While studying at Gordon Conwell, she met Graeme Fisher, from Moraga, California. They were married on June 17, 1997. Terry's daughter Johannah was a flower girl in the wedding. As Fran watched the bridal party come down the aisle, she whispered to John, "Years ago Dottie was a junior bridesmaid for me. Years later Terry was a junior bridesmaid for Dottie, and then Cindy became a junior bridesmaid for Terry, and now Johannah is a flower girl for Cindy. "Is that just the nicest thing?" Fran said. "It sure is," John responded.

Ethel was too weak to attend the wedding, so Andy stayed home with her, and Ella came and stayed with them. That evening, after the wedding reception, Cindy and Graeme came to see Ethel and Andy. Cindy was still in her wedding gown and veil, and Graeme in his tuxedo. Ethel was surprised and positively thrilled.

*****

Ethel had been failing for some time; she reached a point where she could no longer walk. During the past two weeks she had gotten much worse; she barely ate, and she didn't talk much any more. It was breaking Andy's heart to see her like that. It was heartbreaking for the whole family. John or Joe would pick up Sarah and Pat whenever they wanted to come over and visit with Ethel and Andy, but lately seeing Ethel in that condition was more than Sarah could bear.

The NVNA were wonderful; a nurse came to see Ethel every day, and Ella, or another aide came every day also. Fran took care of her mother's needs throughout the nights. Joe and Dottie took turns helping too; they did their best to give Fran a break. For a while Ethel could lightly squeeze someone's hand if they asked her a question, but she couldn't respond at all anymore.

One Saturday at the end of August Fran spent the entire day crying. "I don't know what's wrong with me?" She said to John. "This isn't like me." "I know Hon," he said "You've been very strong Fran, but watching what's happening to your mother is taking its toll on you. This has been a very difficult time for everyone, but for you, it's been a nightmare." Fran continued crying right into the evening. Fran Roberts called to see how everything was. As soon as she heard Fran crying, she said, "we're coming right over." She and Jack got to Fran and John's about forty-five minutes later. They were very kind to Fran, and they prayed over her; then they went into Ethel's room and prayed over her. When they came out, Fran Roberts said, "Your mother looks so different from a week ago Fran; I can understand why you've been so upset today." By the time Fran and Jack left, Fran was doing much better. She couldn't thank Jack and Fran enough for their kindness.

Fran couldn't sleep that night; she spent most of the night talking to her mother and moistening her lips with swabs. She recited the twenty-third Psalm many times, because it was her mother's favorite psalm. She kept telling her mother that Jesus was right there in the room, and that He loved her very much, and He would never leave her.

The next day Fran was a physical and emotional wreck; she was very tired from lack of sleep. By early afternoon she felt she needed to get out of the house for a little while or she'd come apart at the seams. She and John called Joe and Dottie first, but they weren't home. Fran called Jackie, and then Steve and Kellie; they weren't home either. John tried Shaun and Maura, Mark and Renee, Pete and Jacqui, and Claire, but absolutely no one in the family was at home. "It's Sunday," John said. "They're taking advantage of the nice weather." Finally Fran called her friend Jean Taylor. "Debbie and I just rented a video," she said. "We'll watch it at your house. You go out for a couple of hours and enjoy yourselves. We'll watch your mom and dad; don't worry about anything."

Fran and John decided to go to the Christmas Tree Shop; Fran loved browsing through that fascinating store. After about an hour and a half Fran called home. She had left a message on Dottie's answering machine to please go to the house and relieve Jean and Debbie. When Jean answered the phone, Fran said, "Hi Jean, is Dottie there yet?" Jean said, "Yes she is Fran... but Fran?" "Yes?" she answered. Jean said, "I'm so glad you called... I think you'd better come home right away." "We'll be right there," Fran said.

She couldn't seem to bring herself to ask Jean the question that was burning on her tongue, so she simply said, "Bye."

Fran and John raced home. As they walked in Andy and Ethel's front door, Fran knew by the look on Jean's face what had happened. Andy had sat with his darling wife for quite a while that morning. At eighty-eight years old, he wasn't fully grasping what was happening that afternoon. As Fran came in, Jean hugged her and said, "Your dad isn't aware of what's happened, Fran. We're going home now, but if you need me for anything, I'm just a phone call away." Fran was fighting back tears as she thanked Jean and Debbie.

Andy was sitting in the living room watching TV. As Fran and John entered the living room, he said, "Hi Fran, your mother is still sleeping; Dottie's sitting with her." From her parents' bedroom Fran could hear Dottie crying softly. "It's good that Dad's hard of hearing," she said to John, as they walked into the bedroom. Dottie hugged Fran and said, "She's gone, Fran; Mom's gone." "I know, Honey," she said. "She's not sick anymore; she's with the Lord now." Fran went to her mother's side and held her hand. "Fran, you're so brave," Dottie said. "No, Honey," Fran said. "I'm not brave, I'm just all cried out." Fran kissed her mother's still warm cheek and, still holding her hand, she turned to Dottie and said, "Whenever you're ready Dottie, we need to talk to Dad." "I'll be okay," she said. "John," Fran said, "will you please call Joe, and Terry, Jackie and Steve?" "Of course," John said. "He kissed Fran and hugged Dottie. As he was leaving the room, Fran said, "Better call Sarah and Pat, too." *"This is going to be hard for Sarah,"* Fran thought. *"They've been best friends since they were in their teens."*

Surprisingly, Andy took the news well. "I knew it would be soon," he said. "She's in heaven now, isn't she Fran? I mean, she's fine now, right?" "Yes Dad, she's perfect." He was trying to be brave, but he couldn't hold back the tears. Muffled sobs came from deep within him as he walked into the bedroom. When Fran went into her parents' room a few minutes later, Andy was kissing Ethel's hand and crying. He looked at Fran as she put her arm around him, and he said, "She's my darling wife, Fran," as tears ran down his cheeks.

It was Sunday afternoon, August 31, 1997, when Ethel (Dalton) Vitello left this world. She had been the heart and life-blood of the

Vitello family for over six decades. Her husband and family were her entire life, and in her own sweet, gentle way, she made a huge impact in the lives of her children and grandchildren. For all who knew and loved her, Ethel made this world a little nicer place, simply because she had been here.

Fran turned to her Bible to find just the right Scripture to put on the memorial card for Ethel. She knew exactly the verses she wanted. They were the ones she always felt had been written for women like her mother:

"Who can find a virtuous woman? For her worth is far above jewels. Her children call her blessed; her husband praises her saying, 'Many women have done well, but you excel them all.' Charm is deceitful and beauty is vain, but a woman who fears the Lord, she shall be praised."
--Proverbs 31:10, 28-30.

*****

Terry home-schooled the boys for six years. Then they, and a few other home-schooling couples, started a classical Christian school. Fran and John were very concerned that they might be taking on more than they could handle, but if those couples could trust God to make it happen, then she and John could do no less.

With God's help Jonathan Edwards Christian Academy opened their doors for their first school year in September 1997, with thirty-two students, in grades one through five. Andrew was enrolled in the fifth grade and Philip in the fourth. Each year the school added another grade. The following year Nathanael was enrolled in the second grade, and Terry started teaching the Kindergarten class, with Johannah as one of her five pupils. Two years later Terry was teaching the seventh and eighth grades, which included Andrew and Philip. Jonathan Edwards Academy was blessed to have excellent Christian teachers educating the children, and God was doing a great work there.

"I'm so thankful Mom," Terry said to Fran one day. "Each year I have one or more of my own children in my classes; it's the next best thing to home-schooling." " John and I couldn't be happier about that Terry," Fran said. "Being there, taking part in what's being taught to your children is a blessing." "Yes," Terry said. "God's been so faithful."

*****

On September 24, 1997 Jared Thomas Roche was born. He weighed eight pounds, ten ounces, and was twenty-one inches long, and he was just beautiful. Kellie suffered through hard, lower back labor, but came through the delivery admirably. Steve was another story though; he was an absolute wreck. He was very emotional, and felt every pain Kellie had, right up until the moment she was given an epidural.

"You're so much like your grandfather," Fran said to him later. "If Nana were in pain, Papa felt it too; he would literally cry for her." "I hate being like this," Steve said. "I feel like a blubbering idiot." "I know, Honey," Fran said. "Papa hated it too. I think it's that over-whelming feeling of helplessness." "Boy, helplessness is right," Steve said, shaking his head.

Fran and John couldn't have been happier for Steve; he finally had a child of his own. They always felt that he'd be a super dad. Steve was about as happy as any man could ever be with his new little son. "My only regret is that Nana isn't here to see my little boy," he said to Fran. "I mean, only *three weeks* after she died, Mom." "I know Steve," Fran said. "But that's the way of life, isn't it? When there's a death, a new life soon follows. God, in his goodness and mercy planned it that way." "Yeah, I guess," Steve said. "Life goes on, huh?" "Right."

Fran and John were right; Steve became a super dad, and Kellie took to motherhood like a fish to water. "Parenthood is what those two were meant for," John said one day.

*****

"I never thought I'd see this day," Fran whispered to John, as they sat in the front row of St. Francis Xavier Church in Weymouth. It was December 29, 1997, and Jackie was standing with Steve, his best man, at the altar. Sue looked beautiful as she walked down the aisle on her father's arm. Her parents, Peter and Sophie Arendacs, looked very happy. Fran and John were thrilled, as they truly believed that Sue was the best thing that ever happened to Jackie. Jackie smiled as Sue came near. He looked so handsome to Fran that day, and so very happy. It was a lovely wedding ceremony, performed by Jackie's uncle Joe.

Later, the whole family went to The Common Market Restaurant in Milton for the wedding dinner. Then everyone went back to Fran and John's house for wedding cake, champagne and coffee. It was a lovely day from beginning to end. "The only thing missing from this almost perfect day," Jackie said later, "was Nana." "I know, Honey," Fran said, "but you're thirty-six years old, and your eighty-eight year old grandfather was at your wedding; that's something to be thankful for." "You're right Mom; I am *very* thankful for that." The following week Sue's parents had a wedding reception for Jack and Sue in their hometown of Wayne, New Jersey, where Sue grew up, and invited their family and friends.

*****

Andy got together with Pat Provenzano and another friend, Tony Gulinello every Tuesday. They would speak Italian and reminisce. Tony lived in Brockton, and he would pick Andy up around eleven o'clock, and then they'd pick up Pat at his house in Quincy. They would then go to Barry's Deli in Wollaston for lunch. Every week, when Andy came home, he would say, "They make the biggest and the best hot-pastrami sandwiches in the world." Every now and then he would insist on treating Fran to 'the biggest and best hot-pastrami sandwich in the world.' Fran and her dad would go to Barry's, and ooh and aah over their sandwiches. Then Andy would order one to go for John. "Wait 'til John tastes this," Andy would say every time, as if John had never tasted it before. John would never fail to groan in ecstasy over the sandwich. "This is the biggest and the best hot-pastrami sandwich in the world," he'd say. "Ah hah; I knew you'd love it," Andy would say. The strange thing is, it really was the biggest and best hot-pastrami sandwich in the world. At least it was in *their* world.

*****

Andy started having more frequent angina attacks. Sometimes the nitroglycerine took care of the problem, but other times, when it didn't, Fran called an ambulance, and either she or Joe would go to the hospital with him. Sometimes he had fluid in his lungs; when that occurred the doctor put him on Lasix, a very strong diuretic. "His heart has been weakened by the angina attacks," the doctor said. "It's just not doing its job as efficiently as it always has." They would keep Andy in the hospital until he was stable and there was no more fluid in his lungs. The NVNA started sending a nurse to see him once or twice a week, and an aide two or three times a week. The aide would help Andy shower, and help him get dressed; they'd also change his bed. It was only for about an hour and a half, but it meant the world to Fran. It helped her out immensely. Every one of the health aides was excellent, but Fran requested Ella to come as often as possible. Andy cared a great deal for Ella, as did the rest of the family. Ella was a strong Christian, and she was just as kind to Andy as she had been to Ethel. "There's got to be a special place in heaven for her," Fran said to Joe one day; he heartily agreed.

*****

One night, about three months after Ethel passed away, Andy had an angina attack. After three nitroglycerine pills, Fran called an ambulance and then called Joe. Joe came over and went with his dad in the ambulance. Later Joe called from the hospital. "They put him on a nitroglycerine drip, but as soon as they took him off of it, he went right into another attack. They put him back on the drip, and as soon as he was stable they took him off it. Sure enough, he had another attack. He's back on the drip now, but the doctor said the cycle is definitely going to repeat itself." "Oh my goodness," Fran said. "Thank God he's in the hospital. What are they going to do Joe?" "Well, for now they're keeping him on the drip, and giving him Lasix for the fluid in his lungs." "Oh, poor Dad," Fran said. "He's been through so much lately; is he in much pain, Joe?" "No, he doesn't seem to be." "Well, John and I will be there shortly," Fran said. "We'll stay with him and you can go home," "Okay," Joe said. "I'll see you when you get here."

The next day the surgeon asked to speak with Joe, Fran and Dottie. He said, "Angelo's arteries are badly clogged; we were going to do a catheterization procedure on him, but it won't work for him. Your father is going to need a quadruple by-pass." "Oh dear God," Fran said. "He's almost eighty-nine years old. That's an awful operation for someone his age." "We perform by-pass surgery on lots of older people," the doctor said. "Most people who need it *are* old. Other than his clogged arteries, your father is in excellent health. I believe he would do well with this surgery." "I don't know," Dottie said. "I think he's too old to go through that." "I think so too," said Fran. Joe agreed. "Well, you think about it, and discuss it with your father," the doctor said, "but keep in mind, the minute we take him off the nitroglycerine drip, he *will* have another attack." They decided to leave it up to Andy. "After all, it's his body and his life," Joe said. Fran and Dottie agreed.

When they told Andy what the doctor had said, he was adamant. "No! No operation! I just want to go home." "Dad," Fran said. "That's what we want, too, but you...." He cut her off. "I said no operation! For what anyway? I'm not seventy years old; I'm almost eighty-nine. No, just take me home." "Dad, that's the whole issue," Joe said. "You can't go home because every time they take you off the nitroglycerine drip, you have another angina attack. The pills just aren't doing it for you anymore." Andy looked confused and overwhelmed. Fran felt so bad for him. "Dad, the doctor says that you're in excellent health, but your arteries are so clogged that you need this surgery. He believes you'll come through it fine." "All I want is to go home," he said in an almost whisper. "We know Dad," Dottie said, but you can't come home like this. You won't even get out of this room before another attack starts." Just then the doctor came into the room. He explained to Andy just what is done on the operating table in a quadruple by-pass. He was very clear and he pulled no punches. "I want you to know the absolute truth about this surgery, Mr. Vitello," he said. "You're a perfect candidate for this operation, and I believe you'll come through it with flying colors." Andy became quiet, and pensive. The doctor was patient, and waited a few long moments before speaking. Finally, he smiled at Andy, and patted his arm. "Mr. Vitello, you should make a decision as soon as possible." "I *have* made my decision," Andy said. "I want to go home." Fran and Joe and Dottie just looked at each other. "Dad, haven't you heard what we and the doctor have said to you?" Fran asked. "I've heard," he said. "I want to go home, and if I can't do that without the operation… then I'll have the operation." "Are you sure, Dad?" Joe asked. "I mean, do you want to think about it some more before making that decision?" "No," Andy said. "I want to go home; I'll have the operation." Fran hugged her father, and so did Dottie. "You're a brave man, Dad; I'm proud of you," Dottie said. Andy looked at his three children and said, "I want to die in my own home, but if I don't make it through the operation, just bury me beside my darling wife. That's all I want; I miss her so much." "We know Dad, and we will," Fran said, "but don't be thinking like that. Nothing's going to go wrong; you just concentrate on getting well and coming home after the surgery."

Andy was operated on two days later. It was a long operation; Joe, Fran and Dottie waited at the hospital most of the day. They went to the cafeteria for some lunch, took walks around the hospital, read some magazines, and prayed together. John came right from work to the hospital, and waited with them. Finally, the doctor came out to them. "Andy did great, and everything went well." "Oh, thank God," they all said, as they breathed a sigh of relief. They were able to see their father for just a couple of minutes when he came out of the recovery room. They weren't sure he knew they were there, but they prayed over him and reassured him that the operation was a complete success, and that he was going to be fine.

Andy recuperated fairly quickly for his age. He had to go to a rehabilitation facility for physical therapy when he was released from the hospital. He was there for a few weeks, and finally was able to do what he wanted so desperately to do…. he went home.

"We're on our way Fran," Joe said into the phone. She had a pot of coffee and lunch waiting for them when they arrived. As Joe drove down the driveway Andy was close to tears with excitement. "My home, my beautiful home," he kept saying. Joe was close to tears himself.

Fran was at the door as Joe helped Andy out of the car and into the house. "Welcome home, Dad," she said, as she hugged him gently. Andy kept kissing her cheek and saying, "I'm home Fran; I'm back in my beautiful home." "That's right Dad," she said. "This is where you belong. Would you like a cup of coffee, Dad?" Andy answered her the way he always did, "Ah, that would go good right about now." He was happy. He was home.

Later, the house filled up with grandchildren and great-grandchildren.

*****

In March of 1998 Dottie and her friend Donna took a trip to Italy. They had a marvelous time, but the highlight of their trip was going to Sicily. They drove to Riesi, and found the home of Andy's second cousin Rosario Pistoni. Rosario had come to the states a couple of times years ago, and spent time with his great aunt and uncle, Crocifessa and Pietro. He spent some time getting to know his cousins Andy and Charlie, and their families too. "He's just the nicest man," Dottie said about Rosario, when she called Fran one evening. "Sicily is absolutely beautiful, Fran," she said. "I didn't actually expect it to be this beautiful, but it is." "I hope you have the video camera with you," Fran said. "Oh, don't worry; I'm filming everyone and everything," Dottie said.

Rosario took Dottie right to the home that Andy was born in. Dottie stood there with tears streaming down her cheeks. "It's just overwhelming seeing where Grandma and Papa grew up," she said to Fran, "and where Dad was born and lived until he was almost five years old." "Riesi is so lovely, Fran, and the people are so warm and friendly, especially Rosario and his family." Dottie couldn't speak much Italian, and Rosario couldn't speak any English, but Dottie was so thankful that his son Salvatore could speak a little English, and translated for them. Rosario also took Dottie to the church where Peter and Crocifessa were married, and where Andy and Charlie were baptized. Dottie was so happy, and hated saying goodbye to Rosario and his family when it was time for her and Donna to leave. It was a wonderful trip, one that Dottie knew she would remember lovingly for the rest of her life.

Andy and Ethel had traveled quite a bit when they were younger. They visited many states, and Canada, and traveled to Hawaii, England, Germany, Austria, Switzerland, Spain and Morocco. They usually traveled with Sarah and Pat, or Fran and Hal, and sometimes with Joe and Mae. They also went on a couple of cruises. They took a trip to Italy, but never went to Sicily. "Dad, how could you and Mom go to Italy, but not visit Sicily, where you were born?" Fran asked her father after the trip to Italy. "We were on the tour, and it didn't include a side trip to Sicily," he said. "Everything was kind of rushed. We're going to go back to Italy some day," he added. "We'll definitely go to Sicily then." Unfortunately, they never did get to Sicily.

Peter had gone back to Sicily only once, when his mother was dying in 1919, but no one in the family had gone to Sicily since then. Dottie felt proud and privileged to be the first to go there since her grandfather's visit eighty years earlier.

When Dottie showed the video she had taken in Sicily, everyone was excited. Andy didn't actually remember much of Riesi, but the excitement was obvious in him. This is where his ancestors had lived; this is where his parents grew up; this is where *he* was born. "Why the heck didn't I go there when I had the chance?" He said. "But this is wonderful, Dottie." He was thrilled to finally be seeing Riesi, and thrilled that his daughter had actually been there.

*****

The therapist who came to the house to give Andy physical therapy was tough; she didn't let him get away with anything. She was kind to Andy though, and joked with him. Despite her rigidity, Andy liked her a lot. He needed a lot more care than he did before the surgery. The operation saved his life, but the quality of his life was not what it used to be. He couldn't walk as well any longer, and his mind was not sharp anymore. Fran always felt that it had been too much anesthesia going into him for too long a time.

*****

Andy got back to going out for hot pastrami sandwiches on Tuesdays with Pat and Tony, but he needed his walker to get around. Tony was a little younger, but Pat and Andy were close in age. After a couple of months it became too difficult for Pat and Tony to get Andy out and about. Soon the Tuesday outings came to an end. Fran, every now and then, would take her dad to Barry's for the 'best hot pastrami sandwiches in the world'. Once in a while Pat and Tony would bring the sandwiches to Andy, and they'd have lunch together in Andy's dining room. Andy loved those days; they were very special to him. Those outings were a pleasant diversion that kept him, at least for a few hours, from missing Ethel so much.

Tony and his wife Helen were newer friends of Ethel and Andy's. Of course, Pat and Sarah had been Andy and Ethel's closest friends for most of their lives. Tony drove, but neither Sarah or Pat ever learned to drive, so they simply went everywhere by bus or train. Lately it was getting too difficult for them to get around, and getting to see Andy depended on Fran and John or Joe picking them up. Sometimes Dottie would pick them up after work and bring them over.

Pat was a very healthy man all his life; he hated hospitals and didn't believe in going to a doctor, or taking medicines. "Get plenty of rest and drink plenty of fluids, and whatever is ailing you will go away on its own," was Pat's answer to every malady. He always attributed his good health to a diet that included lots of fruits and olive oil. Pat lived to be ninety-one years old; he died in 1999. "Pat was a very good man," Andy said, "and an excellent friend. Poor Sarah; how's she going to get along without him?" Thankfully, Pat's niece Elaine, who had been helping both of them, continued to take care of Sarah. After Pat died, Fran had Sarah over more often, and she and Elaine took turns having her at their homes for holiday dinners. It pleased Andy to have her there, as she helped to keep a little of 'the old days' alive in him. They'd reminisce and speak Italian. They missed Pat and Ethel though; they missed them a lot.

*****

Fran would take Andy out for a ride and for lunch now and then, but Andy was bored; all he did most days was watch TV and fall asleep in his chair. Joe decided to look into senior day centers as a little change for him. He and Fran liked the Deerfield Senior Day Center in Hingham, so they arranged for him to be picked up and driven home in the Center's wheelchair accessible van two days a week. Andy wasn't crazy about going there though. "The lunches are lousy," he said, after a few visits. "Oh Dad, I doubt if they're really that bad," Fran said. "Well, it's nothing like you make," he said. The days he really liked being at the Center were when someone played the piano, and they'd sing the old songs he loved so much. Then, like his father, he'd sing his heart out. Those days at the Center, he loved. Every day when the van brought him home, Fran would be waiting. Andy would say the same thing as he was wheeled into the house..."Where's my beautiful daughter? Aah, here she is." Fran would help him off with his jacket and his cap "Would you like a cup of coffee Dad?" she'd ask. He would always say, "Ah, that would go good right about now."

*****

Gerry Elliott was a gem. She was a young woman in her thirties who lived across the street from Shaun and Maura, and was helping Fran with Andy's care. She came to the house a couple of mornings a week and got Andy washed and dressed and ready to go to the Center. "She certainly makes my work a lot easier," Fran said. "She doesn't charge too much, and it's a good feeling knowing she lives just one street away." Gerry had her husband Joe and four teenagers at home to care for, but she was always there if Fran needed her. With Gerry and Ella helping with Andy's care, things didn't seem so overwhelming to Fran and John, *and* Joe and Dottie.

*****

"Colorado, John!" Fran said, as she and John discussed where they would go on their vacation. "Oh yeah!" John said. "We can fly to Colorado Springs, rent a car, and play it by ear from then on." "Oh John, that'll be wonderful," Fran said, all excited. Ever since Fran read the book "Centennial", by James Michener, she had wanted to go to Colorado. John read it after she did, and seeing the Rocky Mountains became a desire of his heart too. When Centennial was made into a mini-series for TV, Fran and John were positively enchantcd by it; they knew that one day they would go there. The time was right; she and John hadn't had a vacation longer than a weekend in quite a few years. Her mom had passed away almost two years earlier, and taking care of her dad, especially since his surgery, was wearing heavily on her and John. They could use a time to relax and enjoy each other again without constantly worrying about Andy. Joe wanted them to go; between he and Dottie, and a few of the grandchildren, Andy would be in good hands, and, of course Ella or Gerry would be coming in every day. "During April vacation," Terry said, "I can come with Nathanael and Johannah and stay the whole week and take care of Papa." Fran was so thankful for that, and for all of them.

The Norwell Visiting Nurse Association had said, "We take care of the caregivers, too." They felt that Fran and John should have gotten away after Ethel died, but Andy got sick so soon after, that Fran dismissed the thought of a vacation.

Fran hated flying, but she knew if they were going to spend as much time as possible in and around Colorado, they needed to get there quickly. So, on April 7, 1999 they boarded a plane at Logan Airport and flew to Colorado Springs. They picked up the 2000 Dodge Intrepid they had reserved at Avis, and went immediately to the Days Inn where they had a room reservation. The next morning they went to Focus On The Family, where they toured the beautiful facility they had heard and read so much about. They were very impressed, and praised God for the work He was doing through Dr. James Dobson and 'Focus'

They never made another reservation; each morning they got in the car and went wherever the road took them. They asked the locals for suggestions, and headed for towns and cities that seemed interesting. They ate at some wonderful and different restaurants, and stayed at some wonderful, and some *not* so wonderful motels. They went through a few big cities, but mostly they preferred the smaller towns like Ouray, and Leadville, and out of the way places.

The Rockies were everywhere! North, south, east, west; no matter where you looked it seemed, there they were, looming over a town. Fran and John drove up Pike's Peak, which was 14,000 feet above sea level. Forest rangers had set up a blockade at 12,000 feet because of snow at the top which made driving hazardous. The air at 12,000 feet was very thin. Fran, who had asthma, found her breathing very strained. She kept needing to use her inhaler. When they stopped at the gift shops on the way up Pike's Peak, everyone said the same thing; keep drinking lots of water. Fran couldn't understand what that had to do with her breathing, but she did whatever they said.

At one of the gift shops, Fran barely had five words out of her mouth, when the sales woman said, "Oh, you're from Boston, aren't you?" Fran couldn't believe it; she never thought she spoke like a true Bostonian. But there it was, two thousand miles from home, and she was spotted as one who 'pahks her cah at Hahvard Yahd'. "There you go," John said laughing, "I guess you can take us out of Boston, but you can't take the 'Boston' out of us."

At about 11,500 feet, Fran and John pulled off the road. The scenery was so gorgeous that they just had to get out of the car again and take pictures. They looked out over the mountains. It seemed so strange to be standing on solid ground but looking down at the tops of huge trees, and looking down on birds flying. They walked into the woods and looked around. It was very windy where they were, and as they walked Fran said, "It feels like we're the only two people in the world up here." "I know what you mean," John said. "I've never felt quite like this before." John walked a little way from her, just taking it all in, when all of a sudden Fran heard a strange sound from right above her. She looked up and almost froze at the sight of a beautiful golden eagle soaring overhead. She yelled to John, but the wind took her voice in the opposite direction. Finally, she just about screamed his name, "John! Look!" He turned and she pointed upward. He couldn't believe his eyes as the eagle, with wings completely outstretched, soared above his head and was gone. They were both so excited. For a couple of 'Bostonians' to see a golden eagle right over their heads, way up near the top of Pike's Peak, was about as 'unreal' as anything they could imagine. "Were you able to get some good pictures of it?" John asked. "Pictures?" Fran said. She had the camera around her neck, but was so enthralled at the sight of the eagle that she never even thought to take its picture. "Oh, shoot!" She cried. "I don't believe it! I never got a picture of it, John!" As they slowly descended the mountain, they stopped again in the gift shop to use the rest rooms. Fran found a postcard with a golden eagle on it that looked exactly like the one they saw. "Well, here's our picture of the eagle," she said. "Good enough," John said with a smile.

The next day they went to the Garden Of The Gods, which Fran thought, other than looking out over the Rockies, was the most beautiful place she had ever seen. As they drove through it, they were amazed at the color of everything. The mountainous rocks with their unusual and fascinating shapes were actually red; even the soil was red. "I could stay here all day, just basking in the beauty of these rocks," Fran said. "Something almost miraculous happened here at one time," John said. They ate lunch at the Garden Restaurant, and took their time browsing through the largest gift shop they had ever seen.

They spent a night in a cozy log cabin in Buena Vista, with lovely pronghorn antelopes all over the grounds. Fran was furiously taking pictures of everything. Fran asked the owner of the cabin what the name of the beautiful, brilliantly colored birds were that she kept seeing in the trees there. "They're magpies," he said. "Magpies?" Fran said. "How can such a beautiful creature have a name like Magpie?" The owner laughed. "That's its name."

On the road to Glenwood Springs, out of the blue, it started snowing real hard. They were on a mountain road, and the snow was piling up fast. As they drove very slowly, they saw a truck overturned on the side of the road; the police waved them on. "Thank God it's way over on the road," John said, "or we'd be spending the night in the car." A little further down the road a car was on its side, with police and a tow-truck there. It was a very slippery, nerve-wracking ride, with Fran and John praying the entire way.

While they were in Glenwood Springs Fran had a bad fall, and crashed down hard on her left knee. She had been having some pain in that knee even before they started out on their trip, but after the fall the pain was so excruciating that they both knew they had to end their trip and get a flight home in the morning. It was late at night, but the owner of the motel they were staying at gave her an ice pack for her knee. It was beginning to swell up, so John went to the store and bought two packages of frozen peas; they were more flexible than the ice pack. Fran took three aspirin, and then John gently tied the peas to the front and back of her knee, and helped her into bed. He carefully put two pillows under her knee, but they both knew she wouldn't be able to sleep at all. Any movement of her leg caused a stabbing pain to her knee. John slept on a vinyl sofa, and spent the night swimming in perspiration. He kept checking on Fran; he could hear her moaning and whimpering throughout the night. About three o'clock in the morning, John checked on her, and in the dark she said, "How could this happen John? It's been so long since we've taken a vacation. We've wanted to see Colorado for years. It's not fair John. We're here! We're actually here, and we have to go home. How could God let this happen? *Why* would He let this happen?" As bad as the pain in her knee was, it couldn't compare to the disappointment she was feeling.

In the morning John called a place where they could rent medical supplies and rented a walker. The only problem was that one has to be able to 'walk' to use a walker. Fran couldn't even touch her toe to the floor. John returned it and got a wheelchair.

"How's that?" John asked in the morning, as he got Fran settled in the front seat of the car with a pillow under her leg. "Not bad Honey," she said. "In fact, I'm surprisingly comfortable, as long as I don't do anything with this leg." She filled up with tears. "Oh God John," she said. "I just can't believe we're on our way to the airport to go home." "Fran, I've been thinking," John said. "If you thought you'd be all right in the car, and the wheelchair, we may not have to go home. Most places are wheel-chair accessible, and I could push you wherever we go." "Oh Gosh, John, that's just too much for you," Fran said, "and I don't know how my leg will be. Anyway, what kind of vacation is that for you? You work hard, and you've been doing so much for my parents. This is no way for you to spend your vacation. No, Honey." "Fran, we'll both be very disappointed if we go home," John said." I mean, if you can't do it, then we'll have to go, but for my part, it won't be a problem." "Oh John, I don't know," Fran said. "I appreciate what you're trying to do, but..." "Think about it, Fran," he said. "We're in Colorado! I know *I* can do this; if you think *you* can do it, we should at least give it a try. We can *always* go home."

They did give it a try, and were amazed at how well it was working. They went everywhere, and did almost everything they would have done walking. John was wonderful; he maneuvered that wheelchair like he had been doing it all his life. "I've had a lot of practice with your mom and dad," he said. "I know," Fran said. "Too bad you couldn't have had a break from it. I'm sorry this had to happen John." "Don't talk like that, Fran; I'm having a wonderful time. Except for the pain you've been in, I don't regret a thing." "You're much too good to me, John," she said. "You're wrong Fran; *you're* too good to *me*," he said. "I'm just trying to reciprocate a little." Fran smiled. "Well, you certainly have gone way beyond the call of duty. I really appreciate it John, and for convincing me not to cut short our trip."

They went to Durango, where they took a four-hour trip on the Durango-Silverton Narrow Gauge Railroad. It was an old-fashioned mountain train that went along the edge of the mountain, and right through it. It was very exciting and the scenery was positively gorgeous. They looked down on a mountain river that looked like a thin line from seven thousand feet up. "That could be Michener's 'North Platte River," John said. Everyone deboarded the train and ate lunch by a lovely lake in Cascade Canyon before heading back. The ride was a lot of fun, and the conductor and crew were just wonderful to Fran in her wheelchair.

The town of Silverton fascinated Fran and John. It was a true old-western town that looked just like it did a hundred and fifty years ago. The only difference they could make out was, instead of horses on the road there were automobiles. "Silverton is protected by law against changes; everything is kept the same as it was in the old west," Fran told Dottie when she called home later. "The only thing missing in Silverton is John Wayne coming out of the sheriff's office with guns blazing."

One night they ate at the Conestoga Restaurant, where they had roast buffalo. "I thought it would be different from any meat we've ever eaten," she told Joe on the phone, "but it tastes very much like roast beef. It was real good, and tender too."

They found Centennial, but it wasn't even in Colorado. It was actually over the line into Wyoming. Fran expected a bustling town, but it was simply a tiny 'one-horse' town, not at all like the Centennial in Michener's story. The sign, as you entered the town, read, "CENTENNIAL - Population 100 - Elevation 8,450." "Maybe the book wasn't written about *this* Centennial," John said. "That's true," Fran said. "It's more of a 'fictionalized' history of Colorado. It would have been nice though to find Michener's 'Centennial', wouldn't it?" "Yeah," John said, "but what a joy just 'finding' Michener's Colorado."

One of Fran and John's favorite little towns was Chugwater, Wyoming. Chugwater was truly 'the town that time forgot'. It wasn't beautiful; everything was very old, but somehow it had a warm and comfortable feel about it. They stayed at what used to be called the Buffalo Motel. It was now a Motel 8. "I think it's the only somewhat modern building in the entire town," Fran said. It was a nice motel, and the people were very friendly and helpful. They seemed genuinely proud of their little town, and rightfully so.

Fran and John went to what's called the Four Corners. It's a spot where you can stand and have one foot on the line between Colorado and Utah, and the other foot on the line between New Mexico and Arizona. John took a picture of Fran with one wheel on two states, and the other wheel on the other two states.

"Magnificent! Beautiful! Awesome!" were just a few of the words that flowed freely from John and Fran as they looked out over the Grand Canyon. Nothing could have prepared them for the true majesty and splendor of the Canyon. "All atheists should visit the

Grand Canyon," Fran said. "How could anyone not believe in God after seeing this?"

John was terrific; whenever they stopped the car to enjoy the scenery, he carefully maneuvered the wheelchair over rough and rocky ground so that Fran was right at the edge of the Canyon. People often stared at him strangely as he looked so determined to get Fran right to the edge. They would keep their eyes glued on John, as they got closer to the edge. "I believe they think you're going to do away with me," Fran chuckled. "Hah," he laughed. "Well this would certainly be the place to do it, if I were so inclined." "Sooo," he said, in his best Jimmy Cagney voice, "ya better not give me a hard time, Babe, or over ya go." "Hmm, I wonder what they'd do if I started screaming," Fran said. "Don't even think it!" John said. "While you're having fun, I'll be beaten to a bloody pulp, and carted off to the hoosegow... do they still have hoosegows? Do hangings still go on around here?" Fran just laughed.

Fran and John felt sad when it was time to start on their trip home. They had visited so many cities, towns and fascinating places in Colorado, and they had met some real nice and fascinating people, too. Colorado was just as beautiful as they had imagined. They knew they'd watch 'Centennial' again as soon as they got home. They also knew they'd be looking at it through different eyes, now that they had actually seen Colorado's unique beauty.

On the trip home, Fran and John drove through many different states, some beautiful, and others not so beautiful. They went to Branson, Missouri, and to Dolly Parton's "Dixie Stampede". That was a lot of fun and very exciting. It was a barbecue dinner show with lots of horses, cowboys, southern belles and square dancing. It was also part rodeo and part reenactment of a Civil War battle. Fran and John happened to be sitting on the 'South' side, so they were cheering for the confederates.

Virginia was one of the prettiest states they went through, and the Shenandoah Valley was simply beautiful. Fran and John had been noticing a particular kind of tree that seemed to grow everywhere. It had the prettiest deep pink flowers all over it. They saw the trees in Kentucky and all through Virginia, and right into Pennsylvania.

When Fran asked about them, she was told they were Redbud trees. She was determined to find a nursery back home that sold them.

When they got to Pennsylvania, they went on a tour of Gettysburg. Fran and John had seen the movie 'Gettysburg' not long before going on their trip, and seeing and hearing about the battles on the tour had a much deeper meaning for them. Fran was crazy about Colonel Lawrence Joshua Chamberlain in the movie, played by Jeff Daniels, and his battle at Little Round Top. That, and Pickett's Charge seemed to come alive for them on the tour. It was a very moving experience. "Imagine, " Fran said. "Over fifty thousand men died here... and they were all Americans fighting Americans." "Yeah," John said. "Hard to believe."

They stayed the night at Hershey Farms in Strasburg, where they had stayed before, and the next morning set out for home. After being gone for three weeks, they arrived home unexpectedly at six o'clock in the evening on May 1. Joe and Dottie were there.

As much as Fran and John had hated leaving Colorado, and as much as they enjoyed all the states they went through, the long trip home made getting there a pleasure. "It's nice to go away," John said, as they walked in the door, "but it sure is great to get home." Andy was so glad to see them. They all hugged, and Fran said, "Dad, it's so good to be home, and to be back with you." She kissed his forehead and Andy said, "I missed you Fran." "I missed you too, Dad." Fran was surprised at how much her father had declined in the three weeks they were gone. "I was just about to put a pot on," Dottie said. "Oh, I'd love a cup of coffee," Fran said. "Dad, could you go for a cup of coffee?" She knew what he would say. He smiled and said, "Ah, that would go good right about now." Fran and Dottie just smiled. Fran brought gifts and souvenirs for just about everybody. She also had over a hundred pictures to show them.

Andy and Ethel had traveled quite a bit, and Dottie, and Joe and Mae also. Fran and John hadn't traveled much; they had gone to England when Dottie and Chet were there, and to New Brunswick, Canada in 1975 to meet John's relatives. Over the years they would go for a weekend occasionally to New Hampshire, or Vermont. They liked Maine a lot, and Pennsylvania Dutch country was special to them. They had also gone twice to Joe and Mae's condo in Venice

Florida. But seeing Colorado and so many states on the way home, was better than any trip they could ever imagine. But John was right; it is so nice to go away, but it's just *great* to be home.

When family and friends asked them later, "What were the highlights of your trip?" Fran and John answered with no hesitation.... "The Grand Canyon, Pike's Peak, and The Garden of the Gods."

That night Fran and John thanked God for his protection on them, and Fran said, "And thank You Lord, for my husband, who convinced me we could continue with our trip, and did everything possible to make it wonderful. Thank you for blessing us like you did."

Two days later Fran found a nursery that had Redbud trees. She and John bought three of them, and they are growing and thriving on their front lawn. Each April and May, when the trees are in bloom, their beauty takes them right back to the lovely ride home from Colorado.

*****

Claire met Scott Mateus, who lived in Somerset, and it was love at first sight for both of them. They were married on September 25, 1999 at St. Francis Xavier Church in South Weymouth. Although he had to be in a wheelchair, Andy was able to go to his granddaughter's wedding. He was very happy for Claire, although he was very emotional throughout the entire ceremony and reception. He missed his darling wife and everything reminded him of her. He cried as he watched his son Joe perform the wedding ceremony for his daughter and her husband. Claire and Scott have two children, Scott and Bianca. They live in Whitman, Massachusetts.

*****

"John, can I talk to you about something?" Steve asked, when he dropped by one afternoon after work. "Sure," John said. "What's up?" "Well, years ago you wanted to adopt us kids, but it was never the right time," Steve said. "I just want to know if you still want to adopt us, and if you and Mom think that *now* might be the right time." "Wow!" John said. "Where did that come from?" "I've been thinking about it a lot lately," Steve said. "You're the only father I've ever really had; I've always wanted you to be my *legal* father, and Jared's legal grandfather. I want it written down, so to speak; I want it to be real." "Wow!" John said again. "I know this comes as a shock to you John," Steve said, "but what do you think?" "Well, I'm all for it," John said. "But, isn't it a bit unusual, adopting someone in his thirties?" "It may be unusual, but I doubt if it's never done," Fran said. "Mom, how do you feel about it now, so many years later?" "I think it would be wonderful," she said. "It's what John has always wanted. When you were children, I didn't want to have to deal with your 'father' but now you can make that decision yourself. You're the only children John has ever had; he made *that* decision years ago when you and Terry and Jackie were very young. He could see the problems that would have developed, especially with Terry, if he and I had children together." Fran went on, "Nothing could please me more than John adopting you, because I know how much he loves you, and our grandchildren...like you were his own flesh and blood." "Steve," John said, "Other than your mother and I getting married, I can honestly say this is the greatest thing that could ever happen to me. I've *always* wanted to be more than just a stepfather to you kids." John hugged Steve, and then Steve hugged his mother. They were all close to tears. "You never really were a stepfather to me," Steve said. "You were the only father I really knew."

"Have you spoken to Terry and Jackie about this, Steve?" John asked. "Yep, I spoke to Jack last night," he said. "He's all for it." "Wonderful!" John said. "I called Terry last night," Steve said, "but no one was home." "I doubt if Terry will do it," John said. "John," Fran said. "I know how much you would like Terry to do this because of the grandchildren, but...." "It isn't just for them, Fran," John said. "It took many years for me and Terry to have a good relationship, but today, God has given us a better- than-good relationship. I may not be old enough in years to be her father, but emotionally and spir- itually I am. I truly love Terry, and I know she loves me too. I'm not interested in the guy that planted the seed; *I'm* her father, and I'm those four wonderful kids' grandfather. I *know* God arranged this. More than anything in this world, I'd like to be the *legal* father and grandfather to *all* the kids in this family, but if that never happens, it will never change the way I feel."

Fran kissed John on the cheek. "Okay!" she said. "Tomorrow I'll make some phone calls and find out what we have to do to make this happen." "Good!" John said. "I'll call Jackie tonight and talk to him about it. Meanwhile, Steve, you get hold of Terry and find out how she feels about the adoption. If she doesn't feel it's right for her, then so be it, but let her in on what's going on." "Okay! Let's do it!" Steve hollered, as he 'high-fived' John.

After a lot of phone conversations, forms filled out, and letters written to the court by John, Fran, Jack and Steve, they finally got a court date. Sue and Kellie had to write their own letters, saying that they were in favor of the adoption, and attesting to the fact that there was no ulterior motive on anyone's part.

On September 27, 2000 Fran and John, Jack, Sue, and Steve went to the Probate Court in Dedham where John legally adopted Jack and Steve. They were all so excited. John was not his usual wacky self that day; he just seemed to bask in the warmth and love of his family. He was happy, very happy. Jack and Steve were 'all wound up' though. They were hilarious; they even had the judge laughing. The judge was a lovely woman who joined in the excitement and the joy that they were all feeling. "I've never done an adoption on adults before," she said. "This has been an absolute pleasure for me." The judge posed for quite a few pictures that Sue took, some with Jack, some with Steve, and some with Fran and John, as she signed the adoption papers. Then she posed with all of them while the bailiff took a few pictures of them. She made the whole adoption experience wonderful. Later, they drove down to the Cape, to Sandwich, and went to lunch at the Daniel Webster Inn. They invited the judge to join them, but she had a full day of cases ahead of her. She said, "I can't think of anything I'd like better than to walk out those doors and go to lunch with the five of you." She hugged all of them; then she smiled and said, "My day has already peaked; it'll be all downhill from here."

It was a perfect day; they were thrilled with the way it all turned out. Each one of them felt like some unfinished part of their lives had finally been made complete. There was a kind of peace that seemed to settle on all of them. The calm didn't last long; Jack and Steve were in rare form again, keeping them all in stitches. During a rare, quiet moment in the car on the way home, John silently prayed, *"Thank You, Lord; thank You so much for my children. "*

Fran in Centennial, April 1999

Fran and John at Grand Canyon, April 1999

CHAPTER TWENTY-THREE
Twenty-five Years

Andy was failing; after a few ambulance trips to the hospital, he fell one day and broke his hip. He spent a week in the hospital, and then a few weeks at a rehabilitation facility. He just seemed to get weaker and weaker, until he wasn't eating anymore, and drinking very little. The doctor finally said, "The best we can do is to keep him pain free."

That same afternoon a Hospice nurse came into Andy's room and introduced herself to Fran. She said, "The hospital has called us in; if you would like, we'll be glad to take over your father's care from now on." The Hospice nurse was very kind to her. Fran knew that her wonderful father was dying; there was no denying it now. She said to the nurse, "I'm bringing my father home; I thank you for your concern, and if you can come and care for him there, that would be perfect, but if he's ready to die, he's going to die in his own bed, in his own home." Joe had come in the room and heard most of the conversation. "I agree," he said. "Our father needs to be in his own home now." The Hospice nurse touched Fran's arm, and smiled gently at Joe. "I'll make all the arrangements," she said. A little while later she came back into the room and said, "The EMTs will be here shortly; you can take your dad home today." "Thank you so much," Fran said. "I'll follow you to your home and get him settled for the night," the nurse said.

Fran spent as much time in Andy's room as she could. The nights seemed endless. Joe and Dottie did what they could to keep up the vigil. It was a sad time; seeing their once strong and vigorous father lying helpless in his bed was killing them. This was an especially difficult time for Dottie, as her daughter Cindy lived in Beverly, an hour's drive away, and was about to give birth to her first child at any moment. Her doctor had predicted possible complications. Dottie was back and forth between Beverly and Weymouth, needing to be with her daughter, and wanting to be with her dying father.

Steve slept at the house a few nights in a row on the twin bed in Andy's office. Fran and John appreciated him being there; he was a big help to them. The other grandchildren came over or called most days. Terry, and Joe's son Paul, both lived two hours drive away, Terry in Greenfield, and Paul in Connecticut. They called often. Their Papa was so very important to all of the grandkids, and even the older great-grandkids. It was a difficult time; no one wanted to face the inevitable.

For a short while Andy was able to nod his head and squeeze Fran's hand. He would smile when she or Dottie or Joe came close to him. He no longer spoke, or ate or even drank. It was especially hard on everyone who took care of him. Fran wouldn't leave his side for very long; she was determined to be with him when he breathed his last.

Baby Nathaniel John Fisher was born to Cindy and Graeme on February 2, 2001. Dottie was so thrilled with her beautiful little grandson. Sadly, he would never meet his great-grandfather, as Andy passed away the following day.

Fran had sat with her father for a very long time. His breathing was shallow but his pulse was still strong. John had sat with him earlier and read from the Bible to him, and prayed with him. Joe had been in and out during the day, doing the same. The hospice nurse had been there in the morning, and was due to come back in a couple of hours.

As Fran sat with her dad, she kept talking to him; she didn't want him to feel frightened. "Dad, I'm here with you," she said, "you're not alone." She continued holding his hand and checking his pulse; she couldn't see him breathing any more, but when she put her hand near his nose, she could very lightly feel his breath. "Dad, Jesus is here in the room with us," she said. "He's right here watching over you. Remember He said, "I'll never leave you or forsake you?" And remember He also said, "I go to prepare a place for you, that where I am, you will be also?" Well, He's here Dad, waiting to take you to heaven whenever you're ready to go. Mom is there too, Dad."

Fran had to stop for a moment, as she felt like she had a rock in her throat, and tears were streaming down her cheeks. After a moment she continued. "Dad, I just want you to know that you've been a wonderful father to all of us, and a wonderful grandfather, too. You did a good job with us, Dad; you were always there for us, helping us. I know you're worried about Dottie, living alone and having money problems. But you don't need to worry about that any longer. Dottie's doing great; she has a good job and is making decent money. Cindy and Graeme just had a beautiful, healthy baby boy, and Dottie's a grandmother now. Isn't that something Dad? Dottie... a grandmother." Fran went on talking. "Dad, we're *all* doing good; you don't have to worry about your family any more, thanks to all you've done for us. I love you Dad; your whole family loves you, so very much." Fran hesitated for a moment and then said, "Dad, you can go now, if you want. Jesus is standing right here ready to take you home. There's nothing to fear."

Fran stopped talking; she felt paralyzed for a moment, as she realized that the pulse that was beating so strongly in his wrist was no longer there. She could hardly breathe. Finally she reached up to feel the pulse in his neck; it was no longer beating. She felt both wrists, and knew that he had let himself slip away. Her wonderful father had decided that life here on earth was no longer for him, and if Jesus and Ethel were waiting for him, he was ready to go.

Fran sat there holding her dad's hand, with tears pouring down her cheeks. After a few minutes she dried her eyes and kissed his cheek. She said, "Bye Dad; say hi to Mom for me." Then she walked over to the other side of the house. John was sitting in his favorite chair reading. He looked up at Fran, and she said, "He's gone, Hon." John jumped up and put his arms around her. "Are you okay?" He said. "Yes," she said. "John, I felt his life leave his body." "What do you mean Hon?" He asked. "I was holding his hand and talking to him," she said. "I told him that Jesus was there in the room, and that he could go home to heaven with Jesus if he was ready. John,

I had my fingers on his wrist, and I felt his pulse stop beating right there in my hand." "Oh God, Fran," John said. "Are you sure you're okay?" "I'm fine John," she said. "I'm so thankful that I was with my dad when he died, because I wasn't there when Mom died. He left this world just as I was telling him he could go with Jesus. I felt him go, John. I can't begin to explain the peace I'm feeling right now." "Praise God," John said. "John, would you call Terry and Jackie?" Fran said. "I'll call them right now," he said. "I'll use my dad's phone and call Joe and Dottie," Fran said. "Gosh, I hate calling Dottie in the middle of her joy with Cindy, but she wanted me to call her immediately. I'll call Sarah too," Fran said. "She's so fragile these days; she's going to take this hard. I guess you'd better get out the address books Hon, and call everybody."

Angelo Vitello left this world on February 3, 2001; he was ninety-one years old. When he was born, his mother said that he was destined by God to become something special in this world. He *did* become something special; not necessarily the way the world thinks of special, but the kind of special that people who know him never forget. Like his parents, he was from the proverbial 'old school'. He loved America with all his heart, and he spoke good English, but *Andy was Italian* through and through. The culture, the language, the food, the people.... he *loved* being Italian, and thoroughly enjoyed the company of his Italian friends.

Andy was a man who loved his wife the way *all* men should love their wives; he made her the joy of his life. Besides being a loving and devoted husband, he was a strong and loving patriarch to his entire family. His family came before anything else in this world; nothing was more important. Andy was a simple man, but he was the best father and grandfather this world has ever produced... attested to by his children and grandchildren.

Andy adored his mother all of his life, and was like her in many ways. He never saved his money in a sock, but like Crocifessa, he was frugal with money, but extremely caring of, and generous to his family.

He was a unique and precious individual, and he will always be greatly missed. His descendants, generations from now, *should know* that their ancestor Angelo Vitello, *truly was a very special man,* a man they can be proud is a branch on their family tree.

*****

Ever since Fran could remember, she would always start a pot of coffee about twenty minutes before she expected John to arrive home from work. It became a very important part of their day, sitting together at the kitchen table, having coffee and talking about each other's day. They would go straight from chatting about their day's activities to solving all the world's problems in an hour or so right there at the table. They were true 'armchair philosophers', and getting deep into a discussion was more fun than almost anything. "This is the best part of my day," John said many times. "Mine, too," Fran always agreed. When the coffee was gone and the world problems solved, John would take his shower and Fran would start preparing supper.

*****

About a year after Andy passed away, Steve and Kellie separated. They had been married fourteen years. It was a very hard decision for Steve to make, but he knew they couldn't go on any longer the way things were. They had some serious problems that were not going to go away. Steve came to Fran and John's house one day and said, "Would it be alright if I moved into Nana and Papa's side of the house for a while until I can figure out what I'm going to do?" Fran and John were upset about the separation; they were very concerned for Jared, but they had known for quite some time that it was inevitable.

Steve stayed close to Jared, and in a different way, close to Kellie too. He would take Jared out every Wednesday after work and take him to dinner at Friendly's. He'd also pick him up three Saturdays each month and take him overnight. When they weren't together they called each other every night. Jared was Steve's whole life. Although Jared was unhappy and confused in the beginning about his father leaving, in time he adjusted well to the situation. Because of the way his parents handled things, he realized that they both loved him very much, and he would still see his daddy quite often.

After having their home to themselves for a year, Fran and John had lost their privacy once again, but since Steve valued his privacy too, they could just close the kitchen door and forget he was there, and vice-versa. He was quiet and clean, which meant a great deal to Fran. There were a lot of benefits to having Steve there, too. Fran and John were, in Steve's words, "two of the most technically challenged people I have ever seen." Having him there to fix the TV, the VCR, or the DVD player or Fran's laptop computer when she did something 'wrong' was a definite bonus. Fran knew absolutely nothing about computers; the only reason she even had one, and the only thing she used it for, was to write the book that was in her head and in her heart.

Yes, Steve was a handy guy to have around, that's for sure, but he was also a lot of fun. Between him and John, Fran spent a lot of time laughing, which was the thing she loved more than anything to do. They had their differences now and then, to be sure, but thankfully they were rare, and they never stayed upset with each other for long.

When Jack got together with Steve it was non-stop laughing, and were they ever loud. Terry and Jim were relatively quiet people, but when Andrew, Philip, Nathanael and Johannah were in the same room with Jack and Steve, the noise level would rise to a deafening pitch. "Poor Jim," Fran said many times. "He was raised in a nice quiet home; this must be so overwhelming for him." He did seem to be overwhelmed at times, but Jim was a good sport, and he seemed to adopt the attitude, "If you can't fight 'em, join 'em." The yelling, the screaming, the laughing, and the hooting and hollering was just what the kids looked forward to when they knew they were going to see their Uncles Jack and Steve, and Jack and Steve never disappointed them. On holidays, or family cookouts, when Joe's family got together with Fran's family, it was 'heavenly bedlam'. When Ethel and Andy were alive, they loved the jokes, the bantering, and the laughter. This was their family, and being together was their greatest happiness. It *was* loud, but it was good, clean fun.

*****

Fran and John were avid readers. John set his alarm clock for 5:15 every morning; he'd spend about forty minutes reading his Bible before going to work. Fran would do her Bible reading every morning while having her coffee. It was their routine, and they felt it was very important to start their day with God's word in their minds and hearts. They always had a book going too. John loved exciting stories like the twenty-one books of Patrick O'Brian's "Master and Commander" series. He also liked to read history books, and biographies of great Christian leaders. Fran enjoyed stories like Jan Karon's "At Home in Mitford" series, or Bodie Thoene's "The Zion Chronicles." Her favorite all-time author though, was James Michener. She had read almost all of his books, but her favorites were "Hawaii" and "Centennial".

Fran and John also loved the movies. They would go at least once a month. All too often there just wasn't anything they cared to see; sex, nudity, bad language and gory violence was just too common in so many movies. Terry, Jack and Steve had bought them a VCR quite a few years earlier, and Fran and John had a large video collection. They didn't like most of what was on TV, so each night, after reading for a while, one of them would ask, "What movie do you want to watch tonight, Hon?" They'd settle in with snacks and soft drinks and watch a video that they had probably seen once or twice before. They'd always time it so that when the movie was over they'd switch to the ten o'clock news. The kids got them a DVD player for Christmas, so besides reading their Bibles, and the books they loved, they also had their choice of videos or DVDs to watch…"What could be better than this?"

Fran and John also loved dining out; they would go out to eat at least once a week, sometimes alone, sometimes with Jackie and Sue, or Dottie, and other times with friends. Spontaneous outings with Steve were fun. He'd call sometimes on his way home from work and say, "Hey, what are you guys planning for supper?" If Fran said she hadn't decided yet, Steve would say, "Let's go to Christo's, or to Jamie's." Fran loved cooking too, and preparing meals for her family and friends was something she always looked forward to.

Holidays were at her and John's house, and she cooked and planned them just like Ethel and Crocifessa had always done.

She and John loved getting together with Joe and Betty, and Fran and Jack. They took turns, one month dinner at the Murphys, next month at the Hopkins, and then at the Roberts. They had been doing that for years. The three couples went on retreats together, and Fran and John and Joe and Betty went away at least once a year for a fun weekend together. John and Fran considered the friendship of Joe and Betty, and Fran and Jack a special gift from God.

Another couple Fran and John considered a true blessing were Larry and Bertha Clancy. "They are two of the sweetest people God ever created," Fran said. "They truly care about us; Larry does so many things to help us out, and Bertha bakes the best oatmeal cookies we've ever tasted, and makes sure she keeps us well stocked with them around the holidays. The best thing about them though, is the fact that we know we can count on them when we need prayer partners for something; they're very dear to us."

Fran had been leading a women's Bible study on Tuesday mornings for about fifteen years. Two of Fran's closest friends were Jean Taylor and Pat Harvey, "true prayer warriors" as Fran called them. Jean had been very special to Fran for years before she met Pat. Jean and Pat had been coming to the Bible study right from the beginning. Fran so appreciated their faithfulness and devotion. John, for many years led a Bible study in their home on Thursday evenings. It would be impossible to list all the people who attended that Bible study over the years. There were about fifteen regulars, with many others who came for a time and then moved on. Teaching a Bible study was one of Fran and John's greatest passions.

Fran and John lived a simple life, and enjoyed each other's company more than anything. They loved God, each other and their family. They also cared a great deal for the Community Baptist Church in Weymouth, where they worshipped. They enjoyed life... the simpler the better, and as long as it glorified God, they were truly happy.

On September 12, 2004 Terry, Jack and Steve held a Silver Anniversary party for their parents' twenty-fifth anniversary at

Nicole's function room at the Rockland Golf Course. Fran and John had actually been together for thirty-four years.

Fran looked up Richie Famularo, whom they hadn't seen since Terry and Jim's wedding. He said, "Of course I remember you guys; I'd be honored to play for your twenty-fifth anniversary." They were so glad to see Richie. "He's just as nice as he was twenty-five years ago," Fran said, when they got together a week before the party.

Fifty-eight people attended the party, family and old friends, and lots of new friends too. Of course, Dottie, Cindy and Graeme were there. Joe and Mae, Shaun, Paul and Kathy, Mark and Renee, Pete and Jacqui, Claire and Scott were there also. John's family was there too, Bruce and Ann, and their children, and Jim and his children, and Mary. Kellie and Jared were there, and old friends like Rosemarie and Bill Buckley, and Mary Pinciaro came too.

Fran and John read words of thanksgiving to each other, and with their pastor Tom Dagley, renewed their marriage vows. The food was positively fabulous, and the music Richie played was perfect. Fran and John and many other couples enjoyed the dancing, and others just enjoyed chatting together and renewing old acquaintances. Steve read a poem he had written to his parents for the occasion that had everyone howling with laughter. Steve, like his mother, wrote quite a bit of poetry, even had a couple published, but as John said, "It's doubtful that *this* particular poem will ever make it into the archives of classic poetry."

It was a delightful and beautiful celebration, and everyone, especially Fran and John, had a wonderful time. At one point during the party she and John looked around the room at the people they loved most in the world, and John said, "Will you look at those kids; Andrew is getting up near six feet, and Philip's close behind. Nathanael looks like he's going to pass them both in height." "I know," Fran said. "It seems like just yesterday they were shorter than me, and dying to get "taller than Nannie". Remember how they always wanted to stand back-to-back with me to see if they had reached my height yet?" John smiled. "I sure do; being taller than an adult, even if that adult "is only 4'11" was a great achievement for them. I still remember the joy on their faces when they finally did it. 'Course Johannah is going to be a peanut like you." "Yes,"

Fran said, "but it's obvious already that she's going to be taller than me." "She's looking forward to that day," John said. "Even Jared is starting to measure his growth 'according to Nannie'. Man, I love those kids." "They're five of the best kids I've ever known," Fran said. "We sure have been blessed. God has given us so much to be thankful for." Fran and John felt blessed in *so many* ways that day.

*****

Christmas 2004 was wonderful. Christmas Eve Fran and John went to Joe and Mae's like they had been doing for many years. The whole family was there, including Dottie and Cindy and Graeme and their family. On Christmas Day Fran and John, Terry, Jim and the kids, Jack, Sue and Steve, Dottie, Cindy, Graeme and little Nathaniel exchanged presents. A paper fight ensued, with rolled up wrapping paper being tossed at anyone who wasn't looking. Soon everyone joined in on the fight. The noise level kept rising, and so did the laughter.

Later Fran cooked a nice dinner for the family. Before dinner Dottie and Johannah prepared the celery and cream cheese and black olives the way Ethel always did for holidays. Everyone was hungry and enjoyed "Nana's celery". Dinner started with chicken soup, then antipasto salad and fresh Italian bread. "Grandma's famous baked macaroni" was next, with meatballs, sausages and pork chops in the sauce. Everyone was stuffed, so they waited a little while, and then Fran served coffee and desserts. Sue made a pecan pie, and an assortment of Christmas cookies. Terry made an apple crisp, and brought vanilla ice cream, and Cindy brought a strawberry-rhubarb pie. Everything, from beginning to end was delicious. Food was always very important in the Vitello/Murphy household, but, just as wonderful and important as the food, was the fun and the laughter. John, Jack and Steve were in rare form that Christmas day, keeping everyone, especially the kids, in stitches. That evening Joe and Mae and Claire and Scott came by to enjoy coffee and dessert with Fran and John and Dottie and all the kids.

Later that night, after everyone had gone home, John and Fran sat in the sunroom with the stove going. They were each snuggled under their lap robes enjoying a cup of mostly decaffeinated coffee. The house was a wreck, but they were too exhausted to do anything about it. "We'll clean it up together tomorrow," John said. Fran was way too comfortable to argue. They talked about the day and reminisced about Christmases past. They were feeling very warm and nostalgic. "You know something?" John said. "I think this was the best Christmas ever," "Hmm," Fran said, "you sound just like my Dad now." She smiled and said, "but you're right John; I think this *was* the best Christmas ever."

They sipped their coffee, and during a quiet moment John said, "What are you thinking about Fran?" "Well, I was just thinking about how I came to be in this world," Fran said. "Umm, I think we know how you came to be in this world," John said smiling. "No, I don't mean how I was conceived," she said. "I was thinking about Psalm 139, where it says that *God* formed my inward parts inside my mother's womb, and He knew me before I was even conceived." "Yeah, that's pretty great, isn't it?" John said. "Yes," she said, "it is."

"So, if He knew me before I was conceived," Fran said, "then He had it all planned that I had to be born to Angelo Vitello and Ethel Gertrude Dalton. Which means that first Angelo Vitello had to be born to Pietro Vitello and Crocifessa Bellanti, and Ethel Dalton had to be born to Harry Dalton and Ethel Bell, and so on, and so on, and so on, and it's the same with every person who ever lived. I'll bet if we could keep going back farther and farther, we'd find that we're all related, and our ancestors one day were eating fruit they shouldn't have eaten in a garden called Eden." "Whoa now," John said. "Can you substantiate that?" "Well, no, of course not, and I know it's silly," Fran said, "but think about this, John. "I wouldn't be here today if my great-grandparents Bellanti hadn't arranged a marriage for their daughter Crocifessa, with my great-grandparents Vitello, and their son Pietro. Crocifessa and Pietro needed to get married so that my father, Angelo could come into this world."

"Okay, now, in Manchester, England, some years earlier," Fran went on, "my great-grandparents Bell married, probably arranged by *their* parents, and my grandmother Ethel Bell was born. They needed to come to this country so that she could meet my grandfather Harry Dalton so that my mother could come into this world.

So then, my grandparents Vitello left Sicily and came to America, and my great-grandparents Bell, and my grandmother Ethel left Manchester, England and came to America so that my father and mother could meet in this country. Of course none of these people had any idea that they were carrying out some grand master plan when they left their respective countries. My grandfather Harry, who was born in Salem, Massachusetts, and my grandmother Ethel hadn't even met yet, so God had all that arranged too.

Fran continued, "Are you still with me?" "Confused, but yes, I'm still with you." Okay, now, my father grew up in the North End of Boston, and Ethel and Harry moved to South Boston, where my mother was born. Then, very close in time, my father and his family moved to Parker Street in Jamaica Plain, and my mother and her mother moved to Bickford street in Jamaica Plain, which by the way, was one street over from Parker Street. The rest is obvious; Andy and Ethel meet and marry and I am born. There, what do you think?" "Wow!" John said. "You're really something. I can imagine what you'd come up with if you weren't exhausted. But, it *is* amazing, and you are right Fran, only God could conceive such a marvelous plan."

"But, now think about it John," Fran said. I had to start working at O'Brion, Russell Insurance Company in Boston so that I could meet Jack Roche, who lived in Hyde Park but worked at Maryland Casualty Insurance Company in Boston, and marry him so that Terry could be born. Then she had to go out to Amherst to meet Jim from Greenfield, and marry him so that Andrew, Philip, Nathanael and Johannah could be born. And we had to move to Quincy so that Steven could meet and marry Kellie so that Jared could be born. "It's the most marvelous plan imaginable, and yes, only God could conceive of something so perfect. And, you know something John? It *is* a perfect plan; it's people that mess it all up by our greed and lust and self-centeredness." "That's the truth," John said. "So how did I fit into the equation?" "Well, I haven't got that all figured out yet," Fran said. "I know that God knows all things, so He must have known that Jack and I would divorce, and that Jack would want to start a new life. He also knew that Terry, Jackie and Steven needed a full-time father." "Aha!" John said with a grin. "Enter John Murphy." "Well yes, but how were we supposed to meet, let alone fall in love?" Fran said. "I mean, between me being divorced with three children, and you a lot younger than me, I would never have even considered going out with you, and you certainly wouldn't have had any interest in me." "Yeah, but you were quite a looker," John said, raising one eyebrow and twirling his moustache in a lecherous fashion. "Seriously John, the age difference and the fact that we didn't travel in the same circles, how would we ever have met?" "I see where you're going with this," he said. "Your sister Dottie had to start working at Boston University," he said, "and I had to start working at the book store in the University for her and I to meet." "Right!" Fran said.

I believe God had it all arranged beforehand," Fran continued. "He had to work on Dottie to get me to the bookstore. Once there, I started working on you and Dottie to get together, but you guys never moved in that direction. We all became good friends; Dottie met Chet, and 'the rest is history,' as they say. "Wow! Think about it," John said. "If Dottie and I had hit it off, Cindy would never have been born. You're right Fran, it's not all just a series of many coincidences; it's all part of a master plan only God could have conceived, and arranged to happen." "Isn't it wonderful, Hon?" Fran said. "It sure is, Fran, and I thank God for every bit of it." "Mmm, me too," she said.

"You know what, John?" "What's that, Hon?" John asked. "I just love every member of this family," Fran said. "I mean, all the way back, to my great-grandparents in Riesi, Sicily, and Manchester, England. I love them all. It's just a nice family ...a *really* nice family, and I'm proud to be a branch of this family tree." John smiled. "It certainly is a nice family, Hon, and I'm proud to have been grafted in. Do you think we can go to bed now? It's one o'clock in the morning." "Oh, do we have to?" Fran asked. "Isn't this great fun, talking like this?" "It is, but I'm not going to be able to keep my eyes open much longer." "Okay, you're right," Fran said. "Let's go to bed."

They started to get up when Fran said, "Oh, my goodness John, I just thought of something. Do you realize that if Mae hadn't left Nova Scotia to come to this country, and if she hadn't started working at Herman's Health & Beauty Aids that..." "Oh no!" John said. "Don't even go there. It's too late; I'm exhausted, and my brain is mush now as it is. Aren't you exhausted?" "Yes, I guess I am," she said. "Okay, turn out the light."

As they walked up the stairs to their bedroom Fran said, "Tomorrow night Hon, we'll talk about your father coming to this country and marrying your mother after his first wife died. There's a lot of history there." He yawned, and then smiled. He leaned over and kissed her. "I love you Fran." "I love you too John."

****

Jared 2002

Little Nathaniel, Cindy, Dottie (standing) and Fran.

**Standing: Joe, Fran and Mae, seated: Rosemarie,
Mary P. and Bill Buckley
Fran and John's 25th Anniversary, September 2004.**

Clockwise from top: Andrew, Nathanael, Johannah and Philip 2004

Jared and Steve at Jared's First Communion June 2006

John and Fran 2006

EPILOGUE

Today is a good day, and kind of a sad day also; I finished the book today. I tried to write all that was in my heart, but there's so much left out that I wanted to say. But no one wants to read a book with a thousand pages.

Ever since my parents passed away I have been thinking about the fact that I am now the matriarch of my side of the family. It's a strange feeling; I mean my thoughts run to my mother, and my grandmothers. Could I ever be even *close* to the women they were? Crocifessa was sweet, loving, generous, and devoted to her family. Ethel Sr. was strong, capable, devoted to her family, and a lot of fun. My mother Ethel was sweet, strong, capable, and devoted to her family. My husband says I've inherited all of those qualities; he's just being kind. But I shall strive for the rest of my days to earn and own those qualities, with God's help.

To bring you up to date, let me tell you that Joe has semi-retired, and Shaun and Pete are, for the most part, running J. W. Graham Painting Company now; he's still very active in the business though. Joe is very involved in the St. Jerome Parish Constanza ministry in the Dominican Republic. On his last trip there, his son Paul went him. He's also very active in his church, and busy being the patriarch of *his* family. No matter how old we get, I always see Joe as my protector…my *big* brother.

Dottie has opened her own antiques and collectibles shop in Essex, something she's wanted to do for many years. She's also a freelance writer for different newspapers. She's madly in love with her grandchildren and loves being with them. She will probably move to the North Shore some day to be closer to her business, and to Cindy and the kids. Dottie's a lot of fun; I'll miss not having her nearby…after all, she's my *little* sister.

John started out working for my father Andy, and when my dad retired he worked for Joe for many years, and now, after thirty-one years with the company, he's working for Shaun and Pete. They say John's the "backbone of J. W. Graham". John still loves his job, and even better, he has loved all his *employers*. He'll retire in a few years, but he'll probably continue working on a part-time basis, if I know my husband.

Terry is still teaching at Jonathan Edwards Academy. She teaches History and loves reading anything to do with the Civil War. Each year she produces and directs a Shakespearean play for the school. Andrew and Philip have acted in all five of her plays, and Nathanael has acted in three. This year Johannah had a part in the play. Terry is also an avid Jane Austen fan; she has gotten the entire family hooked on Jane Austen books and movies.

Jim is still with Lunt Silversmiths. He's an excellent artist and takes care of the sets and scenery for his wife's plays. He and Terry are active in their church, and *very* active in their children's lives. Their primary goal in life is to raise their children for the Lord.

Jack and Sue have just bought a large, beautiful home by a pond in Pembroke. They have no children, but they have two big dogs, Elwood and Otis. Jack is still painting, and Sue works in the lab at Newton-Wellesley Hospital. Sue's dad passed away a few years ago, and now that they have the room, her mom, Sophie has come to live with them.

Steve is still with ADT Security Systems, and living with us. He sees Jared often and works hard at keeping a close relationship with him. Steve has been a boon to me while I've been writing this book. I said before I know nothing about computers, and I have had to call him over a hundred times to set my computer straight again. He grumbles about me not wanting to learn more about the computer, but I do appreciate his technical knowledge, and his willingness, albeit grumbling, to help me out.

Andrew just turned nineteen, and is a freshman at Calvin College in Grand Rapids, Michigan. He's already involved in the drama programs of the college, and starred in their production of Arcadia. He loves Shakespeare, and acting and acting in his plays. He misses everyone back home, but he looks forward to whatever the Lord has for him.

Philip is seventeen, and a senior at JEA. He's an avid soccer player, but history is his passion, thanks to his mother. He loves Calvin College and has just learned that he and his best friend Daniel have both been accepted there. He's looking forward to being at school with his brother again. Philip has a love of Shakespeare and Jane Austen stories.

Nathanael is fourteen and an excellent student; he's also a terrific soccer player. He hasn't started thinking seriously yet about choosing his college, but wherever he goes, he'll do well. He loves acting in his mother's Shakespearean plays.

Johannah is twelve and isn't thinking about college at all yet. She loves playing soccer and, she too, is good at it. She shares her mother's love of Shakespeare and Jane Austen stories as well.

Jared is eight years old and is a student at Sacred Heart School in Weymouth. Like his father, he loves movies; he's also a whiz at computer games. Jared is also a cub scout.

Shaun and Maura are still living in Weymouth. Maura is a stay-at-home mom during the week with their two boys, Sean 12, and Neil 8. She works as a registered nurse on weekends.

Paul and his wife Kathy are still living in Connecticut with their children, Nicholas, 18, who is a freshman at Worcester Polytechnical Institute, Danielle 16, Leah 14, and Jacob 8. Paul is an engineer for United Technologies in Connecticut, and Kathy teaches school.

Mark and Renee are still living in Weymouth with their three children, Mark Angelo 11, Rachel 8, and Tommy 6. Mark works for Traveler's Insurance Company as a fraud investigator. Renee works part time as concierge at South Shore Hospital.

Peter and Jacqui are still living in Cohasset with their two children, Amanda 7, and Peter 2. Jacqui is a stay-at-home mom at this time.

Claire and Scott are in the process of building a new home in Whitman, where they live with their two children, Scott 4, and Bianca 2. Claire is an esthetician for Ambrosia Day Spa in Norwell, and Scott is a painter for J. W. Graham Painting Company.

Cindy and Graeme live in a lovely home in Peabody, with their two children, Nathaniel 4 ½, and Emily Ethel 2. At this writing Cindy is expecting her third child, a girl, whom they plan to name Camille. Cindy works as a marriage and family psychotherapist in private practice on a part time basis, and Graeme is a software engineer working on a very important program for Raytheon. They are both active in their church, and are kept busy with their careers and their growing family.

Well, that's the family; we're a simple family. Not too many real exciting things go on, but we're rarely bored. One thing we can always count on is laughter. This family has an abundance of very funny people in it. It's the one thing none of us could ever do without.

I truly hope you've enjoyed reading about Crocifessa and Peter, and Ethel Sr. and Harry, and Andy and Ethel, and Joe, Fran and Dottie, and of course John, and all the children and grand-children, uncles, aunts, in-laws, nephews, nieces, cousins and friends as much as I've enjoyed telling you about them.

As you can tell, I like talking about my family. **I can't help it...I'M ITALIAN!**

THE END...*for now.*

Printed in the United States
206445BV00001BA/103-240/A

9 781600 344893